Praise for *Jeff Herman's Guide to Bo...*
Editors & Literary Agent...

"Nothing beats *Jeff Herman's Guide*."
— **Jack Canfield**, coauthor, *Chicken Soup for the Soul* series

"Jeff Herman has done a service to every writer who wants to make a living in this business. Every author should have a copy on their shelf."
— **Chip MacGregor**, literary agent

"Everything you need to get started."
— **Cheryl Richardson**, *New York Times*–bestselling author of *Stand Up for Your Life*

"*Jeff Herman's Guide* remains the Rosetta Stone of writerly success."
— **James Broderick, PhD**, BookPleasures.com

"I got my agent by using this guide!"
— **Meg Cabot**, *New York Times*–bestselling author of *The Princess Diaries*

"When you get to the 'finding the agent' stage, check out *Jeff Herman's Guide*. I found it very useful because it gives more background on agents. Keep in mind that publishing is very personality driven."
— **Emily Giffin**, *New York Times*–bestselling author of *First Comes Love*

"I sent my proposal and sample pages to ten agents selected from *Jeff Herman's Guide* and was shocked to receive interest from three of them. I celebrated when I signed with an agent and again when my first book was sold."
— **Jacqueline Winspear**, *New York Times*–bestselling author of *Maisie Dobbs*

"Here's my two cents: I used *Jeff Herman's Guide*. It includes a huge list of agents, interviews about what they are looking for, and useful info on big and small presses."
— **Kristy Woodson Harvey**, author of *Lies and Other Acts of Love*

"If you are only going to get one book on this subject, *Jeff Herman's Guide* is the one I recommend. When I was looking for an agent, this was the book that showed me how. The only thing is, you have to do what it says."
— **Marie Bostwick**, author of *Between Heaven and Texas*

Also by Jeff Herman

Write the Perfect Book Proposal: 10 That Sold and Why
(with Deborah Levine Herman)

Jeff Herman's GUIDE TO BOOK PUBLISHERS, EDITORS & LITERARY AGENTS

Who They Are, What They Want, How to Win Them Over

Jeff Herman

New World Library
Novato, California

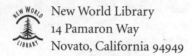 New World Library
14 Pamaron Way
Novato, California 94949

Text design by Tona Pearce Myers
Index by Carol and Nina Roberts

Library of Congress Cataloging-in-Publication Data is available.

First printing, October 2016
ISBN 978-1-60868-404-5
Ebook ISBN 978-1-60868-405-2

Printed in Canada on 100% postconsumer-waste recycled paper

 New World Library is proud to be a Gold Certified Environmentally Responsible Publisher. Publisher certification awarded by Green Press Initiative. www.greenpressinitiative.org

10   9   8   7   6   5   4   3   2   1

You can't be lost if searching.
Truth is a writer's deliverance, and freedom the reward.
When a writer leaps, the universe applauds.

CONTENTS

Part 3. Independent Presses (US)

Part 4. University Presses (US)

Part 5. Canadian Book Publishers

Part 6. Literary Agents

Part 7. Independent Editors

INTRODUCTION

Welcome back, or welcome for the first time. This is the latest edition of the book I've been producing since 1990, and I have invested considerable time and resources into revising almost every aspect of it.

Much has changed and much has remained the same since my journey in publishing began in the 1980s. Dozens of long-lasting independent (mom-and-pop) publishers have either disappeared or been absorbed into a numerically tiny oligarchy of multinational, trillion-dollar conglomerates, and relatively few start-ups have emerged. Digital retailing has displaced physical retailing, and most books will soon be bought in digital form. Though aggregate revenues have been enhanced, ever fewer writers are able to support themselves by writing.

However, millions of Americans from all backgrounds and conditions are writing with as much passion and determination as ever, and self-publishing has become a respectable option for countless writers who previously would have been effectively locked out. While the literary agency community has suffered from what has been a harsh economic culling, hundreds of dedicated independent agents still tenaciously continue to help writers make their dreams come true.

In the beginning, my primary motive for doing this book was to give writers valuable information that was cloaked from them by habit, if not volition. It seemed that the screening process was unduly influenced by factors entirely separate from merit. Those who were fortunate enough to be from certain communities, to have attended certain schools, or to have the right connections were more likely to get published. If access to the process wasn't fairly distributed, it followed that the opportunities were rigged. Clearly, cultural constraints are harmful for society, whether imposed by a government or by inbred subcultures. My vision was, and is, to simply give writers crucial information about the industry and its primary players, blended with accessible road maps and advice about overcoming likely obstacles. Over the years thousands of writers and industry insiders have told me the book helped them, which in turn gives me the inspiration and motivation to keep doing it. And it has given me a special sense of accomplishment to see that some of my methods have become generic over time.

Finally, I view myself as both a teacher and a student. Nothing anyone says will be correct every time, nor can anyone predict every result before it happens. You should be directed and inspired by what you don't know, and be curious about anything that feels easy. If something is effortlessly predictable, it is simply waiting to be altered and improved, if not by you then by someone else, which is why new books are often written about old subjects. Someone once asked me to define the measurement of 1, which I failed to do to her satisfaction. In her world, math was an unnatural limitation, the product of human fear of the unknown and its infinite possibilities. In that light, please use what I and others suggest as a place to begin, not the ground upon which to settle. The realities you dare to conjure will prove to be what's most enduring and meaningful.

Jeff Herman

Part 1

ADVICE FOR WRITERS

**What You (Might) Need to Know
about Publishing, Even If It (Not You)
Is Boring and Stupid**

INTRODUCTION
PERFECTLY IMPERFECT ADVICE AND RANDOM THOUGHTS

Jeff Herman

Except for a few hiatuses, I have been in the book-publishing business since the early 1980s, when I was in my early twenties. I entered the business without any forethought. I wasn't an avid book lover or English major. My primary mission was to be respectfully employed in a Manhattan skyscraper where people wore jackets and ties and performed seemingly important tasks. That was my projection for post-college success, and I imagined it as glamorous and exotic. Reality was a hard, slow grind compared to the glorious images painted by youthful endorphins and innocence, and getting what we wish for tends to be easier than wearing the shoes day in and day out.

I answered countless blind ads in the employment section of the *New York Times* for entry-level office jobs. One day, someone with a harried, high-pitched voice called to schedule an interview. I showered and showed up on time in a decent suit. I said little and tried to smile and nod on cue. The only question I recall was if I could start work the following Monday (it was a Friday) for $200 a week (1981) as a "publicity assistant." It was a small independent book-publishing company with a compelling list and history. I was second-in-command of the firm's two-person publicity department, which entitled me to do the filing, phone answering, and typing — none of which I knew how to do before doing it. I knew nothing about publishing or what the job entailed. My most important attributes may have been a calm persona of sanity and an apparent willingness to follow orders. Or maybe it was just my sincere promise to show up. In a nutshell, that explains how I "chose" the business I am in.

I tell this vignette because people often ask how I got into the business. But there's also a larger reason why I share this. I didn't have much of a plan or fixed direction, but yet I arrived somewhere and along the way made decisions (good or otherwise), grew, and helped make constructive things happen for myself and others. Maybe it's okay to not know what we want or where we are going in order to accomplish what we should. When I was young, a wise man told me that "man plans, god laughs," and I have subsequently heard that phrase many times. Frankly, I had to *grow into* understanding what that meant, and I frequently question it all over again. Perhaps writers shouldn't overplan what they write or will write. For sure, they can't fully control what happens to their work after they write it, short of destroying it.

Because it can be useful to consider what others say about what you do and wish to achieve, I have generated this section of the book. Read what you will with absolute discernment. Not all of it is for you, and all of it is imperfect — same as you and me. The only perfection is that you and I are here now together.

LITERARY AGENTS: WHAT THEY ARE AND WHAT THEY DO

Jeff Herman

Think of a venture capitalist: those people who invest their resources in other people's talents and dreams in exchange for a piece of the glory. The capitalist's skill is the ability to choose wisely and help manifest the endeavor. Literary agents are conceptually similar. For an industry-standard 15 percent commission ("ownership"), we invest considerable measures of time, expertise, and faith in the writers we choose to represent. Our professional credibility is on the line with each pitch we make. We don't directly provide the cash; part of our job is to get the publisher to put its money on the line. If you stick with the trajectory of information that follows, the reasons why most writers elect to have an agent will be made clear.

Publishers Overtly Discourage Unagented/Unsolicited Submissions

A typical publisher's in-house functions include product acquisition and management, back-office administrative tasks, editing, production, distribution, sales and marketing, accounting, and numerous other indispensable aspects related to publishing a book and running a business. However, all editorial content is outsourced and managed from the inside — that is, unlike magazines and newspapers, books are rarely written by in-house staff, which means that they are entirely dependent on "freelance" writers, including you.

If people stopped writing new books, publishers wouldn't have anything new to publish. So it might seem counterintuitive and ironic that most traditional publishers make it difficult, if not impossible, for writers to submit their work for consideration. But from the publisher's perspective, it's about being functional. For every book that gets published at a given moment, there are at least 1,000 manuscripts vying for the same opportunity at the same time. Imagine George Clooney or your favorite heartthrob standing in Times Square and announcing that he's looking for a wife. It would be a chaotic situation, and it's possible he and others would be trampled to death. This illustrates why publishers feel the need to barricade themselves against writers even though they can't exist without them. Not only do publishers lack in-house writers; they also lack an infrastructure for screening and filtering unagented/unsolicited works.

How Do Publishers Find Books to Publish?

Solicitation. Proactive editors sometimes have their own book ideas and will seek people to write them. They might read various literary publications in which virgin content is often debuted, and then contact the writers who impress them. Editors might also scan the news for interesting events and discoveries and then reach out to the people involved. Whenever the editor commences the conversation and offers someone the opportunity to be published, it is solicitation (not the illegal kind).

Agency representation. Editors rely on agents to do hardcore screening and to only represent writers and works that merit publication. Editors don't have time to screen hundreds of works in order to discover one they can publish; they don't have to, because the agents do it for them. When an editor receives a submission from a trusted agent, he or she immediately assumes that the work is professionally qualified and merits quality attention.

Having an agent equals access to editors. Not having an agent usually means the opposite, no matter how good the work might be.

Who Do Agents Work For?

The majority of literary agents are self-employed small-business people. They work for neither the publisher nor the writer but are indispensable to both for different reasons. The agent's constant interest is to generate commissions against the client's advance and subsequent royalties. The healthier the agent can make the client, the healthier the agent can make herself. The agent's revenues are tied to the client's revenues, and this mutuality of interests drives the agent to make the client as successful as possible.

Agents have clear lines that they won't/can't cross on behalf of a client. There are a finite number of publishers and an infinite number of potential clients. An agent can replace an unsatisfied client in a minute and perhaps can never replace an aggrieved publisher. Losing a publisher as a possible customer for future submissions is like permanently losing a large percentage of the business. In practice, it's rare for the agent to be forced into making such choices, and the agent will usually manage to preempt destructive conflicts by simply telling the client what is and isn't acceptable or possible.

The client needs to understand that a literary agent isn't the same as a litigator and won't relentlessly fight for issues that often can't be achieved anyway, such as a 20-city media tour. The agent's interests will stray from the client's interests if the agent-publisher relationship becomes threatened due to the client's actions or demands. However, any author who becomes more problematic than profitable will unilaterally burn all his bridges anyway. An author's profitability must always outpace her negatives, or she will be of diminishing value to both the agent and the publisher. However, agents usually confront publishers if they violate or ignore contracts and what's customary. If a publisher disrespects the client, the agent will feel as if he is being similarly abused and will push back. A key distinction is that for the agent you're a "client," whereas for the publisher you're an "author."

How Do Agents Make Money?

In the context of the agency-client relationship, agents make a 15 percent commission from all the advance and royalty revenues the agent's efforts enable the client to earn.

The above percentage pertains to the moneys received from the US publishers, which usually is the lion's share, if not the only source, of all revenue. The percentages assessed against subsidiary rights from deals made by the agent will vary by agency. For translation deals, most of the time US agents team with foreign agents in the respective countries, and the foreign agent wants at least 10 percent off the top, which generally is charged to the author in addition to the US agent's commission. That's the way it's done. If the US publisher controls the foreign rights, which they often do, the same sub-agent deal is also usually involved, except now the US publisher is also taking a cut. This sounds like a lot of dealings absent the author, but few authors can make these arcane deals unilaterally and they are the primary beneficiaries. Think of it as free money.

How Do False Agents Make Money?

Bogus agents make money in countless ways other than by doing what real agents do. Bogus agents tend not to ever sell works to traditional publishers and don't operate on the basis of earning commissions. Instead, they may offer amazing promises and an itemized menu of nonagent services, like simply reading your work for a fee. Sometimes they will offer a range of editorial services that are not necessarily useful or needed. If someone says she will be your agent if you pay her money, then she isn't a bona fide agent.

Legitimate agencies receive hundreds of unsolicited pitches each month. If a modest fraction of these were converted into a $100 "reading (consideration) fee," it would be a substantial monthly windfall without accountability. Eventually, the internet often exposes such scams, but by that time the bogus agent may have changed their company's name and be exploiting fresh pods of unjaded writers. It's like changing a parking spot if your time limit expires. Sometimes law enforcement will step in, but even then individual monetary losses probably won't ever be recouped, though valuable lessons hopefully will have been learned.

What's the Association of Authors' Representatives (AAR)?

The AAR is nothing like the Bar Association, American Medical Association, or any other mandatory-membership professional organization. Agents don't have to belong to or be licensed by any outside entity to be legal. The AAR can loosely be compared to a nonprofit country club minus a physical address, paid staff, and the usual accoutrements. A large percentage of agents choose to join the AAR because it offers a collegial way to network with other agents and find relief from their cloistered offices. To varying degrees, agents are compelled to be competitive with each other for clients, and AAR meetings serve as a refreshing "no-kill" zone where they can presumably be friends with others who understand what they do for a living.

AAR membership is restricted to agents who have made a specific number of actual book deals within a specific time frame and promise to adhere to the AAR's strict codes of conduct. The majority of codes are generic common sense, and a lot of space could be saved if they simply stated "Don't break the law"; but overeducated people prefer to deliberate over everything, and we have all been conditioned to make work for America's bloated legal establishment. However, some of the codes are archaic and prevent many qualified agencies from wanting to join. For instance, the codes seem to proscribe members from establishing separate divisions dedicated to nonagent services, like editing, collaborating, and helping writers self-publish. The fast-changing nature of publishing has made it impossible for an ever-increasing number of boutique agencies to rely only on commission-based services, and agents are exceptionally qualified to provide these kinds of traditionally fee-based services.

What Services and Assets Do Agents Provide in Exchange for Their Commissions?

1. They deliver access to the appropriate editors at traditional publishing companies. Few writers can achieve the same level of access without an agent because editors don't want to do mass screening; they rely upon the agents to do that on their behalf.

2. The agents know who the appropriate editors and publishers are for the works they represent.

3. Agents can accelerate the sales process by going to many publishers simultaneously with the same project, which sometimes creates a competitive bidding war, called "auction."

4. Agents know how to tweak and improve the work in order to maximize its sale to a publisher.

5. Agents understand publisher contracts and how to modify the language to the writer's advantage.

6. Agents know how to assess a work's potential monetary value and are positioned to negotiate the best terms possible.

7. Agents help clients understand how to interact with editors and publishers after the publisher's contract is signed.

8. Agents can provide valuable consultations about what is marketable.

What Won't Agents Do as Part of Their Commission?

I can't speak for all agents, or even for myself in all situations, but in the context of agenting in general, agents shouldn't be counted on as editors — meaning they don't have much time for perfecting or fixing afflicted manuscripts in detail; nor are they publicists or sales reps. The agent may be able to provide excellent referrals for these and other needs or may even have excellent in-house divisions for generally fee-based services. Though there's nothing wrong with an agent offering fee-based services, the agency should make it clear that these services are absolutely separate from commission-based services and that representation isn't contingent on retaining the fee-based services from the agent or from those specifically recommended by the agent.

How Do You Get an Agent?

Getting an agent might not be as difficult as you think. But if you're not thinking about it, don't expect it to be easy. If it were easy, you'd have no reason to buy this book. Some people make it look easy, but what are you seeing? Observing a person's accomplishments absent their likely struggles is rarely a worthy endeavor. Here are some things to consider when trying to land an agent.

- *Expect rejections.* The prima facie percentages are disconcerting. On average, agents reject about 98 percent of what's pitched. There's no rational reason for them to represent something without believing they can sell it to a publisher. Doing so would simply be a waste of everyone's time and not a good way for the agents to leverage their editor relationships. So the odds are that you will receive rejections.

- *Pitch the right agents.* Most agents have areas of editorial specialization and categories they rarely, if ever, deal with. You might have an excellent romance novel, but if you pitch only to agents who never handle romances, your rejection rate will be 100 percent. Conversely, only pitching to appropriate agents might give you a 100 percent "yes" rate. You need to find out who the right agents are for your work, and there are many proven ways to do that. Start by using the agency section in this book (see page 211), but that doesn't need to be the full extent of your research. Each agency's website will probably include a clear statement about what to pitch and what not to bother them with. Visit physical bookstores that have a large shelf of books in your category and read the acknowledgments sections; most of the time the author's agent will be acknowledged. Join local and national organizations that either specialize in your category or seem to have many like-minded members, and make friends. Friends will often share valuable information and experiences with each other and may even make valuable introductions on your behalf. If you enter the community with a sense of generosity you will receive much generosity in turn.

- **Prepare to become a pitcher.** It won't matter how good your content is if you fail to properly pitch it. Writers can greatly compensate for editorial mediocrity by embellishing via their pitch skills. Fear of rejection prevents many talented people from reaching their full potential. Replacing fear with hunger and determination removes all limitations. It's often not the most talented people who rise to the top of their fields but those who want it the most.

- **Good pitching is power.** The publishing business is about editorial content, so your pitch will need to be expressed in the form of a pitch letter, often referred to in "pub-speak" as a query letter. *Query* means you are asking a question or making a request, which in this context means asking the agent to consider representing your work. Agents receive hundreds to thousands of such queries every year, and reading them can be a mind-numbing process. In order to be competitive it's best to avoid asking for anything while offering everything; a pitch should be an offer of something that will benefit the agent — an enticement, a seduction. For advice on writing the best pitch possible, please refer to the essay dedicated to this subject (see page 19).

- **Pitch by email** and **snail mail.** Use both simultaneously. I'm serious. Agency digital submission boxes are overflowing, and not just with legitimate pitches. The internet is a blessing and a curse for all the obvious reasons. In the early years of the current century, emails were still relatively exotic and appreciated, and not everyone had fully "switched" yet. There was the "You've got mail" announcement each time we booted up and maybe a mere dozen emails every 24 hours, mostly spamless. Dealing with inboxes today is like flossing teeth after a corn-eating orgy. Ironically, hardcopy mail has now become exotic and thus might be seen and read much more quickly than the digital version of the same material. So why not hedge your bet by using both conveyance methods? Yes, some agents say they prefer that you use their digital mailboxes. But what they really prefer is what works out best in the long run. Shoot for best-case results, and everyone will be happy in the end. However, you might want to mention at the end of your letter that you've sent it via both hardcopy and email.

An unimportant side note: Many of my veteran colleagues still refer to receiving submissions "over the transom," which is a dated metaphor for anything that's unrequested. Until about 50 years ago, most New York offices had open windows above hallway entrances, which were called "transoms." Most mail and other deliveries were simply tossed into the offices through the transoms.

- *Pitch in batches.* If you're not in a big hurry to get published, meaning you're willing to wait many years, you should only pitch one agent at a time. Frankly, some agents will never respond, period. Others may take a very, very long time. These are understaffed mom-and-pop businesses, and dealing with recent submissions is often a low priority compared to servicing current clients. Do yourself a favor and pitch about 10 agents at a time. Pitching more than that at a time isn't wise, because you may see ways to constantly upgrade your pitch with each cycle. Every four weeks, if you're still in limbo, go out there with a fresh batch of 10 pitches. Most successful authors have a bloody past of rejections and humiliations; amass your bloody past as efficiently as possible so that you can reach your future while still breathing.

There are obvious exceptions. If you make a connection with a particular agent you like and he invites your submission, then play it out on an exclusive basis, but not forever. If he disappears from your radar for more than four to eight weeks, it may be time to play the field.

- *Sell yourself to the agent.* The agent is already 98 percent sure he doesn't need you. Even if he skips reading your work and goes straight to "reject," there's a less than 2 percent chance that he made a mistake. It's incumbent upon you to make the agent think you could be one of the magic 2 percent and avoid giving the impression you are one of the 98 percent.

- *Put yourself in the shoes of an agent.* What does an agent want? Commission-eligible clients, moron. What doesn't an agent want? If you can't answer this question by yourself, then you really are a moron.

What Else Should You Know about Agents?

Literary agents aren't that smart. Nor are they especially stupid. In other words, they're pretty much like everyone else, and that probably includes you. A combination of geography, respective subculture, and opportunities is what brings people to agenting. I might not have become an agent if I were not a New Yorker and had not been conditioned to be a "mind worker" by family, community, and subculture. Joining the military, for instance, would have marked me as an extreme outlier in my community, as opposed to a conformist if I were from Tennessee. Many agents are former in-house book editors; it's a way for them to move on while still using the skills and connections they already possess. Some agents were nurtured from when they were career virgins, meaning they landed an entry-level job in an agency, instead of in a publishing house, out of college.

Do Agents and Editors Have Similar Traits?

The primary difference is that editors get paychecks, whereas most agents are self-employed and get paid only if they generate commissions. Agents can become millionaires if they strike the right deals, whereas in-house editors can become rich only through marriage, through an inheritance, or by becoming an owner/partner instead of an employee where they work. Agents run businesses and are risk takers, whereas editors serve the needs of the companies they work for.

Do Agents and Editors Make "Sweetheart" Deals?

Yes, all the time, but we prefer not to think about it that way. There are fewer than 1,000 full-time acquisitions editors and agents in total, and an even smaller core of those who are the most active. We have to keep working within this tight circle to get our mutual needs met. The system succeeds for writers because agents must push author revenues in order to push their own revenues. Writers are the conduits through which agents eat, and they're the people who generate the raw material that editors can't live without.

Who Can Be an Agent?

Anyone can self-declare him- or herself a literary agent. Of course, succeeding as an agent is a different story. Finding raw product is actually easy, because so much is generated all the time. But knowing how to discern the tiny fraction of the unfiltered mass content that publishers will pay for is mostly an acquired skill. Forming direct relationships with editors is an unrestricted process, but they won't buy what they don't want, no matter how strong the agent-editor relationship is. Knowing what publishers will pay for is tantamount to knowing what the public will pay for.

What If an Agent Offers You Representation?

Bull's-eye. Mazel tov. Before you commit, settle any unfinished business with other agents who are still considering your work. Tell them you have an offer and need to make an immediate decision. Before accepting an agent's offer, you're entitled to ask reasonable questions and do your due diligence:

- Ask for a list of books the agent has sold to publishers, including the publishers' and authors' names. Some or all of this information might already be posted on her website.
- Check the internet for any "bad news." But be discerning about what you read. Disgruntled people often publicly rant in ways that are unfair.
- Have a conversation about why he likes your book, how he plans to sell it, how much he thinks he can get for it, the time frame, and if he believes in sexual monogamy (just checking if you're awake).

How Do You Know If Your Agent Is Doing a Good Job?

If your agent gets you a book deal with a traditional publisher, then she most likely did a good job for you. However, typically agents can sell only about half the works they represent in any given 12-month period. Having representation should mean your work receives quality access to the right editors, but that doesn't guarantee that any of them will make an offer. In fact, most agented works probably never get published, especially in the literary fiction zone. Editorial quality is just one factor determining what does and doesn't get published. If a particular category or concept is overpublished, for instance, many excellent prospects become surplus content. Timing is very important and impossible to deliberately control, though many people wish they could. You can't get a deal without correct access, but access won't guarantee you a deal.

What If the Agent Is Unable to Sell Your Work?

If your work is unsold after a long time (six months to a year), you should determine what the problem is and what the next steps might be. Upon request, the agent should let you know where the work was submitted, each submission's status, and any available details about rejections received. In consultation with your agent, it might be a good idea to consider some revisions or ways to tweak what editors are seeing.

Try to nail down whether the agent is still confident about selling the work. Sometimes an agent might no longer be confident but is reluctant to release a work he has already invested himself in. The bottom line is, does the agent plan to keep actively pitching the work? In the absence of that crucial intent, there's no good reason for the agent to hold you and your work in limbo, and you should arrange for a friendly release. Getting a new agent requires following the same process you used when getting your first agent.

It might not be your agent's fault that your work is unsold. Often it wouldn't have mattered who was representing it. Putting an unsold manuscript on the back burner for a year or so and working on something else might be the best move to make, instead of permanently burning your agent relationship. Many successful fiction writers were unable to sell the first manuscript(s) they wrote until after they became successful. There's no law that says your works have to be published in the order in which you wrote them.

Agent-jumping is tricky. It's not easy to get an agent in the first place, and agents may not see any reason to be enthusiastic about representing a work that your previous agent failed to sell. But if the work wasn't widely circulated or shown to the right editors, a new agent might see fresh opportunities or ways to fix what's broken. You should be clear with yourself about why you want to switch agents, or you are likely to encounter the same grievances all over again.

What Will Happen to Agents as a Category over the Next Several Years?

This question makes most agents uncomfortable, because trends are not favorable. As I see it, literary agents will continue to be as important as ever in the context of traditional publishing. Actually, their standing and purpose have never been at risk. The problem is that traditional publishing will continue to become a less friendly environment for writers and, by extension, their agents. Writers and agents are in the same beleaguered boat. Each year, more agencies will either close or merge to form larger agencies, and a diminishing number of new agents will enter the business. Those at greatest risk will be the boutique agencies that are most reliant on maintaining a fresh flow of new deals, as opposed to having the luxury of resting on their laurels. Publishers are acquiring fewer books and paying less for most of the books they still acquire. In order to survive, many boutique agencies will be forced to offer related fee-based services, such as editing, collaborating, and helping writers self-publish, in addition to commissionable services.

Do Agents Sell Everything They Represent?

Only if they represent very few projects. Agents usually know at the outset which projects are likely slam dunks and which are comparatively marginal. But this business is loaded with surprises; agents plan, and the process laughs at them. They hedge their bets by signing up more projects than they expect to actually get offers for. In fact, the ratio is probably less than 50/50 for the toughest categories, such as literary fiction. However, no bona fide agent will intentionally represent a project that he doesn't feel is viable, unless there are unseen motives or pressures to do so.

What's the Typical Agent's Sales Process and How Long Does It Take?

Velocity is an agent's and writer's friend. You would presumably prefer not to observe your own book-launch party from heaven, which probably happens more than you realize. (I'm assuming that all writers go to heaven, of course.) Usually, the agent will make a multiple submission, which means selecting approximately a dozen appropriate editors from distinct houses or divisions within the same house. Agents know which houses/divisions and which editors might be inclined to like the project in hand. The agent might make calls to prescreen or sell the project or might just go ahead and email it over and then follow up to see what the early response is.

Email has greatly altered the pitch process for agents. Until 1999 or so, almost all submissions were made in hardcopy. Agents had to run up large photocopying and delivery balances and had to allocate a lot of physical space for storing everything. Now everything tends to go by email, which makes it easier and cheaper to deal with.

Agents typically follow up for some kind of response from each of the editors in cycles of one to four weeks, depending on the project and other circumstances. However, editors can't make instant unilateral decisions without going through in-house protocols. An editor may like a project but be prevented from acquiring it by his colleagues for a variety of possible reasons, such as list redundancies or the sales department vetoes it.

The agent keeps the process from stalling by making subsequent submissions as needed. Often, the agent will use the rejections as a learning opportunity and encourage the client to revise the work accordingly. Sometimes it may be as simple as altering the title to something more compelling or clear. If/when a genuine offer is close at hand, the agent will attempt to provoke a competitive bidding process. If at least two publishers are eager to acquire the same work, the agent might hold a formal auction in which the competing houses are forced to blindly bid against one another until only one house remains standing. But don't get too excited; auctions are the exception, not the rule.

Sometimes an agent will have good reasons to give a specific editor an exclusive or preemptive opportunity to consider and make an offer on a particular project before anyone else. The agent will generally set a deadline by which a verbal deal needs to be made.

How long might all of this take before a verbal deal is in hand? For certain kinds of nonfiction, such as basic how-to books, within eight weeks the agent may have a deal or know there probably won't be a deal. Arcane nonfiction or fiction by unpublished writers might require a much longer time. A slow process doesn't necessarily mean the agent isn't doing the job; some projects compile many rejections over time before finding the right editor at the right publisher at the right time.

How Do Agents Find Their Clients?

Agents need clients in order to function. An agent without clients is like a playboy without girlfriends. Yet some agents seem to be elusive to the point of invisibility, at least from the potential client's point of view. Not all agents want or need new/more clients, so, yes, they will make themselves unavailable. Most agents, to varying degrees, are always looking for new product, which means they are looking for new clients. But follow the sequence of the last sentence: the word *product* precedes *client*, because it's the viability of the product that counts. Writers who write salable products will get agents and publishers. Don't forget that the industry and the reader are interested in the product first and the author second, if at all. Over time successful authors become interesting to their readers as people, but it doesn't start out that way. Of course, the author's ability to help promote her books forms a large part of how agents and publishers assess the value of the product.

Agents discover clients by responding to submissions and referrals; by attending conferences; by writing books or appearing in books; by proactively reaching out to experts and writers with ideas and inducements. Most agents are willing to scan and reject thousands of submissions a year in order to find a few dozen projects they feel confident about selling to publishers.

If You Get 20 Agent Rejections, Is It Unlikely You'll Get an Agent?

Don't answer the above question affirmatively or it will be your truth, and it shouldn't be. Of course, there is the little matter of talent or the lack thereof, and that can't be dismissed as unimportant. But let's get real: a lot of highly talented people live below the poverty line, and a lot of mediocre people are self-made millionaires. On average, unsuccessful people are no smarter or dumber than successful people. Simply being gifted is like being an unmined and uncut diamond. If you want to get published, scratch your way to the surface and struggle to the point of refinement. Countless others have and are, and they have the results to prove it. Success is the great equalizer because you don't have to be the best in order to reach the top. Corruption and nepotism are also perpetual factors, but they benefit only a small fraction of us. I assure you that some of the best-written manuscripts are, and will remain, unpublished simply because their authors did a poor job at trying to get them published. Conversely, some of the most mediocre manuscripts are, or will be, successfully published simply because their authors did a stellar job at getting them published. Hunger and determination frequently overcompensate for raw talent.

Agents aren't in lockstep. We tend to be specialized and often make dumb decisions.

Receiving 20 agent rejections might mean many things. Maybe you've been submitting your romance novel to sci-fi agents. Maybe those first 20 are over capacity and not taking new clients. Maybe you need to rewrite your pitch letter. Babe Ruth had many more strikeouts than hits, and two-thirds of the time Ted Williams didn't get past the batter's box.

How Do Agents Like to Work with Their Clients?

How do you like to work with your significant other, neighbors, children, bosses, and subordinates? Exactly — it depends on the people in question. There is no one way for agents to interact with their clients. Some agents are loquacious and some might be on the autism spectrum. However, there are certain universal professional protocols that should be expected and followed. You're entitled to know what your agent's plan and schedule for selling the work are. It's appropriate for you to know who your project has been submitted to and what the results are. If many weeks go by without any word, you should check in for news. If nothing is happening, you should determine if your agent has lost confidence and hasn't gotten around to telling you yet.

Good clients ask good questions and can discern good answers. Like, "What if I tweak the overview — will that change the way editors are seeing the project?" Or "How about I generate a list of 10 prestigious people who are likely to endorse and recommend the book?" These aren't really questions; they are proactive solutions. It may be on the agent to generate the deal, but the agent will move to the next project if a deal doesn't materialize. As a writer you don't have that luxury. You have the most to gain and the most to lose. Obviously, you don't want to be a nuisance and get in your agent's way or your own way, but there are many cooperative and constructive ways you can help overcome the challenge of getting your book published.

Is It Okay to Switch Agents?

Agent-hopping happens a lot, especially for writers who have already been published. Published writers are at an advantage because agents see them as proven commodities. Unpublished writers seeking to switch are often perceived as having been "fired" by their last agent; at any rate, they still haven't earned their first stripe.

When I hear from a published author who wants to change agents, the first thing I ask is, "Why?" Certain answers are reasonable, and others are alarm bells. I think it's okay if the writer expresses that it's simply not a mutually satisfying relationship. Of course, it's probably a bogus and evasive answer, but that's exactly why it's okay. I respect that the author just wants to move on without any annoying whining or backstabbing (we can always save that for later). An alarm bell rings when the author complains about low advances, low book sales, or lack of publisher support. The first thing that enters my mind is: could I have done better? This question is especially meaningful if I happen to respect the agent in question. Even if the author is a decent commodity, agents are wary of authors who are serial jilters or bigmouths.

What Kind of Client Do Agents Dislike?

That's a loaded question because it meshes business with personal. The real question is: what are the agent's priorities as a businessperson? It's theoretically possible that an agent might tend to release the clients she likes the most. Why would that happen? Because all the likability in the world can't compensate for a book that doesn't sell. If a likable client is dead weight, he's an endangered client. If an obnoxious client is sufficiently and reliably profitable, she's safe. If you are a superstar who generates the rent money, you can get away with behaving like Godzilla. No one will like you, but everyone will want a piece of you.

How Come Rejection Letters Are Generic, and Why Are There No Useful Comments?

Reading and evaluating manuscripts is very time-consuming and requires special expertise. It's impossible for an agent to dedicate any measure of his time to providing that level of service pro bono to the people he is rejecting. Any expectation to the contrary is naive, misguided, and unreasonable.

WRITE THE PERFECT QUERY LETTER

Jeff Herman and Deborah Herman

The query is a short letter of introduction to publishers or agents, encouraging them to request to see your fiction manuscript or nonfiction book proposal. It is a vital tool, often neglected by writers. If done correctly, it can help you avoid endless frustration and wasted effort. The query is the first hurdle of your individual marketing strategy. If you can leap over it successfully, you're well on your way to a sale.

The query letter is your calling card. For every book that makes it to the shelves, thousands of worthy manuscripts, proposals, and ideas are knocked out of the running by poor presentation or inadequate marketing strategies. Don't forget that the book you want to sell is a product that must be packaged correctly to stand above the competition.

A query letter asks the prospective publisher or agent if she would like to see more about the proposed idea. If your book is fiction, you should indicate that a manuscript or sample chapters are available on request. If nonfiction, you should offer to send a proposal and, if you have them, sample chapters.

The query is your first contact with the prospective buyer of your book. To ensure that it's not your last, avoid common mistakes. The letter should be concise and well written. You shouldn't try to impress the reader with your mastery of all words over three syllables. Instead, concentrate on a clear and to-the-point presentation with no fluff.

Think of the letter as an advertisement. You want to make a sale of a product, and you have very limited space and time in which to reach this goal.

The letter should be only one page long, if possible. It will form the basis of a query package that will include supporting materials. Don't waste words in the letter describing material that can be included separately. Your goal is to pique the interest of an agent or editor who has very little time and probably very little patience. You want to entice her to keep reading and ask you for more.

The query package can include a short résumé, media clippings, or other favorable documents. Do not get carried away, or your package will quickly come to resemble junk mail. If you're sending a hardcopy package, include a self-addressed stamped envelope (SASE) with enough postage to return your entire package. This will be particularly appreciated by smaller publishing houses and independent agents.

For fiction writers, a short (one- to five-page), double-spaced synopsis of the manuscript will be helpful and appropriate.

Do not waste money and defeat the purpose of the query by sending an unsolicited manuscript. Agents and editors may be turned off by receiving manuscripts of 1,000-plus pages that were uninvited and that are not even remotely relevant to what they do. Though digital submissions obviously don't consume physical space, nobody enjoys a cluttered, overburdened inbox.

The query follows a simple four-part format (which can be reworked according to your individual preferences):

- Lead
- Supporting material/persuasion
- Biography
- Conclusion/pitch

Your Lead Is Your Hook

The lead can either catch the agent's or editor's attention or turn him off completely. Some writers think getting someone's attention in a short space means having to do something dramatic. Agents and editors appreciate cleverness, but too much contrived writing can work against you. Opt instead for clear conveyance of thoroughly developed ideas, and get right to the point.

Of course, you don't want to be boring and stuffy in the interest of factual presentation. You'll need to determine what is most important about the book you're trying to sell, and write your letter accordingly.

You can begin with a lead similar to what you'd use to grab the reader in an article or a book chapter. You can use an anecdote, a statement of facts, a question, a comparison, or whatever you believe will be most powerful.

You may want to rely on the journalistic technique of the inverted pyramid. This means that you begin with the strongest material and save the details for later in the letter. Don't start slowly and expect to pick up momentum as you proceed. It will be too late.

Do not begin a query letter like this: "I have sent this idea to 20 agents/publishers, none of whom think it will work. I just know you'll be different, enlightened, and insightful and will give it full consideration." There is no room for negatives in a sales pitch. Focus only on positives — unless you can turn negatives to your advantage.

Some writers make the mistake of writing about the book's potential in the first paragraph without ever stating its actual idea or theme. Remember, your letter may never be read beyond the lead, so make that first paragraph your hook.

Avoid bad jokes, clichés, unsubstantiated claims, and dictionary definitions. Don't be condescending; agents and editors have egos, too, and have power over your destiny as a writer.

Supporting Material: Be Persuasive

If you are selling a nonfiction book, you may want to include a brief summary of hard evidence, gleaned from research that will support the merit of your idea. This is where you convince the agent or editor that your book should exist. This is more important for nonfiction than it is for fiction, where the style and storytelling ability are paramount. Nonfiction writers must focus on selling their topic and their credentials.

You should include a few lines showing the agent or editor what the publishing house will gain from the project. Publishers are not charitable institutions; they want to know how they can get the greatest return on their investment. If you have brilliant marketing ideas or know of a well-defined market for your book where sales will be guaranteed, include this rather than other descriptive material.

In rereading your letter, make sure you have shown that you understand your own idea thoroughly. If it appears half-baked, the agents and editors won't want to invest time fleshing out your thoughts. Exude confidence so that the agent or editor will have faith in your ability to carry out the job.

In nonfiction queries, you can include a separate table of contents and brief chapter abstracts. Otherwise, that material can wait for the book proposal.

Your Biography: No Place for Modesty

In the biographical portion of your letter, toot your own horn, but in a carefully calculated, persuasive fashion. Your story of winning the third-grade writing competition (it was then that you knew you wanted to be a world-famous writer!) should be saved for the documentary done on your life after you reach your goal.

In the query, all you want to include are the most important and relevant credentials that will support the sale of your book. You can include, as a separate part of the package, a résumé or biography that will elaborate further.

The separate résumé should list all relevant and recent experiences that support your ability to write the book. Unless you're fairly young, your listing of academic accomplishments should start after high school. Don't overlook hobbies or non-job-related activities if they correspond to your book story or topic. Those experiences are often more valuable than academic achievements.

Other information to include: any impressive print clippings about you; a list of your broadcast interviews and speaking appearances; and copies of articles and reviews about any books you may have written. This information can never hurt your chances and could make the difference in your favor.

There is no room for humility or modesty in the query letter and résumé. When corporations sell toothpaste, they list the product's best attributes and create excitement about the product. If you can't find some way to make yourself exciting as an author, you'd better rethink your career.

Here's the Pitch

At the close of your letter, ask for the sale. This requires a positive and confident conclusion with a phrase such as "I look forward to your speedy response." Such phrases as "I hope" and "I think you will like my book" sound too insecure. This is the part of the letter where you go for the kill.

Be sure to thank the reader for his or her attention in your final sentence.

Finishing Touches

When you're finished, reread and edit your query letter. Cut out any extraneous information that dilutes the strength of your arguments. Make the letter as polished as possible so that the agent or editor will be impressed with you, as well as with your idea. Don't ruin your chances by appearing careless; make certain your letter is not peppered with typos and misspellings. If you don't show pride in your work, you'll create a self-fulfilling prophecy: the agent or editor will take you no more seriously than you take yourself.

Aesthetics are important. If you were pitching a business deal to a corporation, you would want to present yourself in conservative dress, with an air of professionalism. In the writing business, you may never have face-to-face contact with the people who will determine your future. Therefore, your query package is your representative.

For hardcopy submissions, you should invest in a state-of-the-art letterhead — with a logo! — to create an impression of pride, confidence, and professionalism. White, cream, and ivory paper are all acceptable, but you should use only black ink for printing the letter. Anything else looks amateurish. If agents or editors receive a query letter on yellowed paper that looks as if it's been lying around for 20 years, they will wonder if the person sending the letter is a has-been or a never-was.

For electronic submissions, keep your email formatting simple and readable, and be sure to include all your contact information. Also, most agents' websites include detailed guidelines for electronic submissions. Be sure to adhere to them, or your work might be rejected solely because you have not followed the rules.

Don't sabotage yourself by letting your need for instant approval get the best of you. Don't call agents or editors. You have invited them to respond, so be patient. Then prepare yourself for possible rejection. It often takes many nos to get a yes.

One more note: This is a tough business for anyone — and it's especially so for greenhorns. Hang in there.

Query Letter Tips

If you have spent any time at all in this business, the term *query letter* is probably as familiar to you as the back of your hand. Yet no matter how many courses you've attended and books you've read about this important part of the process, you may still feel inadequate when you try to write one that sizzles. If it's any consolation, you're far from being alone in your uncertainties. The purpose of the query letter is to formally introduce your work and yourself to potential agents and editors. The immediate goal is to motivate them to promptly request a look at your work, or at least a portion of it.

In effect, the letter serves as the writer's first hurdle. It's a relatively painless way for agents and editors to screen out unwanted submissions without the added burden of having to manhandle a deluge of unwanted manuscripts. They are more relaxed if their inboxes are filled with 50 unanswered queries as opposed to 50 uninvited 1,000-page manuscripts. The query is a very effective way to control the quality and quantity of the manuscripts that get into the office. And that's why you have to write good ones.

The term *query letter* is part of the lexicon and jargon of the publishing business. This term isn't used in any other industry. I assume it has ancient origins. I can conjure up the image of an English gentleman with a fluffy quill pen composing a most civilized letter to a prospective publisher for the purpose of asking for his work to be read and, perchance, published. Our environments may change, but the nature of our ambitions remains the same.

Let's get contemporary. Whenever you hear the term *query letter*, you should say to yourself "pitch" or "sales" letter. Because that's what it is. You need the letter to sell.

Here are a few more tips to make your query letter the best it can be.

- ***Don't be long-winded.*** Agents/editors receive lots of these things, and they want to mow through them as swiftly as possible. Ideally, the letter should be a single page with short paragraphs. (I must admit I've seen good ones that are longer than a page.) If you lose your reader, you've lost your opportunity.

- *Get to the point; don't pontificate.* Too many letters go off on irrelevant detours, which makes it difficult for the agent/editor to determine what's actually for sale — other than the writer's soapbox.

- *If sending your letter on hardcopy, make it attractive.* When making a first impression, the subliminal impact of aesthetics cannot be overestimated. Use high-quality stationery and typeface. The essence of your words is paramount, but cheap paper and poor print quality will only diminish your impact.

- *Don't say anything negative about yourself or your attempts to get published.* Everyone appreciates victims when it's time to make charitable donations, but not when it's time to make a profit. It's better if you can make editors/agents think that you have to fight them off.

Why Not Simply Submit Your Manuscript?

You might be wondering why you can't bypass the query hurdle and simply submit your manuscript. You may do that — and no one can litigate against you. But if you submit an unsolicited manuscript to a publisher, it's more likely to end up in the so-called slush pile and may never get a fair reading. If it's sent to an agent, nothing negative may come of it. However, most agents prefer to receive a query first.

Sending unsolicited nonfiction book proposals is in the gray zone. Proposals are much more manageable than entire manuscripts, so editors/agents may not particularly mind.

But you may want to avoid wasting time — and, in the case of hardcopy submissions, money — sending unwanted proposals. After all, the query is also an opportunity for you to screen out those who clearly have no interest in your subject.

Also, you shouldn't be overly loose with your ideas and concepts. After all, you can't protect ideas in the context of writing and publishing. You don't want to become overly cautious, but neither do you want to be a runaway train. Focus on pitching your ideas to those who are genuinely qualified to help you manifest them.

These pointers, in combination with the other good information in this book and all the other available resources, should at least give you a solid background for creating a query letter that makes a lasting impression.

For Deborah Herman's biography, see page 53.

YOU (MIGHT) BELONG IN THE SLUSH PILE (OR ELSEWHERE)

Jeff Herman

It's not you per se who might belong in the slush pile; it's your written product. Until about 12 years ago slush piles were almost entirely physical, whereas now they probably exist about 80 percent "in the cloud." Perhaps the term should be changed to *slush cloud*, which sounds much tastier than a *slush pile*. My question is: what are publishers doing with all the extra physical space that was formerly used for slush piles? But let me back up.

Most traditional publishers have a written policy that they won't accept or consider unagented/unsolicited submissions. If not submitted by a literary agent, the work is unagented. If no one at the company invited you to submit your work, it is unsolicited. If your work falls into either category, you're an "Un." In the context of publishing, a Un is a noncitizen or an untouchable. That sounds harsh, but it's the most accurate way to paint it, and it's virtually every writer's starting point. No one is born with or inherits a book deal. The good news is that it's entirely within every writer's power to self-mutate from being a Un to becoming an agented or solicited writer. You most likely already believe that, or you wouldn't be reading this book.

So what happens to Uns' submissions? They get returned, thrown out, or placed in the slush pile with countless other Uns' submissions.

Why does this policy exist? Because for every book traditionally published there are more than 1,000 manuscripts trying to be published at the same point in time. Publishers don't have the in-house staff to screen what's submitted to find the fraction of a percentage they can publish. Instead, they make direct solicitations for writers and experts they might want, or they rely on the several-hundred-strong literary agency community to do the screening and essentially nominate what's publishable.

What happens to the slush pile? That's an interesting question for which I have no scientifically proven answers, but I do have true anecdotes. Every once in a while, a low-level person in the editorial hierarchy will volunteer without prodding to wander through the slush pile and randomly select something to read, and occasionally they find a gem. Excellent books have been discovered in the slush pile and successfully published, and it will keep on happening. But trying to get published through the slush is like trying to pay for college with lottery scratch-offs.

A Random Prediction

Thousands of years from now, a new species or civilization will discover ancient manuscripts and digital archives within the ruins of a once-great metropolis that had been abruptly destroyed by a surging sea. They will have no context for any of it and will ponder and debate its significance at the highest levels. Unknown to them, they will have unsealed a massive slush pile, the unpublished manuscripts written with love and passion by thousands of ordinary people from a lost and little-understood society.

A museum will be constructed for the purpose of housing and displaying the wit, wisdom, and dysfunctions of this period from Earth's beleaguered past. In one fell swoop, an entire slush pile will finally be published.

A True Story

Approximately 20 years ago, there lived a man in Florida who was unable to get an agent or a publisher for his fiction manuscript. Then he had an idea. He was an admirer of a Pulitzer Prize–winning novel named *The Yearling*. The work had been published more than 50 years earlier, sold millions of copies, and was made into a feature film starring a young Gregory Peck. Though no longer a popular book, it still sold tens of thousands of copies each year as a classic reprint.

Our hero repurposed the book into a raw manuscript and changed its title and the author's name. Only someone familiar with the classic book would have recognized the manuscript as blatant plagiarism. He then proceeded to make unagented and unsolicited submissions of "his" work to all the usual publishing prospects. What happened next was easily predictable. In some cases, he never received any response, ever. Some publishers at least returned the manuscript, clearly unread, with an unsigned letter stating that unagented/unsolicited submissions would not be considered, ever.

Refreshingly, he actually received some genuine rejection letters seemingly written by entry-level editors and interns. The letters were brief and dismissive and expressed no appreciation for the work's merits or encouragement for it prospects. One of these rejection letters was from the same publisher that was still profitably publishing *The Yearling*.

What Does the Above Story Tell Us?

Each of my rejection letters includes a job application for my favorite fast-food establishment (if you're not sure whether I'm kidding, try me: submissions@jeffherman.com). Frankly, considering the lack of respect and encouragement that struggling authors tend to experience, such an attachment wouldn't be out of place.

Even though this story is 20 years old, it's no less telling today. At first blush, we see that a bestselling, Pulitzer Prize–winning novel that was made into a major motion picture couldn't even get itself arrested. What's unseen is what's most crucial, which is that the work's merits were worthless in the absence of genuine *access*. Without access, you don't really exist and the game can't begin. The dude didn't have an agent, was unsolicited, and didn't do anything to get quality access. The negative outcome is unsurprising for those who have been to the rodeo.

Publishers have surrounded themselves with firewalls to avoid being trampled by the relentless surge of eager writers. Having an agent is tantamount to a VIP bypass. For editors it's a safe assumption that if agented it merits *access*.

What If You Can't Get an Agent? Join the Battle of the Unsl

If you bang your head against a publisher's firewall, the wall won't move but your head will. Though it makes no sense to throw yourself against the wall, it's wise to remember that all walls have inherent limitations that can be exploited.

What if you can't get an agent? You are far from alone and are in excellent company; many superb writers don't connect with agents when first starting out. Fortunately, there are ways to get access to editors and get published even if you don't have an agent. Here's a big secret: publishers actually will consider unagented/unsolicited submissions, but they don't want you to know that. In fact, they may not even know it. Remember this: the rule exists for their convenience, not yours. If you rigidly follow their rules, you're only serving them, not yourself. It's reasonable for you to consider ways to bypass the rule. Ironically, your success will also be the publisher's success; it's a win-win.

Guess what? Being published isn't only for the best writers, though it's invariably for those who are the best at getting published. Writing and getting your writing published are distinct endeavors. No one can keep you from writing, but you can be prevented from traditionally publishing your work. Guess what? Mediocre writers are frequently published while countless überwriters are left stranded at the gate. How does that happen? Keep reading.

1. No agent? No problem. Appoint yourself as your agent, and be your only client. You can even sign a contract with yourself and assign a 15 percent commission to your doppelgänger agent. What does this mean? Learn what an agent needs to know by finding out who publishes books like yours and who the appropriate editors are at each of those houses. You can do that by using this book, researching on Amazon and bookstore shelves, and reading the acknowledgments sections of similar books for editor names.

2. Cold-call. Another trick is to cold-call publishers asking to be routed to the editorial departments of the divisions/programs in question. Once a live voice says something like "Editorial," you'll have reached your destination. The next step is to cajole this person into giving you the name of an editor for romance titles or for whatever category your manuscript falls into. Accumulating relevant editor names will enable you to bypass the slush pile. Actually submitting your work to a real person who helps make crucial decisions is a tremendous upgrade from sending it to "Editorial Department" or "Submissions." Your work needs to be directed to an actual person with the genuine clout to acquire books. If the editor is interested in your work, you will enter the exalted "solicited" zone, which means you have avoided the knee-jerk deportation to the slush graveyard. You will have achieved access…

3. Know what editors do. You can't deeply understand what someone else does if you have never done it yourself. But gaining superficial knowledge about their basic functions and needs is immensely better than complete ignorance or misinformation. Obviously, editors edit, but not as much as you might think or as much as they might prefer. An accurate job description for today's editor could easily be Product Acquisition and Management. Notice that the word *editor* doesn't even appear? That's because they are not being paid or rewarded for their editing skills. In fact, those secondary tasks are often outsourced (to the chagrin of fussy authors). Book publishers no longer provide the intense fact-checking and word-smashing that urbane publications like the *New Yorker* are still famous for. In fact, some unsatisfied authors use their own funds to hire editors to go beyond what their publishers will do.

An editor's career track is tied to the success of the books that he acquires, not that he edits. Critically acclaimed books that are economic failures are not good for an editor's career unless they also attract commercially successful books to the editor. An editor's career success will match the commercial success of the books he or she acquires, regardless of the books' literary or cultural standing.

What's a successful career for an editor? Frankly, I can't imagine how most of them manage to support a full household in the Northeast unless both spouses are gainfully employed or there's a trust fund. Many years of toil are required before decent six-figure incomes are attained. In 1981 my entry-level publishing job paid $5 per hour, which was okay for a 22-year-old at that time. That same job today probably pays about $15 per hour, but I don't think the 300 percent increase has kept pace with New York's inflation rate. For instance, back then TV was still free and landlines were the only option, at less than $20 per month.

Let's keep our eyes on the ball. Editors need to acquire good product (books) in order to justify their employment. Your job as a writer is to give it to them. If you succeed at giving them what they need, you will get what you want (a deal). It's really that simple, yet too many writers don't seem to get it. They approach editors on their knees asking for mercy and attention, which is also how they confront agents. That's not pitching; that's begging, and it's unappealing. Don't be a beggar; be a giver and a maker. Initiate the process by communicating your intent and power to make everyone else very happy.

You don't have to actually believe it any more than you believed you were really Juliet when you portrayed her in the school play. When you pitch your work, what you feel about yourself doesn't have to match how you want other people to feel about you. In fact, how other people see you might be more accurate than how you see yourself. No one wants losers for clients or authors. Don't ever apologize for being a writer who wants to get published; your apology might be accepted, but your manuscript won't be. When pitching your work, please believe you are offering others a generous opportunity to share your inevitable success. I have been pitched thousands of times by phone, in person, and through written expression. Arrogance, delusions of grandeur, and an unwarranted sense of entitlement are powerful turnoffs. But presenting a negative persona about one's own abilities and prospects can be even worse. Between these extremes there's plenty of space for a compelling blend of humility and confidence.

Editors can't make unilateral decisions about what to acquire or how big an advance to offer. When they discover something they want, they are required to sell and defend it at so-called editorial meetings. Other editors may act like the devil's advocate, testing the editor's resolve and whether she has fully considered the risks. Strong editors can usually get what they want, whereas marginal editors often don't. An editor who mostly fails to get green-lighted should be calling the headhunters, because he's already been marked for failure by his peers.

Also at these meetings is the in-house sales staff. If they say, "We can't sell it," it's game-over for that book. If they call their contacts at Barnes & Noble and Amazon and they say, "We won't order it," it's game-over for that book. If someone calls one of the company's boss-people, and she says, "I don't care what anyone else says, I want that book," it's game-on. So what can you do? Hedge your bet by learning how to impersonate the boss's phone voice and make sure she's heard loud and clear. If you can pull off a con like that, there's no reason you can't also generate a bestseller. Seriously, make sure you give editors (and your agent, if you have one) all the ammunition they might need to get the job done on your behalf.

4. *Know what publishers do.* If you have ever seen a book, then you know what publishers do. More specifically, they curate editorial products that the marketplace will presumably support; they produce them into consumable formats; they make them appealing; they get them into the hands of reviewers, media contacts, and key bloggers; they produce print and digital catalogs for distribution to retail accounts and employ salespeople to generate orders; they maintain inventory, fulfill orders, issue invoices, and manage the accounting; they pay authors varying percentages of revenues received; they sell subsidiary rights; they do what few authors can do by themselves. If I left anything out, *I'm sorry.* You go ahead and spend your spring weekends writing all of this not knowing if anyone will even bother to read it. IS ANYONE ACTUALLY READING THIS? Prove it: jeff@jeffherman.com.

Perhaps the most significant value that traditional publishers provide is credibility. Everyone in the business and throughout the supply chain knows that each traditionally published book is like a lucky sperm, or maybe we should say a "sperm with merit." Forget about sperms. For every book that publishers choose, at least 1,000 have been rejected. And publishing a book isn't cheap. Separate from the advance, the typical book costs at least $25,000 of a publisher's overall resources; much more if large inventories are called for.

By the way, having an agent shouldn't excuse you from learning everything you can about how the business works. The more you know, the better you will be at helping your agent and yourself to get the best results possible.

I am confident that this runaway essay has given everything that was promised and more. The journey continues.

THE KNOCKOUT NONFICTION BOOK PROPOSAL

Jeff Herman

The quality of your nonfiction book proposal will invariably make the difference between success and failure. Before agents and publishers will accept a work of fiction (especially from a newer writer), they require a complete manuscript. But nonfiction projects are different: a proposal alone can do the trick. This is what makes nonfiction writing a much less speculative and often more lucrative endeavor (relatively speaking) than fiction writing.

You may devote five years of long evenings to writing a 1,000-page fiction manuscript, only to receive a thick pile of computer-generated rejections. Clearly, writing nonfiction doesn't entail the same risks, for the simple reason that you don't have to write an entire manuscript before you can begin pitching it. On the other hand, writing fiction is often an emotionally driven endeavor in which rewards are gained through the act of writing and are not necessarily based on rational, practical considerations. Interestingly, many successful nonfiction writers fantasize about being fiction writers.

As you'll learn, the proposal's structure, contents, and size can vary substantially, and it's up to you to decide the best format for your purposes. Still, the guidelines given here serve as excellent general parameters.

Appearance Counts

Much of what follows becomes less relevant, or perhaps not possible, if all your material is conveyed solely through digital transmission. However, even digital items should look as good as possible, and many people greatly prefer to print a hardcopy to read from. In my opinion, physicality is still king (or queen) when it comes to making best impressions.

- Your proposal should be printed in black ink on clean, letter-sized (8½" x 11"), white paper.
- Letter-quality printing is by far the best. Make sure the toner or ink cartridge is fresh and that all photocopies are dark and clear enough to be read easily. Publishing is an image-driven business, and you will be judged, perhaps unconsciously, on the physical and aesthetic merits of your submission.

- Always double-space, or you can virtually guarantee reader antagonism — eye-strain makes people cranky.
- Make sure your proposal appears fresh and new and hasn't been dog-eared, marked up, or abused by previous readers. No editor will be favorably disposed if she thinks that everyone else on the block has already sent you packing. You want editors to think you have lots of other places to go, not nowhere else.
- Contrary to common practice in other industries, editors prefer not to receive bound proposals. If an editor likes your proposal, she will want to photocopy it for her colleagues, and your binding will only be in the way. If you want to keep the material together and neat, use a binder clip; if it's a lengthy proposal, clip each section together separately. Of course, email submissions negate the above issues.

Proposal Contents

A nonfiction proposal should include the following elements, each of which is explained below:

- Title page
- Overview
- Biographical section
- Marketing section
- Author platform
- Competition section
- Promotion section
- Chapter outline
- Sample chapters

Title page. The title page should be the easiest part, but it can also be the most important, since, like your face when you meet someone, it's what is seen first.

Try to think of a title that's attractive and effectively communicates your book's concept. A descriptive subtitle, following a catchy title, can help you achieve both goals.

It's very important that your title and subtitle relate to the book's subject, or an editor might make an inaccurate judgment about your book's focus and automatically dismiss it. For instance, if you're proposing a book about gardening, don't title it *The Greening of America*.

Examples of titles that have worked very well are:

How to Win Friends and Influence People by Dale Carnegie
Think and Grow Rich by Napoleon Hill

Baby and Child Care by Dr. Benjamin Spock

How to Swim with the Sharks without Being Eaten Alive by Harvey Mackay

And, yes, there are notable exceptions: an improbable title that went on to become a perennial success is *What Color Is Your Parachute?* by Richard Bolles. Sure, you may gain confidence and a sense of freedom from such exceptional instances. By all means let your imagination graze during the brainstorming stage.

However, don't bet on the success of an arbitrarily conceived title that has nothing at all to do with the book's essential concept or reader appeal.

A title should be stimulating and, when appropriate, upbeat and optimistic. If your subject is an important historic or current event, the title should be dramatic. If a biography, the title should capture something personal (or even controversial) about the subject. Many good books have been handicapped by poorly conceived titles, and many poor books have been catapulted to success by good titles. A good title is good advertising. Procter & Gamble, for instance, spends thousands of worker hours creating seductive names for its endless array of soap-based products.

The title you choose is referred to as the "working title." Most likely, the book will have a different title when published. There are two reasons for this:

1. A more appropriate and/or arresting title may evolve with time.
2. The publisher has final contractual discretion over the title (as well as over a lot of other things).

The title page should contain only the title, plus your name, address, telephone number, and email address — and the name, address, and phone number of your agent, if you have one. The title page should be neatly and attractively spaced. Eye-catching and tasteful computer graphics and display-type fonts can contribute to the overall aesthetic appeal.

Overview. The overview portion of the proposal is a terse statement (one to three pages) of your overall concept and mission. It sets the stage for what's to follow. Short, concise paragraphs are usually best.

Biographical section. This is where you sell yourself. This section tells who you are and why you're the ideal person to write this book. You should highlight all your relevant experience, including media and public-speaking appearances, and list previous books, articles, or both, published by or about you. Self-flattery is appropriate — so long as you're telling the truth. Many writers prefer to slip into the third person here, to avoid the appearance of egomania.

Marketing section. This is where you justify the book's existence from a commercial perspective. Who will buy it? For instance, if you're proposing a book on sales, state the number of people who earn their living through sales; point out that thousands of large and small companies are sales dependent and spend large sums on sales training, and that all sales professionals are perpetually hungry for fresh, innovative sales books.

Don't just say something like "My book is for adult women, and there are more than 50 million adult women in America." You have to be much more demographically sophisticated than that.

Author platform. The platform has become a crucial piece of the proposal in recent years. It's expected that as a minimum the author is sufficiently savvy about social media to have a large digital network of like-minded "friends" who can be tapped to purchase the book. It's all about the number of relevant people ("communities") you can access, and the expectation that they will either buy your book or at least tell others about it ("viral marketing"). Mention the number of contacts you have through social media, as well as subscribers to your newsletter or professional services, and be as specific as possible about the numbers who visit your website.

Competition section. To the uninitiated, this section may appear to be a setup to self-destruction. However, if handled strategically, and assuming you have a fresh concept, this section wins you points rather than undermining your case.

The competition section is where you describe major published titles with concepts comparable to yours. If you're familiar with your subject, you'll probably know those titles by heart; you may have even read most or all of them. If you're not certain, just check Amazon or AbeBooks, where pretty much anything ever published is listed. If the titles in question are only available through "resellers," and not the original publishers, they are most likely out of print. Don't list everything published on your subject — that could require a book in itself. Just describe the leading half dozen titles or so (backlist classics, as well as recent books) and *explain why yours will be different*.

Getting back to the sales-book example, there is no shortage of good sales books. There's a reason for that — a big market exists for sales books. You can turn that to your advantage by emphasizing the public's substantial, insatiable demand for sales books. Your book will feed that demand with its unique and innovative sales-success program. Salespeople and companies dependent on sales are always looking for new ways to enhance sales skills (it's okay to reiterate key points).

Promotion section. Here you suggest possible ways to promote and market the book. Sometimes this section is unnecessary. It depends on your subject and on what, if any, realistic promotional prospects exist.

If you're proposing a specialized academic book such as *The Mating Habits of Octopi*, the market is a relatively limited one, and elaborate promotions would be wasteful. But if you're proposing a popularly oriented relationship book along the lines of *The Endless Orgasm in One Easy Lesson*, the promotional possibilities are also endless. They would include most major electronic broadcast and print media outlets, advertising, maybe even some weird contests.

You want to guide the publisher toward seeing realistic ways to publicize the book.

Chapter outline. This is the meat of the proposal. Here's where you finally tell what's going to be in the book. Each chapter should be tentatively titled and clearly abstracted.

Some successful proposals have fewer than 100 words per abstracted chapter; others have several hundred words per chapter. Sometimes the length varies from chapter to chapter. There are no hard-and-fast rules here; it's the dealer's choice. Sometimes less is more; at other times a too-brief outline inadequately represents the project.

At their best, the chapter abstracts read like mini-chapters — as opposed to stating "I will do…and I will show…" Visualize the trailer for a forthcoming movie; that's the tantalizing effect you want to create.

Also, it's a good idea to preface the outline with a table of contents. This way, the editor can see your entire road map at the outset.

Sample chapters. Sample chapters are optional. A strong, well-developed proposal will often be enough. However, especially if you're a first-time writer, one or more sample chapters will give you an opportunity to show your stuff and will help dissolve an editor's concerns about your ability to actually write the book, thereby increasing the odds that you'll receive an offer — and you'll probably increase the size of the advance, too.

Nonfiction writers are often wary of investing time to write sample chapters since they view the proposal as a way of avoiding speculative writing. But this can be a short-sighted view; a single sample chapter can make the difference between selling and not selling a marginal proposal. Occasionally, a publisher will request that one or two sample chapters be written before he makes a decision about a particular project. If the publisher seems to have a real interest, writing the sample material is definitely worth the author's time, and the full package can then be shown to additional prospects, too.

Many editors say that they look for reasons to reject books and that being on the fence is a valid reason for rejecting a project. To be sure, there are cases where sample chapters have tilted a proposal on the verge of rejection right back onto the playing field!

Keep in mind that the publisher is speculating that you can and will write the book upon contract. A sample chapter will go far to reduce the publisher's concerns about your ability to deliver a quality work beyond the proposal stage.

What Else?

There are a variety of materials you may wish to attach to the proposal to further bolster your cause. These include:

- Laudatory letters and comments about you
- Laudatory publicity about you
- A headshot (but not if you look like the Fly, unless you're proposing a humor book or a nature book)
- Copies of published articles you've written
- Videos of TV or speaking appearances
- Any and all information that builds you up in a relevant way, but be organized about it — don't create a disheveled, unruly package

Length

The average proposal is probably between 15 and 30 double-spaced pages, and the typical sample chapter an additional 10 to 20 double-spaced pages. But sometimes proposals reach 100 pages, and other times they're 5 pages in total. Extensive proposals are not a handicap.

Whatever it takes!

DUMB-ASS RANDOM QUESTIONS & ANSWERS

Jeff Herman

By being snarky, I bet I got your attention. And now that I have it, hold on to your hat, because there's more to know. By the way, did your grade-school teachers ever say, "There's no such thing as a stupid question," before asking if there were any questions? Well, they were wrong. I've attended a lot of writers' conferences and have entertained many stupid questions. However, I tended to hear the same stupid questions over and over again. It finally dawned on me that a large percentage of writers had the same stupid questions. Besides, where do we draw the line between a stupid and a smart question, and who gets to decide? I came to the decision that stupid isn't bad, but choosing to remain stupid might be. And I concede it's kind of stupid for me to think about stuff like this with such intensity.

What Is an Advance?

The advance is the money that a traditional publisher gives you in exchange for granting them the exclusive right to publish your book. Unless you breach the terms of the publisher's contract, you never have to return the advance, even if your book sells only 3 copies. However, all royalty income will be charged against the advance, so you won't see any more money until your royalties (see below) surpass the advance.

How Are Advances Determined?

The amount of the advance is roughly determined by the publisher's best estimation of how many copies and subsidiary rights they can sell within the first year of publication. Presidential aspirant Hillary Clinton can easily command many millions of dollars as a single advance, because the publisher can count on making a lot of money by publishing her book. At the other extreme, your obscure neighbor Jim James will probably be ecstatic to receive a more typical $5,000 advance for his recipe book about ways to boil water.

What Are Royalties?

Traditional publishers pay their authors a percentage of the book's revenues. Many variables determine the royalty percentage, and publishers don't all offer the same structure. However, the following structure is accurate more than half the time: Hardcovers start at 10 percent of the listed retail price and escalate to 15 percent after 15,000 copies are sold. Paperbacks are usually fixed at 7.5 percent of the list price. However, many retailers are able to force publishers into granting them better than 50 percent discounts. These are known as "high-discount" sales, and every book contract contains fine print allowing the publisher to pay a significantly reduced royalty against copies sold at high discount. Refusing to grant the high discount often means losing the sale and the royalty altogether. The lower royalty is "justified" because the publisher's profit margin is supposedly also reduced. You or your agent can negotiate these kinds of contingencies to a point but won't be able to entirely negate them.

Most independent presses pay royalties on the basis of "net" receipts, which means what the publisher receives from the bookstore. Most of the time, wholesalers, bookstores, and other retailers pay publishers around 50 percent of the list price for print books. However, the independent presses usually manage to equalize the royalty situation for their authors by simply doubling the royalty percentages. For instance, whereas a list royalty might be 7.5 percent, a net royalty might be 15 percent.

Paperback originals are much more common now than they were in the past. Publishers will only issue a hardcover edition if confident about selling a requisite number of units. Library sales were much more robust in the past, and libraries greatly preferred hardcovers because they were more durable. Hardcover profit margins are much higher than those for paperbacks, but only some books can command a $30+ list price, and no one wants to end up losing more revenues than were generated. For obvious reasons, paperbacks sell many more copies, and most hardcovers are converted to paperback after the first year anyway, unless they do not have good sales, in which case they may simply disappear from print without ever migrating to paperback.

Digital sales have surged over the past few years and represent a large percentage of overall sales. However, the rapid growth seems to be leveling off lately, though I'm not sure anyone knows why. It may simply be that most readers who prefer digital jumped on the bandwagon all at once. In any case, authors tend to receive 25 percent of the publisher's net earnings from each digital sale.

What Happens after You Deliver Your Finished Manuscript to Your Publisher?

First, congratulations for having a traditional publishing deal and for meeting your deadline. Your publisher will take 30 to 60 days to have someone read the manuscript and make all kinds of suggestions and demands about what to revise or add. You get to decide if you want to make the suggested changes or if you want to protest them. It's okay to disagree, but unless you convince your publisher to see it your way, by contract it's their way or the highway and you may have to return the advance. The work isn't considered to be accepted until the publisher says so, at which point you'll get another advance payment. In my long experience, serious editorial grievances between authors and publishers are rare.

Next, the manuscript goes into production (including line editing/copyediting, type-setting, and proofreading), which takes several months and is like what happens to a cow that's repurposed into a sirloin steak, except nothing gets killed and rendered. Your publisher will consult with you about cover and title ideas. They get final say, though a consensus is greatly preferred. Then the book is posted in the frontlist of the publisher's catalog (print or digital), which goes to all booksellers.

Will the Publisher Promote Your Book?

If you mean will they pay to send you on a multicity or even a uni-city media tour, the answer is usually no. Every traditional publisher has in-house publicity and marketing departments that will, to varying degrees, try to get you interviewed by relevant media outlets and send the book to prospective reviewers and bloggers. But here's a sobering fact: Fortune 500 companies like Procter & Gamble pay their in-house sales and marketing professionals healthy six-figure incomes, and many of them have MBAs from the top programs. This isn't a model that publishers can even remotely afford to follow. Though talented people work for the publishers, the in-house staffs are small and most titles are neglected. The small number of books that received the biggest advances will consume the most attention, because the publisher needs to recover its relatively huge investments in those titles. In fact, the publisher might even pay to outsource some of the marketing to help maximize sales.

It's wise for most authors to learn how to be a self-marketing machine. One of the attributes that probably made you attractive to your publisher in the first place was the fact that you wouldn't be dependent upon them to drive sales.

There are significant differences between the ways corporate houses and smaller houses market their books. Large publishers can afford to lose money a lot of the time, thanks to their huge backlist catalogs. Smaller presses lack that kind of cash cushion and must be doubly certain that every dollar spent is likely to generate more than $1 in return. They need to make every book as successful as possible, but they can't afford placing big bets.

What's an "Author Platform"?

Platform is one of the more recent terms to enter the publishing world's collective conversation, and, for better or worse, it has become something of an obsession. If misunderstood, a platform can become more like a gallows.

A platform is everything you already possess or can quickly manifest to almost guarantee that your book will be commercially successful. This is where your editorial ability could become secondary to other qualities. Specifically, publishers want to be convinced that you have mature and vibrant social media and professional networks, which need to exist largely in cyberspace for optimal speed, volume, and value. You're expected to receive high-volume, quality traffic to your website, and to appear often and early whenever you or your subject is searched for. Basically, they want you to be able to enter a few clicks and sell 10,000 copies minimum. There are authors who can do that and much more. The good news is that you don't have to spend a lot of money or be a techno-geek to learn how to become an internet player. Furthermore, there are few rules and truly no limitations to what can be done. New marketing paradigms emerge all the time from humble home-based jockeys. When people say, "that won't work," you should assume they might be 100 percent wrong.

When it comes to internet marketing, nothing succeeds until it does. It's simply a matrix of infinite problems and challenges waiting to be manipulated. Human psychology is the ultimate arbiter for what does and doesn't work. For instance, Facebook succeeds because it gives people the feeling of instant connection to friends and family, which is a primal instinct. What people have always wanted the most is what they will always want the most, and technology has not changed that fact.

If you don't have much of a platform, some agents and editors will automatically dismiss you for that reason alone. But please don't throw in the towel, because there are countless ways to compensate for whatever is lacking in your overall package. For obvious reasons, I want my clients to have vibrant platforms. But guess what? I have signed up and sold projects by authors who totally lacked conventional platforms, and their books did well. I'm sure the same is true for most of my colleagues. Caveat: There are many expensive services and products promising to make you a platform avatar. There are also many good books devoted to the subject for less than $25 each.

Fiction writers don't get a break in this regard, though they need to have a different kind of platform than authors who write self-help books. Fiction writers greatly benefit from popular fan pages, for instance.

Why Have Ebooks Changed the Business?

Obviously, it's expensive to print, store, and ship physical books. Because most retail sales are based on consignment, which means that the stores can return unsold books instead of paying the publisher for them, all books are printed at significant risk. Ebooks bypass all of the above, which means publishers potentially save tens of thousands of dollars in speculative overhead. If everyone simply decided to buy only ebooks, it's hard to say how many jobs and functions would disappear. But once the dust settled, stability would eventually return, and many of the same players would still be standing. Digital publishing has made self-publishing much more viable and is a great opportunity for entrepreneurial independent publishers. The real wild card is that no one knows what the eventual balance will be between physical books and ebooks, but recently ebook sales have leveled off in most areas. Fiction and self-published ebooks remain strong, and that's not likely to change.

Physical bookstores have had to readjust what they do and how they attract readers in their community, because if enough sales shift to digital, there simply won't be enough reason for them to continue existing, especially if Amazon continues to gobble up market share of all print sales. Recently, Amazon has opened physical bookstores, and it will be interesting to see what happens with those outlets. Barnes & Noble has had to adjust and close stores, and seemed on the brink of disappearing because of its huge inventory of stores, warehouses, staff, and other capital-draining infrastructure. So far, they have found ways to remain viable, but time will tell if that sort of retail bookstore is sustainable. In contrast, mom-and-pop stores require little capital investment and tend to be embedded in their communities as preferred destinations for recreational book shopping, even if their prices are a bit higher. For many people, selecting and reading books isn't a function; it's a passion. For them, boutique venues and the "book experience" are inviolable. If their love is passed on to future generations, then technology's dictates will be slightly thwarted.

What's Happening with Ebooks?

Tracked ebook sales have leveled off over the past couple of years and currently make up about 25 percent of all book sales. However, *tracked* is the key word here, because most ebooks are self-published, and that makes it difficult to measure aggregate sales. I'm going to go against common wisdom here by predicting that by 2020, overall ebook sales will taper off to about 10 percent of the book market, in favor of enhanced physical books. By *enhanced* I mean that physical books will be exceptionally alluring for reasons beyond mere editorial content. Currently, most paperback editions are only marginally more attractive than a newspaper; they are meant to be discarded. But we are a visual and tactile species. In the near future, digital reading will be equal to digital sex — accessible, better than nothing, and comparatively uncomplicated. But newly upgraded physical editions will be more desirable for the same reasons that people tend not to like blank walls.

Barnes & Noble and thousands of mom-and-pop booksellers must agree that print books are here to stay. The number of independent stores is growing, not shrinking, and

B&N is showing a tenacious spirit. This wouldn't be happening in an atmosphere of doom. Needless to say, every ebook sale and every online sale is at the expense of physical bookstores. But readers love shopping in bookstores, and there's nothing that online sellers can do to match that experience.

Why Do Publishers Fight with Amazon?

During the first decade of this century, publishers were frequently in public contention with Barnes & Noble, and no one had any issues with Amazon. But over the past several years Amazon has become the strongest single force in publishing, while B&N has been struggling to redefine itself.

Publishers squabble with Amazon for reasons similar to those for which European countries squabble with Russia. It's about who will dominate the present and the future. The irony is that Amazon decisively won the fight when they introduced the Kindle ereader several years ago, but some publishers still don't realize that they have already lost the war and that it's time to sue for peace.

Amazon is the only player with an innovative spirit, and that's the essence of the conflict. Oh, Amazon also happens to be rather selfish, greedy, and imperialistic, but that's the nature of corporate competition and combat. Any of the Big 5 publishing houses could have accessed their parent company's deep pockets to internally capitalize the creation of digital readers in advance of the Kindle, or could have partnered with Sony or one of the other early ereader producers. This would have given them unilateral control over the editorial product and a competitive digital delivery system. It's no accident that the early radio and TV set manufacturers were also the first content producers. In fact, self-retailing their own digital products through their own readers might have been a brilliant strategy for the major publishers. But instead they all sat on their hands and conducted business as usual while Amazon created the future, and therefore Amazon now owns it.

Over the past couple of years, the publisher-Amazon wars have mostly dropped from the headlines, and a palatable détente seems to be prevailing by mutual choice. The drama wasn't good for Amazon's image, and unmasked that the publishers can bark but can't actually bite. However, tensions remain high and new contention is potentially around the corner.

When a publisher refuses to comply with Amazon's dictates, Amazon can (and often does) simply stop selling that company's products as part of the free-two-day-shipping Prime program, or explicitly states that delivery will require excessive delays, which hurts the publisher much more than it hurts Amazon. True, consumers can easily buy the embargoed products elsewhere, and many do. However, several million consumers pay $99 (might be more by the time you read this) a year to be Amazon Prime members, which entitles them to free, fast shipping and easy ordering. Most of these consumers won't shop elsewhere unless they *really* want the embargoed product.

Publishers can't exist without Amazon, nor can they defend themselves against Amazon, which is why they also hate Amazon. The largest houses attempted to take a unified stand against Amazon's domination in 2012 by forming an alliance with Apple, and were subsequently sued by the federal government for their troubles. Ultimately, they were collectively fined many millions of dollars as part of a settlement for allegedly acting in concert with one another in violation of antitrust codes. Amazon emerged unscathed and more confident than ever.

When publishers lose sales, their authors lose money. So it's no surprise that the largest author organizations have anti-Amazon tantrums in unison with agents and publishers. But as I said elsewhere, Amazon won the war before it was actually fought. The publishers' best leverage is that Amazon can't afford to kill them; it needs the publishers to generate the books that it sells the most of. A scorched-Earth approach has never been contemplated by either side because they both live from the same soil.

By the way, Amazon has been a godsend for self-publishers because it provides the only comprehensive, full-service retail platform with massive traffic.

What about Self-Publishing?

I've heard self-publishing causes blindness and hair to grow on your palms. This book is about traditional publishing, which will remain the preferred method for the vast majority of writers into the foreseeable future. That said, self-publishing is a viable alternative, but you'd better understand what it is and isn't before choosing it.

I read somewhere that more than 500,000 "books" will be self-published in 2017. Most of them are digital or print-on-demand (POD). But what this staggering figure doesn't reveal is that at least 95 percent of self-published books sell fewer than 10 copies a year. As a self-publisher, are you prepared to invest enough resources to not be one of the 95 percent? Do you even know what that investment means? Sadly, many self-publishers retain an array of expensive services that promise them the moon but end up delivering credit-card debt. Yes, a fraction of self-publishers are exceedingly successful or at least self-satisfied with the results. But most of them have probably leveraged their preexisting business skills and connections to make it work. They probably had a realistic business plan and budget in place before pulling the trigger, the same as they would with any other self-financed venture.

Today, anyone can self-publish anything at any time. That's the easy part, but self-selling/marketing and self-distributing are where most self-publishers fall down the stairs. Brick-and-mortar retailers aren't interested in stocking self-published books. Amazon will give you a webpage, but that will mean nothing if you don't drive sales to the page.

If you know who your customers are likely to be, how many there are, and how to reach them, then self-publishing might make more sense than traditional publishing. And it's better to self-publish than no-publish if you can't get a traditional deal. But don't get bamboozled by expensive self-publishing packages. You can make it happen for less than $1,000 — or even less than $100 if you don't need a professional copyedit and cover design — and take it one frugal step at a time from there. Many excellent books (mostly self-published) are devoted to the subject.

Here's the flip side: self-publishers are filling important editorial niches that traditional publishers neglect. For instance, some of the bestselling craft, hobby, and specialized how-to books are self-published. So are many of the bestselling "fan fiction" titles in such categories as vampires and zombies. Most of these successful self-publishers have figured out online selling and don't want to do business through traditional retailers because they would make much less money going the traditional route. It's likely that the importance of self-publishers as niche micropublishers will explode over the next few years. Maybe you can get a piece of the action.

What about Distribution for Self-Publishers?

Lack of distribution has always been the biggest obstacle for self-publishing, and that's not destined to change. However, most traditionally published books also struggle for meaningful distribution, for the simple reason that store space is extremely limited in comparison to the number of books that are traditionally published. Most published authors are frustrated about the fact that they rarely find their own books in bookstores, even if they have a Big 5 publisher. Publishers can't dictate what gets shelved; stores will stock what they are most likely to sell the most of based on consumer demand. The exception is that retail placement is for sale, meaning that the author and/or publisher can pay for retail visibility. However, publishers will only do this if they think the product will move. Visibility doesn't guarantee that sales will recover the cost.

What's Really Going on in Book Publishing?

A relatively quiet under-the-radar storm is continuing to disrupt the foundations of book publishing. On the surface it seems as if we are in a stable period in which the Big 5 are consolidating their dominance, Amazon continues to dictate how everyone must behave, and independent publishers struggle for market share against the billion-dollar constellations. But most observers are failing to see what's really happening in plain sight. The term *self-publishing* no longer does justice to what many people are accomplishing outside the traditional system. You can become a successful publisher of your own and other people's books without any budget to speak of. In fact, there's little evidence that big spending equals big sales.

Viable content is crucial, but that doesn't mean you have to comply with what the professionals say. Industry insiders were relentlessly critical of the editorial quality of *Fifty Shades of Grey* and even boasted that they would have immediately rejected it. But as we all know, it bypassed the system and became a multimillion-dollar property, because millions of people liked it. Don't make the mistake of assuming that the publishing establishment knows best about what the public wants to read. Your opinion as an experienced reader is no less valid than that of someone who reads and edits for a living.

Obviously, strong content is only the beginning, not the destination. The key is to get people who "talk a lot" to read and like your book. What's most incredible about the internet is that anyone can seemingly become "a person of influence" to millions of like-minded people. A single shout-out about a new sponge by a housewife from Kansas with thousands of kindred followers can generate tremendous ecommerce revenues. And if the conversations continue and customers stay loyal, the success will be self-sustaining.

This is what's happening in publishing as you read this: online reviewers, bloggers, and social media users with big followings are dictating which books succeed. But you probably don't know it yet because no one knows how to measure the numbers. The sole money counter is Nielsen BookScan, but it only measures what flows through established retailers, and much of the book market has migrated elsewhere. However, that "elsewhere" is mostly Amazon. Amazon is an easy sales platform for self-publishers, even though Amazon takes at least 30 percent of the gross revenue. Many readers use Amazon as their first book search engine and preferred sales venue when looking for a title or author they have heard about. Unless your site is easily findable through a Google search, Amazon is probably the only reliable way for people to find and buy your book.

The irony here is that Amazon was initially seen as a godsend for traditional publishers that were desperately trying to break up Barnes & Noble's de facto cartel of the retail book market. Ultimately, publishers unknowingly jumped from the frying pan into the fire. Amazon has become an even tougher taskmaster than B&N, and also offers an ideal way for writers to reject conventional publishers.

Is Self-Publishing Good for Democracy?

The ascent of the internet was supposed to bring down totalitarian governments, which is exactly what happened in the 1980s and 1990s. And self-publishing goes hand-in-hand with the internet, since anything can be uploaded and subsequently downloaded. But throughout the current decade democracies are struggling. Even in the US, basic freedoms are being eroded.

The ability to freely transmit information has proven to have a boomerang impact. Ugly belief systems have poisoned millions of people through the internet. The problem isn't the availability of information, but what people do with the information. The internet is loaded with information telling people not to kill others in the name of their gods, but it doesn't help. Governments can block egregious information from being spread through the internet in territories they control, but there are countless ways for sophisticated users to override those obstructions. The internet is simply an inert channel that has nothing to do with human nature. At the end of the day, individuals have the power to decide who they are and what they will do. Unfortunately, bad information can be more compelling and influential than good information.

Now here's the good news, which you already know: You are your own universe. The world might be insane, but you don't have to be. Writing and publishing is your potential game changer regardless of what's happening all around you. You can create yourself any way you want to. You are free to write, and read, what you will. And you never need to be alone. The fight for decency is far from over. In fact, decency is by far the will of the majority; it just doesn't make for good headlines. The internet is indestructible even if access is vulnerable. Keep yourself free, and follow only yourself. If enough people do only that, the world will be fine.

Will Traditional Publishing Become Extinct Anytime Soon?

That's very unlikely. However, midsize independent publishers are endangered because many of them lack the cash flow to survive a fast-changing environment and can't jettison fixed costs fast enough. Every year, they become fewer and fewer. Small presses will manage to survive simply because they are small and can more easily manage their overhead and shift to digital publishing and POD as needed. The Big 5 can't fail because of their billion-dollar backlist catalogs. In a worst-case scenario, all they have to do is stop acquiring expensive frontlist titles and just rely on midlist acquisitions and backlist sales. Their revenues would plummet, but ironically their profit margins would soar.

WHEN NOTHING HAPPENS TO GOOD (OR BAD) WRITERS
a.k.a. Ignored Writer Syndrome (IWS)

Jeff Herman

"I will not be ignored!" screams Alex Forrest, the book editor played by Glenn Close, to her philandering lover, played by Michael Douglas, in the classic film *Fatal Attraction*.

What perfect karma: a book editor being ignored, even though her job was not relevant to the conflict. Too bad about the rabbit, though.

It's an inalienable truth that any writer who aggressively pitches his or her work will encounter abundant rejections along the way. You know that. But what you may not have been prepared for was the big-loud-deafening nothing at all. You followed the given protocols; have been gracious, humble, and appreciative; and have done nothing egregious. And you would never boil a rabbit. So what's your reward? Absolutely nothing; you have been ignored.

A document stating that your work has been rejected, even if clearly generic, may be a much more welcome outcome than the silence of an empty universe. At least that formal rejection letter reflects that you are part of a genuine process. True, you have been turned away at the gate, but it still seems that you belong to a fraternity of sorts. It's like you're an understudy, or simply wait-listed. Your existence is acknowledged even if unwelcome, whereas to be ignored is proof of nothing. Nature abhors a vacuum, and any writer with nerve endings will understand why soon enough, if not already.

I write this essay because of the frequent feedback I receive from readers complaining about the nonresponsiveness of editors and agents. I have carefully considered this phenomenon and how it must negatively affect the morale and stamina of those who are endeavoring in good faith to be published. I have decided that to be ignored deserves its own category in the travails of writing, and that it inflicts even more pain and frustration than the proverbial rejection. I shall designate it with a logical term: *ignored*.

Why are so many writers ignored by editors and agents? I will respond to that with questions of my own. Why are so many children ignored? Why are so many of the poor and needy ignored? Why are so many social problems ignored? I could ask this question in countless ways, and the primary universal answer would essentially remain the same: it's far easier to do nothing.

Let's get back to our specific context. As I mention elsewhere, agents and editors have demanding, often tedious, workloads that overwhelm the typical 40-hour workweek (they tend to put in way more hours than that, even though they can rarely bill by the hour or receive extra pay). They are rewarded for generating tangible results, which is most often measured in the form of monetary revenues. Taking the time to respond to writers, even in a purely perfunctory manner, might be the courteous thing to do, but neither their businesses nor their bosses will reward their kindness. You may feel that such inaction is a misguided and shortsighted "policy," and you might be right, but it doesn't change the facts as they are.

Does being ignored mean that you have actually been read and rejected? This question can't be answered, because you're being ignored. It's possible that someone did read your work and rejected it, and then simply neglected to reply to your email or threw out your proposal even if an SASE was attached. Why would someone do that? Because it's much easier to, and they can't justify the time it would take to answer as many as 150 submissions per week. It's also possible that your submission has not been read and may never be read, because nobody is available to screen the "incoming" in any organized fashion. It's not out of the question that submissions will accumulate in numerous piles, boxes, and email inboxes for several years before they are simply discarded, never to be opened. Does this strike you as harsh or ridiculous? Whatever; it is the way it is.

What is certain is that if your work is read and accepted, you will hear about it. In closing, my message to you is that you not allow being ignored to diminish your dreams and goals. It's simply a part of the process and part of the emotional overhead you might encounter on your road to success. It's also a crucial reason why you should not put all your manuscripts in "one basket." To do so may be tantamount to placing your entire career in a bottomless pit. Making multiple submissions is reasonable and wise if you consider the possible consequences of granting an exclusive without any deadline or two-way communications. Please refer to the other essays and words of advice in this book to keep yourself from becoming a victim of Ignored Writer Syndrome (IWS).

THE WRITER'S JOURNEY
The Path of the Spiritual Messenger

Deborah Herman

If you have decided to pursue writing as a career instead of as a longing or a dream, you might find yourself focusing on the goal instead of the process. When you have a great book idea, you may envision yourself on a book-signing tour or as a guest on a talk show before you've written a single word.

It's human nature to look into your own future, but too much projection can get in the way of what the writing experience is all about. The process of writing is like a wondrous journey that can help you cross a bridge to the treasures hidden within your own soul. It is a way for you to link with God and the collective storehouse of all wisdom and truth, as it has existed since the beginning of time.

Many methods of writing bring their own rewards. Some people can produce exceptional prose by using their intellect and their mastery of the writing craft. They use research and analytical skills to help them produce works of great importance and merit.

Then there are those who have learned to tap into the wellspring from which all genius flows. They are the inspired ones who write with the intensity of an impassioned lover. I refer to them as "spiritual writers," and they write because they have to. They may not want to, they may not know how to, but something inside them is begging to be let out. It gnaws away at them until they find a way to set it free. Although they may not realize it, spiritual writers are engaged in a larger spiritual journey toward ultimate self-mastery and unification with God.

Spiritual writers often feel as if they're taking dictation. Spiritual writing — in any genre: nonfiction, sci-fi, women's fiction, whatever — has an otherworldly feeling and can teach writers things they would otherwise not have known. It is not uncommon for a spiritual writer to read something after a session in "the zone" and question if indeed she wrote it.

Writing opens you up to new perspectives, much like self-induced psychotherapy. Although journals are the most direct route for self-evaluation, fiction and nonfiction also serve as vehicles for a writer's growth. Writing helps the mind expand to the limits of the imagination.

Anyone can become a spiritual writer, and there are many benefits to doing so, not the least of which is the development of the soul. On a more practical level, it is much less difficult to write with flow and fervor than it is to be bound by the limitations of logic and analysis. If you tap into the universal source, there is no end to your potential creativity.

The greatest barrier to becoming a spiritual writer is the human ego. We treat our words as if they were our children — only we tend to be neurotic parents. Children are not owned by parents, but rather must be loved, guided, and nurtured until they can carry on, on their own.

The same is true for our words. If we try to own and control them like property, they will be limited by our vision for them. We will overprotect them and will not be able to see when we may be taking them in the wrong direction for their ultimate well-being. Another ego problem that creates a barrier to creativity is our need for constant approval and our tendency toward perfectionism. We may feel the tug toward free expression but will erect blockades to ensure appropriate style and structure. We write with a "school-marm" hanging over our shoulders, waiting to tell us what we are doing wrong.

Style and structure are important to ultimate presentation, but that is what editing is for. Ideas and concepts need to flow like water in a running stream. The best way to become a spiritual writer is to relax and have fun. If you are relaxed and pray for guidance, you'll be open to intuition and higher truth. However, writers tend to take themselves too seriously, which causes anxiety, which exacerbates fear, which causes insecurity, which diminishes their self-confidence and leads ultimately to mounds of crumpled papers and lost inspiration. You are worthy. Do not let insecurity prevent you from getting started and following through.

If you have faith in a Supreme Being, the best way to begin a spiritual writing session is with the following writer's prayer:

Almighty God [Jesus, Allah, Great Spirit, etc.], Creator of the Universe, help me to become a vehicle for your wisdom so that what I write is of the highest purpose and will serve the greatest good. I humbly place my [pen/keyboard/recording device] in your hands so that you may guide me.

Prayer helps to connect you to the universal source. It empties the mind of trash, noise, and potential writer's blocks. If you are not comfortable with formal prayer, a few minutes of meditation will serve the same purpose.

Spiritual writing as a process does not necessarily lead to a sale. The fact is that some people and concepts have more commercial potential than others. Knowledge of the business of writing will help you make a career of it. If you combine this with the spiritual process, it can also bring you gratification and inner peace. If you trust the process of writing and make room for the journey, you will grow and achieve far beyond your expectations.

Keep in mind that you are not merely a conduit. You are to be commended and should take pride in the fact that you allow yourself to be used as a vessel for the Divine. You are the one who is taking the difficult steps in a world full of obstacles and challenges. You are the one who is sometimes so pushed to the edge that you have no idea how you go on. But you do. You maintain your faith and you know that there is a reason for everything. You may not have a clue what it is…but you have an innate sense that all your experiences are part of some bigger plan. At minimum they create good material for your book.

In order to be a messenger of the Divine you have to be a vessel willing to get out of the way. You need to be courageous and steadfast in your beliefs because God's truth is your truth. When you find that your inner truth does not match that of other people, you need to be strong enough to stay true to yourself. Your soul, that inner spark that connects you to all creation, is your only reliable guide. You will receive pressure from everywhere. But your relationship with your creator is as personal as your DNA. You will be a house divided if you try to please other people by accepting things they tell you that do not resonate with your spirit.

When you do find your inner truth, your next challenge is to make sure that you do not become the person who tries to tell everyone else what to believe. When a spiritual writer touches that moment of epiphany it is easy to become god-intoxicated. There is no greater bliss than to be transformed by a connection to the source of all creation. It is not something that can be described. It is individual. This is why it is important for a spiritual writer to protect this experience for another seeker. The role of a spiritual messenger who manifests his or her mission through the written word is to guide the readers to the threshold of awakening. Bring them to the gate but allow God to take them the rest of the way. Your job is to make the introduction. From there the relationship is no longer your responsibility. Your task is to shine the light brightly for some other seeker to find it.

It is difficult to believe so strongly in something while feeling unable to find anyone to listen to you. If you try too hard you might find that there are others who will drain your energy and life force while giving nothing in return. They may ridicule you and cause you to step away from your path. You do not have to change the world by yourself. You need to do your part. Whether it is visible or as simple as letting someone know you care, you are participating in elevating the world for the better. Some people like it exactly as it is. There are those who thrive on chaos and the diseases of the soul. Your job as a spiritual writer is to protect your spirit as you would your own child. Do not give away your energy; make it available for those who truly want it and will appreciate it. When you write, expect nothing in return. While following the protocols of the business world, do not set your goal too high, such as transforming people's souls. If you do, you will elevate your responsibility beyond the capability of simple humans. If you do the groundwork, God will do the rest.

The world of the spiritual writer can be a very lonely place. It is easier to love God, creation, and humanity than it is to feel worthy of receiving love in return. Those of us who devote our energy to trying to make a difference through our writing forget that God has given us this gift as a reward for our goodness, faith, and love. It is a two-way street. What we give we can also receive. It maintains the balance. It replenishes our energy so we can continue to grow and fulfill our individual destiny. We are all loved unconditionally. God knows everything we have ever thought, done, or even thought about doing. We judge ourselves far more harshly than God ever would. We come into this world to learn and to fix our "miss"-takes. We only learn through object lessons. We have free will. Sometimes we have to burn our hands on the stove several times before we learn that it is too hot to touch. I personally have lived my life with the two-by-four-to-the-head method. While not recommended, it is the only way I have been able to learn some of my more difficult lessons. I have often considered wearing a helmet.

When we connect with our inner truth we can become intoxicated with our own greatness. Writing is a very heady thing, especially if we are able to see our name in print. If we have people listening to what we have to say, we can believe that we are the message and forget that we are merely the messenger. Spiritual writers need to start every day by praying for humility. If we don't, and there is danger that we are going to put ourselves before the purity of Divine truth, we will not be able to be the pure vessel that we had hoped to become. The universe has methods of protecting itself. We will experience humiliation to knock us down a few pegs, to give us the opportunity to get over ourselves. I have experienced many instances of humorous humiliation, such as feeling amazed with myself only to literally fall splat on my face by tripping over air. No injury except to my inflated pride. God has a sense of humor.

On a more serious note, spiritual messengers who are taken in by their own egos are vulnerable to negativity. The information they convey becomes deceiving and can help take people off their paths. This is why spiritual writers should always begin each session with a prayer to be a vessel for the highest of the high and for the greater good. While readers have the choice to discern the wheat from the chaff, in this time of rapid spiritual growth, it is important to help seekers stay as close to their paths as possible. There is no time for major detours. We all have a lot of work to do.

We are all here to improve the lives of one another. We are blessed to live in an information age, in which we can communicate quickly and clearly with one another. However, technology also serves to make us separate. We all cling to our ideas without respecting the paths of others. We are all headed to the same place, the center of the maze, where there is nothing and everything all at once. We are all headed for the place of pure love that binds all of us to one another. We don't want to get caught up with trivial arguments about who is right and who is wrong. Our goal right now needs to be to foster everyone's path to his or her own higher truth. We share what we have so others can find it, without wasting time arguing the point to win them to our side. Too many battles have been fought over who is the most right. We all come from the same source.

When it comes down to it, spiritual writers are the prophets of today. You are here to express the voice of God in our world in ways that we as human beings can understand. We need to listen to the essence of the message rather than focusing on who is the greater prophet. In the business of writing, there is no sin in profit. But in the mission of writing, we must not forget that we all answer to the same boss and serve the same master.

You are also a messenger. When you agree to be a spiritual writer, you are also agreeing to bring light into the world. This is no small commitment. Remember to keep your ego out of it. While it is important to learn to promote and support your work, you must not forget that you are the messenger and not the message. If you keep this at the center of your heart and remember that you serve the greater good, you are a true spiritual writer who is honoring the call. May God bless you and guide you always.

Deborah Herman, wife and business partner of Jeff Herman, considers herself a mystic literary agent. She is the author of *Spiritual Writing from Inspiration to Publication* (Atria, 2001), which is currently being updated to reflect the digital age. Herman will be self-publishing in her own imprint, Soul-Odyssey Media, a division of www.offthebookshelf.com, the full-service micropublishing platform of which she is CEO and through which she offers book coaching, editing, and marketing consultation. Herman received certification from the Rutgers mini-MBA program in digital marketing, social media, and entrepreneurship, which she uses to help spiritual writers become writer-entrepreneurs. Her Twitter handles are @spiritualagent and @digitaldeborah.

TRIBULATIONS OF THE UNKNOWN WRITER (AND POSSIBLE REMEDIES)

Jeff Herman

Many nations have memorials that pay homage to the remains of their soldiers who died in battle and cannot be identified. In a way, it seems that the legions of unpublished writers are the Unknown Writers. As has been expressed elsewhere in this book, it cannot be assumed that the works of the unknown writer are of any lesser quality than those works that achieve public exposure and consumption, any more than those soldiers who died were less adept than those who got to go home. To the contrary, perhaps they were *more* adept, or at least more daring, and therefore paid the ultimate price.

No warrior aspires to become an unknown soldier, let alone a dead soldier. Every soldier prefers to believe that her remains will be known, that they will perhaps even explain what happened toward the end and will be presented to her loved ones for final and proper farewells. It is much the same for the writer. No writer worth her ink wants to believe that her legacy of expression will be forever unknown. Even if her other accomplishments in life are magnificent, it is still those words on the pages that she wants revealed, preferably while she's still around to experience and enjoy it.

Obviously, in life and beyond, there are many unknown writers. That's just the way it is.

It may just be that the fear of living and dying as an unknown writer is the extra push you need to bring your work to the first step on the road to publication — getting your work noticed by a publishing professional, be it agent or editor. If you are still reading this essay, then it is absolutely true that you are willing to try harder to reach that goal. In recognition and respect for your aspirations and determination, I will provide additional insights and strategies to help you help yourself avoid the fate of the unknown writer.

But let's make sure that your goals, at least in the early stages of your publishing life, are reasonably measured. It is suitable to imagine yourself one day at the top of the publishing food chain. Why not? Genuine humans have to be there at any given moment, so why not you? However, it is improbable that you will arrive there in one step. Your odds will be enhanced through your dedication to learning, calculating, and paying the necessary dues. For the purposes of the lesson at hand, I will encourage you to focus on the more humble goal of simply transitioning to the realm of being a published writer. For sure, there is more to do after that, but we will leave those lessons for other places in this book, and for other books.

Ways to Be Seen in a Crowd

Established literary agencies, including yours truly's, are inundated with unsolicited query letters (both hardcopy and digital), proposals, pieces of manuscripts, and entire manuscripts. This stream of relentless *intake* easily runs from 50 to 150 uninvited submissions per week, depending on how visible the agency in question is to the world of writers at large. These numbers do not account for the many works that the agency has requested or was expecting from existing clients. Frankly, many successful agents are simply not hungry for more than what they already have and make efforts to be as invisible and unavailable as possible.

The above scenario only tells of the agencies. It's likely that the publishers, both big and small, are receiving the same in even greater volumes, which is of dubious value since many publishers prefer not to consider anything that is unsolicited or unrepresented, period.

How can your work go from being an unseen face in the crowd to a jack-in-the-box whose presence cannot be denied? Here are some suggested steps.

1. ***Don't merely do what everyone else is already doing.*** That doesn't mean that you should entirely refrain from doing what's conventional or recommended. After all, the beaten track is beaten for a reason: it has worked before and it will work again. But be open to the possibility of pursuing specific detours along the way. Look upon these excursions as a form of calculated wildcatting. If nothing happens, or if you end up puncturing the equivalent of someone's septic tank, then just take it as a lesson learned.

2. ***Make yourself be seen.*** A pile of no. 10 envelopes is simply that, and none of the component envelopes that form the pile are seen. Someone once sent me a letter shaped like a circle. It could not be grouped with that day's quota of query letters; it demanded to be seen and touched and dealt with, immediately. Another time I received a box designed as a treasure chest, which contained an unsolicited proposal. I did not appreciate receiving a bag of white powder with a certain proposal. The powder was flushed down the toilet and the manuscript returned without being read. Digital queries are even more prone to disappear into a sea of sameness. But maybe that's why the email gods created the subject line: so that you can say something that can't be ignored.

3. **Be generous.** Most submissions are actually a demand for time, attention, and energy. During a long day in the middle of a stressful week in the throes of a month in hell, an agent will see none of those submissions as good-faith opportunities from honorable people. To the contrary, they will feel like innumerable nuisances springing forth from the armpits of manic brain-eating zombies, with drool and odor. I can recall opening a package to find a handwritten card from a stranger telling me how much he appreciated my contributions to the business and how much I have helped him and others, etc., etc. I always remember those kinds of things; wouldn't you?

4. **Don't be a nag, be a gift.** Everyone likes gifts, and nobody likes nags. So why do so many aspiring writers (and others) act like nags? It's counterintuitive. Of course, nature teaches us from the moment we are born that the noisy baby gets the tit. Passivity invites neglect. Noise attracts attention. What an interesting conundrum. Nagging is bad. Passivity leads to death. Noise can't be ignored. Well, all of that is equally valid, and none of it disqualifies the original point that you are a gift, so act like one.

5. **Keep knocking, even after the door is opened.** That does not make sense, and it might not be appreciated. But if someone were to keep knocking on my door even after I opened it, I would simply have to ask that person why he or she is doing that, and therein is the beginning of a conversation. Of course, it may all go downhill from there, but then it may not. What happens next depends on the nature of the conversation that has just been launched, regardless of its weird genesis.

6. **Don't ask for anything, but offer whatever you can.** If that is the energy projected throughout your communications, you will attract due wealth. However, the word *due* is rather crucial in this context. A well-intentioned worm may end up on the end of a fishhook, and a nasty frog may be well fed all summer. Too often people stop at just being nice, and then they become prey. Is it fair that they are eaten for doing nothing at all? Actually, that's exactly what they asked for, to end up nourishing the needs of others. We must all serve a purpose, and we must all consume to survive. If you don't wish to be consumed, then don't present yourself for that. The universe is a layered place of lessons and challenges, and being a writer is just one of many ways to play the game. Don't just give yourself away, any more than you would throw yourself away. If you value the gems you wish to share, you will discern to whom to grant them, and simply refuse to participate with others.

7. **Know your gifts and appreciate them.** I can tell right away when I am reading a query letter from a writer who believes in herself and the quality of her product,

and I can see those who are not so sure that they should even be trying. Sometimes the writer is apologetic, or even goes as far as asking me if he should be trying. Ironically, the writer's quality as a writer cannot be predicted by his native sense of self-worth. In fact, great literature has emerged from the hearts of those who are seemingly committed to a life of losing. But there is a logical explanation for that: To each writer is assigned a muse. Some writers may hate themselves while loving their muse, and it shows.

POST-PUBLICATION DEPRESSION SYNDROME (PPDS)

Jeff Herman

If you're struggling to get published, then this essay isn't for you, yet. If you're currently under contract, now is a good time to read this. If you have already been published and experienced what the above title indicates, then hopefully this essay will help you heal and realize you are far from alone.

You don't need to be reminded how much passion, fortitude, and raw energy goes into crafting your work, followed by the grueling process of getting it published. What you're probably not prepared for is the possibility of post-publication blues.

No one directly discusses or recognizes this genuine condition because newly published authors are expected to be overjoyed and grateful for the achievement of being published. After all, each published author is among the fortunate "one out of a thousand" struggling writers who make it to the Big Show. In reality, people who reach the pinnacle of success in any field of endeavor will often feel an emotional letdown in the wake of their accomplishment. The feeling can be comparable to a state of mourning, as the thrill of chasing the goal instantly evaporates and is replaced by nothing. Writers are especially prone to wallowing alone, as theirs is a solitary process by design, and only other writers who have been through the same cavern can be truly empathetic.

Emotional letdowns happen when results don't fulfill expectations. Everything preceding the point of publication involves drama, excitement, and anticipation. Butterflies flutter in the belly and endorphins soar through the brain. One day the writer's goal will be manifested in the body of a published book, and the self-constructed dreams will be displaced by a reality that seems to lack sizzle. What follows might feel sad and unnourishing. No matter how much is achieved, it might feel as if something crucial were left behind.

Achieving awesome goals is a reward unto itself, but it may not be enough to satisfy what's needed. The writer's imagination may have drawn fantastic pictures of glamorous celebrity parties, profound talk-show appearances, instantaneous fame, and goblets of money. But just as the explosive passions and idealized assumptions of first love might be followed by an anticlimactic consummation, finally receiving the bound book in hand might prove to be surprisingly uneventful.

Sometimes the publication is everything the writer hoped for, which of course is a wonderful outcome. But for many it feels like nothing much happened at all. The media aren't calling; few people show up for signings/readings; and, perhaps most upsetting of all, friends and relatives report that the book can't be found. Meanwhile, no one from the publisher is calling anymore and they act like their job is done. In truth, most of the publishing team is probably absorbed with publishing the endless flow of new books, whereas what's already been published is quickly relegated to "yesterday's list." A chirpy in-house publicist may be available, but she may not appear to be doing or accomplishing much while adeptly saying imprecise things in a glib, patronizing manner.

There's abundant information available about how to be a proactive author and successfully compensate for the universal marketing deficits endemic to the book-publishing business. But that's not the purpose of this essay. For sure, it's constructive to take practical steps for mitigating disappointments and solving existential problems, but such activities may also distract the troubled writer from the tender places crying somewhere inside. These feelings must be recognized and soothed. Even bestselling writers get the blues.

Seeking or initiating communities of "published writers in pain" should be what the doctor ordered. If done right, such personal connections will help level the loneliness and despair that define post-publication depression. However, the community must consciously dedicate itself to a positive process. Nothing useful will be accomplished by reinforcing anger, resentment, or a sense of victimhood. Even worse is unsupportive competitiveness or negativity that pushes people down. And — as can happen in any inbred community — distortions, misinformation, and poor advice might circulate with a bogus badge of credibility.

Life is rarely a clear trail. If it looks to be, then unexpected destinations are likely to prevail. Writers will eat dirt and wear thorns in exchange for self-compassion and self-discovery. Pain isn't punishment but a consequence that expands the writer's integrity, authenticity, and relevance. Post-publication depression is an item on a menu in a script written by the writer for the writer. Never fear the pain; just be prepared to live through it and learn from it, and to help others do the same.

EVERY WRITER NEEDS TO MEET ZERO

Jeff Herman

Hold a simple calculator in your hand and enter 0 + 0. Obviously, the result will be 0. Now enter 0 - 0. Again, the result will be 0. Next, multiply any value by 0 and you end up with 0. And any number subtracted from 0 results in the same number less than 0. (0 - 7 = -7).

On one hand we are taught that zero is nothing ("you're a zero"). But the same rules infuse zero with apocalyptic powers. How can "nothing" also be the most decisive and possibly destructive digit in the numerical tool kit? Any first grader with the insight to ask that question could get sent down to special education. Basic arithmetic forces us to accept a distorted and conflicted reality, which causes a lot of observable phenomena to seem incomprehensible, if not impossible. It's much easier to dismiss the existence of what can't be explained, even if it's right in front of us.

If there's a conspiracy against human potential, it begins with a self-burdened intellectual cult commonly referred to as math, and Ground Zero is its war against the true value and meaning of zero. We are forced to shred our imaginations through a false arbiter that won't tolerate variance. When our children lament how much they despise math, we should listen, because, as taught and used, it holds them back.

Don't blame the calculators. Don't blame anyone. Accepted paradigms are imprinted into us from the moment of birth and can stubbornly prevail for countless generations. An abrupt challenge of what's commonly considered to be real could provoke a spiral of social chaos and cause its promoters to be destroyed. Change is best when done gently in measured doses. Collectively and individually, there's a thin, fragile line between revelation and insanity. Seeing the truth and losing the lie is a painful, unregulated test that flirts with madness.

Albert Einstein and his peers managed to take us far in a relatively short span because enough of us were ready to go for the ride. No one managed to kill the messengers that time. But in his midlife, Einstein hit a theoretical wall that permanently sidelined his progression. Basically, his manipulation of numbers refused to explain observable outcomes, and he refused to accept that his numbers might be the problem. More than six decades later, scientists are struggling mostly against one another to codify what they are seeing.

Nonscientific terms like *randomness*, *spooky*, and *wormhole* are frequently used as a way to categorize the massive list of observable phenomena that defy science's sanctioned laws and methods, not to mention simple logic.

What's especially unfair is that scientists frequently concoct their own mythologies to explain the unexplainable. For instance, we are taught that all energy and matter was compressed into a tiny ball that somehow exploded and became everything that we can see and measure. Maybe that's exactly what happened. But what created the super-ball, and why did it blow up? And why is that any less or more credible than a nameless entity creating everything on a whim? If you subscribe to the ball creation theory, you are called rational. If you subscribe to the entity creation theory, you might be considered ignorant or uneducated.

We are taught that life was somehow formed in some kind of pool of water, and that the same thing might have happened on other planets. But why did that never happen again on Earth? And why are other new "lives" not emerging in the same way as the original one did? I'm not defending religion or debasing science, but I am saying that we don't have to choose between the two, especially since they are birds of the same feather: possible explanations for what we don't know. It follows that you are free to create your own theories, even if you throw them out five minutes later. There are no fixed answers to pretty much any question you ask. What is certain is that your native creativity is part of your design, and you should never let anyone interfere with it, especially your thinking and writing.

Visually, o reflects its mysteries. Its oval shape doesn't have a beginning or an end. We can't accurately measure its circumference without destroying it because we are unable to determine the true value of pi (not even the most powerful computers have figured out that one). Because zero has no value, having zero money means you're flat broke, and adding zero to your wealth won't make you any richer. But if Donald Trump multiplied his wealth by zero, he would be instantaneously broke. How can nothing have the power to destroy everything, and why do we accept this conundrum?

Obviously, something cannot be both nothing and everything. But what if the existence of "nothing" is impossible? What if "something" is invariably everywhere and can be whatever we say it is? When we dream, the impossible often prevails. But it's deemed to be impossible only while we're awake, not while we're experiencing it when asleep. Why is one state more real than the other? Can you prove that it is? The better question is: why bother to prove it? What if you accept that everything is a luscious mystery and that you can morph it however you want to? Just be your own "Alice." This is the kind of liberation that will unbind your mind to create marvelous possibilities in your writing, and in your reality.

Part 2

PUBLISHING CONGLOMERATES

THE BIG 5

Jeff Herman

The term *Big 5* has become the vernacular for referring to the largest book publishers in the US. It was the Big 6 until two of them, Penguin and Random House, got married in 2013. It isn't just size that qualifies for membership in this dubious collective. In fact, a handful of independent publishers are large enough (10-figure revenues) to be included, but several unique characteristics in addition to size separate the Big 5 from the independents.

1. Foreign Ownership

Most of the Big 5 are foreign owned, which is fully legal and transparent. In fact, more than half of America's book-publishing infrastructure is foreign owned. The foreign acquisitions commenced in the 1980s, surged, and then peaked in the early 2000s without much noise or pushback, and publishing wasn't the only industry affected. However, the Big 5 domestic operations have remained staffed by Americans, and the books are still mostly written by Americans.

Is massive foreign ownership something to be concerned about? I suggest we should be watchful without succumbing to prejudice or paranoia. Any country's culture is greatly influenced by the books its people read and write, so it should be disconcerting that foreigners have so much control over important aspects of our society. However, inordinate corporate control in general, regardless of address, should also be carefully observed.

If it's of any relief, pretty much all the attractive American fish have already been gobbled up. For sure, there will still be meaningful acquisitions and mergers over the next few years, but they will occur at a more modest pace and magnitude.

2. Books Are a Small Fraction of the Parent Company's Matrix

Most of the Big 5 are owned by companies for which books are a tiny fraction of overall revenues and profits. Massive and burgeoning commercial enterprises, such as cable TV, computer games, websites, pop-culture magazines, sports teams, music, movies, and

PUBLISHING CONGLOMERATES

much more, are where most of these companies live. Book revenues can't come close to these other income streams, and the imbalance will only become more pronounced in the future.

Most of the corporations are publicly traded, even if there's a "celebrity human face" at the helm. This means that important decisions must ultimately satisfy the board of directors and the major shareholders. Losing money, or failing to make enough of it, in the name of "art" or on the basis of editors' aesthetic tastes and hunches is unacceptable in corporate culture.

A natural question is: why do these multinational corporations want to own retro book companies? The answer: money follows power. Correct, few books make big money; but money isn't the only way to measure power. The top 20 percent of any country's population, in terms of education and income, are culturally and politically dominant. Even the most authoritarian governments must appease, manipulate, or intimidate this decisive strata in order to maintain power. The same 20 percent tend to be the most avid consumers of books. Therefore, book publishing delivers levels of influence, prestige, and credibility way beyond what its paltry revenues suggest.

3. Frequent Reorganization and (Too) Many Imprints/Divisions

It's the nature of multinational conglomerates to keep on eating, which is frequently followed by indigestion. As a result, each of the Big 5 is an obese amalgamation of programs with distinct traditions. Integrating the diversity of formerly rogue asteroids into cooperative orbits is never a simple task. To the contrary, it's messy and contentious. Competitive overlapping programs often end up in the same corporate "family," and because corporations abhor redundancies, perfectly viable programs are often suffocated. Many legacy brands within the Big 5 exist in name only and have ceased reflecting their storied histories apart from their inherited backlists.

What Does the Conglomeration of Publishing Mean?

1. *Less risk taking.* Editors are not encouraged to stray from the corporate mission, which is to make money or face the consequences.

2. *More "sameness."* What worked before becomes the model to follow until it fails, which causes less originality or anything else that doesn't fit proven methods.

3. *Steady irrelevance concealed by apparent success.* The lack of forward motion negates innovation, and banality is rewarded. Lack of competition enables domination of the bestseller lists and therefore compounds in-house complacency.

Suddenly, something fresh and better is born and must be killed, acquired, or copied, or else the game changes and power is shifted.

4. ***You belong, or you don't.*** In China, it helps a lot to be a member of the Communist Party. In America, it helps to be published by the Big 5. However, this being America, opportunities aren't monopolized. The independents, and self-publishers, will always raise their flags high.

THE LISTINGS

HACHETTE BOOK GROUP ❖ www.hachettebookgroup.com

1290 Avenue of the Americas, New York, NY 10104, 212-364-1200

Hachette belongs to Lagardère, a huge French media conglomerate. Frenchly, I mean frankly, I mispronounced this name for many years. I don't speak French, at least not on purpose, but I thought the *t*'s were silent, so I used to say something like "Hachay." Silly me; it turns out it's pronounced more like the tool, so that you hear the *t*'s. Anyway, it's only fair that the French have a place at the table with the British and the Germans in America's media universe, and Time Warner was eager to divest its low-margin book-publishing portfolio.

The transaction was made in 2006, except that the new entity was prevented from using the high-profile brand, Warner, and the relevant imprints had to be retitled. It took the industry a little while to get used to the fact that the name Warner Books was permanently retired, but life went on. Little, Brown was included in the package.

Unless otherwise specified, Hachette editors' email addresses follow this format: firstname.lastname@hbgusa.com.

HACHETTE BOOKS

In 2014 the name Hachette Books displaced the name Grand Central Publishing as the conglomerate's de facto flagship catalog. It includes much of the former Warner backlist and also acquired the rights to most of Disney's Hyperion adult trade list. As of this writing, only a small number of new titles have begun to appear under this imprint, though many titles are under contract. The imprint publishes the usual gamut of commercial fiction and nonfiction works — anything with "universal appeal."

Gretchen Young, Executive Editor. Business, memoir, biography, commercial nonfiction, cooking.

Ben Greenberg, Executive Editor. Memoir, narrative, political/social issues, humor.
Alex Logan, Senior Editor. Fiction focused on romance and women's interest.
Deb Futter, Editor in Chief. Commercial fiction and nonfiction.
Lindsey Rose, Assistant Editor. Mystery, thriller.
Maddie Caldwell, Editor. Cooking, romance.
Dana Hamilton, Editor. Humor, health.
(Ms.) Krishan Trotman, Senior Editor. Nonfiction.

TWELVE ❖ www.twelvebooks.com

Twelve was established in August 2005 with the intention of publishing only 12 books a year, though that's no longer the annual cutoff point. The mostly nonfiction imprint wants to create the intention that each title is extra-super-special, not just another book about whatever.

Deb Futter, Publisher. Nonfiction.
Sean Desmond, Editorial Director. Politics, current events, business, general.

GRAND CENTRAL LIFE & STYLE ❖ www.grandcentrallifeandstyle.com

As might be surmised by its name, this imprint focuses on wellness, beauty, fashion, the home, cooking, diet, fitness, relationships, inspiration, and related subjects.

Karen Murgolo, Editorial Director.
Sarah Pelz, Executive Editor.
(Ms.) Morgan Hedden, Editorial Assistant.

FOREVER ❖ www.forever-romance.com

This is the imprint dedicated to all areas of romance.

Amy Pierpont, Editor in Chief.
Leah Hultenschmidt, Editorial Director.
Lauren Plude, Editor.

ORBIT ❖ www.orbitbooks.net

This is the science fiction and fantasy imprint.

Will Hinton, Editorial Manager.
Devi Pillai, Editorial Director.

FAITHWORDS ❖ www.faithwords.com

10 Cadillac Drive, #220, Brentwood, TN 37027, 615-221-0996

As the name suggests, this program is dedicated to inspirational and Christian-oriented titles. Celebrity preachers and heaven visitors can be found here. Some titles are published under the Center Street imprint.

Kate Hartson, Executive Editor.
Christina Boys, Editor.

LITTLE, BROWN AND COMPANY ❖ www.littlebrown.com

LB began life in 1837 and has been one of America's premier book brands ever since. A few decades ago it was consumed by Time Warner, and then it was inherited by Hachette. Its mission remains unchanged. Its backlist catalogs (adult and children's) are massive and probably generate nine-figure revenues per year without any marketing needed.

(Ms.) Tracy Behar, Executive Editor. Health, psychology, self-help, parenting, science.
(Ms.) Lee Boudreaux, Vice President. Literary fiction, favors Southern themes.
Judy Clain, Editor in Chief. Literary fiction, memoir, suspense; narrative nonfiction.
Ben George, Senior Editor. Fiction; narrative nonfiction.
Joshua Kendall, Executive Editor. Fiction and nonfiction.
Wes Miller, Editor. Literary fiction, mystery, thriller, suspense.
Vanessa Mobley, Executive Editor. Narrative, current events, history.
(Ms.) Asya Muchnick, Executive Editor. Crime fiction; narrative nonfiction, history, biography, cultural history, popular science.
John Parsley, Executive Editor. Journalism, history, narrative, politics, business, pop culture, science, current events.
Michael Szczerban, Executive Editor. Food, cooking, lifestyle.
Malin von Euler-Hogan, Associate Editor. Narrative, memoir, humor, pop culture.

Little, Brown Books for Young Readers

LB began publishing children's books in 1926 and currently issues about 135 new titles a year. It publishes picture books, fiction and nonfiction in both paperback and hardcover for middle grade and young adult. LB Kids produces novelty media-tie-in books. Poppy publishes for teen girls.

Deirdre Jones, Editor. Middle grade.
Alvina Ling, Editor in Chief. Middle grade, young adult.
Pam Gruber, Senior Editor. Young adult.

Megan Tingley, Publisher. Picture books, middle grade.
Andrea Spooner, Executive Editor. Picture books, fantasy, young adult.

THE PERSEUS BOOKS GROUP ❖ www.perseusbooksgroup.com

212-340-8100

Perseus is a large constellation of once-independent presses, now known as imprints. In a much-anticipated acquisition, Hachette bought Perseus in early 2016. However, the details about what this will mean for its several divisions/imprints isn't yet clear. What's presented here reflects the situation as of spring 2016. Please check the Perseus website for the most current information.

Basic Books ❖ www.basicbooks.com

250 West 57th Street, New York, NY 10107, 212-340-8101

Since 1952, Basic has helped explain many conversations and conflicts in the areas of history, science, sociology, psychology, politics, business, and current affairs. Basic Civitas is an imprint within the imprint specializing in African and African American studies.

Editors' email addresses follow this format: firstname.lastname@perseusbooks.com.

Lara Heimert, Publisher. General history, culinary history.
(Mr.) TJ Kelleher, Editorial Director. Science, natural history, computer science, economics.
(Mr.) Alex Littlefield, Senior Editor. Politics, economics, current affairs, history, gardening.
Alison MacKeen, Senior Editor. Social sciences, health, media, technology, parenting, urbanism, education.
Dan Gerstle, Senior Editor. History, politics, education, sports.
Ben Platt, Editor. History, social sciences, current events, futurism, politics.
Brian J. Distelberg, Editor. Politics, law, sociology, technology, media.
(Ms.) Quynh Do, Associate Editor. Technology, philosophy, urban and cultural studies.

Da Capo Press ❖ www.perseusbooksgroup.com/dacapo

250 West 57th Street, 15th Floor, New York, NY 10107, 212-340-8100
44 Farnsworth Street, Boston, MA 02210, 212-340-8100

Da Capo continues its long history of publishing books about general history, pop culture, music, sports, and popular business. Da Capo Lifelong Books — again, an imprint within an imprint — specializes in pregnancy, parenting, health, fitness, and relationships.

PUBLISHING CONGLOMERATES

Editors' email addresses follow this format: firstname.lastname@perseusbooks.com.

Renee Sedliar, Editorial Director, Lifelong Books (MA). Health, fitness, cooking, spiritual wellness.

Bob Pigeon, Executive Editor (NY). History, military history, politics, current affairs.

Ben Schafer, Executive Editor (NY). Culture, entertainment, music, media, science, American counter culture.

Dan Ambrosio, Senior Editor (NY). Popular business, health, wellness, personal improvement.

Nation Books ❖ www.nationbooks.org

116 East 16th Street, New York, NY 10003, 212-822-0250

The Nation Books division has a strong focus on journalistic exposés about important issues and is associated with *The Nation* magazine.

Alessandra Bastagli, Editorial Director; abastagli@nationbooks.org. Domestic and international affairs, politics, economics.

Katy O'Donnell, Editor; katy@nationbooks.org. Social issues and current events.

Public Affairs ❖ www.publicaffairsbooks.com

250 West 57th Street, 15th Floor, New York, NY 10107, 212-340-8100

As implied by its distinctive name, Public Affairs publishes books about current events, government, economics, business, politics, foreign affairs, and investigative journalism/narrative.

Colleen Lawrie, Senior Editor; colleen.lawrie@publicaffairsbooks.com. Business, economics, politics, social justice, women's interest.

Ben Adams, Senior Editor; benjamin.adams@publicaffairsbooks.com. Science, current affairs, economics, history, food.

Running Press ❖ www.perseusbooksgroup.com/runningpress

2300 Chestnut Street, Suite 200, Philadelphia, PA 19103, 215-567-5080

Since 1972, Running Press has been an innovative book packager and merchandiser, meaning that many of their books are unconventionally designed and often show up where other books don't. "Impulse" or "gift" describes their distinctive formula, though conventional is also welcome. They generate a varied list of adult and children's titles in such areas as pop culture, humor, food and cooking, crafts, and lifestyle.

Editors' email addresses follow this format: firstname.lastname@perseusbooks.com.

Kristen Green Wiewora, Editor. Cooking, crafts.

Jennifer Kasius, Editorial Director. Diet, food, cooking, humor, popular reference.

Cindy De La Hoz, Editor. Relationships, parenting, women's self-help.

Seal Press ❖ www.sealpress.com

1700 Fourth Street, Berkeley, CA 94710, 510-809-3800

According to Seal's website, "A book can change a woman's life." I bet people already know that, and I also bet that men are equally susceptible. But the real point is that Seal's books aim to support "women of all ages and backgrounds." They publish self-help and narrative books for and about women. My understanding is that male writers should not apply, regardless of content, which strikes me as an archaic, if not illegal, restriction. But they will work with male agents, and I've never held back from pitching them appropriate projects or shaking hands with their editors at conferences; nor should you.

Editors' email addresses follow this format: firstname.lastname@perseusbooks.com.

Laura Mazer, Executive Editor. Pop culture, concept books, parenting.

Krista Lyons, Publisher. Health and fitness.

Donna Galassi, Associate Publisher. Social issues, travel literature.

Stephanie Knapp, Acquisitions Editor. Gender issues, running, music, TV.

Weinstein Books ❖ weinsteinbooks.com

This boutique imprint is the book affinity program for the Weinstein Company, which is a large feature-film production company. Its catalog reflects subjects and authors that have wide media appeal or derive from existing shows and films.

Amanda Murray, Editorial Director; amanda.murray@weinsteinco.com.

HARPERCOLLINS PUBLISHERS ❖ www.harpercollins.com

195 Broadway, New York, NY 10007, 212-207-7000

HarperCollins is owned by News Corporation, which is technically Australian owned, but its founder and dominant shareholder, Australian Rupert Murdoch, became a naturalized US citizen in 1985. News Corp. is a huge international media conglomerate within which book publishing reflects a tiny fraction of revenues and an even smaller fraction of profits. News Corp.'s monetary heart and other primary organs are tied to its 10-figure Fox TV and film properties.

Rupert Murdoch purchased Harper about 20 years ago and has done a good job at making it into a commercially rational enterprise while still leaving room for important books that don't necessarily make any money. The firm is an amalgam of many legacy brands from the good old days of mom-and-pop publishing. As is often the case in corporate publishing, these brands are mostly maintained to give credibility and gravitas to the firm, even though the respective frontlists often have nothing in common with the brands' precorporate histories.

Unless otherwise specified, Harper editors' email addresses follow this format: firstname.lastname@harpercollins.com.

AMISTAD ❖ www.amistadbooks.com

Amistad publishes works by and about people of African descent.

(Ms.) Tracy Sherrod, Editorial Director.

AVON ❖ www.avonromance.com

Avon has been one of the strongest brand names in mass-market romance and women's fiction for many decades and continues to claim a large piece of market share in these thriving categories. It also publishes erotica, paranormal, and urban fantasy.

Erika Tsang, Editorial Director. Romantic suspense, "dark, angsty" historical romance.
Lucia Macro, Executive Editor. Contemporary and historical romance.
May Chen, Senior Editor. Contemporary and historical romance, paranormal fiction.
Tessa Woodward, Editor. Books with "sexy, dark, dirty heroes."
Amanda Bergeron, Editor. Contemporary romance with angst and drama.
Chelsey Emmelhainz, Editorial Assistant. High-concept romance.
Nicole Fisher, Editorial Assistant. Sexy and contemporary romance.

BOURBON STREET BOOKS

This is a new imprint dedicated to paperback crime novels, thrillers, and mysteries.

Hannah Wood, Editor.

BROADSIDE BOOKS ❖ www.broadsidebooks.com

Specializes in conservative political and public-policy books.

Adam Bellow, Executive Editor.

ECCO BOOKS ❖ www.eccobooks.com

Formerly a small independent press, acquired by Harper in 1999. Currently a "boutique-ish" publisher of wide-ranging quality fiction and nonfiction, including memoir, "new voices," and contemporary cookbooks.

Daniel Halpern, Founder and Publisher.
Megan Lynch, Editorial Director.
Hilary Redmon, Editor.
Zack Wagman, Editor. Thriller; pop culture, political history.
Gabriella Doob, Associate Editor. Cultural history, cooking.

HARPER

The Harper imprint is the heartland of HarperCollins and has existed since the early part of the 19th century. Whether independent or corporate owned, it has always maintained a full range of quality fiction and nonfiction books and carries a deep backlist.

(Ms.) Terry Karten, Executive Editor. General fiction and nonfiction.
Jonathan Jao, Executive Editor. Nonfiction.
Jennifer Barth, Executive Editor. Fiction, mystery/crime; memoir.
Michael Signorelli, Editor. General fiction; pop culture/celebrity stories.
(Ms.) Gail Winston, Editor. General nonfiction, parenting, relationship.

HARPER BUSINESS ❖ www.harperbusiness.com

This boutique imprint specializes in hardcover business biography, memoir, narrative, trends, history, and cutting-edge ideas.

Hollis Heimbouch, Editor.
Stephanie Hitchcock, Editor.

HARPER DESIGN

Exceptionally well-produced illustrated books in a wide range of subjects.

Rebecca Hunt, Executive Editor.

HARPERONE ❖ harperone.hc.com

353 Sacramento Street, San Francisco, CA 94111, 415-477-4400

Formerly named HarperSanFrancisco, this cherished imprint has deliberately been maintained on the "other coast" for more than 30 years. It publishes a deep list of serious books about religion, science, alternative health, and new ideas in business and life.

Michael Maudlin, Executive Editor. Potentially controversial or nonmainstream religious perspectives and spiritual ideas.

Gideon Weil, Executive Editor. New/alternative thoughts about health and living.

Julia Pastore, Executive Editor. All areas relevant to health, wellness, and lifestyle.

Luke Dempsey, Executive Editor. Inspirational memoir, prescriptive self-help.

Kathryn Renz Hamilton, Editor. Religion and spirituality.

Hilary Lawson, Associate Editor. Alternative health and lifestyle, feminism, alternative culture.

HarperElixir

This is a recent imprint within the HarperOne program. Its purpose appears to be publishing fringe spiritual self-help books that are more intuitive in nature and less scientifically or academically rigid.

Libby Edelson, Senior Editor.

Claudia Riemer Boutote, Editor.

HARPER PERENNIAL

This imprint exists mostly for the purpose of reprinting Harper's successful hardcover books into evergreen backlist paperbacks. But it also publishes many quality fiction and nonfiction paperback originals.

Cal Morgan, Editor.

Eric Meyers, Editor.

HARPER VOYAGER ❖ www.harpervoyagerbooks.com

Voyager specializes in science fiction, fantasy, supernatural, and horror.

David Pomelico, Editorial Director.
Kelly O'Connor, Assistant Editor.
Rebecca Lucash, Editorial Assistant.

HARPER WAVE ❖ www.harperwave.com

Wave is a relatively new imprint specializing in new perspectives in mind-body-spirit,

Karen Rinaldi, Publisher.
Julie Will, Executive Editor.
Sarah Murphy, Editor.
Hannah Robinson, Assistant Editor.

WILLIAM MORROW

Founded in 1926, Morrow is one of the major legacy names in American publishing. It continues to publish a vibrant and large list of quality fiction and nonfiction titles.

Deborah Brody, Executive Editor. Health.
Cassie Jones, Executive Editor. Cookbooks.
Rachel Kahan, Executive Editor. Fiction.
Kate Nintzel, Executive Editor. Fiction.
Cara Bedick, Senior Editor. Health, lifestyle.
Tessa Woodward, Senior Editor. Fiction.
David Highfill, Editor. Mystery, crime, thriller.
Emily Krump, Editor. Fiction.
Margaux Weisman, Associate Editor. Literary fiction, crime fiction, mystery.

DEY STREET BOOKS ❖ www.deystreetbooks.com

Dey Street Books is a new imprint formed in 2014 to envelop and displace the It Books imprint, which was launched in 2009 as a home for super-cool books. One of It's limitations was surely the unfortunate name. My first impression was that it was a special home for books by Cousin It and It's freakish cousins.

Harper's new headquarters is adjacent to Dey Street in lower Manhattan, hence the moniker for this division. Dey Street is following in It's footprints, publishing irreverent pop-culture narratives and edgy celebrity memoirs.

(Ms.) Carrie Thornton, Editorial Director. Memoir, lifestyle.

Julia Cheiffetz, Executive Editor. Memoir, narrative, biography.

Mark Chait, Executive Editor.

Denise Oswald, Senior Editor.

Brittany Hamblin, Editor.

Bethany Larson, Assistant Editor.

WITNESS IMPULSE ❖ wmmorrow.hc.com/witnessimpulse

This is a relatively new imprint focused on mysteries and thrillers.

Chelsey Emmelhainz, Editor.

HARLEQUIN ❖ www.harlequin.com

Harlequin is one of the world's leading publishers of romance titles. Their catalog covers every imaginable romance theme in both adult and teen categories. The firm was acquired by HarperCollins in 2014.

Editors' email addresses follow this format: firstname.lastname@harlequin.com.

Blaze

Steamy and lusty.

Dana Hopkins, Editor.

Adrienne Macintosh, Editor.

Laura Barth, Editor.

Kathleen Scheibling, Editor.

Desire

Girl magnets that have it all: wealth, status, looks, power, and a few secrets.

Tahra Seplowin, Editor.

Shana Asaro, Editor.

Stacy Boyd, Senior Editor.

Charles Griemsmann, Editor.

Harlequin Teen

Paranormal, dystopian, horror, and romance.

(Mr.) T. S. Ferguson, Associate Editor.

Heartwarming

Romance based on traditional values; home, family, and community are central.

Dana Grimaldi, Editor.

HQN Books

Publishes mainstream single-title romances, as opposed to serials by a single author.

Margaret O'Neill Marbury, Editorial Director.
Allison Carroll, Editor.
Denise Zaza, Editor.
Margot Lipschultz, Editor.

Intimate Moments

Like it sounds.

Patience Bloom, Senior Editor.

Intrigue

Stories about romantic suspense (people in danger).

Paula Eykelhof, Executive Editor.

Kimani

African American and multicultural romantic themes.

Glenda Howard, Senior Executive Editor.

Love Inspired

Stories of faith, forgiveness, hope, and love prevailing against the odds.

Giselle Regus, Editor.
Tina James, Editor.

Mira Books

Contemporary and historical psychological and suspense thrillers.

Erika Imranyi, Executive Editor.

Superromance

Romance plus a lot more.

Victoria Curran, Editor.

HARPERCOLLINS CHRISTIAN PUBLISHING ❖

www.harpercollinschristian.com

A while back, Harper saw "the light," but not in the same way you might. They saw where the money was. The American Christian community is huge and loves books about faith. Harper knew better than to try to start a religion program from scratch and instead opted to purchase two of the most successful and long-standing firms in the Christian community: Thomas Nelson and Zondervan.

Thomas Nelson ❖ www.thomasnelson.com

501 Nelson Place, Nashville, TN 37220, 615-889-9000

With roots going back to Scotland more than 200 years ago, Nelson may be the oldest Christian publisher in the world and probably has the biggest catalog. Originally known for its Protestant Bibles and church/Sunday school–related products, it publishes a large range of faith-based books for adults and children.

Brian Hampton, Publisher; bhampton@thomasnelson.com. Nonfiction.
Amanda Bostic, Editorial Director; amanda.bostic@harpercollins.com. Inspirational Christian fiction.
Webster Younce, Executive Editor; wyounce@thomasnelson.com. Nonfiction.
Matt Baugher, Editor; mbaugher@thomasnelson.com. Nonfiction.
Daisy Hutton, Editor; dhutton@thomasnelson.com. Inspirational Christian fiction.
Becky Monds, Editor; bmonds@thomasnelson.com. Children's.

Zondervan ❖ www.zondervan.com

5300 Patterson Avenue SE, Grand Rapids, MI 49530, 616-698-6900

For more than 80 years Zondervan has been a powerhouse publisher of Bibles and Christian-themed books for adults and children.

Becky Philpott, Editor; becky.philpott@zondervan.com. Inspirational fiction; nonfiction.
Carolyn McCready, Executive Editor; carolyn.mccready@zondervan.com. Nonfiction.

Zondervan Children's ❖ www.zondervan.com/children.html

Kim Childress, Editor.

HARPERCOLLINS CHILDREN'S BOOKS ❖ www.harpercollins.com/childrens

As would be expected, Harper has a deep children's program consisting of many legacy and relatively recent imprints.

Balzer + Bray

Balzer is best known for its beautifully illustrated and packaged children's and middle grade books and young adult novels.

Alessandra Balzer, Publisher.
Donna Bray, Publisher.
Kristin Daly Rens, Executive Editor.

Greenwillow Books

A well-respected boutique imprint since 1974, Greenwillow publishes quality books for children of all ages.

Martha Mihalick, Associate Editor.

HarperCollins Children's Books

Harper is the flagship within the flagship and the heartbeat of the entire children's program in terms of volume and depth.

Nancy Inteli, Editorial Director.
Kristen Petit, Executive Editor. Young adult.
Margaret Anastas, Editor.

HarperTeen ❖ www.harperteen.com

This imprint was recently created to publish exactly what its name implies.

Jennifer Klonsky, Editorial Director.
Karen Chaplin, Senior Editor.

Emilia Rhodes, Senior Editor.
Alyson Day, Editor.

Katherine Tegen Books

This is a boutique home for books that tell "meaningful stories with memorable characters."

Katherine Tegen, Publisher.
Jill Davis, Editor. Picture books, middle grade through young adult.
Anica Rissi, Executive Editor. Young adult and middle grade.
Ben Rosenthal, Editor. Young adult.
Maria Barbo, Editor. Young adult and middle grade.

MACMILLAN PUBLISHERS ❖ us.macmillan.com

175 Fifth Avenue, New York, NY 10010, 212-674-5151

Macmillan is owned by the large German conglomerate Verlagsgruppe Georg von Holtz-brinck, whose name can't be memorized or said fast by Americans. The firm doesn't have any evident history in the chemical, plumbing fixtures, propagation, or armaments industries. Macmillan serves as the umbrella brand encompassing many other legacy US publishing brands that have been amalgamated and sorted in recent years as part of the corporate creative-destruction of America's publishing assets into foreign-owned vassals. Macmillan is a celebrity brand for book people, but its current incarnation is several generations removed from its origins as a powerful UK book publisher. Like a bouncing ball, rights to the Macmillan name have been bought and sold several times in recent years, and it has been permanently severed from its valuable catalogs. For several years the brand was simply missing and presumably forgotten. Suddenly, it reappeared as the name of the Holtzbrinck folks' US- and UK-based operations, probably because Americans couldn't pronounce its German name unless seriously intoxicated or while lifting a piano.

FARRAR, STRAUS AND GIROUX ❖ www.fsgoriginals.com

1818 West 18th Street, New York, NY 10011, 212-741-6900

This one is a jackpot brand universally recognized for discovering and nurturing excellent works by new writers. In 1946 the firm was partly founded by refugee Euro-Semites who dedicated themselves to publishing edgy new voices whose works may not have been welcomed elsewhere at the time. Its current program hasn't strayed, but it's no longer a particularly unique venue.

Editors' email addresses follow this format: firstname.lastname@fsgbooks.com.

(Ms.) Alex Star, Executive Editor. History, politics, current events.
Amanda Moon, Editor. Popular science, *Scientific American* imprint titles.
Eric Chinski, Editor in Chief. Fiction; current events, history.
Emily Bell, Senior Editor. Fiction; general nonfiction.
Jonathan Galassi, Publisher. Fiction; serious nonfiction.
Paul Elie, Editor. Social issues, politics, current affairs, serious nonfiction.
Ileene Smith, Executive Editor. Memoir, biography.

FLATIRON BOOKS ❖ www.flatironbooks.com

175 Fifth Avenue, New York, NY 10010, 212-674-5151

Flatiron is a relatively new and editorially autonomous boutique imprint that will endeavor to justify its ongoing existence by publishing a full range of frontlist fiction and nonfiction books that enough people will buy. The interesting name is derived from the iconic office building they are in.

Editors' email addresses follow this format: firstname.lastname@flatironbooks.com.

Amy Einhorn, Publisher. Mostly fiction.
Bob Miller, Publisher. Nonfiction.
Colin Dickerman, Editorial Director. Mostly narrative nonfiction.
Christine Kropprasch, Senior Editor. Mostly fiction.
Whitney Frick, Executive Editor. Narrative nonfiction.
Caroline Bleeke, Editor. Fiction.

HENRY HOLT AND COMPANY ❖ www.henryholtbooks.com

175 Fifth Avenue, New York, NY 10010, 212-674-5151

Holt has been a premier publishing brand since 1866. It still carries a strong reputation as a general fiction and nonfiction publisher with genres including mystery, thriller, social sciences, and current events.

Editors' email addresses follow this format: firstname.lastname@hholt.com.

Serena Jones, Senior Editor. Science, history.
Allison Adler, Associate Editor. Narrative nonfiction with millennial sensibilities.
Sarah Bowlin, Senior Editor. Fiction
Barbara Jones, Executive Editor. Current issues.
Michael Signorelli, Senior Editor. Fiction.

Metropolitan Books

This Holt imprint was established in 1995 for the purpose of publishing fiction and nonfiction books with a slightly fringe or quirky orientation — just a little outside the mainstream but often perfectly conventional nonetheless.

Editors' email addresses follow this format: firstname.lastname@hholt.com.

Sara Bershtel, Publisher. Social issues, history.
Riva Hocherman, Executive Editor. Social issues, narratives.

Times Books

This Holt imprint is owned, or at least substantially controlled, by the *New York Times*. In fact, approximately half its books are authored by current or former *NYT* reporters. The imprint is entirely nonfiction and publishes the kinds of subjects you're likely to read about in the *NYT*, even if not authored by an *NYT* reporter, though politics and government seem to be dominant.

Paul Golob, Executive Editor; paul.golob@hholt.com.

ST. MARTIN'S PRESS ❖ us.macmillan.com/omp.aspx

175 Fifth Avenue, New York, NY 10010, 212-674-5151

Here's another one of the well-respected publishing giants that's been conglomerated in recent years. SMP has managed to maintain itself as it was before the plague and tends to have much less editorial turnover/attrition than other publishing programs. In other words, it has been a reliably stable planet in an unpredictable solar system.

Editors' email addresses follow this format: firstname.lastname@stmartins.com.

George Witte, Editor in Chief. Literary fiction; current affairs, investigative journalism.

Nichole Argyres, Editor. Literary and commercial fiction, mystery; narrative nonfiction, paradigm-changing ideas, women's interest, medicine, science, parenting, food, politics.

Tim Bartlett, Executive Editor. Current issues, business stories, narrative.

Elizabeth Beier, Executive Editor. Commercial fiction; problem-solving nonfiction, pop culture, cookbooks.

(Ms.) BJ Berti, Senior Editor. Craft, lifestyle, home, style, fashion, food.

Hannah Braaten, Associate Editor. Mystery, women's fiction; narrative and quirky nonfiction.

Emily Carleton, Senior Editor. Business, economics, current affairs.

Laura Chasen, Associate Editor. Young adult crossover commercial fiction.

Brenda Copeland, Executive Editor. Commercial fiction; slightly eccentric memoir and narrative.

Brendan Deneen, Executive Editor. Horror, science fiction, fantasy; entertainment/celebrity tie-ins.

Hope Dellon, Executive Editor. Contemporary, historical, and crime fiction.

Elisabeth Dyssegaard, Editor. Social history, current issues.

Jennifer Enderlin, Senior Vice President. Commercial fiction, including paperback originals.

Michael Flamini, Executive Editor. History, politics, nature, performing arts, food.

Sara Goodman, Senior Editor. Young adult novels.

Rose Hilliard, Senior Editor. Romance, women's, and paranormal fiction.

Michael Homler, Editor. Crime fiction, thriller; biography, quirky narrative, popular science, sports.

Holly Ingraham, Associate Editor. Adult and young adult commercial fiction.

Keith Kahla, Executive Editor. Commercial fiction.

Silissa Kenney, Associate Editor. Wide-ranging fiction categories; health, parenting.

Elizabeth Lacks, Associate Editor. Crime fiction; personal narrative about compelling experiences.

Vicki Lame, Associate Editor. Women's, literary, and historical fiction.

Matt Martz, Associate Editor. Crime fiction; business, history, science, current affairs.

Monique Patterson, Editorial Director of Romance.

Daniela Rapp, Editor. Narrative nonfiction, pets, quirky, popular science, travel stories, pop culture.

Marc Resnick, Executive Editor. Military narrative, sports, adventure, pop culture.

Eileen Rothschild, Associate Editor. Romance, women's fiction.

Charles Spicer, Executive Editor. Men's and women's commercial fiction, crime fiction; true crime, history.

Anne Marie Tallberg, Associate Publisher. Mass-market and trade paperback fiction.

Dori Weintraub, Editor-at-Large. Literary fiction; memoir, biography.

Jennifer Weis, Executive Editor. General and young adult fiction; health/medicine, women's interest.

Karen Wolny, Executive Editor. Current events, interesting trendy concepts, social issues.

Thomas Dunne Books ❖ us.macmillan.com/thomasdunne.aspx

Dunne is a close sibling to St. Martin's, and they seem to frequently share each other's editors. Perhaps the single distinguishing aspect is that Mr. Dunne still exists and has been laboring as a hands-on editor since before being given his own imprint in 1986.

Editors' email addresses follow this format: firstname.lastname@stmartins.com.

Thomas Dunne, Publisher. British fiction; politics, history, science, current events.

Kat Brzozowski, Associate Editor. Mystery.

Melanie Fried, Associate Editor. Mystery, women's fiction; pop culture narratives and memoirs.

Laurie Chittenden, Executive Editor. Commercial fiction; high-concept narrative.

Peter Joseph, Executive Editor. Literary, crime, and historical fiction; science, history, general nonfiction.

Rob Kirkpatrick, Senior Editor. Sports, pop culture, history.

Marcia Markland, Senior Editor. Commercial and literary fiction; animals, psychology, social/current events, women's interest, science.

Nicole Sohl, Associate Editor. Edgy fiction; entertainment tie-ins.

Peter J. Wolverton, Editor in Chief. Commercial and fantasy fiction; sports, outdoors, adventure.

Minotaur ❖ us.macmillan.com/minotaur.aspx

This imprint publishes many of St. Martin's and Dunne's crime fiction titles.

Editors' email addresses follow this format: firstname.lastname@stmartins.com.

Keith Kahla, Editor.

(Ms.) Kelley Ragland, Associate Publisher.

Charles Spicer, Editor.

Andrew Martin, Publisher.

PICADOR ❖ www.picador.com

Picador was established in 1995 as an imprint for literary fiction and nonfiction. That doesn't sound overly innovative, but hatching imprints is how large houses try to refresh themselves and reward veteran editors who will never earn the salaries they would be worth in other businesses. Picador is also where all the Macmillan divisions repurpose many of their successful titles as paperback cash cows.

Elizabeth Bruce, Editor; elizabeth.bruce@picadorusa.com. Thriller, general fiction.

TOR/FORGE ❖ www.tor.com

175 Fifth Avenue, New York, NY 10010 212-674-5151

Tor publishes a premier line of science fiction and fantasy. Forge publishes fiction, including historical, thriller, mystery, women's, modern Westerns, military, and young adult novels, as well as some nonfiction.

Editors' email addresses follow this format: firstname.lastname@tor.com.

Tom Doherty, Publisher.

Patrick Nielsen Hayden, Senior Editor.

Liz Gorinsky, Editor.

Miriam Weinberg, Editor.

MACMILLAN CHILDREN'S ❖ www.mackidsbooks.com

Encompasses many vibrant and deeply rooted imprints.

Farrar, Straus and Giroux Books for Young Readers ❖

us.macmillan.com/publishers/farrar-straus-giroux#FYR

This program boasts a huge catalog of children's classics going back to the 1950s. Its frontlist program includes everything from preschool to young adult.

Editors' email addresses follow this format: firstname.lastname@fsgbooks.com.

Janine O'Malley, Editor.
Wesley Adams, Editor.
Joy Peskin, Editor.
Grace Kendall, Editor.

Feiwel & Friends ❖ us.macmillan.com/publishers/feiwel-and-friends

Publishes across the board from prereaders to age 16.

Liz Szabla, Editor; liz.szabla@macmillan.com. Picture books, young adult.
Jean Feiwel, Editor; jean.feiwel@macmillan.com. Picture books, middle reader, young adult.

Henry Holt Books for Young Readers

Holt's program is noted for its high-quality picture books, chapter books for young readers, and novels for young adults.

Sally Doherty, Executive Editor; sally.doherty@hholt.com.
Laura Godwin, Editorial Director; laura.godwin@hholt.com.

Roaring Brook Press ❖ us.macmillan.com/publishers/roaring-brook-press

This imprint was founded in 2002 and publishes for young readers of all ages. (Like me, you may be wondering how all these imprints manage to live with one another. The answer is, they just do, and the editors are glad to have their jobs.)

Editors' email addresses follow this format: firstname.lastname@roaringbrookpress.com.

Katherine Jacobs, Associate Editor.
Emily Feinberg, Editor.
Connie Hsu, Senior Editor.

PENGUIN RANDOM HOUSE ❖ www.penguinrandomhouse.com

December 13, 2013, was perhaps both the most anticlimactic and the most meaningful day in the modern history of American and international publishing. On this day, amid the noise of Christmas consumption, Random House and Penguin legally finalized their friendly merger. It was a gentle event that the Justice Department seemingly ignored. The metaphorical equivalent of an old-growth forest abruptly collapsed in the woods. Everyone knew but no one listened.

In fairness, the handwriting had been on the wall for more than a decade. And there's still plenty of handwriting to be parsed about what might follow. There's still room for more compression both within and between the entities. Though both Penguin and Random House maintain a clear American footprint, don't be fooled. Ownership is primarily German and secondarily British, although a plurality, perhaps even a majority, of revenues are American. More important, book sales are a comparatively small fraction of overall revenues and profits for the corporate parent.

What follows is a breakdown of an especially large and fluid matrix of amalgamated divisions and imprints with ancient legacies and new mandates. However, the merger-digestion process is still sorting itself out, and it's possible that by the time you read this some programs will have been reverted to the dust from which everything derives.

RANDOM HOUSE

1745 Broadway, New York, NY 10019, 212-782-9000

CROWN PUBLISHING GROUP ❖ www.crownpublishing.com

Until 1988, Crown was a thriving independent, family-owned house, and there was a noticeable measure of protest and concern when Random House announced its consumption of Crown. People understood that it represented an early stage of the Blob War against mom-and-pop publishing. Today, Crown stands as a large, autonomous division encompassing many distinct imprints. However, Crown is now simply a name without a trace of its former face or personality, which is par for the course.

Editors' email addresses follow this format: firstinitiallastname@randomhouse.com.

Julian Pavia, Executive Editor. Science fiction, fantasy, thriller, general fiction.

Rachel Klayman, Executive Editor. Science, politics, current events.

Amanda Cook, Executive Editor. Science, current affairs, business.

Alexis Washam, Executive Editor. General fiction, mystery.

Domenica Alioto, Senior Editor. Historical narrative.

Hilary Ruben Teeman, Senior Editor. Fiction.

Crown Archetype ❖ crownpublishing.com/imprint/crown-archetype

This imprint appears to be a boutique pocket for high-profile, mainly nonfiction authors and subjects.

Tricia Boczkowski, Editorial Director; tboczkowski@penguinrandomhouse.com.

Crown Business ❖ crownpublishing.com/imprint/crown-business

Like it sounds, it's a boutique imprint specializing in high-end business books by authors with large followings.

Roger Scholl, Editor; rscholl@randomhouse.com.
Talia Krohn, Editor; tkrohn@randomhouse.com.

Crown Forum ❖ crownpublishing.com/imprint/crown-forum

Political and social commentary books with a conservative orientation.

Derek Reed, Associate Editor; dreed@penguinrandomhouse.com.

Clarkson Potter ❖ crownpublishing.com/imprint/clarkson-potter

This imprint has an impressive pre–Random House history. For many years it was where you'd find a huge array of frontlist and backlist books dedicated to food, cooking, lifestyle, craft/hobbies, decorating, and entertaining.

Editors' email addresses follow this format: firstinitiallastname@randomhouse.com.

Rica Allannic, Executive Editor. Cooking, illustrated lifestyle.
Amanda Englander, Editor. Cooking.
Frances Lamb, Editor. Cooking.
Doris Cooper, Editorial Director. Cooking.
Angelin Borsics, Editor. Cooking.

Harmony Books ❖ crownpublishing.com/imprint/harmony-books

This imprint is a long-lived brand whose standing within RH has ebbed and flowed for years. At one time it was the designated New Age, spirituality, mind-body-spirit program. In recent years it tends to avoid fringe topics while focusing on acceptably alternative books about diet, health, relationships, culture, self-help, and popular psychology.

Diana Baroni, Editorial Director; dbaroni@penguinrandomhouse.com.

Ten Speed Press ❖ crownpublishing.com/imprint/ten-speed-press

6001 Shellmound Street, Emeryville, CA 94608, 510-285-3000

Many publishing professionals were sorry to see this formerly independent publisher fall into the corporate abyss. But that tends to happen when a firm's founder/owner retires, dies, or simply wants to cash out while he/she can. TSP was/is famous for its quirky and innovative list of books about food, careers, test prep, humor, health, and perhaps anything else you might think of.

Editors' email addresses follow this format: firstname.lastname@tenspeed.com.

Julie Bennett, Editorial Director. Cookbooks.

Lisa Westmoreland, Senior Editor. Popular reference, test-taking/education guides, writing, how-to, cooking.

Kaitlin Kethchum, Editor. Illustrated and lifestyle how-to books.

Emily Timberlake, Editor. Food and cooking.

Jenny Wapner, Executive Editor. Food and cooking.

Lorena Jones, Editor-at-Large. Self-help business narrative relevant to lifestyle issues.

Three Rivers Press

This is the trade paperback division for the Crown program. Most of its catalog is devoted to evergreen backlist nonfiction titles originally published by Crown. But it also publishes a wide range of trade paperback nonfiction originals.

Amanda Patten, Senior Editor; apatten@randomhouse.com. Celebrity narrative, celebrity humor.

Waterbrook Multnomah Publishing Group ❖ www.waterbrookmultnomah.com

12265 Oracle Boulevard, Suite 200, Colorado Springs, CO 80921, 719-590-4999

Launched by Random House in 1996, this dynamic division exclusively publishes books for evangelical Protestant Christians of all ages. As per routine with corporately owned religious book divisions, the program is based thousands of miles away from the New York parent company's headquarters.

(Ms.) Shannon Marchese, Senior Editor; smarchese@penguinrandomhouse.com. Inspirational fiction, women's fiction, illustrated children's books; faith-based nonfiction.

KNOPF DOUBLEDAY PUBLISHING GROUP ❖ www.knopfdoubleday.com

Both Knopf and Doubleday are distinct legacy brands that ended up as part of Random House for different reasons at different times. RH never really figured out what to do with all its brands. After all, they pretty much do the same things, and it's difficult to keep them from creating fiscally wasteful redundancies, which is the kiss of death in corporate culture. RH may have solved the problem by crashing these two brands together without having to stop using either of them.

Knopf ❖ www.knopfdoubleday.com/imprint/knopf

The firm was founded by Alfred Knopf in 1915 and is still one of the few "Rolls Royce / Cartier"–level brand names in American publishing. Louis C.K. probably wouldn't get published here. People you have never heard of, or never stayed awake reading, might be found here. "Smart people" have always been enthusiastic bookbuyers. In fact, they used to be the only bookbuyers. It's fitting that programs exist essentially for them. Within publishing's circle of circles, getting published by Knopf puts you at the head of the line, though you will probably be more reliant upon your trust fund than your royalties.

Unless otherwise specified, editors' email addresses follow this format: firstinitiallast name@randomhouse.com.

Victoria Wilson, Senior Editor. Fiction; current affairs, interesting narrative.
Tim O'Connell, Editor. Fiction; interesting narrative.
Diana Miller, Editor; dtmiller@randomhouse.com. Fiction.
Andrew Miller, Senior Editor. Journalistic narrative and history.

Doubleday ❖ www.knopfdoubleday.com/imprint/doubleday

Doubleday is one of the great publishing brands. Now it's just one of many brands that were long ago decapitated from their foundational souls. The brand has had a rocky tenure as part of the RH "family." But what is a publisher worth if it can't maintain brand value? The ironic answer is that few readers care who the publisher is when they buy a book; but it still means a lot to the people who work in the book business, especially authors and booksellers. Doubleday continues a wonderful tradition of publishing excellent fiction and nonfiction frontlist books.

Editors' email addresses follow this format: firstinitiallastname@randomhouse.com.

Melissa Danaczko, Senior Editor. General fiction.
William Thomas, Editor in Chief. General fiction; current affairs, history, narrative.
Yaniv Soha, Senior Editor. Popular science, medicine/health, contemporary narrative.

Jason Kaufman, Executive Editor. Fiction.
Jennifer Jackson, Senior Editor. Fiction.

Pantheon ❖ www.knopfdoubleday.com/imprint/pantheon

Pantheon was founded in 1941 by a German refugee and specialized in translating important books by an all-star international roster. The firm was acquired in 1961 by Random House for all the right reasons and was permitted to maintain its special vision for several decades. Though its frontlist has been significantly reduced in recent years, it's still an impressive destination for books.

Erroll McDonald, Executive Editor, emcdonald@randomhouse.com. Culture, science, politics.
Dan Frank, Editorial Director; dfrank@randomhouse.com. Current affairs, American history, science.

Schocken Books ❖ www.knopfdoubleday.com/imprint/schocken

Though lately an obscure and little-heard-from imprint, Schocken has a dramatic and brilliant history. In fact, the entire program is literally a refugee from Nazi Germany. The Schocken family took advantage of the opportunity to gather up their valuable copyrights and make a run for it while still possible. An unintended benefit of the Nazi race laws was that all Jewish writers needed to be consolidated into Jewish-owned publishing houses, so just before they "left the room," the Schockens ended up with the rights to such literary giants as Kafka. Today the firm publishes an annual handful of titles relevant to Jewish cultural history and themes.

Altie Karper, Editor; akarper@randomhouse.com.

RANDOM HOUSE ❖ www.randomhousebooks.com

If you're a little confused, just be glad not to be part of the management team that has to keep figuring out how to align, or keep alive, its wealth of Brahmin brands that have been amalgamated many times over. The RH imprint carries the glory and burden of the Random House history, which has been one of America's premier publishing brands since 1925. RH was a large independent firm until about a generation ago, when it was acquired by the Newhouse family. A few years later it was acquired by the German-owned media goliath Bertelsmann, which made a lot of money during the middle of the 20th century as the Nazi Party's exclusive designated publisher. This assignment was especially lucrative because buying the books was compulsory for millions of people. Not even Donald

Trump can make people buy his books. Today's Random House has one of the biggest and most lucrative backlist catalogs in the world, and its frontlist always consists of a highly respected and diverse assortment of good books.

Editors' email addresses follow this format: firstinitiallastname@randomhouse.com.

Andy Ward, Editor in Chief. Nonfiction, science, sports, business, current events.
Susan Kamil, Publisher. Fiction and nonfiction.
(Mr.) Sam Nicholson, Editor. Fiction and nonfiction.
Will Murphy, Executive Editor. Fiction and nonfiction.
Noah Eaker, Senior Editor. Fiction and nonfiction.
Andrea Walker, Senior Editor. Fiction and nonfiction.
Kara Cesare, Executive Editor. Fiction.
Kate Medina, Executive Editor. Fiction and nonfiction.

ALIBI ❖ www.randomhousebooks.com/alibi

This imprint was established for the sole purpose of publishing genre commercial fiction as digital/print-on-demand originals. Its catalog consists mostly of mysteries, thrillers, crime fiction, and some women's fiction.

Dana Isaacson, Editor; disaacson@randomhouse.com.
Kate Miciak, Editor; kmiciak@randomhouse.com.

BALLANTINE BOOKS

BB was conceived as an innovative unattached firm in 1952 with what at the time was an unusual vision: specializing in mass-market paperback originals, which the old guard disrespected. There was a time not that long ago when paperbacks were the exception. Following WWII, publisher-entrepreneurs broke the cultural glass ceiling by placing paperbacks in unthinkable venues like grocery stores. Somewhere along the line, Random House gobbled up BB, and their destinies have been entwined ever since. BB continues to perform its primary purpose as a publisher of a wide assortment of popular fiction categories and some nonfiction, mostly in paperback. Several recognizable brand names prevail within BB, each with its own rich history.

Pamela Cannon, Executive Editor. Cooking, food, general narrative.
Sara Weiss, Senior Editor. High-concept self-help, popular psychology, memoir.
Marnie Cochran, Executive Editor. High-concept self-help, health, parenting.

BANTAM

Bantam was formerly an independent firm specializing in paperback mass-market fiction. That orientation prevails today, with a sizable assortment of nonfiction hardcover refugees that perhaps got lost in the hallway.

Shauna Summer, Editor. Women's fiction, romance.

DEL REY ❖ sf-fantasy.suvudu.com

According to the imprint's website: "Del Rey Books began as an imprint of Ballantine Books in 1977. Founded by editors Judy Lynn and Lester del Rey, Del Rey is now one of the world's foremost publishers of science fiction, fantasy, and speculative fiction, as well as media and pop culture titles."

Michael Braff, Editor. Science fiction, fantasy.

LOVESWEPT ❖ www.randomhousebooks.com/loveswept-flirt

You won't find how-to books about death or taxes here, unless they include cleavage and abs. Women's fiction/romance, duh. Most of the list seems to be published in digital only.

Sue Grimshaw, Editor.
Junessa Viloria, Editor.

SPIEGEL & GRAU

Some years ago two smart veteran editors were given the space and budget to create and manage their own dedicated list. Large houses often do that as way to maybe shake up internal motivation and creativity, and it's possible something special will bloom. If it doesn't work they just shut it down and move any successful titles into an existing backlist program. Their site also states, "We aim to enhance each author's vision," which I'm sure doesn't mean to imply that no one else wants to do that.

Julie Grau, Co-Publisher. Literary fiction; celebrity books, narrative nonfiction, prescriptive nonfiction.
Cindy Spiegel, Co-Publisher. Fiction; groundbreaking nonfiction.
Christopher Jackson, Executive Editor. Literary fiction; narrative nonfiction, ideas, politics, pop culture.
Laura Van der Veer, Associate Editor. Fiction and nonfiction.

RHCB is arguably the largest and busiest children's publisher in the known universe. Its list includes Dr. Seuss books (game-over), and there are several imprints.

Alfred A. Knopf Books for Young Readers

Full spectrum of children's books. The list and the brand were part of the original Knopf–Random House merger.

Melanie Cecka, Publisher.
Nancy Siscoe, Senior Executive Editor.
Allison Wortche, Senior Editor.
Erin Clarke, Executive Editor.
Katherine Harrison, Associate Editor.
Michelle Frey, Executive Editor.

Crown Children's

Although this imprint retains the Crown name, it was placed within the RH program following the merger. They publish a dynamic and commercial list of titles for all young age groups, ranging from nonreaders (picture books) to young adult.

Emily Easton, Executive Editor.
Phoebe Yeh, Publisher.

Delacorte Press

Publishes a wide range of middle grade and young adult novels and nonfiction.

Wendy Loggia, Publishing Director.
Beverly Horowitz, Publisher.
Krista Marino, Executive Editor.
Kate Sullivan, Senior Editor. Young adult.
Rebecca Weston, Editor. Middle grade.

Random House Books for Young Readers

The flagship imprint within the flagship program, this is where Dr. Seuss and Babar live. The program covers every category and age group.

Maria Modugno, Editorial Director. Picture books.
Michelle Nagler, Associate Publishing Director. Middle grade, young adult.

Mallory Loehr, Publishing Director. All areas.
Caroline Abbey, Editor. All areas.
Diane Landolf, Editor. Middle grade.

Schwartz and Wade

Established in 2005 as a boutique imprint specializing in highly designed illustrated books. Middle grade through young adult; fiction and nonfiction.

Anne Schwartz, Publisher.
(Mr.) Lee Wade, Publisher.
Ann Kelley, Associate Editor.

PENGUIN ❖ www.penguinrandomhouse.com

375 Hudson Street, New York, NY 10014, 212-266-2000

Penguin is the other half of the huge conglomeration of a plurality percentage of America's traditional publishing assets. Ironically, it's not American owned, even though most revenues are generated in America. Needless to say, every kind of book you can imagine is probably published by one or more of the numerous brands, imprints, and divisions found herein.

Unless otherwise specified, editors' email addresses for all Penguin imprints follow this format: firstinitiallastname@penguinrandomhouse.com.

AVERY ❖ www.penguin.com/meet/publishers/avery

Avery was acquired by Penguin in 1999. It had been a successful independent publisher specializing in alternative health and lifestyle books, and that orientation has been maintained.

Caroline Sutton, Editor in Chief.
Lucia Watson, Executive Editor.

BERKLEY/NAL ❖ www.penguin.com/meet/publishers/berkley

This is the amalgamation of two of the most prestigious mass-market book brands in publishing. More than 50 years ago, the companies were created around the revolutionary concept of publishing books that ordinary people would like to read, printing them as affordable paperbacks, and distributing them where real people shopped for nonbook products. Hence, the term *mass-market publishing* was born. Today, Berkley/NAL continues to publish a diverse list of commercial fiction and nonfiction titles as paperback originals.

Cindy Hwang, Editorial Director. Romance.

Claire Zion, Editor in Chief. Romance.

Kate Seaver, Editor. Women's fiction.

(Ms.) Leis Pedersen, Senior Editor. Romance, mystery.

Danielle Perez, Executive Editor. Mystery, thriller.

Kerry Donovan, Executive Editor. Romance.

Laura Fazio, Associate Editor. Romance.

Ace Books ❖ www.penguin.com/meet/publishers/ace

Ace was founded in 1953 as a science fiction publisher. Many of the classics that you have and haven't heard of still prevail on its backlist. The program has been eaten several times by corporations but continues to survive with minimal alterations to its mission.

Jessica Wade, Senior Editor.

Caliber

Caliber is a small imprint dedicated to military history and related themes.

Natalee Rosenstein, Executive Editor.

Roc

Roc is a small imprint dedicated to science fiction and fantasy.

Anne Sowards, Editor.

Jessica Wade, Editor.

BLUE RIDER PRESS ❖ www.penguin.com/meet/publishers/blueriderpress

Blue Rider was created in 2011 for the purpose of generating a special "high-rent" space for some of the veteran editors and their highly esteemed authors, fiction and nonfiction. Beavis and Butt-Head memoirs wouldn't be appreciated here.

David Rosenthal, Publisher. Fiction and nonfiction.

Sara Hochman, Editor in Chief. Fiction and nonfiction.

Becky Cole, Executive Editor. Self-help, how-to, memoir, narrative.

Brandt Rumble, Senior Editor. Sports narrative, popular science.

DAW ❖ www.penguin.com/meet/publishers/daw

DAW was founded as an independent press in 1971 and was the first program to be exclusively dedicated to science fiction and fantasy. That mandate continues to thrive.

Sheila Gilbert, Editor.
Sarah Guan, Editor.

DUTTON ❖ www.penguin.com/meet/publishers/dutton

Dutton's history as a major American publisher can be traced to 1852, when Edward Payson Dutton heard the calling to publish Christian books. Over the generations the firm has been resurrected and reincarnated many times. Today it is a premium imprint specializing in top-selling (that's always the plan) fiction and nonfiction hardcover books.

Ben Sevier, Editor in Chief.
Stephen Morrow, Executive Editor. Science, economics, psychology, investigative journalism.
Jill Schwartzman, Executive Editor. Pop culture, music, narrative, biography, high-profile self-help.
Jessica Renheim, Associate Editor. Mystery, thriller, crime fiction; narrative.
Maya Ziv, Executive Editor. Fiction.

THE PENGUIN PRESS ❖ www.thepenguinpress.com

This is the one that gets to use the flagship brand name, which has a distinguished history originating in London. Today's Penguin Press (US) was rebooted in 2003 as a home for distinguished nonfiction and fiction titles.

Ann Godoff, Editor in Chief. Fiction and nonfiction.
Scott Moyers, Publisher. Current affairs/politics.
Ginny Smith, Senior Editor; vsmith@penguinrandomhouse.com. Biography, narrative.
Ed Park, Executive Editor. Fiction.
Emily Cunningham, Editor. Biography, narrative, social history.

PLUME ❖ www.penguin.com/meet/publishers/plume

Plume was created in 1970 to serve as the paperback reprint division for New American Library. Its backlist boasts numerous classics. Today its frontlist serves a wide range of commercial nonfiction trade paperbacks and some fiction.

Kate Napolitano, Senior Editor. Wide-ranging self-help, how-to, pop culture.

PORTFOLIO ❖ www.penguin.com/meet/publishers/portfolio

Portfolio was established several years ago as a boutique destination for commercial books about business and investing.

(Mr.) Adrian Zackhein, Publisher.
Stephanie Frerich, Senior Editor.
Natalie Horbachevsky, Editor.

G. P. PUTNAM'S SONS ❖ www.penguin.com/meet/publishers/gpputnamssons

Now here's a big brand that was its own domain for more than a century and even had its own skyscraper. Now it's a brand with a marvelous backlist and frontlist that successfully competes for commercial primacy.

Sally Kim, Editorial Director. Commercial fiction.
Mark Tavani, Executive Editor. Thriller; sports stories, current affairs, history, science.
Kerri Kolen, Executive Editor. Wide range of popular nonfiction and narrative, including pop culture, current affairs, humor, investigative journalism.
Christine Pepe, Executive Editor. Mystery, thriller, romantic suspense; parenting/child care.
Sara Minnich, Senior Editor. Contemporary and historical fiction, upmarket mystery and thriller; narrative history, popular science, travel narrative, current affairs.
Tara Singh Carlson, Senior Editor; tsingh@penguinrandomhouse.com. Women's fiction, suspense, magical realism.

RIVERHEAD BOOKS ❖ www.penguin.com/meet/publishers/riverhead

Riverhead was created in 1994 as an editorially autonomous imprint for cutting-edge commercial fiction and high-end nonfiction hardcover originals. It has generated a healthy backlist and is a reliable producer of successful and award-winning frontlist titles.

Rebecca Saletan, Editorial Director. Literary fiction; current events, environmental issues, multicultural subjects, food, travel.
Sarah McGrath, Editor in Chief. Wide range of literary fiction and narrative nonfiction.
Jake Morrissey, Executive Editor. Historical fiction and thrillers; narratives in science, history, culture, religion.
Laura Perciasepe, Editor. Wide range of literary fiction and narrative nonfiction.
Courtney Young, Executive Editor. Natural science, social science, business, technology, culture.

TARCHER PERIGEE ❖ www.penguin.com/meet/publishers/tarcherperigee

The Tarcher and Perigee programs were merged in late 2015. This was a smart consolidation because there was already substantial editorial overlap between the kinds of practical and alternative lifestyle, health, spiritual, and self-help categories that both programs already excelled at. Fortunately, the Tarcher name has been maintained, since it has a strong tradition of publishing innovative works, going back to the days when it was an independent West Coast press.

Stephanie Bowen, Senior Editor. Practical business, how-to, inspiration.
Jeanette Shaw, Editor. Practical business, healthy lifestyle/beauty, pop culture.
Marian Lizzi, Editorial Director. Wide-ranging self-help categories, including popular business, lifestyle, popular psychology, narratives.
Joanna Ng, Associate Editor. Self-help/how-to categories.

VIKING BOOKS ❖ www.penguin.com/meet/publishers/vikingbooks

Viking is an important legacy publishing brand, which has published countless great books for more than 150 years. That level of gravitas is still respected.

Andrea Schulz, Editor in Chief. Mystery, literary fiction; narrative nonfiction.
Wendy Wolf, Associate Publisher. History, science, psychology, politics, culture, current affairs.
Paul Slovak, Executive Editor. High-end commercial fiction; cultural history, natural history.
Carole Desanti, Executive Editor. Literary fiction, commercial fiction; health, psychology.
Rick Kot, Executive Editor. Current affairs, science, business stories, history, arts/culture.
Joy De Menil, Executive Editor. History, politics, economics, science.
Laura Tisdel, Executive Editor. Literary fiction; women's interest, parenting, memoir, narrative.
Allison Lorentzen, Senior Editor. Literary/upmarket fiction; pop culture narrative.
Melanie Tortoroli, Editor. History, science, nature, journalism, travel, food.

PENGUIN YOUNG READERS GROUP ❖ www.penguin.com/children

345 Hudson Street, New York, NY 10014

There are many vibrant historic imprints meshed here from both Penguin and Random House, and each of their antecedents.

Dial Books for Young Readers ❖

www.penguin.com/meet/publishers/dialbooksforyoungreaders

Dial is a busy hardcover program of books for preschool through young adult.

Lauri Hornik, Publisher.
Jessica Garrison, Editor.
Kate Harrison, Senior Editor.
Namrata Tripathi, Editorial Director.

Dutton Children's Books ❖

www.penguin.com/meet/publishers/duttonchildrensbooks

Dutton is the oldest continuously operating children's publisher in America. That may explain why Winnie the Pooh and his friends live here. Today, Dutton is a boutique middle grade/young adult imprint and publishes a relatively small list of new fiction titles.

Andrew Karre, Editor.
Julia Strauss-Gabel, Publisher.

Grosset & Dunlap ❖ www.penguin.com/meet/publishers/grossetdunlap

GD tends to publish nonfiction paperback series for ages 0 to 12.

Francesco Sedita, Publisher.
Eve Adler, Editor.

Philomel Books ❖ www.penguin.com/meet/publishers/philomel

Focuses on picture books for preschoolers, and fiction for middle grade through young adult. One of its specialties is attracting books written from or about other cultures.

Michael Green, Publisher.
Jill Santopolo, Executive Editor.
Liza Kaplan, Editor.

G. P. Putnam's Sons Books for Young Readers ❖

www.penguin.com/meet/publishers/gpputnamssonsbooksforyoungread

This is one of the imprints blessed and/or burdened with a flagship moniker, in this case dating back to 1838. Today Putnam publishes about 50 new titles a year, all of which are hardcover fiction, from picture books to young adult.

Jennifer Besser, Publisher.

(Ms.) Stacey Barney, Editor.

Arianne Lewin, Editor.

Susan Kochan, Associate Editorial Director.

Razorbill ❖ www.penguin.com/meet/publishers/razorbill

Publishes about 50 middle grade to young adult titles a year, both fiction and nonfiction. How many kids (or adults) know what a razorbill is? Part of the program's identity is to be a little more fringe or edgy with its list.

Ben Schrank, Publisher.

Jessica Almon, Editor.

Tiffany Liao, Associate Editor.

Viking Children's Books ❖

www.penguin.com/meet/publishers/vikingchildrensbooks

Needless to say, there's a proud and rich history here. Today, Viking publishes about 50 books a year for prereaders to teenagers, fiction and nonfiction.

Kenneth Wright, Publisher.

Kendra Levin, Editor.

Leila Sales, Editor.

(Ms.) Tracy Gates, Editor.

SIMON & SCHUSTER ❖ www.simonandschuster.com

1230 Avenue of the Americas, New York, NY 10020, 212-698-7000

Simon & Schuster was founded in 1924 by Richard L. Simon and Lincoln Schuster. The firm was sold to Marshall Field (the man, not the store, though he also owned the store) in 1944 and was repurchased by its founders following Field's death in 1957. It was sold to Gulf+Western in 1975, which morphed into Paramount Communications in 1989. In 1994 Paramount was acquired by Viacom. In 2006, CBS was split off with Simon & Schuster from Viacom and made into a separate corporation, though it is still part and parcel of Viacom (it confuses me too). The corporate situation has been uneventful since then. As revealed below, S&S is both an imprint and an umbrella for several distinct programs with varying levels of independence, and there are semiautonomous imprints within the divisions.

Editors' email addresses for all Simon & Schuster imprints follow this format: firstname.lastname@simonandschuster.com.

ATRIA PUBLISHING GROUP ❖ www.atria-books.com

Atria (the plural of *atrium*) are centralized spaces open to Earth's natural elements. Considering I had to look that up even though I know everything about everything, chances are good that most people are as clueless as I was about what that name is supposed to make us feel. In fact, I thought S&S made up that name to sound fancy. Maybe if plebian venues such as malls didn't have atria, the program would have been named Atrium. Atria was formed in 2002 by repackaging several of S&S's trade programs into a coherent universe of wide-ranging fiction and nonfiction subjects. Over time, several divisions have been germinated within Atria's garden.

Peter Borland, Vice President and Editorial Director. Commercial fiction; narrative nonfiction, memoir, biography, pop culture.

Johanna Castillo, Vice President and Executive Editor. Fiction, including women's, thriller, historical; nonfiction, including inspirational, self-help, Spanish translation.

(Ms.) Leslie Meredith, Vice President and Senior Editor. Science, nature, history, spirituality, religion, food/cooking, health/nutrition.

Sarah Branham, Senior Editor. Fiction, including mystery, crime, historical; memoir, cookbooks.

Sarah Cantin, Senior Editor. Fiction, including historical, suspense; nonfiction, including travel stories, pop culture, narrative.

(Ms.) Jhanteigh Kupihea, Senior Editor. Upmarket women's romance and psychological suspense; pop culture.

(Mr.) Rakesh Satyal, Senior Editor. Celebrity, pop culture, digital influencers, emerging trends.

Todd Hunter, Editor. Fiction, including political, suspense, mystery, thriller; African American topics.

Lindsay Newton, Assistant Editor. Upmarket fiction, including mystery/suspense, crime, historical.

Daniella Wexler, Assistant Editor. Literary and upmarket fiction.

Emily Bestler Books ❖ www.simonandschusterpublishing.com/emily-bestler

One way for an editor to reach the top, without starting their own company, is to get their own division named for them within the corporate matrix. Frankly, many veteran editors probably earn this honor, but only a few achieve it. It would simply be impractical to make it a routine event, and what is deserved often has little relation to what is given in any competitive enterprise. When an editor shows her- or himself to be a consistent earner, and an above-average magnet for hot projects, and has formed powerful alliances within the firm, there's an editor in the running for their own imprint.

Emily Bestler, Senior Vice President, Editor in Chief. Upmarket fiction and nonfiction.

37 Ink

Fiction and nonfiction titles with African American themes.

Dawn Davis, Vice President and Publisher.

Howard Books ❖ imprints.simonandschuster.biz/howard

216 Centerview Drive, Suite 303, Brentwood, TN 37027

S&S acquired this independent press in 2006 to gain a footprint in the vibrant Christian/faith-based publishing world and achieve membership in the Evangelical Christian Publishers Association. It's not by accident that the firm has been maintained in Tennessee, as opposed to being relocated to S&S's Manhattan headquarters. The program publishes a large list of theological, inspirational, and pop-culture titles in both fiction and nonfiction. Chelsea Handler's books wouldn't be found here. But *Duck Dynasty* titles thrive due to the Robertson family's frequent Christian-friendly references.

Jonathan Merkh, Vice President and Publisher.

Philis Boultinghouse, Senior Editor. Focuses on celebrity-driven nonfiction inspirational books.

Beth Adams, Senior Editor. Inspirational fiction and nonfiction.

Amanda Demastus, Associate Editor. Biblical/inspirational-based fiction and nonfiction.

Lisa Stillwell, Senior Acquisitions Editor. Fiction and nonfiction.

GALLERY BOOKS ❖ imprints.simonandschuster.biz/gallery-books

This division was established from scratch about 12 years ago. Its purpose is to be a distinct platform for publishing "fresh voices" (picture a gallery with pictures) in both fiction and nonfiction, with a clear focus on pop culture, entertainment, celebrities, and multimedia tie-ins, which makes sense considering that Viacom is a sister company.

Louise Burke, President and Publisher. Major projects.

Jennifer Bergstrom, Publisher and Vice President. Major projects.

Karen Kosztolnyik, Executive Editor. Fiction and nonfiction.

Lauren McKenna, Executive Editor. Women's fiction, historical and contemporary romance; pop culture.

Alison Callahan, Executive Editor. "Ambitious" fiction; narrative nonfiction, memoir.

Mitchell Ivers, Vice President and Senior Editor. Commercial fiction; memoir, popular history, true crime, politics.

Jeremie Ruby-Strauss, Senior Editor. "Blockbuster nonfiction," celebrity, pop culture, diet/fitness, multimedia tie-ins.

(Ms.) Micki Nuding, Senior Editor. Women's, romance, and historical fiction; nondiet health subjects.

Abby Zidle, Senior Editor. Romance, suspense, thriller, women's fiction, historical fiction; pop culture.

Ed Schlesinger, Senior Editor. "Dark" fiction, horror, science fiction, fantasy, crime fiction; media tie-ins.

Adam Wilson, Senior Editor. Supernatural, thriller, romance, urban fiction, fantasy; pop culture.

Marla Daniels, Editorial Assistant. Romance, women's fiction.

Natasha Simons, Associate Editor. Upmarket horror and "women in jeopardy"; pop culture, online personalities.

Kate Dresser, Editor. Women's fiction; self-help, pop culture.

Elana Cohen, Assistant Editor. Women's fiction, romance.

NORTH STAR WAY ❖

www.simonandschusterpublishing.com/northstarway/home2.html

North Star is only a couple of years old and can be viewed as an innovative work in progress, or perhaps as an experiment with room to fail until it succeeds. The concept is that people who have an energetic social media footprint are competitively well positioned to support their book. North Star endeavors to provide these highly qualified authors with a wide range of ancillary nonpublishing benefits that traditional publishers never provide. The program is geared for mass-market self-help/how-to topics.

Michele Martin, Publisher.

POCKET BOOKS

Pocket has mostly reverted to its origins as a mass-market reprint program. Books that succeed in hardcover or quality paperback formats are often repurposed into less expensive mass-market editions where they prosper as backlist legacies, sometimes for eternity.

SCRIBNER ❖ imprints.simonandschuster.biz/scribner

Scribner is one of the extra-holy names in American publishing. When it was founded in 1846 by Charles Scribner and Isaac Baker, the company had a religious orientation. Scribner's sons saw greener, secular pastures, and within a few decades the firm was arguably the number one publisher of nonreligious American literature — which explains why the name became Charles Scribner's Sons as opposed to "& Sons," I assume. The house also launched and managed its own bookstore chain, as New Yorkers over the age of 50 will fondly recall. The forensics for how Scribner became an S&S satellite is a little like tracing the mammalian food chain. In 1984 Macmillan ate Scribner. Several years later Paramount ate Macmillan. Gulf+Western ate Paramount, which then became Viacom, which ate CBS. The sons are long dead, so now it's simply Scribner, and it seemingly struggles to support its autonomy. Without notice, the corporate overlords might decide that Scribner is an unprofitable redundancy, and it will disappear; that's what happened to the Free Press several years ago. However, the Scribner name will always be repurposed somewhere in the realm of publishing, because it's essentially immortal.

Colin Harrison, Vice President and Editor in Chief. Current events, culture, politics, history, sports, science, true crime.

(Ms.) Shannon Welch, Senior Editor. Health, wellness, lifestyle, psychology, spirituality, environment, education, sports, inspirational memoir.

John Glynn, Associate Editor. Literary fiction; sports, pop culture, health and wellness.

Rick Horgan, Executive Editor. Current events, thought-leader books, social issues, business, popular psychology, true crime.

Kathryn Belden, Executive Editor. Social/cultural history.

(Ms.) Liese Mayer, Editor. Literary and commercial fiction; social and cultural history, investigative journalism.

Daniel Loedel, Associate Editor. Literary fiction.
David Lamb, Editorial Assistant. Technology, sociology, politics.

SIMON & SCHUSTER ❖ imprints.simonandschuster.biz/simonandschuster

In addition to being the iconic name of the entire house (mansion), Simon & Schuster is also the name of one of its distinct divisions. Due to the rash of mergers, contractions, and nervous breakdowns endemic to the book business, there are numerous editorial overlaps and shared facilities, and even some healthy competition, between the divisions within each of the corporate entities. The S&S imprint's specialness is marked by the fact that it is the carrier of the nearly century-old name and possesses an immense backlist with many of the best books ever published in the US. In fairness, the same can be said of most of the legacy book brands. S&S's vibrant frontlist program can best be summed up as a wide spectrum of commercial fiction and nonfiction.

Alice Mayhew, Vice President and Editorial Director. History, politics, biography, philosophy, entertainment, pop culture.

Mary Sue Rucci, Vice President and Editor in Chief. Commercial fiction.

Priscilla Painton, Vice President and Executive Editor. Political biography, memoir, narrative, history, politics, science, religion, economics, US current events.

Trish Todd, Vice President and Executive Editor. Popular and literary fiction; practical nonfiction, lifestyle, psychology, humor.

Robert Bender, Vice President and Senior Editor. Biography, autobiography, history, current events, popular science, film, music, business narrative, investing, baseball.

(Mr.) Jofie Ferrari-Adler, Senior Editor. Politics, current affairs, recent history, military history, sports, narrative/investigative journalism, music.

Ben Loehnen, Senior Editor. Business, psychology, science, nature, religion.

Karyn Marcus, Senior Editor. Upmarket suspense; popular science, social trends, animal subjects.

Ira Silverberg, Senior Editor. Literary fiction; serious nonfiction.

Johanna Li, Associate Editor. Literary fiction; art and cultural history.

Emily Graff, Editor. Commercial and literary fiction; US history, current affairs.

Jonathan Cox, Editor. Science fiction; technology, economics, science, business, investigative journalism, sports.

Amar Deol, Assistant Editor. Crime fiction; true crime, business, psychology, sports, current affairs.

Stuart Roberts, Assistant Editor. History, current affairs, business, science, politics.

Sophia Jimenez, Editorial Assistant. Fiction and nonfiction that's "hilarious and quirky"; "minority voices."

Kaitlin Olson, Editorial Assistant. Suspense and historical fiction; popular science, lifestyle.

Julianna Haubner, Editorial Assistant. Historical sagas, investigative journalism.

Zachary Knoll, Editorial Assistant. Culinary/food, illustrated narrative.

Megan Hogan, Publishing Assistant. Strange history, popular science.

THRESHOLD EDITIONS ❖ simonandschusterpublishing.com/threshold-editions

Political- and social-themed books from a conservative perspective.

Mitchell Ivers, Editorial Director.

Natasha Simons, Associate Editor.

TOUCHSTONE BOOKS ❖ imprints.simonandschuster.biz/touchstone

Touchstone can best be described as a fusion catchall program combining frontlist original (fiction and nonfiction) titles and evergreen backlist cash cows. It's common for huge publishers to keep legacy brands alive, even if there's no unique purpose and substantial overlap with other imprints. You can never predict if new divisions will live or die, so bets are hedged through a process of cluttering clusters. Sometimes the new brands fail, and then the old brands become a welcome refuge for the surviving titles and editors, and vice versa.

Michelle Howry, Senior Editor. Practical nonfiction, self-help/how-to, personal finance, popular psychology, relationships, cooking, health, parenting.

Tara Parsons, Editor in Chief. Commercial fiction.

Lauren Spiegel, Senior Editor. Women's fiction; pop culture, celebrity.

Elaine Wilson, Editorial Assistant. Historical fiction; food memoir, cookbooks.

Matthew Benjamin, Senior Editor. Narrative and prescriptive nonfiction, investigative journalism, self-help, diet/fitness, men's interest.

Miya Kumangai, Editorial Assistant. Historical fiction and mystery.

(Ms.) Etinosa Agbonlahor, Editorial Assistant. Fiction with international themes.

SIMON & SCHUSTER CHILDREN'S

S&S is especially noted for its large and wide-ranging children's program, which includes several distinct divisions/imprints.

Aladdin ❖ imprints.simonandschuster.biz/aladdin

This dynamic imprint specializes in fiction and nonfiction picture books and chapter books from prereaders to middle grade.

Liesa Abrams, Editorial Director.
Alyson Heller, Editor. Picture books.
Emma Sector, Editorial Assistant. Fantasy, adventure, zany plots.
Karen Nagel, Executive Editor. Picture and chapter books.
Amy Cloud, Editor. All areas.

Atheneum Books for Young Readers ❖
imprints.simonandschuster.biz/atheneum

Publishes a full range of picture books, middle grade books, and teen titles.

Caitlyn Dlouhy, Vice President and Editorial Director.
Richard Jackson, Editorial Director.
(Ms.) Reka Simonsen, Executive Editor.
Emma Ledbetter, Associate Editor.
Alexa Pastor, Editorial Assistant.
Jessica Sit, Assistant Editor.
Natascha Morris, Editorial Assistant.

Little Simon ❖ imprints.simonandschuster.biz/little-simon

Noted for innovative and attractive books for young children.

Jeffrey Salane, Editorial Director.
Hannah Lambert, Editor.

Margaret K. McElderry Books ❖
imprints.simonandschuster.biz/margaret-k-mcelderry-books

A boutique imprint formed in 1972 by its legendary namesake. Well respected for a full range of author- and character-driven works for all ages in all formats.

Karen Wojtyla, Vice President and Editorial Director.
Annie Nybo, Assistant Editor.
Ruta Rimas, Editor.

Paula Wiseman Books ❖
imprints.simonandschuster.biz/paula-wiseman-books

A special imprint noted for high-quality novelty, illustrated, and gift books.

Paula Wiseman, Publisher.
Sylvie Frank, Editor.
Sarah Jane Abbott, Editorial Assistant.

Saga Press ❖ www.sagapress.com

Young adult science fiction, fantasy, and supernatural titles.

Joe Monti, Executive Editor.
(Ms.) Navah Wolfe. Editor.
Justin Chanda, Publisher.

Simon Pulse ❖ imprints.simonandschuster.biz/simon-pulse/home

Boundary-pushing fiction for teenagers.

Mara Anastas, Publisher.

Simon & Schuster Books for Young Readers ❖
imprints.simonandschuster.biz/bfyr

That's correct, Simon & Schuster is also the name of one of its distinct children's divisions. Its large program covers all ages and formats. As mentioned elsewhere, it's common for large houses to maintain multiple overlapping divisions. In most cases, the divisions pre-dated corporate mergers, and allowing them to prevail makes the most sense. Also, it's a way for houses to hedge their bets in case any of the new divisions falter.

David Gale, Vice President and Editorial Director. Contemporary middle grade and teen fiction.
(Ms.) Zareen Jaffery, Executive Editor. Commercial and literary fiction for teens and middle grade; teen nonfiction.
(Mr.) Christian Trimmer, Senior Editor. Picture books, middle grade and young adult fiction.
Kristin Ostby, Editor. Picture books, middle grade fiction and nonfiction.
Liz Kossnar, Editorial Assistant. Contemporary young adult fiction.
Catherine Laudone, Editorial Assistant. Literary and fantasy young adult, adventurous middle grade fiction.

Part 3

INDEPENDENT PRESSES (US)

PLANET INDEPENDENT

Jeff Herman

Here's the other half of publishing. Any publisher, no matter how large, that's not owned by one of the Big 5 corporate houses is by default an independent publisher. Some of them are micropublishers with revenues in the four figures, and some are huge, with revenues well into the 10 figures. See my introduction to the Big 5 section (page 65) for a fuller discussion about what separates the two categories.

The number of seven-figure independent houses has greatly declined since I produced the first edition of this book in 1990. Most of those entities were merged into one of the Big 5, and some simply went out of business as their owners retired or couldn't make payroll. Losing those houses has had serious consequences for readers and writers. A huge portion of an invaluable subspecies of book curators has abruptly disappeared and not been replaced — and perhaps it can't be adequately replaced in the current environment. As a direct result, writers have significantly fewer traditional opportunities for publishing their work. However, there's always an upside: the partial extinction, combined with digital technology, has made self-publishing indispensable and inevitable.

Which Publishers Are and Aren't Listed Here?

I have made my best effort to include all the many independent publishers I'm sufficiently familiar with. I'm confident these houses represent a strong cross section of regions, specialties, and subcultures. I welcome your suggestions for additional publishers to include in future editions (jeff@jeffherman.com).

What Advantages Do Independent Houses Offer Compared to the Big 5?

Let's begin by saying that most independent houses are able to do everything the corporate houses do in terms of marketing, quality production, editing, sales, and distribution. It's unusual for the bestseller lists not to include a decent number of independently published books.

The primary advantage is that the vast majority of independent publishers are actually owned and operated by a select group of human beings, not 20,000 shareholders.

Decisions are made on the basis of people's hearts and guts, not technical modalities. There are far fewer obstacles to editors' taking calculated risks and innovating, and authors are less likely to get lost in bureaucracy. Most successful ideas are generated and germinated by independent operators.

Independent houses are more likely to consider unagented/unsolicited submissions, for the simple reason that they don't receive as many agented submissions as the Big 5.

What Are the Disadvantages?

Frankly, I feel they are minimal. The primary disadvantage is that the Big 5 can and do pay large advances. The irony is that in practice this rarely happens. In fact, most Big 5 advances are on par with what the independents pay for comparable titles. More important, I'm not aware of any evidence showing a difference in total earnings (advance plus royalties) over a book's lifetime between corporate and independent houses for comparable titles. Nor am I aware of any evidence that the Big 5 sell more copies on average over a book's lifetime than the independents do for comparable titles.

Agents definitely prefer selling books to the Big 5 because the potential for a larger advance is always there, and each of the Big 5 acquires many, many more books than most of the independents can afford to.

Keep in mind that typical John Grisham, Stephen King, Danielle Steel, etc., fans neither know nor care who the publishers are. Readers are only focused on the author, not his/her publisher. They also care about price and perhaps what store they give their business to. Only industry insiders pay attention to who someone's publisher is. No writer should ever feel second-class because they are with a relatively obscure publisher. It's not a step down and might even be a step up considering the extra attention indie books often receive. As I said above, it's common for the bestseller lists to be populated by more than a few independently published titles. You probably don't know that because, like most people, you don't care, which further proves the point.

Independent publishing is one of the crucial safety nets against the industry's possible intellectual and creative suffocation. Current economic realities mandate the existence of multinational corporate empires. Naturally, these entities are no more or less enlightened than governments. Collateral damage only matters when it interferes with profits and market share. Destruction is laudable for the purposes of conquest and control. Innovations are driven by fear and greed, not generosity. One of Abraham Lincoln's greatest quotes was that people are more likely to be ruined by power than by adversity.

It's plausible that 10 years from now 90 percent of the book business will be controlled by three entities. In that case, the remaining 10 percent, and those whom they publish, will be on the front lines in a war against conformity. Approach this section with the wisdom that independent publishing is both a practical option and a philosophical mission.

THE LISTINGS

ABBEVILLE PRESS ❖ www.abbeville.com

116 West 23rd Street, New York, NY 10010, 646-375-2359

Founded in 1977, Abbeville publishes fine-art and illustrated books. Subjects include design and decorative arts, fashion, jewelry, food, nature and gardening, design, film, culture, music, sports, and travel. Their website states that they won't be acquiring new projects for the "next several seasons." However, never say "never."

Susan Costello, Editorial Director.

ABC-CLIO ❖ www.abc-clio.com

130 Cremona Drive, Santa Barbara, CA 93117, 805-968-1911

This company is over 50 years old, and I don't know what all the letters actually stand for, which probably doesn't matter. However, they publish an impressive list of reference and academic books for educators and students in all age ranges, covering many subjects. Their products are organized within several imprints and subsidiaries, some of which were formerly independent presses before being acquired by ABC.

ABC-CLIO/Greenwood ❖ www.abc-clio.com/ABC-CLIOGreenwood.aspx

This program covers a wide universe of subjects and identifies itself as "Your source for essential reference.... Books that improve the research experience by providing innovative content with directly relevant resources to enhance critical thinking."

Vince Burns, Vice President of Editorial; vburns@abc-clio.com.

Praeger ❖ www.abc-clio.com/Praeger.aspx

Praeger focuses on academic books about psychology, education, health, politics, current events, history, military issues, business, and religion.

Anthony Chiffolo, Editorial Director; achiffolo@abc-clio.com.

ABINGDON PRESS ❖ www.abingdonpress.com

201 Eighth Avenue South, Nashville, TN 37202, 800-251-3320

Founded in 1789, Abingdon is the official publisher of the United Methodist Church. As would be expected, it publishes a wide range of faith-, inspiration-, and curriculum-based books, including fiction. Its fiction program includes contemporary and historical romances, suspense, mystery, and Amish themes. The program prides itself on publishing a diversity of religious opinions.

Constance Stella, Senior Acquisitions Editor; cstella@abingdonpress.com.

AKASHIC BOOKS ❖ www.akashicbooks.com

232 Third Street, Suite A115, Brooklyn, NY 11215, 718-643-9193

Dedicated to publishing urban-themed literary fiction and political nonfiction by writers whom the establishment has "ignored" or refused to publish.

Ibrahim Ahmad, Senior Editor; info@akashicbooks.com.

AMACOM BOOKS ❖ www.amacombooks.org

1601 Broadway, New York, NY 10019, 212-586-8100

Amacom is the publishing division of the American Management Association, which if taken literally sounds like its purpose is to manage America. It publishes an excellent list of books for business professionals about management, leadership, motivation, training, marketing, public relations, sales, customer service, and finance. Surprisingly, it also publishes a modest number of nonbusiness self-help reference titles.

Editors' email addresses follow this format: firstinitiallastname@amanet.org.

Ellen Kadin, Executive Editor. Marketing, career development, communications, personal development.

Stephen S. Power, Senior Editor. Management, leadership, human resources.
Airie Stuart, Senior Editor. Small business, entrepreneurship, sales/marketing.

AMERICAN ACADEMY OF PEDIATRICS ❖ www.aap.org

Division of Consumer Publishing, 141 Northwest Point Boulevard,
Elk Grove Village, IL 60007, 847-434-7394

This program was created to provide quality educational information for parents and caregivers on a wide variety of health issues.

Kathryn Sparks, Editorial Manager; ksparks@aap.org.

ANDREWS MCMEEL PUBLISHING ❖ www.andrewsmcmeel.com

1130 Walnut Street, Kansas City, MO 64106, 816-581-7500

AM was founded in 1970 and originally named Universal Press Syndicate. The firm became extremely successful at syndicating a huge roster of illustrators, cartoonists, and columnists to an archaic physical-content delivery vehicle referred to as "newspapers." The book program was founded as an organic way to repurpose its talented clients. The firm is also famous for its calendar and gift book programs. In recent years, the frontlist program has been downsized to a tight list of mostly cookbooks and gift books, with some humor and middle grade fiction titles.

Patty Rice, Editor; price@amuniversal.com. Humor, gift, and illustrated gift.
Jean Lucas, Editor; jlucas@amuniversal.com. Illustrated cookbooks.

ARTE PUBLICO PRESS ❖ www.artepublicopress.com

4902 Gulf Freeway, Building 19, Room 100, Houston, TX 77204, 713-743-2843

This is the most established publisher of books by US-based Hispanic writers in fiction, nonfiction, and children's categories.

Writers are requested to follow the submission guidelines on the company's website.

BAEN BOOKS ❖ www.baen.com

PO Box 1188, Wake Forest, NC 27588

Baen is a veteran independent publisher of quality science fiction and fantasy books. The good news is that they actually welcome unsolicited manuscripts for acquisition consideration. However, they don't want it to be a particularly personal process where authors get to interact with real people — not a unique preference. The best method is to visit their website and follow the stated submission protocol.

BAKER PUBLISHING GROUP ❖ www.bakerpublishinggroup.com

6030 East Fulton Road, Ada, MI 49301, 616-676-9185

Baker claims to publish books that represent historic Christianity and the diverse interests of evangelical readers. The firm was founded in 1924 by a recent Dutch immigrant, Herman Baker, and became a thriving enterprise. Today's Baker comprises several imprints, most of which have their own storied histories.

Editors' email addresses follow this format: firstinitiallastname@bakerbooks.com.

Baker Books ❖ www.bakerpublishinggroup.com/bakerbooks

Baker publishes a large list of Christ-centered nonfiction self-help and reference books for laity and clergy.

Brian Thomasson, Editor.

Bethany House ❖ www.bakerpublishinggroup.com/bethanyhouse

Bethany began more than 50 years ago and is a leader in inspirational fiction, including romance and suspense. Its nonfiction program includes Christian living, theology, and "eternity."

(Ms.) Raela Schoenherr, Editor. Fiction.
Jeff Braun, Editor. Nonfiction.

Revell ❖ www.bakerpublishinggroup.com/revell

Revell has been publishing Christian books for more than 125 years. Subjects include inspirational and educational fiction, self-help, marriage/family issues, and youth books.

Vicki Crumpton, Editor. Nonfiction and fiction programs.

BEACON PRESS ❖ www.beacon.org

24 Farnsworth Street, Boston, MA 02210, 617-742-2110

Beacon has been a breath of independent air since 1854. It currently publishes books that seem to be about causes, social conditions, theories, and events that have affected, or are affecting, our lives. Women's and environmental subjects are welcome. Health-care issues receive a lot of attention. Although it would be unfair to say that the firm has any political or social agendas, it's clear that many of their books wouldn't be welcome by the Far Right or fundamental-religious communities.

Editors' email addresses follow this format: firstinitiallastname@beacon.org.

Helen Atwan, Editorial Director. Public health and legal issues.

Amy Caldwell, Executive Editor. Religion from a cultural and historical perspective, science and society, women's studies.

(Ms.) Gayatri Patnaik, Executive Editor. African American issues and history, LGBT issues, alternative views of American history.

Alexis Rizzuto, Contributing Editor. Environmental and educational issues.

Joanna Green, Editor. Social justice, environmental, economic, and judicial issues.

Rakia A. Clark, Senior Editor. Social issues.

Jill Petty, Senior Editor. Social issues.

Rachael Marks, Associate Editor. Educational issues.

Will Myers, Associate Editor. Environmental sustainability issues.

Melissa Nasson, Acquisitions Editor. Legal/judicial issues, women's interest.

BENBELLA BOOKS ❖ www.benbellabooks.com

10300 North Central Expressway, Suite 530, Dallas, TX 75231, 214-750-3600

BenBella is a successful, independent, outside-the-NYC-box boutique publisher. They tend to publish commercial self-help nonfiction books on timely subjects or by writers with self-marketing skill sets. They also publish narratives and true crime.

Editors' email addresses follow this format: firstname@benbellabooks.com.

Glenn Yeffeth, Publisher.

Debbie Harmsen, Editor in Chief.

Heather Butterfield, Editor.

Erin Kelley, Editor.

Leah Wilson, Executive Editor.

BERRETT-KOEHLER PUBLISHERS ❖ www.bkpub.com

235 Montgomery Street, Suite 650, San Francisco, CA 94104, 415-288-0260

This successful West Coast independent press publishes an eclectic and interesting list of business-oriented books that large publishers might pass over for the wrong reasons.

Their books are practical and traditional, and author "platforms" are of course critical. However, if the late Abbie Hoffman had written a real self-help business book, this is one of the venues he might have seriously considered.

Neal Maillet, Editorial Director; nmaillet@bkpub.com. .

BEYOND WORDS PUBLISHING ❖ www.beyondword.com

20827 NW Cornell Road, Suite 55, Hillsboro, OR 97124, 503-531-8700

Beyond Words has actually been a division of Simon & Schuster for many years. However, their origins are independent, and their current editorial process appears to be separate from that of their corporate overlord, so I've made an executive decision to list them as independent. If you've heard of *The Secret*, you'll understand what this boutique player is capable of accomplishing; it's plausible that the New York publishing matrix would have reflexively rejected that book with comments like "trite" or "too down-market." BW tends to publish books that are generally designated as mind-body-spirit.

Richard Cohn, Publisher; richard@beyondword.com.

BIBLIOMOTION ❖ www.bibliomotion.com

39 Harvard Street, Brookline, MA 02445, 617-934-2427

Bibliomotion is a recent start-up by two industry veterans. They promise to provide a crucial competitive advantage by integrating the author into every aspect of the publishing process, whereas almost all publishers prefer the opposite approach. They also promise to help their authors understand and use digital marketing. Their list appears to be 90 percent high-quality self-help business books and 10 percent general parenting books.

Erika Heilman, Cofounder and Publisher; erika@bibliomotion.com.

BLOOMSBURY PUBLISHING ❖ www.bloomsbury.com/us

1385 Broadway, New York, NY 10018, 212-419-5300

Bloomsbury qualifies as a multinational independent press with active English-language programs in England, Australia, and India. They publish a varied list of mostly narrative nonfiction books that most sentient beings would be impressed by, even if not inclined to read. They also publish some cookbooks and literary fiction. It's possible that many

Bloomsbury books would be rejected by corporate houses as "noncommercial" or too academic. Fortunately, the big players are often wrong about what books readers will indeed buy when given the chance.

Editors' email addresses follow this format: firstname.lastname@bloomsbury.com.

George Gibson, Publishing Director. History, current events, science.
Anton Mueller, Executive Editor. Current affairs, politics.
Nancy Miller, Editorial Director. Serious nonfiction subjects.
Lea Beresford, Senior Editor. Fiction and nonfiction.
Rachel Mannheimer, Editor. Fiction and nonfiction.

CAREER PRESS/NEW PAGE BOOKS ❖ www.careerpress.com
www.newpagebooks.com
12 Parish Drive, Wayne, NJ 07470, 800-227-3371

Career Press publishes the kind of business and personal-development books that real people (as opposed to MBA zombies) buy and read. Its hopping New Page division ranges from pedestrian self-help books about how to organize a traditional wedding to titles on how to organize Wiccan ceremonies. Anything you want to know about selling, extraterrestrials, and much more can be found here.

Michael Pye, Senior Acquisitions Editor; mpye@careerpress.com.
Adam Schwartz, Editor; aschwartz@careerpress.com.

CENTRAL RECOVERY PRESS ❖ www.centralrecoverypress.com
321 North Buffalo Drive, Suite 275, Las Vegas, NV 89129, 702-868-5830

This publisher specializes in books about addiction recovery, behavioral therapies, and general wellness. I'm surprised the casinos don't run them out of town. But then again, it makes sense to have a place to refer "clients" to after they lose their shirts.

Editors' email addresses follow this format: firstinitiallastname@centralrecovery press.com.

Nancy Schenck, Executive Editor.
Eliza Tutellier, Acquisitions Editor.
Vallery Killeen, Editor.

CHELSEA GREEN PUBLISHING ❖ www.chelseagreen.com

85 North Main Street, Suite 120, White River Junction, VT 05001, 802-295-6300

Founded in 1984 (which, prior to 1984, seemed like it would be an important year), Chelsea is a top-notch publisher of books about sustainable/green living, which can be summarized as "consumption minus destruction."

Editors' email addresses follow this format: firstinitiallastname@chelseagreen.com.

Joni Praded, Senior Editor. Books about political, social, and environmental issues.
Ben Watson, Senior Editor. Sustainability, human culture.
Michael Metivier, Associate Editor.
Fern Marshall Bradley, Senior Editor. Farming, gardening, community action.

CHICAGO REVIEW PRESS ❖ www.chicagoreviewpress.com

814 North Franklin Street, Chicago, IL 60610, 312-337-0747

The press was founded in 1973, has nearly 1,000 titles in print, and owns five distinct imprints. Subjects include crafts, film, food, history, music, parenting, pop culture, popular science, sports, travel, women's interest, and children's books.

Editors' email addresses follow this format: firstinitiallastname@chicagoreview press.com.

Cynthia Sherry, Publisher. Nonfiction children's books, travel, popular science.
Jerome Pohlen, Senior Editor. History, gardening, education, popular science, young adult nonfiction.
(Mr.) Yuval Taylor, Senior Editor. Music, film, history.
Lisa Reardon, Senior Editor. Children's and young adult nonfiction, parenting.

Lawrence Hill Books

This imprint was acquired by CRP in 1993. It was founded in 1973 in Brooklyn, New York, and is noted for its books about African American issues, urban subjects, civil rights, progressive politics, and history.

The same editors as above acquire for this program.

Ball Publishing

Specializes in professional horticulture.

Cynthia Sherry, Publisher.
Jerome Pohlen, Senior Editor.

Zephyr Press

Specializes in professional books for educators.

Jerome Pohlen, Senior Editor.

Academy Chicago Publishers

Started as a regional independent press many decades ago and still specializes in fiction and nonfiction books relevant to Chicago.

Anita Miller, Editor-at-Large.
(Mr.) Jordan Miller, Editor-at-Large.

CHRONICLE BOOKS ❖ www.chroniclebooks.com

680 Second Street, San Francisco, CA 94107, 415-537-4200

Chronicle claims to have been born on the day that paper was invented in the year 105 CE, even though there's no record of the firm's existence prior to 1967 CE. The nature of their claim accurately reflects Chronicle's irreverent publishing personality. Though some of their books are arguably absurd, profits are a reasonable justification after the fact, especially if you're one of the company's owners. Here you will find a delightful array of cleverly packaged and designed theme-oriented books/products for children, adults, and anyone who likes things that are silly and/or useful.

Editors' email addresses follow this format: firstname_lastname@chroniclebooks.com.

Melissa Manlove, Editor. Children's picture books.
Ginee Seo, Director of Children's Division.
Wynn Rankin, Editor. Illustrated books.
Sarah Billingsley, Editor. Food and cooking.
Tamra Tuller, Editor. Children's.
Elizabeth Yarborough, Editor. Health, reference, self-help.
Laura Lee Mattingly, Senior Editor. Lifestyle, parenting, self-help/how-to.
Sarah Malarkey, Publishing Director. Pop culture, humor, reference.
Amy Treadwell, Senior Editor. Food and drink.

CLEIS PRESS ❖ www.cleispress.com

101 Hudson Street, Suite 3705, Jersey City, NJ 07302, 646-257-4343

This publisher could also be named Over-the-Top Press. Cleis outs itself as "the largest sexuality and queer publisher in America." But their catalog seems to have something for everyone and even offers a lot of books that aren't about orgasms.

Karen Thomas, Editor; acquistions@cleispress.com.

COFFEE HOUSE PRESS ❖ www.coffeehousepress.org

79 Thirteenth Avenue NE, #110, Minneapolis, MN 55413, 612-338-0125

I'm very happy that there's a publisher with this perky name. Coffee House is a nonprofit company, something many publishers would never admit to. They publish books, poetry included, that their editors deem to be genuine works of art. Guess what? There's a market for that.

(Mr.) Chris Fischbach, Publisher; fish@coffeehousepress.org.

DEVORSS & COMPANY ❖ www.devorss.com

PO Box 1389, Camarillo, CA 93011

Since 1929, DeVorss has been publishing books about metaphysics, spirituality, and New Thought concepts, which can also be captioned as mind-body-spirit. The company also distributes and markets titles published by others that are in harmony with its own catalog.

Editorial@devorss.com.

EERDMANS PUBLISHING CO. ❖ www.eerdmans.com

2140 Oak Industrial Drive NE, Grand Rapids, MI 49505, 616-459-4591

Founded in 1911, Eerdmans is an independent publisher of Christian books ranging from academics to theology, Bible studies, and religious history and reference. The firm prides itself on publishing objective viewpoints throughout the "Christian spectrum" without favoring any single Christian perspective. They also have a Young Readers program.

Editors' email addresses follow this format: firstinitiallastname@eerdmans.com.

James Ernest, Editor in Chief.

Anita Eermans, Publisher. Children's program.

Gayle Brown, Editor and Art Director. Young Readers program.

Kathleen Merz, Editor. Children's program.

ENTREPRENEUR PRESS ❖ www.entrepreneur.com/entrepreneurpress

18061 Fitch, Irvine, CA 92614, 949-622-7106

Entrepreneur Press is a division of the popular magazine named *Entrepreneur*. As would be expected, they publish books about zoology and proctology. That was a test to see if anyone actually reads what I break my finger bones writing. Per their website, their books "aim to provide actionable solutions to help entrepreneurs excel in all ventures they take on." In fact, they generate a rich assortment of cutting-edge how-to/self-help and reference books for anyone in business, even if not self-employed.

Jennifer Dorsey, Editor; jdorsey@entrepreneur.com.

EUROPA EDITIONS ❖ www.europaeditions.com

214 West 29th Street, Suite 1003, New York, NY 10001, 212-868-6844

Europa is an independent publisher of literary fiction, nonfiction, and "high-end crime" fiction. Founded in 2005, the firm specializes in bringing some of Europe's best books to American readers, and vice versa. Authors from several dozen nations, including the US, are published by Europa. It's safe to assume that the firm favors books by Americans that will have international appeal and relevance.

Kent Carroll, Publisher; kentcarroll@europaeditions.com.

Michael Reynolds, Editor in Chief; michaelreynolds@europaeditions.com.

F+W MEDIA ❖ www.fwmedia.com

F+W Media is the umbrella for several craft- and hobby-specific book, seminar, and magazine divisions.

Adams Media ❖ www.adamsmedia.com

57 Littlefield Street, Avon, MA 02311, 508-427-7100

Adams was acquired by F+W in 2003 and has continued its successful tradition of generating commercial and practical self-help titles in most areas that typical Americans do or will encounter.

Editors' email addresses follow this format: firstname.lastname@adamsmedia.com.

Peter Archer, Editor. Nonfiction, including popular business.
Christine Dore, Editor. Cooking, parenting.
Jacqueline Musser, Editor. Lifestyle, self-help.

Writer's Digest Books ❖ www.writersdigest.com

10151 Carver Road, Blue Ash, OH 45242, 513-531-2690

For many decades WD has published a huge list of reference, self-help, and inspiration titles for writers about writing and publishing. Most writers are familiar with the magazine of the same name.

Phillip Sexton, Publisher; phillip.sexton@fwcommunity.com.

GRAYWOLF PRESS ❖ www.graywolfpress.org

250 Third Avenue North, Suite 600, Minneapolis, MN 55401, 651-641-0077

Graywolf is committed to "discovering and energetically publishing" contemporary American and international literature (fiction and nonfiction). They "champion writers in all stages of their careers" and look for "diverse voices." In other words, this is a not-for-profit publisher that won't let potential lack of sales dissuade them from publishing what they deem to be great books. However, in practice, because their catalog is known to be carefully curated by exceptionally astute people, anything they publish is immediately considered to be wonderful by a core community of devoted readers; which is a little like running for mayor of New York City once you get the Democratic nomination. Of course, it's a subjective process, but like-minded communities are by definition homogenously subjective.

Ethan Nosowsky, Editorial Director; nosowsky@graywolfpress.org.

GROVE ATLANTIC ❖ www.groveatlantic.com

154 West 14th Street, New York, NY 10011, 212-614-7850

"An independent literary publisher since 1917." Several imprints coexist under this revered umbrella, though they appear to share the same editorial team. Corporate houses would quickly dismiss many books published here due to a commercially risk-averse culture.

Editors' email addresses follow this format: firstinitiallastname@groveatlantic.com.

(Mr.) Morgan Entreken, Publisher. Fiction; current events/issues, politics.
Otto Penzler, Editor for the Mysterious Press imprint.
Amy Hundley, Senior Editor. Fiction.
Peter Blackstock, Senior Editor. Fiction; social history.
Joan Bingham, Senior Editor. Fiction, mystery; social history and issues.
Jamison Stoltz, Editor. History, current events.
Elizabeth Schmitz, Editorial Director. Fiction.

Grove Press ❖ www.groveatlantic.com/#page=infogrove

Grove was founded in 1947 in America's bohemian heartland (at that time), Greenwich Village, and quickly made a name for itself by publishing numerous bad boys who used foul language, practiced unorthodox sexual methodologies, liked to induce hallucinations, and even tended to compulsively "typewrite" (meant as a cutting criticism at the time). Much ground has been covered along the road since then. In 1993 Grove and Atlantic Monthly Press merged their DNA to become a perfectly respectful and self-supporting publisher of wide-ranging fiction and nonfiction works that tend to have intriguing titles by authors with exotic or sensuous names, which you'll definitely want to read in the absence of noise or other enticements for nimble brains and bodies.

Atlantic Monthly Press ❖ www.groveatlantic.com/#page=infoatlantic

The only obvious distinction (in these times) between the Atlantic and Grove imprints is that Atlantic publishes only hardcover books, whereas Grove also publishes paperback originals and reprints.

The Mysterious Press ❖ www.groveatlantic.com/#page=infomysterious

Here you will find hardcore noir and adrenaline stimulation, both the old-time classics and new titles by those who dare to attempt following in their footsteps.

HARVEST HOUSE ❖ www.harvesthousepublishers.com

990 Owen Loop North, Eugene, OR 97402, 800-547-8979

From the publisher's mission statement: "To glorify God by providing high-quality books and products that affirm biblical values…and proclaim Jesus Christ as the answer to every human need." This nondenominational Christian press publishes a large list of practical and accessible self-help books for adults and children about how to confront life's challenges in Christian ways. They also publish inspirational fiction.

Kathleen Kerr, Editor; kathleen.kerr@harvesthousepublishers.com. Fiction and nonfiction.

LaRae Weikert, Editor; larae.weikert@harvesthousepublishers.com. Fiction, children's; nonfiction.

HAY HOUSE ❖ www.hayhouse.com

PO Box 5100, Carlsbad, CA 92018, 760-431-7695

Hay House is a pacesetter in the mind-body-spirit book categories. Many of the most financially successful self-help gurus are published by Hay House (not to be confused with their subsidy/vanity division, Balboa Press). They publish a diversity of nonfiction titles relevant to self-improvement with a spiritual or metaphysical slant. They also publish kindred nonbook merchandise.

Patty Gift, Director of Acquisitions; pgift@hayhouse.com.

HAZELDEN PUBLISHING ❖

www.hazelden.org/web/public/publishing.page

PO Box 176, Center City, MN 55012, 651-213-4213

Hazelden's stated mission is to help people recognize, understand, and overcome addiction and related problems and challenges. This is the in-house publishing arm of one of the most respected and pioneering recovery facilities in the world. Their books are consistent with the proverbial 12-step approach.

Sid Farrar, Editor; sfarrar@hazelden.org.

HEALTH COMMUNICATIONS, INC. ❖ www.hcibooks.com

3201 SW 15th Street, Deerfield Beach, FL 33442, 945-360-0909

"Changing lives one book at a time" (from publisher's website), HCI claims to select books that help readers achieve abundance, consolation, and healing through a huge range of self-help subjects for adults and teens. HCI enjoyed many years in the sun publishing the *Chicken Soup for the Soul* series.

Allison Janse, Editor.
Christine Belleris, Editorial Director; christineb@hcibooks.com.

HIPPOCRENE BOOKS ❖ www.hippocrenebooks.com

171 Madison Avenue, New York, NY 10016, 212-685-4373

For more than 40 years, Hippocrene has been a leading publisher of ethnic-food cookbooks, foreign-language dictionaries, and translations.

Anne McBride, Editor in Chief; annemcbride@yahoo.com.

HOUGHTON MIFFLIN HARCOURT ❖ www.houghtonmifflinbooks.com

222 Berkeley Street, Boston, MA 02116, 617-351-5000
3 Park Avenue, New York, NY 10016, 212-420-5800

HMH is an amalgamation of several revered houses with deep American roots. It qualifies as one of the largest independent firms, as opposed to a corporate firm, because its owners only publish books; there are no other, more lucrative priorities. They publish a wide commercial list of fiction and nonfiction for adults and children.

Editors' email addresses follow this format: firstname.lastname@hmhco.com.

Alexander Littlefield, Senior Editor (NY). Food, science, social history.
Justin Schwartz, Executive Editor (NY). Cookbooks, food, lifestyle.
Susan Canavan, Senior Executive Editor (MA). Sports history, contemporary history.
Jenna Johnson, Executive Editor (NY). Fiction; quirky humorous reference titles.
Bruce Nichols, Publisher (NY). Political history, current events, health issues.
Lauren Wein, Executive Editor (NY). Fiction.
Deanne Urmy, Senior Executive Editor (MA). Politics, current affairs, health, women's interest.

Rick Wolff, Senior Executive Editor (NY). Business subjects, sports.

Naomi Gibbs, Associate Editor (NY). Thriller; science.

Nicole Angeloro, Editor (MA). Fiction.

HOUGHTON MIFFLIN HARCOURT CHILDREN'S

Picture books, middle grade through young adult.

Margaret Raymo, Senior Executive Editor (MA).

Ann Rider, Executive Editor (MA).

Kate O'Sullivan, Senior Editor (MA).

Elizabeth Bewley, Executive Editor (NY).

Jeannette Larson, Editorial Director (NY).

Julie Tibbott, Editor (NY).

Clarion

Dinah Stevenson, Publisher (NY).

Lynne Polvino, Editor (NY).

Anne Hoppe, Associate Publisher (NY).

HUMAN KINETICS PUBLISHERS, INC. ❖ www.humankinetics.com

PO Box 5076, Champaign, IL 61825, 800-747-4457

HK is a well-established publisher of books, journals, and educational content relevant to health, physical education, sport sciences, recreation, and dance.

acquisitions@hkusa.com

INNER TRADITIONS/BEAR & COMPANY ❖ www.innertraditions.com

PO Box 388, 1 Park Street, Rochester, VT 05767, 802-767-3174

For more than 30 years, these two recently merged firms have published a rich list of books about ancient mysteries, Celtic studies, Eastern religions, healing arts, martial arts, Tantra, tarot, and many related subjects.

Jon Graham, Editor; jon@innertraditions.com.

KENSINGTON PUBLISHING ❖ www.kensingtonbooks.com

119 West 40th Street, New York, NY 10018, 800-221-2647

Founded in 1974, Kensington is one of the largest independent publishing houses in the US today, best known for its dense lists of category/genre mass-market fiction and some nonfiction, all divided into several imprints.

Editors' email addresses follow this format: firstinitiallastname@kensingtonbooks.com.

Dafina

African American–themed romance titles.

Selena James, Editor.

Kensington

Kensington covers the whole waterfront of category commercial fiction.

John Scognamiglio, Editor in Chief. Mystery, romance.
Alicia Condon, Editorial Director. All fiction categories.
(Ms.) Esi Sogah, Editor. Romance.
Michaela Hamilton, Executive Editor. Mystery, thriller; true crime, pets, pop culture.
Martin Biro, Editor. All fiction areas.
Peter Senftleben, Associate Editor. All fiction areas.
Wendy McCurdy, Editorial Director. All fiction areas.

LLEWELLYN WORLDWIDE ❖ www.llewellyn.com

2143 Wooddale Drive, Woodbury, MN 55125, 651-291-1970

Founded in 1901, Llewellyn is one of the largest independent mind-body-spirit publishers. Specific topics include Wiccan, New Age, metaphysics, wellness, and kindred nonbook products.

Editors' email addresses follow this format: firstnamelastinitial@llewellyn.com.

Amy Glazer, Acquisition Editor. Animals, paranormal.
Elysia Gallo, Editor. Occult.
Angela Wix, Editor. Self-help, reference, spirituality.

MANIC D PRESS ❖ www.manicdpress.com

Box 410804, San Francisco, CA 94141, 415-648-8288

I'm sorry, but I'm at a loss for how to reflect what this publisher is about, but I'll give it my best shot. If you wrote a heavily illustrated book, fiction or nonfiction, that June Cleaver, Donna Reed, or Ted Cruz would consider unacceptably perverse, then you have found a possible home.

mss@manicdpress.com

MCGRAW-HILL PROFESSIONAL ❖ www.mhprofessional.com

2 Penn Plaza, New York, NY 10121, 212-512-2000

McGraw-Hill is a huge corporation comprising many nonbook divisions. However, everything the firm does is dedicated to generating and distributing content for educators and professionals about many subjects, and their trade book program continues to be an important piece of the corporate matrix. They publish a wide list of titles relevant to all areas of business, personal finance, investing, and entrepreneurship.

Editors' email addresses follow this format: firstname_lastname@mcgraw-hill.com.

Donya Dickerson, Editorial Director. All business categories.
Knox Huston, Senior Editor. Leadership, management, investment.
(Ms.) Casey Ebro, Senior Editor. Popular business, how-to, reference.
Cheryl Ringer, Editor. All business categories.

MILKWEED EDITIONS ❖ www.milkweed.org

1011 Washington Avenue South, Suite 300, Minneapolis, MN 55415, 612-332-3192

Founded in 1980, Milkweed calls itself an independent publisher of literature and proclaims that its purpose is to "identify, nurture and publish transformative literature [poetry, fiction and nonfiction, and young adult], and build an engaged community around it." The company depends on donations in addition to revenues for its survival. Having that safety net obviously enables its editors to be extra-risky and not entirely beholden to traditional profit-and-loss protocols.

Daniel Slager, Publisher; daniel_slager@milkweed.org.
(Ms.) Joey McGarvey, Editor; joey_mcgarvey@milkweed.org.

NAVAL INSTITUTE PRESS ❖ www.usni.org

291 Wood Road, Annapolis, MD 21402, 410-268-6110

From the website: "to advance the professional, literary and scientific understanding of sea power and issues critical to national defense and its historic traditions." Though the press is entirely independent of the Defense Department, its primary markets are the Navy, merchant marines, and relevant communities. Their biggest commercial success was as Tom Clancy's original fiction publisher (he was a Navy alumnus).

Richard Latture, Editor in Chief.

NEW HARBINGER PUBLICATIONS ❖ www.newharbinger.com

5674 Shattuck Avenue, Oakland, CA 94609, 800-748-6273

New Harbinger prides itself on generating a primo catalog of scientifically sound yet cutting-edge self-help books in many areas of physical and mental health and personal growth.

Melissa Kirk, Acquisitions Editor; melissa@newharbinger.com.

NEW HORIZON PRESS ❖ www.newhorizonpressbooks.com

PO Box 669, Far Hills, NJ 07931, 908-604-6311

NHP focuses on true crime, "battles for justice," medical drama, incredible true stories, women's and men's interest, and parenting. Many of its books are optioned for TV and film.

Joan Dunphy, Publisher; nhp@newhorizonpressbooks.com.

THE NEW PRESS ❖ www.thenewpress.com

120 Wall Street, 31st floor, New York, NY 10005, 212-629-8802

The New Press claims to publish serious books that promote a better understanding of vital domestic and international issues, and strives to publish books that mainstream commercial houses aren't modeled to deal with. They can afford to do this because they are a nonprofit subsidized by private-sector donors (I don't know who). I feel it's safe to say that most of their books would be considered left of center both politically and socially, though they don't appear to be aligned with any specific parties or organizations.

Carl Bromley, Editorial Director; cbromley@thenewpress.com.

NEW WORLD LIBRARY ❖ www.newworldlibrary.com

14 Pamaron Way, Novato, CA 94949, 415-884-2100

In 1977, on a kitchen table, Whatever Publishing was born. Today it's an eight-figure enterprise. The firm publishes about three dozen new titles each year in the areas of personal consciousness, personal growth, creativity, prosperity, philosophy, spirituality, wellness, nature/environment, and many related subjects — even book publishing.

Georgia Hughes, Editorial Director; georgia@newworldlibrary.com.

Jason Gardner, Executive Editor; jason@newworldlibrary.com.

W.W. NORTON & COMPANY, INC. ❖ www.wwnorton.com

500 Fifth Avenue, New York, NY 10110, 212-354-5500

What began in someone's living room more than 90 years ago has become the largest publishing company entirely owned by its employees. That sounds like a kibbutz, though I'm sure there's an economic/political hierarchy. The firm strives to publish books about influential issues and events that cross into all conceivable areas of human endeavor and discovery. If the Public Broadcasting System had a book division, Norton might be it. They also publish a respected fiction list.

Editors' email addresses follow this format: firstinitiallastname@wwnorton.com.

Matt Weiland, Senior Editor. History, literary biography, sports.

John Glusman, Editor in Chief. Military, political, and American history.

Brendan Curry, Senior Editor. Current events, political history, science, technology.

Maria Guarnaschelli, Editor. Unusual food and cookbooks, cultural history.

Jill Bialosky, Editor. Fiction; science.

Jeff Shreve, Editor. Science, political issues.

Tom Mayer, Senior Editor. Fiction; science, psychology.

Alane Mason, Executive Editor. Cultural and political history.

Amy Cherry, Senior Editor. Social history and themes.

NO STARCH PRESS ❖ www.nostarch.com

245 8th Street, San Francisco, CA 94103, 415-863-9900

No Starch claims to be "the finest in geek entertainment." Maybe you know what that means better than I. They have an excellent list of books about all areas of computing that appear to be both entertaining and educational. They also have a lot of books about games, LEGO, science, and math.

Tyler Ortman, Editor; tyler@nostarch.com.

Jennifer Griffith-Delgado, Editor; jennifer@nostarch.com.

THE OVERLOOK PRESS ❖ www.overlookpress.com

141 Wooster Street, New York, NY 10012, 212-673-2526

Founded in 1971, Overlook successfully publishes a large, eclectic list of fiction and non-fiction titles in such areas as history and culture.

Peter Mayer, Publisher; pmayer@overlookny.com.

PAULIST PRESS ❖ www.paulistpress.com

997 Macarthur Boulevard, Mahwah, NJ 07430, 800-218-1903

According to its website, Paulist "publishes the best in Catholic thought since 1972." The company is part of the Paulist Fathers and strives to bring Catholic-based education, wisdom, healing, growth, and inspiration to all peoples.

Rev. Mark-David Janus, CSP, Editorial Director; submissions@paulistpress.com.

PEACHTREE PUBLISHERS ❖ www.peachtree-online.com

1700 Chattahoochee Avenue, Atlanta, GA 30318, 404-876-8761

Peachtree publishes quality children's books, from picture books to young adult fiction and nonfiction. In adult categories they publish titles about parenting, health, and anything about the American South.

Helen Harriss, Acquisitions Editor; requests hardcopy submissions — don't submit by email.

PEGASUS BOOKS ❖ www.pegasusbooks.com

80 Broad Street, 5th Floor, New York, NY 10004, 212-504-2924

Pegasus publishes a wide-ranging list including history, philosophy, culture, and literary fiction.

Editors' email addresses follow this format: firstname@pegasusbooks.us.

Jessica Case, Associate Publisher. Upmarket crime and suspense fiction; history, popular science, culture.

Iris Blasi, Senior Editor. Fiction, mystery, thriller; quirky journalistic narrative.

Maia Larson, Associate Editor. Historical, crime, and suspense fiction, fantasy, science fiction; true crime.

PELICAN PUBLISHING COMPANY ❖ www.pelicanpub.com

1000 Burmaster Street, Gretna, LA 70053, 504-368-1175

Pelican is best known for travel guides, architectural reviews, holiday-themed books, specialized cookbooks, some fiction, and children's books. As might be expected, many of its titles are relevant to the Gulf Coast. In fact, surviving natural disasters, not to mention the economy, has often been the company's greatest challenge.

Nina Kooij, Editor in Chief; editorial@pelicanpub.com.

THE PERMANENT PRESS ❖ www.thepermanentpress.com

4170 Noyac Road, Sag Harbor, NY 11963, 631-725-1101

Since 1978, this micropublisher sustains itself by publishing literary fiction, and some nonfiction, that serious readers can't ignore. Near zero capitalization has never been a worthy excuse for failure in the book business, for the simple reason that quality will outlast all the hype that money can buy. The key has always been patience and the ability to resist making risky expenditures. During times of easy credit it's only too easy to overspend and overborrow, which is why so many worthy independent presses ultimately disappear. We should all pay attention to why some small presses, like this one, prevail.

Martin Shepard, Publisher; shepard@thepermanentpress.com.

PROMETHEUS BOOKS ❖ www.prometheusbooks.com

59 John Glenn Drive, Amherst, NY 14228, 716-691-0133

Prometheus defines itself as a leading publisher of popular science, philosophy, humanism, psychology, and perhaps any other topic you can think of. In actuality, this is a somewhat controversial publisher that tends to publish deliberately confrontational and provocative content. For instance, if you want to challenge organized religion, New Age concepts, or unproven alternative-health protocols, this might be your home. The house can't be nailed down as politically left-wing or right-wing. They simply seem to like material that's supported by logic and hard science, as opposed to emotions, sentimentality, or wishful thinking.

Dan Mayer, Editorial Director, dmayer@prometheusbooks.com.

QUARTO PUBLISHING GROUP ❖ www.quartoknows.com

100 Cummings Center, Beverly, MA 01915, 800-328-0590

Quarto is a UK-based firm and claims to be "the world's leading illustrated book publisher and distributor." I don't know if that's an accurate statement, but it at least explains what they are about. The firm has been expanding its US footprint in recent years and publishes its titles under a range of imprints, the most active of which are identified below.

Fair Winds Press

A large and growing list of books about health, beauty, fitness, parenting, and lifestyle.

Jill Alexander, Acquisitions Editor; jill@rockpub.com.

Harvard Common Press ❖ www.harvardcommonpress.com

535 Albany Street, Boston, MA 02118, 617-423-5803

This well-established independent press was acquired by the Quarto Group in early 2016, which means that much of the available information as of press time, including location, may have changed. The company has never had anything to do with Harvard, but is named for Harvard Common, which is an actual place that anyone can name their company after without permission. Since 1976, the company has been a successful producer of high-quality and uniquely positioned food books and cookbooks. They are also noted for their excellent taste in parenting and childbirth titles.

editorial@harvardcommonpress.com.

QUIRK BOOKS ❖ www.quirkbooks.com

215 Church Street, Philadelphia, PA 19106, 215-627-3581

In view of their name, it would be appalling for any of their books to be ordinary, not to mention dull. Quirk's website welcomes "off-the-wall" novels, "playful" cooking and craft books, and "cool photography or crazy illustrations." They have a strong children's program and also publish nonbook merchandise.

Jason Rekulak, Publisher; jason@quirkbooks.com. Adult and children's fiction; humor, pop culture, sports, sex, monsters, "guy stuff."

Tiffany Hill, Editor; tiffany@quirkbooks.com. Food, drink, parenting, pets, creative reference, making stuff, "girl stuff."

RED WHEEL/WEISER/CONARI ❖ www.redwheelweiser.com

665 Third Street, Suite 400, San Francisco, CA 94107, 415-978-2665

What we have here is a synergistic consolidation of several legacy metaphysical/esoteric/spiritual/New Age publishing brands. These forced communities generally work out well enough; the only potential downside being that the resulting amoeba might disrespect the various colonies within its realm. Red Wheel and its imprints publish books in a wide range of mind-body-spirit categories, including metaphysics, alternative health, yoga, relationships, and New Age. The Weiser imprint seems to have a tighter focus on the occult, esoteric philosophies, and the "old" religions. Conari Press has a strong footprint in women's interest.

Greg Brandenburgh, Editor in Chief; gbrandenburgh@rwwbooks.com.

REGAN ARTS ❖ www.reganarts.com

65 Bleecker Street, 8th floor, New York, NY 10012, 646-448-6611

This is a very new press founded by industry veteran Judith Regan. Its first catalogs are focused on solid nonfiction subjects and narratives powered by big-name/celebrity authors with reliable media platforms.

Editors' email addresses follow this format: firstname@reganarts.com.

Judith Regan, President.

Alexis Gargagliano, Executive Editor.

Lucas Wittmann, Executive Editor.

Jordana Tusman, Senior Editor.

REGNERY PUBLISHING, INC. ❖ www.regnery.com

300 New Jersey Avenue NW, Washington, DC 20001, 202-216-0600

Fidel Castro will never be a Regnery author. Neither will Hillary Clinton. But their names are frequently referenced in unflattering ways in many of Regnery's books. Without going to the blatant extremes of fascism, this is where right-wingers are at home, and more than a few of them have landed on the *New York Times* bestseller list. Regnery likes publishing toothy exposés about public figures and issues that tend to liberally draw from hearsay, gossip, and anonymous sources.

Editors' email addresses follow this format: firstinitiallastname@eaglepub.com.

(Mr.) Alex Novak, Associate Publisher.
Marji Ross, Publisher.
Harry Crocker, Executive Editor.

RODALE BOOKS ❖ www.rodaleinc.com

733 Third Avenue, New York, NY 10017, 212-697-2040

Rodale Books is the book-publishing division of Rodale, which is internationally respected as a multimedia content generator in the areas of healthy living. Naturally and organically, the book program reflects and supports the company's mission.

Editors' email addresses follow this format: firstname.lastname@rodale.com.

(Ms.) Dervla Kelly, Senior Editor. Lifestyle, cooking, illustrated books.
Jennifer Levesque, Editorial Director. Diet, fitness, cooking, sports, parenting, lifestyle.
Ursula Cary Ziemba, Senior Editor. Sustainable lifestyle.
Marisa Vigilante, Senior Editor. Health, diet, wellness, lifestyle.
Leah Miller, Senior Editor. Mind-body-spirit, inspiration, psychology, new ideas.
Mollie Thomas, Assistant Editor. Simplified sustainable living.
Mark Weinstein, Executive Editor. Sports, fitness, men's health.
Jeff Csatari, Executive Editor. Practical health and fitness, men's health.

ROWMAN & LITTLEFIELD ❖ www.rowman.com

4501 Forbes Boulevard, Lanham, MD 20706, 301-459-3366
5360 Manhattan Circle, Boulder, CO 80303, 303-543-7835
200 Park Avenue South, Suite 1109, New York, NY 10003, 212-529-3888

In recent years, Rowman has accumulated an impressive portfolio of independent presses with strong positions in their respective professional and academic communities (including

Globe Pequot and Lyons Press). Under its own name, Rowman publishes a huge list of nonfiction titles for scholars and consumers in the humanities and social sciences.

Editors' email addresses follow this format: firstinitiallastname@rowman.com.

Susan McEachern, Editorial Director (CO). International studies, geography, history, regional studies.

Suzanne Staszak-Silva, Executive Editor (NY). Health, psychology, sexuality, food studies, military life studies, criminal justice, crime studies.

Marie-Claire Antoine, Senior Acquisitions Editor (NY). Security, terrorism, intelligence, diplomacy, Middle Eastern and African politics.

Sarah Stanton, Senior Acquisitions Editor (CO). Sociology, religion, criminology.

Leanne Silverman, Acquisitions Editor (CO). Anthropology, archaeology, communications.

Susanne Canavan, Acquisitions Editor (MD). Education.

Tom Koerner, Publisher (MD). Educational market.

Charles Harmon, Executive Editor (CO). Library/information sciences, museum studies.

Jonathan Sisk, Senior Executive Editor (MD). American government, US history.

Stephen Ryan, Senior Acquisitions Editor (MD). Arts, entertainment, pop culture for adult and young adult markets.

Christen Karniski, Editor. Sports.

Kathryn Knigge, Associate Editor (MD). Military life, green living, criminal justice, true crime.

Audra Figgins, Assistant Editor (CO). Geography.

Monica Saviglia, Assistant Editor (MD). Military history, intelligence studies, Mid-East and African politics.

Globe Pequot ❖ www.globepequot.com

246 Goose Lane, Guilford, CT 06437, 203-458-4500

Specializes in regional travel guides throughout the US, books of regional interest and regional history, and popular reference.

Rick Rinehart, Editor (MD). All above areas.

Erin Turner, Executive Editor (CT). Regional history and stories.

Amy Lyons, Editorial Director (CT). Regional reference and interest.

Holly Rubino, Senior Editor (CT). Pets, animals.

Keith Wallman, Editor (CT). American, military, and sports history.

Gene Brissie, Editor (CT). American history.

SASQUATCH BOOKS ❖ www.sasquatchbooks.com

1904 Third Avenue, Suite 710, Seattle, WA 98101, 206-467-4300

Sasquatch is known for its innovative and eclectic list of nonfiction books about food and wine, travel, lifestyle, gardening, and nature. Many of its books are relevant to the Pacific Northwest region.

Gary Luke, Editor; gluke@sasquatchbooks.com.
Hannah Elnan, Editor; helnan@sasquatchbooks.com.

SCHOLASTIC INC. ❖ www.scholastic.com

557 Broadway, New York, NY 10012, 212-343-6100

Scholastic is the largest publisher of children's and young adult editorial products in the world. They publish for both consumer distribution and classroom adoption.

Editors' email addresses follow this format: firstinitiallastname@scholastic.com.

Aimee Friedman, Executive Editor.
Mallory Kass, Editor.
Emily Seife, Editor.

Arthur A. Levine Books ❖ www.arthuralevinebooks.com

This boutique imprint was created by Mr. Levine in 1996. They are highly respected for the production and editorial quality of the books they publish.

Cheryl Klein, Editor; cklein@scholastic.com.
Arthur Levine, Editorial Director; alevine@scholastic.com.

SEVEN STORIES PRESS ❖ www.sevenstories.com

140 Watts Street, New York, NY 10013, 212-226-8760

Founded in 1995, Seven Stories was named for the seven original authors who took a leap of faith to be published by this untested start-up. In the nonfiction zone, SS is proud of its large list of political and social-advocacy books. In fiction, the house has been a champion for new voices.

Dan Simon, Publisher; dansimon@sevenstories.com.

SHAMBHALA PUBLICATIONS ❖ www.shambhala.com

4720 Walnut Street, Boulder, CO 80301, 888-424-2329

This house was conceived during the hippie sixties in San Francisco by a group of devout Mormons who ingested LSD that had been inserted into a batch of Big Macs as part of a CIA experiment. Well, the San Francisco part is true, anyway. To sum it up, this is a successful publisher of books that are compatible with Eastern philosophies and religions. Specific subjects include yoga, martial arts, natural health, crafts, creativity, and green living.

Dave O'Neal, Publisher; daveo@shambhala.com.

SKYHORSE PUBLISHING ❖ www.skyhorsepublishing.com

307 West 36th Street, 11th Floor, New York, NY 10018, 212-643-6816

Skyhorse is a gutsy horse, in that they entered independent publishing when many others were leaving (that is, in 2006): Their founder had the requisite experience and connections to survive, expand, and thrive as an independent publisher. Their eclectic list includes history, politics, rural living, sports, health, humor, hobbies, self-help, conspiracy theories, and even some fiction.

Editors' email addresses follow this format: firstinitiallastname@skyhorsepublishing.com.

Mark Gompertz, Editorial Director. American history, social issues.
Bethany Buck, Editorial Director, Sky Pony (Children's Program). Picture Books, middle grade, young adult.
Nicole Frail, Editor. Romance; relationships, lifestyle, popular reference, pets.
Joseph Craig, Editor. Social issues, history, true crime.
Maxim Brown, Editor. Fiction; current events, politics.
Leah Zarra, Editor. Cooking.
Kim Lim, Editor. Travel narrative.
Jason Katzman, Editor. Science fiction/fantasy.
Lilly Golden, Editor. Thriller.

SMITHSONIAN BOOKS ❖ www.smithsonianbooks.com

600 Maryland Avenue SW, Suite 6001, Washington, DC 20024

SB publishes a variety of nonfiction titles, many of which are illustrated, about the kinds of subjects relevant to the museum's amazing exhibits, such as American history, technology, culture, science, and space/aviation.

Carolyn Gleason, Director; cgleason@si.edu.

SOHO PRESS ❖ www.sohopress.com

853 Broadway, New York, NY 10003, 212-260-1900

Soho endeavors to publish bold new literary voices, international crime fiction, and young adult fiction. Most of their books are fiction with the occasional memoir or narrative.

Mark Doten, Senior Editor; mdoten@sohopress.com.
Juliet Grames, Associate Publisher; jgrames@sohopress.com.

SOUNDS TRUE, INC. ❖ www.soundstrue.com

413 S. Arthur Avenue, Louisville, CO 80027, 800-333-9185

ST was founded in 1985, and "to disseminate spiritual wisdom" is their stated mission. Audio was its only format for many years, which explains the firm's name. The company grew and thrived, and successfully entered the traditional print fray in 2005. Its most popular categories include health, meditation, music, self-empowerment, spirituality, and yoga.

Jennifer Y. Brown, Acquisitions Editor; jenniferb@soundstrue.com.

SOURCEBOOKS ❖ www.sourcebooks.com

1935 Brookdale Road, Naperville, IL 60563, 630-961-3900
232 Madison Avenue, Suite 1100, New York, NY 10018, 212-414-1701
18 Cherry Street, Milford, CT 06460, 203-876-9790

Launched in 1987, Sourcebooks has managed to become one of the most dynamic and fastest-growing independent presses in the country. They have been a little ahead of the curve by acquiring even smaller presses with proven niches and by discovering authors with preexisting marketing and sales connections and corporate tie-ins. Sourcebooks has not been coy about helping to discover the digital future. They are especially strong in children's and romance categories and have a large footprint in all areas of nonfiction, including gift books and calendars. Basically, this is a risk-tolerant publisher that knows how to see and follow the money.

Editors' email addresses follow this format: firstname.lastname@sourcebooks.com.

Deb Werksman, Editorial Director (CT). Romance (all categories), women's fiction.
Mary Altman, Editor (NY). Romance (all categories).
Cat Clyne, Assistant Editor (NY). Romance, women's fiction, erotica.
Shana Drehs, Editorial Director (IL). Women's and historical fiction; women's interest, parenting, relationships, self-help, pop culture, gift items, inspiration.

Steve Geck, Editorial Manager (NY). Children's book programs.

Todd Stocke, Editorial Director (IL). Books that include impressive multimedia applications and author platforms.

Anna Michels, Editor. Literary fiction, mystery, thriller; practical and prescriptive nonfiction, gift books, inspiration, humor, quirky history.

Grace Menary-Winefield, Assistant Editor (NY). Quirky self-help, weird history.

Annette Pollert-Morgan, Editorial Manager (NY). Books for teens and young adult.

Barla Bejan-Negru, Editor (IL). Gift, calendars.

Meaghan Gibbons, Editor (IL). Business books that aren't focused on the bottom line.

SQUARE ONE PUBLISHERS, INC. ❖ www.squareonepublishers.com

115 Herricks Road, Garden City Park, NY 11040, 516-535-2010

SQ1 was founded in 2000 by veteran publishing innovator Rudy Shur. Most of his titles are self-help-/how-to-oriented by experts in their respective fields, with a strong emphasis on alternative health and lifestyle titles. But there's also an assortment of general fiction and nonfiction titles, as well as cookbooks. As with most independent publishers, acquisitions often depend upon the editor's heart and intuition, as opposed to mere statistics. Actually, statistics would suggest that most small presses shouldn't even exist.

Rudy Shur, Founder and Publisher; sq1info@aol.com.

TIN HOUSE BOOKS ❖ www.tinhouse.com/books

2617 NW Thurman Street, Portland, OR 97210, 503-473-8663

Tin House Books follows the same tradition as the company's much-loved magazine of the same name, which is to carefully curate an eclectic list of fiction and nonfiction, as well as some poetry. The firm isn't averse to introducing new voices. It seems that their primary criterion is the depth and uniqueness of the writing. This isn't where you'll find a how-to book about salesmanship, but you might discover the next Kerouac.

Editors' email addresses follow this format: firstname@tinhouse.com.

Meg Storey, Editor.

Tony Perez, Editor.

Masie Cochran, Editor.

TURNER PUBLISHING COMPANY ❖ www.turnerpublishing.com

424 Church Street, Suite 2240, Nashville, TN 37219, 615-255-2665
445 Park Avenue, 9th Floor, New York, NY 10022, 646-291-8961

It may sound like a cliché, but Turner (no relation to Ted) is one to watch. While many large and small presses are standing still or withering away, Turner is quickly expanding. Though fast growth is often the kiss of death in any business, digital technology has become publishing's great equalizer, because content doesn't have to be solely printed and physically managed, and the content generators (authors) provide outsourced, low-cost labor. Turner recently grabbed a lot of attention by purchasing the rights to several thousand general nonfiction titles that Wiley no longer wanted to carry. With a single signature, Turner became a midsize publisher that few insiders were familiar with, yet. They appear to be on the prowl for all kinds of nonfiction and fiction titles, though specific subject preferences may become clearer in the near future.

Stephanie Beard, Editor (TN); sbeard@turnerpublishing.com.

TYNDALE HOUSE PUBLISHERS, INC. ❖ www.tyndale.com

351 Executive Drive, Carol Stream, IL 60188, 800-323-9400

Stated purpose: "Minister to the needs of people through literature consistent with biblical principles." They publish a wide list of Christian-based fiction, nonfiction, and children's books. Many of the top names in Christian publishing are Tyndale authors. Their most famous (some might say infamous) and successful program was the *Left Behind* fiction series.

Karen Watson, Director; karenwatson@tyndale.com. Fiction.
Carol Traver, Editor; caroltraver@tyndale.com. Nonfiction.

ULYSSES PRESS ❖ www.ulyssespress.com

Acquisitions Office: 167 West 21st Street, New York, NY 10011, 510-601-8301

The firm seems to be publishing something for every nonfiction category you can think of, so it's difficult, if not impossible, to clearly define what they won't consider. One overriding attribute is made evident by viewing their catalog: every book seems to have a clear title and is for a well-focused market.

Casie Vogel, Editor; casievogel@ulyssespress.com.
Bridget Thoreson, Editor; bridgetthoreson@ulyssespress.com.

VERSO BOOKS ❖ www.versobooks.com

20 Jay Street, Suite 1010, Brooklyn, NY 11201, 718-246-8160

Long story short, Verso publishes the kinds of books that Bernie Sanders reads and that Paul Ryan does not.

Andrew Hsiao, Editor; submissions@versobooks.com.

WILEY ❖ www.wiley.com

111 River Street, Hoboken, NJ 07030, 201-748-6000

Though Wiley isn't listed as one of the corporate houses, it is an international billion-dollar content generator. In recent years, the firm seems to have been selling off its consumer trade book assets and focusing more on the high-ticket professional and academic markets. Many of its $100+ books have such arcane titles and content that I could never accurately paraphrase what they are about. However, Wiley is still publishing a large list of trade books in the areas of finance, banking, marketing, investing, and general business. A compelling side note: Wiley family members have been actively engaged in the operation since the company's foundation more than 200 years ago.

Richard Narramore, Senior Editor; richard.narramore@wiley.com. General business subjects with strong author platforms.
(Ms.) Shannon Vargo, Editor; svargo@wiley.com. General practical business subjects.
Bill Falloon, Executive Editor; bfalloon@wiley.com. Investing and personal finance.
(Mr.) Sheck Cho, Executive Editor; scho@wiley.com. Technology.
Tula Batanchiev, Editor; tbatanchie@wiley.com. Investing.

WORKMAN PUBLISHING COMPANY ❖ www.workman.com

225 Varick Street, New York, NY 10014, 212-254-5900

Workman has been a bold independent innovator since 1968. Its clever calendars, humor titles, and gift/illustrated products have always profitably complemented its traditional books. The company has frequently excelled at capturing an inordinate measure of market share in cluttered categories. This is especially true for its *What to Expect* pregnancy and parenting series. Workman's books run the full gamut of nonfiction categories and children's books; for them the key seems to be how to differentiate what they publish in the eyes of the consumer, even if the content is conservative. Ordinary isn't their model.

Editors' email addresses follow this format: firstname@workman.com.

Bruce Tracy, Senior Editor. Clever illustrated books for adults.
Megan Nicolay, Editor. Cooking, crafts, hobbies, humor.
Suzie Bolotin, Editor in Chief. Interesting nonfiction titles consistent with catalog.
Justin Krasner, Editor. Children's.
Maisie Tivnan, Editor. Interesting nonfiction.
Margot Herrera, Senior Editor. Health, women's interest.
Kylie Foxx McDonald, Editor. Food, cookbooks.
Samantha O'Brien, Associate Editor. Nonfiction.

Algonquin Books ❖ www.algonquin.com

PO Box 2225, Chapel Hill, NC 27515

This formerly independent publisher has been allowed to maintain its special fingerprints since being acquired by Workman many years ago. And they still hold to their stated mission to "publish quality fiction and nonfiction by undiscovered writers." Many of their books have a distinct Southern feel and flavor. They also publish children's books.

Editors' email addresses follow this format: firstname@algonquin.com.

Amy Gash, Senior Editor. Nonfiction, advice, pop culture, food.
Andra Miller, Editor. Fiction and nonfiction.
Krestyna Lypen, Editor. Children's.
Chuck Adams, Executive Editor. Fiction.
Elyse Howard, Publisher. Algonquin Young Readers division.

Artisan ❖ www.workman.com/artisanbooks

Artisan specializes in publishing nicely packaged and illustrated books about fashion, decorating, food, dining, and cooking.

Judy Pray, Executive Editor.

Storey Publishing ❖ www.storey.com

210 Mass MoCA Way, North Adams, MA 01247, 413-346-2100

Storey's stated mission is to publish "practical information that encourages personal independence in harmony with the environment." This publisher may have been ahead of its time and is now clearly on time, since many of its books are dedicated to all aspects of sustainable/green living. They also publish an excellent assortment of books about small farming, pet care, crafts, gardening, and nature.

Editors' email addresses follow this format: firstname.lastname@storey.com.

Deborah Balmuth, Editor. Mind-body-spirit.

Deborah Burns, Editor. Equine, pets, nature.

Gwen Steege, Editor. Crafts.

Carleen Madigan, Editor. Gardening.

Margaret Sutherland, Editor. Cooking, wine, beer.

Part 4

UNIVERSITY PRESSES (US)

INTRODUCTION
THE UNIVERSITY AS PUBLISHER
From Academic Press to Commercial Presence

William Hamilton

University presses publish much more than scholarly monographs and academic tomes. Although the monograph is — and will always be — the bread and butter of the university press, several factors over the past quarter century have compelled university presses to look beyond their primary publishing mission of disseminating scholarship. The reductions in financial support from parent institutions, library-budget cutbacks by federal and local governments, and the increasing scarcity of grants to underwrite the costs of publishing monographs have put these presses under severe financial pressure. The watchword for university presses is always *survive*.

While university presses were fighting for their lives, their commercial counterparts also experienced difficult changes. The commercial sector responded by selling off unprofitable and incompatible lists or merging with other publishers; many houses were bought out by larger concerns. Publishers began to concentrate their editorial and marketing resources on a few new titles that would generate larger revenues. Books that commercial publishers now categorized as financial risks, the university presses saw as means of entry into new markets and opportunities to revive sagging publishing programs.

Take a look through one of the really good bookstores in your area. You'll find university press imprints on regional cookbooks, popular fiction, serious nonfiction, calendars, literature in translation, reference works, finely produced art books, and a considerable number of upper-division textbooks. Books and other items normally associated with commercial publishers are now a regular and important part of university press publishing.

There are approximately 100 university presses in North America, including US branches of the venerable Oxford University Press and Cambridge University Press. Of the largest American university presses — California, Chicago, Columbia, Harvard, MIT, Princeton, Texas, and Yale — each publishes well over 100 books per year. Many of these titles are trade books that are sold in retail outlets throughout the world.

The medium-sized university presses — approximately 20 fit this category — publish between 50 and 100 books a year. Presses such as Washington, Indiana, Cornell, North Carolina, Johns Hopkins, and Stanford are well established as publishers of important works worthy of broad circulation.

UNIVERSITY PRESSES (US)

153

All but the smallest university presses have developed extensive channels of distribution, which ensure that their books will be widely available in bookstores and wherever serious books are sold. Small university presses usually retain larger university presses or commissioned sales firms to represent them.

University Press Trade Publishing

The two most common trade areas in which university presses publish are (1) regional titles and (2) nonfiction titles that reflect the research interests of their parent universities.

For example, University of Hawaiʻi Press publishes approximately 30 new books a year with Asian or Pacific Rim themes. Typically, 8 to 10 of these books are trade titles. Recent titles have included Japanese literature in translation, a lavishly illustrated book on Thai textiles, books on forms of Chinese architecture, and a historical guide to ancient Burmese temples. This is a typical university press trade list — a diverse, intellectually stimulating selection of books that will be read by a variety of well-informed, responsive general readers.

For projects with special trade potential, some of the major university presses enter into copublishing arrangements with commercial publishers — notably in the fields of art books and serious nonfiction with a current-issues slant — and there seem to be more of these high-profile projects lately.

Certain of the larger and medium-sized university presses have in the past few years hired editors with experience in commercial publishing to add extra dimensions and impact to the portion of their program with a trade orientation.

University Press Authors

Where do university press authors come from? The majority of them are involved in one way or another with a university, research center, or public agency or are experts in a particular academic field. Very few would list their primary occupation as author. Most of the books they write are the result of years of research or reflect years of experience in their fields.

The university press is not overly concerned about the number of academic degrees following its trade book authors' names. What matters is the author's thoroughness in addressing the topic, regardless of his or her residence, age, or amount of formal education. A rigorous evaluation of content and style determines whether the manuscript meets the university press's standards.

The University Press Acquisition Process

Several of the other essays in this volume provide specific strategies for you to follow to ensure that your book idea receives consideration from your publisher of choice — but let me interject a cautionary note: the major commercial publishers are extremely difficult to approach unless you have an agent, and obtaining an agent can be more difficult than finding a publisher!

The commercial publishers are so overwhelmed by unsolicited manuscripts that you would be among the fortunate few if your proposal or manuscript even received a thorough reading. Your unagented proposal or manuscript will most likely be read by an editorial assistant, returned unread, or thrown on the slush pile unread and unreturned.

An alternative to the commercial publisher is the university press. Not only will the university press respond, but the response will also generally come from the decision maker — the acquisitions editor.

Before approaching any publisher, however, you must perform a personal assessment of your expectations for your book. If you are writing because you want your book to be on the bestseller list, go to a medium to large commercial press. If you are writing to make a financial killing, go to a large commercial publisher. If you are writing in the hope that your book will be a literary success, contribute to knowledge, be widely distributed, provide a modest royalty, and be in print for several years, you should consider a university press.

Should a University Press Be Your First Choice?

That depends on the subject matter. It is very difficult to sell a commercial publisher on what appears on the surface to be a book with a limited market. For example, the late Tom Clancy was unable to sell *The Hunt for Red October* to a commercial publisher because the content was considered too technical for the average reader of action-adventure books. Clancy sent the manuscript to a university press that specialized in military-related topics. As they say, the rest is history. Tom Clancy created the present-day technothriller genre and has accumulated royalties well into the millions of dollars. Once Clancy became a known commodity, the commercial publishers began courting him. All his subsequent books have been published by commercial houses.

How do you find the university press that is suitable for you? You must research the university press industry. Start by finding out something about university presses. In addition to the listings appearing in this book, a more complete source is *The Association of American University Presses Directory*. The AAUP directory offers a detailed description of each AAUP member press, with a summary of its publishing program. The directory lists the names and responsibilities of each press's key staff, including the acquisitions editors. Each press states its editorial program — what it will consider for publication. A section on submitting manuscripts provides a detailed description of what the university press expects a proposal to contain. Another useful feature is the comprehensive subject grid, which identifies more than 125 subject areas and lists the university presses that publish in each of them.

An updated edition of *The Association of American University Presses Directory* is published every fall and is available for a nominal charge from the AAUP central offices in New York City or through its distributor, University of Chicago Press.

Most university presses are also regional publishers. They publish titles that reflect local interests and tastes and are intended for sale primarily in the university press's local region. For example, University of Hawai'i Press has more than 250 titles on Hawai'i. The books — both trade and scholarly — cover practically every topic one can think of. Books on native birds, trees, marine life, local history, native culture, and an endless variety of other topics can be found in local stores, including chain bookstores.

Almost all university presses publish important regional nonfiction. If your book naturally fits a particular region, you should do everything possible to get a university press located in that region to evaluate your manuscript.

Do not mistake the regional nature of the university press for an inability to sell books nationally — or globally. As mentioned earlier, most university presses have established channels of distribution and use the same resources that commercial publishers use for book distribution. The major difference is that the primary retail outlets for university press books tend to be bookstores associated with universities, smaller academic bookstores, specialized literary bookstores, and independent bookstores that carry a large number of titles.

What to Expect at a University Press

You should expect a personal reply from the acquisitions editor. If the acquisitions editor expresses interest, you can expect the evaluation process to take as long as six to eight months. For reasons known only to editorial staffs — commercial, as well as those of university presses — manuscripts sit and sit and sit. Then they go out for review, come back, and go out for review again!

Once a favorable evaluation is received, the editor must submit the book to the press's editorial board. It is not until the editorial board approves the manuscript for publication that a university press is authorized to publish the book under its imprint.

A word about editorial boards: The imprint of a university press is typically controlled by an editorial board appointed from the faculty. Each project presented to the editorial board is accompanied by a set of peer reviews, the acquisitions editor's summary of the reviews, and the author's replies to the reviews. The project is discussed with the press's management and voted upon.

Decisions from the editorial board range from approval, through conditional approval, to flat rejection. Most university presses present to the editorial board only those projects they feel stand a strong chance of acceptance — approximately 10 to 15 percent of the projects submitted annually. So if you have been told that your book is being submitted to the editorial board, there's a good chance that the book will be accepted.

Once a book has been accepted by the editorial board, the acquisitions editor is authorized to offer the author a publishing contract. The publishing contract of a university press is quite similar to a commercial publisher's contract. The majority of the paragraphs read the same. The difference is most apparent in two areas — submission of the manuscript and financial terms.

University presses view publishing schedules as very flexible. If the author needs an extra six to twelve months to polish the manuscript, the market is not going to be affected too much. If the author needs additional time to proofread the galleys or page proofs, the press is willing to go along. Why? Because a university press is publishing for the long term. The book is going to be in print for several years. It is not unusual for a first printing of a university press title to be available for 10 or more years. Under normal circumstances the topic will be timeless, enduring, and therefore of lasting interest.

University presses go to great lengths to ensure that a book is as close to error-free as possible. The academic and stylistic integrity of the work is foremost in the editor's mind. Not only the body of the book, but the notes, references, bibliography, and index should be flawless — and all charts, graphs, maps, and other illustrations perfectly keyed.

It does not matter whether the book is a limited-market monograph or serious non-fiction for a popular trade. The university press devotes the same amount of care to the editorial and production processes to ensure that the book is as accurate and complete as possible. Which leads us to the second difference — the financial terms.

Commercial publishers follow the maxim that time is money. The goal of the organization is to maximize shareholder wealth. Often the decision to publish a book is based solely on financial considerations. If a book must be available for a specific season in order to meet its financial goals, pressure may be applied to editorial by marketing, and editorial in turn puts pressure on the author to meet the agreed-upon schedule. This pressure may result in mistakes, typos, and inaccuracies — but will also assure timely publication and provide the publisher with the opportunity to earn its expected profit. At the commercial publishing house, senior management is measured by its ability to meet annual financial goals.

University presses are not-for-profit organizations. Their basic mission is to publish books of high merit that contribute to universal knowledge. Financial considerations are secondary to what the author has to say. Producing a thoroughly researched, meticulously documented, and clearly written book is more important than meeting a specific publication date. The university press market will accept the book when it appears.

Do not get the impression that university presses are entirely insensitive to schedules or market conditions. University presses are aware that certain books — primarily text-books and topical trade titles — must be published at specific times of the year if sales are to be maximized. But less than 20 percent of any year's list would fall into such a category.

University Presses and Author Remuneration

What about advances? Royalties? Surely, university presses offer these amenities — which is not to suggest they must be commensurate with the rates paid by commercial houses.

No and yes. No royalties are paid on a predetermined number of copies of scholarly monographs — usually 1,000 to 2,000.

A royalty is usually paid on textbooks and trade books. The royalty will be based on the title's sales revenue (net sales) and will usually be a sliding-scale royalty, ranging from as low as 5 percent to as high as 15 percent.

As with commercial publishers, royalties are entirely negotiable. Do not be afraid or embarrassed to discuss them with your publisher. Just remember that university presses rarely have surplus funds to apply to generous advances or high royalty rates. However, the larger the university press, the more likely you are to get an advance for a trade book.

Never expect an advance for a monograph or supplemental textbook.

When Considering a University Press

When you're deciding where to submit your manuscript, keep the following in mind. University presses produce approximately 10 percent of the books published in the United States each year. University presses win approximately 20 percent of the annual major book awards. Yet university presses generate just 2 percent of the annual sales revenue.

So if you want your book to be taken seriously and reviewed and edited carefully; if you want to be treated as an important part of the publishing process and want your book to have a good chance to win an award; and if you are not too concerned about the financial rewards — then a university press may very well be the publisher for you.

William Hamilton was the director and publisher of the University of Hawaiʻi Press for 25 years. He retired in December 2012.

THE LISTINGS

CAMBRIDGE UNIVERSITY PRESS ❖ www.cambridge.org/us

1 Liberty Plaza, Floor 20, New York, NY 1000632, 212-337-5000,
newyork@cambridge.org

Dating back to 1534, Cambridge University Press publishes books in many areas of the humanities and social sciences, with particular focus on subjects including law, history, political science, and economics; it is also active across a broad spectrum of scientific and medical publishing. It administers some of the prestigious journals issued by the press, and it also publishes an extremely successful list of books aimed at those learning American English as a foreign or second language.

Though obviously UK based, CUP's North American acquisitions program is very robust, and a large part of their revenues is derived in the US. Five hundred years is a long time in this business, considering that the printing press is only a few years older. And it seems that CUP rarely puts anything out of print, as its backlist catalog carries 53,000 titles available for sale, many of which are several hundred years old.

CUP expanded common law copyright structures in the early 17th century by printing its own editions of the Bible in defiance of another printer that had claimed exclusive rights to print the Bible in Britain. In the same century, CUP proved that commercially publishing original nonfiction books, like the compilations of Isaac Newton's latest scientific discoveries, could be profitable.

In some ways, CUP can be compared to today's technological trendsetters. For many decades the press continually set new qualitative standards and economics for the mass printing of books and pamphlets, which quickly replaced word of mouth as the primary means of distributing information. The transformation rapidly lifted literacy from a hobby to a requirement, much as computer literacy became essential in the 1990s.

Robert Dreesen; rdreesen@cambridge.org. Political science, sociology, political
philosophy and theory.

Ray Ryan; rryan@cambridge.org. Literature.

Vince Higgs; vhiggs@cambridge.org. Astronomy and physics.

Matt Lloyd; mlloyd@cambridge.org. Earth and environmental science.

Beatrice Rehl; brehl@cambridge.org. Philosophy, classical art and archaeology.

John Berger; jberger@cambridge.org. Law.

Lewis Bateman; lbateman@cambridge.org. Political science, history.

Lauren Cowles; lcowles@cambridge.org. Academic computer science, statistics.

Matt Galloway; mgallowa@cambridge.org. Current issues, law.

Michael Watson; mwatson@cambridge.org. International issues, politics.

COLUMBIA UNIVERSITY PRESS ❖ www.cup.columbia.edu

61 West 62nd Street, New York, NY 10023, 212-459-0600

Columbia University Press publishes in the areas of Asian studies, literature, biology, business, culinary history, current affairs, economics, environmental sciences, film and media studies, finance, history, international affairs, literary studies, Middle Eastern studies, New York City history, philosophy, neuroscience, paleontology, political theory, religion, and social work.

Jennifer Crewe, President and Editorial Director; jc373@columbia.edu. Asian humanities, film, food history, New York City.

Patrick Fitzgerald, Publisher for the Life Sciences; pf2134@columbia.edu. Conservation biology, environmental sciences, ecology, neuroscience, paleobiology, public health, biomedical sciences.

Bridget Flannery-McCoy, Editor; bmf2119@columbia.edu. Health economics, sustainability economics, labor economics.

Philip Leventhal, Editor; pl2164@columbia.edu. Literary studies, cultural studies, US history, journalism, media, New York City history and culture.

Wendy Lochner, Publisher for Philosophy and Religion; wl2003@columbia.edu. Animal studies, religion, philosophy.

Jennifer Perillo, Senior Executive Editor; jp3187@columbia.edu. Criminology, gerontology, psychology, social work.

Anne Routon, Editor; akr36@columbia.edu. Asian history, international relations, Middle East studies.

Myles Thompson, Publisher, Finance and Economics; mt2312@columbia.edu. Finance, economics.

CORNELL UNIVERSITY PRESS ❖ www.cornellpress.cornell.edu

Sage House, 512 East State Street, Ithaca, NY 14850, 607-277-2338

Cornell University Press was established in 1869, giving it the distinction of being the first university press to be established in America. The house offers 150 new titles a year in many disciplines, including anthropology, Asian studies, biological sciences, classics, cultural studies, history, industrial relations, literary criticism and theory, medieval studies, philosophy, politics and international relations, psychology and psychiatry, veterinary subjects, and women's studies. Submissions are not invited in poetry or fiction.

Mahinder Kingra, Editor in Chief; msk55@cornell.edu. Medieval studies, ancient history, classics, European history.

Roger Haydon, Executive Editor; rmh11@cornell.edu. Political science, international relations, Asian studies, philosophy.

Michael J. McGandy, Senior Editor; mjm475@cornell.edu. American history, American politics, law, New York State, regional books.

Emily Powers, Acquisitions Assistant; ep375@cornell.edu.

James Lance, Senior Editor; jml554@cornell.edu. Anthropology, social sciences

Comstock Publishing Associates

CUP's many books in the life sciences and natural history are published under the Comstock Publishing Associates imprint.

Kitty Liu, Editor. Biology and natural history, ornithology, herpetology and ichthyology, mammalogy, entomology, botany and plant sciences, environmental studies.

ILR Press

A list of books in industrial and labor relations is offered under the ILR Press imprint.

Frances Benson, Editorial Director; fgb2@cornell.edu. Workplace issues, labor, business, health care, sociology, anthropology.

DUKE UNIVERSITY PRESS ❖ www.dukeupress.edu

905 West Main Street, Suite 18B, Durham, NC 27701, 919-687-3600

Duke University Press publishes primarily in the humanities and social sciences and issues a few publications for primarily professional audiences (e.g., in law or medicine). It is best known for its publications in the broad and interdisciplinary area of theory and history of cultural production, and it is known in general as a publisher willing to take chances with nontraditional and interdisciplinary publications, both books and journals.

Ken Wissoker, Editorial Director; kwiss@duke.edu. Anthropology; cultural studies; post-colonial theory; lesbian and gay studies; construction of race, gender, and national identity; social studies of science; new media; literary criticism; film and television; popular music; visual studies.

Courtney Berger, Editor; cberger@dukeupress.edu. Political theory, social theory, film and television, geography, gender studies, American studies, Asian American studies, cultural studies of food.

Miriam Angress, Associate Editor; mangress@dukeupress.edu. Religion, women's studies, world history, humanities, cultural studies.

THE FEMINIST PRESS AT THE CITY UNIVERSITY OF NEW YORK ❖

www.feministpress.org

365 Fifth Avenue, Suite 5406, New York, NY 10016, 212-817-7915

The mission of the Feminist Press is to publish and promote the most potent voices of women from all eras and all regions of the globe. Founded in 1970, the press has brought more than 300 critically acclaimed works by and about women into print, enriching the literary canon, expanding the historical record, and influencing public discourse about issues fundamental to women.

To submit, send an email of no more than 200 words describing your book project with the word *submission* in the subject line. Send email query to: editor@feministpress.org.

FORDHAM UNIVERSITY PRESS ❖ www.fordhampress.com

2546 Belmont Avenue, University Box L, Bronx, NY 10458, 718-817-4795

Fordham University Press publishes primarily in the humanities and the social sciences, with an emphasis on the fields of philosophy, theology, history, classics, communications, economics, sociology, business, political science, and law, as well as literature and the fine arts. Additionally, the press publishes books focusing on the metropolitan New York region and books of interest to the general public.

Fredric Nachbaur, Director; fnachbaur@fordham.edu.

Tom Lay, Editor; tlay@fordham.edu. Humanities.

GEORGETOWN UNIVERSITY PRESS ❖ www.press.georgetown.edu

3240 Prospect Street NW, Suite 250, Washington, DC 20007, 202-687-5889

Georgetown University Press publishes in the areas of bioethics; international affairs and human rights; languages and linguistics; political science, public policy, and public management; and religion and ethics.

Richard Brown, PhD, Director; reb7@georgetown.edu. Bioethics, international affairs and human rights, religion and politics, and religion and ethics.

Hope J. LeGro, Assistant Director; hjs6@georgetown.edu. Languages, linguistics. Director, Georgetown Languages.

Donald Jacobs, Acquisitions Editor; dpj5@georgetown.edu. International affairs, human rights, public policy, public management.

Clara Totten, Acquisitions Editor; cls86@georgetown.edu. Languages.

HARVARD UNIVERSITY PRESS ❖ www.hup.harvard.edu

79 Garden Street, Cambridge, MA 02138, 617-495-2600, contact_hup@harvard.edu

HUP publishes scholarly books and thoughtful books for the educated general reader in history, philosophy, American literature, law, economics, public policy, natural science, history of science, psychology, and education, and reference books in all the above fields. The HUP website offers photographs of the editors that you may or may not wish to peruse prior to submitting, as well as detailed submission guidelines that you will not want to miss.

Andrew Kinney, Editor. Human behavior, education.

John Kulka, Executive Editor-at-Large — American, English, and world literature; modernism; history of criticism; theory; the American publishing industry; political journalism; globalization; democracy; and human dignity.

Ian Malcolm, Executive Editor-at-Large. International economics.

Kathleen McDermott, Executive Editor for History. American history, Atlantic history, European history from late medieval to modern, Russian and Central European history, Asian history, international relations, global history, military history, US western history, Native American history, legal history.

Joyce Seltzer, Senior Executive Editor for History and Contemporary Affairs. Serious and scholarly nonfiction that appeals to a general intellectual audience as well as to students and scholars in a variety of disciplines, especially history across a broad spectrum, American studies, contemporary politics, social problems, and biography.

Shamila Sen, Executive Editor-at-Large. World religions, classics, ancient history, religion.

(Mr.) Lindsay Waters, Executive Editor for the Humanities. Philosophy, literary studies, cultural studies, film, Asian cultural studies, pop culture, conflicting relations among the races in the United States and around the world.

Janice Audet, Executive Editor. Life Sciences.

Jeff Dean, Executive Editor. Physical sciences and technology.

Belknap Press

HUP's Belknap Press imprint strives to publish books of long-lasting importance and superior scholarship and production, chosen whether or not they might be profitable, thanks to the bequest of Waldron Phoenix Belknap, Jr.

INDIANA UNIVERSITY PRESS ❖ www.iupress.indiana.edu

1320 E. 10th Street, Bloomington, IN 47405, 812-855-8817

IU Press is a leading academic publisher specializing in the humanities and social sciences. It produces more than 140 new books annually. Major subject areas include African, African American, Asian, cultural, Jewish and Holocaust, Middle East, Russian and East European, and gender studies; anthropology, film, history, bioethics, music, paleontology, philanthropy, philosophy, and religion.

Dee Mortensen, Editorial Director; mortense@indiana.edu. African studies, religion, philosophy, Judaism.

Jennika Baines, Acquiring Editor; bainesj@indiana.edu. International studies, Russian studies, Eastern European studies.

Janice Frisch, Acquisitions Editor; frischj@indiana.edu. Film, music, media studies, folklore, gender/sexuality studies.

Ashley Runyon, Acquisitions Editor; asrunyon@iu.edu. Regional interest in nonfiction and fiction.

Quarry Books

Quarry Books focuses on everything about Indiana and the Midwest, exploring subjects such as photography, history, gardening, cooking, sports, leisure, people, and places.

JOHNS HOPKINS UNIVERSITY PRESS ❖ www.press.jhu.edu

2715 North Charles Street, Baltimore, MD 21218-4363, 410-516-6900

JHU Press is one of the world's largest and most diverse university presses.

Gregory M. Britton, Editorial Director; gb@press.jhu.edu. Higher education.

Jacqueline C. Wehmueller, Executive Editor; jcw@press.jhu.edu. Consumer health, psychology and psychiatry, history of medicine.

Vincent J. Burke, Executive Editor; vjb@press.jhu.edu. Life sciences, mathematics, physics.

Robert J. Brugger, Editor Emeritus; rjb@press.jhu.edu. American history, American studies, history of technology, regional books.

Matthew McAdam, Editor; mxm@press.jhu.edu. Humanities, literary studies.

Suzanne Flinchbaugh, Associate Editor. Political science, health policy, Copublishing Liaison.

Elizabeth Sherburn Demers, Senior Acquisition Editor; ed@press.jhu.edu. American history, American studies, history of technology.

Robin W. Coleman, Acquisitions Editor; rwc@press.jhu.edu. Public health issues.

KENT STATE UNIVERSITY PRESS ❖

www.kentstateuniversitypress.com

1118 University Library, 1125 Risman Drive, PO Box 5190, Kent, OH 44242-0001, 330-672-7913

Kent State University Press is interested in scholarly works about history, including military, Civil War, US diplomatic, American cultural, women's, and art history; literary studies; titles of regional interest for Ohio; scholarly biographies; archaeological research; the arts; and general nonfiction.

Will Underwood, Director; wunderwo@kent.edu.

LOUISIANA STATE UNIVERSITY PRESS ❖ www.lsupress.org

338 Johnston Hall, 3rd Floor, LSU, Baton Rouge, LA 70803, 225-578-6294

LSU Press is dedicated to publishing scholarly, general-interest, and regional books. It's one of the oldest and largest university presses in the South and the only university press to have won Pulitzer Prizes in both fiction and poetry.

Rand Dotson, Executive Editor. Slavery, Civil War, Reconstruction, nineteenth- and twentieth-century South, Louisiana roots music.

James W. Long, Acquisitions Editor; jlong12@lsu.edu. Media studies.

Margaret Lovecraft, Acquisitions Editor. Regional books, literary studies, landscape architecture.

MASSACHUSETTS INSTITUTE OF TECHNOLOGY/THE MIT PRESS ❖

www.mitpress.mit.edu

1 Rogers Street, Cambridge, MA 02142, 617-253-5646

Science and technology is MIT's strong suit, but its list is broader than the college's name might imply.

Gita Manaktala, Editorial Director; manak@mit.edu. Information science, communication.

Philip Laughlin, Senior Acquisitions Editor; laughlin@mit.edu. Cognitive science, philosophy, bioethics.

Jane Macdonald, Acquisitions Editor; janem@mit.edu. Economics, finance, business.

Robert Prior, Executive Editor; prior@mit.edu. Life sciences, neuroscience, biology.

Doug Sery, Senior Acquisitions Editor; dsery@mit.edu. Digital humanities, new media, game studies.

Roger Conover, Executive Editor; conover@mit.edu. Art, architecture, visual and cultural studies.

Christopher Eyer, Assistant Acquisitions Editor; cweyer@mit.edu. Life sciences, neuroscience, engineering, cognitive science, philosophy, bioethics.

Emily Taber, Acquisitions Editor; etaber@mit.edu. Economics, finance, business.

Susan Buckley, Associate Acquisitions Editor; susanb@mit.edu. Digital media and learning.

Marc Lowenthaul, Acquisitions Editor; lowentha@mit.edu. Computer science, linguistics, Semiotext(e).

Justin Kehoe, Assistant Acquisitions Editor; jkehoe@mit.edu. Science, technology, society.

Beth Clevenger, Acquisitions Editor; eclev@mit.edu. Environmental studies, urbanism, food.

Victoria Hindley, Associate Acquisitions Editor; vhindley@mit.edu. Art and architecture.

Marie Lee, Executive Editor; marielee@mit.edu. Computer science.

Katie Helke, Associate Acquisitions Editor; helkekat@mit.edu. Technology and society.

Anthony Zannino, Editorial Assistant; zannino@mit.edu. Environmental studies, urbanism, linguistics.

Jeremy N. A. Matthews, Acquisitions Editor; jnamatt@mit.edu. Physical sciences, mathematics, engineering.

Kathleen Hensley, Acquisitions Assistant; khensley@mit.edu. Computer science.

Laura Keeler, Editorial Assistant; lkeeler@mit.edu. Finance, business, economics.

Jesús J. Hernández, Acquisitions Assistant; jesush@mit.edu. Information science, communications.

NEW YORK UNIVERSITY PRESS ❖ www.nyupress.org

838 Broadway, 3rd Floor, New York, NY 10003-4812, 212-998-2575

NYU Press is interested in titles that explore issues of race and ethnicity. They are also interested in media studies and American studies.

Eric Zinner, Editor in Chief; eric.zinner@nyu.edu. Literary criticism and cultural studies, media studies, American history.

Ilene Kalish, Executive Editor; ilene.kalish@nyu.edu. Sociology, criminology, politics.

Jennifer Hammer, Editor; jennifer.hammer@nyu.edu. Religion, psychology, anthropology.

Clara Platter, Editor; clara.platter@nyu.edu. Law.

Chip Rossetti, Managing Editor; chip.rossetti@nyu.edu. Arabic literature.

Caelyn Cobb, Assistant Editor; caelyn.cobb@nyu.edu. Sociology, criminology, politics, women's studies.

Alicia Nadkarni, Assistant Editor; alicia.nadkarni@nyu.edu. Media studies.

Amy Klopfenstein, Editorial Assistant; amy.klopfenstein@nyu.edu. Religion, psychology, anthropology, law.

OHIO STATE UNIVERSITY PRESS ❖ ohiostatepress.org

180 Pressey Hall, 1070 Carmack Road, Columbus, OH 43210-1002, 614-292-6930

Ohio State University Press's areas of specialization include literary studies, including narrative theory; history, including business history, medieval history, and history of crime; political science, including legislative studies; and Victorian studies, urban studies, and women's health. They also publish annual winners of short fiction and poetry prizes, the details of which are available at www.ohiostatepress.org.

Lindsay Martin, Acquisitions Editor; lindsay@osupress.org. Literary studies.

Eugene O'Connor, PhD, Acquisitions Editor; eugene@osupress.org. Classics, medieval studies, language and linguistics.

Tara Cyphers, Managing Editor/Acquisitions Editor; tara@osupress.org. Rhetoric.

OXFORD UNIVERSITY PRESS ❖ www.oup.com/us

198 Madison Avenue, New York, NY 10016, 212-726-6000

Oxford University Press, Inc. (OUP USA), is by far the largest American university press and perhaps the most diverse publisher of its type. The press had its origins in the information technology revolution of the late fifteenth century, which began with the invention of printing from movable type. Oxford's New York office is editorially independent of the British home office and handles distribution of its own list, as well as titles originating from Oxford's branches worldwide. OUP USA publishes at a variety of levels, for a wide range of audiences in almost every academic discipline.

Editors' email addresses follow this format: firstname.lastname@oup.com.

Tim Bent, Editor. History.

Jamie Berezin, Product Development Editor. Academic and professional law.

Adina Popescu Berk, Editor. History, classics, archaeology.

(Mr.) Dana Bliss, Senior Editor. Social work.

Joan Bossert, Associate Publisher. Neuroscience, consumer health, psychological and behavioral sciences.

Ada Brunstein, Editor. Neuroscience, psychology.

Theo Calderara, Editor. Religion (academic).

Angela Chnapko, Editor. Politics.

James Cook, Editor. Criminology.

Alexandra Dauler, History Editor. World history, business history, history of science.

Anne Dellinger, Associate Editor. Comparative politics, area studies.

Susan Ferber, Editor. American history, world history, art history, academic art and architecture.

Alex Flach, Senior Commissioning Editor. Academic and professional law.

Allan Graubard, Editor. Earth science, environmental sciences.

Abby Gross, Senior Editor. Psychology, social work.

Sarah Harrington, Editor. Developmental psychology.

Norm Hirschy, Editor. Dance, music.

Andrea Knobloch, Editor. Clinical medicine, anesthesiology.

Julia Kostova, Editor. Literature, film, linguistics, religion, philosophy.

Donald Kraus, Executive Editor. Bibles.

Alodie Larson, Editor. Art, art history.

Jeremy Lewis, Editor. Earth sciences, life sciences, physics.

David McBride, Editor. Current affairs, political science, law (trade), sociology (trade).

Peter Ohlin, Editor. Bioethics, linguistics, philosophy.

Craig Panner, Editor. Neurology.

Scott Parris, Editor. Business/management, economics, finance.

David Pervin, Editor. Economics, business and management, political science.

Sarah Pirovitz, Editor. American studies, literature, archaeology, classical studies.

Lucy Randall, Editor. Bioethics, philosophy.

Blake Ratcliff, Editor. Law, terrorism and global justice.

Cynthia Read, Senior Editor. Religion (trade).

Christopher Reid, Editor. Clinical medicine.

Suzanne Ryan, Editor. Music.

Anna-Lise Santella, Editor. Music.

Max Sinsheimer, Editor. Reference.

Hallie Stebbins, Linguistics Editor. Linguistics, communication and media studies.

Rebecca Suzan, Commissioning Editor. Emergency medicine, palliative medicine.

Nancy Toff, Editor. History.

Stefan Vranka, Editor. Classical studies.

Steve Wiggins, Associate Editor. Biblical studies.

Chad Zimmerman, Editor. Epidemiology, genetics, infectious diseases, public health.

PENN STATE UNIVERSITY PRESS ❖ www.psupress.org

820 North University Drive, University Support Building 1, Suite C,
University Park, PA 16802-1003, 814-865-1327

Penn State University Press's strengths include core areas such as art history and literary criticism as well as fields such as philosophy, religion, history (mainly US and European), and some of the social sciences (especially political science and sociology).

Patrick H. Alexander, Director; pha3@psu.edu. American studies, European history and culture, history, medieval and early modern studies, philosophy, regional studies, religion, religious studies, romance studies, and Slavic studies.

Eleanor Goodman, PhD, Executive Editor for the Arts & Humanities; ehg11@psu.edu. Art and art history, architectural history, European history and culture (Spanish, French), literature, medieval and early modern studies, visual culture.

PRINCETON UNIVERSITY PRESS ❖ www.press.princeton.edu

41 William Street, Princeton, NJ 08540-5237, 609-258-4900

Princeton University Press, which celebrated its 100th anniversary in 2005, is one of the country's largest and oldest university presses. With a goal to disseminate scholarship both within academia and to society at large, the press produces publications that range across more than 40 disciplines, from art history to ornithology and political science to philosophy.

Fred Appel, Executive Editor. Anthropology, religion.

Al Bertrand, Editor. Humanities.

Eric Crahan, Senior Editor. Political science, American history.

Seth Ditchik, Executive Editor. Economics, finance.

Alison Kalett, Senior Editor. Biology, earth sciences.

Vickie Kearn, Executive Editor. Mathematics.

Robert Kirk, Executive Editor. Natural history, biology, ornithology, field guides.

Michelle Komie, Executive Editor. Art, architecture.

Anne Savarese, Executive Editor. Literature.

Robert Tempio, Executive Editor. Philosophy, classics, ancient world, political theory.

RUTGERS UNIVERSITY PRESS ❖ www.rutgerspress.rutgers.edu

106 Somerset Street, 3rd Floor, New Brunswick, NJ 08901, 848-445-7762

Rutgers University Press publishes books in a broad array of disciplines across the humanities, social sciences, and sciences. Fulfilling a mandate to serve the people of New Jersey, it also publishes books of scholarly and popular interest on the state and surrounding region. Strengths include history, sociology, anthropology, religion, media, film studies, women's studies, African American studies, Asian American studies, public health, history of medicine, evolutionary biology, the environment, and books about the mid-Atlantic region.

(Mr.) Micah Kleit, Director; micah.kleit@rutgers.edu. Jewish studies, mid-Atlantic region.

(Ms.) Leslie Mitchner, Associate Director and Editor in Chief; lmitch@rutgers.edu. Humanities, literature, film, communications.

Peter Mickulas, Senior Editor; mickulas@rutgers.edu. Social sciences, environment, criminology, *Critical Issues in Health and Medicine* series.

Lisa Banning, Assistant Editor; lmb333@rutgers.edu. New media studies, Asian American studies.

Kimberly Guinta, Executive Editor; kimberly.guinta@rutgers.edu. Caribbean studies, higher education, anthropology, women's studies, gender studies.

Rivergate Books

Rivergate Books is a recent imprint devoted to New Jersey and surrounding states.

STANFORD UNIVERSITY PRESS ❖ www.sup.org

425 Broadway Street, Redwood City, CA 94063, 650-723-9434

Stanford University Press publishes about 130 books per year. Roughly two-thirds of these books are scholarly monographs and textbooks in the humanities and the social sciences, with strong concentrations in history, literature, philosophy, and Asian studies, and growing lists in politics, sociology, anthropology, and religion. The remaining one-third are textbooks, professional reference works, and monographs in law, business, economics, public policy, and education.

Kate Wahl, Publishing Director and Editor in Chief; kwahl@stanford.edu. Sociology, law, Middle East studies.

Margo Beth Fleming, Senior Editor; mbfleming@stanford.edu. Business, economics, organizational studies.

Emily-Jane Cohen, Senior Editor; beatrice@stanford.edu. Literature, philosophy, religion.

Michelle Lipinski, Acquisitions Editor; mlipinsk@stanford.edu. Anthropology, law.

Margo Irvin, Acquisitions Editor; mcirvin@stanford.edu. Jewish Studies.

Friederike Sundaram, Acquisitions Editor; fsundaram@stanford.edu. Digital humanities and social sciences.

STATE UNIVERSITY OF NEW YORK PRESS ❖ www.sunypress.edu

353 Broadway, State University Plaza, Albany, NY 12246-0001 (USPS mailing address), info@sunypress.edu

SUNY Press is one of the largest public university presses in the United States, with an annual output of some 170 books and a backlist of more than 4,000 titles. The press publishes chiefly in the humanities and social sciences and has attained national recognition in the areas of education, philosophy, religion, Jewish studies, Asian studies, political science, and sociology, with increasing growth in the areas of literature, film studies, communication, women's studies, and environmental studies.

Editors' email addresses follow this format: firstname.lastname@sunypress.edu.

Dr. Michael Rinella, Senior Acquisitions Editor. Political science, African American studies.

Andrew Kenyon, Acquisitions Editor. Philosophy.

Dr. Beth Bouloukos, Senior Acquisitions Editor. Education, Hispanic studies, queer studies, women's studies.

Christopher Ahn, Senior Acquisitions Editor. Asian studies, religion.

Rafael Chaiken, Assistant Acquisitions Editor. Jewish studies.

Excelsior Editions

Excelsior Editions showcases the history of New York and surrounding states while at the same time making available noteworthy and essential popular books, both classic and contemporary.

James Peltz, Codirector, Excelsior Editions. Film studies, Italian American studies, Jewish studies.

SYRACUSE UNIVERSITY PRESS ❖

www.syracuseuniversitypress.syr.edu

621 Skytop Road, Suite 110, Syracuse, NY 13244-5290, 315-443-5534

Syracuse University Press publishes new books in specialized areas including New York State, Middle East studies, Judaica, geography, Irish studies, Native American studies, religion, television, and pop culture.

Suzanne Guiod, Editor in Chief; seguiod@syr.edu. Disability studies, peace studies, politics, religion, Middle East studies.

Deborah Manion, Acquisitions Editor; dmmanion@syr.edu. Irish studies, Jewish history and culture, television and pop culture, writing and community.

Kelly Balenske, Editorial Assistant; klbalens@syr.edu.

TEXAS BOOK CONSORTIUM

The "consortium" of Texas's public and university presses was founded in 1974, and each program is editorially distinct.

Texas A&M University Press ❖ www.tamupress.com

John H. Lindsey Building, Lewis Street, 4354 TAMU, College Station, TX 77843-4354, 979-845-1436

Texas A&M University Press's primary editorial interests span a range of significant fields, including agriculture, anthropology, nautical archaeology, architecture, borderland studies, Eastern Europe, economics, military history, natural history, presidential studies, veterinary medicine, and works on the history and culture of Texas and the surrounding region.

Jay Dew, Editor in Chief; jaydew@tamu.edu.

(Ms.) Shannon Davies, Senior Editor, Natural Sciences; sdavies@tamu.edu.

Thom Lemmons, Managing Editor; thom.lemmons@tamu.edu.

State House Press/McWhiney Foundation Press ❖

tfhcc.com/state-house-press

PO Box 818, Buffalo Gap, TX 79508, 325-572-3974

State House Press and the McWhiney Foundation Press see their missions as making history approachable, accessible, and interesting, with special emphasis on Texas, West Texas, the Civil War, military, and Southern history.

Texas Christian University Press ❖ www.prs.tcu.edu

3000 Sandage, Fort Worth, TX 76109, 817-257-7822

Texas Christian University Press is among the smallest university publishers in the nation and focuses on the history and literature of the American Southwest.

Texas Review Press ❖ texasreviewpress.org

PO Box 2146, SHSU Division of English and Foreign Languages, Evans Building, Room #152, Huntsville, TX 77341-2146, 936-294-1992, texasreview@shsu.edu

Texas Review Press was established in 1979 but published only chapbooks and an occasional anthology until 1992, when it introduced the *Southern and Southwestern Writers Breakthrough* Series. It now publishes six to eight books a year and has over 40 titles in print in fiction, poetry, and prose nonfiction.

UNIVERSITY OF ALABAMA PRESS ❖ www.uapress.ua.edu

USPS address: Box 870380, Tuscaloosa, AL 35487-0380
Physical/shipping address: 200 Hackberry Lane, 2nd Floor McMillan Bldg., Tuscaloosa, AL 35401, 205-348-5180

The University of Alabama Press publishes in the following areas: American history; Southern history and culture; American religious history; Latin American history; American archaeology; southeastern archaeology; Caribbean archaeology; historical archaeology; ethnohistory; anthropology; American literature and criticism; rhetoric and communication; creative nonfiction; linguistics, especially dialectology; African American studies; Native American studies; Judaic studies; public administration; theater; natural history and environmental studies; American social and cultural history; sports history; military history; and regional studies of Alabama and the southern United States, including trade titles. Submissions are not invited in poetry, fiction, or drama.

Daniel Waterman, Editor in Chief; waterman@uapress.ua.edu. American literature and criticism, rhetoric and communication, creative nonfiction, linguistics, African American studies, public administration, theater, natural history and environmental studies.

Elizabeth Motherwell, Acquisitions Editor for Natural History and the Environment; emother@uapress.ua.edu.

Donna Cox Baker, History Editor; donna.baker@ua.edu.

Wendi Schnaufer, Senior Acquisitions Editor; wschnaufer@uapress.ua.edu. Archaeology, anthropology, food studies, Latin American–Caribbean studies, ethnohistory.

UNIVERSITY OF ARIZONA PRESS ❖ www.uapress.arizona.edu

Main Library Building, 5th Floor, 1510 E. University Boulevard, PO Box 210055, Tucson, AZ 85721-0055, 520-621-1441

The University of Arizona Press publishes about 55 books annually. These include scholarly titles in American Indian studies, anthropology, archaeology, environmental studies, geography, Chicano studies, history, Latin American studies, and the space sciences. UA Press also publishes general-interest books on Arizona and the Southwest borderlands.

Allyson Carter, Editor in Chief, Social Sciences and Sciences; acarter@uapress.arizona .edu. Anthropology, archaeology, ecology, geography, natural history, environmental science, astronomy and space sciences, related regional titles.

Kristen Buckles, Acquiring Editor; kbuckles@uapress.arizona.edu. Native American literature and studies, Latin American studies, US West history.

UNIVERSITY OF ARKANSAS PRESS ❖ www.uapress.com

McIlroy House, 105 N. McIlroy Avenue, Fayetteville, AR 72701, 479-575-3246

University of Arkansas Press publishes approximately 20 titles a year in the following subjects: history, Southern history, African American history, Civil War studies, poetics and literary criticism, Middle East studies, Arkansas and regional studies, music, and cultural studies. About a third of its titles fall under the general heading of Arkansas and Regional Studies.

David Scott Cunningham, Senior Editor; dscunnin@uark.edu.

UNIVERSITY OF CALIFORNIA PRESS ❖ www.ucpress.edu

155 Grand Avenue, Suite 400, Oakland, CA 94612–3758, 510-883-8232

Founded in 1893, University of California Press (UC Press) publishes in the areas of art, music, cinema and media studies, classics, literature, anthropology, sociology, archaeology, history, religious studies, Asian studies, biological sciences, food studies, natural history, and public health.

Niels Hooper, Executive Editor. History (except Asia), American studies, Middle East studies.

Reed Malcolm, Senior Editor. Anthropology, Asian studies.

Kim Robinson, Editorial Director. California issues/studies.

Maura Roessner, Senior Editor. Social sciences.

Eric A. Schmidt, Editor. Religion, ancient world.

Naomi Schneider, Executive Editor. Sociology, politics, anthropology, social issues.

Merrik Bush-Pirkle, Environmental Science Editor.

Seth Dobrin, Senior Editor. Social sciences.

Christopher Johnson, Executive Editor. Psychology.

Nadine Little, Art History Editor.

Kate Marshall, Acquisitions Editor. Food and wine, Latin American studies.

Raina Polivka, Music/Film/Media Editor.

UNIVERSITY OF CHICAGO PRESS ❖ www.press.uchicago.edu

1427 East 60th Street, Chicago, IL 60637, 773-702-7700

University of Chicago Press is noted for its large and diverse program of scholarly and occasionally commercial books.

Alan G. Thomas, Editorial Director, Humanities and Sciences; athomas2@uchicago.edu. Literary criticism and theory, religious studies.

John Tryneski, Editorial Director; tryn@uchicago.edu. Political science, law and society.

Timothy Mennel, Senior Editor; tmennel@uchicago.edu. American history, Chicago history.

Mary E. Laur, Senior Project Editor; mlaur@uchicago.edu. Books about writing and general reference.

Joe Jackson, Editor; joejackson@uchicago.edu. Economics, business, finance.

Marta Tonegutti, Editor; mtonegutti@uchicago.edu. Music studies.

Susan Bielstein, Executive Editor; smb1@uchicago.edu. Art, architecture, ancient archaeology, classics, film studies.

T. David Brent, Executive Editor; tbrent@uchicago.edu. Anthropology, paleoanthropology, philosophy, psychology.

Karen Merikangas Darling, Senior Editor; darling@uchicago.edu. Science studies (history, philosophy, social studies of science, medicine, technology).

Elizabeth Branch Dyson, Editor; ebd@uchicago.edu. Ethnomusicology, interdisciplinary philosophy, education.

Christie Henry, Editorial Director; chenry@uchicago.edu. Biological science, behavior, conservation, ecology, environment, evolution, natural history, paleobiology, geography, earth sciences.

Douglas Mitchell, Executive Editor; dmitchel@uchicago.edu. Sociology, history, sexuality studies, rhetoric.

David Morrow, Senior Editor; dmorrow@uchicago.edu. Reference works, including regional reference, intellectual property.

Priya Nelson, Associate Editor; pnelson@uchicago.edu. Anthropology, history, linguistics.

Randolph Petilos, Assistant Editor; rpetilos@uchicago.edu. Medieval studies, poetry in translation.

UNIVERSITY OF GEORGIA PRESS ❖ www.ugapress.org

320 South Jackson Street, Athens, GA 30602, 706-542-6770

University of Georgia Press publishes 70 to 80 titles each year, in a range of academic disciplines as well as books of interest to the general reader, and is committed to publishing important new scholarship in the following subject areas: American and Southern history and literature, African American studies, civil rights history, legal history, Civil War studies, Native American studies, folklore and material culture, women's studies, and environmental studies. Their regional publishing program includes architectural guides, state histories, field guides to the region's flora and fauna, biographies, editions of diaries and letters, outdoor guides, and the work of some of the state's most accomplished artists, photographers, poets, and fiction writers.

Mick Gusinde-Duffy, Editor in Chief; mickgd@uga.edu.

Walter Biggins, Senior Acquisitions Editor; wbiggins@uga.edu.

Pat Allen, Acquisitions Editor; pallen@uga.edu.

Beth Snead, Assistant Acquisitions Editor; bsnead@uga.edu.

UNIVERSITY OF HAWAI'I PRESS ❖ www.uhpress.hawaii.edu

2840 Kolowalu Street, Honolulu, HI 96822-1888, 808-956-8255

Areas of University of Hawai'i Press (UHP) publishing interest include cultural history, economics, social history, travel, arts and crafts, costumes, marine biology, natural history, botany, ecology, religion, law, political science, anthropology, and general reference; particular UHP emphasis is on regional topics relating to Hawai'i, and scholarly and academic books on East Asia, South and Southeast Asia, and Hawai'i and the Pacific.

Masako Ikeda, Acquisitions Editor; masakoi@hawaii.edu. Hawai'ian and Pacific studies (all disciplines), Asian American studies (all disciplines), general-interest books on Hawai'i and the Pacific.

Pamela Kelley, Acquisitions Editor; pkelley@hawaii.edu. Southeast Asian studies (all disciplines), East Asian literature.

Stephanie Chun, Acquisitions Editor; chuns@hawaii.edu. East Asian language and reference, religion, Buddhist studies, history, philosophy.

UNIVERSITY OF ILLINOIS PRESS ❖ www.press.uillinois.edu

1325 South Oak Street, Champaign, IL 61820-6903, 217-333-0950

The University of Illinois Press is one of the founding members of the Association of American University Presses. They publish scholarly books and serious nonfiction, with special interests in Abraham Lincoln studies, African American studies, American history, anthropology, Appalachian studies, archaeology, architecture, Asian American studies, communications, folklore, food studies, immigration and ethnic history, Judaic studies, labor history, literature, military history, Mormon history, music, Native American studies, philosophy, poetry, political science, religious studies, sociology, Southern history, sport history, translations, transnational cultural studies, Western history, and women's studies.

Laurie Matheson, Director; lmatheso@uillinois.edu. History, Appalachian studies, labor studies, music, folklore.

Daniel Nasset, Acquisitions Editor; dnasset@uillinois.edu. Film studies, anthropology, communication studies, military history.

Dawn M. Durante, Acquisitions Editor; durante9@uillinois.edu. African American studies, women's studies, American studies, religion.

Marika Christofides, Assistant Acquisitions Editor; mchristo@uillinois.edu.

UNIVERSITY OF IOWA PRESS ❖ www.uiowapress.org

119 West Park Road, 100 Kuhl House, Iowa City, IA 52242-1000, 319-335-2000

As one of the few book publishers in the state of Iowa, the press considers it a mission to publish excellent books on Iowa and the Midwest. But since the press's role is much broader than that of a regional press, the bulk of its list appeals to a wider audience in the following categories: literary studies, including Whitman studies and poetics; letters and diaries; American studies; literary nonfiction and thematic edited anthologies, particularly poetry anthologies; the craft of writing; literature and medicine; theater studies; archaeology; the natural history of the Upper Midwest; and regional history and culture.

James McCoy, Director; james-mccoy@uiowa.edu.
Catherine Cocks, Acquisitions Editor; cath-campbell@uiowa.edu.

UNIVERSITY OF MICHIGAN PRESS ❖ www.press.umich.edu

839 Greene Street, Ann Arbor, MI 48104-3209, 734-764-4388

University of Michigan Press publishes trade nonfiction and works of scholarly and academic interest. Topic areas and categories include African American studies, anthropology, archaeology, Asian studies, classical studies, literary criticism and theory, economics, education, German studies, history, linguistics, law, literary biography, literature, Michigan and the Great Lakes region, music, physical sciences, philosophy and religion, poetry, political science, psychology, sociology, theater and drama, women's studies, disability studies, and gay and lesbian studies.

LeAnn Fields, Senior Executive Editor; lfields@umich.edu. Class studies, disability studies, theater, performance studies.
Ellen Bauerle, Executive Editor; bauerle@umich.edu. Classics, archaeology, German studies, music, fiction, early modern history, African studies.
Kelly Sippell, Executive Editor; ksippell@umich.edu. ESL, applied linguistics.
Christopher J. Hebert, Editor-at-Large; hebertc@umich.edu. Popular music, jazz.
Scott Ham, Acquiring Editor; scottom@umich.edu. Michigan and the Great Lakes.

UNIVERSITY OF MINNESOTA PRESS ❖ www.upress.umn.edu

111 Third Avenue South, Suite 290, Minneapolis, MN 55401, 612-627-1970

The University of Minnesota Press's areas of emphasis include American studies, anthropology, art and aesthetics, cultural theory, film and media studies, gay and lesbian studies, geography, literary theory, political and social theory, race and ethnic studies, sociology, and urban studies. The press is among the most active publishers of translations of works of European and Latin American thought and scholarship. The press also maintains a long-standing commitment to publish books that focus on Minnesota and the Upper Midwest, including regional nonfiction, history, and natural science.

Jason Weidemann, Editorial Director; weide007@umn.edu. Anthropology, Asian culture, cinema and media studies, geography, native studies, sociology.

Pieter Martin, Senior Editor; marti190@umn.edu. Architecture, legal studies, politics and international studies, Scandinavian studies, urban studies.

Erik Anderson, Regional Trade Editor; mntrade@umn.edu. Regional, Scandinavian, music, trade paperback reprints.

Danielle Kasprzak, Associate Editor. Cinema and media studies.

UNIVERSITY OF MISSOURI PRESS ❖ www.umsystem.edu/upress

113 Heinkel Building, 201 South 7th Street, Columbia, MO 65211

The University of Missouri Press publishes more than 70 titles per year in the areas of American and world history, including intellectual history and biography; African American studies; women's studies; American, British, and Latin American literary criticism; journalism; political science, particularly philosophy and ethics; regional studies of the American heartland; short fiction; and creative nonfiction.

Clair Willcox, Editor in Chief; willcoxc@missouri.edu.

Sara Davis, Managing Editor; davissd@missouri.edu.

Gary Kass, Acquisitions Editor; kassg@missouri.edu.

UNIVERSITY OF NEBRASKA PRESS ❖ www.nebraskapress.unl.edu

1111 Lincoln Mall, Lincoln, NE 68588-0630, 402-472-3581

UNP publishes in a wide variety of subject areas, including western Americana, Native American history and culture, military history, sports, philosophy, and religion.

Alicia Christensen, Editor; achristensen6@unl.edu. American studies.

Matt Bokovoy, Editor; mbokovoy2@unl.edu. Native studies.

Bridget Barry, Editor; bbarry2@unl.edu. Military history, geography, environmental studies.

Rob Taylor, Sports Editor; rtaylor6@unl.edu.

UNIVERSITY OF NEW MEXICO PRESS ❖ www.unmpress.com

1717 Roma Avenue NE, Albuquerque, NM 87106, 505-277-2346

University of New Mexico Press's areas of strong interest are anthropology, archaeology, cultures of the American West, folkways, Latin American studies, literature, art and architecture, photography, crafts, biography, women's studies, travel, and the outdoors. UNM Press offers a robust list of books in subject areas pertinent to the American Southwest, including native Anasazi, Navajo, Hopi, Zuni, and Apache cultures; Nuevomexicano (New Mexican) culture; the pre-Columbian Americas; and Latin American affairs. UNM Press also publishes works of regional fiction and belles lettres, both contemporary and classical.

W. Clark Whitehorn, Executive Editor; clarkw@unm.edu.

Elise M. McHugh, Senior Acquisitions Editor; elisemc@unm.edu.

Sonia Dickey, Acquisitions Assistant; soniad@unm.edu.

UNIVERSITY OF NORTH CAROLINA PRESS ❖ www.uncpress.unc.edu

116 South Boundary Street, Chapel Hill, NC 27514-3808, 919-966-3561

University of North Carolina Press's areas of interest include American studies, African American studies, American history, literature, anthropology, business/economic history, Civil War history, classics, ancient history, European history, folklore, gender studies, Latin American and Caribbean studies, legal history, media studies, Native American studies, political science, public policy, regional books, religious studies, rural studies, social medicine, Southern studies, and urban studies.

Mark Simpson-Vos, Editorial Director. American studies, gender and sexuality, literary studies, Native American studies, Civil War and military history, Southern culture and history.

Charles Grench, Assistant Director and Senior Editor; charles_grench@unc.edu. American history, European history, law and legal studies, classics and ancient history, business and economic history, political science, social science, African American history, craft history.

Elaine Maisner, Senior Executive Editor; elaine_maisner@unc.edu. Religious studies, Latin American studies, Caribbean studies, regional trade.

Joseph Parsons, Senior Editor. Social science, humanities, business and entrepreneurship, health and medicine.

Brandon Proia, Acquisitions Editor. Current affairs, African American studies.

UNIVERSITY OF OKLAHOMA PRESS ❖ www.oupress.com

2800 Venture Drive, Norman, OK 73069, 405-325-2000

OUP is a preeminent publisher of books about the American West and American Indians. Its other scholarly disciplines include classical studies, military history, political science, and natural science.

Charles E. Rankin, Associate Director, Editor in Chief; cerankin@ou.edu. American West, military history.

Alessandra Jacobi-Tamulevich, Editor; jacobi@ou.edu. American Indian, Mesoamerican, and Latin American studies.

Kathleen Kelly, Editor. Women's history.

UNIVERSITY OF SOUTH CAROLINA PRESS ❖ www.sc.edu/uscpress

718 Devine Street, Columbia, SC 29208, 803-777-5245

University of South Carolina Press publishes works of original scholarship in the fields of history (American, African American, Southern, Civil War, culinary, maritime, and women's), regional studies, literature, religious studies, rhetoric, and social work.

Jim Denton, Acquisitions Editor; dentoja@mailbox.sc.edu. Literature, religious studies, rhetoric, social work.

Linda Haines Fogle, Assistant Director; lfogle@mailbox.sc.edu. Regional studies.

UNIVERSITY OF TENNESSEE PRESS ❖ www.utpress.org

110 Conference Center, 600 Henley Street, Knoxville, TN 37996-4108, 865-974-3321

University of Tennessee Press is dedicated to publishing high-quality works of original scholarship in regional studies.

Scot Danforth, Acquisitions Director; danforth@utk.edu. American Civil War, American religion, special projects.

Thomas Wells, Acquisitions Editor; twells@utk.edu. Archaeology, Native American studies.

UNIVERSITY OF TEXAS PRESS ❖ www.utexas.edu/utpress

PO Box 7819, Austin, TX 78713-7819, 512-471-7233

UTP produces books of general interest about Texas, African and Native Americans, Latinos, and women. Major areas of concentration are anthropology, Old and New World archaeology, architecture, art history, botany, classics and the Ancient World, conservation and the environment, Egyptology, film and media studies, geography, landscape, Latin American and Latino studies, literary modernism, Mexican American studies, marine science, Middle Eastern studies, ornithology, pre-Columbian studies, Texas and western studies, and women's studies.

Robert Devens, Editor in Chief; rdevens@utpress.utexas.edu.

Jim Burr, Senior Editor; jburr@utpress.utexas.edu. Classics and ancient world, film and media studies, Middle East studies, Jewish studies, Old World archaeology, architecture, applied languages.

Casey Kittrell, Sponsoring Editor; ckittrell@utpress.utexas.edu. Fiction in translation.

Kerry Webb, Senior Editor; kwebb@utpress.utexas.edu.

UNIVERSITY OF VIRGINIA PRESS ❖ www.upress.virginia.edu

Box 400318, Charlottesville, VA 22904, 434-924-3468, vapress@virginia.edu

The UVaP editorial program focuses primarily on the humanities and social sciences with special concentrations in American history, African American studies, Southern studies, literature, and regional books.

Richard K. Holway, History and Social Sciences Editor; rkh2a@virginia.edu.

Boyd Zenner, Architecture and Environmental Editor; bz2v@virginia.edu.

Eric Brandt, Humanities Editor; eab7fb@virginia.edu.

Angie Hogan, Associate Editor; arh2h@virginia.edu. Eighteenth-century studies.

UNIVERSITY OF WASHINGTON PRESS ❖

www.washington.edu/uwpress

PO Box 35970, Seattle, WA 98195, 206-543-4050

UW Press publishes titles that cover a wide variety of academic fields, with especially distinguished lists in Asian studies, Middle Eastern studies, environmental history, biography, anthropology, Western history, natural history, marine studies, architectural history, and art.

Lorri Hagman, Executive Editor; lhagman@uw.edu. Asian studies, cultural and environmental anthropology.

Regan Huff, Senior Acquisitions Editor; rhuff@uw.edu. Environment, art history, Northwest studies.

(Ms.) Larin McLaughlin, Editor in Chief; lmclaugh@uw.edu. American studies, Native American studies, gender/sexuality studies.

UNIVERSITY OF WISCONSIN PRESS ❖ www.uwpress.wisc.edu

1930 Monroe Street, 3rd Floor, Madison, WI 53711-2059, 608-263-1110

University of Wisconsin Press publishes a large range of general-interest books (biography, fiction, natural history, poetry, photography, fishing, food, travel), scholarly books (American studies, anthropology, art, classics, environmental studies, ethnic studies, film, gay and lesbian studies, history, Jewish studies, literary criticism, Slavic studies, etc.), and regional books about Wisconsin and the Upper Midwest.

Raphael Kadushin, Executive Editor; kadushin@wisc.edu. Autobiography/memoir, biography, classical studies, dance, performance, film, food, gender studies, LGBT studies, Jewish studies, Latino/a memoirs, travel.

Gwen Walker, PhD, Editorial Director; gcwalker@wisc.edu. African studies, anthropology, environmental studies, Irish studies, Latin American studies, Slavic studies, Southeast Asian studies, US history.

UNIVERSITY PRESS OF FLORIDA ❖ www.upf.com

15 NW 15th Street, Gainesville, FL 32603, 352-392-1351, press@upf.com

University Press of Florida publishes books of regional interest and usefulness to the people of Florida, reflecting its rich historical, cultural, and intellectual heritage and resources.

Subjects include African studies, anthropology and archaeology, art, dance, music, law, literature, Middle Eastern studies, natural history, Russian studies, history, Florida, Latin American studies, political science, science and technology, and sociology.

Meredith Morris-Babb, Interim Editor in Chief.
Sian Hunter, Senior Acquisitions Editor.
Stephanye Hunter, Acquisitions Editor.
Shannon McCarthy, Acquisitions Editor.
Judith Knight, Editor-at-Large.

UNIVERSITY PRESS OF KANSAS ❖ www.kansaspress.ku.edu

2502 Westbrooke Circle, Lawrence, KS 66045-4444, 785-864-4154

University Press of Kansas publishes regional books that contribute to the understanding of Kansas, the Great Plains, and the Midwest.

Michael Briggs, Editor in Chief; mbriggs@ku.edu. Military history, intelligence studies.
Charles T. Myers, Director; ctmyers@ku.edu. American politics, legal history, presidential studies.
Kim Hogeland, Acquisitions Editor; khogeland@ku.edu. US western history, Native American studies.

UNIVERSITY PRESS OF MISSISSIPPI ❖ www.upress.state.ms.us

3825 Ridgewood Road, Jackson, MS 39211-6492, 601-432-6205

UPM publishes books that interpret the South and its culture to the nation and the world.

Leila W. Salisbury, Director; lsalisbury@mississippi.edu. American studies, film studies, pop culture.
Craig Gill, Assistant Director and Editor in Chief; cgill@mississippi.edu. Art, architecture, folklore and folk art, history, music, natural sciences, photography, Southern studies.
(Mr.) Vijay Shah, Acquiring Editor; vshah@mississippi.edu. American literature, comics studies, Caribbean studies.

UNIVERSITY PRESS OF NEW ENGLAND ❖ www.upne.com

1 Court Street, Suite 250, Lebanon, NH 03766, 603-448-1533

University Press of New England (UPNE) is supported by a consortium of schools — Brandeis University, Dartmouth College, University of New Hampshire, Northeastern University, Tufts University, and University of Vermont — and based at Dartmouth College. The publishing program reflects strengths in the humanities; liberal arts; fine, decorative, and performing arts; literature; New England culture; and interdisciplinary studies.

Michael P. Burton, Director; michael.p.burton@dartmouth.edu. Art, photography, decorative arts, material culture, historic preservation, distribution titles.

Phyllis Deutsch, Editor in Chief; phyllis.d.deutsch@dartmouth.edu. Jewish studies, nature and environment, environment and health, sustainability studies, 19th-century studies, American studies, criminology with a gendered component.

Stephen Hull, Acquisitions Editor; stephen.p.hull@dartmouth.edu. New England regional, African American studies, New England sports, sports and society, music and technology, international studies with a civil society component.

Richard Pult, Acquisitions Editor; richard.pult@dartmouth.edu. New England regional/Boston, New England sports, marine biology/ecology, criminology, music/opera, Native American studies, American studies, visual culture, institutional histories.

VANDERBILT UNIVERSITY PRESS ❖

www.vanderbiltuniversitypress.com

2014 Broadway, Nashville, TN 37203, 615-322-3585

The editorial interests of Vanderbilt University Press include most areas of the humanities and social sciences, as well as health care and education. The press seeks intellectually provocative and socially significant works in these areas, as well as works that are interdisciplinary or that blend scholarly and practical concerns.

Michael Ames, Director; vupress@vanderbilt.edu.

Beth Kressel Itkin, Acquisitions Editor; beth.itkin@vanderbilt.edu.

Joell Smith-Borne, Managing Editor; joell.smith-borne@vanderbilt.edu.

UNIVERSITY PRESSES (US)

185

WAYNE STATE UNIVERSITY PRESS ❖ www.wsupress.wayne.edu

4809 Woodward Avenue, Detroit, MI 48201-1309, 313-577-6120

Wayne State University Press is a distinctive urban publisher with a strong presence in African American studies, Armenian studies, children's studies, classical studies, fairy-tale and folklore studies, film and television studies, German studies, the Great Lakes and Michigan, humor studies, Jewish studies, labor and urban studies, literature, and speech and language pathology.

Kathryn Wildfong, Acquisitions Manager; k.wildfong@wayne.edu. Africana studies, Jewish studies, Great Lakes and Michigan.

Annie Martin, Acquisitions Editor; annie.martin@wayne.edu. Film and TV studies, fairy-tale studies, children's studies, *Made in Michigan Writers Series*, speech and language pathology.

WESLEYAN UNIVERSITY PRESS ❖ www.wesleyan.edu/wespress

215 Long Lane, Middletown, CT 06459, 860-685-7711

Wesleyan University Press publishes in the areas of art and culture.

Suzanna Tamminen, Director and Editor in Chief; stamminen@wesleyan.edu. Dance.

Marla Zubel, Acquisitions Editor; mzubel@wesleyan.edu. Musicology, film studies, science fiction studies, regional Connecticut trade.

YALE UNIVERSITY PRESS ❖ yalebooks.com

302 Temple Street, New Haven, CT 06511, PO Box 209040, New Haven, CT 06520-9040, 203-432-0960

YUP is one of the largest and most diverse academic publishers in the world.

(Ms.) Jean E. Thomson Black, Executive Editor; jean.black@yale.edu. Life sciences, physical sciences, environmental sciences, medicine.

Jennifer Banks, Executive Editor; jennifer.banks@yale.edu. Literature in translation, religion, psychology.

Katherine Boller, Editor; katherine.boller@yale.edu. Art and Architecture.

Joseph Calamia, Editor; joseph.calamia@yale.edu. Physical sciences, environmental sciences, geology, applied mathematics, engineering.

Jaya Aninda Chatterjee, Assistant Editor; jaya.chatterjee@yale.edu. Politics, international relations, Russian/Eurasian studies.

Patricia Fidler, Publisher; patricia.fidler@yale.edu. Art and architecture.

William Frucht, Executive Editor; william.frucht@yale.edu. Political science,
   international relations, law, economics.
Heather Gold, Assistant Editor; heather.gold@yale.edu. Religion.
Erica Hanson, Assistant Editor; erica.hanson@yale.edu. History.
Sarah Miller, Editor; sarah.miller@yale.edu. Literature, language, performing arts.
Christopher Rogers, Executive Director; chris.rogers@yale.edu. History, current events.
Steve Wasserman, Executive Editor-at-Large; steve.wasserman@yale.edu. Trade books.

Part 5

CANADIAN BOOK PUBLISHERS

INTRODUCTION
CANADIAN BOOK PUBLISHING AND THE CANADIAN MARKET

Greg Ioannou

There's good and bad news about the Canadian publishing industry for writers. First, the bad: breaking in isn't easy. The good news: most Canadian publishers are interested in new writers. They have to be, because small to midsize Canadian houses operate mainly on government grant money. In order to get that grant money, houses must publish Canadian authors. They also can't afford bidding wars. Instead, they often find new authors, develop them, and hope that they stay — or that their fame will add value to the house's backlist.

The key to getting published is to make sure that you're sending the right manuscript to the right publisher, using an appropriate style for submissions. Publishers are less frustrated by poor writing than they are by poorly executed submissions.

If you've written a nonfiction book about rural Nova Scotia, don't send your manuscript to a children's publisher in Vancouver. Research the publishers first instead of spamming busy editors with manuscripts that don't fit their house's list.

The internet is a fantastic tool for writers. It's easier to research potential publishers online than it is to sit at the library and search through *Quill & Quire's Canadian Publishers Directory* — though that is still a valuable resource.

If you want more information than what's included in the listings that follow, do an online search for Canadian publishers. A few places to start are the Association of Canadian Publishers — which provides a search form by genre and province — and the Canadian Publishers' Council. The Canadian Children's Book Centre is particularly focused and has an annual publication that lists publishers that accept unsolicited manuscripts and artwork. If you see a publisher whose mandate seems to match your book idea, visit their website and locate their submission requirements, or contact a Canadian agent.

Rather than sending your manuscript everywhere, write custom proposals that show the publisher that you know what they publish, you've read their submission guidelines thoroughly, and your manuscript adheres to those requirements. It is okay to show enthusiasm for the press or to suggest where you think your manuscript fits on their list. But don't act as though the publisher would be lucky to get your book. Do not threaten publishers with deadlines; you may bully yourself into an automatic rejection. Take the time to write a brief but informative proposal, including a chapter-by-chapter outline if appropriate, and send a sample of your work. Include in the cover letter the approximate word count, genre, and reading level. Consider contacting the Canadian Authors Association or the Writers' Union of Canada for more information on writing for the Canadian market.

If you're a foreign writer hoping to be published in Canada, offer some form of subject-matter expertise. It's like immigrating to another country: you need to have a skill that a Canadian doesn't have.

American writers should remember that Canada is not part of the United States; Canadian publishers cannot use US stamps to return manuscripts. Use International Reply Coupons (available at any post office) instead, or, if the editor accepts electronic submissions, submit your manuscript via email.

Greg Ioannou is the president of Colborne Communications, which provides a full range of services to the book-publishing industry, taking books from initial conception through writing, editing, design, layout, and print production.

Colborne Communications

Toronto, 416-214-0183, www.colcomm.ca, greg@colcomm.ca

THE LISTINGS

ANNICK PRESS LIMITED ❖ www.annickpress.com

15 Patricia Avenue, Toronto, ON M2M 1H9, Canada, 416-221-4802,
Twitter: @AnnickPress

Annick Press publishes children's literature, specifically picture books, nonfiction, and juvenile and young adult novels. The company has won many prestigious design and publishing awards, including the Canadian Booksellers Association's Publisher of the Year award. Annick publishes approximately 30 titles annually and seeks titles that speak to issues young people deal with every day, such as bullying, teen sexuality, advertising, and alienation, as well as books on science, fantasy, pop culture, and world conflict.

Colleen MacMillan, Associate Publisher.

ANVIL PRESS ❖ www.anvilpress.com

PO Box 3008, MPO, Vancouver, BC V6B 3X5, Canada, 604-876-8710,
info@anvilpress.com

Anvil is a literary publisher interested in contemporary, progressive literature in all genres, whose mission is to discover, nurture, and promote new and established Canadian literary talent. It was created in 1988 to publish *subTERRAIN* magazine, which explores alternative literature and art; three years later, the press moved into publishing books as well. It publishes 8 to 10 titles per year and is not interested in publishing genre novels (science fiction, horror, romance, etc.).

Brian Kaufman, Publisher.

ARSENAL PULP PRESS ❖ www.arsenalpulp.com

#202–211 East Georgia Street, Vancouver, BC V6A 1Z6, Canada, 604-687-4233, info@arsenalpulp.com, Twitter: @Arsenalpulp

Arsenal Pulp Press publishes provocative and stimulating books that challenge the status quo in the following genres: cultural studies, political/sociological studies, regional studies and guides (particularly for British Columbia), cookbooks, gay and lesbian literature, visual art, multicultural literature, literary fiction, youth culture, and health. It has been a four-time nominee for Small Press Publisher of the Year, given by the Canadian Booksellers Association (2004, 2008, 2010, 2012). No genre fiction, such as science fiction, thriller, or romance. It has had particular success with cookbooks and publishes 14 to 20 new titles a year.

Brian Lam, Publisher.
Robert Ballantyne, Associate Publisher.
Susan Safyan, Editor. Fiction, continuing education, various nonfiction.

BRICK BOOKS ❖ www.brickbooks.ca

431 Boler Road, Box 20081, London, ON N6K 4G6, Canada, 519-657-8579, brick.books@sympatico.ca, Twitter: @BrickBooks

Brick Books is a small literary press that seeks to foster interesting, ambitious, and compelling work by Canadian poets. The only press in Canada that specializes in publishing poetry books, Brick was nominated for the prestigious Canadian Booksellers Association Libris Award for Best Small Press Publisher of the Year, 2006. It publishes seven new books and an average of nine reprints every year.

Barry Dempster, Acquisitions Editor; barrydempster@rogers.com.

CORMORANT BOOKS ❖ www.cormorantbooks.com

10 St. Mary Street, Suite 615, Toronto, ON M4Y 1P9, Canada, 416-925-8887

Established by Jan and Gary Geddes in 1986, Cormorant Books seeks to publish the best new work in the areas of literary fiction and creative nonfiction for the adult market. This award-winning house publishes a select list of literary fiction, trade nonfiction, and works of fiction in translation.

Robyn Sarah, Poetry Editor; r.sarah@cormorantbooks.com.
Barry Jowett, Associate Publisher; b.jowett@cormorantbooks.com.
Bryan J. Ibeas, Acquisitions and Marketing; b.ibeas@cormorantbooks.com.

COTEAU BOOKS ❖ www.coteaubooks.com

2517 Victoria Avenue, Regina, SK S4P 0T2, Canada, 306-777-0170, coteau@coteaubooks.com, Twitter: @CoteauBooks

Coteau publishes novels, juvenile fiction, regional and creative nonfiction, and drama by authors from all parts of Canada. The press seeks to give literary voice to its community and places a special emphasis on Saskatchewan and prairie writers. It also has an active program of presenting and developing new writers. Coteau releases more than a dozen new titles each year. It publishes novels for young readers ages 9 to 12, ages 13 to 15, and 16 and up. It docs not publish kids' picture books.

John Agnew, Publisher; publisher@coteaubooks.com.

DRAWN AND QUARTERLY ❖ www.drawnandquarterly.com

PO Box 48056, Montréal, QC H2V 4S8, Canada, 514-279-2221, Twitter: @DandQ

Drawn and Quarterly is an award-winning publisher of graphic novels, comic books, and comic book series, with over 20 new titles per year. The publisher acquires new comic books, art books, and graphic novels by renowned cartoonists and newcomers from around the globe.

(Mr.) Chris Oliveros, Publisher; chris@drawnandquarterly.com.
Peggy Burns, Associate Publisher; peggy@drawnandquarterly.com.

DUNDURN PRESS ❖ www.dundurn.com

500-3 Church Street, Toronto, ON M5E 1M2, Canada, 416-214-5544, submissions@dundurn.com, Twitter: @dundurnpress

Dundurn was established in 1972 to bring Canadian history and biography to a general readership. Politics, history, and biography were the original mandate, which quickly expanded to include literary and art criticism and large illustrated art books. In the 1990s, Dundurn acquired three other Canadian publishing houses, and since 2007 it has acquired the assets of several more, broadening Dundurn's editorial range to include literary fiction, young adult books, mysteries, and popular nonfiction. It publishes 75 to 80 new titles a year and is now one of the largest publishers of adult and children's fiction and nonfiction in Canada.

Kirk Howard, President and Publisher.
Carrie Gleason, Editorial Director.

ECW PRESS ❖ www.ecwpress.com

665 Gerrard Street East, Toronto, ON M4M 1Y2, Canada, 416-694-3348,
info@ecwpress.com, Twitter: @ecwpress

ECW (Entertainment, Culture, Writing) Press publishes nonfiction and fiction for the adult market. ECW has published close to 1,000 books, which have been distributed throughout the English-speaking world and translated into dozens of languages. Its list includes poetry and fiction, pop culture, political analysis, sports, biography, and travel guides. ECW releases around 50 new titles per year.

Jack David, Copublisher; jack@ecwpress.com.
Michael Holmes, Senior Editor; michael@ecwpress.com.
Susan Renouf, Executive Editor at Large; susan@ecwpress.com.
Jennifer Knoch, Editor; jenk@ecwpress.com.
Laura Pastore, Editor; laura@ecwpress.com.

FITZHENRY & WHITESIDE LTD. ❖ www.fitzhenry.ca

195 Allstate Parkway, Markham, ON L3R 4T8, Canada, 905-477-9700,
godwit@fitzhenry.ca

Fitzhenry & Whiteside Ltd. specializes in trade nonfiction and children's books. The firm also offers a textbook list and a small list of literary fiction. It publishes or reprints 60 to 80 titles per year, specializing in history, natural sciences, forestry, ecology, biography, psychology, reference, Canadiana, antiques, art, photography, and children's and young adult fiction and nonfiction. The children's book list includes early readers, picture books, and middle grade and young adult novels.

Sharon Fitzhenry, President; sfitz@fitzhenry.ca.
Cheryl Chen, Publisher. Children's books; cheryl.chen@fitzhenry.ca.

Fifth House Publishers ❖ www.fifthhousepublishers.ca

FHP publishes children's through adult fiction and nonfiction on subjects that are entirely "Canadian," including books about Native/Aboriginal peoples. The list includes art, culture, history, current events, and the environment.

Sharon Fitzhenry, Publisher; sfitz@fitzhenry.ca.

GASPEREAU PRESS ❖ www.gaspereau.com

47 Church Avenue, Kentville, NS B4N 2M7, Canada, 902-678-6002, info@gaspereau.com

Gaspereau Press is a Nova Scotia–owned and –operated trade publisher specializing in short-run editions of both literary and regional interest for the Canadian market. Its list includes poetry, local history, literary essays, novels, and short story collections. Gaspereau was nominated for the prestigious Canadian Booksellers Association's Libris Award for Best Small Press Publisher of the Year, 2006. Gaspereau is one of a handful of Canadian trade publishers that prints and binds books in-house. With only 16 paces between the editor's desk and the printing press, Gaspereau practices a form of "craft" publishing that is influenced more by William Morris and the private press movement of the nineteenth century than by the contemporary publishing culture.

Gaspereau accepts hardcopy submissions only; electronic submissions will be deleted without being opened.

Andrew Steeves, Publisher.

GOOSE LANE EDITIONS ❖ www.gooselane.com

500 Beaverbrook Court, Suite 330, Fredericton, NB E3B 5X4, Canada, 506-450-4251, info@gooselane.com

Canada's oldest independent publisher, Goose Lane Editions is a small publishing house that specializes in literary fiction, poetry, and a select list of nonfiction titles on subjects including history, biography, Canadiana, and fine art. It does not publish commercial fiction, genre fiction, or confessional works of any kind. Nor does it publish for the children's market.

Susanne Alexander, Publisher; s.alexander@gooselane.com.
Angela Williams, Publishing Assistant; awilliams@gooselane.com.
Ross Leckie, Editor; rleckie@gooselane.com. Poetry.
Bethany Gibson, Editor; bgibson@gooselane.com. Fiction.
Brent Wilson, Editor; nbmhp@gooselane.com. Military history.
Karen Pinchin, Editor; kpinchin@gooselane.com. Nonfiction.

GREAT PLAINS PUBLICATIONS ❖ www.greatplains.mb.ca

233 Garfield Street South, Winnipeg, MB R3G 2M1, Canada, 204-475-6799, info@greatplains.mb.ca

Great Plains Publications is an award-winning prairie-based general trade publisher specializing in regional history and biography. Its mandate is to publish books that are written by Canadian prairie authors. It also publishes books by Canadian authors not living on the prairies that are of specific interest to people living in this region (content, setting).

Gregg Shilliday, Publisher.

(Ms.) Ingeborg Boyens, Executive Editor.

Enfield & Wizenty ❖ www.greatplains.mb.ca/enfield-wizenty

The Enfield & Wizenty imprint publishes "original novels and short story collections by Canadian writers at all career stages."

Maurice Mierau, Consulting Editor.

Great Plains Teen Fiction ❖ www.greatplains.mb.ca/great-plains-teen-fiction

Great Plains Teen Fiction publishes contemporary and historical fiction from authors across the country for readers ages 14 to 18.

Anita Daher, Consulting Editor.

HARBOUR PUBLISHING ❖ www.harbourpublishing.com

PO Box 219, Madeira Park, BC V0N 2H0, Canada, 604-883-2730, submissions@harbourpublishing.com

Harbour focuses on British Columbia's history, culture, fishing, and hunting.

Howard and Mary White, Publishers.

Douglas & McIntyre (2013) Ltd. ❖ www.douglas-mcintyre.com

4437 Rondeview Road, PO Box 219, Madeira Park, BC V0N 2H0, Canada, 800-667-2988, submissions@douglas-mcintyre.com

Douglas & McIntyre publishes a broad general program of adult fiction and nonfiction, with an emphasis on art and architecture, First Nations issues, Pacific Northwest history, cookbooks, and current events. It publishes around 35 nonfiction books a year while maintaining a distinguished literary fiction list.

Howard White, Publisher.

HERITAGE HOUSE PUBLISHING CO. LTD. ❖ www.heritagehouse.ca

#103–1075 Pendergast Street, Victoria, BC V8V 0A1, Canada, 250-360-0829, heritage@heritagehouse.ca

Since 1969, Heritage House has striven to be "Canada's storyteller," especially as it relates to the Northwest, also known as the "Cariboo region." Their list covers a wide range of categories, including travel, culture, pioneer history, and young adult.

Rodger Touchie, Publisher.
Lara Kordic, Senior Editor.

Greystone Books Ltd. ❖ www.greystonebooks.com

343 Railway Street, Suite 201, Vancouver, BC V6A 1A4, Canada, 604-875-1550, submissions@greystonebooks.com

Greystone Books titles focus on natural history and science, the environment, pop culture, sports, and outdoor recreation. The firm publishes around 30 new books a year.

Rob Sanders, Publisher.
Nancy Flight, Associate Publisher.

HOUSE OF ANANSI PRESS ❖ www.houseofanansi.com

128 Sterling Road, Lower Level, Toronto, ON M6R 2B7, Canada, 416-363-4343

House of Anansi Press specializes in finding and developing Canada's new writers and in maintaining a culturally significant backlist that has accumulated since the house was founded in 1967. Anansi publishes Canadian and international writers of literary fiction, poetry, and serious nonfiction, releasing five new fiction titles, eight new nonfiction titles, and four new poetry titles per year. It does not publish genre fiction (mystery, thriller, science fiction, or romance) or self-help nonfiction. The company launched Spiderline, a crime fiction imprint, in 2010. The same year, the imprint Anansi International was started to reflect the company's commitment to publishing voices from around the world.

Sarah MacLachlan, President; sarah@anansi.ca.

Groundwood Books ❖ www.groundwoodbooks.com

Groundwood Books, an independent imprint of House of Anansi Press, publishes children's books for all ages, including fiction, picture books, and nonfiction. It primarily focuses on works by Canadians, though it sometimes also buys manuscripts from international authors. Many of its books tell the stories of people whose voices are not always heard. Books by the First Peoples of this hemisphere have always been a special interest, as well as French-Canadian works in translation. Since 1998, Groundwood has been publishing works by Latino authors, in both English and Spanish, under its Libro Tigrillo imprint. Groundwood is always looking for new authors of novel-length fiction for children in all age areas but does not accept unsolicited manuscripts for picture books. They like character-driven literary fiction and do not publish high-interest/low-vocabulary fiction or stories with anthropomorphic animals or elves/fairies as their main characters.

Sheila Barry, Publisher.

INSOMNIAC PRESS ❖ www.insomniacpress.com

520 Princess Avenue, London, ON N6B 2B8, Canada, 416-504-6270,
Twitter: @InsomniacPress

Insomniac Press is a midsize independent press that publishes nonfiction, fiction, and poetry for adults. Insomniac always strives to publish the most exciting new writers it can find. While it publishes a broad range of titles, Insomniac has also developed special niche areas, including black studies books, gay and lesbian books, celebrity musician–authored books, and gay mysteries. Insomniac is actively seeking commercial and creative nonfiction on a wide range of subjects, including business, personal finance, gay and lesbian studies, and black Canadian studies.

Mike O'Connor, Publisher; mike@insomniacpress.com.
Dan Varrette, Managing Editor; dan@insomniacpress.com.

JAMES LORIMER & COMPANY LIMITED ❖ www.lorimer.ca

317 Adelaide Street West, Suite 1002, Toronto, ON M5V 1P9, Canada, 416-362-4762,
Twitter: @LorimerBooks

James Lorimer is a publisher of nonfiction, children's books, young adult novels, and illustrated guidebooks. It publishes Canadian authors for a Canadian audience and seeks manuscripts in the following genres: cultural or social history, natural history, cookbooks with a Canadian or regional focus, education, public issues, travel and recreation, and biography. It is especially interested in projects for the southwestern Ontario marketplace.

Lorimer accepts hardcopy submissions only.

James Lorimer, Publisher; jlorimer@lorimer.ca.
Pam Hickman, Acquisitions Editor; pamhickmankidsbooks@formac.ca.
Dana Hopkins, Editor; editor@lorimer.ca.

MCGILL-QUEEN'S UNIVERSITY PRESS ❖ www.mqup.ca

Montréal office: 1010 Sherbrooke West, Suite 1720, Montréal, QC H3A 2R7, Canada, 514-398-3750, mqup@mcgill.ca
Kingston office: 93 University Avenue, Kingston, ON K7L 5C4, Canada, 613-533-2155, mqup@queensu.ca

MQUP publishes original scholarly books and well-researched general-interest books in all areas of the social sciences and humanities. While its emphasis is on providing an outlet for Canadian authors and scholarship, some of its authors are from outside Canada. More than half of its sales are international.

Philip J. Cercone, Executive Director and Senior Editor (Montréal); philip.cercone@mcgill.ca. American history, economics, philosophy.

Kyla Madden, Senior Editor (Montréal); kyla.madden@mcgill.ca. World history, religion, history of medicine.

Mark Abley, Editor (Montréal); mark.abley@mcgill.ca. Philosophy, linguistics.

Jonathon Crago, Editor (Montréal); jonathan.crago@mcgill.ca. Art history, architecture, communication studies, film, music, Quebec history.

Jacqueline Mason, Editor (Montréal); jacqueline.mason@mcgill.ca. Political science, public policy, international studies, law, psychology.

Khadija Coxon, Editor (Kingston); khadija.coxon@queensu.ca. Philosophy, science and technology, food studies, sociology, geography.

Joanne Pisano, Editorial Assistant (Montréal); joanne.pisano@mcgill.ca.

MCGRAW-HILL RYERSON LTD. ❖ www.mcgrawhill.ca

300 Water Street, Whitby, ON L1N 9B6, Canada, 905-430-5000, 800-565-5758, Twitter: @McGrawHillCDN

One of the 111 McGraw-Hill Companies around the globe, McGraw-Hill Ryerson is staffed and managed by Canadians but reports to its parent company in New York. Though primarily an educational division, McGraw-Hill Ryerson also has a thriving trade arm, which publishes and distributes reference books on a wide array of subjects, including business, computing, engineering, science, travel, and self-study foreign-language programs. Other areas include outdoor recreation, child care, parenting, health, fine arts, music, sports, fitness, cooking, and crafts.

Unsolicited/unagented proposals may be submitted through the Proposal Submissions page on the company's website.

CANADIAN BOOK PUBLISHERS

NEW SOCIETY PUBLISHERS ❖ www.newsociety.com

PO Box 189, Gabriola Island, BC V0R 1X0, Canada, 250-247-9737,
Twitter: @NewSocietyPub

New Society Publishers is an activist press focused on social justice and ecological issues. Its mission is to publish books that contribute in fundamental ways to building an ecologically sustainable and just society. It publishes books on food, gardening, health and wellness, energy, sustainable living, urban issues, green building, education, and parenting. All its books are printed on 100 percent postconsumer recycled paper with vegetable-based inks.

Sue Custance, Publishing Director; editor@newsociety.com.

NOVALIS ❖ www.novalis.ca

10 Lower Spadina Avenue, Suite 400, Toronto, ON M5V 2Z2, Canada, 416-363-3303

Novalis is a religious publishing house that publishes and distributes books and other resources touching on all aspects of spiritual life, especially from the Christian and Jewish traditions. While most of its titles are for the general public, Novalis also publishes more specialized works in the area of theology and religious studies. Subjects include personal growth, self-help, spirituality and prayer, children's books, gardening, meditation, Church history, and Celtic spirituality, among others. The largest bilingual religious publisher in Canada, Novalis has equally strong publishing programs in both English and French.

Joseph Sinasac, Publishing Director; joseph.sinasac@novalis.ca.
Anne-Louise Mahoney, Managing Editor; anne-louise.mahoney@novalis.ca.
Don Beyers, Acquisitions Editor; don.beyers@novalis.ca.

Owlkids Books ❖ www.owlkids.com/books

10 Lower Spadina Avenue, Suite 400, Toronto, ON M5V 2Z2, Canada, 416-340-2700,
owlkids@owlkids.com

Owlkids Books has been publishing children's books for more than 35 years. It specializes in science and nature titles but also looks for nonfiction in a wide range of subjects, including Canadian culture, sports, crafts, activities, history, humor, and picture books.

Karen Boersma, Publisher.
Angela Keenlyside, Associate Publisher.
Karen Li, Editorial Director.
Faith Cochran, Creative Director.

OOLICHAN BOOKS ❖ www.oolichan.com

PO Box 2278, Fernie, BC V0B 1M0, Canada, 250-423-6113, info@oolichan.com, Twitter: @OolichanBooks

Oolichan Books is a literary press publishing poetry, fiction, and creative nonfiction titles, including literary criticism, memoir, and books on regional history, First Nations, and policy issues. The press is named after the small fish that was once plentiful in West Coast waters and a dietary staple of First Nations people, to whom it was sacred.

Randal Macnair, Publisher.
Carolyn Nikodym, Assistant to the Publisher.
Ron Smith, Editor.
(Ms.) Pat Smith, Consulting Editor.

ORCA BOOK PUBLISHERS ❖ www.orcabook.com

PO Box 5626, Station B, Victoria, BC V8R 6S4, Canada, 800-210-5277, info@orcabook.com, Twitter: @orcabook

Orca focuses on children's books: picture books and juvenile and young adult fiction. Its limited adult list focuses on general trade nonfiction, including travel and recreational guides, regional history, and biography. The Orca Currents line seeks short novels with contemporary themes written for middle-school students reading below grade level. The Orca Sports line features sports action combined with mystery/suspense. For ages 10 and up, Orca Sports seeks strong plots, credible characters, simple language, and high-interest chapters. The Orca Echoes line features early chapter books for readers ages 7 to 9 at a grade 2 reading level. The Orca Young Readers line has historical and contemporary stories for ages 8 to 11, with age-appropriate plots and storylines.

Andrew Woolridge, Publisher; andrew@orcabook.com.
Bob Tyrrell, President.
Sarah Harvey, Senior Editor.
Ruth Linka, Associate Publisher.
Amy Collins, Editor.
Tanya Trafford, Editor.

PENGUIN RANDOM HOUSE CANADA ❖ penguinrandomhouse.ca

320 Front Street West, Suite 1400, Toronto, ON M5V 3B6, Canada, 416-364-4449

Penguin Canada completed its international merger with Random House in 2013.

Penguin Canada ❖ penguinrandomhouse.ca/imprints/penguin-canada

Initially a distribution arm for Penguin International, Penguin Books began publishing indigenous Canadian work in 1982 with such notable titles as Peter C. Newman's landmark history of the Hudson's Bay Company, *Company of Adventurers*, and fiction by Robertson Davies, Timothy Findley, Alice Munro, and Mordecai Richler. It also publishes books under other imprints, including Hamish Hamilton Canada, Puffin Canada, and Viking Canada. Penguin Canada's books cover subjects as diverse as Canadian nationalism, homelessness and mental illness, and health care and education.

Nicole Winstanley, Publisher.
Diane Turbide, Editorial Director.
Lynne Missen, Editor.

Random House Canada ❖

penguinrandomhouse.ca/imprints/random-house-canada

Random House Canada was established in 1944, and in 1986 the company established its own indigenous Canadian publishing program. The Random House Canada imprint features a diverse list of literary and commercial fiction, Canadian and international cookbooks, and nonfiction.

Anne Collins, Vice President, Penguin Random House Canada.

Doubleday Canada ❖ penguinrandomhouse.ca/imprints/doubleday-canada

Doubleday Canada marked its 75th anniversary in 2012. One of Canada's most prominent publishers, it is committed to producing fine fiction from both established and new voices, and developing challenging and entertaining nonfiction. It also maintains a young adult publishing program.

Kristin Cochrane, President & Publisher, Penguin Random House Canada.
Martha Kanya-Forstner, Editor. Fiction and non-fiction.
Bhavna Chauhan, Editor. Fiction.
Amy Black, Editor. Fiction.

Hamish Hamilton Canada ❖ www.hamishhamilton.ca

The Canadian counterpart of one of Britain's most distinguished literary lists, Hamish Hamilton Canada has provided a home for an exciting and eclectic group of authors united by the distinctiveness and excellence of their writing. It maintains a deep commitment to literary value, embracing both young and old, the experimental and the new, and continues to be selective with a list of 5 to 10 titles a year.

Nicole Winstanley, Publisher.

Knopf Canada ❖ penguinrandomhouse.ca/imprints/knopf-canada

Knopf Canada was launched in 1991, when Sonny Mehta, president of Alfred A. Knopf, approached prominent editor Louise Denny to create and run a Canadian arm of Knopf in the offices of Random House Canada. It is interested in thoughtful nonfiction and fiction with literary merit and strong commercial potential.

Amanda Lewis, Editor. Fiction and nonfiction.
Lynn Henry, Editor. Fiction and nonfiction.
Pamela Murray, Editor. Fiction.
Anne Collins, Editor. Fiction and nonfiction.

Mcclelland & Stewart ❖ penguinrandomhouse.ca/imprints/mcclelland-stewart

75 Sherbourne Street, 5th floor, Toronto, ON M5A 2P9, Canada, 416-364-4449, Twitter: @mcClelland Books

Established in 1906, M&S is something of a Canadian institution and was an early publisher of Lucy Maud Montgomery's *Anne of Green Gables* and Winston Churchill's *History of the English Speaking Peoples*. Today, it publishes a wide range of poetry, fiction, and nonfiction.

Anita Chong, Senior Editor. Fiction.

Tundra Books ❖ penguinrandomhouse.ca/imprints/tundra-books

1 Toronto Street, Suite 300, Toronto, ON M5C 2V6, Canada, 416-364-4449, Twitter: @tundraBooks

Tundra is a children's book publisher famous for its extremely well-produced and -illustrated books for young readers.

Tara Walker, Publisher, Penguin Random House Canada Children's Publishing Group.
Samantha Swenson, Editor.

PLAYWRIGHTS CANADA PRESS ❖ www.playwrightscanada.com

269 Richmond Street West, Suite 202, Toronto, ON M5V 1X1, Canada, 416-703-0013, info@playwrightscanada.com, Twitter: @PlayCanPress

Playwrights Canada Press is the largest exclusive publisher of Canadian drama, publishing roughly 30 books of plays, theater history, criticism, biography, and memoir every year. It exists to raise the profile of Canadian playwrights, theater, and theater practitioners. French plays by Canadian authors are published in translation, and the press's mandate includes printing plays for young audiences.

Annie Gibson, Publisher; annie@playwrightscanada.com.
Stephanie Nuñez, Managing Editor; stephanie@playwrightscanada.com.

RED DEER PRESS ❖ www.reddeerpress.com

195 Allstate Parkway, Markham, ON L3R 4T8, Canada, 800-387-9776, rdp@reddeerpress.com, Twitter: @RedDeerPress

Red Deer Press is an award-winning publisher of literary fiction, nonfiction, children's illustrated books, juvenile fiction, teen fiction, drama, and poetry. Its mandate is to publish books by, about, or of interest to Canadians, with special emphasis on the Prairie West. The press publishes 18 to 20 new books per year, all written or illustrated by Canadians. Approximately 20 percent of their program is composed of first-time authors and illustrators.

Richard Dionne, Publisher; dionne@reddeerpress.com.
Peter Carver, Children's Editor.

RONSDALE PRESS ❖ www.ronsdalepress.com

3350 West 21st Avenue, Vancouver, BC V6S 1G7, Canada, 604-738-4688, ronsdale@shaw.ca, Twitter: @ronsdalepress

A literary publishing house, Ronsdale Press is dedicated to publishing books from across Canada and books that give Canadians new insights into their country. Ronsdale publishes fiction, poetry, regional history, biography and autobiography, plays, books of ideas about Canada, and children's books. The press looks for thoughtful works by authors who have read deeply in contemporary and earlier literature and whose texts offer genuinely new insights. Ronsdale accepts submissions only from Canadian authors.

Ronald B. Hatch, General Acquisitions Editor.
Veronica Hatch, Children's Acquisitions Editor.

SECOND STORY PRESS ❖ www.secondstorypress.ca

20 Maud Street, Suite 401, Toronto, ON M5V 2M5, Canada, 416-537-7850, info@secondstorypress.ca, Twitter: @_secondstory

The Second Story Press list spans adult fiction and nonfiction; children's fiction, nonfiction, and picture books; and young adult fiction and nonfiction. As a feminist press, it looks for manuscripts dealing with the many diverse and varied aspects of the lives of girls and women. Some of its special-interest areas include Judaica, ability issues, coping with cancer, and queer rights. They publish about 16 new books per year, primarily from Canadian authors.

Margie Wolfe, Publisher.
Kathryn Cole, Managing Editor.
Carolyn Jackson, Managing Editor.

TALON BOOKS LTD. ❖ www.talonbooks.com

PO Box 2076, Vancouver, BC V6B 3S3, Canada, 604-444-4889, info@talonbooks.com, Twitter: @Talonbooks

Talon Books was founded as a poetry magazine at Magee High School in Vancouver in 1963. Since then it has grown into one of Canada's largest independent presses. It publishes drama, fiction, and nonfiction of the political, social, critical, and ethnographic variety.

Kevin Williams, President; kevin@talonbooks.com.

UNIVERSITY OF ALBERTA PRESS ❖ www.uap.ualberta.ca

Ring House 2, University of Alberta, Edmonton, AB T6G 2E1, Canada, 780-492-3662

University of Alberta Press publishes in the areas of biography, history, language, literature, natural history, regional interest, travel narratives, and reference books. The press seeks to contribute to the intellectual and cultural life of Alberta and Canada. Canadian works that are analytical in nature are especially welcome, as are works by scholars who wish to interpret Canada, both past and present.

Linda Cameron, Director; linda.cameron@ualberta.ca.
Peter Midgley, Senior Acquisitions Editor; pmidgley@ualberta.ca.
Roger Epp, Acquiring Editor; roger.epp@ualberta.ca.
Mary Lou Roy, Editor/Production; marylou.roy@ualberta.ca.

UNIVERSITY OF BRITISH COLUMBIA PRESS ❖ www.ubcpress.ubc.ca

2029 West Mall, Vancouver, BC V6T 1Z2, Canada, 604-822-5959, Twitter: @UBCPress

UBC Press is the publishing branch of the University of British Columbia. Established in 1971, it is among the largest university presses in Canada, publishing 70 new books annually, with an active backlist of more than 800 titles. UBC Press is widely acknowledged as one of the foremost publishers of political science, Native studies, and forestry books. Other areas of particular strength are Asian studies, Canadian history, environmental studies, planning, and urban studies.

Peter Milroy, Director Emeritus; milroy@ubcpress.ca. Special projects, international rights.

Randy Schmidt, Senior Editor; schmidt@ubcpress.ca. Forestry, environmental studies, urban studies and planning, sustainable development, geography, law and society.

Darcy Cullen, Acquisitions Editor; cullen@ubcpress.ca. Canadian history, regional, native studies, sexuality studies, northern and Arctic studies, health studies, education.

UNIVERSITY OF MANITOBA PRESS ❖ www.umanitoba.ca/uofmpress

301 St. John's College, University of Manitoba, Winnipeg, MB R3T 2M5, Canada, 204-474-9495, uofmpress@umanitoba.ca, Twitter: @umanitobapress

Founded in 1967, University of Manitoba Press publishes innovative and exceptional books of scholarship and serious Canadian nonfiction. Its list includes books on Native studies, Canadian history, women's studies, Icelandic studies, aboriginal languages, film studies, biography, geography, nature, and Canadian literature and culture. It publishes five to eight books a year, meaning each book receives the concentrated focus and attention that are often not possible at a larger press.

David Carr, Director; carr@cc.umanitoba.ca.

Glenn Bergen, Managing Editor; d.bergen@umanitoba.ca.

Jill McConkey, Acquisitions Editor; jill.mcconkey@umanitoba.ca

UNIVERSITY OF OTTAWA PRESS/LES PRESSES DE L'UNIVERSITÉ D'OTTAWA ❖ www.press.uottawa.ca

542 King Edward, Ottawa, ON K1N 6N5, Canada, 613-562-5246, puo-uop@uottawa.ca, Twitter: @uOttawaPress

As Canada's only officially bilingual university press, the UOP is both uniquely Canadian and unique in Canada. Since 1936, UOP has supported cultural development through the publication of books in both French and English aimed at a general public interested in serious nonfiction.

Lara Mainville, Director; lara.mainville@uottawa.ca.
Dominike Thomas, Acquisitions Editor; dthomas@uottawa.ca.

UNIVERSITY OF TORONTO PRESS ❖ www.utpress.utoronto.ca

10 Saint Mary Street, Suite 700, Toronto, ON M4Y 2W8, Canada, 416-978-2239, info@utpress.utoronto.ca, Twitter: @utpress

University of Toronto Press is Canada's oldest and largest scholarly publisher and is among the 15 largest university presses in North America. Established in 1901, the press publishes scholarly, reference, and general-interest books on Canadian history and literature, medieval studies, and social sciences, among other subjects. Approximately 200 new titles are released each year, and the backlist includes more than 3,500 titles. The house publishes in a range of fields, including history and politics; women's studies; health, family, and society; law and crime; economics; workplace communication; theory/culture; language, literature, semiotics, and drama; medieval studies; Renaissance studies; Erasmus studies; Italian-language studies; East European studies; classics; and nature. The list includes topical titles in Canadian studies, Native studies, sociology, anthropology, urban studies, modern languages, and music.

Anne Brackenbury, Executive Editor; brackenbury@utphighereducation.com. Anthropology, criminology, geography, native studies, Latin/North American studies, sociology.
Natalie Fingerhut, Editor; fingerhut@utphighereducation.com. International relations, Jewish history, Canadian and European history, security studies, non-Western history.
Jennifer DiDomenico, Acquisitions Editor; jdidomenico@utpress.utoronto.ca. Economics.
Douglas Hildebrand, Acquisitions Editor; dhildebrand@utpress.utoronto.ca. Anthropology, criminology, education, LGBTQ studies, geography, Native studies, race and diaspora studies, urban studies.
Len Husband, Acquisitions Editor; lhusband@utpress.utoronto.ca. Canadian history, natural science, philosophy.
Richard Ratzlaff, Acquisitions Editor; rratzlaff@utpress.utoronto.ca. Book history, English literature, modern languages, Victorian studies.

Suzanne Rancourt, Executive Editor; srancourt@utpress.utoronto.ca. Humanities, classics, medieval and renaissance studies.

Daniel Quinlan, Acquisitions Editor; dquinlan@utpress.utoronto.ca. Political science, law.

Mat Buntin, Acquisitions Editor; mbuntin@utphighereducation.com. Politics, international development studies, human rights, security studies.

Mark Thompson, Acquisitions Editor; mthompson@utpress.utoronto.ca. Literature, book history, film, cultural studies, communications.

Stephen Shapiro, Associate Acquisitions Editor; sshapiro@utpress.utoronto.ca. Health, medicine, social work.

VÉHICULE PRESS ❖ www.vehiculepress.com

PO Box 42094 BP Roy, Montréal, QC H2W 2T3, Canada, 514-844-6073, admin@vehiculepress.com, Twitter: @VehiculePress

For more than 35 years, Véhicule Press has been publishing prize-winning poetry, fiction, social history, Quebec studies, Jewish studies, jazz history, and restaurant guides.

Simon Dardick, Editor. Nonfiction.
Dimitri Nasrallah, Editor. Fiction.
Carmine Starnino, Editor. Poetry.

WHITECAP BOOKS ❖ www.whitecap.ca

314 West Cordova Street, Suite 210, Vancouver, BC V6B 1E8, Canada, 604-681-6181, Twitter: whitecapbooks

Whitecap Books is one of Canada's largest independent publishers. In addition to the cookbooks, gift books, and coffee-table books that it is primarily known for, Whitecap publishes gardening and crafts, photo-scenic, history, arts and entertainment, children's fiction and nonfiction, travel, sports, and transportation books. Its Walrus Books division publishes children's books.

Nick Rundall, Publisher; nickr@whitecap.ca.
Abby Wiseman, Associate Publisher; abbyw@whitecap.ca.
Jordie Yow, Editor; jordiey@whitecap.ca.

Part 6

LITERARY AGENTS

PLANET LITERARY AGENT

Jeff Herman

Here are the listings for 130 literary agencies and 185 individual agents, most of whom provide the information you need to make intelligent choices about whom to pitch and how to do it.

Who Is and Isn't Listed in This Edition?

To the best of my knowledge, only qualified agents are included. Please let me know if you disagree (jeff@jeffherman.com). I invited more agents than are here and would have gladly included most of them, but to be included, agents must respond to my survey, even if they only list name and website, and many did not. Some agents are at full capacity and don't want to receive unsolicited submissions, and I didn't make adequate contact with everyone I tried to. As you know or soon will, spam filters and unfriendly agency mailboxes can be impenetrable. By the way, I received more than a few boilerplate rejection letters from agents in response to my invitation to include them in this book.

Bottom line: I can confidently say that at least 98 percent of the agents in this section are legitimate. But just because someone isn't here doesn't mean they aren't a real agent.

What's a "Fee-Charging" Agent?

I hope there are no reading-fee agents in this listing. If there are, it's because they conned me, and you need to let me know (jeff@jeffherman.com). A legitimate agent shouldn't charge for the simple purpose of considering your work for representation. Anyone who does is probably not really an agent, which means they never actually sell anything to legitimate publishers.

Think about this: I receive several hundred unsolicited queries each month, as do many of my peers. If I converted a fraction of them into check-stuffed envelopes and PayPal credits, I'd have a nice revenue stream and wouldn't have to rely on commissions. Real agents don't make money from reading your work; they make it from successfully selling your work to a traditional publisher for a 15 percent commission. However, there are a few acceptable exceptions to this rule. A small number of legitimate agents request a modest fee (less than $100) in order to defray the cost of employing people to do first reads. I have included one or two of them because their policies are transparent, they have genuine track records, and you can easily bypass them.

THE LISTINGS

ANDREA BROWN LITERARY AGENCY, INC. ❖ www.andreabrownlit.com

Agents' names and contact info: Andrea Brown, President, andrea@andreabrownlit.com; Jamie Weiss Chilton, Agent, jamie@andrea brownlit.com; Jennifer Laughran, Senior Agent, jennl@andreabrownlit.com; Jennifer Mattson, Agent, jmatt@andreabrownlit.com; Lara Perkins, Associate Agent, lara@andreabrownlit.com; Laura Rennert, Executive Agent, lauraqueries@gmail.com; Jennifer Rofe, Senior Agent, jennifer@andrea brownlit.com; Kelly Sonnack, Agent, kelly@andreabrownlit.com; Caryn Wiseman, Senior Agent, caryn@andreabrownlit.com

Describe the kinds of works you want to represent. Children's books and young adult, both fiction and nonfiction.

How do you want writers to pitch you? We accept e-queries only. Please see our website for submission guidelines.

ANDREA HURST & ASSOCIATES LITERARY MANAGEMENT ❖

andreahurst.com

PO Box 1467, Coupeville, WA 98239

Agent's name and contact info: Andrea Hurst, President, info@andreahurst.com

Describe the kinds of works you want to represent. I am closed to unsolicited queries, unless you are a well-published author or referred by a publisher or literary agent. I represent book-club or contemporary women's fiction, mystery/thriller/suspense, cookbooks, prescriptive nonfiction.

Describe what you definitely don't want to represent. Children's and middle grade, memoir, authors who are unpublished or not referred by an agent or publisher.

How do you want writers to pitch you? Authors *must follow submission guidelines on the website* and query to info@andreahurst.com.

Describe your education and professional history. BA, expressive arts; 30 years in publishing in various capacities, including literary agent, bestselling author, developmental editor, webinar presenter for *Writer's Digest.*

Knowing what you do now, would you do it again? If not, what might you do instead? I've loved my career in book publishing, and there is nothing I'd do differently. I look to the future and hope to write and publish more books and help authors have successful careers.

Do you charge fees? If yes, please explain. The literary agency does not charge fees; however, we do have a completely separate editing and consulting side of the business that offers paid services. We do not offer representation to any clients we edit or consult for in any capacity.

What do you like to do when you're not working? Read, write, take walks along the beautiful Puget Sound, and watch a few select TV shows or movies. I also like spending time in the Monterey/Carmel area.

List some of the titles you have recently placed with publishers. *The Buried Book* and *The Rejected Writers Book Club* (Lake Union), *Canon Cocktail Book* (Houghton Mifflin), *Wild Cookbook* (Running Press), *Tiki Cookbook* (Sterling Press), *Pancakes in Paris* (Sourcebooks), *Death of a Chocolate Cheater* (NAL/Penguin), *Story Fix* (Writer's Digest Press).

Do you think the business has changed a lot over the past few years? If yes, please explain. The business has changed so much over the past few years it's hardly recognizable. However, there are so many new and exciting opportunities for authors now. From ebooks to audiobooks and beyond, there are plenty of new ways to extend readership. It makes for a new and exciting world of publishing.

What do the "Big 5" mean to you? New York.

How do you feel about independent/small presses? If they do a good job, I am all for them, including digital publishers.

What are your feelings about self-publishing? For many people, including myself, self-publishing has been an amazing way to reach new readership and build audience. We do scout the successful self-published books for representation.

Do you think Amazon is good or bad — or both — for the book business? All businesses change, and for me Amazon has been extremely helpful for reaching my readers and promoting my books.

What do you like and dislike about your job? We really dislike it when writers don't go to our website first and follow directions!

What are ways prospective clients can impress you, and what are ways they can turn you off? Follow directions on our website, and all will be well. Learn the book-publishing business and be professional. Always have a well-edited and high-quality product.

How would you describe the "writer from hell"? We all know that answer.

Describe a book you would like to write. Many!

Is there anything you wish to express beyond the parameters of the preceding questions? Please respect our time and follow the directions on our website. If we are interested in seeing more of your work, we will contact you.

Agent's name and contact info: Sean Fletcher, Agent Scout, sean@andreahurst.com

Describe the kinds of works you want to represent. I represent adult and young adult science fiction/fantasy, contemporary young adult, middle grade (all genres). I am looking only for serious authors with works that are well crafted and professionally edited or authors with a strong platform.

Describe what you definitely don't want to represent. Romance, children's picture books, horror, erotica, nonfiction.

How do you want writers to pitch you? Send a query and the first 10 pages pasted into an email to sean@andreahurst.com.

How did you become an agent? I am an avid reader and started writing novels in college, publishing my first novel in 2015. After finishing my degree, I began an editorial internship with Andrea Hurst & Associates. After extensive internship and training, I became an assistant editor and agent scout. I speak and teach at writers' conferences and just completed my seventh novel. I enjoy working with writers and am looking for new talent to expand my client base.

What do you like to do when you're not working? When not editing or writing my own novels, I enjoy hiking, biking, and traveling.

ANNIE BOMKE LITERARY AGENCY ❖ www.abliterary.com

PO Box 3759, San Diego, CA 92163, 619-634-3415

Agent's name and contact info: Annie Bomke, submissions@abliterary.com

Describe the kinds of works you want to represent. On the fiction side, I love character-driven works; mystery (cozies, psychological thrillers, and everything in between); historical, women's, literary and upmarket, contemporary young adult, and new adult fiction; and books with multicultural or LGBT characters. So if you have a literary psychological thriller set in Nazi Germany with a gay protagonist, I'd love to see it. I'm a sucker for books set in the Victorian era, retellings of *Hamlet*, and books about famous historical figures. I also love ridiculously funny novels and literary psychological horror.

For nonfiction, I'm looking for fresh prescriptive business, self-help, and health/diet books with a great platform. I also love memoir with a fresh voice (funny or serious), narrative nonfiction on an unusual topic, and big-concept popular psychology books. I'm fascinated by topics, like behavioral economics (for example, *Predictably Irrational* by Dan Ariely), that explore some aspect of why people do the things they do from either a psychological or biological perspective.

Describe what you definitely don't want to represent. I don't represent romance, poetry, children's picture books and chapter books, mid-grade, short story collections, or screenplays. I'm also not a big fan of genre fiction like sci-fi, fantasy, or paranormal, though I like some novels with a slight twist in those areas.

How do you want writers to pitch you? Although I love an interesting concept, for me it really comes down to the writing, so the best way for authors to pitch me a novel is to send me a query, synopsis, and the first two chapters of their book. For nonfiction books, I ask that authors send me a book proposal. (Proposal guidelines are on my website.) Then I'll see if I'm pulled in by the writing and if I want to request more. I take submissions through email and hardcopy. (For hardcopy submissions, please include an SASE.) Authors can also pitch to me during writers' conferences at designated pitch appointments or panels.

Describe your education and professional history. I have a BA in rhetoric from UC Berkeley. During college, I interned at *Zoetrope: All-Story*, a literary magazine founded by Francis Ford Coppola. Then I worked at Margret McBride Literary Agency for seven and a half years, first as an intern, then as the royalties and foreign-rights agent.

How did you become an agent? When I was in high school and college, I wanted to be a writer, but I knew I needed a day job. I had worked briefly as a technical writer, so I figured I'd do that. My last year in college I got an internship at a literary magazine (*Zoetrope: All-Story*), and I absolutely fell in love with publishing. There was just something so thrilling about helping bring writers' voices into the world. I moved back home to San Diego after college, because I had no money, and the only publishing jobs in San Diego were at literary agencies. So I applied to a whole bunch of them and got an internship at Margret McBride Agency. And the rest is history.

Knowing what you do now, would you do it again? If not, what might you do instead? I would definitely do it all over again. It's been over 10 years since my internship at *Zoetrope: All-Story*, and I'm still in love with publishing.

Do you charge fees? If yes, please explain. No.

When and where were you born, and where have you lived? I was born in a small town in Ohio in the early 1980s. My parents literally lived on a farm. We moved to San Diego when I was three, and I've lived here most of my life, apart from my stint in Berkeley.

What do you like to do when you're not working? I love playing Sudoku (25 by 25) and going for walks in nature and trying to spot hawks. (The best is watching crows try to dive-bomb hawks. It's hilarious.) I love watching true-crime documentaries and having solo impromptu dance parties. And I kinda like reading.

List some of the titles you have recently placed with publishers. The Introvert Entrepreneur by Beth Buelow (Perigee, 2015).

Describe your personality. I aspire to be like the woman in the Cake song "Short Skirt/Long Jacket": "With fingernails that shine like justice, and a voice that is dark like tinted glass, she is fast, thorough, and sharp as a tack. She's touring the facilities and picking up slack."

What do you like reading/watching/listening to on your own time? In my spare time, I read a pretty wide range of books (mostly fiction), from funny young adult novels to psychology books, though mostly I read literary fiction, mystery, and psychological thrillers. My favorite TV shows are *Project Runway*, *Chopped*, *The Great British Baking Show*, *Portlandia*, *It's Always Sunny in Philadelphia*, *Modern Family*, *Aqua Teen Hunger Force*, and *Law & Order* in all its incarnations. I'm a sucker for any kind of character-driven police-procedural show like *Luther*, *The Fall*, *Broadchurch*, *River*, and *The Killing*. (Thank you, Netflix!) I listen to a pretty wide range of music, including crappy dance music and '90s R&B.

Do you think the business has changed a lot over the past few years? If yes, please explain. I feel the business went through major changes about 8 to 10 years ago, between the rise of ebooks and the drop in the economy. Things have gotten better since then, but publishers still are more selective now than they were 10 years ago.

What do the "Big 5" mean to you? The Big 5 are solid publishers who can offer excellent opportunities to a writer. I always try to work with the Big 5 when I can.

How do you feel about independent/small presses? Independent presses are also a fabulous publishing option for many writers. Independent presses are often more open to experimental books and books that are outside of the box of mainstream publishing, and they're continually coming up with fresh, out-of-the-box ways of promoting their books.

What are your feelings about self-publishing? Self-publishing is a great option for authors who have had trouble finding an agent and want to get their work out there. I just always tell authors to promote the hell out of their self-published books, because if they want a traditional publisher for their future books, their sales figures will make all the difference in the world.

Do you think Amazon is good or bad — or both — for the book business? There is only so much space in brick-and-mortar stores, and it's impossible for any store to carry every book that comes out, so I think that Amazon provides an excellent, streamlined platform that makes it easy for people to buy books. In that sense, it's great for the book business, especially for smaller presses, which have a harder time getting their books in stores.

I also think that Amazon is bad for the book business in the sense that it has a monopoly on the market and acts like a bully to get what it wants. All the dirty tricks Amazon pulled while it was negotiating ebook prices with publishers have really turned me off the site. I try not to buy any books there (unless I have a gift certificate), though admittedly I still buy other stuff there. It's just so convenient!

What do you like and dislike about your job? What I love about my job is helping authors bring their fabulous ideas and stories into the world. I also love that every day is different. Every day there are new queries to read, new ideas to learn about.

What I don't like about my job is getting rejections on my authors' work and then relaying the news to them. I also don't enjoy writing rejections, especially if I've had some back-and-forth with the author already.

What are ways prospective clients can impress you, and what are ways they can turn you off? It sounds simple, but I'm impressed by authors who behave professionally. The littlest things, like being polite and respectful and following my submission guidelines, go a long way with me.

Conversely, I'm turned off by people who don't behave professionally. People who send hardcopy queries without an SASE, people who query me through Facebook, people who call me to ask what an agent does, people who send me a link to check out their writing on their website in lieu of attaching sample chapters, etc. It's not difficult to follow my guidelines, so when authors don't, it says to me that they think the rules don't apply to them or that they haven't invested the time to learn what the rules are.

The early stages of interacting with an agent are a lot like applying for a job. You wouldn't email an HR manager with a link to your LinkedIn page and expect the manager to offer you a job or apply for a job through the company's Facebook page (unless directed to do so). Publishing is a business, and I appreciate authors who treat it as such.

How would you describe the "writer from hell"? An author who refuses to take feedback and doesn't listen. Also authors who send angry emails to their editors at 3 AM. It's important for the agent to be clear about what (if any) major changes he or she expects before signing an author. Agents and authors have to make sure they're on the same page, or else they're going to be fighting the whole way. So a warning sign is if authors hem and haw about what changes they're willing to make and won't give a straight answer, or if they make half-assed attempts to address the agent's concerns that don't actually do anything. I once worked with an author who, instead of making changes to address my feedback or telling me why she didn't agree with it, would argue why it was unnecessary to address such concerns in the actual manuscript. For example, if I asked her to expand on an idea, she would write in the manuscript itself something like, "If some want a more thorough explanation of X, they can refer to my earlier chapter where I addressed it." Talk about passive aggressive!

Describe a book you would like to write. Once I had a dream that I had written this amazing young adult novel. It was about two sisters who become wards of Edgar Allan Poe. In one scene, they watch Poe perform alchemy or some other kind of dark magical ceremony, spying down on him from a high garden wall. It was all very eerie and mysterious. I might write it someday, if nobody beats me to it.

Do you believe in a higher and/or lower "power"? If by "higher power" you mean unicorns, then yes, yes I do.

ANN TOBIAS, A LITERARY AGENCY FOR CHILDREN'S BOOKS

520 East 84th Street, 4L, New York, NY 10028, 212-452-1949

Agent's name and contact info: Ann Tobias, atqueries@gmail.com

Describe the kinds of works you want to represent. I specialize in works for children: young (3–6, 4–8), mid-level (8–12), and young adult (13 and up). In the area of picture books, I prefer to represent work that is both written and illustrated by the same person. Children's book editors do not want to see work written and illustrated by collaborators, so if you are an artist, I hope you will also write your own text, and if you are a writer, do your own art. In a picture book or a longer work for older kids, I want to be stunned by writing that is strong and beautiful, whether it's a light, rollicking story or a dark and serious one.

Describe what you definitely don't want to represent. I avoid vampires, horror, and paranormal as well as material that aims to educate or improve children — no life lessons, please.

How do you want writers to pitch you? What I want to learn from a pitch/query are simple facts: What have you written that you want me to read — picture book, middle grade or young adult novel? Fantasy? Realism? A mystery? Historical fiction? What is the length? What is the age group? What is the age of the protagonist? Give me a sense of the plot in one sentence and the theme in another sentence. If your project is nonfiction, please list your credentials. When sending a query, please include one to two pages of your manuscript in the body of your email (no attachments, please).

Describe your education and professional history. After college (Northwestern), I worked in children's book publishing — on-staff at Harper, William Morrow, and Scholastic. When my children were born, I edited freelance for Dial, Crown, Morrow Jr. Books, Hyperion, and others. Working for so many publishers enabled me to make the jump from editing to agenting, which I did in 1988 when I moved to Washington, DC, and realized that, although it was a lovely city in many ways, there were no publishers. Washington held very little opportunity for a displaced children's book editor. There were five or six agents in Washington who represented writers of adult material, but no one represented children's writers, so I did.

Knowing what you do now, would you do it again? If not, what might you do instead? Would I choose agenting again, knowing what I know now? Yes. I loved editing, but the reality of publishing these days is that, no matter how talented an editor may be, holding on to a job in publishing is uncertain at best. Agents who are sole proprietors can't fire themselves, and even more important, I am glad to be my own boss, taking responsibility for my decisions and being free to try new ways of doing things, some of which work and some of which don't, so I won't get into examples here.

Do you charge fees? If yes, please explain. No fees.

What do you like to do when you're not working? It would be nice to say that I have an intense interest in something unusual and dramatic, but my overwhelming interest is reading. And I like to cook something delicious for myself and others.

List some of the titles you have recently placed with publishers. A few examples of my clients' work recently placed: A debut middle grade fantasy, *The Power of Poppy Pendle*, has been followed by its sequel, *The Courage of Cat Campbell*, and both titles will be brought to a conclusion in the recently contracted-for *The Marvelous Magic of Miss Mabel* by Natasha Lowe (Paula Wiseman Books, Simon & Schuster). A third book in the *Red Kayak* series aimed at the upper end of the middle grade age group by Priscilla Cummings, *Cheating for the Chicken Man*, has been published recently by Dutton. Abby Hanlon's first book, *Dory Fantasmagory*, an extremely young middle grade has been followed by *Dory and the Real True Friend*. A third untitled *Dory* book has recently been contracted for (all Penguin).

Describe your personality. I think I am a great team player, so why am I on my own and why do I enjoy it? A mystery. I definitely miss not reacting to coworkers' manuscripts and hearing them react to those I am interested in. I definitely like earning my agent's fees and keeping all the money!!! (Not that there's that much, considering that I make 15 percent of very little, but it is a good feeling to own it, whatever it is.)

What do you like reading/watching/listening to on your own time? I cannot list the number of writers who are important to me — too many to fit on these pages. I don't watch much TV, and music is wonderful but sometimes disrupts the lovely sound of pages turning.

Do you think the business has changed a lot over the past few years? If yes, please explain. I think the business of publishing reflects our economy — a few people have everything and most people are scraping by. That's the big picture. There are myriad smaller examples, such as contracts that used to be 12 pages are now 40, most of it due to ebooks. Wading through them is time-consuming and difficult. I never used to wish I was a lawyer, but now a day does not pass that I think to be a successful, effective agent, a legal degree is necessary — this from a person who craves reading books and manuscripts (not documents).

What do the "Big 5" mean to you? To me, the Big 5 mean the large publishing houses that are considered most mainstream. They used to be the publishers people most wanted to be published by and still may be, but I think that is changing as self-publishing and ebooks are creating a more fluid atmosphere in the industry.

What are your feelings about self-publishing? Self-publishing in children's books has been a little slower to arrive than in adult books, and although there have been some successful self-published children's books, there has been nothing to match the success of adult self-published books. For the most part, I am unimpressed by the quality of the concepts, the writing, and the appearance of self-published children's books that are submitted to me. I haven't been even slightly tempted to take on the author of a self-published children's book.

Do you think Amazon is good or bad — or both — for the book business? Amazon is a phenom. As a store, it is great to buy from — Amazon is efficient and convinces me it wants to be helpful. As a publisher, it has little understanding of the publishing process. Will somebody please show Amazon how to write a royalty statement? Will someone please convince Amazon to install a few phones so we can actually talk to the personnel who so cavalierly make decisions about matters they have convinced me they know little or nothing about?

What do you like and dislike about your job? I want to work closely with my clients to bring their manuscripts to a point where editors find their material irresistible. I worry when clients are too quick to follow my direction and never argue, and I worry when they fight me every inch of the way. Somehow, there is an ideal give-and-take in our editorial discussions that leads to each author or author-artist producing a marvelous manuscript, and for the most part my clients and I achieve it. When this does not happen, I am seized by a deep desire to move to California and become a surfer.

My primary job, I think, is to see that my clients stay in the business and flourish. It's often difficult to get published for the first time, but it's very much harder to stay published and turn that first book into 10 more. I love the excitement that accompanies starting out a client's new manuscript — I am full of energy and hope for the project, and it is fun. I don't like the realization that a project is not going to succeed. I don't like having to give a client bad news of any kind — a book is going out of print, sales are falling, a manuscript has been rejected.

What are ways prospective clients can impress you, and what are ways they can turn you off? Prospective clients impress me when I can tell they have done their homework. By that, I mean when a new, unpublished writer of children's books shows me she has read actual published children's books — classics, recent, and everything in between. The number of would-be children's book writers who write manuscripts without having picked up a kid's book in many decades is truly surprising. And their manuscripts sound old, tired, boring.

I recommend that potential writers of children's books read at least 200 books in the age group they wish to address in their own manuscript. They must *think* about them and compare them with the classic titles that I am assuming they have already read (and remember) such as *Tom Sawyer*, *Heidi*, *Little Women*, the work of E. B. White, *Babar*, the *Angus* books, books by E. Nesbit, *Treasure Island* (oldies but goodies). After reading 200 recently published books in their chosen age group, I strongly suggest they read 100 more published books for children in other age groups, just to get an idea of the scope of publishing for children. I really want people to do this before sending me a manuscript, and here's fair warning: I can always tell when they haven't — a huge turnoff!

How would you describe the "writer from hell"? The "writer from hell" appeared much more frequently when I edited in publishing houses. They were most often authors my bosses assigned to me. I am sure the authors wanted my boss, not me, to be their editor. It was awkward and no fun but sometimes ended with respect on both sides — not always, but often enough. As an agent, I choose my clients myself, spend a lot of time reading their work, and have in-depth discussions with them before taking them on. It works much better!

Describe a book you would like to write. Agents and editors for the most part do not write books. They leave that to authors and instead have this small talent for finding and helping authors achieve publication. Writing my own book is just not in my DNA.

Is there anything you wish to express beyond the parameters of the preceding questions?
I cannot resist asking readers who are serious about writing for children to back up and reread (and act on) the question about what impresses me and what turns me off.

THE AUGUST AGENCY LLC ❖ www.augustagency.com

Agent's name: Cricket Freeman

Describe the kinds of works you want to represent. We are a discreet agency that has worked quietly since 2001, in the US and internationally, offering highly personalized service to an exclusive group of exceptional writers. Primarily we handle mainstream nonfiction, creative nonfiction, narrative nonfiction, memoir, and crime fiction. We favor persuasive and prescriptive nonfiction works, each with a full-bodied narrative command and an undeniable contemporary relevance. We enjoy untangling literary Gordian knots — the intricate story operating on multiple levels — whether historical crime thrillers, narrative memoir, contemporary creative nonfiction, or anything in between.

Describe what you definitely don't want to represent. We do *not* handle children's books, screenplays, poetry, short stories, romance, Westerns, horror, fantasy, or sci-fi.

How do you want writers to pitch you? More than three-quarters of our clients have come to us through writers' conferences, so it's obvious that's the best way for us to connect. In fact, invite me to your conference to teach a workshop and hear pitches, and in a scheduled one-on-one or even during the ride from the airport you can pitch your book and pick my brain mercilessly, and we'll plot your career objectives. Note: We only accept submissions at a conference or by referral. However, occasionally we open up to over-the-transom submissions through the submission form on our website. Unfortunately, we cannot consider queries that come to us any other way. Tip: The best queries are easier said than done. They're simple, but also slippery. They only have two paragraphs: one about the book and one about you — but those paragraphs have to be golden.

Describe your education and professional history. How did you become an agent? I didn't go to university to be a literary agent. After all, who does? You wander through the back door from somewhere close at hand: a publishing house, a law office, a media company — and usually because someone opened the door and invited you in. In my case, I was an experienced freelance writer and former national magazine editor in chief who knew my way around the publishing world; plus I'd been a real-estate broker who boogied through contracts. When I pitched a book at a conference, the agent recognized my value and recruited me. A year later, when I was up to my eyeballs in intriguing work, he wandered out the door. I stayed. Being an entrepreneur, I then founded my own agency.

Knowing what you do now, would you do it again? If not, what might you do instead?
Mmmmmm. Of course I would. Being an agent has brought me considerable rare gifts: friendships with delightful, generous, and spellbinding people from all over the globe, many my clients. My life is infinitely richer for it. And the best gift of all: while in Oregon for a writers' conference, I first met my Mr. Freeman on a hilltop under a meteoric sky. Destiny? Methinks so.

Do you charge fees? If yes, please explain. We do not charge fees for our literary representation services. We earn standard commissions on payments, advances, and royalties.

When and where were you born, and where have you lived? I'm a baby boomer, a proud fifth-generation Floridian, what locals call a "skeeter beater" (someone whose intrepid family was brave enough, wild enough, or criminal enough to be there before the advent of mosquito control, when a palm broom hung by each front door to beat the skeeters off your body before entering). When it comes to my writing and business creativity, I don't grow where bananas don't grow, so my agency is based in South Florida. At the time I founded the August Agency, locating an agency anywhere outside New York City was considered foolhardy, so we maintained a NYC branch for many years. By the time the recession rolled around and the internet ruled business, we all opted for sunshine and more fiscal efficiency.

What do you like to do when you're not working? I write. Other than that, sometimes I can squeeze in time to read, watch movies, design, travel, hike, canoe, walk the beach, or visit with other writers, my favorite people.

List some of the titles you have recently placed with publishers. Not all our clients' projects are books, although that is how they first come to us. We have sold their works for hardcover, trade paper, and mass-market paperback editions, but also as digital, film, audio, serial, reprint, gaming, and foreign rights. Outlets have included academic presses, genre presses, regional houses, content providers, educational testing services as well as traditional advance-paying publishers, such as Career Press, Wiley, Praeger, Gale, and AMACOM Books. A typical title might be *The Office Politics Handbook* by Jack Godwin, PhD.

Describe your personality. Creative, complex, artistic, loving, funny, nurturing, mushy, straightforward, easy, generous, bawdy, Southern, spirited. How long need I fuss about such fripperies?

What do you like reading/watching/listening to on your own time? Of course, books will always be my best friends. I like discovering a ray of light through nonfiction, but love getting lost in a novel late at night. And at heart I'm a rhythm & blues baby, so anything from Billie Holiday to Keb Mo to John Mayer will get me rockin'. Then there's streaming media, offering up a bounty of stories with a click. I'm discovering my favorite TV series and movies are often from outside the US, such as from New Zealand, bringing an out-of-the-ordinary perspective on story construction and delivery.

Do you think the business has changed a lot over the past few years? If yes, please explain. *Egads!* When I became an agent, I was one of the few agencies to even have a website. All business was conducted in hardcopy — all queries came by mail (by the bushel basket every day); every manuscript was printed, boxed, and FedExed to publishers; and contracts were faxed back and forth. By contrast, today nothing is handled in hardcopy; everything is digital and handled in the blink of an eye. With distance comes perspective, so I can see trends in my literary crystal ball. These are heady times, ripe with possibility, an amazing new playground with lots that's new and exciting, but be cautious of bullies lurking in the shadows ready to pocket your lunch money. I see that opportunities for writers are growing with each year, that having an agent is becoming more necessary in some areas yet less so in others, and that boutique agencies who foster authors' careers, like the August Agency, are becoming scarcer each year.

What do the "Big 5" mean to you? The major publishers will always be the gold standard for authors, the definition of having arrived, of being a success at writing — no matter what this free-wheeling publishing environment brings to surprise us, and no matter how many readers authors have, how many books they sell, or how much money lands in their pockets.

How do you feel about independent/small presses? I have always believed in the gift of small presses to discover, develop, appreciate, and publish those fabulous, entertaining, and invaluable books we all adore but the big guys can't be bothered with and thus ignore. This past year we expanded our literary services, becoming one such small commercial press: August Words Publishing — unique books by exceptional authors for select readers. (Now a shameless plug: please visit www.augustwordspublishing.com.)

What are your feelings about self-publishing? Decades ago, before digital publishing and long before the August Agency, I had Possibilities Press, which provided prepublication preparation for small publishers and self-publishers: ghostwriting, editing, book design, cover design, printing, binding, and market analysis. Even with a professionally produced book, many self-published authors discovered a steep uphill climb. We've come so far since then, from glue pots and typesetting to the click of a mouse, from a social shunning in literary circles to encouragement and acceptance. But some things still remain true for self-published books: Is it ready for prime time? Remember, you only get one shot at your reader with this book, whether an agent, editor, or buyer. At last, from the reader's viewpoint every book is on equal ground, no matter if it is published by one of the major houses, an academic press, a small regional publisher, a few-books-a-year micropress, or directly by the author. One thing I have seen is that large publishers today are now viewing self-published books as test-marketed: low sales numbers brand a book as not testing well, but books with high sales are deemed as having test-marketed well and are worthy of a look.

Do you think Amazon is good or bad — or both — for the book business? Amazon is at once a blessing and a curse. It has allowed little upstart August Words Publishing to offer its books on equal footing with other publishers and in 14 countries. It is an amazing research tool, a bargain-hunter's paradise, a self-pubbed author's champion, a midlist author's savior, and an industry revolutionizer. But it can also be a competition smasher, an industry monopolizer, a literary bully, and a mom-and-pop, hometown-bookstore assassin. When Amazon coughs, the industry holds its breath. So one day I adore it, the next I loathe it — much like spinach.

What do you like and dislike about your job? I don't see being an agent so much as a job as it is a lifestyle, like being a professional writer, artist, or musician. A lifestyle is your passion.

What are ways prospective clients can impress you, and what are ways they can turn you off? When a literary agent accepts you as a client you will be in the deep end of the publishing ocean and will be expected to be able to swim on your own. Agents expect to be working with confident professionals who can produce the professional-level materials and information necessary so agents can do their job effectively. We look for that professionalism in every interaction with prospective clients: queries, emails, phone calls, personal interactions with us and others. Listen to your grandma here: be prepared, do your homework, be kind, bring joy. And heed Miss Aretha, too: R-E-S-P-E-C-T. Any less than 100 percent professionalism simply will not cut it. Ever.

How would you describe the "writer from hell"? Have you heard about the writer whose career got snuffed?

There's this writer. An insecure, desperate writer. But also a skilled, impassioned writer. A writer who's as deft with her pen as a musketeer with his sword, and with as much heart. Fueled by her hopes, this writer pushes forward in her quest till she discovers an agent who believes in her pen. The writer thinks she's finally arrived as a writer. Nothing can stop her now. She dreams of buzzing up the *New York Times* bestseller list, touring the world amid exploding flashbulbs, and laughing it up with Ellen and Kimmel.

But then one day, before the writer finds her place in the sun, she overreacts and goes off on her agent. She jumps to a crooked conclusion, blames her agent for anything and everything, has a bad hair day, gets cursed by an evil witch — take your pick. Whatever triggers it, she acts like a screaming, kicking two-year-old. She shrieks at her agent, she sends flaming emails, she resorts to name-calling, ad nauseam. Even if the agent tries to reach out to her, the writer refuses to see it, much less apologize. Somehow, in her convoluted thinking, her bizarre actions and blistering words are justified.

Once the storm is over, all the writer hears is a deafening silence. The agent casts her adrift. The writer's career is over before it truly begins, she doesn't understand why, and her heart is broken. Moreover, the agent cries at such a loss on the rocks of shortsightedness.

The moral of this tragic tale? Throw a temper tantrum and you commit career suicide. Remember, publishing at this level is a relatively small community. It doesn't take too many tantrums, large or small, before word gets around branding you "difficult," "unpredictable," "psychotic."

Why does this singlehandedly kill off an otherwise promising career? Trust, from which everything else flows. When a writer throws a conniption fit, the agent immediately asks herself: "Would she throw a tantrum with an editor? Or — oh, my — with a reader at a book signing?" Such embarrassment is something an agent or editor will not accept, despite the writer's talent. Remember, agents are looking for not only good writers, but *professional* writers.

Describe a book you would like to write. For the past several years I've been researching and writing a creative nonfiction book, and I'm currently neck-deep in early aviation history and the effervescent 1920s.

Do you believe in a higher and/or lower "power"? I just don't see the relevance of this question to business.

BALDI AGENCY ❖ www.baldibooks.com

233 West 99th Street, 19C, New York, NY 10025, 212-222-3213, baldibooks@gmail.com

Agent's name: Malaga Baldi

Describe the kinds of works you want to represent. I consider the following: general fiction, reference, biography, computers/technology, business/investing/finance, history, mind-body-spirit, travel, lifestyle, cookbooks, science, memoir, cultural history, literary fiction, creative/hybrid nonfiction, LGBTQ fiction and nonfiction.

Describe what you definitely don't want to represent. I do not have experience with category/genre fiction such as: Westerns, mystery, thrillers, romances, science fiction, fantasy, etc. In general, I do not represent young adult, children's or middle grade books, new adult, poetry, or film projects.

How do you want writers to pitch you? Please see www.baldibooks.com for submission information; email baldibooks@gmail.com.

Describe your education and professional history. In the early 1980s I worked for literary agents Candida Donadio and Elaine Markson. I worked as a publicity assistant at Ballantine Books and a clerk at the Gotham Book Mart. I received an MA from Antioch, March 1980, and a BA from Hampshire College, January 1977.

How did you become an agent? In 1974 I took a year off from Hampshire College. I was a mother's helper for Lois Wallace, a powerful and independent agent. Wallace had just left William Morris to start her own agency with a British partner. During the time I worked for her I met Joan Didion, John Gregory Dunne, and Erica Jong. One afternoon there was a knock at her apartment door. We opened the door to Erich Segal. His hard-lens contact had popped out. We found ourselves on our knees…six hands gently tapping the marble floor for a hard contact lens. A lightbulb went off in my head: I can do this.

Knowing what you do now, would you do it again? If not, what might you do instead? I would do it all over again.

Do you charge fees? If yes, please explain. No.

When and where were you born, and where have you lived? Born in Philadelphia in the last century, grew up in Madrid, Spain. My formative — grammar-, middle-, and high-school — years were spent in New Jersey and Connecticut. I lived in Amherst, Northampton, and London for several years. NYC resident since 1979.

What do you like to do when you're not working? I love to go to art galleries. I am a weekend warrior in the spring, summer, and fall — toiling away in a little garden plot. Walking the circumference of NYC in installments has been one of my favorite recent activities. Theater, music, dance, and spoken word occupy my free evenings. *Reading!!!!*

List some of the titles you have recently placed with publishers. Nonfiction: *Flying Cars, Zombie Dogs, and Robot Overlords* by Charles Pappas (Rowman & Littlefield, 2016), *The Sound of Music Story* by Tom Santopietro (St. Martin's, 2015), *Of Men & Beards* by Christopher Oldstone-Moore (University of Chicago Press, 2015), *Then and Now: A Memoir* by Barbara Cook with Tom Santopietro (HarperCollins, 2016), *Sticking It Out: A Drummer's Memoir* by Patti Niemi (ECW, 2016), *The Contender: A Biography of Marlon Brando* by William J. Mann (HarperCollins, 2018). Fiction: *Walking the Dog* by Elizabeth Swados (Feminist Press, 2016), *The Castle Cross the Magnet Carter* by Kia Corthron (7 Stories Press, 2016), *Jazz Moon* by Joe Okonkwo (Kensington, 2016).

Describe your personality. Funny, serious, judgmental, introspective, awkward, insecure, loyal, stubborn, proud, and given to bouts of despair. Paralleling my American mongrel multiethnic background — a little bit of everything.

What do you like reading/watching/listening to on your own time? I have no time.... Maybe next year.

Do you think the business has changed a lot over the past few years? If yes, please explain. Fewer phone calls, more face time. Lots of conferences. Electronic books. Fewer print books at home. Fewer places to donate books. More book-to-film synergy.

How do you feel about independent/small presses? I love them.

What are your feelings about self-publishing? This is hard work, and occasionally it is very successful. The publicity and distribution that a traditional publisher can offer are hard to replicate.

Do you think Amazon is good or bad — or both — for the book business? Amazon is here to stay in some form or another. Of course, I encourage all to buy from their local independent bookstore.

What do you like and dislike about your job? I love working with new writers, gaining their confidence, and explaining the industry and the publishing process. I love closing a deal. I also enjoy the downside — talking to authors after a stinging bad review or a rejection on the next book from their home-base publisher. These are the bumps that make for a strong relationship between author and agent. Talking it through, coming up with a plan, and rising from the ashes can be transformative. I have learned more from disappointment than triumph.

The things I don't like about it: (1) I wish I controlled the publisher's purse strings. For example, the release of a check on particular contract payouts is taking an excruciatingly long time lately. Why is this taking so long? (2) I do not enjoy being told something is too small or it does not have a platform. Small is beautiful. Many of my books are small. I once called an editor at a Big 5 house to follow up on a book I had recently submitted. The assistant asked me what the platform was. Novels do not have platforms. (As far as I know...Do they?)

What are ways prospective clients can impress you, and what are ways they can turn you off? I am impressed and blown away by great books. What I advise writers is: Stick to your guns. *Number your pages.* Never, ever start a book with "The natives were restless." Edit, edit, edit. Make every word, sentence, paragraph count. Read everything out loud. Write the book out in long hand at some point during your book-writing process. Read the masters. Be patient. Do not call your novel a fiction novel. Join a writers' group for feedback/encouragement/criticism. Do your research about publishers, agents, contracts. Write every day. Tell the truth.

How would you describe the "writer from hell"? I have yet to experience a client from hell. It is a big deal to write a book. You have to have high expectations. It is important to be transparent. Being a dreamer and being realistic can work together.

Describe a book you would like to write. I have no time.

BJ ROBBINS LITERARY AGENCY

5130 Bellaire Avenue, North Hollywood, CA 91607, 818-760-6602

Agent's name and contact info: BJ Robbins, robbinsliterary@gmail.com

Describe the kinds of works you want to represent. I love character-driven fiction with a strong voice and compelling story, both contemporary and historical. I'm also open to crime fiction and psychological suspense. In nonfiction I'm looking for narrative history, memoir, current affairs, popular science, biography, pop culture, travel/adventure, and self-help if the author has great credentials and a strong platform.

Describe what you definitely don't want to represent. No romance, sci-fi/fantasy, poetry, screenplays, plays, picture books, religious tracts, or technothrillers.

How do you want writers to pitch you? Via email. Write a strong and engaging query letter that tells me why you're querying my agency, a brief description of your project, a short bio, and perhaps the first couple of pages in the body of the email.

Describe your education and professional history. Graduated from University of Rochester with a BA in English, spent my junior year abroad at the University of Sussex. First job out of college was in the publicity department at Simon & Schuster. Spent a year at M. Evans, then moved to Harcourt Brace Jovanovich, where I was marketing director and later senior editor. I moved to Los Angeles in 1991 and started my agency in 1992.

Knowing what you do now, would you do it again? If not, what might you do instead? I can't imagine doing anything else, so yes, I would do it again.

Do you charge fees? If yes, please explain. No.

When and where were you born, and where have you lived? Born in Manhattan, grew up in Larchmont, New York. Have lived in New York and LA, mostly, with a couple of years in San Diego when I worked for Harcourt.

What do you like to do when you're not working? Tap dance, play basketball, watch movies, and occasionally binge-watch TV. And read purely for fun, not for work.

List some of the titles you have recently placed with publishers. *Mongrels* by Stephen Graham Jones (William Morrow), *Blood Brothers* by Deanne Stillman (Simon & Schuster), *Reliance, Illinois* by Mary Volmer (Soho Press), *Planet Earth 2050* by J. Maarten Troost (Holt), *Shoot for the Moon* by James Donovan (Little, Brown).

BLUE RIDGE LITERARY AGENCY, LLC ❖ www.blueridgeagency.com

133 Marvin Place, Lynchburg, VA 24503, 434-239-6303,
www.facebook.com/BRLAAgency

Agent's name: Dawn Dowdle

Describe the kinds of works you want to represent. Primarily romance and mystery (especially cozy mysteries). Also consider thrillers and suspense.

Describe what you definitely don't want to represent. Young adult, nonfiction, sci-fi, fantasy.

How do you want writers to pitch you? Please send the first three chapters and the synopsis as Word attachments. Please also provide word count, genre, bio, and marketing plans. Instructions are at www.blueridgeagency.com.

Describe your education and professional history. After many years of fiction reading and being detail-oriented, I began a freelance editing service. After about five years, I switched and opened my literary agency to work with newer writers. When I look back at the various occupations I had before this, I can see where I am using skills from each of those in my work as an agent.

How did you become an agent? I edited a friend's manuscript. She sent it out to agents. This was back when most were still wanting them mailed. She got back a half piece of paper with the name of her manuscript incorrect. She said to me, "I wish I could just do this myself." It started me thinking. I began investigating becoming an agent, so I could help authors get started in publishing.

Knowing what you do now, would you do it again? If not, what might you do instead? Definitely, but I would prefer it not be right when publishing was going through a major change (ebooks entering) and the economy was in such a downturn.

Do you charge fees? If yes, please explain. No.

When and where were you born, and where have you lived? I was born and raised in Wenatchee, Washington, one year in grade school. We moved around a lot. Other than that, I've lived in Washington State and DC and Virginia. We moved from northern Virginia to Lynchburg eight years ago.

What do you like to do when you're not working? Shopping, putting together jigsaw puzzles, watching TV, reading, spending time with family, going to plays, watching *House Hunters*.

List some of the titles you have recently placed with publishers. *Booked 4 Murder* plus books 2 and 3 (Kensington), *Picture Past the Fire* plus two additional romances (Harlequin Superromance), *Port Fairlight Summer* plus books 2 and 3 (Forever Yours), *Dragons Among Them* plus books 2 and 3 (Samhain), *The Wedding Date* plus books 2 and 3 (Forever Yours), *Death in a Hot Sea* plus books 2 and 3 (Torrey House), *Murder at Morningside* plus books 2 and 3 (Lyrical Underground).

Describe your personality. Tenacious, friendly, caring, and honest.

What do you like reading/watching/listening to on your own time? *House Hunters*, *NCIS New Orleans*, *Scorpion*, *CSI Cyber*, *Limitless*, *Castle*, *Rosewood*, and *Blindspot*.

Do you think the business has changed a lot over the past few years? If yes, please explain. Very much so. With the onset of ebooks, many of the bigger publishers have now opened ebook imprints. This has helped many newer authors get published. This is especially true in romance, not quite so much in mystery yet. So many books are now published on a regular basis, it is making it harder. Books have to stand out even more.

What do the "Big 5" mean to you? The Big 5 are where most authors strive to be published. Most want print but aren't ready for it yet. Even in the ebook imprints, it is hard, as you are usually the small fish in a big pond. Marketing dollars are not usually spent on newer authors' books, or at least the larger dollars are not spent on these books. So even when you get a contract with a bigger publisher, it doesn't mean your book will get the promotion it may need.

How do you feel about independent/small presses? I work with many independent/small presses. You have to be careful. Some are pretty small. I like working with the more established ones. They do a great job in helping the authors promote their work. And many of these publishers are always striving to make their company better and help the authors' books get noticed.

What are your feelings about self-publishing? Many authors/books need to be self-published. They may not have the audience needed to make it with a publisher. I do not assist authors in self-publishing at this time, but I will work with hybrid authors.

Do you think Amazon is good or bad — or both — for the book business? Both. It is a large bookstore. It's where most people look for books. At times they have had great programs that have helped newer authors get their books noticed. They keep changing their programs, and right now they are not as helpful. I don't like that they are taking down many reviews as well. Reviews are so important to get sales.

What do you like and dislike about your job? I like interaction with authors, reading books, helping authors get published and grow their careers, and meeting my authors when I travel. I dislike the lack of response to communication in this industry, the inability to see sales for my authors' books, and the long delay in getting payments.

What are ways prospective clients can impress you, and what are ways they can turn you off? To impress me, follow query instructions, send a great story that is well edited, and respond quickly when I email. What turns me off is not following query instructions, not responding to my emails, and responding negatively to my rejection email.

How would you describe the "writer from hell"? Someone who is very demanding, especially for things they aren't ready for. Speaking out on the internet. Once it's out there, it can't be retrieved.

Describe a book you would like to write. A cozy mystery.

Do you believe in a higher and/or lower "power"? I am a Christian and believe in God.

Is there anything you wish to express beyond the parameters of the preceding questions? I love working with authors, seeing a book come to fruition and become published. I enjoy going to conferences and talking to authors. When I travel, I try to meet as many of my authors as I can. It really puts a personality with a name.

BLUMER LITERARY AGENCY

809 West 181st Street, Suite 201, New York, NY 10033, 212-947-3040
(no phone queries, please)

Agent's name and contact info: Liv Blumer, livblumer@earthlink.net

Describe the kinds of works you want to represent. Story-driven fiction, practical nonfiction, memoir (so long as it's about something more than the author).

Describe what you definitely don't want to represent. No category fiction, no children's books (young adult okay), no politics, no polemics of any kind.

How do you want writers to pitch you? Let me put it this way. I tend to read carefully written snail mail queries, but find that it is entirely too easy to glance at and hit the Delete key for email queries. No telephone queries.

Describe your education and professional history. College degree (Goucher), 25 years working at mainstream publishers in editorial and subsidiary rights followed by 20 years as an agent.

How did you become an agent? I couldn't take another minute as a good corporate citizen. When you hit the wall, it's better to leave than tarnish your good reputation.

Knowing what you do now, would you do it again? If not, what might you do instead? My one regret is never having a job working outdoors.

Do you charge fees? If yes, please explain. No fees.

When and where were you born, and where have you lived? Born on Long Island, lived in Manhattan, Queens, and Baltimore.

What do you like to do when you're not working? Garden, cook, play Words with Friends and cards, daydream, and yes, read.

List some of the titles you have recently placed with publishers. An untitled novel set in 1940s in Massachusetts and a low-cost wedding planner.

Describe your personality. My rheumatologist says I'm a pain in the ass. I like to think that I'm dogged.

What do you like reading/watching/listening to on your own time? Mostly fiction, although I just finished a very good memoir about a woman who studied snails.

Do you think the business has changed a lot over the past few years? If yes, please explain. Yes. Fewer eccentrics, alas, and more bureaucrats. Less passion and more imitation.

What do the "Big 5" mean to you? Hachette, Penguin Random House, HarperCollins, Simon & Schuster, Macmillan.

How do you feel about independent/small presses? They are inherently risk takers. God bless them.

What are your feelings about self-publishing? Often necessary and sometimes lucrative.

Do you think Amazon is good or bad — or both — for the book business? Both.

What do you like and dislike about your job? The thrill of discovery and the agony of rejection.

What are ways prospective clients can impress you, and what are ways they can turn you off? I appreciate a succinct, literate query letter from someone who is not looking for a new best friend.

How would you describe the "writer from hell"? Someone who doesn't take advice because they think they know everything.

Describe a book you would like to write. I'm not a writer.

Do you believe in a higher and/or lower "power"? Nature is my higher power.

BONEDGES LITERARY AGENCY

6060 North Central Expressway, Dallas, TX 75206, 214-613-8415,
bonedges001@aol.com

Agents' names: Bonnie James, John Grassley, Mike Macafee

Describe the kinds of works you want to represent. We are a hands-on agency specializing in quality fiction and nonfiction. As a new agency, it is imperative that we develop relationships with good writers who are smart and hardworking and understand what's required of them to promote their books.

Describe what you definitely don't want to represent. Children's books, young adult, cooking, poetry, crafts, photography.

How do you want writers to pitch you? Please send a query letter via email with one to three sample chapters (double-spaced) in Word, a profile of the competition, the intended audience and market, and an author bio. *Email submissions only. Do not send any unsolicited submissions to the above address.*

How did you become an agent? Bonnie: After years on the publishing and editorial side of the business, I was ready for a more entrepreneurial challenge. Now I enjoy being able to spend my time on books and authors.

Knowing what you do now, would you do it again? If not, what might you do instead? Yes, I love what I do.

Do you charge fees? If yes, please explain. No fees.

What do you like to do when you're not working? Play tennis, cook, and travel.

Describe your personality. Warm, intense, focused, able to listen and connect with my clients.

Do you think the business has changed a lot over the past few years? If yes, please explain. Yes, the publishing industry is rapidly changing. There are different start-ups, new ereaders, and self-publishers becoming millionaires.

What are your feelings about self-publishing? There is now a wider understanding of what publishing is, and it is more difficult than it looks.

Do you think Amazon is good or bad — or both — for the book business? Amazon is both good and bad for the book business.

How would you describe the "writer from hell"? The client from hell is never satisfied and has expectations that exceed all possibilities of realization.

BRADFORD LITERARY AGENCY ❖ www.bradfordlit.com

5694 Mission Center Road, #347, San Diego, CA 92108, 619-521-1201

Agent's name and contact info: Laura Bradford, laura@bradfordlit.com

Describe the kinds of works you want to represent. I handle commercial fiction, specifically genre fiction. I love romance (all subgenres), mystery, thrillers, women's fiction, urban fantasy/speculative fiction, new adult, young adult. I do some select nonfiction as well.

Describe what you definitely don't want to represent. I don't handle screenplays, children's books, poetry, Westerns, New Age, religion, horror, or epic fantasy.

How do you want writers to pitch you? A simple, professional query letter is very important, one that is specific, articulate, and concise. I don't need an author to be zany to grab my attention; just cut right to the heart of what your manuscript is about and give me a strong hook. Don't be vague. As far as submissions go, please email a query letter along with the first chapter of your manuscript and a synopsis (all pasted into the body of the email) to queries@bradfordlit.com. Please be sure to include the genre and word count in your cover letter. To avoid having your email fall into spam, the subject line should begin as follows: "QUERY:" (the title of the manuscript and any *short* message you would like us to see should follow).

Describe your education and professional history. I have a BA in English literature from the University of California at San Diego. I came to agenting pretty much straight out of college. I became an intern at my first agency less than six months after I graduated. I started my own agency in 2001.

How did you become an agent? Once upon a time, I thought I might like to be a novelist, and I joined Romance Writers of America so I could learn what was what. At my first meeting, the speaker was a literary agent, which was something I had never heard of before. I was instantly fascinated. I researched what the job was and how to go about getting started. It seemed like the perfect job for someone who loved books and business, and it would allow me to be around my favorite people: authors. Despite the fact that one of the agents I called about an internship told me that agenting was the worst job on earth and that I shouldn't pursue it, I persevered. Within a couple of months, I had landed an internship with Manus and Associates (500 miles away from where I was living). I quit my job and moved. I worked as a bookstore manager to support myself while I was an unpaid intern. I lived in a relative's house for free until I finally got officially hired at the agency as an assistant. A few years later, after becoming an agent, I struck out on my own, so I could focus on genre fiction.

Knowing what you do now, would you do it again? If not, what might you do instead? I would do it all over again in a heartbeat. I totally adore my job.

Do you charge fees? If yes, please explain. No.

When and where were you born, and where have you lived? February 6, in the San Francisco Bay Area.

List some of the titles you have recently placed with publishers. *Shoot 'Em Up* by Janey Mack (Kensington), *Downtown Devil* by Cara McKenna (Berkley), *Waking Up with a Billionaire* by Katie Lane (Grand Central), *Slow Goodbye* by Soraya Lane (Montlake Romance), *Under the Surface* by Anne Calhoun (St. Martin's), *Didn't I Warn You* by Amber Bardan (Carina Press), *Infinite Risk* by Ann Aguirre (Feiwel & Friends), *Baron* by Joanna Shupe (Kensington), *Blank Canvas* by Adriana Anders (Sourcebooks), *The Silver Gate* by Kristin Bailey (Katherine Tegen), *Whiskey Sharp* by Lauren Dane (HQN), *Tailored for Trouble* by Mimi Jean Pamfiloff (Ballantine), *Disorderly Conduct* by Tessa Bailey (Avon), *Alex, Approximately* by Jenn Bennett (Simon Pulse).

Describe your personality. I am pretty even-tempered and patient. I am organized (because an agent has to be). I am flexible (because an agent has to be). Kind of bossy. I have a deep appreciation for whimsy. I'm an optimist. I like to think I have a good sense of humor, but I'm probably not the right person to ask about that.

What do you like reading/watching/listening to on your own time? I read the kinds of books I represent, actually. Mostly romances. I am actually more likely to listen to an audiobook for fun, though, than to read for fun. Since I read for work all the time, I find I don't as often have an urge to pick up a book for fun anymore. Audiobooks are my workaround. I watch a lot of Discovery and HGTV. And I prefer hour-long dramas to sitcoms.

What are your feelings about self-publishing? I think it is a growing part of the publishing landscape, and it can be a wonderful thing. I like that authors have more options, access, and control than they ever have before. Some authors are self-publishing in a smart way and finding a lot of success with it. Other authors are not being smart about it but still finding success. Still others are not finding that they enjoy being entrepreneurial or that they are not happy with the amount of return they are getting for the work they put in. I think it is ideal for some authors and not for others, but it is nice that it is a viable option for all. I have many authors who are publishing traditionally as well as self-publishing. I don't think it has to be an either/or thing. And I do think that agents have a place in that landscape.

Do you think Amazon is good or bad — or both — for the book business? Honestly? As a businessperson, I can admire their success. As a consumer, I can appreciate their convenience. As a former brick-and-mortar bookstore bookseller, boy, was I annoyed with them when they were up-and-coming. I do hate that brick-and-mortar bookstores seem to be going the way of the dodo, but I feel it may really be the changing times that I hate, not Amazon. If it hadn't been Amazon changing the retail landscape, it would have been someone else. My authors sell a gazillion books through Amazon, so how can I resent that?

What do you like and dislike about your job? I love that my days are totally varied. I love the fellowship of being around creative, talented people. I love the satisfaction of being part of something special when I see my authors' books on the bookshelves. As far as what I dislike, I don't think anyone really likes to be a part of disappointing people, and agents hand out a *lot* of rejection. I *really* don't like getting a nastygram from authors who are angry about my passing on their work. It is surprisingly common, and it is unnecessary, unprofessional, and unpleasant.

What are ways prospective clients can impress you, and what are ways they can turn you off? Exhibiting professionalism and organization is good. Being thoughtful about career strategy and being forward-thinking are good. Authors who generally don't come across like team players send up big red flags for me. Also, those who come off as super-entitled and act as though they aren't interested in doing a lot of work (as in they plan to sit back and wait for the publisher to do everything).

How would you describe the "writer from hell"? I think writers come in infinite variety, and I am pleased to work with a lot of different "types." As for some of the characteristics I don't particularly love, it is hard to work with someone with unrealistic expectations, someone who isn't a team player (and publishing *is* a team sport), someone who does not respect deadlines. My least favorite characteristic of all? Those who don't comport themselves professionally in public. That includes online dealings.

Agent's name and contact info: Natalie Lakosil, natalie@bradfordlit.com

Describe the kinds of works you want to represent. My specialties are children's literature (from picture books through teen and new adult), romance (contemporary and historical), cozy mystery/crime, upmarket women's fiction, general fiction, and select children's nonfiction. Within those genres my interests include historical, multicultural, and magical realism; sci-fi/fantasy; gritty, thrilling, and darker contemporary novels; middle grade with heart; and short, quirky, or character-driven picture books.

Describe what you definitely don't want to represent. I am not looking for inspirational novels, memoir, adult thrillers, poetry, or screenplays.

How do you want writers to pitch you? Please email your query letter, synopsis, and first 10 pages in the body of an email to queries@bradfordlit.com. No attachments are accepted, and the subject line must begin with the word *Query* to avoid the spam filters.

Picture-book authors are welcome to submit the entire picture book in the body of the email.

Describe your education and professional history. I am an honors graduate of the University of San Diego, California, with a BA in literature/writing. After nearly four years at the Sandra Dijkstra Literary Agency and a brief dabble in writing author profiles and book reviews for the *San Diego Union Tribune*, I joined the Bradford Agency in February 2011. I currently also manage the licensing department, handling permissions and subsidiary rights, for Cognella, Inc.

How did you become an agent? I became an agent through an internship with an agency, which led to an office job at that agency, which led to building my own client list. I started out looking to be a writer and realized quickly after my internship that it wasn't the path for me, but being an agent was. Being an agent allowed me the perfect marriage of business, management, and literature I was craving.

Knowing what you do now, would you do it again? If not, what might you do instead? I'd do it all over again in a heartbeat.

Do you charge fees? If yes, please explain. No.

What do you like to do when you're not working? Spend time with my husband and young son.

List some of the titles you have recently placed with publishers. *Murder on the Last Frontier* by Cathy Pegau (Kensington), *Blood and Bone* by Tara Brown (Montlake), *Piper Morgan Joins the Circus* by Stephanie Faris (Aladdin), *Skinny Dipping with Murder* by Auralee Wallace (St. Martin's), *Monster Mia* by Andria Rosenbaum (Scholastic), *Allegedly* by Tiffany Jackson (Katherine Tegen), *You Throw like a Girl* by Rachele Alpine (Aladdin), *Let the Children March* by Monica Clark-Robinson (Houghton Mifflin Harcourt), *That Thing You Do* by Katie McGee (St. Martin's), *Doll Soldiers* by Sarah Raughley (Simon Pulse).

Describe your personality. Driven, responsive, passionate, organized, and honest.

What do you like reading/watching/listening to on your own time? Most recently I've enjoyed watching *Bones*, *Once Upon a Time*, and *Orange Is the New Black*. I am addicted to romance novels, historical romance in particular, and love to read any published novel getting buzz to simply absorb and enjoy.

Do you think the business has changed a lot over the past few years? If yes, please explain. Oh, yes; houses have merged, digital offers abound, paperless is preferred, and genres are in and out.

How do you feel about independent/small presses? There are some wonderful ones out there and some that are best avoided.

What are your feelings about self-publishing? It has created a slew of new opportunities for writers, agents, and publishers, but is still largely a gamble. It's definitely not an instantaneous moneymaker for all authors, nor is it a sure way for authors to break into traditional publishing.

Do you think Amazon is good or bad — or both — for the book business? Both. I've seen Amazon really push an author to big sales success by taking full advantage of its website, which is great. I have also loved the opportunities and new genres generated from the self-publishing boom it aided in starting. However, I do fear the potential consequences if Amazon does monopolize the bookselling world.

What do you like and dislike about your job? I once heard a colleague describe the agent business as "finding buyers for sellers." I think it's somewhere between that and the magical "making dreams come true." I love selling, contract negotiation, pitching, networking, and reading. I hate rejection, and I hate having to share bad news.

What are ways prospective clients can impress you, and what are ways they can turn you off? I am always impressed when prospective clients have done their research on me and know what I like or mention my blog. Turnoffs are a pleading, self-deprecating approach and not following submission guidelines.

How would you describe the "writer from hell"? A client from hell has unrealistic expectations and gets incredibly upset, even abusive, in correspondence and actions when these expectations aren't met. She or he is unethical, misses deadlines consistently, breaches contract terms, is rude and unprofessional when approached, entitled, demanding, and manipulative. I'd put up red warning flags if a client started questioning or ignoring my advice, especially if legal in nature, flying off the handle on social media, or aggressively emailing with nasty comments several times a day or week.

Do you believe in a higher and/or lower "power"? Yes.

Is there anything you wish to express beyond the parameters of the preceding questions? Don't give up.

Agent's name and contact info: Monica Odom, monica@bradfordlit.com

Describe the kinds of works you want to represent. Nonfiction by authors with demonstrable platforms in the areas of pop culture, illustrated/graphic design, food and cooking, humor, history, and social issues. Narrative nonfiction in these areas, and some memoir. Fiction in the areas of literary fiction, upmarket commercial fiction, compelling speculative fiction and magic realism, historical fiction, alternative histories, dark and edgy fiction, literary psychological thrillers, and illustrated/picture books.

I am most actively seeking adult projects, but am open to all levels of children's projects and hold the same criteria no matter the age group: original storytelling, incredible voice, compelling characters, and vivid, detailed setting. I also like to see a strong sense of narrative tension. I am serious about the fact that *we need diverse books* and am looking for authentic representation of all characters, diverse or otherwise.

Describe what you definitely don't want to represent. I am not looking for genre fiction (sci-fi, fantasy, romance, erotica, etc.), military stories, poetry, or inspirational/spiritual works.

How do you want writers to pitch you? Please email your query to: monica@bradfordlit .com. To avoid having your email fall into spam, the subject line should begin as follows: "QUERY:" (the title of the manuscript and any *short* message you would like us to see should follow). Fiction: a query letter along with the first chapter and a synopsis; include the genre and word count in your cover letter. Picture books: short query along with entire manuscript in the body of the email. Nonfiction: full nonfiction proposal including a query letter and a sample chapter.

Describe your education and professional history. I joined Bradford Literary Agency in 2015. Prior to joining Team Bradford, I worked for five years managing finance, subrights, and social media at Liza Dawson Associates and became an associate agent there in 2013. I have a BA in English from Montclair State University and earned a master's in Publishing: Digital & Print Media from New York University in 2014.

List some of the titles you have recently placed with publishers. *Women* by Carol Rossetti (Skyhorse), *Women in Science* by Rachel Ignotofsky (Ten Speed Press).

CARNICELLI LITERARY MANAGEMENT ❖ www.carnicellilit.com

7 Kipp Road, Rhinebeck, NY 12572

Agent's name and contact info: Matthew Carnicelli, President, queries@carnicellilit.com

Describe the kinds of works you want to represent. I'm always looking for new nonfiction submissions from authors with the appropriate credentials in the areas of current events, biography, memoir, history, business, health, science, self-help, psychology, sports, and pop culture. For fiction, I'm mainly interested in accessible literary fiction and, from time to time, good political and medical thrillers.

Describe what you definitely don't want to represent. I'm not interested in receiving submissions in the areas of plays, screenplays, children's literature, or poetry.

How do you want writers to pitch you? I hope that writers will spend some time reviewing my website to familiarize themselves with the types of books I represent. Then, please write a clear, straightforward query letter that will make me beg to see your proposal or manuscript. Please limit your query to one page in the body of the email and know that I won't open any email queries with attachments. Tell me why your project is so important, timely, and salable and why you are the only author with the right credentials to write it. Convince me to ask you to send me more.

Describe your education and professional history. I began my publishing career at Dutton, where as an editor I worked with many great writers of fiction, history, and current events, including Christopher Bram, Sandra Mackey, Martin Duberman, Vice President Al Gore, William J. Mann, Judith Warner, Cornel West, and Cathleen Schine. At Contemporary Books and McGraw-Hill, I became enthralled with strong health writing and business and sports books, working with such authors as John Wooden, Victoria Moran, Dr. Robert Brooks, Gail Ferguson, Roland Lazenby, and Robert Kurson. I became an agent in 2004 in order to have more control over the depth of my work with clients and to focus only in areas that interested me intellectually and creatively, and over the past decade I've represented such notable authors as *Sports Illustrated* reporter Jim Gorant, brain and movement expert Anat Baniel, political pundit Dave "Mudcat" Saunders, historian Brian McGinty, *Meet the Press* moderator Chuck Todd, economist Joseph P. Quinlan, and graphic novelist Derf Backderf.

I graduated from Washington University in St. Louis and received a master's degree in English literature from the University of Toronto. I have taught college-level nonfiction writing and enjoy leading writing workshops. I've been on panels at numerous writers' conferences and lectured on publishing at places like Georgetown University, and the *Wall Street Journal* and Bloomberg regularly call upon me to comment on publishing and other topics.

Do you charge fees? If yes, please explain. I offer editing and consulting services for fees, but this is a distinct and separate business from my literary agency. Clients with whom I work in this capacity will not be considered as possible candidates for representation.

List some of the titles you have recently placed with publishers. *Through the Keyhole: Debunking the Biggest Sexual Myths and What It Means for Modern Relationships* by Michael Aaron, PhD (Rowman & Littlefield), *Trashed: A Graphic Novel* by Derf Backderf (Abrams ComicArts), *A Storm of Witchcraft: The Salem Trials and the American Experience* by Emerson W. Baker, PhD (Oxford), *Kids Beyond Limits: The Anat Baniel Method for Awakening the Brain and Transforming the Life of Your Child with Special Needs* by Anat Baniel (Perigee), *Lost Girl Found: A Novel* by Leah Bassoff and Laura DeLuca (Groundwood), *Gold Rush in the Jungle: The Race to Discover and Defend the Rarest Animals in Vietnam's "Lost World"* by Daniel Drollette (Crown), *Street Poison: The Biography of Iceberg Slim* by Justin Gifford, PhD (Doubleday), *The Double V: How Wars, Protest, and Harry*

Truman Desegregated America's Military by Rawn James, Jr. (Bloomsbury), *Spurrier: How the Ball Coach Taught the South to Play Football* by Ran Henry (Lyons Press), *Showboat: The Life of Kobe Bryant* by Roland Lazenby (Little, Brown), *The Rest I Will Kill: William Tillman and the Unforgettable Story of How a Free Black Man Refused to Become a Slave* by Brian McGinty (Norton/Liveright), *Shooting Lincoln: Two Men, an Assassination, and the Conspiracy That Birthed Modern Media* by Nicholas J.C. Pistor (Da Capo), *Kicking Cancer in the Kitchen: The Girlfriend's Cookbook and Guide to Using Real Food to Fight Cancer* by Annette Ramke and Kendall Scott (Running Press), *Shetani's Sister: A Novel* by Iceberg Slim (Vintage), *Follow Me into the Dark: A Novel* by Felicia C. Sullivan (Feminist Press), *The Stranger: Barack Obama in the White House* by Chuck Todd (Little, Brown), *Rocket Fuel: The One Essential Combination That Will Get You More of What You Want from Your Business* by Gino Wickman and Mark C. Winters (BenBella), *The End Is Near and It's Going to Be Awesome: How Going Broke Will Leave America Richer, Happier, and More Secure* by Kevin Williamson (HarperCollins).

Is there anything you wish to express beyond the parameters of the preceding questions? Over the past two decades, first as an editor and then as a literary agent, I've had the good fortune to work with a vast array of prominent journalists, business leaders, health experts, media figures, and policy makers, and I've always been on the lookout for breakthrough new talent, too. My goal as a literary agent is to help provocative thinkers and great writers express themselves more clearly and navigate the tricky terrain to get their books out into the world. I've always been a big believer in the power of breakthrough ideas and stories to change the world in a big way.

CAROL MANN AGENCY ❖ www.carolmannagency.com

55 Fifth Avenue, 18th Floor, New York, NY 10003

Agents' names and contact info: Gareth Esersky, gesersky@verizon.net; Carol Mann, carol@carolmannagency.com; Thomas W. Miller, tom@carolmannagency.com; Lydia Shamah, lydia@carolmannagency.com; Myrsini Stephanides, myrsini@carolmannagency.com; Joanne Wyckoff, joanne@carolmannagency.com; Laura Yorke, laura@carolmannagency.com

Describe the kinds of works you want to represent. Nonfiction: wellness, spirituality, self-help, parenting, current affairs, history, narrative nonfiction, psychology, memoir, pop culture, music, humor, popular science, business, relationships, gift books. Fiction: offbeat literary, graphic, middle grade, young adult, psychological thrillers, upmarket women's fiction with a twist.

How do you want writers to pitch you? Please submit to us via email at submissions@ carolmannagency.com.

Do you charge fees? If yes, please explain. No.

Is there anything you wish to express beyond the parameters of the preceding questions? For more about the Carol Mann Agency, please visit our website, www.carolmannagency .com.

CAROLYN JENKS AGENCY ❖ www.carolynjenksagency.com

30 Cambridge Park Drive, Cambridge, MA 02140, 617-354-5099

Agent's name: Carolyn Jenks

Describe the kinds of works you want to represent. Seeking adult literary-commercial, historical, thriller, mystery, young adult and new adult fiction, and narrative nonfiction, original screenplays, brilliant plays for the theater.

Describe what you definitely don't want to represent. No longer seeking picture books, science fiction, chick lit, or cookbooks.

How do you want writers to pitch you? Query via our webpage contact form. Pitches matter. No cold calls.

Describe your education and professional history. Professional acting career began in Chicago at age 12. Studied with Herbert Berghof in NYC at HB Studio. BA in comparative literature from the University of Wisconsin, MA in theology from Emmanuel College in Boston, MSW from University of Connecticut, Diplomate in clinical social work from NASW. Courses in film production and film history at Columbia University. Courses in predicament and problems of personal freedom at The New School for Social Research. Literature, theater, publishing, and film have been the driving passions of my life to date.

How did you become an agent? I believe it was divine providence, serendipity, or punishment for past sins. I'll go into detail when it comes time to write my memoir.

Knowing what you do now, would you do it again? If not, what might you do instead? Of course, I would do it again.

Do you charge fees? If yes, please explain. No fees charged.

When and where were you born, and where have you lived? Born in Evanston, Illinois; lived in Dallas, Chicago, New York, and Boston.

What do you like to do when you're not working? Work.

List some of the titles you have recently placed with publishers. *Esther* by Rebecca Kanner (biblical fiction, Simon & Schuster), *The Christ Mosaic* by Vincent Czyz (thriller, Blank Slate Press), *Black Bird Fly* and *Land of the Forgotten Girls* by Erin Entrada Kelly (middle grade fiction, HarperCollins), *Magnolia City* by Duncan Alderson (historical fiction, Kensington).

Describe your personality. An extraverted introvert. I learned from my acting days that you cannot be successful alone. Every artist requires a team. I thrive on building successful teams that launch enduring writers.

What do you like reading/watching/listening to on your own time? Biography, literary fiction, commercial series on TV, films by new directors and emerging genius actors. Music is a daily food.

Do you think the business has changed a lot over the past few years? If yes, please explain. We are currently celebrating the 20th-anniversary edition of *The Red Tent* by Anita Diamant. Talking about the changes in our industry is one of my favorite subjects.

What do the "Big 5" mean to you? Over the span of several decades I have seen awesome professionals start in beginning positions and rise to the top of their profession. Within the keen competition exists a community of passionate and talented editors and executives that I wouldn't trade for the world. Resilient, wise, and ultimately survivors, the Big 5 are challenging and always the best and the brightest to work with.

How do you feel about independent/small presses? They, too, have changed or gone by the wayside. Many of our authors debut with small presses.

What are your feelings about self-publishing? I'm totally for this option if the platform is understood as a bridge to a larger audience and a deal with a Big 5 publisher.

Do you think Amazon is good or bad — or both — for the book business? My experience is that it is good. Amazon can build a platform.

What do you like and dislike about your job? I dislike that there are only so many hours in a day.

What are ways prospective clients can impress you, and what are ways they can turn you off? The writer who shows an ability to take a leap of faith with a new agent and reveals wit and teamwork with our staff earns my respect.

How would you describe the "writer from hell"? One who doesn't understand that revision is part of writing. The writer who shows us the "What did you do for me today?" syndrome.

Describe a book you would like to write. I'm a constant lover of fictionalized biography. I know, it sounds strange.

Do you believe in a higher and/or lower "power"? "I would rather live my life as if there were a God and die to find out there isn't, than to live as if there isn't and find out after death there is." — Camus.

THE CHARLOTTE GUSAY LITERARY AGENCY ❖ www.gusay.com

10532 Blythe Avenue, Los Angeles, CA 90064, 310-559-0831, fax: 310-559-2639, gusay1@ca.rr.com (for queries and general questions)

Agent's name and contact info: Charlotte Gusay, Owner and Founder, gusay1@ca.rr.com

Describe the kinds of works you want to represent. I enjoy both fiction and nonfiction and books-to-film. Prefer commercial, mainstream but quality material. Also like material that is innovative, unusual, eclectic, quirky, literary. Always looking for up-and-coming writers — African American or Hispanic writers, multiethnic or works in translation. Will consider literary fiction especially with crossover potential. TCGLA often partners with agents who are signatories to the Writers Guild; hence the agency represents screenplays and screenwriters very selectively. Especially like to find books to market to film. I'll sometimes look at unusual or unique children's books and illustrators, but very selectively limit children's projects to young adult, teen, and new adult.

Describe what you definitely don't want to represent. Not too fond of science fiction or horror. (Although, I would not turn down the next *Blade Runner*.) And poetry or short stories (with a few exceptions) are almost impossible to sell. I do not represent romance genres per se, but don't put it past me to fall in love with a novel that is a corny love story or something outrageous or quirky.

How do you want writers to pitch you? I love to get queries. But please bear in mind, I am very selective. Here's what to do if you wish to query the agency: Send a query, *one page only*, by either snail mail or email (gusay1@ca.rr.com), that includes *complete* contact information: name, snail mail address, phone, email. If fiction, describe your book (novel, story, collection) and tell us how you think it fits into the current book/publishing market (i.e., is it literary, a thriller, a mainstream novel?). Or perhaps it doesn't exactly fit into the current market, and that may be a good thing. We need to know how you see it. It helps for you to tell us a little about yourself, no more than a paragraph or so. If nonfiction, we need one or two paragraphs describing your book and one or two paragraphs describing your author credentials for writing this particular nonfiction book.

If we are interested, we will *then* request to see your book project, and we'll send you complete instructions for submitting it to us. We usually send such instructions by snail

JEFF HERMAN'S GUIDE

mail. If you receive such instructions, you will discover that, for fiction, we ask for a one-page synopsis and the first 50 pages and, for nonfiction, we ask for a complete proposal with title, subtitle, overview, table of contents, marketing and promotion, author platform, author bio with publishing history, and one to three sample chapters (one of which should be the first chapter). Even for a memoir or narrative nonfiction, this information helps us gain insight into your breadth and depth as an author.

If you are interested in more on the agency's submission process and some notes on our philosophy of business, please see www.gusay.com/contact/default.php.

Describe your education and professional history. I hold a BA in English literature/theater and a General Secondary Life Teaching Credential. I have taken graduate-level courses in education and studied dance, fashion, and film. I have had several careers prior to becoming a literary agent, the first of which was teaching in secondary schools. Soon, interest in filmmaking developed. I founded (with partners) a documentary film company in the early 1970s and made several documentaries. Soon I became interested in the fledgling audio-publishing business and worked as the managing editor for the Center for Cassette Studies/Scanfax, producing audio programs, interviews, and documentaries. Soon thereafter I launched headlong into the business of books and publishing and founded George Sand, Books, in West Hollywood, one of the most prestigious and popular bookshops in Los Angeles. It specialized in fiction and poetry and sponsored readings, events, and a much-loved Sunday literary salon. Patronized by the Hollywood community's glitterati and literati, George Sand, Books, was the go-to place when looking for the "best" literature and quality books and a good chat about books. It was here that the marketing of books was preeminent. After 12 successful years, it closed in the late 1980s, a year after my new little daughter came into my life. Two years later the Charlotte Gusay Literary Agency was opened.

How did you become an agent? I started in the book business with a great entrepreneurial spirit, cold calls, and seat-of-the-pants daring after 12 years in the retail book business (as founder and owner of a prestigious bookshop in Los Angeles called George Sand, Books) and years of business experience, including editing and producing films and spoken-word audio programs. However, agenting is the most challenging and rewarding experience I've ever had.

Knowing what you do now, would you do it again? If not, what might you do instead? Were I to change my career? Fashion is rather much ingrained in me. I really should have gone into fashion. It's a bit late now, I think.

Do you charge fees? If yes, please explain. No reading fee. No editorial fees.

When and where were you born, and where have you lived? I was born in the Midwest and grew up in California. I love Los Angeles and have lived here for many years.

What do you like to do when you're not working? Gardens and gardening, cooking, touring architecture (especially mid-century modern houses and furniture), following fashion, going to movies, reading good fiction (especially juicy novels and delicious memoirs), and, well, reading in general. But traveling has taken over my interests. In the last few years, I've traveled the globe here and there: Europe, of course, South Africa (Zambia, Zambezi, Johannesburg, just prior to Mandela's death), Alaska (landed on a glacier in a teeny plane on Denali), the Galapagos, Greece every summer (sailed to Odysseus's home, Ithaca island, and to Onassis's island, Skorpios), the Czech Republic and Poland (with my countess friend who owns a castle in Opochno and a hunting lodge nearby), China, and Kent, England, for the UK launch of my client Anthony Russell's book *Outrageous Fortune: Growing Up at Leeds Castle* (St. Martin's). Went to Merida, Mexico, on the Yucatan this year. Going to Russia next year.

List some of the titles you have recently placed with publishers. The agency represents such books-to-film rights as David Shields and Caleb Powell's *I Think You're Totally Wrong: A Quarrel* (Knopf) and Shields's *New York Times* bestseller *The Thing About Life Is That One Day You'll Be Dead*. Both books were optioned by actor-director-writer James Franco for his production company, Rabbit Bandini Productions. TCGLA represented recently the film rights to popular Irish novelist Maeve Binchy's first novel, *Light a Penny Candle* (Viking/NAL/Signet).

Other representative titles: *Everything I Need to Know I Learned in The Twilight Zone* (St. Martin's); *Mark Twain's Guide to Diet, Exercise, Beauty, Fashion, Investment, Romance, Health and Happiness* (Prospect Park Books); *Mark Twain for Cat Lovers* and *Mark Twain for Dog Lovers* (Lyons Press); *The Burma Spring: Aung San Suu Kyi and the Struggle for the Soul of Burma* by former State Department speechwriter and journalist Rena Pederson, foreword by Laura Bush (Pegasus); *The Reputation Economy: How to Become Rich in a World Where Your Digital Footprint Is as Valuable as the Cash in Your Wallet* (Crown Business); a debut literary novel entitled *Dancing in the Baron's Shadow* by Haitian American writer Fabienne Josaphat (Unnamed Press); *US (a)* by poet Saul Williams (Gallery/MTV Books); *Jacky's Diary* (Yoe Books/IDW); *Outrageous Fortune: Growing Up at Leeds Castle* (St. Martin's); *Chorus: A Literary Mixtape* by Saul Williams (Gallery); *Wild West 2.0: How to Protect and Restore Your Reputation on the Untamed Social Frontier* (AMACOM); *American Fugue* by National Endowment of the Arts International Award Recipient Alexis Stamatis (Etruscan Press); *Honesty Sells: How to Make More Money and Increase Business Profits* (Wiley); *Forty-One Seconds: From Terror to Freedom* (Presidio Press/Ballantine); *Richard Landry Estates* (Oro Editions); *Beachglass* (St. Martin's); *The Dead Emcee Scrolls: The Lost Teachings of Hip Hop* (MTV Books/Simon & Schuster); *Said the Shotgun to the Head* (MTV Books/Simon & Schuster); *Meeting Across the River: Stories Inspired by the Haunting Bruce Springsteen Song*, story contributed by Randy Michael

Signor (Bloomsbury); *Other Sorrows, Other Joys: The Marriage of Catherine Sophia Boucher* and *William Blake: A Novel* (St. Martin's); *Imperial Mongolian Cooking: Recipes from the Kingdoms of Genghis Khan* by Marc Cramer (Hippocrene); *Somebody's Child: Stories from the Private Files of an Adoption Attorney* by Randi Barrow (Perigee/Penguin Putnam); *Retro Chic: A Guide to Fabulous Vintage and Designer Resale Shopping in North America & Online* by Diana Eden and Gloria Lintermans (Really Great Books); *Loteria and Other Stories* (St. Martin's); *The Spoken Word Revolution: An Essay, Poem and an Audio Contribution* by Saul Williams (Sourcebooks); *Rio L.A.: Tales from the Los Angeles River* by Patt Morrison, with photographs by Mark Lamonica (Angel City Press).

Other film options: *What Angels Know: The Story of Elizabeth Barrett and Robert Browning*, screenplay optioned by producer Marta Anderson, also developed as a novel; *Somebody's Child: Stories from the Private Files of an Adoption Attorney* by Randi Barrow (Perigee/Penguin Putnam), optioned by Green/Epstein/Bacino Productions for a television series; *A Place Called Waco: A Survivor's Story* by David Thibodeau and Leon Whiteson (Public Affairs/Perseus Book Group), optioned by a well-known film developer for television; *Love Groucho: Letters from Groucho Marx to His Daughter Miriam*, edited by Miriam Marx Allen (Faber & Faber; Farrar, Straus and Giroux US; and Faber & Faber UK), sold to CBS.

Many books and several film projects are in submission and in development at any given time. As of this moment, we are developing books on, for example, the state of health and medicine today by an internist, a humor book on dogs, a novel by a well-known actress, a music memoir by the founder of a 1960s band, a humor book on old films, and a number of novels. Please check the agency website for more complete descriptions: www.gusay.com.

Describe your personality. People like my intelligence, enthusiasm, and humor. I'm creative, and often if an author's book doesn't get a positive reception from an editor at first, I rethink titles and slants and suggest revisions. This works often to sell books. On the other hand, when I am in my agent mode, people don't like or don't understand my selectivity. If I reject a project, often the writer feels bleak and, well, rejected. I hope writers will come to understand my selectivity — I absolutely must have enthusiasm coupled with a conviction that I can sell any given project. I try to be honest and straightforward, transparent, and positive.

What do you like reading/watching/listening to on your own time? Recent and not-so-recent films I like: *Slam* (my client Saul Williams's film that made him an underground bestselling performance poet/musician/actor), *The Paper Chase*, Bas Luhrman's *Romeo and Juliet*, Monty Python and Marx Brothers films, and 1940s and 1950s films, often for the clothes. A few of my all-time favorite films are *Runaway Train*, *The English Patient*, *Dr. Zhivago*, *Cabaret*, *Rebel without a Cause*, *Woman in the Dunes*, and many more. A few favorite television shows: *Masterpiece Theatre* (there's a new one: *Indian Summers*), *Homeland, Breaking Bad, True Detective, Girls, The Good Wife*. And many, many books — a few all-time favorites: Austen's *Pride and Prejudice*, Hemingway's *The Sun Also Rises, The English Patient, Dr. Zhivago, Housekeeping, Out of Africa*, Keats's poetry, and many more. I like memoirs if really, really well written, for example, *The Glass Castle*. Last year I read Sterling Lord's memoir, *Lord of Publishing*. I read Edwidge Danticat's new book *Claire of the Sea Light*. The one thing these have in common for me: they held my attention, I was moved in some important way, and the writing is always superb and swept me away. I listen to pop music, jazz, rock and roll, and classical. I hate to have to admit it, but I like Taylor Swift; I listen to 1950s and 1960s jazz, and I still love the Beatles, the Rolling Stones, and more. I love to listen to books.

Do you think the business has changed a lot over the past few years? If yes, please explain.
Essentially publishing is the same as always. Writers write; books are published. The digital, electronic aspect of the publishing business has dictated our MO, no question, but the rest remains the same.

What do the "Big 5" mean to you? Here they are exactly: Hachette, HarperCollins, Macmillan, Penguin Random House, Simon & Schuster. These or any number of their imprints are the first tier of submissions of almost any writer's book project. Good luck.

How do you feel about independent/small presses? Small/independent publishers are very important, especially for fiction and poetry. If any of the Big 5 or midlist publishers won't publish a writer's exquisite piece of fiction, then often a small independent will publish it.

What are your feelings about self-publishing? Self-publishing is good and not good. The good: I'm so happy when a client can self-publish a book I tried so hard but was unable to sell. The writer often seems very pleased to have his or her book published, no matter who published it. The not-so-good part: the agent — after working a long time, months, sometimes even years, trying so hard to sell such a book to a traditional or even a small or digital publisher — gets no commission whatsoever. The agent loses. Time and money are lost. Of course, a dream client who publishes his or her own book would step up and offer the agent her share of any sales. Also, so many times self-published books are not well edited, full of typos and errors, sloppy formatting, and just amateurish all the way around. As long as self-published books are well developed, well written, and then edited and the final rendering is totally professional, self-publishing is a positive way to go. But bear in mind, the average sales of a self-published book is 100 copies.

Do you think Amazon is good or bad — or both — for the book business? Amazon and I have a love/hate relationship. I love, love, love it, because I can research titles, get books in an instant on my Kindle/iPad or at my door. (Way too easy for my pocketbook.) But then the downside is that Amazon is putting brick-and-mortar bookstores out of business. Bookstores are very important places that contribute to our culture. I know, because that's how I began in the book business with my beloved bookshop in West Hollywood — George Sand, Books. How sad is that when there is nowhere to go to browse the books and talk to people about books?

What do you like and dislike about your job? An agent's job in the publishing business is essentially that of a bookseller. I sell books. To publishers, producers, and ultimately to the retail book trade. Sometimes I develop a book idea. Sometimes I develop someone's story, help the writer get a proposal written. I help to find a coauthor for a story or nonfiction book if such a writer is needed. I've even written proposals myself, because I believed strongly in the book, the person's story, or the salability of an idea. For fiction writers with potential, I sometimes make cursory suggestions. However, I must be clear — I am not an editor and certainly not a fiction editor. Most often I help writers find a professional editor to work on their novel *before* it is submitted to a publishing house. That is key. The manuscript must be pristine. Flawless. I repeat: a manuscript must be complete, polished, and professional.

I love, love, love to get to know writers. I'm excited every day to see what will come in next on my query line. I do not like to "edit." However, I will do nonfiction proposal editing or reviewing when it's not too big of a job. I do not like to have to "reject" writers. So often books being considered by my agency are borderline ready. No matter how good they are, if they're not ready, I have to decline to represent them. If writers will work with a professional editor to get their manuscript ready to submit, then I will certainly reconsider.

What are ways prospective clients can impress you, and what are ways they can turn you off? Simply put: professionalism is key to impressing me. That will always seduce me. However, if I begin to hear complaints about my agency policies, or if a prospective client refuses to understand how I work and then begins to denigrate my agency, I often cannot tolerate such and disengage immediately.

How would you describe the "writer from hell"? The client from hell is the one who does not understand the hard work we do for our clients. Or the one who refuses to build a career in a cumulative manner, but rather goes from one agent to the next and so on. Or clients who circulate their manuscripts without cooperating with their agents. Or those who think it all happens by magic. Or those who have not done their homework and who do not understand the nuts and bolts of the business or who are overly demanding and thoughtless. The warning signs when we know this may be a difficult client: demanding telephone calls, rude notes or emails, impoliteness, unprofessional behavior.

The perfect client, however, is the one who cooperates. The one who appreciates how hard we work for our clients. The one who submits everything on time, in clean, edited, proofed, professional copies of manuscripts (either hardcopy or digital) and professionally prepared proposals. Clients who understand the crucial necessity of promoting their own books until the last one in the publisher's warehouse is gone. Those who work hard on their bookselling in tandem with the agent. The author-agent relationship, like a marriage, is a cooperative affair built on mutual trust, and it is cumulative. The dream client will happily do absolutely whatever is necessary to reach the goal.

Describe a book you would like to write. I've been working on a book for quite a while: a pop-culture book on a well-known woman icon in the world of politics and fashion. I think I'm too busy to get really serious about it.

Do you believe in a higher and/or lower "power"? Not sure what this is referring to with regard to the publishing business. Is this by chance referring to a "God"? I am an existentialist. Is that a lower power?

Is there anything you wish to express beyond the parameters of the preceding questions? To the writers who come to my agency for representation: I want you to know that I have the deepest admiration for your willingness to write books, stories, nonfiction, novels, anything. Whether you're published or not, you must keep writing. And if you wish to be published, you must not give up, even after many rejections. It's just part of the deal. Getting published? I compare this god-awful process to getting pregnant: it only takes one publisher who says yes. Keep on keeping on!

CORVISIERO LITERARY AGENCY ❖ www.corvisieroagency.com

275 Madison Avenue, 14th Floor, New York, NY 10016, 646-942-8396, fax: 646-217-3758, query@corvisieroagency.com

Agent's name and contact info: Marisa Corvisiero, Founder and Senior Literary Agent, marisa@corvisieroagency.com

Describe the kinds of works you want to represent. I seek creative stories with well-developed plots and rich characters with unique voices. For adults, new adults, and young adults, I will consider contemporary romance, thrillers, adventure, paranormal, urban fantasy, science fiction, or any combination thereof. For middle grade, I like very unique concepts in fantasy, adventure, and science fiction. I love picture books with special stories that deliver a subtle, nondidactic message. (Illustrations not needed.) I especially enjoy stories with Christmas, time-travel, and space science fiction themes. In nonfiction, I enjoy out-of-the-box and high-concept spiritual, self-improvement, science, and business books for all ages. Yes, that includes business books for kids! They are needed.

Describe what you definitely don't want to represent. I represent a very selective niche of nonfiction categories, memoirs, and picture books. They must be very unique and outstanding. A platform for nonfiction is usually a must, unless the topic itself is very timely and the story or subject matter must be shared.

How do you want writers to pitch you? A query email with a one- to two-page synopsis (double-spaced) and the first five pages of the manuscript attached as a separate doc or docx file. Picture-book submissions require the full manuscript. Your query letter should include links to your social-media profiles in your email signature and a brief description of your writing career goals. No paper or faxed submissions will be reviewed. Please *do not* query Marisa via her personal agency email unless specifically requested to do so. Send all queries to query@corvisieroagency.com.

Describe your education and professional history. I received my bachelor's degree in business administration in international business and marketing from Hofstra University in 1995, where I was the president of the Phi Alpha Delta law fraternity chapter, and the president of the Pre Law Society during my last year. I received my JD from Pace University School of Law in 2000 and earned the school's prestigious International Law Certificate for my studies in international law. During my legal studies, I held several board positions on the Student Bar Association, where I was also the treasurer of the Environmental Law Society, the chair of the Social Committee, and the coeditor of the Pace University School of Law yearbook in 1999 and 2000. I held positions in several law firms and companies since 1995 in different capacities. In such positions, I attained the knowledge and experience necessary to properly and dynamically represent my clients. These stellar firms and companies include Paul, Hastings, Janofsky & Walker, LLP, a top global law firm; Windels, Marx, Lane & Mittendorf, LLP, a white-shoe boutique law firm; and Avaya, Inc., a Fortune 500 telecommunications company; among several distinguished others. I then founded the Corvisiero Law Practice, PC. Since the law firm's inception, it has achieved incredible success and growth, and continues on its high-speed trajectory toward excellence. The firm now provides assistance in a number of practice areas as a comprehensive package of legal services for existing and new clients.

I am also the founder of the Corvisiero Literary Agency and am our senior literary agent. During the few years prior to starting my own agency, I worked with the L. Perkins Agency, where I learned invaluable lessons and made a name for myself in the industry. I am also a literary consultant, speaker, author, and an attorney practicing law with a focus on corporate law and estate planning in New York City. I am licensed to practice in New York state and have been in good standing for the duration of my admission to the Bar. I belong to the New York City Bar Association, New York State Bar Association, and the American Bar Association.

I am fluent in Italian and Spanish and have some working knowledge of Portuguese and Japanese.

How did you become an agent? As a writer, I had a lot of author friends and some publishing connections. I started helping authors get deals…the rest is history.

Knowing what you do now, would you do it again, or what might you do instead? There are some things one can only learn with experience. In hindsight there are a few small things that I'd do differently…

Do you charge fees? If yes, please explain. We do not charge fees to agented clients for representation, services, and support. We do offer consultations and services to nonclients pursuant to standard pricing models. I also practice law and represent authors on publishing deals, copyrights, trust and estates, and other business matters on a per-hour basis.

List some of the titles you have recently placed with publishers. J.A. Dennam, *Sexual Integrity* (Cleis Press); Heidi McLaughlin, *Boys of Summer* series, three-book deal (Grand Central); Sienna Snow, *Arya's Absolution*, three-book deal (Forever Yours); Harper Sloan, new Western series, three-book deal (Pocket); Steve Bohls, *Jed and the Junkyard Wars*, two-book deal (Disney Hyperion); Stina Lindenblatt, *New Rockers* series, three-book deal (Loveswept); Michael Ventrella and Jonathan Maberry, *Alternate Sherlock Holmes Anthology*, two-book deal (Diversion); Kerry Vail, *Shifter* series, three-book deal (Carina Press); Nicole Jaqueline, *Unbreak My Heart*, two-book deal (Grand Central); Megan Erickson, *Trust the Focus*, two-plus-one deal (Intermix); L.P. Dover, *Second Chances* series, three-book deal (Loveswept).

Describe your personality. Hardworking, demanding, and no-nonsense, but always fair and kind.

What do you like reading/watching/listening to on your own time? I have very eclectic tastes.

What do the "Big 5" mean to you? The Big 4 — HarperCollins, Penguin Random House, Simon & Schuster, Macmillan, plus reputable publishers that sell good books.

How do you feel about independent/small presses? Not all publishers are created equal.

What are your feelings about self-publishing? If done properly, it can be successful.

Agent's name and contact info: Saritza Hernandez, Senior Literary Agent, saritza@corvisieroagency.com

Describe the kinds of works you want to represent. Romance, erotica, LGBT fiction.

Describe what you definitely don't want to represent. Inspirational/religious fiction, memoir, nonfiction, children's books (picture/chapter/middle grade).

How do you want writers to pitch you? Check our submission guidelines on our website for details, but make sure your work is ready to go out to editors on the day you submit your query.

Describe your education and professional history. I was one of those annoying kids who loved being in school, so when I stopped my college plans to marry the man of my dreams at the ripe young age of 20 with just my Associate of Arts, my parents likely thought me crazy. A romantic at heart, I knew I would eventually finish my schooling, but three kids, two dogs, and a decade of working for the government later, I yearned for books, learning, and more books. I signed up for online courses at University of Phoenix to finish the 20 credits I needed to obtain my BS degree.

I worked in the publishing industry for 13 years doing pretty much every job you can think of until 5 years ago, when I decided to learn the job from the other side of the desk. I fell in love with the learning and the books all over again. As an agent, you're constantly learning about the industry and changing trends. There are books everywhere and, even better, there are authors writing new ones every day! It's the best job in the world, and I've enjoyed every minute of my 5 years as a literary agent.

How did you become an agent? One of my closest friends had written an amazing book and asked me to help her get it published. The more I researched what literary agents did and what it meant to be on the business side of the desk, the more I wanted to be an agent. I started looking for a mentor in the industry, and one day, on Twitter, Lori Perkins said she was looking for apprentices for her agency. She took me under her wing as the epub agent. I started representing clients whose primary focus was digital publishing and became the first literary agent to represent and sell books in the digital market.

Knowing what you do now, would you do it again? If not, what might you do instead? I wish I'd done it earlier! I see some of the new blood in the industry, young men and women who go to school to learn about the publishing industry and go from being interns at publishing houses, literary agencies, and publicity firms to being some of the top literary agents in the field, and I love it!

Do you charge fees? If yes, please explain. Nope, never.

When and where were you born, and where have you lived? I was one of the last babies delivered at the Ramey Air Force Base Hospital in Aguadilla, Puerto Rico, on June 9, 1973.

What do you like to do when you're not working? Binge-watching Netflix originals like *Jessica Jones* and *Transparent* or reruns of favorite series like *Star Trek: The Next Generation.*

List some of the titles you have recently placed with publishers. *Status Update* by Annabeth Albert (male-male erotic romance fiction, Carina Press), *Gravity* by Juliann Rich Books (gay young adult fiction, Bold Strokes), *Do-Gooder* by j. leigh bailey (gay young adult fiction, Harmony Ink Press), *The Reformation of Micah Johnson* by Sean Kennedy (gay young adult fiction, Harmony Ink Press), *Dreadnought* by April Daniels (LGBTQIA young adult fiction, Diversion Books), *Beauty, Inc.* by Tara Lain (male-male contemporary romance, Dreamspinner Press), *Such a Dance* by Kate McMurray (historical male-male romance, Kensington), *Pent Up* by Damon Suede (male-male contemporary romance, Dreamspinner Press).

Describe your personality. Quirky. I'm a fan of many things and expert on very little. I'm a proverbial student of life and devoted wife and mother. I will discuss (at length) anything having to do with my children or spouse and most people describe me as fun-sized and funny.

What do you like reading/watching/listening to on your own time? I have eclectic tastes. I read primarily what I represent, so favorites are LGBT fiction (David Levithan, Alex Sanchez, etc.), but I love male-male romance the most and have been a fan of many of the authors who are now my clients writing in the genre. My Kindle app on my iPad is loaded with everything from middle grade titles to heavy erotica. I just love to be transported. I'm rather eclectic when it comes to TV, too, as I'm a huge *Downton Abbey* fan but love the fantasy world of *Game of Thrones*, too. Guilty pleasures include *Star Trek: The Next Generation*, *Star Trek: Deep Space Nine*, and *How to Get Away with Murder*. If my Kindle and DVR are eclectic, you can bet my iTunes is a mishmash of everything from Etta James to Disney movie soundtracks. Favorite bands at the moment are OneRepublic and Fun. Favorite solo artist is Sam Smith. Favorite song on repeat is "I Lived" by OneRepublic.

Do you think the business has changed a lot over the past few years? If yes, please explain. Not as much as people think it has. We are finally seeing the fruits of the evolution of publishing in this big, digitally driven world and have found that, although many will ask for Kindles this year for Christmas, many more will ask for printed books they can devour before their hot chocolates turn cold.

What do the "Big 5" mean to you? Wider distribution and exposure for my clients, especially those writing LGBTQIA fiction.

How do you feel about independent/small presses? Love, love, love them!

What are your feelings about self-publishing? I love it and hate it! Love that it's another opportunity for authors to present their work and expand their repertoire. I hate that it is getting more difficult to find the diamonds in the rough among the ocean of rocks.

Do you think Amazon is good or bad — or both — for the book business? Did I mention my ebook hoarding problem? I blame Amazon for my ebook and coffee addiction, as they make it so easy with their one-click shopping for me to spend my money on six new ebooks and two 24-pack boxes of Jet Fuel Coffee K-Cups. I suppose I should prepare to be assimilated soon. As a publishing and distribution opportunity for my clients, they're a valuable tool, as many of my clients make a substantial amount of money from their ebook sales monthly.

What do you like and dislike about your job? I love my job! Discovering talent, reading amazing books, and seeing an author's career flourish are almost as fulfilling as seeing my own children succeed. I don't like chasing money owed to my clients.

What are ways prospective clients can impress you, and what are ways they can turn you off? They should impress me with their writing, make me fall in love with their words, and seduce my mind with masterfully crafted work that makes me stand up and take notice.

How would you describe the "writer from hell"? I'm very blessed to not have experienced a client from hell, but that's why I think "the call" is so important for both the author and the agent. If a client is argumentative, defiant, or unwilling to work, we're not going to mesh well. So I ask a lot of questions to get a feel for how we're going to work together and offer representation if I feel we're a good match. I suppose the worst clients are those who "demand" work and address me as their employee rather than their partner. If you're looking for someone to boss around, become a parent or get a pet, not an agent.

Describe a book you would like to write. Funny thing is, I've started several and never get around to finishing them, which is why I admire writers who can win NaNoWriMo. Maybe one day, I'll finish one of mine. It will likely be a romance.

Do you believe in a higher and/or lower "power"? Absolutely, I do. I wouldn't be here, had I not had some higher power watching over me and keeping me from getting in my own way.

Is there anything you wish to express beyond the parameters of the preceding questions? I quote movie lines like Scripture, especially *Ghostbusters 2*: "Everything you're doing is bad. I want you to know this." — Janosz

Agent's name and contact info: Doreen Thistle, doreen@corvisieroagency.com

Describe the kinds of works you want to represent. I prefer to represent mystery, thrillers, urban fantasy, paranormal, historical literary fiction, and memoir in novel-length projects.

Describe what you definitely don't want to represent. No science fiction and no horror, please — I'm too imaginative!

How do you want writers to pitch you? Please send an email to queries@corvisieroagency .com with "Query for Doreen" in the subject line. The email should include: (1) the query letter, (2) the first 15–30 pages of the manuscript (3) a 1–2-page synopsis that tells the full story. Paste it in the body of the email, thank you; no attachments.

Describe your education and professional history. Learning disabilities kept me from a traditional degree program, but my parents helped me access internships with mentors in PR and marketing, editing and research. I used this education to run nonprofit organizations for women in crisis and special-ed programs for kids who needed nontraditional learning environments as well as for developmental editing of manuscripts and writing family histories for publication in the private sector.

How did you become an agent? While I was helping a physician friend edit his first novel, I attended the SEAK Fiction Writing for Physicians Conference to meet agents on his behalf. I was befriended there by the late, great medical thriller author Michael Palmer, who suggested that I submit the manuscript query to Marisa Corvisiero, saying that she was an agent "who was different in a wonderful way." Marisa and I corresponded, and I discovered that Michael was absolutely right! It's an honor to have been invited to join the Corvisiero Literary Agency.

Knowing what you do now, would you do it again? If not, what might you do instead? I love people's stories, and I deeply respect their dreams. This is a great profession for helping them express both successfully.

Do you charge fees? If yes, please explain. No.

When and where were you born, and where have you lived? I was born in New York state, grew up on the Space Coast in Florida, spent five amazing years living in Bavaria and England and traveling in Austria, Italy, and France, and have had the joy of raising my son in beautiful Colorado.

What do you like to do when you're not working? I'm one of nine children from a very close family, with four generations of people I love to hang out with, especially my own son. They're mostly athletes, and I'm not, so I always have a book in hand when the touch football game begins.

List some of the titles you have recently placed with publishers. As a newly apprenticed agent, I'm delighted to have signed Dr. Barbara Golder's medical thriller *Dying for Revenge* (Full Quiver Publishing), to be released spring 2016. It's the first novel in her new mystery series, *The Lady Doc Murders*, with a dozen books planned. Several exciting projects with other great clients are also pending!

Describe your personality. I'm six of one, half a dozen of the other; joyful, outgoing, hopeful — and, being Irish, sure the world will end tomorrow. I intend to be reading when that happens.

What do you like reading/watching/listening to on your own time? I've always loved listening to radio theater and live jazz. I'm intrigued by mystery in books and on TV and keenly interested in biographies and memoirs of people I've admired.

Do you think the business has changed a lot over the past few years? If yes, please explain. I'm so new to the world of publishing that I can only imagine I would also have enjoyed the pre-internet leisured camaraderie of this business.

What do the "Big 5" mean to you? Olympic Gold for author and agent!

How do you feel about independent/small presses? I like them. Because they are "independent," one can work closely with the decision makers and enjoy participating more fully in the process of publication.

What are your feelings about self-publishing? I know people who have done it successfully because they knew how to market; I think that is the key. Options make the world work!

Do you think Amazon is good or bad — or both — for the book business? I think that Amazon has vast potential to simplify and benefit the book business for readers, authors, and agents.

What do you like and dislike about your job? I like the thrill of receiving a synopsis and the first pages of a manuscript. I like the hunt for the right publisher. I like telling a client that the manuscript has been requested for reading. I don't like telling a client that "it didn't fit the list."

What are ways prospective clients can impress you, and what are ways they can turn you off? The hallmarks of clients I will enthusiastically represent are good manners, a project that has been impeccably edited and professionally prepared, and an appreciation of how hard a serious agent works for them. These are also clients who commit to the critical necessity of promoting their books and do so with intelligent energy.

How would you describe the "writer from hell"? No sense of humor. That's hell.

Describe a book you would like to write. Anyone's family history. To paraphrase Will Rogers, I haven't met a life that's boring.

Do you believe in a higher and/or lower "power"? I've experienced the presence of both.

CSG LITERARY PARTNERS/MDM MANAGEMENT ❖

www.csgliterary.com

127 Hillside Avenue, Cresskill, NJ 07626, 201-569-9213

Agent's name and contact info: Steven Harris, steven@csgliterary.com

Describe the kinds of works you want to represent. We are interested in current events, career, reference, biography, business/investing/finance, cookbooks, history, humor, mind-body-spirit/inspiration, health, lifestyle, memoir, and children's nonfiction (but only if heavily platformed!), pop culture, self-help, sports, science.

Describe what you definitely don't want to represent. We do *not* handle poetry, fiction, computer science, religion, children's, or memoir (again, unless there is a sizable platform associated with it).

How do you want writers to pitch you? Brief emailed query letter, with a book proposal attached.

Describe your education and professional history. College educated. In the book business since 1972.

How did you become an agent? Love selling books for authors.

Knowing what you do now, would you do it again? If not, what might you do instead? Absolutely!

Do you charge fees? If yes, please explain. The only fee we charge is 15 percent of all monies received from the publisher's advance and royalties.

List some of the titles you have recently placed with publishers. *How to Be an Ultra-Spiritualist, How Churchill Saved Civilization, What the Dickens: Distinctly Dickensian Words and How to Use Them, The Well Life: Balance Does Exist, Sleeping Your Way to the Top: How to Get the Sleep You Need to Succeed, Bring Your Whole Self to Work, When Your Child Is Gay: What You Need to Know, The Power Job Hunt: A 21-Day Guide to Insider Tips and Foolproof Tactics to Help Land Your Dream Job, Bridging Two Worlds: Insights from an Authentic Medium about Connecting with the Afterlife.*

Do you think the business has changed a lot over the past few years? If yes, please explain. Except for the emergence of ebooks, the reemergence of the independent bookstore, and the further erosion of the midlist book, it's still the same business.

What do the "Big 5" mean to you? Fewer editors and publishers to sell books to.

How do you feel about independent/small presses? Many of them publish as well as the majors.

What are your feelings about self-publishing? Authors with a very strong platform should certainly consider the profitability aspect of self-publishing if they can drive enough sales themselves. However, authors should realize that publishing is a full-time job, and they may be served better by the support of a full-time publisher. Self-publishing has not yet evolved to a point where it's an easy solution for authors.

Do you think Amazon is good or bad — or both — for the book business? Amazon is as bad as Walden Books and B. Dalton were in the '80s and as bad as Barnes & Noble was in the '90s. But the book business survived those chains; it will survive Amazon.

What are ways prospective clients can impress you, and what are ways they can turn you off? Unique subjects, short query letters, and, most important, a book proposal that is organized and extremely well written with no typos or grammatical errors.

CURTIS BROWN AUSTRALIA PTY LTD ❖ www.curtisbrown.com.au

10 Heeley Street, Paddington, NSW 2021, Australia, 00-61-2-9361-6161,
fax: 00-61-2-9360-3935

Agents' names and contact info: Clare Forster, clare@curtisbrown.com.au;
Grace Heifetz, grace@curtisbrown.com.au; Fiona Inglis, fiona@curtisbrown
.com.au; Pippa Masson, pippa@curtisbrown.com.au; Tara Wynne,
tara@curtisbrown.com.au

Describe the kinds of works you want to represent. We represent a broad range of fiction and nonfiction for adults and children.

Describe what you definitely don't want to represent. Poetry, most picture books.

How do you want writers to pitch you? Three sample chapters and a synopsis or sample and chapter breakdown for nonfiction via email to info@curtisbrown.com.au or post to PO Box 19, Paddington, NSW 2021; include return postage.

Describe your education and professional history. Tara: I have always been an agent; graduate degree in English literature at Edinburgh University.

How did you become an agent? I applied for available positions the first summer after university. Made it to three interviews and was offered one job!

Knowing what you do now, would you do it again? If not, what might you do instead? I love what I do, just wish we were all paid more.

Do you charge fees? If yes, please explain. No fees.

When and where were you born, and where have you lived? Kuwait, but grew up in Ireland and the UK.

What do you like to do when you're not working? Yoga, ocean swimming, walking the dog, and spending time with family.

List some of the titles you have recently placed with publishers. Butterfly on a Pin by Alannah Hill (Australian fashion designer), *Born to Rule: Unauthorised Biography of Malcolm Turnbull* (Australian prime minister), *Women I've Undressed* by Orry-Kelly (Hollywood Golden Age costume designer), *Foreign Soil* by Maxine Beneba Clarke (short stories), *Whimsy and Woe* by Rebecca McRitchie (Gaiman/Burton-esque junior fiction).

Describe your personality. Loyal, self-depreciating, patient to a point, then fiery.

What do you like reading/watching/listening to on your own time? Brilliant TV series like *True Detective* and *Hannibal* or *Fargo*; reading historical and literary fiction and current bestsellers; rereading classics and poetry.

What do the "Big 5" mean to you? We are all wondering if the Big 5 will become the Big 1 or 2 in the not-too-distant future.

How do you feel about independent/small presses? Love working with indies that have good distribution and a firm grasp of marketing.

What are your feelings about self-publishing? It can be the best solution for certain projects that won't sell sufficient numbers in other territories but can at least be made available. Same with backlist titles — best option.

Do you think Amazon is good or bad — or both — for the book business? Has forced us to dumb down.

What are ways prospective clients can impress you, and what are ways they can turn you off? I am impressed by great writing and a professional approach to one's career and to agents and publishers. I am turned off by too much flattery and constantly chasing or emailing.

How would you describe the "writer from hell"? Always telling you by phone or email how to do your job, but not leaving you alone for long enough to actually get on with it!

Describe a book you would like to write. A brilliant crime novel or book-club historical.

Do you believe in a higher and/or lower "power"? Some sort of higher power.

DANA NEWMAN LITERARY, LLC ❖ dananewman.com

9720 Wilshire Boulevard, 5th Floor, Beverly Hills, CA 90212

Agent's name and contact info: Dana Newman, dananewmanliterary@gmail.com

Describe the kinds of works you want to represent. I'm interested in representing practical nonfiction (business, health and wellness, self-help, psychology, parenting, technology) by authors with smart, unique perspectives and established platforms. I love compelling, inspiring narrative nonfiction in the areas of memoir, biography, history, pop culture, current affairs, women's interest, social trends, science, and sports. My favorite genre is literary nonfiction: true stories, well told, that read like a novel you can't put down. On the fiction side I'm looking for a very select amount of literary fiction and upmarket women's fiction (contemporary and historical).

Describe what you definitely don't want to represent. Please don't send me any genre fiction (mystery, thriller, fantasy, horror, science fiction, romance), poetry, screenplays, religion, or children's or young adult projects.

How do you want writers to pitch you? Email a query letter to dananewmanliterary@ gmail.com that identifies the category, gives title and word count, and provides a brief overview of your project, credentials, platform, and previous publishing history, if any. For fiction submissions, please send a query letter and the first 5 pages of your book in the body of the email (no attachments). If I'm interested in your material, I'll email you a request for a full proposal (for nonfiction) or a synopsis and the first 20 pages (for fiction). Be sure to include your contact details (email address and phone number). If you have relevant writing experience (articles, books) and/or have received writing awards, please include details in your cover letter.

Describe your education and professional history. I have a BA in comparative literature from University of California at Berkeley and a JD from University of San Francisco School of Law. I founded my literary agency in 2010. Prior to becoming a literary agent, I worked for 14 years as in-house counsel for the Moviola companies in Hollywood, California, providers of entertainment and communications technologies. In addition to representing authors as a literary agent, I'm also a transactional and intellectual property attorney, advising content creators and entrepreneurs on contracts, copyrights, trademarks, and licensing.

How did you become an agent? I'm a lifelong book lover, and after working as an in-house attorney in the entertainment industry for many years I knew I wanted to bring those skills and my passion for reading to a position in publishing. Having worked in entertainment during the transition from analog to digital platforms in film editing and audio recording, I was excited about the new technologies and business models for the creation and distribution of books that were emerging.

Knowing what you do now, would you do it again? If not, what might you do instead? I would absolutely do it again — I wish I'd started sooner.

Do you charge fees? If yes, please explain. No.

When and where were you born, and where have you lived? I'm a proud member of Generation X, born in Los Angeles. I've lived in LA and in the Bay Area (Berkeley and San Francisco).

What do you like to do when you're not working? Read (of course), run, practice yoga, hike LA's canyons, travel, spend time with my family and friends, see live music, and try the latest foodie restaurant.

List some of the titles you have recently placed with publishers. *A Stray Cat Struts: My Life as a Rockabilly Rebel* by Slim Jim Phantom (Thomas Dunne); *Aldous Huxley's Hands: The Untold Story of Huxley's Quest for Perception and the Birth, Death and Rebirth of Psychedelic Science* by Allene Symons (Prometheus); *Tuff Juice: My Journey from the Streets* *to the NBA* by Caron Butler with Steve Springer (Lyons Press); *Breakthrough: The Making of America's First Woman President* by Nancy L. Cohen (Counterpoint); *That's Gotta Hurt: How Sports Injuries Are Transforming the Games We Watch and the Athletes Who Play Them* by Dr. David Geier (ForeEdge); *The Moment: A Practical Guide to Creating a Mindful Life in a Distracted World* by Achim Nowak (New Page Books); *Selma & Nelly: Two Nobel Women* by Marlene Wagman-Geller (Bleeding Heart, 2016); *Yoga's Healing Power: Looking Inward for Change, Growth, and Peace* by Ally Hamilton (Llewellyn); *Surviving Lesbian Love Addiction* by Lauren D. Costine, PhD (Rowman & Littlefield); *Food Truths from Farm to Table* by Michele Payn-Knoper (Praeger).

Describe your personality. I'm endlessly curious, happiest when I'm learning or experiencing something new or engaged in a lively conversation. I tend to be logical and analytical (I am a lawyer after all), but also love working with creative people and collaborating on a project. I'm a passionate and diligent advocate for people and things I believe in.

What do you like reading/watching/listening to on your own time? Too many to list, but I'm usually reading literary fiction or memoir when I have time to read for pleasure. I like character-driven, edgy TV dramas and comedies like *Homeland, House of Cards, Orange Is the New Black, Togetherness, The Affair,* and *Transparent.* I listen to my teenage daughters' playlists mostly and like health and wellness podcasts.

Do you think the business has changed a lot over the past few years? If yes, please explain. Publishing has changed in the last few years as the market adjusted to the rise of ebooks and a reduction in physical bookstores. Ebook sales have leveled off, though, and print books still represent the majority of sales. The marketing and promotion of books now includes a greater focus on online strategies, as that's where most books are discovered and purchased.

What do the "Big 5" mean to you? The Big 5 mean the current five largest publishing conglomerates and all of their various imprints, the top tier in trade publishing. One path for publishing a book, with publishers that have extensive editorial expertise and marketing and publicity resources, but sometimes lack the agility of smaller or midsize publishers.

How do you feel about independent/small presses? I think independent and small presses serve an important role in the publishing ecosystem and can be a great fit for certain projects. They don't have the budgets or marketing and publicity muscle that the larger publishers have, but they're usually staffed by hardworking, dedicated people who are passionate about publishing good books and can take risks that larger publishers can't.

What are your feelings about self-publishing? Self-publishing is a great option for those writers who have the means and ability to handle all aspects of the publishing process or put together a team of experts to help them. It's easier than ever to upload an ebook and have it distributed to major online retailers, but it's another thing to have that book be well edited with a striking professional cover, receive impactful reviews and media attention, and sell a lot of copies. The success stories are wonderful, but they represent a very small percentage of all the self-published books out there, most of which don't find an audience and fail to sell.

Do you think Amazon is good or bad — or both — for the book business? Both. Amazon plays a big role in a book's success, and authors are well advised to take advantage of its platform as much as possible. However, I believe that competition is essential to innovation and a healthy marketplace and am concerned about the pressures facing other retailers, especially independent bookstores, as a result of Amazon's position.

What do you like and dislike about your job? My work varies from day to day, which I love. Things I enjoy include: assisting writers in polishing their proposals and manuscripts; submitting projects to editors; following up on submissions; negotiating publishing agreements; drafting coauthor agreements; running interference on delivery and production scheduling issues; facilitating cover image discussions; advising on copyright, trademark, and permission issues; working with authors on executing their marketing plan; reading queries, proposals, and manuscripts; attending writers' conferences, where I present workshops on publishing agreements, digital rights, and copyright and trademark issues. The only thing I really don't like about agenting is all the rejection — both having to decline to represent writers' projects and dealing with the rejections from editors I've submitted to.

What are ways prospective clients can impress you, and what are ways they can turn you off? Prospective clients can impress me by doing their homework, educating themselves about the publishing business, following query and submission instructions, and handling communications in a professional and respectful manner. I'm turned off by rudeness, unprofessionalism, emails that are filled with typos and grammatical mistakes, and queries that are sent for the kinds of projects I don't represent.

How would you describe the "writer from hell"? A writer who has unreasonable expectations about the realities of the book business, won't accept any feedback on their work, has no interest in marketing and promoting their work, is unprofessional, is disrespectful of the author-agent and author-editor relationships, and has no sense of humor. I can usually tell if writers are going to be challenging to work with based on the way they communicate — both what they say and how they say it.

Describe a book you would like to write. My dream would be to write the next *Born to Run* or *The Immortal Life of Henrietta Lacks*.

Do you believe in a higher and/or lower "power"? No, but I do believe in spirituality.

DANIEL LITERARY GROUP ❖ www.danielliterarygroup.com

601 Old Hickory Boulevard, #56, Brentwood, TN 37027, 615-730-8207

Agent's name and contact info: Greg Daniel; all submissions should be emailed to submissions@danielliterarygroup.com

Describe the kinds of works you want to represent. Nonfiction of all kinds.

Describe what you definitely don't want to represent. Fiction, children's books, poetry.

How do you want writers to pitch you? Email only.

Describe your education and professional history. Twenty years in publishing. Founded the agency in 2007.

Do you charge fees? If yes, please explain. No.

List some of the titles you have recently placed with publishers. Accidental Saints by Nadia Bolz-Weber (Penguin Random House), *American Heresy* by Benjamin L. Corey (Harper-One), *The Third Reconstruction* by William L. Barber and Jonathan Wilson-Hartgrove (Beacon Press), *Outlaw Christian* by Jacqueline Bussie (Thomas Nelson), *The Catholic Catalogue* by Anna Keating and Melissa Musick (Penguin Random House).

DEFIORE AND COMPANY ❖ www.defliterary.com

47 East 19th Street, 3rd Floor, New York, NY 10003, 212-925-7744

Agent's name and contact info: Miriam Altshuler, querymiriam@defliterary.com

Describe the kinds of works you want to represent. I specialize in adult literary and commercial fiction, narrative nonfiction, and books for children. First and foremost, I respond to voice and stories that are character-driven, books that draw me in and give me a new perspective on a world I didn't know, or make me think more deeply about a world I do know. I seek books with a heart and writers with wonderful storytelling abilities. In fiction, I am most interested in family sagas, historical novels, and stories that offer a new twist or retelling of some kind. In nonfiction, I love memoir, narrative nonfiction, and self-help (as long as it is not too prescriptive). I particularly respond to books that carry an important cultural, social, or psychological message. For children's books, I focus primarily on young adult and middle grade, and my tastes vary broadly in those areas. It always comes back to the voice and the heart of a story for me.

Describe what you definitely don't want to represent. I do not work with adult romance, sci-fi, or fantasy.

How do you want writers to pitch you? Please follow the guidelines on the website. (Please do not call the office.) Send a query via email with a short description/synopsis of your book and what it is about (think flap copy of a book; I want content and ideas) and any relevant information about you I should know. Keep it short and concise, and please do not include any attachments. I also like to have the first chapter of a book, so I can get a sense of the writing, but include it in the body of the email below the query.

Describe your education and professional history. I graduated from Middlebury College as an English major with a minor in creative writing and sociology. My first job out of college was as the assistant to Timothy Seldes at Russell & Volkening Literary Agency, which at that time was one of the oldest and most prestigious agencies. I became an agent at Russell & Volkening 2 years later and in 1994 left to start my own agency, which I ran for 21 years until I joined DeFiore and Company in 2016. I have always been a literary agent and always will be.

How did you become an agent? I love reading, books, and working with people. I am also a great problem solver and love to connect people.

Knowing what you do now, would you do it again? If not, what might you do instead? No question, I would do it again. This is the most interesting job with the most interesting and dedicated people.

Do you charge fees? If yes, please explain. I am an active member of the AAR and do not charge any reading fees.

What do you like to do when you're not working? Like everyone in publishing, I love to read. I am also an avid outdoors person, and I love horseback riding (my daughter is a competitive horseback rider), skiing, and hiking. I also love to travel and go to movies and concerts. And most of all, I love spending time with my husband and two children.

List some of the titles you have recently placed with publishers. *The Keepers* series by Ted Sanders (HarperCollins Children's Books), *The Trouble with Twins* by Kathryn Siebel (Knopf Books for Young Readers), *Stoopid Is As Stoopid Does* by Leslie Connor (Katherine Tegen), *Rethinking Narcissism: The Bad — and Surprising Good — about Feeling Special* by Dr. Craig Malkin (Harper Wave), *Till We Have Built Jerusalem: Architects of a New City* by Adina Hoffman (Farrar, Straus and Giroux), *Tree of Treasures: A Life in Ornaments* by Bonnie Mackay (Penguin Books), *Primates of Park Avenue: A Memoir* by Wednesday Martin (Simon & Schuster), *Electric City* by Elizabeth Rosner (Counterpoint Press).

How would you describe the "writer from hell"? What I prefer to say here is who great clients are: those who respect the art of writing, who work diligently to make the book the best it can be, and who believe in their craft; those who respect my time as an agent and all the various things I do for everyone; those who respect that I work night and day and weekends and understand the boundaries of my work, family, and reading time; those who are collaborative in their thinking and the promoting of their work and understand that publishing has changed, so they have to be part of the process from beginning to end; those who have a sense of humor and understand I am committed to them and believe in their work.

Agent's name and contact info: Brian DeFiore, querybrian@defliterary.com

Describe the kinds of works you want to represent. I have a tough time limiting myself to genres. I love any original authorial voice that grabs me and won't let go. But that's not easy: I bore pretty easily and have a very low tolerance for cliché. For me, it's all about creativity and narrative drive. But I tend to respond positively more often to mainstream fiction for adults and young adults, memoir, pop culture, popular science, and psychology.

Describe what you definitely don't want to represent. Anything that is written to capitalize on a trend.

How do you want writers to pitch you? Creatively. I say to people here all the time: if a writer can't keep you captivated for the length of a letter, do you really believe that he or she will be able to do so for the length of a novel? The best query letter I ever received was about three lines long, but they were three brilliant lines. I sold that book for six figures.

Describe your education and professional history. Started as a young editor at St. Martin's Press and rose through editorial ranks there, and then at Dell/Delacorte (editorial director), Hyperion (VP and editor in chief), and Villard/Random House (SVP and publisher).

How did you become an agent? After hitting a wall after a corporate takeover at my last job, I decided I'd had my fill of corporate life. Working with authors was what I was good at. And I also decided, perhaps unwisely at the start, that I could do it as well on my own as I could working with others in a bigger operation. It was pretty lonely those first few months.

Knowing what you do now, would you do it again? If not, what might you do instead? Sadly, I'd probably do it again. I have a hard time thinking of something I'd like more. And I worry that there are plenty of things that I'd hate. And I have no other clearly monetizable talents.

Do you charge fees? If yes, please explain. No. Straight commission.

When and where were you born, and where have you lived? New York City born and bred. Grew up in Queens; high school in Brooklyn; college upstate. Briefly lived in upstate New York and in Connecticut but got DTs within a year.

What do you like to do when you're not working? Pleasure reading, movies, theater, cooking, bicycling.

List some of the titles you have recently placed with publishers. *Humans of New York* by Brandon Stanton, *The 5th Wave* by Rick Yancey, *The Cheese Trap* by Neal Barnard, *Bridges to Brilliance* by Nadia Lopez, *Don't Give Up, Don't Give In* by Louis Zamperini and David Rensin.

Describe your personality. Mostly even-keeled, with a true wonder for creative brilliance and a low tolerance for stupidity and arrogance.

What do you like reading/watching/listening to on your own time? Excellence in all things. Have been lately knocked out by these books: *All the Light We Cannot See, Middlesex, Hold Still, Lonesome Dove* (I know, decades late!!). Movies: *Brooklyn, The Big Short, Grandma, Mad Max Fury Road, Inside Out.* Theater: *Hamilton, Curious Incident of the Dog in the Nighttime, An American in Paris.*

Do you think the business has changed a lot over the past few years? If yes, please explain. In some ways, yes; in many ways, no. Obviously, the retail sector has changed enormously with fewer bookstores and more books being bought online, whether in print or ebook form. But surprisingly the fundamentals are shockingly unchanged: an industry built around trying to find and develop a surprisingly small number of hit books. The thing that has been overlooked in all of the endless discussion about how digitization would kill the industry is that it is *really damned hard* to find and develop those books. Making them available for download or purchase is maybe 3 percent of the job. The other 97 percent is where the hard work of the industry comes in: finding, selecting, acquiring, developing, packaging, and distributing those titles; and then most crucially: finding ways to get the public to hear about, *desire*, and then purchase something that is going to cost them a lot of money and take days or weeks of their precious time. And do so without the luxury of huge Hollywood-style marketing budgets. It's a daunting task.

What do the "Big 5" mean to you? Dealing with the big leagues is always the most fun: they play with the biggest advances and the biggest promo budgets and give your authors the best shot at a hit. That said, they're huge and can be lumbering, and if a book is clearly *not* rising to the top of their pile during the long developing and selling process, it can very easily get lost or dismissed and that is very frustrating. But if something *is* rising to the top, they have the best shot of making it go on to achieve orbit.

How do you feel about independent/small presses? There are great ones and there are not-so-great ones, so I can't really generalize. They tend to work very hard and can be great at developing authors and getting attention for smaller titles, and that attention can sometimes make a less obvious title a hit in a way that would be impossible at a Big 5 house.

What are your feelings about self-publishing? Clearly some authors have ma
them, mostly in genres where volume and price are drivers. I think the car
against new people trying it, as millions of books are being self-published,
quite bad, making it much harder to work the system and to get the good b
Ultimately, the job of publishing has always mostly been about finding way
noticed, not about efficient distribution, and I think publishers do it a whol
the vast majority of good writers.

Do you think Amazon is good or bad — or both — for the book busin
never been a more definitive "both." Amazon's ability to find readers and
areas underserved by stores has been a wonderful boon. It is unquestio
have broadened the market for books. However, their hardball tactics
and retailers combined with their power as a near monopoly in ebooks (a
via Audible) as well as online retailing of print books gives them an unp
in the industry that has not, as far as I can see, been altogether good for
literary world. In their ecosystem creative works are often used as an inex
to give away at cost or below in order to encourage more expensive purch
memberships, which of course is something no other retailer can do. It's
ing field and one that undervalues books and ultimately, I think, has a h
hurt authors. And in many cases it already has (six months' worth of al
published by Little, Brown and Grand Central, for one glaring example). I
corporation that works without competition can ultimately be a force for

What do you like and dislike about your job? I like that I spend most of
with interesting people who are passionate about what they do. I dislike
of what I do is saying no to some people, while being told no by different

What are ways prospective clients can impress you, and what are ways t
off? Pretty much the only thing they can impress me with is a unique abi
or pictures to tell a story. And they can turn me off by demonstrating eith
no such ability or that they have it but are nevertheless too unpleasant f
spend at least a year of my life with.

How would you describe the "writer from hell"? Someone who doesn'
gain insight from the experience of others.

Do you believe in a higher and/or lower "power"? No, but I do believ
The Force.

Is there anything you wish to express beyond the parameters of the pre
Good guys usually come out on top. And good writers.

Agent's name and contact info: Reiko Davis, reiko@defliterary.com

Describe the kinds of works you want to represent. My interests are varied, but I am particularly drawn to adult literary and upmarket fiction, narrative nonfiction, and young adult and middle grade fiction. Above all, I want to discover books that surprise and move me with their irresistible characters and language.

I love a strong narrative voice; smart, funny heroines; narrowly located settings (especially towns in the South and Midwest); family sagas; darkly suspenseful novels; and stories of remarkable friendships or that explore the often perilous terrain of human relationships. For children's books, I'm actively looking for young adult and middle grade fiction — whether contemporary, historical, fantasy, or simply a story with a timeless quality and vibrant characters. For nonfiction, I'm most interested in cultural, social, and literary history; fascinating tours through niche subjects; narrative science; psychology; guides on creativity; and memoir.

Describe what you definitely don't want to represent. I do not work with any kind of adult genre fiction. I also do not represent children's picture books.

How do you want writers to pitch you? Follow the guidelines on my page on DeFiore's website. Please do not call the office. Send me a query by email with a short description of your book and a brief relevant bio. For fiction, please include the first chapter of your book pasted in the body of your email. Please do not include any attachments — I will not open them.

Describe your education and professional history. I went to Brown University, where I studied comparative literature and art history. I then attended the Columbia Publishing Course, which was a wonderful introduction to the publishing industry. My first job was as an editorial assistant at a small poetry publisher. I then got a job at Miriam Altshuler Literary Agency. I worked there for four years, first as an assistant to Miriam and then as an associate agent, until her agency merged with DeFiore and Company in early 2016. I'm now an agent at DeFiore.

How did you become an agent? I've loved reading for as long as I can remember. I love thinking about and discussing stories. I love helping writers hone their craft and make their books the best they can be. It means a lot to me to be able to support authors' creative visions, help them find the right publisher, and present their work to the largest possible readership.

Do you charge fees? If yes, please explain. No.

When and where were you born, and where have you lived? I was born in Kansas City, Missouri, in 1987. I grew up in Kansas City and spent my four years as an undergrad in

Providence, Rhode Island. I lived in the Hudson Valley for five years after college, first in Rhinebeck and then in Hudson, New York. I now live in Brooklyn.

What do you like to do when you're not working? When I'm not reading manuscripts for work, I love to curl up with a novel or a book of poems. I'm a tennis player, skier, and crocheter (and by extension, yarn shopper). I love watching movies, going to music shows, and enjoying a jazz record in front of a fire with my family. I love dogs (coonhounds in particular). I'm still waiting for the day when I can go backpacking in Greece and the Greek islands.

List some of the titles you have recently placed with publishers. *The Marked Girl* and *The Broken World* by Lindsey Klingele (HarperTeen), *Having the Last Say: Capturing Your Legacy in One Small Story* (Tarcher/Penguin) and *Conquering the College Admissions Essay in Ten Steps* by Alan Gelb (Ten Speed Press), *Vow of Celibacy* by Erin Judge (Rare Bird Books), *Fighter Girl* by Kathryn James (Month9Books), *A Thin Bright Line* by Lucy Jane Bledsoe (University of Wisconsin Press).

How would you describe the "writer from hell"? I'd prefer to describe the ideal writer. I love working with writers dedicated to the art of writing and making their books the best they can be. I take my work seriously and spend an enormous amount of time editing and providing feedback, so I love writers who are open to ideas and collaboration and who respect my efforts to sell and promote their work. When I sign writers, it means I am passionately committed to helping them get their book published and advance their career.

Agent's name and contact info: Caryn Karmatz Rudy, caryn@defliterary.com

Describe the kinds of works you want to represent. Literary and commercial fiction — I'm always looking for that perfect reading-group novel! — and nonfiction in the areas of lifestyle, beauty, health and fitness, relationships, and narrative nonfiction.

Describe what you definitely don't want to represent. Science fiction, fantasy, horror, romance.

How do you want writers to pitch you? A query letter plus the first five pages of the work pasted in the email, *not* as an attachment.

Describe your education and professional history. I graduated from the University of Pennsylvania and spent 17 years as an editor at Grand Central Publishing and Warner Books.

Do you charge fees? If yes, please explain. Never.

When and where were you born, and where have you lived? I was born in Philadelphia in 1970, spent some time in Washington, DC, after college, lived in New York for a decade, and moved back to the Philadelphia suburbs with my husband and children in 2011.

Agent's name and contact info: Adam Schear, adam@defliterary.com

Describe the kinds of works you want to represent. I am most interested in seeing inspired literary novels, hysterical comedies, smart thrillers with sharp dialogue, quirky debuts, and exceptional short story collections. Send me unlikable, unreliable narrators so magnetic that you can't help but love them and believe their half-truths. I have a soft spot for sci-fi and fantasy, especially when it breaks the mold, and young adult with an honest and compelling voice. For nonfiction, I adore popular science and big-idea books. I'm always looking for a writer who can explain a complicated concept in a way that's gripping. Across the board, I'm looking for the type of book that you're compelled to recommend to everyone you know and then secretly feel jealous that they get to read it for the first time.

How do you want writers to pitch you? Please email me at adam@defliterary.com with a query letter containing info on the book, your bio, and the first five pages in the body of the email.

Describe your education and professional history. I am a graduate of Tulane University and the Benjamin N. Cardozo School of Law. I began my publishing career at the William Morris Agency and joined DeFiore and Company in 2009.

Do you charge fees? If yes, please explain. No.

DENISE MARCIL LITERARY AGENCY, LLC ❖

www.denisemarcilagency.com

483 Westover Road, Stamford, CT 06902, 203-327-9970

Agent's name and contact info: Denise Marcil, denise@denisemarcilagency.com

Describe the kinds of works you want to represent. Nonfiction only. I look for informative and inspirational books that help people's lives. Categories of interest are health and wellness, women's interest, self-help, popular reference and how-to, popular psychology, education, human behavior, personal growth and motivation. Authors seeking representation must have extensive traditional and social-media platforms and seminar and/or speaking-event schedules.

Describe what you definitely don't want to represent. Fiction, memoir, biography, narrative nonfiction, history, science, sports, cookbooks, young adult, middle grade, children's, picture books.

How do you want writers to pitch you? Study the information, submission guidelines, and types of books I want to represent. Send a 200-word (maximum) query letter via email to dmla@denisemarcilagency.com. Your letter should be engaging, informative, persuasive.

Convince me there is a need for your book and demonstrate with details the audience for your book. As noted above, authors must have an extensive platform with media outreach and credibility if they are to be considered for representation.

How did you become an agent? Following a few years working for publishers, a job offer by an agent opened that side of the business to me. I discovered I enjoyed selling, which coincided with my talent for persuasion. Combined with my editorial skills, I discovered a career that became a passion and successful business.

Describe your education and professional history. I was an English major at Skidmore College who loved reading, analysis of literature, and creative writing. I knew in my junior year that I wanted to go into publishing. I joined Avon Books when I graduated and loved my job as an editorial assistant during the heyday of mass-market publishing. I moved to Simon & Schuster as assistant editor to expand my knowledge and experience in hardcover publishing.

Later I worked for a literary agent briefly, but decided I wanted to run my own business. I began my agency as a solo practice. I expanded the agency with a support staff and other agents, and we grew to represent hundreds of authors. In 2008, I founded a second agency, Marcil-O'Farrell Literary (www.marcilofarrellagency.com), with Anne Marie O'Farrell, who had worked with me at DMLA. Now I take on new authors at Marcil-O'Farrell, while at DMLA I continue to represent a small list of longtime clients.

Knowing what you do now, would you do it again? If not, what might you do instead? Of course I'd do it again, and I'd be smarter and prescient since I'd know what I know now. I like my role as an agent who works closely with my authors to develop and shape their careers. That's why I'm still in the business. I could have been a dancer, an art historian, or an innovation and ideation creative executive.

When and where were you born, and where have you lived? I was born in Troy, New York, but grew up in the South — Georgia and South Carolina — and later in New Jersey. I moved to New York City after college and now live there and Connecticut.

What do you like to do when you're not working? When I'm not working, I stay busy with social ballroom dancing with my husband, attending dance performances from contemporary to classical ballet, enjoying the cultural wonderland of New York: museums, lectures, theater, discovering neighborhoods I've not been to. I love to travel and enjoy outdoor adventures, especially in our national parks. I volunteer in the agent world for the AAR, for my alma mater (Skidmore), at my library, my church, and for a ballroom dance group. Giving back is vital!

Describe your personality. Competitive, driven, disciplined. Confident. Optimistic, happy, friendly, generous. Direct. Honest.

Do you think the business has changed a lot over the past few years? If yes, please explain. Yes, but the industry has always changed every few years. That's what keeps it vital. Now, more than ever, authors must promote and sell their own books. That's not completely negative for the authors, as those with platforms and established social-media audiences have more power than before. Publishers, especially of nonfiction, expect it. Publishers spend their money on coop advertising and placement of books in stores and for space with online retailers more than publicizing their books and authors. Editors are more cautious about their acquisitions. There are far more agents now than 10 years ago, so the business is more diverse.

What do the "Big 5" mean to you? I do most of my business with the Big 5, so they are important to me and my authors. They have the clout when you need it.

What are ways prospective clients can impress you, and what are ways they can turn you off? Prospective authors would be wise to do their homework about our agency and my list of authors and read the information about submissions on our website. Send me an individual query with a formal salutation, i.e., Dear Ms. Marcil. Then demonstrate that you've studied the authors and the categories I represent.

DH LITERARY, INC.

PO Box 805, Nyack, NY 10960

Agent's name and contact info: David Hendin, dhendin@gmail.com

How do you want writers to pitch you? We are not accepting new clients.

Describe your education and professional history. World Almanac/Pharos Books, President (last title), 1970–1993; United Feature Syndicate, Inc., Senior VP and Editorial Director (last title), 1970–1993 (both divisions of Scripps Howard/EW Scripps). MA, journalism, University of Missouri, 1970. BS, biology/education, University of Missouri, 1967.

When and where were you born, and where have you lived? St. Louis, Missouri; Be'er Sheva and Ashkelon, Israel; New York.

What do you like to do when you're not working? Read and write.

List some of the titles you have recently placed with publishers. *Miss Manners* books and columns and *Big Nate* comic strips and books.

DIANA FINCH LITERARY AGENCY ❖

dianafinchliteraryagency.blogspot.com

**116 West 23rd Street, Suite 500, New York, NY 10011, 917-544-4470
(no queries by phone, please), diana.finch@verizon.net**

Agent's name and contact info: Diana Finch, diana.finch@verizon.net

Describe the kinds of works you want to represent. I love to represent wonderfully imaginative, gripping stories written in distinctive, engaging voices. For nonfiction, I am excited about popular science and social justice, and I love math, history, progressive politics, narrative nonfiction, sports, journalism, environmentalism from all angles including business and lifestyle, smart business advice, and health. Because I've always been successful at selling foreign rights, I love to handle both novels and nonfiction that will appeal to translation publishers as well as to the global English-speaking market.

Describe what you definitely don't want to represent. I don't handle some genre fiction: romance, historical romance, Westerns, horror. I also don't handle illustrated children's books now, although I did sell some special ones early in my career.

How do you want writers to pitch you? First choice: Through my site at dianafinch literaryagency.blogspot.com The submission form asks for a query letter and the first 10 pages (for fiction) or proposal and pages (for nonfiction). Submitting this way allows writers to easily check on the status of their query.

Second choice: By email, with the text of the query in the body of the email and not as an attachment and with a subject heading that includes the word *query*. The first 10 pages for fiction, and the proposal and pages for nonfiction, may be included with the query as an attachment. Word files are hugely preferred to PDFs.

Describe your education and professional history. I'm a faculty brat — my father chaired the English and drama departments at Dartmouth College — and have a BA cum laude from Harvard in English, where as field hockey cocaptain I worked with my teammates to see the benefits of Title IX come to women's collegiate sports. I earned an MA in American literature from Leeds University, England, because after Harvard, where the reading lists in American lit courses featured authors who were alumni of Harvard, I wanted to study the field from a bit more of a distance.

I started out in publishing as an editorial assistant at the very collegial St. Martin's Press, where I acquired my first books and learned from the inside about all the operations of a publishing house — invaluable experience for an agent. I then trained as an agent at Sanford Greenburger Associates and then the Ellen Levine Literary Agency, where I handled foreign and serial rights in addition to my own clients, before opening my own agency in 2003.

How did you become an agent? I became an agent when it was time to move up from the assistant editor ranks, and the older editors I knew all advised me that if they were my age, they'd become agents, because agents flourish when their authors do, and opportunities are unlimited. In my first job as an agent I saw that while the editor is often caught in the middle — as the author's champion at the publishing house, but always an employee of the publisher — the agent is wholly on the side of the author, and that is where I want to be.

Knowing what you do now, would you do it again? If not, what might you do instead? Yes, if I were to relive my life, I would definitely do it over again, and follow my passions and instincts even more closely. However, if I were starting my career now, I think my college experience would have been very different, less traditional; I would have missed out on the 1980s and 1990s, which I consider the golden age of print magazines, especially for emerging writers, and which saw the rise of the chain bookstores (precursors to Amazon), a factor that has so shaped the publishing business of recent years. Without the grounding of those experiences, I wonder if book publishing would feel a lot more transient and less consequential to me.

Do you charge fees? If yes, please explain. I don't charge my clients or potential clients reading, handling, or marketing fees. I do sometimes offer to handle contract negotiations on a per-project fee basis, rather than agenting the project for the life of the deal for a commission on earnings.

When and where were you born, and where have you lived? I was born during the baby boom, in Hanover, NH. In my first winter the snow was three feet deep, which must be why I've always loved winter. I summered on Nantucket Island, where I was the first female fire-truck driver one year — well before it became vacationland for billionaires. In college and immediately after, I lived in Cambridge and Boston and thought New York City was the last place on earth I'd want to live — but I have lived here happily for 30 years, on the Upper West Side, in Park Slope, and now I am a pioneer in the Northeast Bronx, not far from the banks of the Bronx River.

What do you like to do when you're not working? Sports! Watching them and playing them — although now the "playing" is largely running and yoga, and bodysurfing in the summer. I love both soccer, which is such a window on the world, and football — local high school, college, pro! And you name it: baseball, basketball, ice hockey, field hockey, lacrosse, skiing, tennis, even golf!

List some of the titles you have recently placed with publishers. *Merchants of Men* by Loretta Napoleoni, *Stealing Schooling: Apartheid Schools and the Big Business of Unmaking Public Education* by Cornell professor Noliwe Rooks, and *Not by Wages Alone* by Jonathan Rosenblum; plus, Dutch rights to *A Lesson before Dying* by Ernest Gaines, Malaysian rights to *Islam without Extremes* by Mustafa Akyol, and Russian rights to *Word of Mouth Marketing* by Andy Sernovitz.

Describe your personality. Thoughtful, curious, supportive.

What do you like reading/watching/listening to on your own time? Here's my current strategy: I follow a number of people with varied enthusiasms on Goodreads and look to see what they are most enthusiastic about, then make sure to request those titles at my local public library and read at least some of them. I also try to read at least some of the most successful books and the ones that get great reviews from the most exacting professional book reviewers. My online reading is mostly politics and environmental activism. My daughter and I are fans of *The Voice* and love that the strange and talented seem to win this competition. And see above: sports!

Do you think the business has changed a lot over the past few years? If yes, please explain. Yes, of course — due to the rise of social media, the rise of self-publishing made possible by online selling opportunities, and the consolidation of the large publishers, leading to the exodus of many longtime book editors from publishing houses. For me, the change has been conceptual but also personal, with the departure of so many editors and other publishing professionals, including many of the ones I started out with.

What do the "Big 5" mean to you? Consolidation. One of the biggest differences between the Big 5 and smaller publishers are the Big 5's New York zeitgeist — and at the same time they are increasingly global English-language publishers. I hope they won't soon be the Big 4. Although one of the Big 5 just got bigger by acquiring one of the Medium 5.

How do you feel about independent/small presses? On the plus side: passion, clear mandates and small teams relying on teamwork. On the minus side: companies dealing with limitations, often financial ones.

What are your feelings about self-publishing? Whether or not it's successful depends a great deal on personality and on genre. The bloom is off the rose; people are realizing how difficult it is to do well, and the novelty factor is gone. Strategies that can make self-published books successful — such as fast, frequent publication — often don't work for books published traditionally.

Do you think Amazon is good or bad — or both — for the book business? Good for research and visibility. Bad in so many ways — publishing successfully when Amazon is the major player is like trying to stage operas on national broadcast TV channels or sell fine art and specialized scientific equipment in a huge chain store that discounts.

What do you like and dislike about your job? What I dislike are the limitations — everyone is overworked, and there are not enough of us. Not every book can be a bestseller, alas, and discoverability is hard — so many books go unnoticed by readers who would love them! What I like: being in on the genesis of a book, having a chance to make the difference between a book getting published and not, and between a book being published well and not — all of this is always exciting.

What are ways prospective clients can impress you, and what are ways they can turn you off? (1) Demonstrate in your query that you have done some research, are genuinely familiar with books I've represented, and have some specific reasons for querying me. (2) Not being realistic enough about your own book — not every book is going to be a huge bestseller, nor does it need to be.

How would you describe the "writer from hell"? None of my clients, I am glad to say.

Describe a book you would like to write. I'd have to be utterly compelled to write a book myself; I see how hard it is.

Do you believe in a higher and/or lower "power"? Yes, I believe that both exist and are in constant opposition.

Is there anything you wish to express beyond the parameters of the preceding questions? The conflict between a higher power and a lower power is at the core of many great works of fiction.

DOMINICK ABEL LITERARY AGENCY, INC. ❖ dalainc.com

146 West 82nd Street, #1A, New York, NY 10024, 212-877-0710, fax: 212-595-3133, agency@dalainc.com

Agent's name and contact info: Dominick Abel, President, dominick@dalainc.com

Describe the kinds of works you want to represent. Mostly fiction, primarily suspense and mystery. Some narrative nonfiction and business books.

Describe what you definitely don't want to represent. How-to books, science fiction, fantasy.

How do you want writers to pitch you? Email a query letter with, at the writer's option, a synopsis and the first three chapters (all in the body of the email, not as attachments).

Describe your education and professional history. Dominick Abel Literary Agency, Inc., has been in operation since 1975.

Do you charge fees? If yes, please explain. No.

DON CONGDON ASSOCIATES, INC. ❖ www.doncongdon.com

110 William Street, Suite 2202, New York, NY 10038, 212-645-1229, fax: 212-727-2688

Agent's name and contact info: Michael Congdon,
mcongdon@doncongdon.com

Describe the kinds of works you want to represent. Nonfiction, such as history, military history, biography, memoir, and narrative nonfiction (adventure, medicine, nature, science, politics, and true crime), and commercial and literary fiction, including suspense novels, mysteries, and thrillers.

Describe what you definitely don't want to represent. Romance, young adult/children's, how-to, self-help, business.

How do you want writers to pitch you? Via email (without attachments, paste into email instead) or snail mail.

Describe your education and professional history. Cofounder (in 1983) and President of Don Congdon Associates.

How did you become an agent? Began working as an assistant to a literary agent in 1977.

Knowing what you do now, would you do it again? If not, what might you do instead? Would do it again.

Do you charge fees? If yes, please explain. No reading fees. Will charge for overseas postage, purchasing copies of books, and unusual expenses subject to author's prior approval.

What do the "Big 5" mean to you? A source of steady income and support from Bertelsmann-Pearson/Penguin Random House, CBS/Simon & Schuster, Lagardère/Hachette, News Corp./HarperCollins, von Holtzbrinck/Macmillan.

How do you feel about independent/small presses? Ardently support them.

What are your feelings about self-publishing? Support it.

Do you think Amazon is good or bad — or both — for the book business? Both.

Agent's name: Katie Kotchman

Describe the kinds of works you want to represent. I represent both fiction and nonfiction, but my list is focused primarily on the latter. In nonfiction, I specialize in business (all categories), narrative nonfiction (particularly popular science and social/cultural issues), how-to (general self-help in areas of success, motivation, and psychology), and pop culture. I'm actively seeking new nonfiction clients with built-in platforms from whom I can learn something new. In fiction, I'm looking to represent women's fiction, realistic young adult, literary fiction, and psychological thrillers. In all areas, I'm particularly interested in characters who struggle with dualities of nature and/or culture, as the topics of cognitive dissonance and those who straddle two different worlds fascinate me. I have soft spots for the Midwest, family secrets, and a good underdog story.

Describe what you definitely don't want to represent. Thrillers in which the plot revolves around terrorism, medical thrillers, high fantasy, and anything paranormal. No screenplays or poetry either.

How do you want writers to pitch you? Email queries should be sent to dca@don congdon.com, with the subject line "Query: Katie Kotchman."

Describe your education and professional history. I grew up in a small town in North Dakota before heading east to attend Vassar College. I majored in English with a concentration on late 19th- and early 20th-century American literature, but I ended up writing my thesis on Shakespeare's *Richard II* tetralogy. After graduation, I interned at Denise Marcil Literary Agency before being hired full-time as Denise's assistant. That role quickly expanded to include duties as business manager as well as selling audio rights, managing digital rights, and vetting domestic contracts. In 2008, I joined Don Congdon Associates to build my own list as an agent. I act as the agency's digital rights manager, and I'm also a member of the Association of Authors' Representatives' Digital Innovation Committee.

Knowing what you do now, would you do it again? If not, what might you do instead? I'd definitely do it all over again, but I would have made sure to complete an internship or two before graduating from college.

Do you charge fees? If yes, please explain. No. I don't get paid unless my client gets paid.

When and where were you born, and where have you lived? North Dakota, New York, New Jersey, and Connecticut, in that order.

What do you like to do when you're not working? I'm often curled up on my couch reading, whether that's a novel, blogs, news, long-form essays, or social-media posts. Reality TV and crime series are a guilty pleasure, and I watch far more than I should probably admit to in print. And I like to travel and explore — both near and far.

List some of the titles you have recently placed with publishers. Matt Mayberry's *Winning Plays: A Top Athlete's Advice to Tackle Adversity and Achieve Success*, which shares Matt's personal struggle to overcome addiction and achieve his dream of playing in the NFL, only to sustain what would become a career-ending injury in his first game with the Chicago Bears; he's now a successful motivational speaker and maximum performance strategist for Fortune 500 companies, universities, and other organizations (Center Street, Hachette); Inc.com contributing editor, LinkedIn Influencer, and ghostwriter Jeff Haden's *Become*, which debunks the frequently touted maxim that willpower is the key to reaching your biggest goals and instead offers a practical methodology for success (Portfolio/Penguin Random House); *New York Times* and *USA Today* bestselling author Joan Johnston's next three books, a continuation of her long-running *Bitter Creek* series (Bantam Dell/Penguin Random House); Robert P. Crease's *In Einstein We Trust?: How Science Gained, Then Lost, Its Authority*, which traces the history of science to explain how we've ended up at our current cultural moment of crisis and divisiveness where science is often regarded with skepticism and even contempt (Norton).

Describe your personality. Tenacious, thoughtful, detail-oriented, ambivert — this is starting to sound like keywords you should include in a job application, so I'll stop there.

DOUG GRAD LITERARY AGENCY, INC. ❖ www.dgliterary.com

68 Jay Street, Suite N3, Brooklyn, NY 11201, 718-788-6067

Agent's name and contact info: Doug Grad, doug.grad@dgliterary.com

Describe the kinds of works you want to represent. Multigazillion-dollar bestsellers written by the world's nicest celebrities. Failing that, commercial fiction and nonfiction along these lines: thriller, mystery (and all subgenres of both), literary fiction, historical fiction, romantic comedy (sort of romance lite, but not chick lit), military fiction, memoir, military history, sports, music, business, history, humor, popular reference, popular science, etc.

Describe what you definitely don't want to represent. Children's illustrated books, young adult fiction, fantasy, religion, boring books, or books written by truly crazy people.

How do you want writers to pitch you? Email query to query@dgliterary.com.

Describe your education and professional history. I have a BS degree (that's Bachelor of Science, not Bull Shit) in speech from Northwestern University (that's in Chicago, not Boston — the one in Boston is Northeastern). What the heck is a BS in speech? I was a theater major — an actor, to be more precise, which was excellent training to become a book editor, at least for fiction. For four years I studied character, plot, dialogue, pacing, structure, and history.

Professionally, my first job was in a ladies' lingerie shop in Jackson Heights, Queens, owned by the father of a friend of mine who asked me the $64 question: "How'd you like to get into women's underwear?" Little did I know that meant I'd be a stock boy lugging size 44 girdles from the basement to the second floor. (All true, by the way.)

I got my start in book publishing as a temp for Michael Korda at Simon & Schuster in 1986. I started as an editorial assistant at Pocket Books (Simon & Schuster) in 1987, then was promoted to associate editor in 1990. I moved to Ballantine (Random House) in 1995 as an editor, and to New American Library (Penguin) in 1998 as a senior editor. I went to ReganBooks (HarperCollins) in 2005 as a senior editor, and then opened my agency after a 22-year editorial career in 2008.

How did you become an agent? It was either that or sell insurance for New York Life with my late uncle's brother.

Knowing what you do now, would you do it again? If not, what might you do instead? Well, what I would do differently would be to become an agent 10 years earlier, when there was a lot of money to be made in publishing. Let me put it this way: I wouldn't be worried about putting my kids through college if I'd done that. What might I have done instead? I'm still trying to figure out what I want to be when I grow up, and since I'm too old to play center field for the Mets, I'll have to get back to you on that when I come up with an answer.

Do you charge fees? If yes, please explain. I don't, but I should charge an idiocy fee to people who can't be bothered to read what I'm looking for. It's amazing how many people submit young adult fantasy to me. Or send me obvious mass emailings addressed to "Dear Agent." I have a name, people!

When and where were you born, and where have you lived? I was born in Queens, New York, in 1962, 10 days before the Mets played their first game. I grew up in Forest Hills, and my 90-year-old dad still lives in the same apartment in which I grew up. I lived in Chicago (well, Evanston, Illinois) for my four years of college, then came back to New York, where I got an apartment in Astoria before it was cool. I live in Park Slope, Brooklyn, now, which is a beautiful but weird place to live.

What do you like to do when you're not working? I love to play golf. I've played more the last couple of years than I had for a couple of decades. I greatly enjoy playing with my 13-year-old son, who hits the ball about 180 yards off the tee. I told him he has to hit from the regular tee — no more ladies' tees for him! I also love jazz — classic jazz. I play the saxophone and have a pretty good LP and CD collection. I don't get to see as much live jazz as I'd like, however. I also enjoy going to the theater and to baseball and hockey games. Let's go, Mets! Let's go, Rangers!

List some of the titles you have recently placed with publishers. I've recently sold a couple of romantic comedies to Kensington by Sue Pethick — *Boomer's Bucket List* and *The Dog Who Came for Christmas*. These books came out of a conversation with Sue's editor, whom I've known and been friends with for 25 years. He basically said, "I have an idea for a book about a dog who saves a couple's troubled relationship. Do you have a writer who could write that?" And I did! The result was Sue's first book under her own name: *Pet Friendly*. I'm very excited about it, and the new contract is for her third and fourth books — all stand-alones around a dog theme.

I've also sold a memoir of Hall of Fame hockey great Pat LaFontaine to Triumph Books, written with *New York Times* hockey writer Allan Kreda. Pat is the only player in the NHL who ever played his entire career with all three New York State teams — the Islanders, the Rangers, and the Buffalo Sabres. He has great stories, and Pat's share of the income will all go to charity for children's hospitals. Pat is a true gentleman, and it's an honor to work with him.

Describe your personality. Easygoing and fun-loving until I'm pushed around. Then I'm your worst nightmare. Go ahead, make my day.

What do you like reading//watching/listening to on your own time? I have an eclectic list of books on my nightstand. I recently finished hockey player Tie Domi's memoir, *Shift Work* (Simon & Schuster Canada). It's number one in Canada! Short book, but a lot of fun, and very insightful into the mind of the man with the third-most penalty minutes in NHL history. I'm also reading a bio of choreographer Hermes Pan published by Oxford University Press — the guy who worked on all the Fred Astaire–Ginger Rogers movies back in the 1930s. It's kind of dry, though. I just started *Inside of a Dog: What Dogs See, Smell, and Know* by Alexandria Horowitz (Scribner), because I want to figure out what makes my dog (a pug named Winston) tick. It's pretty cool. Earlier this year I read *The Smoke at Dawn* by Jeff Shaara (Ballantine), a novel about the Civil War in the west — the west being Chattanooga, Tennessee. I also read a very cool and crazy noirish science fiction novel called *The Dark Side* by Anthony O'Neill (Simon & Schuster). I'm all over the place! What's fun is that when I have lunch with editors, they give me their favorite books they've recently published, and sometimes I find the time to read them.

Do you think the business has changed a lot over the past few years? If yes, please explain. Oh, yes. There's a desperation out there felt by authors and agents (maybe not so much by editors). Ebooks are not growing — they've leveled off. Book sales have stopped falling, but they're not what they were pre-ebook. Amazon is the 500-pound gorilla in the room with seemingly nothing stopping it. On the other hand, I'm seeing a good amount of growth in smaller publishers and start-ups, picking up the slack and filling the holes.

What do the "Big 5" mean to you? Three things: money, money, and money. That and resources (which is kind of like money). They often spend more on covers, they have great distribution, and they certainly spend more on advances. But they're inflexible on royalties, option clauses, etc., don't do a wonderful job with promotion or publicity unless you're a celebrity or bestselling author, and aren't the be-all and end-all. Unless you like money. As the great Max Bialystock said, "Money is honey."

How do you feel about independent/small presses? Mixed — some do a great job. Some are freakin' disasters. And believe me, I know what I'm talking about — I've made my share of no-advance deals, of tiny-advance deals, I've heard all the promises, seen all the results, and run into all the problems. But as they say about the lottery, you've got to be in to win it.

What are your feelings about self-publishing? It's not the panacea that authors think it is. For some authors, it's the only way they'll ever get published. For a very small number, it's a way to incredible riches. For most, it's an ego stroke that will actually hurt their chances of getting picked up by a larger house and getting paid. My advice to good authors — unless you're writing some really weird stuff that won't find a home except for self-publishing — is don't do it.

Do you think Amazon is good or bad — or both — for the book business? Both. No explanation needed.

What do you like and dislike about your job? I am so lonely. Won't someone please come and work with me? All kidding aside, I do miss working in a big office full of like-minded people. Being on email and the phone just isn't the same. That's why lunches with editors are so important.

I dislike the fact that it's now so hard to make a living doing this. I'm crazy busy most of the time, all in the hope that one of my projects will hit big. It's at the point that I don't even want to talk about what I'm working on anymore, because if it doesn't sell, I just sound like a jackass.

I really love my authors. And I'll only work with people I like. I call that my "Life's too short" philosophy. I won't work with jerks. Because I'm my own boss, and I don't have to! I love my freedom, and my lack of having to be in meetings all day and leaving all the corporate BS behind that I had to deal with when I was an editor, like office politics. It was sometimes like being in high school! Also, if I want to go play golf on a summer Friday, I can just go do it, assuming my wife isn't using the car.

What are ways prospective clients can impress you, and what are ways they can turn you off? Prospective clients can impress me by writing great material and being cool and realistic and fun. They can turn me off by writing rotten material, being egotistical jerkwads, or being needy nutjobs. But I'm not standoffish and unapproachable — I don't bite. Best place to impress me — writers' conferences. Don't be shy, but don't think I'm suddenly your best friend. And please, don't send me a friend request after we've met once and spoken for five minutes at a book-signing event. I mean, really.

How would you describe the "writer from hell"? The writer from hell calls me all the time. Doesn't deliver on time. Complains about everything — advance, publicity, editor, etc. Tells me how to do my job. Yet I see the writer on Facebook posting all kinds of meaningless crap instead of putting butt to chair and fingers to keyboard. Be a professional and write — don't be an amateur and talk about writing.

Describe a book you would like to write. I'd love to write about the crazy era of big New York book publishing in the 1980s when I came up — it would be like *Mad Men* only with bigger egos, more celebrities, and more drugs and less booze. Same amount of sex, though. Yeah, that'll never happen. And the only people who'd want to read it would be the same people who'd sue me for writing it!

Do you believe in a higher and/or lower "power"? I was bar mitzvahed. That has to count for something.

Is there anything you wish to express beyond the parameters of the preceding questions? I would like authors to realize that what an agent does is indeed worth the 15 percent commission. I don't just negotiate a contract. I'm a marriage broker, and if things go wrong, a marriage counselor. I want both editors and authors to have good relationships, which means I get dumped on by both so that they can maintain a good working vibe. It's really hard to do. Some young agents don't understand or have much respect for authors — especially older authors who have published many books. Wow, that is a hard one to negotiate. I bring nearly 30 years of experience to what I do, experience that was gained the hard way. Authors, you're paying for your agents' expertise and advice — make good use of it!

DUNHAM LITERARY, INC. ❖ www.dunhamlit.com

110 William Street, Suite 2202, New York, NY 10038

Agent's name and contact info: Bridget Smith, query@dunhamlit.com

Describe the kinds of works you want to represent. I represent middle grade, young adult, and adult fiction. I love stories that take place in another world, whether speculative or historical, but those that shed light on our contemporary world grip me, too. I want the focus to be on the characters, and I like a literary style. I'm more inclined toward stories about women, or at least with lots of complex female characters in them. I'm also interested in diversity of all kinds.

Describe what you definitely don't want to represent. I don't want thrillers or romances for adults: they aren't genres that speak to me. In general, I don't connect with books that are very commercial in style or stories that play old tropes straight. I don't want prescriptive nonfiction. And I *definitely* don't want screenplays — please stop sending them.

How do you want writers to pitch you? By email, please! Query and first five pages in the body of the email to query@dunhamlit.com. No attachments.

Describe your education and professional history. I graduated from Brown University in 2010 with a degree in anthropology. Subsequently, I interned at Don Congdon Associates, worked in a secondhand bookstore, and read short-story slush for Tor.com. I started as the assistant at Dunham Literary in 2011 and began building my own list of clients a year later.

How did you become an agent? I worked in radio during college, so I applied to a variety of media jobs after graduation, and publishing was a natural choice for this lifelong book lover. I got an internship at an agency and loved it. Several months later, the agency they shared office space with needed a new assistant, and they recommended me for the job. I've been here ever since!

Knowing what you do now, would you do it again? If not, what might you do instead? Probably! Publishing has its frustrations, but I can't imagine any other job that would be so rewarding, interesting, and filled with people I like.

Do you charge fees? If yes, please explain. No.

When and where were you born, and where have you lived? I was born in New Haven, Connecticut, and grew up in the suburbs nearby, a few blocks from where my parents grew up. I lived in Providence, Rhode Island, during college (and loved it), had a brief study-abroad stint in Paris, and then moved to New York afterward. I currently live on the Upper West Side.

What do you like to do when you're not working? I'm learning the violin and brushing up on my French. I was a competitive athlete from the age of four, so I still like to keep in shape, and I took up running a few years ago. I am also very fond of Netflix.

List some of the titles you have recently placed with publishers. I sold a debut young adult by Emma Mills titled *First & Then* to Macmillan, who published it in 2015. I then sold them her next two young adult novels, *This Adventure Ends* and one as yet untitled. Another recent sale was a debut middle grade by Lee Gjertsen Malone titled *The Last Boy at St. Edith's* to Simon & Schuster.

Describe your personality. Geeky, goofy, opinionated, optimistic.

What do you like reading/watching/listening to on your own time? For the most part, what I represent is what I like to read for fun. It's why I rep those categories! In TV and movies, though, I'm a little more wide-ranging. I love a good romantic comedy or cozy mystery or workplace comedy — but I was also obsessed with *Hannibal* and *Battlestar Galactica*. Anything featuring characters I want to spend a lot of time with can win my heart.

Do you think the business has changed a lot over the past few years? If yes, please explain. I didn't get into publishing until after the ebook boom, so the changes I've seen have been subtler. It seems like publishers are being a little more conservative with what they're willing to take on, but then I've still seen big deals for brilliant debut novels.

How do you feel about independent/small presses? Some are wonderful! They can garner all the respect of a major publisher with more personal attention (though perhaps less money). Some are not. But I'm always willing to consider them! There are some wonderful independent children's publishers in particular.

What are your feelings about self-publishing? It can be the perfect choice for some people, particularly those who are great at self-promotion and like to have control over the process or those in genres that aren't breaking out at the big publishing houses (see, for example, the boom in new adult). But I also see a lot of people who think of it as a shortcut to a traditional deal, and those people are approaching both traditional and self-publishing the wrong way.

Do you think Amazon is good or bad — or both — for the book business? I haven't bought anything from them in years, apart from the Kindle I use for manuscripts — but I also have three bookstores within walking distance of my apartment, including two wonderful indies and a Barnes & Noble. I'm glad Amazon can sell books to people who can't otherwise get to a bookstore. I'm less happy with the way they've taken over bookselling and the pressure they can subsequently put on publishers.

What do you like and dislike about your job? I love working with authors. I love finding books that blow me away and getting to have some say in their development and shape. But the counterpoint to this is that I don't like getting rejections any more than writers do! Once I've chosen a project and invested time in it, the rejection feels personal to me, too.

What are ways prospective clients can impress you, and what are ways they can turn you off? I am really impressed when writers take revision suggestions and run with them. I like when they are open to suggestions but also have articulate, thoughtful reasons for the storytelling choices they've made. I admire optimism and resilience in an industry that says no a lot. But I'm always looking for the writing first!

How would you describe the "writer from hell"? Someone who is needy, impatient, angry, entitled, and far less brilliant than they think they are. Basically, picture the kind of person who responds angrily to a rejection letter.

Describe a book you would like to write. I don't want to be a writer! I like being on this side of the desk. But I often tweet ideas for books I'd like to rep using #mswl (short for manuscript wish list).

EBELING & ASSOCIATES ❖ www.ebelingagency.com

898 Pioneer Road, Lyons, CO 80540, 303-823-6963

Agent's name: Michael Ebeling

Describe the kinds of works you want to represent. Prescriptive nonfiction including health, diet, nutrition, self-help, personal growth, mind-body-spirit, humor, business, career books.

Describe what you definitely don't want to represent. Fiction, memoir, history, children's.

How do you want writers to pitch you? Via email with a solid query letter and a book proposal attached as a Word document or a PDF.

Describe your education and professional history. BS in business from the University of Colorado; MA in holistic health and wellness from Naropa University. Ten years as an author manager and 10 years as a literary agent.

How did you become an agent? I was in the business of managing authors, and I had so many authors coming to me to pitch their books, I decided to make it an extension of my business model.

Knowing what you do now, would you do it again? If not, what might you do instead? I *love* what I do, and now that the publishing world has gone to more of a digital model, it is even more of an exciting time to be in the business.

Do you charge fees? If yes, please explain. No.

When and where were you born, and where have you lived? Born in Escondido, California. Lived in Boulder and Lyons, Colorado, and Maui, Hawaii.

What do you like to do when you're not working? Yoga, mountain biking, motorcycle riding, surfing, and meditating.

List some of the titles you have recently placed with publishers. *The Complete Book of Juicing* by Dr. Michael Murray (500,000 copies in print), *The Wallet Allocation Rule*, *Recipe Hacker 2* (BenBella), *Get It* (BenBella).

Describe your personality. I am very passionate about my authors and their messages and brands. I love living in the mountains with my dog, breathing the fresh air, traveling the world. I *love* life!

What do you like reading/watching/listening to on your own time? Health podcasts and reads, books on meditation and consciousness, all kinds of music and concerts.

Do you think the business has changed a lot over the past few years? If yes, please explain. Yes, the playing field is being leveled with all the advances in the digital world. Anyone can become an author now and build their brand with all the tools available on the net. It is a very exciting time for authors and not the "exclusive club" it used to be.

What do the "Big 5" mean to you? Not sure what your Big 5 are, but mine are platform, brand, message, writing, and concept.

How do you feel about independent/small presses? Love them — they fill a great niche.

What are your feelings about self-publishing? Great. Again, a book is more of a glorified business card these days to help an author build their brand and platform. Get your book out and use it to start promoting yourself.

Do you think Amazon is good or bad — or both — for the book business? I would say it is both good and bad.

What do you like and dislike about your job? I dislike authors who do not respect the process and think their message is the most important in the world. I also don't appreciate the lack of response, which is rampant throughout the industry.

What are ways prospective clients can impress you, and what are ways they can turn you off? They can impress me with a kick-ass query letter with an even better proposal attached. What turns me off is when they are pushy, calling me all the time and otherwise not being respectful of my time.

Describe a book you would like to write. Books on marketing, brand building, achieving your highest calling, and seeing the world through a different lens.

Do you believe in a higher and/or lower "power"? Higher, of course, but not religious. Only spiritual.

Is there anything you wish to express beyond the parameters of the preceding questions? Love the process, deliver the message you were put here to share. Do not play small, as that is actually egotism. Be humble and shine your biggest light!

EDITE KROLL LITERARY AGENCY, INC.

20 Cross Street, Saco, ME 04072, 207-283-8797

Agent's name and contact info: Edite Kroll, ekroll@maine.rr.com

Describe the kinds of works you want to represent. Children's fiction as well as picture books written and illustrated by the same artist; adult nonfiction of interest to general readers, especially women; books by women of international backgrounds; feminist books that are not tracts.

Describe what you definitely don't want to represent. No diet, how-to, cookery, gardening, science fiction and fantasy, adult mystery/suspense, romance, coffee-table books, star-focused memoir.

How do you want writers to pitch you? Brief email describing book and pertinent background.

Describe your education and professional history. German-born British/American; children's book editor at British and US publishers before becoming an agent in NYC over 30 years ago.

How did you become an agent? Decided to become an agent after a brief stint in consumer package-goods marketing. Instead of running a publishing department, I felt being an agent would allow me to continue working directly with writers, both for adults and children.

Do you charge fees? If yes, please explain. I only charge mutually agreed-upon legal fees and high copying/scanning fees.

When and where were you born, and where have you lived? Born in Germany and lived there through high school, after which I spent years in London and Paris, before moving to New York City in the late 1960s.

What do you like to do when you're not working? Reading, meeting with friends, being involved in political action, travel.

List some of the titles you have recently placed with publishers. Maria Padian's fourth young adult (Algonquin, fall 2017); a critical biography of Eqbal Ahmad by Stuart Schaar (Columbia University Press, October 2016); a fifth picture book in the *Pig in a Wig* series by Emma Virjan (HarperCollins, 2018); several US and 6 foreign reissues of books by Charlotte Zolotow; 12 foreign sales of books by Shel Silverstein.

Describe your personality. Ever curious, open to different people and experiences, direct, an optimist.

What do you like reading/watching/listening to on your own time? Reading adult literary fiction and mystery/suspense. Classical music and music by singer-songwriters.

Do you think the business has changed a lot over the past few years? If yes, please explain. I think the business has become one of less personal contact and more control over editorial decisions exerted by marketing and sales departments.

How do you feel about independent/small presses? I like and support them.

What are your feelings about self-publishing? Fine, if authors are willing to put in the necessary time for promotion.

Do you think Amazon is good or bad — or both — for the book business? Good in that it makes it easier for readers to acquire books; bad because it wields such enormous influence and focuses so much on commercial books.

What do you like and dislike about your job? Love working to help writers realize their passion. Dislike the endless follow-up needed to get anything done by publishers.

What are ways prospective clients can impress you, and what are ways they can turn you off? Writers impress me with good writing, and they turn me off by querying me on books I specifically do *not* want/look for.

Describe a book you would like to write. None.

EDWARD B. CLAFLIN LITERARY AGENCY, LLC

128 High Avenue, Suite #2, Nyack, NY 10960

Agent's name and contact info: Ed Claflin, ebclaflin@gmail.com

Describe the kinds of works you want to represent. Nonfiction only: narrative history, popular psychology, consumer health, food, business.

Describe what you definitely don't want to represent. No poetry or fiction.

How do you want writers to pitch you? Online queries or proposals.

Describe your professional history. Twelve years in business with an eclectic list.

How did you become an agent? I am a former editor of fiction and nonfiction.

Knowing what you do now, would you do it again? If not, what might you do instead? There is nothing more satisfying than working with authors who are constantly seeking new approaches and are open to new ideas.

Do you charge fees? If yes, please explain. No reading fees.

When and where were you born, and where have you lived? I was born in Stamford, Connecticut, and have lived in Cleveland, Philadelphia, and New York City.

What do you like to do when you're not working? Sailing, skiing, hiking, theater, movies.

List some of the titles you have recently placed with publishers. *The Battle of the Somme* (Lyons), *The Craft Beer Revolution* (Palgrave), *The New Iron Skillet Cookbook* (Sterling), *The Wisdom We're Born With* (Sterling), *Donut Nation* (Running Press), *The Leadership Campaign* (Career Press), *Dinosaur Derivatives and Other Trades* (Wiley).

What are your feelings about self-publishing? Self-publishing is an excellent way to publish memoirs that do not have a commercial "hook," but are life stories that deserve recognition.

What do you like and dislike about your job? Authors become friends, and we are engaged in a shared mission — to get their books into print.

What are ways prospective clients can impress you, and what are ways they can turn you off? If a writer is unwilling or unable to create a salable proposal, we're stuck. Very few editors want to read a whole manuscript before making a decision.

How would you describe the "writer from hell"? A writer who demands perfection in the editing and publishing process, but fails to follow through with the advocacy and promotion of his or her published title.

THE ETHAN ELLENBERG LITERARY AGENCY ❖

ethanellenberg.com

155 Suffolk Street, #2R, New York, NY 10002, 212-431-4554

Agents' names: Ethan Ellenberg, Evan Gregory, Bibi Lewis

Describe the kinds of works you want to represent. *Ethan*: I love commercial fiction. I acquire science fiction/fantasy, romance, suspense and would consider almost anything that is a compelling read. I also have a children's list and actively seek middle grade and young adult writers and author-illustrators. In nonfiction, I prefer storytellers, so it has to be narrative nonfiction.

Describe what you definitely don't want to represent. No poetry.

How do you want writers to pitch you? The best submission is an introductory letter, a synopsis, and the first three chapters by email (see website).

Describe your education and professional history. I have a degree in philosophy from Queens College. My whole career has been in professional book publishing — Berkley first, then Bantam, then this agency.

How did you become an agent? I was working at Bantam and decided this was the best job in the business and an ideal match for my skills.

Knowing what you do now, would you do it again? If not, what might you do instead? It was rocky, and I would have benefited from working at an established agency, but I have no regrets.

Do you charge fees? If yes, please explain. No. But banks do, so there is some friction in money transmittal.

When and where were you born, and where have you lived? Native New Yorker, haven't left much.

What do you like to do when you're not working? Ironically I read a lot — what I don't represent, serious history, religion, and philosophy. It's a nice break.

List some of the titles you have recently placed with publishers. I represented John Scalzi for his sale of 13 properties to both Tor and Audible. Please see the website's news columns; we are very active and continue to make sales for both established and new clients. We've sold recent work for MaryJanice Davidson, Christine Warren, Bertrice Small estate, Eric Rohmann, Candy Fleming, Marthe Jocelyn, Ian Douglas, Shelly Laurenston, Sharon Shinn, Tony Peak, James Cambias, and Gail Martin.

Describe your personality. An unfair question, but an enthusiast for books and authors should interest those seeking an agent.

What do you like reading/watching/listening to on your own time? Per above, history, philosophy, religion, and lots of good fiction.

Do you think the business has changed a lot over the past few years? If yes, please explain. It's gone through a revolution. We still license many books to the Big 5 and others, and selling translation rights has always been a big focus here. But now audio has emerged as a key format and with our own publishing arm, "agent-supported publishing," we are publishing many books in eformat. So there are four key areas now: traditional licenses, translation, audio, and agent-supported publication. The market has dramatically reshaped itself. Print is still key, but the parallel universe of ebooks is also key.

What do the "Big 5" mean to you? I don't think it's debatable; it's the five big publishing conglomerates that control most of the market for print books.

How do you feel about independent/small presses? They're great. I hope this area thrives.

What are your feelings about self-publishing? It has its place. I respect any author who is simply trying to succeed. It's created some marketplace issues, but that is for everyone to contemplate.

Do you think Amazon is good or bad — or both — for the book business? Amazon is great, they've created the marketplace for ebooks, and they are generating great income for the entire industry. But their market share is too large; it's unhealthy. It's the job of all other players not to let a single player dominate.

What do you like and dislike about your job? I like almost everything. Too busy sometimes, but that's the price.

What are ways prospective clients can impress you, and what are ways they can turn you off? It's talent-driven. We love the work; we don't have to love the writer. The more professional you are, the more impressed we are. We're cordial, professional, reasonable, and focused, and we'd like you to be that way, too.

How would you describe the "writer from hell"? We don't represent anyone like that. If you are unreasonable, most likely things wouldn't work out here.

Describe a book you would like to write. Can't give away my secrets.

Do you believe in a higher and/or lower "power"? Not sure what you have going here.

Is there anything you wish to express beyond the parameters of the preceding questions? Anyone who loves storytelling can be happy here. We never run out of excitement and enthusiasm for great work. It's a challenging life; we try to make it easier and we try to get you paid. We are your business partner and adviser, and we never forget that.

THE EVAN MARSHALL AGENCY ❖ www.evanmarshallagency.com

1 Pacio Court, Roseland, NJ 07068-1121, 973-287-6216

**Agent's name and contact info: Evan Marshall,
evan@evanmarshallagency.com**

Describe the kinds of works you want to represent. Full-length adult and young adult fiction in all genres.

How do you want writers to pitch you? Email to evan@evanmarshallagency.com. In the body of the email: a query letter, the first three chapters of the novel, and a synopsis of the entire novel.

Describe your education and professional history. I received my bachelor's degree from Boston College and then attended the Radcliffe Publishing Procedures Course. I began my publishing career as a book editor, working at Houghton Mifflin, Ariel Books, New American Library, Everest House, and Dodd, Mead. I then became a literary agent, working at the Sterling Lord Agency for three years before founding my own agency in 1987. I am the author of several nonfiction books, including *The Marshall Plan for Novel Writing* (now available as software), and 10 mystery novels.

How did you become an agent? I started on the editorial side, wanted to work on a broader range of books, and switched to the agenting side.

Knowing what you do now, would you do it again? If not, what might you do instead? Yes, I'm glad I made the switch. I love working with authors, helping them grow their careers and achieve their goals.

Do you charge fees? If yes, please explain. No.

When and where were you born, and where have you lived? I was born in Boston in 1956 and raised in Sharon, Massachusetts. I have lived in New York City and several towns in New Jersey; I now live in Roseland, New Jersey.

What do you like to do when you're not working? Read, travel, paint.

List some of the titles you have recently placed with publishers. *Kill without Mercy* by Alexandra Ivy, *Highland Master* by Hannah Howell, *My Very Best Friend* by Cathy Lamb, *Murder at the Breakers* by Alyssa Maxwell, *Silence of the Lamps* by Karen Rose Smith.

Describe your personality. I am outgoing, energetic, prompt, and creative. I am a people person and enjoy working with and getting to know the authors I represent. I see my relationship with a client as a creative collaboration.

What do you like reading/watching/listening to on your own time? Suspense novels, mystery, narrative nonfiction, self-improvement books.

Do you think the business has changed a lot over the past few years? If yes, please explain.
Yes! It's all about digital, and the new avenues for success make the business more exciting than ever.

What do the "Big 5" mean to you? Hachette Book Group, HarperCollins, Macmillan, Penguin Random House, Simon & Schuster.

How do you feel about independent/small presses? The playing field has been leveled to a large extent, so that independent/small presses have the opportunity to achieve the same success with their titles as the big players. I enjoy working with smaller publishers that work hard on marketing, distribution, publicity, and promotion. They must bring something to the table; otherwise an author might as well self-publish.

What are your feelings about self-publishing? Self-publishing has made it possible for millions of authors who couldn't get through the New York gates to make their work available to the world; many authors are not even bothering to try the traditional publishers. In self-publishing, strict categories in fiction are not as important, and a lot of fresh new work is being done. Authors have far more control over how their work is marketed and sold. I have recently started a new division in my agency to handle subsidiary rights for the top indie authors: Indie Rights Agency. We are always looking for new talent to work with.

FELICIA ETH LITERARY REPRESENTATION ❖ www.ethliterary.com

555 Bryant Street, Suite 350, Palo Alto, CA 94301

Agent's name: Felicia Eth

Describe the kinds of works you want to represent. I represent nonfiction and adult fiction. Nonfiction tends to be varied: narrative nonfiction dealing with history, science, nature, social issues, travel, biography, cultural issues, food, new trends; business books on big-concept ideas; journalism; and lots of other areas too eclectic to mention, plus some big-idea psychology and offbeat quirky ideas.

Fiction is all adult, on the literary rather than commercial side. I have a strong interest in international settings and unique voices and am open to magical realism that's not traditional fantasy. I look for fresh takes on any kind of story regardless of what the book is — women's, thrillers, multigenerational.

Describe what you definitely don't want to represent. I don't do poetry, young adult or children's, genre novels (sci-fi/fantasy), mysteries, big-scope thrillers, and Westerns and rarely do historicals, though open to them. I don't handle "merchandise" kinds of books, photography books, too much in parenting, how-to, autobiography, etc.

How do you want writers to pitch you? Prefer a query letter to begin with.

Describe your education and professional history. I have a BA in English from Brandeis University, with additional coursework at McGill University. I am Phi Beta Kappa, summa cum laude. I've worked in varied ends of this business, an agent on both coasts, 10 years with Writers House in New York, more years based on the West Coast with my own agency. Previously I worked in the movie business in New York story departments, with Palomar Pictures and Warner Brothers. Additionally I served briefly as West Coast acquiring editor for St. Martin's Press.

How did you become an agent? Working in the story departments of two movie companies, I covered the book business, reading properties for movie/TV potential, and realized I was more interested in the original work than in its ability to convert to the screen. Additionally I'd deferred going to journalism school, but realized I could have as much influence on what "stories" got out in this regard.

Knowing what you do now, would you do it again? If not, what might you do instead? Who's to say — no question the business has changed enormously.

Do you charge fees? If yes, please explain. No fees charged.

When and where were you born, and where have you lived? I was born in New York, a typical baby boomer, who moved to Teaneck, New Jersey, where I grew up very much a New Yorker in sensibility. However, I have since lived in Boston, Montreal, Washington, DC, and San Francisco, so I have a wider scope of personal experiences and attitudes, though admittedly of a "coastal nature."

What do you like to do when you're not working? Love to garden, travel, hang out with animals and friends.

List some of the titles you have recently placed with publishers. A Shift of Mind: A Quantum Approach to Personal Life Mastery, Walking with Abel: Journeys with Nomads, The Thin Place, Snowblind: Stories of Alpine Obsession.

Describe your personality. Direct, funny, demanding, tenacious, slightly irreverent.

What do you like reading/watching/listening to on your own time? Anything good, though not so into "big pop-culture stuff."

Do you think the business has changed a lot over the past few years? If yes, please explain. Absolutely, but this would take way more time and space than we have here to discuss. Suffice it to say that there have been so many changes. Major trade houses are first focused on big books that have strong commercial possibility; the contribution they have to make is a secondary consideration. Publishers fear it's difficult to break something out and so often pass on wonderful projects. Smaller houses and university presses have become part of the mix, doing lots of interesting publishing that might have gotten left behind otherwise. But despite these plusses, getting major attention is often more difficult than for bigger houses, particularly in light of reduced review possibilities. It is a very challenging publishing climate.

What do the "Big 5" mean to you? Come on — it's obviously the major conglomerates that between them account for most of the larger publishing imprints.

How do you feel about independent/small presses? Depends on which ones. Some are terrific, doing great publishing, and I submit to them all the time. Others are barely scraping by, paying substandard everything, and not supplying the supposed "individual attention" they claim to. So it's a case-by-case answer.

What are your feelings about self-publishing? Ah, a perfectly viable alternative for lots of people who are writing books for diverse reasons. But it's very hard to get any commercial traction unless you devote yourself to it unflinchingly, have a background yourself in marketing/publicity, and have either an enormous family or incredible outreach through social-media, professional, or avocational contacts.

Do you think Amazon is good or bad — or both — for the book business? Both of course. They have transformed this business and to see them only as bad would be foolhardy, but does that mean they're concerned about writers? Of course not.

What do you like and dislike about your job? The good is the same as always — reading something incredible, learning about something new, interacting with terrifically talented and interesting people, and feeling you've made the difference in getting it out there for others.

The bad — well, it's tough now for sure. Lots of well-done, important work seems to too easily fall through the cracks these days, for all sorts of reasons. Editors seem to be under tremendous pressure, and this impacts what they can do. It makes it very tough for agents and writers, and so there's a lot of frustration, which I have to deal with.

What are ways prospective clients can impress you, and what are ways they can turn you off? A strong intro letter, with impressive background whether in publishing or otherwise, lots of specifics about past publications, talks, degrees — all in all something that feels unlike every other letter that crosses my desk.

How would you describe the "writer from hell"? Someone who is relentless but doesn't hear what I'm saying. It's important to be tenacious but also to know when to back off. Also someone who's not up-front in sharing all the information I need to know to be effective or who goes behind my back when I'm working on their behalf.

Describe a book you would like to write. Honestly I don't want to be a writer — there are plenty of them out there in the world; that is not my forte.

Do you believe in a higher and/or lower "power"? Seems highly unnecessary for this questionnaire, but that reminds me, I don't handle religious or inspirational books. Nor stories that would be better off being a lawsuit.

Is there anything you wish to express beyond the parameters of the preceding questions? There are lots of terrific agents out there, so don't despair. But likewise agents are unique, so go with one you feel simpatico with.

FINEPRINT LITERARY MANAGEMENT ❖ fineprintlit.com

115 West 29th Street, Third Floor, New York, NY 10001

Agent's name and contact info: Janet Reid, janet@fineprintlit.com

Describe the kinds of works you want to represent. Fiction: crime, thrillers, suspense. Nonfiction: history, biography.

Describe what you definitely don't want to represent. Poetry, screenplays, New Age, health, wellness, spirituality.

How do you want writers to pitch you? Query letter via email.

Describe your education and professional history. Agent for 20 plus years.

How did you become an agent? Sold my soul to a guy at the crossroads.

Knowing what you do now, would you do it again? If not, what might you do instead? Yes. If I couldn't do this job, I'd apply to be a fact checker at the *New Yorker*.

Do you charge fees? If yes, please explain. No.

When and where were you born, and where have you lived? My real life began when I moved to New York City.

What do you like to do when you're not working? Read. Paint my apartment.

List some of the titles you have recently placed with publishers. *Runner* by Patrick Lee and an untitled biography of Adrienne Rich by Hillary Holladay.

Describe your personality. Brusque.

What do you like reading/watching/listening to on your own time? Crime novels.

Do you think the business has changed a lot over the past few years? If yes, please explain. Yes.

What do the "Big 5" mean to you? Half of the Pac-10, right?

How do you feel about independent/small presses? I think they're doing amazing things with little money and a lot of heart.

What are your feelings about self-publishing? I think self-published memoir will be the original source material for many of the next century's historians' works on how people lived in this century. Self-published novels will continue to break readers' hearts.

Do you think Amazon is good or bad — or both — for the book business? I think Amazon is a big retail outlet. It behaves like a big store. Anyone who is surprised or shocked by that isn't paying attention.

What do you like and dislike about your job? I love helping authors get published. I'm not so keen on helping authors adjust to not being published.

What are ways prospective clients can impress you, and what are ways they can turn you off? Send a good query. Send a terrible query.

How would you describe the "writer from hell"? Since I am Satan's literary agent, I describe him as "mine."

Describe a book you would like to write. Well, until Amal beat me to it, *The Autobiography of Mrs. George Clooney.*

Do you believe in a higher and/or lower "power"? Yes. I don't care if you don't, though.

Is there anything you wish to express beyond the parameters of the preceding questions? I keep a blog at jetreidliterary.blogspot.com that answers questions about publishing, particularly about how to query effectively, and at queryshark.blogspot.com that helps authors revise their queries.

Agent's name and contact info: Peter Rubie, peter@fineprintlit.com

Describe the kinds of works you want to represent. Original narrative nonfiction, history, popular science, current events, innovative business and technology, some memoir, spirituality, commercial women's fiction, thrillers, crime, offbeat literary sci-fi and fantasy, middle grade children's fiction and nonfiction, boy-focused young adult, things that excite and interest me.

Describe what you definitely don't want to represent. No romance, screenplays, plays, short stories, or poetry.

How do you want writers to pitch you? By email query letter.

Describe your education and professional history. After college I worked in local and regional newspapers before moving to London to work in Fleet Street and then BBC Radio News. In 1981 I moved to the US and worked a variety of jobs including editor in chief of a local Manhattan newspaper and then freelance editor in publishing before becoming the fiction editor at Walker and Co. for six years or so. I left to become a partner in a boutique literary agency and started my own agency in 2000. In 2007 I merged my company with Stephany Evans's Imprint Agency to form FinePrint, of which I'm the CEO and Stephany is the president.

How did you become an agent? After my boss at Walker drowned unexpectedly (of course), I was invited to become an agent by my then own personal agent and found the work suited me.

Knowing what you do now, would you do it again? If not, what might you do instead? Working with books and authors has always been a passion of mine, and I continue to enjoy the editorial side of things immensely.

Do you charge fees? If yes, please explain. We are a commission-only company.

When and where were you born, and where have you lived? I was born in Taplow, a small village outside London, and have lived in London and Miami and New York, my current city of residence.

What do you like to do when you're not working? I love to write and am a working jazz musician.

List some of the titles you have recently placed with publishers. *No God but Gain* by Stephen Chambers (Verso); *The Man from Berlin* and *The Pale House* by Luke McCallin (Berkley); *Dark Waters* by Chris Goff (Crooked Lane Books); *Pulse, Tremor,* and *Quake* by Patrick Carman (Katherine Tegen); *Backyard* and *Frontyard* by Norman Draper (Kensington); *Sudden Impact* by William P. Wood (Turner); *#OccupytheBible: What Jesus Really Said (and Did) About Money and Power* by Rev. Dr. Susan Thistlethwaite (Astor + Blue); *The Natanz Directive* (Thomas Dunne); *Grimm City: Death's Apprentice* by K. W. Jeter and Gareth Jefferson Jones (Thomas Dunne); *Benedict Hall* by Cate Campbell (a.k.a. Louise Marley; Kensington).

Describe your personality. I'm fairly laid-back these days; enjoy reading, writing, and playing and listening to music.

What do you like reading/watching/listening to on your own time? I'm a *Game of Thrones, Breaking Bad* kind of reader and viewer. But I do have an unspoken vice, Chinese historical epics and martial arts films. I love good historical novels, literate thrillers, crime stories, and intelligent, thought-provoking sci-fi.

Do you think the business has changed a lot over the past few years? If yes, please explain. The business has changed radically in the past few years. Although things are settling down, the impact of digital technology and ebooks has been substantial. This has also accelerated the focus on authors' need not only to be comfortable learning how to write, but also to know how best to market and promote themselves and their work. The loss of bookstores (though they are making a comeback, thankfully) has also radically changed how people find and buy books.

What do the "Big 5" mean to you? This is what we call mainstream publishing, although the medium-size and even smaller-size presses have a place in this field. Self-publishing or independent publishing occupies a large part of the alternative universe of publishing these days, but really does not seriously challenge or alter the dynamics of modern publishing in any substantial way. The number of indie publishers/authors who have broken out from this pack is remarkably small and for the most part is limited to authors who already have a platform they wish to control more carefully and exploit or successful authors unhappy with their experiences with publishers who believe they can get a better return on their work than going through a Big 5 publisher.

How do you feel about independent/small presses? In many cases these presses offer no money up front, so it is difficult for agents to deal with them and make a living at the same time. They can also be exploitive and ineffective in promoting an author's work. But there are also many positive aspects to them, including bringing back into print books that have languished in a limbo of forgotten fame and helping skilled and ambitious authors launch writing careers.

What are your feelings about self-publishing? It clearly has its place and can help authors establish themselves, though it is a hard row to hoe.

Do you think Amazon is good or bad — or both — for the book business? Amazon sort of just "is" these days. It is something we just have to cope with. As a retailer they undeniably dominate book sales and distribution outside of the indie bookstores and chains, but their approach and attitude toward writers and writing can be both deceptive and disingenuous. Overall, their approach to "disrupting the industry" has impacted the industry negatively, and slowly but surely they are coming around to doing business the way it has been done over the years. (For example, they have just opened a physical bookstore.)

What do you like and dislike about your job? Creating books, coming up with ideas, and helping those who have worked hard at their craft get their moment in the sun are deeply rewarding. Dealing with nakedly ambitious people, fearful they will "lose it all," can be draining. The collegial pace of publishing is eroding, and the pace of work has sped up, to the detriment of the industry, I believe.

What are ways prospective clients can impress you, and what are ways they can turn you off? The best way to impress me (and I dare say my colleagues, too) is just to write really well. If you're genuinely prepared to work with me to help you get published, you are my kind of writer. Knowing it all and thinking I am the butler or worse is a serious turnoff for me. I'm a partner, not a servant.

How would you describe the "writer from hell"? They think they know it all and are ambitious to the point that they have no appreciation or loyalty to those who have helped them become a success.

Describe a book you would like to write. A historical crime novel — in fact I'm working on one now.

Do you believe in a higher and/or lower "power"? I believe, if he exists, God helps those who help themselves. And he certainly is not some old man with a beard peering down at us judgmentally and helping or hindering our endeavors.

Additional agents at FinePrint Literary Management: Stephany Evans stephany@fineprintlit.com; Laura Wood, laura@fineprintlit.com; June Clark, june@fineprintlit.com; Penny Moore, penny@fineprintlit.com

FOLIO LITERARY MANAGEMENT, LLC/FOLIO JR. ❖

www.foliolit.com, www.foliojr.com

630 Ninth Avenue, Suite 1101, New York, NY 10036, 212-400-1494

Agent's name and contact info: John Cusick, john@foliolit.com

Describe the kinds of works you want to represent. I represent picture books, middle grade, young adult, and everything in between. I'm seeking unique voices, stories that move readers, moments that make me look up and say, "Wow, yes. I've felt that." I want books that keep me turning the page. I love proactive protagonists, kids and teens chasing a dream or a hero who swings in with a song in her heart and a knife in her teeth. In young adult and middle grade I'm drawn to contemporary realistic stories with strong hooks as well as fresh fantasy set in our world and others. I love stories told in alternate formats (letters, texts, sticky notes?). Give me villains with vulnerability, bad decisions made with the best intentions, flawed heroes, and impossible odds. I love stories about siblings, the arts, and I have a particular soft spot for anything set in the culinary world (restaurants, diners, food trucks, etc.). I'm also seeking innovative, funny, quirky, and vibrant illustrators and author-illustrators. In picture books I'm seeking unforgettable characters, as well as story-driven texts. Some favorites (not represented by me) are *Secret Pizza Party* by Adam Rubin and Daniel Salmieri, *Sparky!* by Jenny Offill and Chris Appelhans, and *That's Not a Good Idea* by Mo Willems.

Describe what you definitely don't want to represent. I do not represent material for adults. I am not currently seeking picture book texts and tend to shy away from sports stories, poetry, and novels with talking animals.

How do you want writers to pitch you? Please send your query along with the first 2,500 words of your manuscript to john@foliolit.com. Please include the word *Query* in the subject line. I try to respond to all queries; however, if you do not hear from me within six weeks, please consider it a pass.

Describe your education and professional history. I began my career in publishing as an agent's assistant with Scott Treimel NY, where I was fortunate enough to learn, along with dog walking and coffee fetching, the ins and outs of publishing. I soon began representing a small list of clients, including Sharon Biggs Waller (*A Mad, Wicked Folly*, Viking Books for Young Readers), Ryan Gebhart (*There Will Be Bears*, Candlewick Press), and Hannah Moskowitz (*A History of Glitter and Blood*, Chronicle Books).

In 2013 I joined Greenhouse Literary and grew my list to include many more critically acclaimed and bestselling authors, including *New York Times* bestseller Tommy Wallach (*We All Looked Up*, Simon & Schuster Books for Young Readers), Courtney Alameda (*Shutter*, Feiwel & Friends), and Gina Ciocca (*Last Year's Mistake*, Simon Pulse). I also began representing picture book authors and illustrators, including Chana Stiefel (*Daddy Depot*, Feiwel & Friends), Julie Bayless (*Roar!* Running Press Kids), and Eric Chase Anderson (*Chuck Dugan Is AWOL*, Chronicle Books).

At Folio Jr. I'll continue to represent a diverse list of iconoclastic voices in picture books, middle grade, young adult, and everything in between.

How did you become an agent? Craigslist! I answered an ad for an agent's assistant/dog walker and began my career at Scott Treimel NY. To begin with, I focused on selling foreign right and subrights and negotiating contracts and soon began representing my own clients. In 2013, I had a small stable of excellent writers, including Ryan Gebhart, Sharon Biggs Waller, and Hannah Moskowitz.

Knowing what you do now, would you do it again? If not, what might you do instead? I love being an agent, advocating for authors and illustrators, working with publishers to find that amazing breakout novel. It really is my dream job.

List some of the titles you have recently placed with publishers. This spring, Tommy Wallach's gorgeous debut *We All Looked Up* was published by Simon & Schuster, and since its release, it has become a *New York Times* bestseller, is sold in thirteen countries, and has been optioned for film by Paramount Pictures. Tommy's follow-up, *Thanks for the Trouble*, is coming out next year, and I cannot wait. I'm also excited about Hannah Moskowitz's new book, *A History of Glitter and Blood*, which is coming from Chronicle Books in August. It's a gritty fantasy that follows a group of fairies in a war-torn city and is truly unlike anything I've ever read. Chronicle's done a beautiful job with the cover and internal artwork; I can't wait to hear what readers think.

Agent's name and contact info: Erin Harris, eharris@foliolitmanagement.com; for queries: www.foliolit.com/erinharris

Describe the kinds of works you want to represent. The short version: I represent literary and upmarket fiction, young adult, and narrative nonfiction. The longer version: Literary and upmarket fiction: I'm seeking novels set against the backdrop of another time, place, or culture; beautifully written contemporary novels about love, friendship, family, and overcoming adversity; novels that incorporate some kind of surreal or fantastical element; novels with mystery and suspense in their DNA. Some favorite nonclient authors: Zadie Smith, Salman Rushdie, Orhan Pamuk, Jennifer Egan, Maria Semple, Tana French, Haruki Murakami, Margaret Atwood, Karen Russell, Téa Obrecht, Sue Monk Kidd, Paula McLain.

Young adult: I'm seeking across the board: diverse characters, engrossing love stories, propulsive plots, and strong prose; contemporary young adult novels with a fresh concept and a singular voice; young adult psychological suspense/mystery; young adult fantasy; speculative young adult or young adult with a touch of magical realism; young adult retellings of classic tales. Some favorite nonclient authors: Gayle Forman, Jandy Nelson, Laurie Halse Anderson, Peter Cameron, John Green, John Corey Whaley, A.S. King, Maggie Stiefvater, Holly Black, Victoria Aveyard, Sabaa Tahir, Danielle Paige.

Nonfiction: I'm seeking memoirs that illuminate another culture or explore cross-cultural conflict; "big idea" books that reveal underlying yet unexpected truths about our society; microhistories. I especially enjoy working with journalists. Some favorite nonclient authors: Geraldine Brooks, Barbara Ehrenreich, Cheryl Strayed, Patti Smith, Roxanne Gay, Leslie Jamison, Jennifer Percy.

Describe what you definitely don't want to represent. I don't represent paranormal romance, romance, chick lit, new adult, screenplays, poetry, flash fiction, or prescriptive nonfiction.

How do you want writers to pitch you? Please query me at eharris@foliolitmanagement.com. You should include your query letter and the first 10 pages of your manuscript or nonfiction proposal pasted into the body of the email. For more information about how to submit, please visit my page on Folio's site: www.foliolit.com/erinharris.

Describe your education and professional history. My life in publishing began in 2007, when I interned for the literary agent William Clark of WM Clark Associates. In 2008, I joined the Irene Skolnick Literary Agency, where I first experienced the thrill of advocating for books I believed in and writers I admired. I worked there for four and a half years, representing my own projects and selling subsidiary rights on behalf of the agency.

Early on, it became apparent to me that there was a need for agents who could think like writers. I'd majored in English at Trinity College (Hartford, CT), studying literature from a critical/academic perspective, but I was eager to hone my creative and editorial skills. This desire led me to pursue an MFA in Creative Writing at The New School. There I studied fiction and nonfiction with Susan Cheever, Sigrid Nunez, Ann Hood, and James Lasdun. I now see myself as a kind of interpreter, an agent conversant in both the language of the writer and the language of the industry, whose job it is to help authors navigate publishing's shifting landscape.

Outside the office, I'm an active participant in New York's literary community. I'm a member of PEN American Center and Women's Media Group as well as a founder and host of H.I.P. Lit, a literary event series based in Brooklyn.

How did you become an agent? I answered a Craigslist ad for an internship at a literary agency. I wound up falling in love with the work and stayed at that agency for almost five years. That's where I got my start and learned the ropes.

Knowing what you do now, would you do it again? If not, what might you do instead? Knowing what I know now, I would absolutely do it again. I have a background in the theater, and I remember a teacher once telling my acting class, "If there's something else you want to do professionally other than act, you should go do that other thing!" I think the same advice applies to agenting. There were other things I wanted to do aside from being a working actor, but there's nothing else I'd rather do than be a literary agent.

Do you charge fees? If yes, please explain. No. At Folio we observe the standards set by the AAR.

When and where were you born, and where have you lived? I was born in Southampton, New York, in the 1980s during a blizzard. I've lived in the Hamptons, Manhattan, Connecticut, and New Jersey.

What do you like to do when you're not working? I like to travel, have dinner parties with friends, go to the movies, visit art museums, swim, binge-watch engrossing television, go to the theater, take long walks in the park, enjoy a glass of wine, and (yes) read!

List some of the titles you have recently placed with publishers. Boston University MFA graduate Erica Ferencik's *The River at Night*, a literary thriller set against the harsh beauty of the Maine wilderness, about four female friends whose idyllic rafting trip descends into an all-too-real nightmare, testing their loyalties and their willingness to fight for survival, pitched as a fictional *Wild* meets *Deliverance* (Gallery); *New York Times* Editor's Choice novelist Daniel Levine's *Hyde*, a reimagining of *The Strange Case of Dr. Jekyll and Mr. Hyde* from the villain's perspective that takes us into the dark backstreets of his 19th-century London (Houghton Mifflin Harcourt); Jennifer Laam's *The Tsarina's Legacy*, a companion novel to *The Secret Daughter of the Tsar* in which a present-day historian claims her birthright as heiress to the lost Romanov throne and transforms Russia by completing a project that Empress Catherine and her prince began two hundred years earlier, told in intertwining historical and contemporary strands (St. Martin's); National Book Award finalist Carla Power's *If the Oceans Were Ink*, built around the year she spent studying the Koran with the renowned Islamic scholar Mohammad Akram Nadwi, providing an exploration of a text that is shaping our world yet remains mysterious to most Westerners and chronicling a friendship between a conservative sheikh and a secular woman (Holt); young adult BEA Buzz Panel author of *Dream Things True* Marie Marquardt's *The Radius of Us*, about a powerful romance between a boy fleeing gang violence in El Salvador, a girl coming to grips with a harrowing assault, and the power of love to transcend (St. Martin's, in a two-book deal). VCFA graduate Katie Bayerl's debut young adult novel *A Psalm for Lost Girls*, pitched in the vein of Jandy Nelson's *The Sky Is Everywhere* meets *True Detective*, set in a small, fictionalized New England city, centering on an abduction that forever alters the lives of three remarkable girls — one who's been missing, one who is living, and one who is dead and rumored to be a saint (Putnam Children's, in a two-book deal); Emiko Jean's young adult debut *We'll Never Be Apart*, about a 17-year-old girl who is committed to a mental institution after her boyfriend dies in a fire set by her troubled twin; to cope, she begins writing the story of her past in foster care — a past she barely understands — and as the truth unravels, she discovers that everything she thought she knew was a lie (Houghton Mifflin Harcourt Children's).

Describe your personality. I'm ambitious, dedicated, hardworking, fun-loving, friendly, and loyal. I present as an extrovert, but I'm secretly an introvert.

What do you like reading/watching/listening to on your own time? I'm fortunate to represent the kinds of books I love to read for pleasure. I think the books on my nightstand right now, which range from literary to upmarket commercial adult fiction to young adult to narrative nonfiction, are emblematic of my tastes. Literary: Lauren Groff's *Fates and Furies*, Helen Phillips's *The Beautiful Bureaucrat*. Upmarket commercial: The galley of Molly Prentiss's forthcoming *Tuesday Nights in 1980*, the galley of Caroline Kepnes's *Hidden Bodies*. Young adult: A. S. King's *I Crawl through It*, Leigh Bardugo's *Shadow and Bone*. Nonfiction: Molly Crabapple's *Drawing Blood*.

Recently I've watched and loved: *Homeland*, *The Affair* (the second season is even better than the first), *Flesh and Bone* (the best! I love ballet, and this show is so dark and daring), *Shameless*, *Game of Thrones*, *The Walking Dead*, *The End of the Tour* (the David Foster Wallace film), *The Experimenter* (about the experiments of Stanley Milgram), *Spotlight*.

I recently inherited a record collection from the 1960s and 1970s, so at home I've been listening to a lot of Joni Mitchell, Van Morrison, James Taylor, and Crosby, Stills, Nash, and Young — but my taste in music is wide-ranging.

Do you think the business has changed a lot over the past few years? If yes, please explain.
I think agents do more editing these days than in years past, especially prior to submitting the work of debut writers to publishers. I also think authors are called upon to be more active participants in their publicity campaigns than perhaps was once the case.

What do the "Big 5" mean to you? The Big 5 (Penguin Random House, Simon & Schuster, Macmillan, Hachette, and HarperCollins) are the publishers I submit to most regularly in a round 1 submissions list, but also in a round 1 submissions list — depending on the type of book — I will likely have included these essential independents: Norton, Grove/Atlantic, Bloomsbury, Graywolf, Houghton Mifflin Harcourt, Candlewick, Chronicle, and Sourcebooks.

How do you feel about independent/small presses? I think they are a truly vital component of our publishing ecosystem! I don't know what we'd do without them.

What are your feelings about self-publishing? If authors have the marketing muscle it takes to promote their own book, then I think self-publishing can be a good alternative for writers who haven't found a home with a traditional publisher.

Do you think Amazon is good or bad — or both — for the book business? I plead the fifth.

What do you like and dislike about your job? I love just about everything about my job, from the thrill of discovering new talent to working with authors in an editorial capacity, so that their manuscripts or proposals are as strong as possible before we go out on submission. I love doing deals, negotiating on behalf of my authors to get the most favorable terms, and finding my authors the perfect home and editor for their book(s). I also love exploiting ancillary rights, whether that's translation, film/TV, audio, or first serial, and I enjoy helping my authors to brainstorm and pursue creative publicity opportunities. I dislike the volume of emails I receive on a daily basis, though by and large I think they're a necessary evil.

What are ways prospective clients can impress you, and what are ways they can turn you off? The number-one way that prospective clients can impress me is by writing an incredible manuscript with a strong concept. At the end of the day, it's all about what's on the page.

Beyond that, I look for writers who conduct themselves in a professional manner, have some knowledge of the industry and how it all works, have carefully researched my agenting practice and are reaching out to me based on that research, have published in well-respected literary magazines, attended residencies, conferences, or MFA programs or worked with a critique group — really, anyone who demonstrates commitment to the craft and treats writing like a job, because it is one.

Writers can turn me off by being unprofessional, by querying me about work that doesn't align with my interests, or by cold-calling me. Agents appreciate authors who can follow the rules, so please make a good first impression by following the submission guidelines on Folio's website.

How would you describe the "writer from hell"? Fortunately, I haven't encountered the "writer from hell" yet, as I'm careful about who I choose to work with! But to piggyback off my last response, I think a "writer from hell" is someone who can't take reasonable direction or instruction. I always think about that great quote from *Jerry Maguire*, "Help me help you." A "writer from hell" is someone who won't let you help them.

Describe a book you would like to write. Though I have an MFA in creative writing, I don't have any aspirations to write, merely to work with my authors in an editorial capacity and to find and sell their great books.

Do you believe in a higher and/or lower "power"? I believe that we all possess a tremendous power for both good and evil, if I can use those big terms. So for me, I believe the "higher" and "lower" powers exist within, not necessarily without.

Agent's name and contact info: Molly Jaffa, molly@foliolit.com

Describe the kinds of works you want to represent. Picture books, middle grade, young adult fiction.

Describe what you definitely don't want to represent. Anything not under the above umbrella.

How do you want writers your novel to molly@foli.

Describe your education an.. .ofessional history. I graduated from Sarah Lawrence College and have been at Folio since 2009. I represent my own list of children's books and codirect the International Rights Department, for which I attend all major international book fairs.

How did you become an agent? I started at Folio as an intern when I was in college and fell in love with the business.

Do you charge fees? If yes, please explain. No.

When and where were you born, and where have you lived? I was born in Dallas, Texas; I now live in Brooklyn, New York.

What do you like to do when you're not working? I love to cook and bake. It's nice to do something that nets immediate results!

List some of the titles you have recently placed with publishers. Julie Murphy's *Ramona Drowning* (Balzer + Bray), Paula Garner's *Phantom Limbs* (Candlewick), Kayla Cagan's *The Pieces of Piper Perish* (Chronicle), Mahtab Narsimhan's *Mission Mumbai* (Scholastic).

What do you like reading/watching/listening to on your own time? TV: *Master Chef* and *Master Chef Jr.*, *Jessica Jones*, *The Walking Dead*, *Empire*, *Scandal*, anything hosted by my hero, Anthony Bourdain. Reading: I try to read a new hardcover a week to stay on top of what's selling well in every category.

How do you feel about independent/small presses? I'm happy to submit to any publisher with a proven track record, strong distribution, and standard payment systems. I don't submit to ebook-only start-ups or to any publishers that don't compensate my authors with a fair advance.

What are your feelings about self-publishing? It can be a great option for some writers, depending on what their publishing goals are. Unfortunately, if a writer has already self-published something and it hasn't become a bestseller, there's not much I can do for them in the way of traditional publishing for that particular project.

What do you like and dislike about your job? I love being an advocate for my authors and negotiating the best possible deals for them. I hate hurting people's feelings when I have to reject projects.

What are ways prospective clients can impress you, and what are ways they can turn you off? Be well read in their genre of choice and have good social-media etiquette.

How would you describe the "writer from hell"? Anyone who's not willing to communicate openly about what they want and need from their publishing career and our relationship. There has to be a solid foundation of trust and honesty between agent and author.

Agent's name and contact info: Jeff Kleinman, jeff@foliolit.com, www.publishersmarketplace.com/members/jkleinman

Describe the kinds of works you want to represent. Fiction: I'm looking for extremely well-written, character-driven books that make me absolutely fall in love with the characters and their world. I represent book-club fiction (not genre commercial, like mystery or romance) and literary fiction and am particularly on the lookout for very well-written thrillers and suspense novels or novels with a great quirky, fun voice — like Melissa DeCarlo's *The Art of Crash Landing*. Nonfiction: I'm particularly interested in narrative nonfiction and memoir and have sold projects in a wide variety of subjects.

Types of projects I'm on the lookout for:

- Books that make a difference. I really love books that make me realize something new about the world or myself — books that will change me for the better. Maybe they celebrate some aspect of life or inspire the reader to try harder. This doesn't mean "inspirational books" (which tend to have a more religious slant and would be better suited to other agents at Folio) as much as inspiring books.

I like well-written, solid stories that charm me to try to do better and be a better person.

- Books with a distinctive, special voice (not sure what I mean? Pick up *The Art of Racing in the Rain* today!).
- Books with a very unique, special, "I haven't seen this before" premise that can be summed up in a sentence or two, but also that don't sound totally crazy. Try telling your book idea to someone who doesn't know you. If, after you do, the person says, "Wow!" that's the kind of thing I'd love to see.
- Upmarket literary suspense/thrillers. I'd love to find upmarket psychological suspense stories with unique concepts and really strong writing.
- Escape stories that take us totally out of our world and into another — for instance, *The Snow Child*, set in the far reaches of 1920s Alaska. (But keep in mind that I don't represent science fiction or fantasy.)
- Upbeat subjects. I avoid "misery memoirs" and books about terrorists bent on destroying civilization.
- History has always been a passion, so I'm on the lookout for something that brings the past to life and makes it relevant.
- Animals are another interest; I grew up in a house that had a lot of animals underfoot, so not surprisingly I find myself doing a lot of animal-oriented books today.

Describe what you definitely don't want to represent. I don't represent children's, middle grade, young adult, Christian, prescriptive (how-to), travel, genre commercial fiction (science fiction/fantasy, Westerns, mystery, romance), poetry, plays, teleplays, screenplays, books on serial killers or children in peril (kidnapped, murdered, victimized, and so forth), or books dealing with the events of September 11, 2001. I also avoid subjects like rape, suicide, and manic-depression and thrillers in which there's some terrorist organization bent on destroying America or the world.

How do you want writers to pitch you? Email only. In your subject line, make it clear this is a submission — include *Query* with your name and the title of the work. Like everybody else these days, I'm besieged with spam and junk email, a lot of which I delete unopened, or it gets sucked into the spam filter without my even seeing it first. I don't want to delete your email by mistake, so try to make it clear that you're contacting me requesting that I review your project. Paste in the first page or so of your material at the bottom of the cover letter (no attachments, please). I generally try to respond to all my email within one minute to a couple of weeks, so if you haven't heard from me within a couple of weeks, please send a follow-up email.

Describe your education and professional history. I have a BA in English and modern studies from the University of Virginia, an MA in Italian from the University of Chicago, and a JD from the Case Western Reserve University School of Law. After practicing law for a couple of years, I teamed up with some literary agents who shared office space with my law firm. After that, it was all downhill. ☺

Knowing what you do now, would you do it again? If not, what might you do instead? If I could do it all over again, I'd buy or steal an RV and drive around all the national parks for the rest of my life. (I haven't figure out the details — like how I could afford gas and food, but it's a pipe dream I'm loathe to let go of.)

Do you charge fees? If yes, please explain. No. At Folio we observe the standards set by the AAR.

When and where were you born, and where have you lived? Born in Cleveland, Ohio. Lived in Chagrin Falls, Ohio (yes, that's a real place; look it up if you don't believe me), Chicago, Minnesota, Virginia, Italy, and probably other places I can't remember anymore.

What do you like to do when you're not working? My wife will tell you that I'm *never* not working.

List some of the titles you have recently placed with publishers. YouTube Head of Culture and Trends Kevin Allocca's *When We Press Play*, an examination of the democratization of culture and art (Bloomsbury); actor and singer-songwriter Val Emmich's debut novel, *The Highs and Lows of Never Forgetting*, the laugh-out-loud, heartbreaking story of a little girl who can't forget befriending a man desperate to remember (Little, Brown; sold on an aggressive preempt, and translation rights already sold to seven countries); the "Sleep Whisperer" W. Chris Winter, MD's *Sleep Revolution*, a game-changing approach to fixing your sleep, once and for all (Berkley); *52 Lessons from a Christmas Carol* author Bob Welch's *Christmas Every Day*, the true story of the founding of America's first theme park, Santa's Workshop — heartwarming inspiration for the dreamer in all of us, highlighting enduring values like hope, joy, faith, wonder, giving back, and reaching for the stars (Convergent); celebrity dog trainer and star of the Emmy-winning CBS show *Lucky Dog* Brandon McMillan's *Make Your Dog a Lucky Dog*, which uses the author's seven Common Commands to train — playfully, carefully, and kindly — any dog, of any age or breed, even the most problematic, in just seven days (HarperOne); journalist Herb Frazier, historian and College of Charleston professor Bernard Edward Powers Jr., and Poet Laureate of South Carolina Marjory Wentworth's *Finding Grace: The Story of Mother Emanuel A.M.E. Church & The Story of All of Us*, which examines the Charleston Church's seminal role in US history to understand the extraordinary selflessness and perseverance of its congregants, with in-depth interviews of victims' families and the survivors of the recent massacre, with a percentage of all proceeds going to the Pinckney Scholarship Fund (Thomas Nelson); Ethel Rohan's *The Kingdom Keepers*, the story of a morbidly obese man who in the wake of his teenage son's inexplicable suicide, begins a weight-loss campaign as the first step in his ambitious plan to rid the world of suicide, a plan that embarrasses his family and shocks his neighbors, but ultimately proves that with courage and love, one big man's small acts can change the world (St. Martin's); American literature professor J. Aaron Sanders's *Speakers of the Dead: A Walt Whitman Mystery* (the first in a planned series featuring Walt Whitman as the protagonist), in which a young Walt Whitman struggles to exonerate his friends from murder charges as he uncovers the dark world of grave robbers who steal corpses for medical colleges (Plume).

Do you think the business has changed a lot over the past few years? If yes, please explain. It's changed in a lot of ways — let's use the word *Amazon*, for instance, since it now controls maybe 70 percent of the book-buying market. But in other ways people — editors, publishers, agents, and readers — are still looking for a great, vivid read.

How do you feel about independent/small presses? Depending on the press, they're a critical component of the publishing ecosystem.

What are your feelings about self-publishing? See Erin Harris's answer (page 310).

Do you think Amazon is good or bad — or both — for the book business? Amazon who?

What do you like and dislike about your job? I love making authors' dreams come true. I hate the constant rejection.

What are ways prospective clients can impress you, and what are ways they can turn you off? For fiction, write a fabulous book with a fresh voice and a compelling, unique perspective and be able to sum up that book in a single, smart, intriguing sentence or two. For nonfiction, *enhance your credentials*. Get published or have some kind of platform or fresh perspective that really stands out above the crowd. Show me (so I can show a publisher) that you're a good risk for publication. Turnoffs include groveling (just pretend this is a job application and act like a professional); providing too much information, telling too much about the project rather than being able to succinctly summarize it; and sending a poorly formatted, difficult-to-read manuscript.

How would you describe the "writer from hell"? Someone who doesn't listen, doesn't incorporate suggestions, and believes the world "owes" him or her a bestseller.

Describe a book you would like to write. I have a list. Now I just need to find some great writers to write them for me!

Do you believe in a higher and/or lower "power"? Yes. My wife.

Is there anything you wish to express beyond the parameters of the preceding questions? A great story can allow you to enter other people's thoughts and lives — and, when you close the book with a sigh, transform you: maybe you're a little more grateful, or a little kinder, or a little wiser. I love books that inspire me to become better, smarter, more present. This has been the case with many of the books I've represented, and it's something

I seek in new projects. I believe strongly that books can make a difference. Good writing and smart ideas can change our world.

Agent's name and contact info: Marcy Posner, marcy@foliolit.com

Describe the kinds of works you want to represent. I straddle the line between adult and children's books (middle grade and young adult only). In the adult world, I'm looking for commercial women's fiction, historical fiction, mystery, biography, history, health, lifestyle — and especially thoughtfully written commercial novels, thrillers with international settings, and narrative nonfiction. In the children's world, I'm looking for smart, contemporary young adult and middle grade novels. A great new mystery series for boys would be fun. I will look at historical fiction and fantasy but am not taking on much in those areas.

Describe what you definitely don't want to represent. Genre romance and mystery, memoir, traditional fantasy, science fiction.

How do you want writers to pitch you? By email, but I'm currently closed to queries.

Describe your education and professional history. I've been in publishing on one side of the fence or the other for 40 years.

How did you become an agent? Sheer luck!

Knowing what you do now, would you do it again? If not, what might you do instead? Yes, I would do it again. If not, Wall Street.

Do you charge fees? If yes, please explain. No.

When and where were you born, and where have you lived? New York, New York, New York.

What do you like to do when you're not working? Spend my time with my grandchildren.

List some of the titles you have recently placed with publishers. *Beauty Sick* by Dr. Renee Engeln, *What Is Baby Doing?* (baby gorilla board books) by Christina Nippert-Eng.

Describe your personality. Outgoing.

What do you like reading/watching/listening to on your own time? Thrillers, mysteries, crime novels.

Do you think the business has changed a lot over the past few years? If yes, please explain. Yes — there is now more than one way for a reader to read a book.

What do the "Big 5" mean to you? It is the big five publishers.

How do you feel about independent/small presses? They are very necessary.

What are your feelings about self-publishing? Don't do it.

Do you think Amazon is good or bad — or both — for the book business? Started out good, now bad.

What do you like and dislike about your job? I dislike rejection — I take everything personally.

What are ways prospective clients can impress you, and what are ways they can turn you off? Good writing impresses me. Not understanding the rules turns me off.

How would you describe the "writer from hell"? Someone who sends me revisions a day after I ask for them. No one can fix things that quickly.

Describe a book you would like to write. None.

FULL CIRCLE LITERARY ❖ www.fullcircleliterary.com

858-824-9269, info@fullcircleliterary.com

Agent's name: Adriana Domínguez

Describe the kinds of works you want to represent. I represent children's books for all ages and select adult fiction and nonfiction. I have a long trajectory of publishing underrepresented authors and illustrators and welcome submissions that offer diverse points of view. Books I have edited or represented have been awarded the Pura Belpré Medal, the Coretta Scott King Honor, and the MPIBA's Reading the West Award, among others; others have been finalists for the National Book Critics Circle Award and the NAACP Award. My list includes national and international bestsellers and titles counted among the "Best of the Year" by Amazon, *Kirkus Reviews, School Library Journal*, the New York Public Library, the Chicago Public Library, Parents.com, Salon.com, and others. On the children's side, I represent fiction and narrative nonfiction as well as author-illustrators. On the adult side, I am looking for diverse fiction that features characters with unique voices telling unforgettable stories with broad appeal. In the area of nonfiction, I seek narrative and pop-culture titles written by authors with rock-solid platforms.

How do you want writers to pitch you? Please see our submission form on our website, www.fullcircleliterary.com. We accept query letters and sample writing, but no attachments. We can't wait to see your project!

Describe your education and professional history. I have 20 years of experience in publishing. Prior to becoming an agent, I was an executive editor at HarperCollins Children's Books, where I managed the children's division of the Rayo imprint. Before that, I was the children's reviews editor at *Críticas* magazine, published by *Library Journal*. I have performed editorial work for both children's and adult publishers. I am also a professional translator; a member of the Brooklyn Literary Council, which organizes the Brooklyn Book Festival; and one of the founders of the Comadres and Compadres Writers Conference in New York City. I am based on the East Coast.

Do you charge fees? If yes, please explain. Full Circle Literary follows standard industry commission rates.

What do you like to do when you're not working? When not working — which is rare — I can be found at the nearest airport, waiting to be whisked away from it all; along with publishing and my family, travel is my biggest passion! Twitter: @VocesBlog.

List some of the titles you have recently placed with publishers. *Darkroom* author Lila Quintero Weaver's *That Year in the Middle Row*, set in Alabama in 1970 against the backdrop of school integration and the Wallace/Brewer gubernatorial primary, in which a girl who is the school's only Latina student discovers a love for running and figures out who she wants to be — and what kind of friends she wants to have — during one tumultuous school year (Candlewick). My growing list of author-illustrators also includes Lorena Siminovich, Rafael López, John Parra, Ana Aranda, and Tony Piedra. My author client list includes award winners and such bestselling writers as Michaela and Elaine DePrince, Katheryn Russell-Brown, Angela Cervantes, and Eric Pierpoint. Adult clients include award-winning authors Reyna Grande and Tim Z. Hernandez.

Agent's name: Lilly Ghahremani

Describe the kinds of works you want to represent. Prescriptive nonfiction from an author with a strong and growing audience. I love books that teach someone how to do something new or live a better life, written in an engaging way. If you are an expert and can prove it and are a great writer and can prove it, I'd love to hear from you! Some areas that are of interest to me right now, in no particular order: health and fitness, self-help, parenting, business, relationships, craft, design, cooking, pop culture and entertainment, humor and gift books, smart and suspenseful fiction (I haven't represented it to date, but I'd love to!), literary fiction (I take on very limited fiction but literary is my sweet spot as a reader), multicultural fiction (especially fiction by and about Middle Eastern women), anything from a University of Michigan graduate — my loyalty is fierce!

How do you want writers to pitch you? Please see our submission form on our website.

Describe your education and professional history. A graduate of the University of Michigan, Ann Arbor (Go Blue!), UCLA School of Law (JD), and San Diego State University's School of Business (MBA), I cofounded Full Circle Literary with Stefanie. But here's how it really began for me: After graduating from UCLA School of Law, I joined a small law firm that represented authors. I soon realized that, although I loved finessing the perfect deal, I wanted to be involved much earlier in helping authors grow and manage their careers. I sold my first book a decade ago to Random House. Since then, I have helped my authors find their way to the perfect house for *them*, whether it is Random House, Penguin, Perseus, Chronicle Books, Simon & Schuster, or many of the other fabulous houses they have to choose from. I work closely with authors on shaping a writing career with longevity, guiding them in how to brand, protect, and market their work throughout the world. I love working with debut authors who show promise, as the thrill of telling authors they have an offer just never gets old.

What do you like to do when you're not working? Whenever time allows, I'm off on a plane to explore somewhere new.

List some of the titles you have recently placed with publishers. James Beard nominee chef Rob Connolly's *Acorns & Cattails: A Modern Cookbook of Forest, Field & Farm*, offering a vibrant palate of modern recipes for the home cook featuring foraged plants, hunted animals, and farmed vegetables (Skyhorse). Most recently, I represented Dawn Dais in multivolume and audio deals for her hilarious parenting series *The Sh!t No One Tells You* and *The Sh!t No One Tells You About Toddlers*.

Agent's name: Taylor Martindale Kean

Describe the kinds of works you want to represent. I am looking for young adult fiction, literary middle grade fiction, and young adult and middle grade nonfiction, all genres. I am interested in finding unique and unforgettable voices in contemporary, fantasy, historical, and multicultural novels. I seek books that demand to be read. More than anything, I am looking for diverse, character-driven stories that bring their worlds vividly to life, voices that are honest, original, and interesting. When considering nonfiction projects, I use much the same approach and hope to find authors with fresh ideas and perspectives, with writing that is accessible, entertaining, and compelling.

How do you want writers to pitch you? Please see our submission form on our website.

Describe your education and professional history. I graduated from the College of William and Mary, where I studied English and Hispanic studies.

What do you like to do when you're not working? When not working, I can be found traveling, cooking, spending time with loved ones, or (surprise!) lost in a good book.

List some of the titles you have recently placed with publishers. Diana Rodriguez Wallach's new *Anastasia Phoenix* series, in which a girl goes on an international hunt for her missing sister who everyone says is dead and finds that everything she knows about her family is not only a lie but embroiled in criminal espionage (Entangled Teen); Sally

Pla's debut, *Someday Birds*, in which a bird-loving boy with OCD and Asperger's reluctantly travels cross-country with his siblings to see his dad, who is hospitalized after a brain injury, and bargains with the universe that if he can spot along the way all the rare birds that the two had been hoping to see someday, then everything might just turn out okay (Harper Children's). Clients include Annie Cardi, Emery Lord, Aisha Saeed, Debra Driza, Anna-Marie McLemore, Lois Miner Huey, Tim Bradley, Sally J. Pla, and more.

Agent's name: Stefanie Von Borstel

Describe the kinds of works you want to represent. I represent children's books from toddler to teen, both fiction and nonfiction, and adult nonfiction. On the adult side, my focus is on design, lifestyle, art, how-to, family interest, and narrative nonfiction. I love to tap into my publicity and marketing background to champion writers and artists. I am always thrilled to work with creatives who have a distinct style or expertise that can cross over to both the children's and adult markets.

How do you want writers to pitch you? Please see our submission form on our website.

Describe your education and professional history. I am cofounder of Full Circle Literary, an entrepreneur, and mom with more than 20 years of experience in the book-publishing industry. Prior to agenting, I worked in editorial and marketing with Penguin and Harcourt Children's Books.

What do you like to do when you're not working? When not reading, I am probably searching for green fig beetles or tide-pooling with my family.

List some of the titles you have recently placed with publishers. Two picture books written and illustrated by boygirlparty artist Susie Ghahremani (Abrams); Jennifer Ward's *How to Find a Bird*, celebrating the joy in finding and observing the many types of birds in nature (Beach Lane Books); Susan Verde's *Hey, Wall!*, a celebration of urban art in which a boy brings his community together to create a mural, illustrated by Pura Belpré Honor and Golden Kite Award winner John Parra (Paula Wiseman Books). Recent adult nonfiction I represent includes *ART INC: The Essential Guide for Building Your Career as an Artist* by Lisa Congdon and Meg Mateo Ilasco (Chronicle Books), *The New Bohemians* by designer Justina Blakeney (Abrams), *Furniture Makes the Room* by Barb Blair (Chronicle Books), and *Knitting without Needles: A Stylish Introduction to Finger and Arm Knitting* by Anne Weil (Potter/Random House). Children's books I have represented have been awarded the Charlotte Zolotow Award for Best Picture Book, Pura Belpré Honors, the Christopher Award, NCTE Orbis Pictus Honor for Best Nonfiction, and the Agatha Award for Best Mystery Novel. I am honored to work with Monica Brown, Sarah O'Leary Burningham, Toni Buzzeo, Diana López, Cindy Jenson-Elliott, Carmen Tafolla, to name a few. Some new releases in 2016 include Diana Lopez's new middle grade novel *Nothing Up My Sleeve* (Little, Brown); Cindy Jenson-Elliot's picture book biography *Antsy Ansel: Ansel Adams a Life in Nature*, illustrated by Christy Hale (Henry Holt); and Monica Brown's *Lola Levine* chapter book series (Little, Brown).

Is there anything you wish to express beyond the parameters of the preceding questions? Full Circle Literary is a full-service literary agency, offering a full-circle approach to literary representation. Our team has diverse experience in book publishing including editorial, marketing, publicity, legal and rights, which we use collectively to build careers book by book.

We work with both award-winning veteran and debut writers and artists, and our team has a knack for finding and developing new and diverse talent. Our titles have received awards and honors from the American Library Association, National Book Critics' Circle, Children's Book Council, Society of Children's Books Writers and Illustrators, National Council of Teachers of English, International Reading Association, and many more.

FUSE LITERARY ❖ www.fuseliterary.com

PO Box 258, La Honda, CA 94020, www.facebook.com/FuseLiterary, www.fuseliterary.com/newsletter

Agent's name and contact info: Gordon Warnock, Partner, querygordon@fuseliterary.com, Twitter: @gordonwarnock

Describe the kinds of works you want to represent. Most of my list is nonfiction by recognized experts with a significant platform (see www.fuseliterary.com for more info). I have a soft spot for quirky nonfiction steeped in pop culture, nerd culture, or punk culture; bonus points if the book is part of a larger project backed by celebrities and an established fan base. I also represent literary and upmarket fiction for adults through young adult and graphic novels for adults through middle grade.

Describe what you definitely don't want to represent. Religious fiction, genre fiction, satire, legal thrillers, New Age, spiritual journeys, family histories, anything younger than middle grade, novellas, collections of short stories or poetry by authors who don't write novels.

How do you want writers to pitch you? Email is best, but also feel free if you meet me at a conference or an online pitch fest. Follow my submission guidelines. I love it when folks follow directions. The most current info can always be found at www.fuseliterary.com.

Describe your education and professional history. I am an honors graduate of Cal State, Sacramento, with a degree in creative and professional writing. I've been working for agencies since I was an undergrad, and I've had numerous other ventures in the industry including editing and running marketing for independent publishers, freelance editorial and author coaching, speaking and teaching for MFA programs and industry publications, and my current favorite, heading our Short Fuse Publishing program.

How did you become an agent? I started interning at an agency for my own personal use as a writer, and I fell in love with it. I found success fairly early, and they fast-tracked me to senior agent. After way too long with that company, Laurie and I started Fuse, and we've since grown to a thriving team of eight sharp and diverse agents covering most of the trade market.

Knowing what you do now, would you do it again? If not, what might you do instead? Of course, silly. I freaking love my job.

Do you charge fees? If yes, please explain. Fuse Literary and Short Fuse Publishing never charge up-front fees. We make a percentage of what authors make when they make it, no more.

When and where were you born, and where have you lived? I was born in Chicago, and I've since lived all around California and in Vancouver, BC.

What do you like to do when you're not working? I love cooking, kayaking, home renovation, and caring for the most adorable white Doberman on the planet.

List some of the titles you have recently placed with publishers. *This Is What a Librarian Looks Like* by Kyle Cassidy, *Draw with a Vengeance* by Helen Wrath, *Everything We Keep* by Kerry Lonsdale, *Creative Visualization for Writers* by Nina Amir, *Sweet Carolina Morning* by Susan Schild, *Cooking for Ghosts* by Patricia V. Davis.

Describe your personality. My editorial notes often cite George Carlin, Mary Poppins, and Stephen King.

What do you like reading/watching/listening to on your own time? I'm a big fan of stand-up comedy. I think writers (especially novelists) can learn a lot by analyzing the narrative methods of seasoned comedians.

Do you think the business has changed a lot over the past few years? If yes, please explain. Definitely. That's one reason why I enjoy it so much. At Fuse, we've made a point of being the change rather than the ones who struggle to catch up. It's done wonders for us and our clients (and it's a lot of fun).

What do the "Big 5" mean to you? One of many facets of the grand ecosystem of publishing, they play an important role as the industry currently stands.

How do you feel about independent/small presses? I'm so glad that today's publishing ecosystem includes a thriving body of independent publishers. They release some of the most daring and cutting-edge work, a lot of what I read for fun.

What are your feelings about self-publishing? Another interesting facet of the grand ecosystem of publishing. I've long been fascinated with how it can work hand in hand with traditional publishing to foster sustained, successful writing careers.

Do you think Amazon is good or bad — or both — for the book business? I like that they're shaking up the industry and actively innovating. That's long overdue, it's what I try to do as an agent, and I hope it continues. Overall, we need to keep in mind that the state of things today will not be the state of things forever, and we need to act accordingly.

What do you like and dislike about your job? I love how active and scientific we're allowed to be at Fuse, truly managing an author's career over the long term rather than just flipping contracts. I also love how we've embraced technology to be able to get work done wherever and whenever, which, of course, is a double-edged sword. I tend to be that asshole who is always looking at his phone.

What are ways prospective clients can impress you, and what are ways they can turn you off? Have goals, have a plan, and have several pieces in the works. Actively and consistently pursue publications, awards, and publicity opportunities in areas that agents don't typically handle. A successful writing career requires all involved parties to do everything they can possibly do. I'm not about to take on authors who think their work ends with the manuscript.

How would you describe the "writer from hell"? Hunched, moaning, pungent, with an incessant hunger for brains.

Describe a book you would like to write. Ha! I'm way too busy with my clients' books, but that's a nice thought.

Agent's name and contact info: Connor Goldsmith, queryconnor@fuseliterary.com

Describe the kinds of works you want to represent. I'm primarily seeking adult sci-fi/fantasy/horror with a fresh new hook and great prose. I'm especially interested in work by and about marginalized people (people of color, the LGBT community, religious minorities, people with disabilities, etc.). I'm also interested in thrillers and crime novels from marginalized perspectives, though I am *not* interested in counterterrorism Middle East thrillers.

Describe what you definitely don't want to represent. I do not represent young adult or children's fiction. I do not represent memoir unless I solicit the clients personally based on their platform. In nonfiction, anything of a right-wing political bent is probably not going to interest me.

How do you want writers to pitch you? I accept a query letter with a 1–2-page full-plot synopsis and the first 10 pages of the manuscript. All content must be pasted into the email; emails with attachments will be deleted unread.

Describe your education and professional history. I got my bachelor's degree in English and the classics at Oberlin College and a master's in media studies at The New School. Before joining Fuse I was an associate agent at Lowenstein Associates, working with the celebrated Barbara Lowenstein.

How did you become an agent? I began my career interning in film and television agenting and fell into literary agenting almost by chance when a job opportunity opened up. I fell in love immediately, though, and I'd never take any of it back. There's so much more freedom and creativity in the world of books.

Do you charge fees? If yes, please explain. No, and you should never sign with an agent who charges any fees. Agents are paid on commission.

When and where were you born, and where have you lived? I was born in New York City and raised both there and in the surrounding suburbs. Apart from my college years, I've always been a New Yorker.

What do you like to do when you're not working? I'm an avid reader, because you have to be in this business, but sometimes after reading all day for work I like to turn on some really, really brainless reality television and let my mind relax.

List some of the titles you have recently placed with publishers. S. J. Sindu's *Marriage of a Thousand Lies*, about a Tamil American lesbian married to a gay male friend to satisfy their traditional Sri Lankan families, who cannot bring herself to continue the sham after her first love agrees to her own arranged marriage with a man (Soho Press); Cass Morris's *Aven*, set in an ancient Rome built on elemental magic, about three determined noble sisters and the charismatic but secretive senator who will either save the Republic or bring it to ruin as war approaches (Daw; in a three-book deal); Lara Elena Donnelly's *Amberlough*, about a gay spy who must compromise all his ideals and beliefs to protect his smuggler lover from a fascist coup (Tor).

Do you think the business has changed a lot over the past few years? If yes, please explain. This is a business that is *always* changing. What we are seeing now is the emergence of multiple publishing marketplaces, each with its own opportunities and its own pros and cons for different kinds of stories and different kinds of authors.

How do you feel about independent/small presses? I think they're just wonderful, but they're not my focus as an agent.

What are your feelings about self-publishing? Self-publishing can be a very viable and rewarding path, but it's important to remember that when you self-publish, you are taking on about a hundred other jobs beyond "author" — editor, production designer, publicist, marketer, accountant, and so on. Make sure you're prepared to wear all those hats. I do not represent self-published authors unless they are querying with an entirely new work (not one set in the same world as the already self-pubbed material).

What are ways prospective clients can impress you, and what are ways they can turn you off? Spelling my name right is always a good first impression! After that, give me a query letter that answers the most important questions: who, what, when, where, why, and why I should care. Tell me the premise, the conflict, and the stakes. I am turned off by overly familiar query letters, though if we've met before or you follow me on social media, do feel free to mention that.

Agent's name and contact info: Michelle Richter, querymichelle@fuseliterary.com

Describe the kinds of works you want to represent. I represent women's commercial fiction, book-club fiction, mystery, suspense, thrillers (more like Harlan Coben than Tom Clancy), and select historical fiction. I also seek the following nonfiction: pop culture, science, medicine, economics, and sociology from recognized experts in their fields. See www.fuseliterary.com for more information. I'm open to young adult contemporary or young adult crime fiction as well.

Describe what you definitely don't want to represent. I definitely don't want children's books, sci-fi, fantasy, inspirational or religious themes (in fiction or nonfiction), memoir, cookbooks, or self-help.

How do you want writers to pitch you? Pitch me at conferences or query me at query michelle@fuseliterary.com. My submission guidelines are on the agency's website.

Describe your education and professional history. I graduated from the University of Massachusetts at Boston with a degree in economics and a minor in Russian. I spent a number of years working in banking and finance in Boston and Baltimore before moving to New York City to attend Pace University's publishing program, where I obtained a master's degree. I then joined St. Martin's Press and worked there eight years.

How did you become an agent? I liked and respected the Fuse partners, having met them at conferences and interacted on social media, so I reached out and was thrilled to be welcomed aboard.

Knowing what you do now, would you do it again? If not, what might you do instead? Yes, I'd do it again.

Do you charge fees? If yes, please explain. No.

When and where were you born, and where have you lived? I was born in Massachusetts in a year ending in 0. I have lived in the Boston area; Washington, DC; Baltimore; Brooklyn; and Albany, New York.

What do you like to do when you're not working? Movies are a great escape for me. I am always up for karaoke. I love travel both within the US and abroad — favorites include Barcelona and Reykjavik. In 2015, I began teaching at Pace's publishing program as an adjunct lecturer, and I love it.

List some of the titles you have recently placed with publishers. *You're as Good as Dead* by E. A. Aymar.

Describe your personality. I'm very forthright and will always tell it like it is. I'm gregarious and snarky.

What do you like reading/watching/listening to on your own time? My pop-culture tastes are diverse. British crime TV is an obsession (*Luther, Sherlock, The Fall, Above Suspicion, Prime Suspect, The Escape Artist, Broadchurch*). I love a good sitcom or reality show, too (*The Mindy Project, Master Chef*). Documentaries about fashion, the media, or food are hard for me to resist (*Jiro Dreams of Sushi, The September Issue*). I read a lot of crime fiction, but love a good book-club read or a thoughtful biography that teaches me something.

Do you think the business has changed a lot over the past few years? If yes, please explain. Sure. There's a lot more digital content and self-published content than ever before. Publishers big and small start up and shut down all the time. It's an ever-changing landscape that we have to keep our eyes on. There are a lot of projects competing for contracting shelf space.

What do the "Big 5" mean to you? The Big 5 are the major-league teams in a sense, but they're not the only imprints to pitch. They may have greater financial resources and connections and certainly some prestige and market strength.

How do you feel about independent/small presses? Some of them are great. There are so many indie presses, in all different sizes. I definitely pitch my clients' work to them and think they can be great homes for authors' work. I always want to know what they'll offer to support the book, not just the advance and royalties, but publicity, marketing, and distribution.

What are your feelings about self-publishing? It can be a good fit for an author, whether for all their work or just one project. But writers must realize that they need to put out a polished project to be taken seriously. So they need to hire an editor, a cover designer, perhaps a publicist and/or marketing manager if they lack those skills (and they likely do). And they need to figure out distribution if it's a print book and not just an ebook.

Do you think Amazon is good or bad — or both — for the book business? I have mixed feelings. I think there are some great editors there who make their authors very happy. As a consumer, I love the pricing and the innovations and inventory. But it's a tricky business model to sustain, and their sheer size and power are a little scary to me.

What do you like and dislike about your job? I love discovering and working with talented writers, going to conferences, networking with editors, and having someone agree to read my clients' work. But it's tough when editors don't see the potential I do.

What are ways prospective clients can impress you, and what are ways they can turn you off? I love motivated, hardworking writers who've got an original concept, are open to editorial suggestions, and have a vision for their career and ideas about how to promote their work. They know the market and who their comparison titles are. They ask smart questions when I offer representation. They'd turn me off if they refused to make changes to their work, if they insisted they knew better than I did, or if they're nonresponsive to communication or are flaky.

How would you describe the "writer from hell"? A person who can't write well but thinks he or she can, bad-mouths industry professionals, has no filter on social media. Not that I've met this person.

Describe a book you would like to write. I've been joking with an editor friend that I should write a travel memoir about the ups and downs of traveling with my spouse, but I don't really feel the writing bug is in me.

Do you believe in a higher and/or lower "power"? Maybe. If that higher power is Stephen King and the bible is his book *On Writing*.

Agent's name and contact info: Tricia Skinner, Assistant Agent, query email: querytricia@fuseliterary.com, nonquery email: tricia@fuseliterary.com

Describe the kinds of works you want to represent. Romance is everything! I love it. I need it. I want the best authors of it to represent. Within that vastness, for young adult, new adult, and adult, in no particular order (and all heat settings), are certain subgenres that I'm excited to read. *Contemporary and inspirational romance*: fresh, gripping, and complex modern love stories with diverse characters or cultures in lead roles; authors who break away from the "same old, same old" trends will win me over. *Multicultural historical romance*: love in "olden times" didn't stop at the borders of a handful of European countries; my preference is for novels set from ancient times to 1900. *Fantasy and science fiction romance*: I'm open to almost any creature, mythology, solar system, or alien-cyborg-sentient-virus spreader, but the world must include a sense of diversity; make me wish for a different future or place (or make me fear it). *Romantic suspense*: I adore thrillers and suspense with eye-bugging "that did not just happen" moments. In all, I want authors who rise above the usual trends and who include multicultural elements to blow my mind.

Describe what you definitely don't want to represent. Within the romance subgenres I adore are certain elements I'm *not* seeking. The breakdown is as follows. *Contemporary and inspirational romance*: any novel that's a version of *Friends* or *Sex in the City*; diversity-absent worlds; light, sweet, funny, or white-collar-only careers; anything where religion or religious beliefs are integral to the story. *Historical romance*: Regency era, American Revolutionary, or Civil War "slave loves master" or vice versa stories; anything in the 1920s through the 1970s. *Fantasy and science fiction romance*: anything with high fantasy, time travel, or goofy "creatures" (platypus shifters, hibiscus people, sentient chalk, etc.). *Romantic suspense*: anything with a "hint" of romantic suspense versus the real deal, for example, cozy mysteries with "elements of romantic suspense."

How do you want writers to pitch you? Email a brief query letter, a 1- or 2-page synopsis, and the first 10 pages (no prologues!) to querytricia@fuseliterary.com. No attachments. Use only my Fuse Literary query address unless I specifically request material be sent elsewhere.

Describe your education and professional history. I'm a former newspaper reporter who also spent over a decade working in industry relations within the video-game industry. I have a bachelor's and master's degree.

How did you become an agent? After accepting representation for my own writing career with Laurie McLean, founder of Fuse Literary, I found myself fascinated by the business side of publishing. I've always been happiest when I could use my talents and skills to help others. Laurie saw that in me and gave me the opportunity to do the two things I love: write books and help other authors.

What do you like to do when you're not working? I'm raising my very own antihero. He currently thinks Darth Vader is awesome and Loki was misunderstood. Our family loves computer games, but we have a blast playing classic card and board games. We have three Great Danes (so far) that I call my fur babies. When I take time for myself, I read until my eyes burn.

Describe your personality. I can do you one better. I'm an INFJ type to my bones (www.16personalities.com/infj-personality).

What do you like reading/watching/listening to on your own time? I'm catching up on TV shows right now. Normally, I don't watch a show from week to week. I prefer to binge-watch because that's less disruptive to my busy life. Plus, who wouldn't want to spend a day staring at Dean and Sam Winchester from *Supernatural*?

Agent's name and contact info: Jennifer Chen Tran, Associate Agent, queryjennifer@fuseliterary.com, agentjen.co

Describe the kinds of works you want to represent. I acquire both fiction and nonfiction. For fiction, I am seeking literary, commercial, women's, and upmarket fiction, contemporary romance, mature young adult, new adult, suspense/thriller, and select graphic novels (adult, young adult, or middle grade). I am particularly interested in voices from underrepresented and marginalized communities, strong and conflicted female characters, war and post-war fiction, and writers who are adept at creating a developed sense of place. I admire writers who have an ear for dialogue and who are not afraid to take emotional risks. For nonfiction, I seek memoir and narrative nonfiction in the areas of adventure, biography, business, current affairs, medical, history, how-to, pop culture, psychology, social entrepreneurism, social justice, travel, and lifestyle (home, design, fashion, food). I believe in creating books that will have a positive impact on the world and that inform and entertain.

Describe what you definitely don't want to represent. I do not represent science fiction or fantasy.

How do you want writers to pitch you? For fiction, send the first 20 pages (pasted into the email, no attachments) and a query letter. For nonfiction, submit your nonfiction proposal and query letter. Electronic submissions only, to queryjennifer@fuseliterary.com.

Describe your education and professional history. I obtained my BA in English literature with a minor in legal studies from Washington University in St. Louis and my JD from Northeastern School of Law in Boston. Originally a visual arts major turned English major, I appreciate creativity in all its incarnations. I was also managing editor of *Student Life*, Washington University's independent student paper, and studied comparative literature with Emma Kafalenos while I was an undergraduate. I am a lifelong reader and New York native. Prior to joining Fuse Literary, I was principal and owner of Penumbra Literary LLC and served as Of Counsel at the New Press. I have also interned at Zachary Shuster Harmsworth literary agency, was an editorial and publicity intern at Hunger House Publishers (since acquired by Turner Publishing), and an editorial intern at *Terrain* magazine.

Do you charge fees? If yes, please explain. No.

When and where were you born, and where have you lived? I was born in New Orleans but remember very little of it since we moved to New York when I was young. I have lived in St. Louis, Boston, San Francisco, New York, and now just north of Sacramento.

What do you like to do when you're not working? Read, go to art museums, watch independent films, try to become outdoorsy, and spend time with my family.

List some of the titles you have recently placed with publishers. M. F. Alvarez's *The Paradox of Suicide and Creativity*, a study spanning over a decade that seeks to humanize rather than medicalize the intimate connection between creativity and suicide, via a close look at Iris Chang, Alan Turing, Kurt Cobain, Robin Williams, and other eminently creative individuals who ended their own lives, arguing that diagnoses of mental illness are overly simplistic, often overshadowing each individual's lasting contributions to society, and that by humanizing death we are also revitalizing life (Lexington Books); board-game start-up entrepreneur, crowdfunding authority, and blogger Jamey Stegmaier's *People Not Pawns: How I Kickstarted My Dream Company*, part business memoir and part nuts-and-bolts insider tips on how to build a successful Kickstarter campaign from the ground up, connect with your core audience, and pave the road to crowdfunding success, featuring interviews with the creators of major Kickstarter campaigns including Studio Neat, 1 Second Everyday, and Quinn Popcorn (Berrett-Koehler).

Describe your personality. I am introverted but can seem like an extrovert, depending on the occasion. I've been told that I'm a good listener, creative, and perceptive. I like to help people and create beauty in the world. It's important for me to live with purpose and part of my purpose in life is to help others achieve their creative dreams.

What do you like reading/watching/listening to on your own time? Some of my favorite reads include: *The Unwanted* by Kien Nguyen, *Into Thin Air* by Jon Krakauer, *The Language of Flowers* by Vanessa Diffenbaugh, *Chronology of Water* by Lidia Yuknavitch, *The Year of Magical Thinking* by Joan Didion, *Never Let Me Go* by Kazuo Ishiguro, *American Born Chinese* by Gene Luen Yang, *The Unbearable Lightness of Being* by Milan Kundera, and *Word Freak* by Stefan Fastis.

Do you think the business has changed a lot over the past few years? If yes, please explain. I think the way that readers receive content has changed a lot. Readers can receive content in a plethora of ways, but we will always need good content. So as much as things change, some things never change. I think both agents and writers need to be more creative in how they reach their audiences and tailor their marketing and promotional plans accordingly.

How do you feel about independent/small presses? I am a big fan of independent and small presses with regard to the high-quality content they are acquiring. Where I think they could be better is in the area of marketing, but that's a given since they don't often have the budgets that bigger publishers do. I admire that independent and small presses nurture talent and give authors an ability to reach their audience, so that authors can continue to grow their careers.

What do you like and dislike about your job? What I like about it is that every day is different, and it is always a challenge. It pushes me to think creatively on behalf of my clients. I like the relational aspect of it and that it is largely a very positive industry to be in. You are building each other up. What is sometimes difficult to deal with is lack of predictability, and sometimes as an agent you are frustrated when editors don't see the vision or feel the same for your client's book. It's part of the business to remain resilient, however.

How would you describe the "writer from hell"? The writer who calls or emails me every second to make sure I'm doing my job instead of trusting me to do it. Micromanaging doesn't really work and will eventually cause resentment. Trust your agent to get results!

GLASS LITERARY MANAGEMENT ❖ www.glassliterary.com

138 West 25th Street, 10th Floor, New York, NY 10001, 646-237-4881

Agent's name and contact info: Alex Glass, submissions@glassliterary.com

Describe the kinds of works you want to represent. Literary and mainstream commercial fiction for adults, middle grade and young adult fiction, nonfiction in a variety of categories (narrative, memoir and biography, history, health and wellness, lifestyle, sports, pop culture).

Describe what you definitely don't want to represent. Romance, science fiction, fantasy for adults, picture books for children.

How do you want writers to pitch you? Via email only.

Describe your education and professional history. BA, political science, and writing seminars from Johns Hopkins University; MFA, creative writing, from American University. I was the ad/promo assistant at the Putnam Berkley Publishing Group for a year, worked in the literature program at the National Endowment for the Arts for 3 years, and spent 13 years as an agent at Trident Media Group before founding my own agency in 2014.

How did you become an agent? Worked my way up at Trident under Robert Gottlieb.

Knowing what you do now, would you do it again? If not, what might you do instead? Absolutely.

Do you charge fees? If yes, please explain. No.

When and where were you born, and where have you lived? I was born in New York City and have lived here my entire life except for seven years in the Baltimore/Washington area for college, grad school, and work at the NEA.

What do you like to do when you're not working? Music, sports, spend time with my wife and baby daughter.

List some of the titles you have recently placed with publishers. Actress Jennifer Esposito's cookbook, *Jennifer's Way* (Grand Central Life & Style); Blake J. Harris's narrative nonfiction about the rise of virtual reality (Dey Street); novelist Marcy Dermansky's third book, *The Red Car* (Norton).

GRACE FREEDSON'S PUBLISHING NETWORK

7600 Jericho Turnpike, Suite 300, Woodbury, NY 11797, 516-931-7757

Agent's name and contact info: Grace Freedson, gfreedson@gmail.com

Describe the kinds of works you want to represent. Predominately adult nonfiction (all categories) written by authors who have their platforms in place.

Describe what you definitely don't want to represent. Fiction, science fiction.

How do you want writers to pitch you? Email queries.

Describe your education and professional history. Thirty years publishing experience; 15 years in-house at all managerial levels.

How did you become an agent? Decided to put my comprehensive experiences to use working with authors with whom I could develop long-standing relationships.

Knowing what you do now, would you do it again? If not, what might you do instead? Timing is everything. I was lucky to launch my own agency in 2000 and establish myself before the advent of ebooks, self-publishing, and digitalization. It's a different business today, but I have loved every minute of it.

When and where were you born, and where have you lived? Native New Yorker.

What do you like to do when you're not working? Travel, ski, bike.

List some of the titles you have recently placed with publishers. *Seed to Supper* by John Tullock, *The 25 Most Influential Aircraft of All Time* by Col. Walt Boyne and Philip Handleman, *Extreme Brain Workout* by Marcel Danesi, PhD, *The Running Diet* by Jason Karp, PhD.

Describe your personality. Curious about everything, eclectic interests, outgoing personality, and love the great outdoors.

What do you like reading/watching/listening to on your own time? News junkie, mixed bag of fiction, movies.

Do you think the business has changed a lot over the past few years? If yes, please explain. It has changed immensely. Now we must work with authors who are experts not only in their field, but also in self-promotion. I miss the opportunity to personally discuss projects with editors.

What do the "Big 5" mean to you? Not much.

How do you feel about independent/small presses? I enjoy working with them.

What are your feelings about self-publishing? I am not impressed by the quality of what I see, but understand an author's rationale for pursuing this.

HAROLD MATSON CO., INC.

31 West 34th Street, Suite 7034, New York, NY 10001, 212-679-4490; direct line to Ben Camardi: 212-679-4491

Agents' names and contact info: Ben Camardi and Jonathan Matson, hmatsco@aol.com (agency's general email)

Describe the kinds of works you want to represent. High-quality fiction and nonfiction. Most of those we take on are referred by clients or are professional writers in need of a new agent (though we will not consider a writer who has a current agent).

Describe what you definitely don't want to represent. Screenplays, stage plays, TV scripts, romance, graphic novels, poetry, children's books.

How do you want writers to pitch you? Query letter by snail mail. All queries sent by email are ignored.

List some of the titles you have recently placed with publishers. That Man in Our Lives by Xu Xi, *Bitter Creek* by Peter Bowen, *Manana* by William Hjortsberg, *Little Cloud* by Dorothy Fabian.

Do you think the business has changed a lot over the past few years? If yes, please explain. Yes, primarily in the electronic sense.

What do the "Big 5" mean to you? They are where the money is.

How do you feel about independent/small presses? The good ones are terrific.

What are your feelings about self-publishing? These days, a good idea if all else fails and a bona fide book doctor is used for final draft.

Do you think Amazon is good or bad — or both — for the book business? Good.

What do you like and dislike about your job? No dislikes.

What are ways prospective clients can impress you, and what are ways they can turn you off? Writers impress us by dint of what they do; the only thing that can be a turnoff is when sales do not happen quickly and the writer makes frequent telephone calls to find out what is going on. When there is news, an agent will track down a client to the ends of the universe to shout the news.

How would you describe the "writer from hell"? Not really hellish, but sometimes writers will accept terms that do not enable them to write the book and then they complain, whine, and blame the agent for a bad deal. We always ask if the terms are affordable before encouraging a signing. The only thing worse than no deal is a bad one.

HARTLINE LITERARY AGENCY ❖ www.hartlineliterary.com

123 Queenston Drive, Pittsburgh, PA 15235, 412-829-2483

Agent's name and contact info: Diana Flegal, diana@hartlineliterary.com

Describe the kinds of works you want to represent. I am currently looking for nonfiction authors with a substantial platform and expertise in their topic as well as upmarket fiction, contemporary women's fiction, and inspirational formula romance.

Describe what you definitely don't want to represent. I represent mainstream and inspirational titles, but nothing that conflicts with the Christian worldview. I am not interested in New Age, sci-fi, erotica, or children's picture books.

How do you want writers to pitch you? Our submission guidelines are posted on our website along with what we are looking for. I prefer a full proposal that includes three sample chapters instead of a query.

Describe your education and professional history. I have been an agent with Hartline Literary Agency for nine years. I previously worked in human resources and sales and provided medical/dental assistance in Haiti while living there for a year and a half.

How did you become an agent? An avid book reader, I met Joyce Hart, CEO and founder of Hartline Literary Agency, through her book club. I applied for and became the editorial assistant to Joyce and held that position three years before coming on board as a literary agent with Hartline.

Knowing what you do now, would you do it again? If not, what might you do instead? Yes, I'd do it again. Some weeks I do imagine winning the lottery, then hosting an annual month long getaway writers' conference on a beautiful island in the Caribbean. ☺

Do you charge fees? If yes, please explain. No, we do not charge any fees for our services. Once a book is placed with a publisher, Hartline Literary Agency earns a 15 percent commission on the sale and all subsequent royalties for every book sold.

When and where were you born, and where have you lived? I am a native of Pennsylvania and have lived in Massachusetts, Florida, Haiti, South Dakota, and North Carolina.

What do you like to do when you're not working? When I am not reading submissions or stealing away with a recreational read, I enjoy hiking in the mountains of North Carolina or kayaking the state's many lakes. Creating paper collage art is also an enjoyable way for me to step away from my computer.

List some of the titles you have recently placed with publishers. *A Fiction Lover's Devotional Series*: *21 Days of Grace* (2015), *21 Days of Christmas* (2015), *21 Days of Love* (2016), and *21 Days of Joy* (2016), compiled by Kathy Ide; *Reclaiming Sanity* (David C. Cook, 2017) and a second "to be titled" book by Dr. Laurel Shaler; *Wedding Express* by Jody Day (Pelican Ventures). Recent releases: *Shock the Clock: Time Management for Writers and Other Creatives* by Jeanette Levellie (Lighthouse Publishing of the Carolinas, 2015), *Holiday Homecoming* by Jean Gordon (Harlequin Love), *Inspired 21 Days of Christmas: A Fiction Lover's Devotional* compiled by Kathy Ide (Broadstreet). Awards: *The Redemption of Caralynne Hayman* by Carole Brown was named USA Best Book Award Winner. *Falling for Chloe* by David Stearman (Lighthouse Publishing of the Carolinas) and *Mercy's Rain* by Cindy Sproles (Kregel Publications) were nominated for the Christian Inspirational 2015 Christy Award.

Describe your personality. Easygoing, I am an ENFJ. I enjoy networking and helping authors connect with their readers through social-media outlets.

What do you like reading/watching/listening to on your own time? I enjoy reading upmarket fiction, women's contemporary fiction, mystery, and all manner of nonfiction (self-help) titles. I also enjoy watching *The Voice*, *American Idol*, Pittsburgh Steeler football, *NCIS*, and good movies. A few favorites are *The Lone Ranger* (remake, starring Johnny Depp), *While You Were Sleeping*, *Overboard*.

Do you think the business has changed a lot over the past few years? If yes, please explain. Publishing has gone through large changes since the economic downturn of 2006. The downsizing and buyout of many midsize publishers and the merging of imprints in the larger houses have impacted the number of open doors for agents, especially for placing new authors. Ebooks have also impacted traditional markets, and everyone on all sides of the desk has scrambled to learn a new way of doing business via social media. A great upside is it has forced writers to hone their skills and step up their writing level in order to gain a foothold in a tight marketplace.

What do the "Big 5" mean to you? Many submission opportunities, within the multitude of imprints within each of them.

How do you feel about independent/small presses? Although I am grateful for the option of small presses, I hesitate to send my clients their way mainly because their marketing budget is small and they have a hard time helping titles find their target readers.

What are your feelings about self-publishing? The stigma has shrunk, but I still see self-publishing as a good option only if authors have a large speaking platform and will be able to sell their books at the "back of the room." All too often we see impatient authors self-publish their book before it is ready for print, bypassing the necessary edit every title needs.

Do you think Amazon is good or bad — or both — for the book business? Whether it is good or bad, we must play ball with them. I tend to be a "glass half full" girl.

What do you like and dislike about your job? I enjoy mentoring and encouraging writers. Networking and teaching writing-conference workshops are a joy. I see a literary agent as being part matchmaker and part doula. We connect the book to a publisher and then help launch the baby (book) out into the arms of the target readers. It is a privilege and honor.

What are ways prospective clients can impress you, and what are ways they can turn you off? Submitting to me a professionally prepared proposal according to our submission guidelines in a genre I have listed as one I am interested in is the best way to get my attention. The biggest turnoff is telling me, "God told me you are to be my agent" or sending me an email telling me I should take the sender on as a client or I will miss out on making a lot of money, bypassing the proper protocol listed on our website.

How would you describe the "writer from hell"? A high-maintenance author would be the one emailing me every day, asking me if I have read the proposal or the revisions yet, while failing to do the simple things I have asked of him or her.

Describe a book you would like to write. I would like to write a book similar to Maeve Binchy's titles set in England — only basing the story here in the States, most likely near Pittsburgh or Asheville, North Carolina. Maeve's characters stay with me for months after reading one of her books. She had a real gift. I am told the tour guides in the area she most often wrote about must continually remind their guests that Quentin's Restaurant does not exist, that her stories were fiction. ☺

Do you believe in a higher and/or lower "power"? Absolutely, a higher power.

Is there anything you wish to express beyond the parameters of the preceding questions? Writers, do your homework. Research what an agent is looking for before you submit to that agent. Be willing to revise and rewrite if asked to. Then be patient. This is a business that moves slowly.

Agent's name and contact info: Linda S. Glaz, linda@hartlineliterary.com, lindaglaz.com

Describe the kinds of works you want to represent. Predominantly fiction.

Describe what you definitely don't want to represent. No children's, no spec fiction, no erotica or novels sprinkled with four-letter words.

How do you want writers to pitch you? See the proposal on our website.

Describe your education and professional history. I have been an agent five years and am also a writer of fiction.

How did you become an agent? I was a reviewer, proofreader, and then an editorial assistant to an agent. Agenting was the next step.

Knowing what you do now, would you do it again? If not, what might you do instead? In a second. I love it!

Do you charge fees? If yes, please explain. No!

When and where were you born, and where have you lived? Other than a three-year stint in Spain, I've lived in Michigan most of my life.

What do you like to do when you're not working? Write!

List some of the titles you have recently placed with publishers. For Such a Time by Kate Breslin, *Friend Me* by Jay Faubion, and numerous others.

Describe your personality. Quad-A personality.

What do you like reading/watching/listening to on your own time? Suspense and more suspense.

What are ways prospective clients can impress you, and what are ways they can turn you off? Do an extremely professional proposal as outlined on our website. Meet me at conferences. A huge turnoff is a proposal for something we don't even handle.

Describe a book you would like to write. One that would have the reader scrambling when the story ends — looking for more pages.

Agent's name and contact info: Cyle Young, 412-656-5464 (cell)

Describe the kinds of works you want to represent. I am seeking young adult, middle grade, and chapter books; genre fiction, especially romance, love stories, and speculative (sci-fi and fantasy); easy readers picture books and board books; nonfiction (parenting, leadership, ministry, and self-help); screenplays.

Describe what you definitely don't want to represent. Works that include swearing or unmarried sex.

How do you want writers to pitch you? A proposal and three sample chapters.

Describe your education and professional history. I hold two master's degrees in leadership and religious education. I have worked in pastoral ministry for 15 years.

How did you become an agent? By building relationships with agents and editors over a period of years.

Knowing what you do now, would you do it again? If not, what might you do instead? Yes.

Do you charge fees? If yes, please explain. No.

When and where were you born, and where have you lived? I was born in Ohio, and except for four years at the University of Michigan, I have lived in Ohio my entire life.

What do you like to do when you're not working? Play board games and video games with my children, and write.

List some of the titles you have recently placed with publishers. Just starting out.

Describe your personality. I love to laugh and joke around, and I like to work hard and stay busy.

What do you like reading/watching/listening to on your own time? I love watching fantasy/adventure and sci-fi movies.

Do you think the business has changed a lot over the past few years? If yes, please explain. No.

What do the "Big 5" mean to you? They are the larger body of the industry.

How do you feel about independent/small presses? Love them; they are the heart of the industry.

What are your feelings about self-publishing? If you do it, do it well.

Do you think Amazon is good or bad — or both — for the book business? More good than bad.

What do you like and dislike about your job? I dislike when people submit without editing.

What are ways prospective clients can impress you, and what are ways they can turn you off? The easiest way to impress me is to write well. Pestering me will not cause me to view you favorably.

How would you describe the "writer from hell"? Someone who doesn't improve or heed advice.

Describe a book you would like to write. A book that creates a following that lasts long after I have died, like *The Hobbit*.

Do you believe in a higher and/or lower "power"? Yes to both.

HARVEY KLINGER, INC. ❖ www.harveyklinger.com

300 West 55 Street, New York, NY 10019, 212-581-7068

Agents' names and contact info: Harvey Klinger, harvey@harveyklinger.com; David Dunton, david@harveyklinger.com; Sara Crowe, sara@harveyklinger .com; Andrea Somberg, andrea@harveyklinger.com; Wendy Levinson, wendy@harveyklinger.com

Describe the kinds of works you want to represent. Quality fiction, both literary and commercial; interesting nonfiction by those who are already known authorities in their respective fields.

Describe what you definitely don't want to represent. Religion, computer science, photography, poetry.

How do you want writers to pitch you? Email.

Describe your education and professional history. Harvey: BA, New College; MA, Johns Hopkins University. My professional history as a literary agent goes back 40 years now.

How did you become an agent? I worked for one who taught me how not to be an agent, then worked under the aegis of a publicist for two years, and then went independent after that.

Knowing what you do now, would you do it again? If not, what might you do instead? I have absolutely no idea what I might have done instead.

Do you charge fees? If yes, please explain. Only for postage and overseas mailings or bank wires.

When and where were you born, and where have you lived? I was born in Mineola, New York, and now live principally in NYC, Pennsylvania, and Florida.

What do you like to do when you're not working? Anything on the water; on land, hiking, walking, eating, and drinking good vodka.

List some of the titles you have recently placed with publishers. Me, Myself & Us by Brian Little (Public Affairs); *Cajun Waltz* by Robert H. Patton (Thomas Dunne); *Land of the Afternoon Sun* by Barbara Wood (Turner); *Séance Infernale* by Jonathan Skariton (Knopf); *The Anatomy of Addiction* by Dr. Akikur Mohammad (Tarcher Perigee).

Describe your personality. Very terrier-like.

What do you like reading/watching/listening to on your own time? Great fiction, good movies, jazz and classical music.

Do you think the business has changed a lot over the past few years? If yes, please explain. The continued consolidation of the business is worrisome, and the fears that ebooks would make the industry crash and burn have not borne out.

What do the "Big 5" mean to you? The Big 5 publishers still standing.

How do you feel about independent/small presses? I love 'em!

What are your feelings about self-publishing? Not worth doing unless you already have an amazing presence on social media.

Do you think Amazon is good or bad — or both — for the book business? It's the devil we know — until a new one comes along.

What do you like and dislike about your job? I like that I can accomplish so much remotely nowadays. I dislike that I can seldom get away from business and shut down my computer or iPad.

What are ways prospective clients can impress you, and what are ways they can turn you off? Those who submit writing credits and blurbs from others — they turn me off by trying to be salespeople instead of writers.

How would you describe the "writer from hell"? Someone for whom nothing's ever good enough.

Describe a book you would like to write. My memoir one fine day.

Do you believe in a higher and/or lower "power"? No.

HOPKINS LITERARY ASSOCIATES

2117 Buffalo Road, Suite 327, Rochester, NY 14624, 585-352-6268

Agent's name and contact info: Pam Hopkins, hlasubmissions@rochester.rr.com

Describe the kinds of works you want to represent. Women's fiction, historical romance, contemporary romance, inspirational romance, historical fiction, mainstream fiction.

Describe what you definitely don't want to represent. No science fiction, horror, children's, nonfiction.

How do you want writers to pitch you? Email only, at hlasubmissions@rochester.rr.com.

ICM/SAGALYN ❖ www.sagalyn.com

info@sagalyn.com

Agent's name: Raphael Sagalyn

Describe the kinds of works you want to represent. Upmarket fiction and nonfiction.

How do you want writers to pitch you? A great cover letter and a great proposal; see our website for submission info.

List some of the titles you have recently placed with publishers. See www.sagalyn.com.

Do you think the business has changed a lot over the past few years? If yes, please explain. Until 2008 or so, you could find a retail bookstore at most any mall in the country. The demise of Borders was a transforming event.

INKLINGS LITERARY AGENCY ❖ www.inklingsliterary.com

3419 Virginia Beach Boulevard, #183, Virginia Beach, VA 23452, 757-340-1070

Agent's name and contact info: Michelle Johnson, michelle@inklingsliterary.com

Describe the kinds of works you want to represent. In young adult and adult: contemporary, suspense, thriller, mystery, romance, horror, fantasy, light sci-fi.

Describe what you definitely don't want to represent. Textbooks, cookbooks, short stories, picture books, poetry, coffee-table books, Christian fiction, screenplays, steampunk.

How do you want writers to pitch you? A query letter that includes the title, genre, word count, a brief blurb about the story, a short bio including any publishing credits, a brief synopsis (1–2 pages), and the first 10 pages of the manuscript.

Describe your education and professional history. I have an education in business management, with a Creative Writing Certificate from the University of Calgary. I have had a lifelong obsession with books. After a career in business management/ownership, including bookstores and community writing centers and a few years with small presses in an editorial capacity, I am now in my fourth year as a literary agent, representing many *New York Times* bestsellers, debut authors, and indie authors alike.

How did you become an agent? While running my writers' center in Virginia Beach, I did a lot of work promoting authors. That turned into a lot of research and advocating for authors. My editing clients were asking me for advice with their contracts, and I ended up doing for them almost everything an agent would do. Several of my editing clients as well as friends and family suggested that I look into a career as a literary agent.

Frankly, literary agents always intimidated me. When I met Marisa Corvisiero at a conference some years ago, she was so lovely and approachable (and human!) that I started really pondering the idea. The experiences that I have had with publishing companies made me more determined to get out there and be a voice for authors, and when the opportunity to join Marisa's agency came along, I jumped on it.

Knowing what you do now, would you do it again? If not, what might you do instead? If I knew then what I know now, of course I would do some things differently, but I'm certain I'd still be where I am today, though the road would have been less bumpy.

Do you charge fees? If yes, please explain. No.

When and where were you born, and where have you lived? I was born in Ohio and have lived all over North America.

What do you like to do when you're not working? There is no such thing as not working.

List some of the titles you have recently placed with publishers. Sawyer Bennett's next books in the *Cold Fury* series (Random House); *Loveswept*, Scott Hildreth's new mafia series (Harlequin Carina); Elliott James's next books in the *Charming* (*Pax Arcana*) series (Hachette Orbit).

Describe your personality. Workaholic, funny, fiercely loyal, freedom fighter.

What do you like reading/watching/listening to on your own time? This is an ever-evolving list of whatever I can fit in. Lately I listen to a lot of Pitbull when I work out. I watch a lot of mystery/thrillers on television when I eat dinner (*Bones*, *Criminal Minds*, *How to Get Away with Murder*, *Blacklist*, *Blindspot*, etc.). I read a lot of bestsellers when I travel so I can stay current.

Do you think the business has changed a lot over the past few years? If yes, please explain. Yes. Obviously Amazon's platform has changed a lot of things. Ebooks have changed the face of the business a bit, but not the heart. Authors now have an easy way to get their work out there, and there are so many more options for them than there used to be. Of course, that means that there are so many more authors out there than there used to be, so the competition is fierce.

What do the "Big 5" mean to you? Hachette, HarperCollins, Penguin Random House, Macmillan, Simon & Schuster — these are the biggest publishing houses that really represent what traditional publishing is.

How do you feel about independent/small presses? There are a lot of great indies out there, providing even more options for authors. Some of them are really wonderful and do some amazing things for their authors.

What are your feelings about self-publishing? I have a lot of authors who started out as self-published authors and are now traditionally published as well. I think they are my most successful authors. Self-publishing, when done properly, can be a wonderful thing for readers and authors alike.

Do you think Amazon is good or bad — or both — for the book business? Amazon has done a lot of amazing and innovative things for the industry as a whole. I also think that they are a business and that their decisions are made strictly from that point of view.

What do you like and dislike about your job? I love talking with authors about the things that make their eyes sparkle. I love the amazing things that come out of their minds, and I love being able to make their dreams come true. I dislike the inability to help everyone. I dislike that often authors forget that we are real people working a job, and it hurts us just as much as them when we have to reject them.

What are ways prospective clients can impress you, and what are ways they can turn you off? Impress: Do the homework, follow the guidelines, write from the heart — not to the trend — and keep participating in conferences and other things in the writing community. Show that you're not afraid to keep learning. Turn off: Hounding, arrogance, disrespectfulness.

How would you describe the "writer from hell"? Imagine if someone gave Dr. House a typewriter instead of a stethoscope. Yeah, him.

Describe a book you would like to write. I can't give away all my ideas, now, can I?

Do you believe in a higher and/or lower "power"? I believe in treating people with kindness, even when they don't necessarily deserve it. I also believe in not discussing my religious beliefs publicly.

IRENE GOODMAN LITERARY AGENCY ❖ irenegoodman.com

Agent's name and contact info: Irene Goodman, irene.queries@irenegoodman.com

Describe the kinds of works you want to represent. Women's fiction, historical fiction, mystery, thrillers, young adult, middle grade.

Describe what you definitely don't want to represent. Poetry, fantasy, children's picture books.

How do you want writers to pitch you? With a query through my website.

Describe your education and professional history. BA and MA from the University of Michigan.

How did you become an agent? I started as an editorial assistant at a publisher. I got to see up close what agents did, and I said, "I know I can do that and be good at it." So I did.

Knowing what you do now, would you do it again? If not, what might you do instead? It's been a great ride, but if I didn't do this, I think I would want to work on the broadcasts of the Metropolitan Opera or run political campaigns.

Do you charge fees? If yes, please explain. No.

When and where were you born, and where have you lived? I was born in Detroit, and I'm still trying to lose the accent. I have also lived in San Francisco and Boston before moving to New York and the Berkshires.

What do you like to do when you're not working? I'm always working. I can't stop. But I love to ride my bike, bake, sit under a tree and read, talk to my sisters and friends on the phone for hours at a time, and go to the theater and the opera.

List some of the titles you have recently placed with publishers. *The Survivors Club* by Michael Bornstein and Debbie Bornstein Holinstat, *And Then We Danced* by Loretta Ellsworth, *WTF (What the French?)* by Olivier Magny, *Don't You Trust Me?* by Patrice Kindl.

Describe your personality. Jeez, I don't know. Ask someone who knows me.

What do you like reading/watching/listening to on your own time? All kinds of novels, light nonfiction, girlie TV such as *What Not to Wear*, brilliant dramas such as *Dexter*, chick flicks, Mafia flicks, classic rock, and the Met Channel on Sirius XM.

What are your feelings about self-publishing? It's a good thing for some people.

Do you think Amazon is good or bad — or both — for the book business? Both. They sell lots of books, and that's good. But they want to take over the world, and they don't play nicely with others.

What do you like and dislike about your job? I am addicted to it. Everyone in my office may feel the need to do an intervention. I'm typing this at 10:00 at night, and I find that quite normal.

What are ways prospective clients can impress you, and what are ways they can turn you off? Professionalism and excellence never get old. Write a great story and the rest will follow. It's okay not to know things. Just don't be an asshole.

How would you describe the "writer from hell"? I'm too polite to say, but I've seen them.

Describe a book you would like to write. I don't want to write a book. I want to sell books.

Do you believe in a higher and/or lower "power"? I believe in life.

JABBERWOCKY LITERARY AGENCY, INC. ❖ www.awfulagent.com

49 West 45th Street, #12N, New York, NY 10036-4603, 917-388-3010

Agent's name and contact info: Sam Morgan, sam@awfulagent.com. But if you're querying me, see below and send to querysam@awfulagent.com.

Describe the kinds of works you want to represent. I work mostly in fantasy and science fiction (preference in that order). I also enjoy general commercial fiction, but nothing too literary. I have a healthy sense of humor and always look for something that puts a smile on your face. However, I could probably write a dissertation on how your sense of humor reflects your point of view on life. I take comedy a little too seriously. So although I will probably understand your humor, I'm more likely to say "that's funny" than actually laugh at your satire. If you do make me laugh, then we'll probably be friends. All of my clients have incredibly strong writing voices and approach their stories with a weird and unique eye.

Describe what you definitely don't want to represent. I am in no way, shape, or form representing young adult, middle grade, picture books, or new adult. Do not send me those. As soon as I read that your book is young adult, I immediately reject it. I don't have time for it, so do not waste yours by sending it to me.

How do you want writers to pitch you? Via email (querysam@awfulagent.com), standard query letter, and include the first five pages pasted into the body of the email. No attachments. I understand and respect how difficult it is to write a book and how sending it out to be judged is its own little battle. I respect that, so I try to respond to each and every query. But there are so many to get through that I need a little respect back, and if you do not follow these rules, you get deleted with no response.

Describe your education and professional history. I graduated from the University of North Carolina at Chapel Hill (Go Tar Heels!) and I am still in my first job in the publishing industry. But I've been here a few years now, and things seem to be going well enough.

How did you become an agent? Completely by accident, to be honest. I didn't even know what a literary agent was before I started working at JABberwocky. I had a friend from college who was hired to do foreign rights here and a few months later he asked if I was free to do some data entry. I had found myself with an abundance of free time and a desire for a consistent cash flow (read: I was unemployed) and said yes. So that's how I got started, filling royalty statements into a spreadsheet. But I got to talking to the people in the office about science fiction and fantasy, which I had a natural taste for, and then about story structure and tropes (which I studied in college and can nerd out on all day), and eventually the boss let me try to be an agent after I got promoted to his assistant. Apparently I have a knack for it (it helps being the child of three generations of lawyers past in reading contracts), and I've been doing it ever since.

Knowing what you do now, would you do it again? If not, what might you do instead? This is a dangerous question because all my answers seem to have me turning into Biff from *Back to the Future II*.

Do you charge fees? If yes, please explain. Nope!

When and where were you born, and where have you lived? I was born and raised in Shelby, North Carolina. We have the best BBQ, and be prepared for a very strongly worded rebuttal should you choose to argue that point. I lived there my entire life before the four years I spent in Chapel Hill for college. Ten days after I graduated, I moved to New York City and have been living here ever since. Did I have a job lined up or any idea what I'd be doing once I got up here? Not a clue. Did my parents think that was a good idea? Not even the slightest. But I showed them.

What do you like to do when you're not working? Sit in silence and ponder the career choices of Matthew McConaughey.

List some of the titles you have recently placed with publishers. Gladly! *The Unnoticeables* by Robert Brockway (Tor), *Steal the Sky* by Megan E. O'Keefe (Angry Robot), *Warlock Holmes* by G. S. Denning (Titan), *Windswept* by Adam Rakunas (Angry Robot), *Waypoint Kangaroo* by Curtis C. Chen (Thomas Dunne), *Duskfall* by Christopher Husberg (Titan). I also am in charge of the audio rights for the agency and have placed clients with all the major audio publishers including but not limited to Audible, Recorded, Cutting, and Tantor.

Describe your personality. I am ridiculously handsome, gut-bustingly witty, and prone to hyperbole.

What do you like reading/watching/listening to on your own time? All the TV! I'm usually up to speed on most of the critic-darling shows, the off-kilter cult favorites, and those weird little genre shows that no one else has heard about but I still watch.

Do you think the business has changed a lot over the past few years? If yes, please explain. If an industry doesn't change, it stagnates, and if it stagnates, it dies. So yes, it has changed and will change even more. All that means is that we have to adjust our methods as well.

What do the "Big 5" mean to you? Boilerplates. Black holes of nonresponsive submissions. Giant stacks of royalty reports. Incredible individuals whom I consider some of my close friends.

How do you feel about independent/small presses? In battle facing a formidable foe, even the smallest among us, with the feeblest weapon but the most indomitable spirit, can change the tide of war.

What are your feelings about self-publishing? Hey, I believe in "you do you." But if you're constantly rejected by traditional publishing, there is probably a reason and you just can't see it. By all means prove us wrong, though.

Do you think Amazon is good or bad — or both — for the book business? They could be better. A whole lot better.

What do you like and dislike about your job? I like being the first champion of the next great novel, turning an aspiring novelist's dream into a reality, seeing a book I found in the slush pile on the bookshelves next to the greats. I dislike crushing dreams daily, not being able to directly control the process once the book is out of my hands, readers/editors /reviewers not believing me when I tell them I represent the world's greatest books.

What are ways prospective clients can impress you, and what are ways they can turn you off? Free booze always works. Serious answer: being yourself, being confident, but also being cool is the best way to impress me. Turnoffs include selfishness, not following submission guidelines, and generally being a butthead.

How would you describe the "writer from hell"? Anyone who uses "lol" in a query letter.

Describe a book you would like to write. A finished one.

Do you believe in a higher and/or lower "power"? Whoa, this survey got *deep*. I believe that humanity has achieved a unique perspective in the universe that allows us to be self-aware enough to know that our time, energy, and space are limited and rapidly shrinking, but delusional and mad enough to face that fact and laugh in the universe's face. I consider that a power we all share.

Is there anything you wish to express beyond the parameters of the preceding questions? Have fun! 👍

Agent's name and contact info: Lisa Rodgers, lisa@awfulagent.com

Describe the kinds of works you want to represent. I represent works of science fiction, fantasy, and romance for adult, young adult, and middle grade audiences.

Describe what you definitely don't want to represent. I don't represent screenplays, scripts, short fiction, and most nonfiction.

How do you want writers to pitch you? Via email, following our submission guidelines (awfulagent.com/submissions-2).

Describe your education and professional history. I graduated from California State University, Sacramento, in 2011 with a bachelor's degree in English literature and a minor in German literature-in-translation, history, and culture. I've previously volunteered as a submissions reader for *Lightspeed Magazine*, interned at Levine Greenberg Rostan Literary Agency, and was an associate editor at *San Francisco Book Review*.

How did you become an agent? I moved to NYC in 2012 to attend NYU's Summer Publishing Institute. From there, I went on to intern at Levine Greenberg Rostan, where I continued to hone my editorial skills while also learning about the administrative side of agenting. I eventually accepted a position as an agent with JABberwocky Literary Agency, where I'm building my own client list as well as handling the agency's growing ebook program.

Knowing what you do now, would you do it again? If not, what might you do instead? Attending the NYU summer program was critical to my path; it allowed me to relocate and put me in contact with those who would eventually help me find my current position. It's not a path that works for everyone, though. If I had previously lived somewhere that was more publishing-centric, I likely would have done my best to secure internships while I was in college to build work experience and connections instead.

Do you charge fees? If yes, please explain. No.

When and where were you born, and where have you lived? In California, I've lived in the San Francisco Bay Area and Sacramento. In New York, I've lived in Brooklyn and Queens. I also spent a semester living in Perth, Western Australia.

What do you like to do when you're not working? I like to knit (mostly socks) and catch up on TV shows. I also enjoy playing video games. My all-time favorites are *The Legend of Zelda: Ocarina of Time* and *Final Fantasy III/VI*.

List some of the titles you have recently placed with publishers. *A Lady's Guide to Ruin* by Kathleen Kimmel, *Enemy* by K. Eason.

What do you like reading/watching/listening to on your own time? Romance novels currently fit my schedule the best right now for leisure reading. They're fun and fast-paced, and I know there will be a happy ever after! Science fiction and fantasy require a bit more mental energy to keep track of the world-building, so I tend to reserve them for vacation time, when I know I'll have a bit more time to invest.

How do you feel about independent/small presses? Independent and small presses serve a very important role in publishing. I think having more options for authors is a good thing. Not every author wants or needs to be traditionally published by the Big 5 publishers.

What are your feelings about self-publishing? Like independent/small presses, self-publishing is a very important option available to authors in today's publishing environment. It gives authors options they wouldn't otherwise have.

JAKE BARTOK LITERARY ASSOCIATES ❖ www.virgointacta.com

211 East 42nd Street, Suite 1109, New York, NY 10017, 929-241-9057 ext. 1241, fax: 929-241-9063

Agents' names and contact info: Jake Bartok, jake_bartok@virgointacta.com; Faustina King, faustina@virgointacta.com; David San Giorgio, david-san-g@virgointacta.com

Describe the kinds of works you want to represent. *Jake*: I represent fiction and nonfiction. I generally won't represent novels that are thinly veiled autobiographies or autobiographies that are thinly veiled novels.

Describe what you definitely don't want to represent. We've been seeing novels whose size is about 30 percent of what a novel should be, i.e., we've been seeing novelettes proffered as novels by writers used to the ebook marketplace. We've also been seeing so-called ebooks with resell rights, generic novels sold to aspiring authors to which they append their bylines and call them their own. Just two examples of what we don't want to represent, but there are more.

How do you want writers to pitch you? Contact me with a brief email message describing the project. I'll read it and reply. If I'd like to see more, I'll ask for it.

Describe your education and professional history. I was educated in Paris and London on full academic scholarships and received a Bachelor of Commerce (magna cum laude) from Oxford University. I went on to earn an MBA from Baruch College in New York. Building on my successful career as a business entrepreneur, I began devoting a growing portion of my time and energies to agenting.

How did you become an agent? I got into agenting in order to nurture talent and balance the scales. By this I mean that my aim is to ensure that writing worth publishing sees publication and is not summarily cast into obscurity.

Knowing what you do now, would you do it again? If not, what might you do instead? I haven't finished doing it yet. In fact, in many respects I've only begun.

Do you charge fees? If yes, please explain. No fees charged.

When and where were you born, and where have you lived? I was born in New York City. I've also lived in Europe, principally Paris, France.

What do you like to do when you're not working? My hobby is repairing things, which have ranged from cars to electric coffee percolators. I have several personal interests, but literature ranks at the top.

List some of the titles you have recently placed with publishers. I try to keep my client list between myself and my direct professional contacts, so please forgive my not listing titles here.

Describe your personality. I find myself amazingly reasonable and rational, at least when compared to many others I've encountered. I grant this may be my own conceit.

What do you like reading/watching/listening to on your own time? I'm a billy goat when it comes to reading, watching, and listening, and this includes dietary information on bags of potato chips and VCR tapes other people have the sense to throw away.

Do you think the business has changed a lot over the past few years? If yes, please explain. I do. Corporate dominance on the print side has meant emphasis on corporate balance sheets. On the digital side, I see growing marketplace commoditization.

What do the "Big 5" mean to you? Maybe tomorrow's Big 2, or fewer.

How do you feel about independent/small presses? Hobby horses, at best; for their owners, that is. The shelves of boutique stores in Manhattan (to name one place I've found them) bulge with their offerings. It's great to see this outpouring. But where is all of it going?

What are your feelings about self-publishing? Self-publishing has always been around and has always been an option for even authors of repute. I would need to approach the subject on a case-by-case basis. I have no overarching opinion on the subject in general.

Do you think Amazon is good or bad — or both — for the book business? That depends on what day of the week it happens to be.

What do you like and dislike about your job? I have liked living much of the time in Paris and being able to interact directly with both US and EU publishers. I'm not as sure today as I was a year or two ago. I dislike professional situations in which I'm subject to vacillation from the editorial side.

What are ways prospective clients can impress you, and what are ways they can turn you off? I'm usually turned off by people who are either arrogant or subservient. Both traits tend to show both in person and in written contacts. I try to avoid being overly judgmental, however, as people are often afraid to be themselves and instead strike poses.

How would you describe the "writer from hell"? I couldn't. I've never actually represented one. This is probably because, if there are signs that someone may be that sort of individual, they're obvious from the start, and any astute person can spot them and take whatever action is necessary. I know I have, before such persons have had a chance to become clients.

Describe a book you would like to write. If I told you, I couldn't be an agent anymore.

Do you believe in a higher and/or lower "power"? I'll have to think that one over awhile, after I finish praying.

Is there anything you wish to express beyond the parameters of the preceding questions? Ask me again after I figure out why I can't see my reflection anymore.

JEANNE FREDERICKS LITERARY AGENCY, INC. ❖

www.jeannefredericks.com

221 Benedict Hill Road, New Canaan, CT 06840, 203-972-9011

Agent's name and contact info: Jeanne Fredericks, jeanne.fredericks@gmail.com

Describe the kinds of works you want to represent. I like to represent practical, popular reference by authorities, especially in health, science, fitness, gardening, and women's interest. I'm also interested in cooking, elite sports, parenting, environment, lifestyle, and antiques/decorative arts.

Describe what you definitely don't want to represent. I do not represent genre fiction (e.g. horror, occult fiction, true crime, romance, Westerns, and sci-fi), juvenile, textbooks, poetry, essays, plays, short stories, pop culture, guides to computers and software, politics, pornography, overly depressing or violent topics, memoirs that are more suitable for one's family or that are not compelling enough for the trade market, manuals for teachers, or workbooks. I rarely represent fiction, and only for existing clients whose novels are a normal outgrowth of their nonfiction writing.

How do you want writers to pitch you? Please query by email without attachments to jeanne.fredericks@gmail.com or by mail with an SASE. No phone calls, faxes, or deliveries that require signatures please.

Describe your education and professional history. BA, Mount Holyoke College, 1972, major in English, Phi Beta Kappa; Radcliffe Publishing Procedures Course, 1972; MBA, NYU Graduate School of Business (now called Stern), major in marketing, 1979. Career history: I established my own agency in 1997 after being an agent and acting director for Susan P. Urstadt, Inc. (1990–96). Prior to that, I was an editorial director for Ziff-Davis Books (1980–81); acquiring editor, the first female managing editor, and assistant managing editor for Macmillan's Trade Division (1974–80); assistant to the editorial director and foreign/subsidiary rights director of Basic Books (1972–74). Member of AAR and Authors Guild.

How did you become an agent? I reentered publishing as an agent because the flexible hours and home-based office were compatible with raising young children. I enjoy working with creative authors who need my talents to find the right publishers for their proposed books and to negotiate fair contracts on their behalf. I am still thrilled when I open a box of newly published books by one of my authors, knowing that I had a small role in making it happen. I'm also ever hopeful that the books I represent will make a positive difference in the lives of many people.

Knowing what you do now, would you do it again? If not, what might you do instead? Yes, I would do it again. I enjoy the long-term relationships I have with my authors, the daily challenges of learning something new, such as ebook publishing, reviewing promising proposals, pitching proposals that I love to publishers, and managing auctions.

Do you charge fees? If yes, please explain. I do not charge any fees.

When and where were you born, and where have you lived? April 19, 1950, Mineola, New York. I have also lived in Louisiana, Michigan, British Columbia, California, New Jersey, Massachusetts, England, and Connecticut.

What do you like to do when you're not working? I enjoy swimming, yoga, hiking, walking with friends and my Lab, reading, traveling, casual entertaining, gardening, photography, family activities, volunteering at church and other local organizations, and good conversations with friends. I am hoping to return to crew, which was my key outside interest for 10 years.

List some of the titles you have recently placed with publishers. Last-Minute Entertaining with America's Best Chefs by Maria Isabella (Page Street), *Growing Vegetables in Drought, Desert & Dry Times* and *Colorful Landscaping for Drought, Desert & Dry Times* by Maureen Gilmer (Sasquatch), *For Sale — American Paradise: How Our Nation Was Sold an Impossible Dream in Florida* by Willie Drye (Lyons), *The New England Catch* by Martha Murphy (Globe Pequot), *Yoga Therapy: The Ultimate Guide to Yoga for Health and Wellness* by Larry Payne, PhD, Eden Goldman, DC, and Terra Gold, DOM (Basic Health), *Yoga Nidra for Stress Relief* by Julie Lush (New Harbinger), *Treasure Ship: The Legend and Legacy of the S. S. Brother Jonathan* and *The Raging Sea* and *Sentinel of the Seas* by Dennis M. Powers (Sea Ventures Press), *The Creativity Cure: A Do-It-Yourself Prescription to Happiness* by Carrie Barron, MD, and Alton Barron, MD (Scribner), *The Scarlett Letters: The Making of the Film* Gone with the Wind by John Wiley, Jr. (Taylor), *Jumping the Fence: A Legacy of Race and Family Secrets in Antebellum New Orleans through the Era of Jim Crow and Beyond* by Maureen Gilmer (Cedar Fort), *The American Quilt* by Robert Shaw (Sterling), *Waking the Warrior Goddess: Dr. Christine Horner's Program to Protect Against and Fight Breast Cancer* by Christine Horner, MD (Basic Health), *Lilias! Yoga: Your Guide to Enhancing Body, Mind, and Spirit in Midlife and Beyond* by Lilias Folan (Skyhorse), *Artful Watercolor* by Carolyn Janik and Lou Bonamarte (Sterling), *Smart Guide to Single Malt Whisky* by Elizabeth Riley Bell and *Smart Guide to Understanding Your Cat* by Carolyn Janik (Smart Guides), *A Woman's Guide to Pelvic Health: Expert Advice for Women of All Ages* by Elizabeth E. Houser, MD, and Stephanie Riley Hahn, PT (Johns Hopkins University Press).

Describe your personality. I love to learn about many subjects, so I continue to be enthused about working with authors who want to share their expertise with others. I favor building and nurturing long-term relationships with authors, but remain open to new talent. I'm an optimist who likes to work with people who see problems as challenges to overcome, and I know that good results in publishing stem from insight, monitoring trends, hard work, and attention to detail as well as keeping up with new technologies and ways of doing things. My background makes me think on many levels — as an MBA, editor, agent, and enthusiastic reader — when representing clients. Though I can be firm and persistent in negotiations, I believe in old-fashioned courtesy and respect among colleagues and love working on a team in creating and marketing a book that will have lasting value.

What do you like reading/watching/listening to on your own time? I am an eclectic reader who enjoys literary fiction, groundbreaking research-based nonfiction that makes me think in new ways, inspirational books, tempting cookbooks, gardening books, and ones with breathtaking photos. I enjoy classical music as a background to reading and editing (Beethoven, Mozart, Chopin, Brahms, Bach), but I love to dance to classic rock, ethnic music, jazz — anything with a good beat that makes me want to move to the music. I'm a big fan of *Downton Abbey*, *Foyle's War*, *Northern Exposure*, *Doc Martin*, *The Midwives*, *Poirot*, films of Jane Austen's classics, and other PBS productions. I lived in England during my college vacations, and my mother was raised there, so I am quite an Anglophile.

Do you think the business has changed a lot over the past few years? If yes, please explain. Yes, there has been quite a dramatic change in what publishers expect from an author. It used to be that if a nonfiction author had authority, could write well, chose a fresh angle on a subject of interest to enough people, and was "promotable," he or she had a good shot at getting a contract. Now publishers also require authors to bring ready-made markets with them, especially in terms of social media. Even smaller publishers expect this. The practical reality behind these new requirements is that the bookstores and chains focus on carrying books by authors who are already known. My concern is that this is leading to contracts being given to too many people who are simply popular online and to too few well-qualified authors who haven't managed to create a following online. Building an online presence requires time and a certain amount of extroversion, which doesn't necessarily jive with the typical reserved writer or the busy professional who doesn't have time to spend on such pursuits. I am somewhat nostalgic for the days when books were acquired on the basis of an experienced editor's judgment that someone could write well about something worth reading and had the potential to learn from the publicity department how to promote the book.

What do the "Big 5" mean to you? A necessary concentration of power and economies to scale in back-office, selling, and inventory functions due to the competition of Amazon and other forms of entertainment. From the perspective of an agent, though, it means fewer publishers to pitch, fewer auctions, and less leverage for securing higher advances, better royalties, and improved contractual language.

How do you feel about independent/small presses? I believe that they can sometimes do a better job publishing a book long term than the Big 5 when they focus on niche markets and actively sell and promote their backlists. Some of my authors who have published with small publishers have sold more copies than authors published with the Big 5.

What are your feelings about self-publishing? Self-publishing opens up opportunities for many aspiring writers and levels the playing field to a certain extent, since self-published authors can sometimes publish successfully and earn more money than with publishers. They can also have more control over the key decisions in publishing. The problem is discoverability in a world where there are far too many books being published. Unless the self-published author has written a high-quality book and is willing to put in the time to build a marketing platform and fine-tune the metadata for discoverability, the book may sell so few copies that all the effort put into writing and publishing will seem worthless. Also if authors aspire to publish POD (print-on-demand) paperbacks, they may be surprised by what they need to know and do to prepare a book for publication.

Do you think Amazon is good or bad — or both — for the book business? I used to feel that Amazon was the hated behemoth that used its clout to drive out small publishers and independent booksellers who couldn't compete with their discounted pricing and speedy fulfillment of orders. I still think that there is some truth to that statement, but over time I realized I had to admit that I liked the convenience and low prices of buying on their site and that I found the site an excellent tool for research. I admire how Amazon staff continually learn and improve their ways of doing business and take the time to meet with agents to educate them about their way of publishing. Now that I am involved with publishing some ebooks and POD books with them, I have respect for their quick sizing-up of opportunities, taking the steps to make publishing seem understandable and doable, and their one-on-one support to agents who are publishing books in their "White Glove" program. To remain competitive, publishers and other book retailers are going to have to be proactive in keeping pace by finding ways to offer more or something better or different than Amazon; otherwise, they may find that they will go the way of so many independent bookstores.

What do you like and dislike about your job? I feel honored to work with smart, persevering authors to help them achieve their dream of being published and then to help them build their writing career. I find auctions thrilling, since they generally yield the highest advances for my authors. Negotiating contracts, though tedious, is satisfying at the end when I know I've used my experience to get the best terms and contractual language for my client. I feel energized by meeting with editors and learning what they like and want. I also enjoy the role of diplomat, since I know the publishing side of the business and can therefore more easily help the author and publisher resolve issues that inevitably arise during the publishing process. What I don't like is rejecting queries and proposals (especially ones that are good, but by authors with insufficient marketing platforms). I also dislike feeling that I can never be caught up, since there is an endless flow of emails that keep tugging me away from the more substantive work such as reading proposals I've requested or helping an author fine-tune a submission package.

What are ways prospective clients can impress you, and what are ways they can turn you off? I am impressed by authors who are true authorities on the subject of their book, have a fresh angle or new research, and can convincingly explain why the proposed book is different, better, and needed by large defined audiences. I am drawn to authors who are sought-after speakers not only by their peers, but also by the public. Due to the current expectations by publishers, I also take notice of authors who have already established a search engine–optimized website and who regularly engage online with their anticipated trade audiences. I prefer working with authors who are polite, patient, and willing to work hard to make their proposal ready for submission. I also appreciate authors who are familiar with my website and therefore know what kinds of books I like and what I like to see in a proposal.

What turns me off is a cold call or query from someone who tells me about a book that is totally unsuited for my line of books. I am repelled by queries that seem grandiose, complaining, gross, depressing, uninformed about the competition, poorly written, or sloppily proofread.

How would you describe the "writer from hell"? An arrogant, pushy, self-centered, unreliable writer who does not understand publishing or respect my time and who vents anger in an unprofessional way. Fortunately, I've rarely encountered such a person in this business. When I sense an overly inflated ego in the initial correspondence and communication, I steer clear of the person.

Describe a book you would like to write. Hmm, no idea! My head is too full of the books that others have written or aspire to write. Maybe I will write my own sometime in the future when I have more time to reflect on the life I've lived and what I want to pass on to the next generation.

Do you believe in a higher and/or lower "power"? Yes, I believe in God, but I also believe that a person needs to work to make opportunities and achieve success in life. I have been active in my church for decades and as the trustee of a new foundation that fosters small-group ministries and Bible study for people from any denomination.

Is there anything you wish to express beyond the parameters of the preceding questions? Just that I urge authors to be resilient in the face of the inevitable rejections, learn from constructive criticism, and embrace learning new technologies and marketing methods.

JEAN V. NAGGAR LITERARY AGENCY, INC. ❖ www.jvnla.com

216 East 75th Street, Suite 1E, New York, NY 10021

Agent's name and contact info: Laura Biagi, lbiagi@jvnla.com, Twitter: @LauraJBiagi

Describe the kinds of works you want to represent. In adult fiction, I am especially interested in literary fiction, magical realism, cultural themes, social issues, and debut authors. I'm drawn to strong voices, complex narrative arcs, dynamic and well-developed characters, psychological twists, and apocalyptic literary fiction. In the young readers' realm, I look for young adult novels, middle grade novels, and picture books. I love young readers' books that have a magical tinge to them and vivid writing. In both adult and young readers' books, I'm also looking for titles that incorporate high-concept, dark/edgy, and quirky elements as well as titles that challenge the way we typically view the world. I occasionally do memoir, but it has to be the right project, as I typically don't go for it. Our primary nonfiction agent is Elizabeth Evans.

Describe what you definitely don't want to represent. I'm probably not the right person for high fantasy, sci-fi, or hard-boiled detective mysteries. I just don't love them as much as other types of fiction.

How do you want writers to pitch you? I prefer to receive submissions via our website (jvnla.com/submissions), but I also accept submissions sent directly to my email address (lbiagi@jvnla.com). If you're submitting via the website or by email, please always include the first page of your manuscript, as this is extremely helpful for me when I'm considering your project.

When and where were you born, and where have you lived? I was born in Louisville, Kentucky, but I grew up in a smaller town 30 minutes away, Shelbyville.

Do you charge fees? If yes, please explain. No, our agency does not charge reading fees.

Describe your education and professional history. I attended college at Northwestern

University, where I studied creative writing (fiction) and anthropology (cultural; I did an eight-week research study in Guatemala for my thesis). My start in publishing was with the Jean Naggar Agency, where I began as an intern. From there, I got hired on as an assistant and now work as an agent! I've also had a brief stint at Barnes & Noble.

What do you like to do when you're not working? I personally like to write adult literary fiction on all topics, especially involving magical realism, absurdism, and/or social issues. This also means that adult literary fiction involving these is right up my alley, so I'm always looking for submissions involving them!

How did you become an agent? The roots of how I came to be an agent could probably be traced back to my college studies in creative writing. I loved critiquing manuscripts in writing workshops so much that I chose to enter an industry in which I could read and critique manuscripts for a living! I was also attracted to how collaborative and creative the industry is and how everyone involved in publishing is driven by a passion for good writing and good stories. My official start in the book-publishing industry began with my internship at the Jean Naggar Agency. Soon after, I was hired on full-time. As an assistant, I worked closely with Jean Naggar and Jennifer Weltz on their titles. I also worked a great deal on our international rights; I created rights lists for international book fairs and sent materials and reviews to our coagents. I am still involved in our international rights and, in that vein, now sell ANZ rights for our published books. In 2012 I began taking on my own clients. I am very excited to be building up a list of adult literary fiction authors and kids' book authors (young adult, middle grade, and picture books).

THE JEFF HERMAN AGENCY LLC ❖ www.jeffherman.com

PO Box 1522, Stockbridge, MA 01262, 413-298-0077

Agent's name and contact info: Jeff Herman, jeff@jeffherman.com

Describe the kinds of works you want to represent. Though I'll never absolutely say "never" to any category, my strong suit is and has always been adult nonfiction.

Describe what you definitely don't want to represent. I just can't bring myself to answer this question, even though I wrote it.

How do you want writers to pitch you? Email seems to be working just fine. I open my box every day and don't delete anything without at least a cursory look. Physical submissions seem more likely to get short shrift. It used to be the other way around until I reached an organic level of digital comfort several years ago. I held out as long as I could, and then I finally drank the digital Kool-Aid.

Describe your education and professional history. I got a liberal arts degree a long time ago from Syracuse University. And then I began my education. I answered a variety of blind employment ads in the *New York Times*, which was the best go-to job source in NYC back then (maybe still is?). By chance, I scored an interview with Schocken Books, which at the time was an independent house with a very rich history that I knew nothing about. It wasn't much of an interview. I think the only question was "Can you start tomorrow?" and the only right answer was "Yes." It was 1981, I was 22 years old, and I'm still in the book business. This experience taught me that planning one's life isn't a requirement, because at the time I didn't have a fixed direction or goal. But I did have a natural passion for discovering what I could about the world around me.

How did you become an agent? In my latter 20s I went out on my own and found I was able to find clients, meet editors, and make deals. The '80s and '90s were a relatively expansive time in book publishing, or at least that's the way I experienced it.

Knowing what you do now, would you do it again? If not, what might you do instead? I think I would have to do it differently today. Thirty years ago, fax machines, voicemail, and word processors were the big innovations. Cell phones didn't work well in Manhattan, and per-minute rates were very high. I read books about "teleselling" and pitch-letter writing to hone my skills. Terms like social media obviously didn't exist yet. I'm sure I'd do it again, just differently.

Do you charge fees? If yes, please explain. No.

When and where were you born, and where have you lived? I'm a Long Island kid and lived most of my life in the New York area. I migrated to the hills about 15 years ago (western Massachusetts).

What do you like to do when you're not working? I don't know how to answer this, which makes me feel like maybe there's something wrong with me. I like watching TV and reading and "bumming around." I like eating basic comfort foods. I'm not complicated.

List some of the titles you have recently placed with publishers. I've agented more than 1,000 books into publication. I post a partial list at www.jeffherman.com.

Describe your personality. I bore easily. Don't really like socializing much. I like to kid around and be provocative without being mean or offensive.

What do you like reading/watching/listening to on your own time? I tend to prefer independently produced films, edgy literature, and anything that challenges the status quo.

Do you think the business has changed a lot over the past few years? If yes, please explain.
There seems to be less money in the middle. There are some very large advances and many shitty advances. I don't mean to be dark, but I think the economics were more abundant and equitable in the recent past.

What do the "Big 5" mean to you? Domination and reality.

How do you feel about independent/small presses? I pray for them. And I predict a resurgence in the near future.

What are your feelings about self-publishing? We must not underestimate its future. In fact, one day it might become the dog that wags the tail.

Do you think Amazon is good or bad — or both — for the book business? I think to a large extent it defines the book business, and has become an invaluable platform for free expression in the form of books by anyone, regardless of resources or social standing, and makes money from doing so.

What do you like and dislike about your job? I don't like it so much when it becomes raw work. I like it more when I feel I'm making a positive difference for and with the people I work with.

What are ways prospective clients can impress you, and what are ways they can turn you off? They impress me when they express themselves in ways I and others can easily understand and connect to, and when they are as eager to give as to receive.

How would you describe the "writer from hell"? Consumption in the absence of production. Hunger in the absence of appreciation.

Describe a book you would like to write. How to Survive the Zombie Apocalypse.

Do you believe in a higher and/or lower "power"? I think so.

Is there anything you wish to express beyond the parameters of the preceding questions?
Be free.

THE JENNIFER DE CHIARA LITERARY AGENCY ❖ www.jdlit.com

31 East 32nd Street, Suite 300, New York, NY 10016, 212-481-8484

Agent's name and contact info: Jennifer De Chiara, jenndec@aol.com

Describe the kinds of works you want to represent. I'm passionate about representing children's literature (picture books, middle grade, and young adult) in every genre (I also represent illustrators), adult literary fiction (writers with something special to say and a special way of saying it), commercial fiction, mystery, thrillers, and horror. In nonfiction, I love to represent celebrity bios (my past and current clients include Danny Aiello, Tippi Hedren, Eric Braeden, Linda Blair, Leif Garrett, Jeanne Cooper, Sylvia Browne, Michael Learned, Julie Newmar, Catherine Hickland, Beth Maitland, Dick Gautier, Jeff Conaway, James Brown, Artemis Pyle, Toni Tennille, and many others) and anything and everything about Hollywood, (entertainment, theater, dance, behind-the-scenes), memoir, biography, pop culture, true crime, self-help, parenting, and humor. In general, I'm open to any well-written book, either fiction or nonfiction, in any genre.

Describe what you definitely don't want to represent. I don't represent poetry, Westerns, romance, or erotica.

How do you want writers to pitch you? Email only; follow the submission guidelines on my agency website, www.jdlit.com.

Describe your education and professional history. Brooklyn College, New York University. I've been a dancer and actress, writing consultant, freelance editor for Random House and Simon & Schuster, literary agent for two established New York City literary agencies. I've been a literary agent for 18 years and started my own literary agency in 2001.

How did you become an agent? How I became an agent is too long a story to tell, but I started my own agency because I wanted to make a difference; I wanted to help put great books out into the world, and I wanted to help make writers' dreams come true. It was an accidental career for me, but it's what I believe I was put on this planet to do.

Knowing what you do now, would you do it again? If not, what might you do instead? Absolutely!

Do you charge fees? If yes, please explain. No.

When and where were you born, and where have you lived? I was born in New York City and have lived here my entire life.

What do you like to do when you're not working? It's a struggle for me to do any of the following because I have so little free time these days, but I'm passionate about reading (everything), writing (working on a screenplay at the moment), ballet (someday I vow to get back to it and take classes just for the fun of it), skiing (love schussing down the slopes, but equally love sipping hot cocoa by a roaring fire), travel (I'm in love with Italy and spent several months there recently), movies/theater (what I could have done with that role, oy!), piano (been taking lessons for close to 20 years and will keep at it until I croak or until the neighbors sign a petition to make me stop).

List some of the titles you have recently placed with publishers. *Elf on the Shelf* by Carol Aebersold and Chanda Bell; *Toni Tennille, A Memoir* by Toni Tennille and Caroline St.

Clair Tennille; *Skynned Alive: Keeping the Beat in Lynyrd Skynyrd, the World's Greatest Rock and Roll Band* (memoir) by Artemis Pyle with Dean Goodman; *Hazy Bloom*, the first three books in a middle grade series by Jennifer Hamburg; *Billy Boo Is Stuck in Goo* (picture book) by Jennifer Hamburg; *I'll Be Damned* (memoir) by Eric Braeden; *Three Truths and a Lie* (young adult) by Brent Hartinger.

Describe your personality. Compassionate, hardworking, ambitious, positive, strong. I care about people and making the world a better place.

What are your feelings about self-publishing? A good option in some cases, a bad one in others.

How would you describe the "writer from hell"? Someone who calls or emails constantly for news, expects a phone call from me when there's nothing to discuss, expects me to perform according to their timetable, has no knowledge of the publishing business and wants to call the shots; can't accept rejection or criticism, has a lack of appreciation for my efforts, fails to work as part of a team. Every once in a while a client from hell slips into the agency, but once they show us their horns, we send them back to the inferno.

Describe a book you would like to write. Literary fiction, definitely, and probably an underdog story.

Agent's name and contact info: Linda Epstein, querylindaepstein@gmail.com

Describe the kinds of works you want to represent. I represent children's literature — picture books, middle grade, young adult, both fiction and nonfiction.

Describe what you definitely don't want to represent. Adult literature.

How do you want writers to pitch you? I accept email queries only.

Describe your education and professional history. I was an English major as an undergraduate and did some graduate work in creative writing. I've always been a writer. I took a circuitous route on the road to becoming a literary agent, but ended up exactly where I belong.

How did you become an agent? I had the best midlife crisis ever. Then I began working toward becoming an agent and did the things one needs to do to get into the field, including reading for other agents (for free) for a few years, interning, and reading in my field.

Knowing what you do now, would you do it again? If not, what might you do instead? Absolutely. I'd just start earlier.

Do you charge fees? If yes, please explain. No.

When and where were you born, and where have you lived? Born and raised in New York. I've lived here my whole life.

What do you like to do when you're not working? Spend time with my family, cook, travel, write, read for pleasure.

List some of the titles you have recently placed with publishers. *Girl Mans Up* by M-E Girard (Katherine Tegen Books/HarperCollins, 2016), *The Fix* by Natasha Sinel (Sky Pony Press, 2015), the sequel to *Peanut Butter and Brains* by Joe McGee (Abrams, 2017), *Honestly Ben* by Bill Konigsberg (Scholastic, 2017), *Where Are the Words?* by Jodi McKay (Albert A. Whitman, 2017).

Describe your personality. I'm a glass-half-full kind of person. I'm loyal and a good friend. Although I can be a scatterbrain, I'm also dependable.

What do you like reading/watching/listening to on your own time? I read lots and lots of children's literature, with brief forays into select favorite adult authors. I'm also very selective regarding my television/movie watching. I mostly listen to rock and roll ('60s through '90s) and alt/indie music.

Do you think the business has changed a lot over the past few years? If yes, please explain. Yes. I could write a book about it.

How do you feel about independent/small presses? As long as they take care of my clients (financially, distribution-wise, and promoting their work), I *love* small presses!

What are your feelings about self-publishing? I think self-publishing can be a good option for people who can put the time, energy, and money into promotion and publicity, which is not everyone. The kink in the self-publishing model is that because there's nobody vetting what gets published, there's quite a lot of self-published work that's just not that good.

Do you think Amazon is good or bad — or both — for the book business? I think Amazon has done a lot to change the landscape of publishing. Some of that has been good for the book business and some of that hasn't. I don't think it's a simple good/bad question, though.

What do you like and dislike about your job? I like most things about my job, except for when I can't sell a project that I love. Also, publishing moves at glacial speed, which can be quite frustrating.

What are ways prospective clients can impress you, and what are ways they can turn you off? Prospective clients can always impress me with fabulous writing and creative ideas. They turn me off when they act entitled, overly confident (when it's unwarranted), and rude.

How would you describe the "writer from hell"? The "writer from hell" is somebody who can't write in the first place, doesn't know how to revise or take criticism, and doesn't have self-awareness.

Describe a book you would like to write. A middle grade mystery that incorporates yarn bombing.

Do you believe in a higher and/or lower "power"? I believe in a higher power. I don't know what a "lower power" even means.

Agent's name and contact info: Stephen Fraser, fraserstephena@gmail.com

Describe the kinds of works you want to represent. Mostly children's and teens', all genres.

Describe what you definitely don't want to represent. No medical, military, erotica, or gross-out.

How do you want writers to pitch you? Via email with excerpt (or full picture book).

Describe your education and professional history. Middlebury College; master's degree in children's literature from Simmons College.

How did you become an agent? After 25 years as an editor (HarperCollins, Simon & Schuster).

Knowing what you do now, would you do it again? If not, what might you do instead? Yes.

Do you charge fees? If yes, please explain. No fees charged.

When and where were you born, and where have you lived? Born on Cape Cod, grew up in Boston, currently live in Manhattan.

What do you like to do when you're not working? Reading, movies, and travel.

List some of the titles you have recently placed with publishers. *The Bamboo Sword* by Margi Preus, *Arctic Code* by Matthew Kirby, *The Green Umbrella* by Jackie Kramer, *Pure Grit* by Mary Cronk Farrell.

Describe your personality. Patient, upbeat.

What do you like reading/watching/listening to on your own time? Biographies of writers or artists, classical music.

Do you think the business has changed a lot over the past few years? If yes, please explain. More cautious; more bottom line–oriented; still fascinating and enriching.

What do the "Big 5" mean to you? Are there still 5?

How do you feel about independent/small presses? I made a lot of sales to medium and small places recently because they seem hungrier for manuscripts.

What are your feelings about self-publishing? For the most part, self-publishing = impatience.

Do you think Amazon is good or bad — or both — for the book business? Not sure about their publishing arm yet, but as a retailer they are good.

What do you like and dislike about your job? I like discovering new talent and working with creative people (writers and editors). I dislike chasing checks and contracts.

What are ways prospective clients can impress you, and what are ways they can turn you off? The first, with a great manuscript. The second, with a rude or bad attitude.

How would you describe the "writer from hell"? Someone who embarrasses his or her agent with bad behavior.

Describe a book you would like to write. A classic middle grade novel for the ages.

Do you believe in a higher and/or lower "power"? Yes.

Agent's name and contact info: Marie Lamba, marie.jdlit@gmail.com

Describe the kinds of works you want to represent. Picture books by established writers and illustrators. Also chapter books, middle grade, adult and women's fiction, and memoir by new and established authors. I especially like books that make me laugh and/or cry. Overall, I'm seeking a blend of highly intriguing story and fine writing.

Describe what you definitely don't want to represent. Genre fiction, including category romance, high fantasy, gory horror, science fiction. But romantic and speculative elements *are* welcome, and I always enjoy a spooky ghost story.

How do you want writers to pitch you? Via email. Put *Query* in the subject line and include the first 20 pages of the manuscript pasted in (not attached) following the query letter.

Describe your education and professional history. I received a BA in English and in literary art (an individualized major blending writing and fine art) from the University of Pennsylvania. I've worked in publishing as a publisher's assistant, an editor, and a book-promotions manager. I'm also an award-winning public relations writer, and a published author of three young adult novels and a picture book. My articles have appeared in more than 100 publications, and I'm a frequent contributor to *Writer's Digest Magazine*.

How did you become an agent? Jennifer De Chiara is my agent and has been representing my work for a number of years. After seeing me in action as both a writer and a promoter, she invited me to join her firm as an associate agent.

Knowing what you do now, would you do it again? If not, what might you do instead? Yes! Agenting is the perfect blend for me of treasure hunting, mentoring, and promoting talent — all things I love to do.

Do you charge fees? If yes, please explain. Never.

When and where were you born, and where have you lived? Born in New York, grew up in northern New Jersey, and lived in Pennsylvania.

What do you like to do when you're not working? Watch chick flicks, eat great food, travel as much as possible, and act silly with my family.

List some of the titles you have recently placed with publishers. *The Jumbies* by Tracey Baptiste (Algonquin); *Harvest Party!* by Jennifer O'Connell (Scholastic); *Daughter of Australia* by Harmony Verna (Kensington); *The Friendship Experiment* by Erin Teagan (Houghton Mifflin Harcourt); *Turkey Trick or Treat*, illustrated by Lee Harper (Two Lions); *Mending Horses* by M.P. Barker (Holiday House); *To the Stars!* by Carmella Van Vleet and Dr. Kathy Sullivan (Charlesbridge); *Eliza Bing Is (Not) a Big Fat Quitter* by Carmella Van Vleet (Holiday House).

Describe your personality. Positive and determined — with a sense of humor!

What do you like reading/watching/listening to on your own time? Humorous or imaginative or soul-changing fiction chick flick movies and entertaining TV like *The Bachelor*, *Greek*, and *Gilmore Girls*.

What do you like and dislike about your job? I really enjoy discovering and championing talent and connecting with so many interesting people. And, of course, I especially love making a writer's dreams come true.

What are ways prospective clients can impress you, and what are ways they can turn you off? They can impress me by being both talented and professional. And following the submission guidelines, please.

Agent's name and contact info: Victoria Selvaggio, Associate Agent, vselvaggio@windstream.net, www.victoriaselvaggio.com

Describe the kinds of works you want to represent. For any genre — a story that will remain with me forever. As with my favorite books and movies listed below, the genre doesn't matter — the story and how I feel about it days, months, and years later is what's most important. I'm all about the journey, the experience — captivate me, educate me, inspire me!

I'm currently looking for all genres (picture books, middle grade and young adult fiction, mystery, suspense, thrillers, paranormal, fantasy, narrative nonfiction, adult fiction), but find I'm particularly drawn to middle grade and young adult. I especially love thrillers and all elements of weird, creepy stuff. I also yearn for manuscripts that make me laugh, cry, and wonder about the world.

Describe what you definitely don't want to represent. Although I'm quite open about what I'm willing to review, I would not want to represent something that may be potentially harmful to someone's character or misleading to the public.

How do you want writers to pitch you? Submission guidelines are available on both the agency's website (www.jdlit.com) and mine (www.victoriaselvaggio.com).

Describe your education and professional history. I received a real estate license in 1987. A few years later, I started, owned, and operated a successful business before pursuing my dream of becoming a published author. I was also quite active for several years as the regional adviser for the Northern Ohio Region of the Society of Children's Book Writers and Illustrators (SCBWI), an international professional organization. Currently, I remain on SCBWI: Northern Ohio's executive board.

How did you become an agent? In 2013, at the SCBWI: Northern Ohio conference, I had the privilege of meeting Karen Grencik, an agent with Red Fox Literary, and Linda Epstein, an associate agent with the Jennifer De Chiara Literary Agency. Before meeting them, my ability to help writers and illustrators reach their publishing goals was limited. As a regional adviser, I could do only so much. Both Karen and Linda provided wonderful insight, and a few months after the conference Linda introduced me to Jennifer De Chiara, president and owner of the Jennifer De Chiara Literary Agency. We connected instantly, and soon I started to read manuscripts for the agency. This only added to my desire to help writers and illustrators, and within a short time I joined this wonderful agency.

Knowing what you do now, would you do it again? If not, what might you do instead? Absolutely. Although I've had my share of challenges, each challenge has been a learning experience. I'm not one to have regrets on the decisions I've made — each decision has helped mold me into the person I am today.

Do you charge fees? If yes, please explain. No.

When and where were you born, and where have you lived? I was born in Cleveland, Ohio, in 1969. Currently I reside in Twinsburg, Ohio.

What do you like to do when you're not working? This is a hard question, as I'm always working. Hobbies include refurbishing/refinishing antiques — currently I'm refurbishing antique wooden ladders that will soon become a coffee table. I love remodeling and painting and gardening. I also love spending time with my children, husband, and our two crazy cats that think they're dogs, and my dog that thinks he's a cat. And of course, writing — when I'm not reading compelling manuscripts, I'm busy creating my own.

List some of the titles you have recently placed with publishers. I'm currently building my client list.

Describe your personality. I'm a Taurus — not that I faithfully follow astrology or read my horoscope, but the traits of this zodiac sign do fit my personality. I tend to pride myself on my willingness to help others. I'm compassionate and sensitive, and I don't hold grudges. My family and close friends know that I'm easygoing and approachable. I have a strong work ethic — determined, motivated, and devoted. And I can be quite aggressive when necessary.

What do you like reading/watching/listening to on your own time? Another hard question, as I don't have a lot of spare time (I do a lot of recording)! Television: I love watching *The Walking Dead*, and I'm starting to find *Fear the Walking Dead* compelling. *Major Crimes* — I enjoy the mystery, humor, and wonderful cast of actors. *Bates Motel* — I want "poor" Norman to be normal. The writers have done such a good job making you feel compassion for him when he's murdering people left and right. Movies: *King Kong* — I know, I know this is an oldie, but I'm still so fascinated with this idea. *The Sixth Sense* — another oldie, but right up my alley. *The Hunger Games* — the scene where Katniss volunteers in Prim's place, that's what I look for in a manuscript: captivating emotion. Books: What I like to read is hard to answer, as I'm constantly falling in love with one book after another, so I'll share books from my childhood. These stories remain vivid in my memory as if I've read them yesterday; they've encouraged me and set me on my own writing path. As a child I loved *The Giving Tree* by Shel Silverstein; as an adult and parent, I understand it completely. I have yet to read it without having a sense of empathy wash over me; this story brings me to tears. I have an older sister, and *A Summer to Die* by Lois Lowry opened my eyes to how quickly life can change. I did (and still do) argue with my sister, and yes, back then I wanted to draw my own line many times, but no line would ever stop my sister from being my sister. Back then and now, I am truly blessed! Stephen King influenced my path as an author. He encouraged me to find my own voice, to continue pushing until I reached my own goals and beyond. I've read almost everything he's penned (that's in print): *Dolores Claiborne*, *The Talisman*, *Pet Sematary*, *Cujo*, *Christine*, *It* — I could go on. Although I absolutely *can't* pick a favorite, *Dolores Claiborne* is the perfect example to show how a story can work *without* (or *with limited*) dialogue. It shows that mastering the art of writing is a skill, and if perfected, regardless of how one portrays a story, a reader will fall in love!

Do you think the business has changed a lot over the past few years? If yes, please explain. The publishing industry has changed in some ways, but I think it's wise for all of us in this profession to expect that. Self-publishing, ebooks, digital distributors (and all the things in between) have influenced consumers, independent bookstores, publishing houses, and more. Although the industry has changed, it's important to note that manuscripts are still being written by creative individuals, publishers are still publishing compelling manuscripts, and readers of all ages are still falling in love.

What do the "Big 5" mean to you? As it's a goal for every writer to be published by a major trade book publishing company, it is a goal for every agent. The Big 5 major trade book publishing companies play an important part in the success of a manuscript, from editing, to packaging and production, to marketing and publicity.

How do you feel about independent/small presses? I feel independent/small presses play an important role as an alternative to the Big 5. But some do vary in their publishing protocol when it comes to agented submissions, advances, distribution, etc.

What are your feelings about self-publishing? My background also includes some self-published titles; although I'm happy for the experiences they've brought, I do find myself wishing I had learned more about the publishing industry and the writing process. Although neither title was ever submitted to an agency or editor, neither title was ever revised (revision is a huge part of the writing process). I do wish I knew back then what I know now. If a writer wishes to follow this path, I usually encourage lots of research (there are scams out there) and revision and editing before publication.

Do you think Amazon is good or bad — or both — for the book business? If answering this as a consumer, my answer may be different, but as an agent understanding the influence that Amazon has had over the publishing industry, I do find myself searching for the positive over the negative.

What do you like and dislike about your job? We are all destined for the "right" path. Becoming an agent was mine! After several years as regional adviser for SCBWI: Northern Ohio and becoming a published author myself, I found myself limited in what I could do to help writers and illustrators reach their goals. I was able to provide tools (education, motivation, inspiration), but building careers was out of reach, so I strived to make it reachable. For me, I love, love, *love* working one-on-one with my clients! All jobs have their disadvantages, but I can't seem to find many as an agent. I love going to work every day. It's as simple as that!

Regarding my response time to queries, I will note this as my least favorite thing about my job. I receive an overwhelming number of emails and queries, and my protocol (as an author knowing what it's like to be on the waiting side) is to respond personally to each one. Unfortunately, this takes time.

What are ways prospective clients can impress you, and what are ways they can turn you off? Most important, be yourself! Impress me with your writing. Show me that you've spent time researching the Jennifer De Chiara Literary Agency and me. Instead of just noting "we'd be a good fit," tell me why you feel that way. Be professional and address your query/cover letter appropriately. Be respectful of my submission guidelines and response time. If I haven't responded to your query, don't get frustrated or upset. Please follow up — it's possible I didn't receive it! Show confidence — don't ever apologize for the lack of publishing credits. And always be professional when commenting about me (and *everyone* else) on social media.

How would you describe the "writer from hell"? As I tend to be positive, looking for the good qualities in a writer, I'm not a huge fan of someone who is unprofessional and arrogant. I'm also not a huge fan of someone who becomes defensive when having work critiqued and/or as a response to a rejection.

Describe a book you would like to write. A modern *King Kong* — he lives on, in this one.

Do you believe in a higher and/or lower "power"? Although I tend to keep my personal beliefs to myself, I will note that I believe in a higher power and I pray often.

Is there anything you wish to express beyond the parameters of the preceding questions? Nope. ☺ I was quite thorough!

Agent's name and contact info: Roseanne Wells, queryroseanne@gmail.com, Twitter: @RivetingRosie

Describe the kinds of works you want to represent. I represent adult fiction (sci-fi, fantasy, upmarket mystery, literary fiction), adult nonfiction (narrative nonfiction, pop culture, popular science, popular psychology/anthropology/sociology — books, like *Quiet* by Susan Cain, that mix studies, personal narrative, and larger contexts — travel, food, humor, select memoir), children's fiction (young adult and middle grade), and very select children's nonfiction. I'm really interested in stories told with a unique narrative structure that is integrated into the story (*Please Ignore Vera Dietz*, *The Time Traveler's Wife*, etc.), books written by diverse authors about diverse subjects (POC, LGBTQ, nonbinary, disabled, mental illness, etc.) in any category or genre that I represent. I'd also love to find a great con or heist story about tech, jewels, art, or valuable food items. I update my interests with the #MSWL hashtag on Twitter and mswishlist.com.

Describe what you definitely don't want to represent. I'm not interested in thrillers, cozy mystery, romance, or inspirational books.

How do you want writers to pitch you? Please follow the guidelines on jdlit.com or meet me at a conference.

Describe your education and professional history. I graduated from Sarah Lawrence College with a BA in dance and literature. I interned at several magazines before I interned at W. W. Norton, which led me to book publishing as a career. I've worked for a magazine group as a proofreader, a small illustrated publisher as an editorial and special sales assistant, and a literary agency, focusing on nonfiction, before I joined JDLA.

How did you become an agent? I was looking for a job in editorial at a publisher during the 2008 economic crash. It was very disheartening, and I felt as though I was hitting my head against the wall. My boss at the magazine group had been an agent very briefly, and she suggested that I might do better as an agent. As I started to learn more about agenting, I realized that it would include what I wanted from working in editorial and then so much more. So I switched my focus to agenting.

Knowing what you do now, would you do it again? If not, what might you do instead? I would definitely be an agent, hands down. If the position didn't exist, I would be in publishing somehow.

Do you charge fees? If yes, please explain. No.

What do you like to do when you're not working? I love cooking and baking (while I sing off-key), dancing, having fun with friends, sometimes binge-watching TV. Oh, and reading, of course.

How do you feel about independent/small presses? I think they have an important place in the ecosystem of publishing. If I'm going to place a book with a smaller press, however, I want to make sure that they are adding benefits that the client wouldn't get otherwise.

What are your feelings about self-publishing? I think self-publishing can be great if it's done well. It can build a readership, help strengthen your platform, etc. But if it's done as a market test for your book or uploaded without a plan, it won't work.

What are ways prospective clients can impress you, and what are ways they can turn you off? I love clients who are professional, have done their research, are open to improving their craft, and understand generally how publishing works and the realities of the current publishing climate. I like it when I feel that I've known a client forever or that we'd be friends outside of publishing. I consider myself to be always learning and growing as a person and an agent, and if a client has a similar attitude, that definitely helps. And I love puns and smart wordplay.

People who are demanding, pushy, or generally rude are on my no list. I don't consider manuscripts or clients who put other writers down to help themselves get noticed, and I don't respond well to manuscripts that are racist, sexist, ableist, or antiqueer or to writers who try to harm someone to further their own agenda.

JENNIFER LYONS LITERARY AGENCY ❖

www.jenniferlyonsliteraryagency.com

151 West 19th Street, 3rd Floor, New York, NY 10011, 212-368-2812

Agent's name and contact info: Jeff Ourvan, jeff@jenniferlyonsliteraryagency.com

Describe the kinds of works you want to represent. Nonfiction: narrative nonfiction, history, biography, science, sports, cookbooks, lifestyle. Fiction: young adult, middle grade, literary, romance, thriller, mystery, fantasy, science fiction.

Describe what you definitely don't want to represent. Memoir, children's picture books.

How do you want writers to pitch you? Queries by email only.

Describe your education and professional history. JD from New York Law School. Currently a licensed attorney, literary agent, editor, and writing instructor; formerly a public-relations consultant, geologist, and commercial fisherman.

How did you become an agent? I met Jennifer Lyons and wanted to work with her.

Knowing what you do now, would you do it again? If not, what might you do instead? I would definitely do it again and intend to continue to do it.

Do you charge fees? If yes, please explain. Commissions on sales for literary agency work.

When and where were you born, and where have you lived? Born in NYC when JFK was president; I've lived in New York, Los Angeles, Tokyo, and Alaska (10 weeks in a tent).

What do you like to do when you're not working? I'm president of the Peter Stuyvesant Little League, so when not working, I'm on a baseball field. Or maybe in a swimming pool.

List some of the titles you have recently placed with publishers. *Masters of the Formula* (BenBella), *The Princess and the Page* (Scholastic), *Rise and Fall of the Cattle Kingdom* (Houghton Mifflin Harcourt), *Under a Sardinian Sky* (Kensington).

Describe your personality. An easygoing Buddhist dude. Unless I'm not. Love to collaborate with my authors on their works.

What do you like reading/watching/listening to on your own time? I read a lot of narrative nonfiction, biography, history, science, young adult, mystery, and thrillers. And watch a lot of baseball and hockey.

Do you think the business has changed a lot over the past few years? If yes, please explain. I'm about four years into agenting. No nostalgia for the old days.

What do the "Big 5" mean to you? Generally, happiness for my authors.

How do you feel about independent/small presses? Love 'em. Wish there were more, and hope the small ones grow larger.

What are your feelings about self-publishing? Go for it if you're prepared to seriously market yourself.

Do you think Amazon is good or bad — or both — for the book business? Generally I like Amazon. They have provided extraordinary marketing plans for authors I've placed with their imprints.

What do you like and dislike about your job? I like my authors, and I like the creative spirit that permeates my work. With my lawyer blood, I like negotiating contracts. I can't think of what I dislike. I did dislike working as a corporate lawyer, though.

What are ways prospective clients can impress you, and what are ways they can turn you off? Impress me with a clever, well-written query; impress me with page-turning writing; impress me by living a bold and value-creative life. Don't immediately send me a query for "another" book you have if I've just declined your first, and presumably better, one.

How would you describe the "writer from hell"? Terminated.

Describe a book you would like to write. I'm writing it now. It's a secret. But it's about New York. And history. And baseball.

Do you believe in a higher and/or lower "power"? Yes. I'll go Buddhist on this one: within you and within me.

JERNIGAN LITERARY AGENCY

PO Box 741624, Dallas, TX 75374, 972-722-4838

Agent's name and contact info: Barry Jernigan, jerniganliterary@gmail.com

Describe the kinds of works you want to represent. Eclectic tastes in nonfiction and fiction. Nonfiction interests include women's interest, gay/lesbian, ethnic/cultural, memoir, true crime; fiction interests include mystery, suspense, thrillers.

Describe what you definitely don't want to represent. Poetry collections, short stories, technology/computers.

How do you want writers to pitch you? Email your query with a synopsis, brief bio, and the first few pages embedded (no attachments). We do not accept unsolicited manuscripts. We accept submissions *via email only* — no snail mail.

Describe your education and professional history. BS, University of Texas.

How did you become an agent? Spent many years in the book department at the William Morris Agency as a career counselor and agent.

Knowing what you do now, would you do it again? If not, what might you do instead? Yes, I would do it again in a minute.

Do you charge fees? If yes, please explain. No fees.

When and where were you born, and where have you lived? Florida.

What do you like to do when you're not working? Travel and cooking.

Describe your personality. Outgoing.

What do you like reading/watching/listening to on your own time? Tops on my book list are the ones that impact me the most. I like to read books that make me laugh.

Do you think the business has changed a lot over the past few years? If yes, please explain. Yes, the impact of the internet has changed everything.

JILL COHEN ASSOCIATES, LLC ❖ www.jillcohenassociates.com

Agent's name and contact info: Jill Cohen, jcohen.ny@gmail.com

Describe the kinds of works you want to represent. Illustrated nonfiction, lifestyle, fashion, beauty, interiors, architecture, food, entertaining.

Describe what you definitely don't want to represent. No fiction, no children's books.

How do you want writers to pitch you? Email first with a description of the project and outline of the platform.

Describe your education and professional history. BA in English, graduate degree in publishing, 30 years as president and publisher of Conde Nast Books, Random House Direct, Time Warner Bulfinch Press.

How did you become an agent? Started my agency in 2006 with several clients — former authors.

Knowing what you do now, would you do it again? If not, what might you do instead? Yes, absolutely would do it again.

Do you charge fees? If yes, please explain. My agency specializes in full packaging of illustrated books, and we do charge a packaging fee.

When and where were you born, and where have you lived? Born in Pennsylvania, educated in New York, and have lived in New York since.

What do you like to do when you're not working? When am I not working?

List some of the titles you have recently placed with publishers. *Bunny Williams Interiors*, Carolyne Roehm's *At Home in the Garden*, Trish McEvoy's *Makeup of a Confident Woman*, Preston Bailey's *Flowers*, Aerin Lauder's *Beauty at Home*, India Hicks's *Island Style*.

Describe your personality. Outgoing, creative, talkative.

What do you like reading/watching/listening to on your own time? *House of Cards*, *Breaking Bad*, alternative music.

Do you think the business has changed a lot over the past few years? If yes, please explain. Yes, of course — Kindle and the iPad have changed everything.

What do the "Big 5" mean to you? I like doing business with a big house — it gives authors a sense of security.

How do you feel about independent/small presses? Love the ones that are well run with a strong brand identity.

What are your feelings about self-publishing? Very good for the authors who are on speaking tours or who connect with audiences and can sell direct.

Do you think Amazon is good or bad — or both — for the book business? Somewhere in between. It's useful, but we need more physical bookstores.

What do you like and dislike about your job? It's 24/7 — there is no time off. I live and breathe it, so I have to discipline myself to take breaks.

What are ways prospective clients can impress you, and what are ways they can turn you off? A turn-on is having authors willing to work to build their platform and understanding how to synergistically grow their business in tandem with their publishing program. A turnoff is someone who has too many advisers.

How would you describe the "writer from hell"? Texting constantly and expecting responses.

Describe a book you would like to write. *Brand Building 101*.

Do you believe in a higher and/or lower "power"? Yes.

Is there anything you wish to express beyond the parameters of the preceding questions? Yes. I believe in the power of intention.

JILL CORCORAN LITERARY AGENCY ❖

jillcorcoranliteraryagency.com

PO Box 4116, Palos Verdes Peninsula, CA 90274, 310-469-2090

Agent's name and contact info: Eve Porinchak, eve@jillcorcoranliteraryagency.com

Describe the kinds of works you want to represent. I am accepting submissions for picture books, middle grade, young adult novels and nonfiction, and adult novels and nonfiction. I am primarily interested in contemporary, somewhat edgy, realistic fiction for young adults and adults. Anything involving crime, speculative fiction, and psychologically intriguing plots is a plus. I love stories that really make me think in a way I hadn't previously or keep me awake with shocking twists. Anything in any genre that makes me laugh out loud is welcomed.

Describe what you definitely don't want to represent. Never a fan of high fantasy, I am not representing epic *Lord of the Rings*–esque manuscripts; however, I do adore the *Hunger Games* series and that type of speculative fiction with some fantasy elements. I also do not represent erotica, religiously themed stories, self-help, how-to, or craft books.

How do you want writers to pitch you? Please submit a brief query letter with a short bio, synopsis of your work, and the first 10 pages to eve@jillcorcoranliteraryagency.com. Or, if submitting a picture book, please paste the entire manuscript in the email. Attachments will be deleted, unless we specifically request them.

Describe your education and professional history. I graduated from UCLA with a bachelor's degree in psychology and biology, then attended medical school anticipating a career in pediatrics, but decided I loved sleep and creative outlets too much to continue doctoring (not to mention those baggy white lab coats — such a fashion *don't*). I then earned my degree in early childhood education. Always working with children in some capacity, I taught preschool, kindergarten, and first grade and served as a foster-care case manager and court-appointed guardian ad litem in New Hampshire and Vermont. Currently, I serve as an aid worker in Tijuana orphanages and teach creative writing to incarcerated teens in Los Angeles. Because I've worked with young adults who are presently or formerly incarcerated for so long — and I *love* this work — many of the manuscripts I'm drawn to examine the potential criminal side in all of us, if we are pushed to the limit or born into unfortunate circumstances. On the lighter side, I've been painting and selling bright cheerful acrylic paintings for many years — that's the puppies-hearts-and-rainbows portion of my life. It all balances out!

How did you become an agent? Having been a writer in an exceptional critique group for seven years (*Hello, SLO for Children!*), I had the privilege of working closely with friends who went on to become *New York Times* bestselling authors. Following friends from pre-published status through the journey to publication was as exciting for me as if it were my own book! During those years, I attended every class, seminar, Boot Camp, SCBWI conference, and Writer's Day event, every meeting, every schmooze, anything writing-related that was available within driving distance. In networking at these events, I met dozens of agents, editors, and fellow authors with whom I've remained close friends. In studying my craft all those years, I learned that I am quite adept at teaching plot structure, editing other people's manuscripts, and helping create submission lists. Also, I've always enjoyed teaching and encouraging both new and veteran authors and helping them weigh giant career decisions. I worked as Jill Corcoran's assistant while I was phasing out of teaching young children, and after a while I quit teaching and joined JCLA full-time, taking on my own clients. After diving in full speed, scurrying back and forth from LA to NYC a few times, I sold my first two books after six months on the job. I'm lucky that in this competitive business Jill recognized my limitless enthusiasm and gave me this opportunity. She's been my Yoda. Literary agenting is somewhat like being a teacher, mother, cheerleader, film producer, therapist, life coach, and business manager all at once. Multifaceted this job is (said in Yoda-voice).

When and where were you born, and where have you lived? Born outside of London to a military family, I'm fortunate to have lived all over the planet, from the sticks of New England, to the 'burbs of DC, to the beaches of Grenada, to the rain forest of Yucatan, Mexico. Finally, I'm settled in sunny southern California and could not be happier!

What do you like to do when you're not working? I travel the world with my adventurous family any chance I get. When home and not working, I read, run long distance, golf, surf (terribly), play softball (decently), play poker with my college buddies, bike to happy hour, paint hearts and flowers, and scour Los Angeles for the perfect cupcake.

List some of the titles you have recently placed with publishers. Ah, as a new agent, I'm learning the art of patience with the publishing business. I have two books coming out in 2017: book #1, which shall not be named or announced yet, and book #2, also a secret until the publisher gives me the okay to broadcast it to everybody in the universe. And, believe me, I will!

Describe your personality. Silly, sarcastic, even-keeled, loyal, optimistic, liberal, easily amused.

What do you like and dislike about your job? I have the privilege of reading an endless supply of stories, editing manuscripts, discussing and obsessing over things like "inciting incidents" and "turning points," meeting collaborative and fascinating people, traveling to conferences all over the country, and gazing out into the SoCal ocean as I work. What's not to love?

JILL GRINBERG LITERARY MANAGEMENT ❖

www.jillgrinbergliterary.com

392 Vanderbilt Avenue, Brooklyn, NY 11238, 212-620-5883

Agents' names and contact info: Katelyn Detweiler, katelyn@jillgrinbergliterary.com; Jill Grinberg, jill@jillgrinbergliterary.com; Cheryl Pientka, cheryl@jillgrinbergliterary.com

Describe the kinds of works you want to represent. The award-winning and bestselling authors we represent span nearly every genre and age group, and we continue to seek out new works in this vein. Some of our notable clients include: Laurie Berkner (acclaimed children's musician, forthcoming picture book series from Simon & Schuster), Sara Donati (*Into the Wilderness* series, *The Gilded Hour*), Henry Gee (*The Accidental Species*), Alison Goodman (*Eon, Eona, The Dark Days Club*), Andy Griffiths (*Treehouse* series [*13-Story Treehouse*]), Christopher Healy (*The Heroes Guide* series), Jennifer L. Holm (*Our Only May Amelia, Babymouse* series, *The Fourteenth Goldfish*), Margo Lanagan (*Black Juice, Tender Morsels*), Justine Larbalestier (*Liar, Razorhurst*), Kirby Larson (*Hattie Big Sky, Duke, Dash*), Melina Marchetta (*Jellicoe Road, The Lumatere Chronicles*), Marissa Meyer (*Cinder, The Lunar Chronicles*), Garth Nix (The *Old Kingdom* series), T. J. Stiles (*The First Tycoon, Custer's Trials*), Gerry Swallow (*The Whole Nother Story* series, *Blue in the Face*), Scott Westerfeld (*Uglies* series, *Leviathan* series, *Afterworlds, Zeroes*), Colin Woodard (*The Republic of Pirates, American Nations*).

Describe what you definitely don't want to represent. We do not accept unsolicited queries for screenplays.

How do you want writers to pitch you? Please send queries via email to info@jillgrinbergliterary.com. Include your query letter, addressed to the agent of your choice, along with the first 50 pages of your manuscript pasted into the body of the email or attached as a doc or docx file.

We also accept queries via mail. Please send your query letter and the first 50 pages of your manuscript by mail, along with an SASE, to the attention of your agent of choice, at

392 Vanderbilt Avenue, Brooklyn, NY 11238. Please note that unless an SASE with sufficient postage is provided, your materials will not be returned.

Do you charge fees? If yes, please explain. No.

List some of the titles you have recently placed with publishers. Children's music performer Laurie Berkner's picture books *We Are the Dinosaurs* (to be illustrated by Ben Clanton), *Pillowland* (to be illustrated by Camille Garoche), and *Monster Boogie* (also to be illustrated by Ben Clanton) (Simon & Schuster Children's); Lissa Dawkins's *Stolen with a Kiss*, the first book in the *Penhallow Dynasty* series, which follows the romantic adventures of members of the strong-minded Penhallow family, set during the Regency era (Avon); Jon Skovron's *Hope and Red*, the first book in the Empire of Storms trilogy, a saga that follows a warrior who has dedicated her life to avenging the massacre of her small village, and a roguish thief who will stop at nothing to protect the urban slum neighborhood that raised him, as they form an alliance to defeat the mystical biomancers, servants of the emperor bent on controlling the underclasses and using them as fodder for their cruel experiments (Orbit; three-book deal); Beth Ain's *A Friend like You*, about a fourth grader and the small moments in her year that add up to big surprises (Random House Children's); Senior Editor at *Nature* Henry Gee's *Across the Bridge: Understanding the Origin of Vertebrates*, seeking to solve the puzzle that has stumped scientists since the time of Aristotle — the origin of backboned animals, including humans, from the rest of the animal world (University of Chicago Press); young adult author Melina Marchetta's adult debut *Shaming the Devil*, about a police inspector who rushes to investigate the deadly bombing of a busload of students when he learns that his daughter was on the bus, and that a teenage girl on board — whose family was linked to a bombing in the past — is the prime suspect (Little, Brown); *A Babymouse Christmas* by Jennifer Holm, illustrated by Matthew Holm, in which Babymouse celebrates Christmas (Random House Children's); Scott Westerfeld, Margo Lanagan, and Deborah Biancotti's trilogy, starting with *Zeroes*, about six teens born in the year 2000 with new kinds of superpowers, whose abilities make them anything but heroes until a high-stakes crisis changes everything (Simon Pulse); S. Jae-Jones's *The Goblin King*, about a young woman who sets forth on a journey from our world above and risks all to save her sister from the clutches of the Goblin King, only to discover that she might be the one who needs saving (Thomas Dunne Books); Lori Fusaro and Laura Coffey's *My Old Dog: Rescued Pets with Remarkable Second Acts*, a book showcasing rescued and retired senior dogs, written by Coffey, a writer, producer, and editor for TODAY.com, with photos by Fusaro (New World Library).

Is there anything you wish to express beyond the parameters of the preceding questions? Our authors are novelists, historians, and scientists; memoirists and journalists; illustrators and musicians; cultural critics and humanitarians. They are passionate about what they write. They have strong, authentic voices, whether they are writing fiction or nonfiction. They are brilliant storytellers. Our authors have won the American Book Award, the National Book Award, and the Pulitzer Prize as well as the Printz Award and Newbery Honor award. They appear on the *New York Times* and international bestseller lists.

We don't make a habit of dividing our list by category — our authors transcend category. Our authors write for every audience, picture book to adult. They are not easily boxed or contained within any neat, singular label. They often cross categories, are "genre busting." We love books, but we take on authors. Our authors are career authors. We are deeply invested in their careers and in making every book count. We are committed to developing ongoing relationships with writers and have represented a good number of our authors for over 10 years.

We understand the importance of the author-publisher connection and put great focus on matching our authors to the right editors and publishers. We fiercely advocate for our authors while maintaining a strong network of top editors and publishers. We have many years of publicity and marketing experience between us, and we give tremendous thought to positioning. Every project requires a tailored, personalized plan. Every author is unique. Every author has a different path.

We are globally minded. Our authors are based around the world. We sell around the world in over 30 countries and cultivate global relationships. Many of our books "travel" well, because they speak to readers of all different ages, different backgrounds, different walks of life.

We are, first and foremost, passionate about what we do. Agenting is a vocation and a lifestyle. We take on new clients and new projects from a place of passion and admiration. We are also extremely business minded. Agenting is not a science, but rather an alchemy of skill sets — legal know-how, editing, publicity and marketing, diplomacy, negotiation, counseling, career management. We bring all of these skills to bear in giving our clients the best possible representation.

JODY REIN BOOKS, INC. ❖ jodyreinbooks.com

7741 South Ash Court, Centennial, CO 80122

Agent's name: Jody Rein

Describe the kinds of works you want to represent. Primarily narrative and commercial nonfiction and occasionally rare and wonderful novels. Occasionally coagent literary fiction, literary crime novels — not too bloody — and high-end historical fiction. Would consider coagenting amazing young adult fiction — not too dark; I like a world with hope in it.

Describe what you definitely don't want to represent. Genre fiction, poetry.

How do you want writers to pitch you? We're not currently open to unsolicited submissions.

Describe your education and professional history. I have a BA in English, with honors, from the University of Michigan. I began my career with Contemporary Books in Chicago in the 1980s as an editorial assistant. As Contemporary rarely worked with New York agents, I sought other ways to find publishable books. My first acquisition was a self-published book about the Three Stooges, which I read about in the *Wall Street Journal*. I acquired the rights to traditionally publish that book, the authors became successful "hybrid" authors long before there was a name for it, and I embarked on a career marked by innovative ways to find and publish good books.

I moved to New York to head up Contemporary's new branch office and eventually became an executive editor with divisions of what are now Penguin Random House and HarperCollins. I published books that came through agents, acquired paperback rights for hardcovers published by other companies (old-fashioned "hybrid" publishing), and published many originally self-published or small-press books, such as the bestseller *Do What You Love* by Marsha Sinetar.

When I moved to Colorado and opened the Jody Rein Books literary agency, my first stop was the Tattered Cover bookstore to scout for successfully published small-press books. I found *You Mean I'm Not Lazy, Crazy or Stupid?!* by Kate Kelly and Peggy Ramundo, sold it to Simon & Schuster, and established myself as what the *Denver Post* termed an "überagent" in Denver. *Lazy, Crazy* remains in print and has sold more than 250,000 copies.

I am now both literary agent and publishing consultant. In these roles I have guided authors through pretty much every possible path to successful publication. My bestselling books include *The Big Year* by Mark Obmascik, which became a Fox Studios movie, Bruce Cameron's *8 Simple Rules for Dating My Teenage Daughter*, and the perennial bestseller *You Can Draw in 30 Days* by Mark Kistler. I created a small agent-facilitated self-publishing company for my clients called Author Planet Press and a publishing consulting company called Author Planet. Author Planet helps writers and small publishers build websites and platforms and provides other publishing-related services.

How did you become an agent? I moved to Denver to get married and wanted to continue to creatively collaborate in book development. Opening my agency was an ideal way to promote the publication of excellent books while working with my long-standing colleagues in New York.

Knowing what you do now, would you do it again? If not, what might you do instead? I would have worked with coagents sooner. I like having colleagues.

Do you charge fees? If yes, please explain. Not in my role as an agent. My consulting company does charge for its services.

When and where were you born, and where have you lived? Kokomo, Indiana; Skokie, Illinois; Ann Arbor, Michigan; Chicago; NYC; Denver.

Is there anything you wish to express beyond the parameters of the preceding questions? I have never believed there is one generally right path to publication. I strongly believe that there is a "best" path for each individual book, and that quality and integrity matter.

JULIA LORD LITERARY MANAGEMENT ❖

www.julialordliterarymgt.com

38 West 9th Street, #4, New York, NY 10011, 212-995-2333

Agents' names and contact info: Julia Lord, julia@julialordliterarymgt.com; Ginger Curwen, ginger@julialordliterarymgt.com

Describe the kinds of works you want to represent. Nonfiction: narrative, reference, biography, history, humor, science, adventure, philosophy, military. Fiction: general, literary, historical, young adult, suspense, mystery, thrillers.

Describe what you definitely don't want to represent. No children's younger than young adult, no sci-fi or fantasy. *Please read our website* to see what we represent.

How do you want writers to pitch you? Follow our guidelines on the website and query us at query@julialordliterarymgt.com.

Describe your education and professional history. *Julia*: I began my agenting career in 1985 working for actors. I opened the talent agency's literary department representing writers for film, television, and theater. I moved to books, eventually opening Julia Lord Literary Management in 1999. My mission is very hands-on: to work with writers to develop their careers, to work with them from idea through publication and marketing. Our office is known for our steadfast commitment to each and every author and book project.

Ginger: I represent thrillers and mystery. My previous publishing experience includes positions at Barnes & Noble, HarperCollins, American Booksellers Association, Bantam Books, and Random House.

Knowing what you do now, would you choose agenting as a career again? If not, what might you do instead? Of course. It's great work for those with voracious and eclectic interests.

Do you charge fees? If yes, please explain. No.

When and where were you born, and where have you lived? Julia has lived in Massachusetts, LA, Rome, and NYC. Ginger has lived in Massachusetts, Connecticut, and NYC.

What do you like to do when you're not working? *Julia*: Reading! Travel, hiking, classical music, piano, theater. *Ginger*: Reading! Travel, tennis, cross-country skiing, drawing, walking my dog.

List some of the titles you have recently placed with publishers. *The Last Four Days of Paddy Buckley* by Jeremy Massey (Riverhead/Penguin), *Frank & Ava* by John Brady (Macmillan), *Shadow Work* by Craig Lambert (Counterpoint/Perseus), *Plato and a Platypus Walk into a Bar: Understanding Philosophy through Jokes* by Thomas Cathcart and Daniel Klein (Abrams/Penguin), *How Not to Write a Novel* by Howard Mittelmark and Sandra Newman (HarperCollins), *The Dark Side of the Enlightenment* by John Fleming (Norton), *Seal Target Geronimo* by Chuck Pfarrer (St. Martin's), *The Trolley Problem* by Thomas Cathcart (Workman), *Travels with Epicurus* by Daniel Klein (Penguin), *NYPD Confidential* by Leonard Levitt (Thomas Dunne).

Describe your personality. *Julia*: People say I am tenacious, so I suppose I am. I also care deeply about my work, my clients. *Ginger*: I would describe myself as an enthusiast, and when I find a book I love, I want everyone to know about it and read it.

What do you like reading/watching/listening to on your own time? *Julia*: history, politics, and classics. *Ginger*: fiction, mystery, and thrillers.

How do you feel about independent/small presses? We like them.

What do you like and dislike about your job? We love finding a new writer — a new voice, new story, new ideas! Writers are creative and talented people who are so often the first to take financial hits in this marketplace. Writers need a team — and that includes a tough agent. We enjoy fighting for their work and their rights.

JULIE HILL LITERARY AGENCY

12997 Caminito del Pasaje, Del Mar, CA 92014, 858-259-2595

**Agent's name and contact info: Julie Hill, hillagent@aol.com
(I welcome hardcopy, though)**

Describe the kinds of works you want to represent. Nonfiction only: self-help, advice, travel essay, memoir, business leadership, business forecasting. Actually all forecasting is interesting to me. Books about the afterlife have always been an interest, but it is hard to find authors who have a real following and something new to say. If you are out there let me hear from you, please.

Describe what you definitely don't want to represent. Horror, sci-fi, fiction of any kind.

How do you want writers to pitch you? Full proposal at the outset. Queries are okay, but why not get right to it? Please, please, please include a market survey with publisher and year of competitive titles. Please also include your established audience numbers (books in print, blog and website numbers, Facebook followers, audience size of any ongoing program you are a part of).

Describe your education and professional history. University of Arizona bachelor's degree, UC Berkeley Publishing Program, graduate work in marketing at UCLA.

How did you become an agent? Other writer friends suggested it. I was doing food and travel writing at the time and having lots of fun, but wanted to be on the road less.

Knowing what you do now, would you do it again? If not, what might you do instead? I would do it again. I love my books, all of them. I am proud of the volumes that line my shelves and that have changed the lives of others.

Do you charge fees? If yes, please explain. Only if I am hired as a consultant, which I do a lot of, actually. This year I spent a number of hours consulting on some independent projects for businesspeople. As an agent I am commission-only and delighted to be so.

When and where were you born, and where have you lived? Born in Los Angeles, lived in Arizona and La Jolla, Del Mar, San Francisco, Berkeley.

What do you like to do when you're not working? Garden and read, read, read. Also cook if I have a willing audience. I will feed you if you will do the dishes.

List some of the titles you have recently placed with publishers. *Leadership Secrets of the Wizard of Oz*, with Workbook, by B. J. Gallagher (author of over 30 books), with full rights from Warner Brothers for movie characters, music, the works (Simple Truths, a division of Sourcebooks). I spent most of my time this year consulting on books yet to be released.

And depositing checks. *Data Crush* (AMACOM) was last year, but I have to mention it won a Business Book of the Year award.

Describe your personality. Impatient, but charming. More fun than most agents I know. Hmm, well, any agents I know.

What do you like reading/watching/listening to on your own time? *Ray Donovan, CBS Sunday Morning, Masterpiece Theatre, Mom.* The Sunday *New York Times* is my favorite thing ever. Takes me until Wednesday to finish, but what an adventure it is. I also love, love, love *New York Magazine.* I once loved the *New Yorker* over everything, but now I mostly read the jokes and cherry-pick the rest. Classical music is almost exclusively my listening favorite. Mozart still rules.

Do you think the business has changed a lot over the past few years? If yes, please explain. Yes, Amazon has sliced all tradition to hell. But if it means more readers keep reading, then I guess I am all for it. I like that publishers report that physical books are rising in popularity again, so change can be pleasant sometimes!

What do the "Big 5" mean to you? Bigger money, better distribution usually.

How do you feel about independent/small presses? I love them. They are all about the art of the book.

What are your feelings about self-publishing? If it makes sense for the author in given circumstances, then go for it. It's a bigger job for the author than selling the work to a traditional publisher, however. I prefer creating a physical artifact of culture with wide distribution and life beyond the Delete button, but it isn't always possible to get the trifecta.

Do you think Amazon is good or bad — or both — for the book business? Both. I hear toddler Jeff Bezos once took his crib apart during naptime. May be a metaphor.

What do you like and dislike about your job? I dislike authors who want to chat instead of deliver a salable product at the outset. I like everything else about it, except maybe when a wonderful publisher goes out of business. It happens. I mourn for days, weeks.

What are ways prospective clients can impress you, and what are ways they can turn you off? What pushes my "On" button is prepared proposals with perfect research and popular websites. And if the authors respect my time…well, they are gold to me.

How would you describe the "writer from hell"? Chatty, not ready to deliver the goods. Wants to invite me to all social events. Does not want to learn how to read a royalty statements, let alone a contract. Calls every time he or she has a new thought or experience. Sometimes people do not realize that writing is best accomplished from a rich interior life, and phones and the internet should be used sparingly if the fire is to remain on high.

Describe a book you would like to write. I am thrilled to represent those who wish to do this, but I am not a candidate myself.

Do you believe in a higher and/or lower "power"? Sure. I was raised a Catholic and married people from other denominations. I believe in an afterlife, and religion fascinates me. I have friends and family in AA. "Power" may be another term for that which is not physical but is still a force in our lives. I am also an astrologer, and planets have power, too. Not overwhelming power, but they do impel rather than compel.

Is there anything you wish to express beyond the parameters of the preceding questions? I'm also an astrologer, and I have a blog called "Astrology for Writers (and Editors too)" at www.publishersmarketplace.com/members/destiny.

KATHRYN GREEN LITERARY AGENCY, LLC ❖

www.kathryngreenliteraryagency.com

157 Columbus Avenue, New York, NY 10023, 212-245-4225

Agent's name and contact info: Kathryn Green, kathy@kgreenagency.com

Describe the kinds of works you want to represent. I am happy and excited to represent young adult and middle grade fiction, women's fiction, quirky nonfiction, memoir, biography, historical fiction, mystery.

Describe what you definitely don't want to represent. Science fiction.

How do you want writers to pitch you? I love a quick query letter sent to my email address (query@kgreenagency.com) describing the project and any salient platform information.

Describe your education and professional history. I have a degree in journalism from George Washington University. My first job was in the publications department of the Girl Scouts of America. After that I became an editorial assistant at *Penthouse* magazine. A year or so later I became fiction editor and later senior editor. After leaving the magazine, I freelanced as an editor for a number of years before starting my own agency.

Do you charge fees? If yes, please explain. No, I don't charge fees.

When and where were you born, and where have you lived? I've lived in Manhattan and London, but I was born in Brooklyn.

What do you like to do when you're not working? Like traveling, daydreaming.

List some of the titles you have recently placed with publishers. *Sit Stay Heal* by Mel Miskimen, *Shutter* by Laurie Stolarz, *The Business of Good* by Jason Haber, *The American West in Color* by John Gunselman.

What do you like reading/watching/listening to on your own time? Love watching Netflix, reading narrative nonfiction, and listening to country music.

How do you feel about independent/small presses? I wish there were more of them.

What are your feelings about self-publishing? It gives writers another outlet, but discoverability remains the drawback.

What do you like and dislike about your job? I love the fact that on any given day I can discover a book or an author with the potential to change readers' lives or at least their viewpoint. I don't like the fact that it is so difficult to break out new authors.

What are ways prospective clients can impress you, and what are ways they can turn you off? I really like succinct letters that tell what the book is about and a bit about the author. I don't like cold calls from authors.

How would you describe the "writer from hell"? Actually I have never met one, so I wouldn't be able to describe him or her.

KIMBERLEY CAMERON & ASSOCIATES ❖

www.kimberleycameron.com

1550 Tiburon Boulevard, #704, Tiburon, CA 94920, 415-789-9191

Agent's name and contact info: Amy Cloughley, amyc@kimberleycameron .com, Twitter: @amycloughley

Describe the kinds of works you want to represent. I look for unique, clear voices with smart, tightly written prose. I have a soft spot for distinctive, strong, contemporary characters set in small towns and always look for an unexpected story arc, a suitable pace, and a compelling protagonist. I am actively building my client list with both debut and veteran writers. Fiction: literary and upmarket fiction as well as commercial, including well-researched historical (prefer 1800s or later) and well-told women's fiction. Also love a page-turning mystery or suspense with sharp wit and unexpected twists and turns. Nonfiction: narrative nonfiction when the plot and characters are immersed in a culture, lifestyle, discipline, or industry; travel or adventure memoir.

Describe what you definitely don't want to represent. Not currently focusing on military/government thrillers, fantasy, sci-fi, or young adult projects.

How do you want writers to pitch you? Please send a query letter in the body of an email to amyc@kimberleycameron.com. Include "Author Submission" in the subject line. Fiction: attach a 1-page synopsis and the first 50 pages of your manuscript as separate Word or PDF documents. Nonfiction: attach a full book proposal as well as sample chapters as separate Word or PDF documents. (Sample chapters should include the first chapter of the book and should not exceed 50 pages.)

Describe your education and professional history. After studying creative writing and earning a BS in magazine journalism, I held positions that straddled the line between editorial and marketing — managing a magazine, advertising campaigns, and marketing projects. I first got into book publishing via an internship at my agency until I ultimately started taking on my own clients, coaching writers through classes and conferences, and participating in the myriad of opportunities that agenting has opened up. Certainly my journalism background laid the groundwork for my appreciation of tightly written prose and love of a unique story; and my marketing background provided a base for the business side of book publishing. Now I can leverage my background in both words and business to benefit my clients.

Why do you think you became an agent and how did you become one? Working as a literary agent is a lovely balance of all my favorite things: providing editorial feedback, pitching to the editors, negotiating deals, and helping writers reach their goals (there really is nothing better than that!). It is truly a business of relationships at every stage. I enjoy the business side of agenting as much as the creative, and I think that all of the positions I have held (and the many, many books I have read) have proven to be the perfect base for this career.

Do you charge fees? If yes, please explain. No.

When and where were you born, and where have you lived? I was born and went to school in the Midwest and have been in the San Francisco Bay Area for 15 years.

List some of the titles you have recently placed with publishers. Since I am a newer agent, I am still in the process of developing my list, but I have placed my first client's book, Allen Esken's *The Life We Bury* (Seventh Street Books).

Describe your personality. What you see is what you get. I am pretty practical and direct, but, true to my Midwestern roots, I always try to be nice. I am passionate about my work and want nothing more than to support my clients and help them reach their goals. Professionally, I suppose it is the "former project manager" in me, but I am all about developing a plan, documenting that plan, and executing that plan, so all parties know what is going on.

What do you like reading/watching/listening to on your own time? With literary/ upmarket fiction as well as narrative nonfiction, I want to learn something new and feel like I have been immersed in a life and circumstance that the author has made compelling and engrossing. The characters' interiors need to come through in a way that allows me to understand their points of view — I don't have to agree with them, but it has to be completely believable and interesting. For commercial projects, I look for a well-paced page-turner that has layers and keeps me guessing; a commercial manuscript that has too much backstory up front rarely works for me. When it comes to TV, I like shows that make me laugh or (am I really admitting this?) reality shows. I can't help myself.

What do the "Big 5" mean to you? For many writers, success with the Big 5 is the ultimate goal. Since my job is to support my clients, that becomes my ultimate goal for them. But for others, independent presses are truly a better fit — whether that is because of the types of books they write or the type of attention that a smaller press can give the clients and their books. Publishing is certainly not a "one size fits all" business.

What are your feelings about self-publishing? Self-publishing is a good option for the writers who want to control and manage every aspect of their projects — hiring private editors, cover and book design, distribution, promotion, etc. — but it isn't for everyone.

Describe your job and what you like and don't like about it. My job is to be my client's advocate. Through the editorial process, submissions, contract negotiation, publishing, and career development, I am the go-to person for questions and for keeping the momentum moving forward. Whether the author is a debut author or seasoned veteran, each milestone is rewarding and each stall is disappointing. We are in it together.

How would you describe the "writer from hell"? As long as clients understand that I have other clients (and a personal life!), we are usually fine. I also treat all my clients as business professionals and partners in this endeavor, and I really need the same courtesy returned.

What do you want to tell new/unpublished writers? It is wonderful to have people in your life that support your writing and love you, but it is also important to have beta readers whom you trust to give you honest, helpful feedback on your project. These two groups are often mutually exclusive. It is nearly impossible to create a publishable novel in isolation (especially for first-time authors). Although you may decide to cherry-pick from the advice you receive (it is still your book after all!), it can be amazing what a fresh perspective can sometimes lead to. Take advantage of their feedback to help you tighten and polish your manuscript before you take your next step toward publishing.

Agent's name: Mary C. Moore

Describe the kinds of works you want to represent. Adult and young adult fantasy and science fiction except dystopian. In sci-fi/fantasy, I prefer upmarket writing and settings /characters that operate outside sci-fi/fantasy tropes, especially earthy female-based characters. If submitting urban fantasy, please no demons, vampires, angels, or were-wolves. Also literary fiction, especially magical realism that highlights a particular culture or surreal intellectual humor; historical, if the voice is strong (please no WWII narratives); genre romance; cozy mystery.

Describe what you definitely don't want to represent. No memoir, picture books, middle grade, military, or nonfiction.

How do you want writers to pitch you? For submissions, please see my website: marycmoore.com/index.php/submissions.

Describe your education and professional history. See my bio on my website: marycmoore.com.

How did you become an agent? Did an internship to learn more about the industry for my own writing and fell in love. Never looked back.

Knowing what you do now, would you do it again? If not, what might you do instead? Start my career in publishing at an earlier age.

Do you charge fees? If yes, please explain. No.

List some of the titles you have recently placed with publishers. *Admiral* by Sean Danker (Ace/Roc), *Dissension* by Stacey Berg (Voyager Impulse).

What do the "Big 5" mean to you? The companies in which most of the traditional publishing industry is consolidated. They have the financial advantage of a big company and thus can put more resources into producing and selling a book. I prefer to sell projects to these companies.

How do you feel about independent/small presses? I think they can be great for debut authors, more personal and hands-on, but I would prefer to sell to the Big 5, if possible, as I work off commission only, and if I only made sales to indies, I wouldn't survive in this business. I usually discuss with my clients which route they want to go if we don't get picked up by the Big 5.

What are your feelings about self-publishing? I appreciate that it has opened doors for many writers, but I believe a lot of newbies think it's the answer to their career, and they end up disappointed. I don't represent self-published titles, but I will consider a new unpublished project by a self-published author. To read my personal experience with self-publishing, see relentlesswriters.blogspot.com/2015/11/self-publishing-and-literary-agent.html.

Do you think Amazon is good or bad — or both — for the book business? Both. Still watching to see how it shakes out.

What do you like and dislike about your job? Like: I get to read for a living. Dislike: how slowly the publishing industry moves.

What are ways prospective clients can impress you, and what are ways they can turn you off? Impress me with professionalism, patience, and the ability to move on from a project to write something new. Most clients I've signed are on their third or fourth manuscript. Turn me off with demands and taking advantage of my time. I also get frustrated with writers who respond to my rejections with requests for feedback or questions about the industry, especially if I gave a bit of it in the initial response. I couldn't possibly respond to every email I get like that, which makes me feel guilty and unhappy that I responded in the first place.

How would you describe the "writer from hell"? A writer with high expectations that the publishing industry is going to do all the work. Needy and insecure and constantly checking in. A diva.

THE KNIGHT AGENCY ❖ knightagency.net

570 East Avenue, Madison, GA 30650

Agent's name and contact info: Pamela Harty, pamela.harty@knightagency.net, 706-473-0994

Describe the kinds of works you want to represent. Romance, women's fiction, nonfiction including business, health, true crime, pop culture, memoir.

Describe what you definitely don't want to represent. Sci-fi and occult.

How do you want writers to pitch you? Through our website guidelines.

KRAAS LITERARY AGENCY

Agent's name and contact info: Irene W. Kraas, ikraas@yahoo.com

Describe the kinds of works you want to represent. Big and unique psychological thrillers (military, alternate history, women sociopaths, etc.; *unique* is the key).

Describe what you definitely don't want to represent. Science fiction, fantasy, young adult, romance, and anything else that is not listed above.

How do you want writers to pitch you? Please send the first 10 pages of your completed manuscript in the body of an email. I do not open attachments unless I request them.

Describe your education and professional history. Bachelor's and master's degrees. I have worked in major businesses and served as a Washington, DC, consultant for many years. Have been in the agency business for 25 years.

How did you become an agent? Fell into it after I thought I had written (a) the great American novel and (b) the most unique science fiction work ever. ☺

Knowing what you do now, would you do it again? If not, what might you do instead? I would do this again in a heartbeat, but would have started younger. I do, however, think my years of business experience with major corporations and consulting firms have added a depth to my understanding of the business from both sides.

Do you charge fees? If yes, please explain. No. Not for at least 20 years. When I first opened and everything was done by mail, I did charge copying and mailing fees.

When and where were you born, and where have you lived? I was born in New York and have lived all over the world including Denmark, Belgium, Costa Rica, and Mexico as well as many states such as Georgia, New Mexico, Texas, Washington, DC, Virginia, and Maryland.

What do you like to do when you're not working? Read, travel, read, paint, read, eat, and so on!

List some of the titles you have recently placed with publishers. I have cut back quite a bit and am semiretired. I sold six works to Random House: four for Paula Paul and two other works for a new writer, Sarah Hobart.

Describe your personality. I am 100 percent loyal and trustworthy, and all of my dealings with both client and publisher are straightforward. I am extremely tenacious and will fight on behalf of my clients and their best interests.

What do you like reading/watching/listening to on your own time? I love David Baldacci, Lee Child, Robert Crais, and John Sanford. I also love Brian Greene's *The Fabric of the Universe* (and other works), and I love literary works as well.

Do you think the business has changed a lot over the past few years? If yes, please explain. Absolutely! Ebooks and all things to do with the internet, movies, and gaming have changed the business drastically. And if I may point out my deepest concern — writers are getting less and less for working harder (if possible), and the publishers are getting more and more.

What do the "Big 5" mean to you? Bottom line–driven corporations — *not* publishers.

How do you feel about independent/small presses? The ones who have been in business many years are wonderful, and it is a pleasure to work with them.

What are your feelings about self-publishing? I think if you want to do it, fine. I think it's pretty much 99 percent a waste of time, and the newest caveat is that if you've self-published, some houses won't even consider taking on that work. This has happened twice to me in the last few months. I have pitched something to an editor who was excited to read the work, but when I mentioned it had been self-published, the editor said, "We do not consider books that have been self-published." I think this is strange, since both works had done extremely well. Anyway, I think self-publishing might be a big thing, but I'm not crazy about it.

Do you think Amazon is good or bad — or both — for the book business? Believe it or not, I think it's mostly good. Yes, it has too much power, and yes, it can be spiteful, but, most important, it can take an order and sell a book in less than 30 seconds. In sales data you can't beat a closing that can be done so quickly and so often on a day-to-day basis. There are no "casual" browsers found online — almost everyone buys!

What do you like and dislike about your job? I dislike clients who always know better than I do. If I was good enough to pick them out of the pile, why do I become stupid because I say their second (or third) book isn't working?

What are ways prospective clients can impress you, and what are ways they can turn you off? Good writing is the only thing that really impresses me. I really don't care who you are, how many degrees you have (or don't have), or what your life history is. All I do is read! I am turned off completely (and won't even read) an email that starts "Dear Agent" or any email that has a list of agents on the "To" line.

How would you describe the "writer from hell"? Are you kidding???

Describe a book you would like to write. Anything that would be fun and fabulously well written.

Do you believe in a higher and/or lower "power"? Are we talking about advances here? ☺

Is there anything you wish to express beyond the parameters of the preceding questions? I urge all writers to write — published or not. Do what you love — that's what we're here for!

THE LA LITERARY AGENCY ❖ www.laliteraryagency.com

PO Box 46370, Los Angeles, CA 90046, 323-654-5288

Agent's name and contact info: Maureen Lasher, maureen.laliterary@mac.com, maureen@laliteraryagency.com

Describe the kinds of works you want to represent. I like to represent the same kind of books that I buy for myself from a bookstore. At the top of my nonfiction list is narrative nonfiction, which is storytelling. The subjects are eclectic and I can't put them in one category, so here are some of our narrative nonfiction books that illustrate what I like to represent. *Light My Fire* by Ray Manzarek (Putnam): Ray re-creates how he founded the

Doors with Jim Morrison and takes you on their trip; he wrote the first draft by pencil on yellow legal pads. *Beyond the Limits* by Stacy Allison (Little, Brown): Stacy tells how she became the first American woman to crest Mt. Everest; her sample chapter focused on the moment when she and two other climbers realized that they had enough oxygen for only one person to summit. *Where the Money Is* by FBI Special Agent William Rehder (W. W. Norton), who is the world's foremost expert on bank robberies. *Uppity* by Bill White (Grand Central): professional baseball player, voice of the New York Yankees for 18 years, and president of the National League for 5 years — the first African American to reach that level in any sport. *Sweet Life* by Barry Manilow (McGraw-Hill), an intelligent, funny, talented writer. *Never Too Late* by Bobby DeLaughter (Scribner): a criminal prosecutor, DeLaughter solved the mystery of Medgar Evers's murder 30 years after the crime when, by chance, he found the missing weapon in the closet of a judge — his father-in-law; the judge wasn't hiding the gun — he didn't know that it was the missing piece of evidence in the case.

In addition to those types of narrative nonfiction, we are interested in biography, autobiography, sports, cooking, science, history, adventure, health, and lifestyle. Fiction is both easier and harder to define. Like everyone in publishing, we long for compelling, beautifully written novels. They can be historical, contemporary, literary, commercial, mystery, or suspense. Reality check: it's difficult to sell a debut novel, but it happens every day.

Describe what you definitely don't want to represent. We don't work with romance novels (although they're huge now), horror, Westerns, science fiction, juvenile and young adult (also huge), or books on how to solve world problems. Our website will give you a broader overview of our books.

Describe your education and professional history. Following my graduation from Brown University with a concentration in history, I moved to New York and got my first job at Prentice Hall. I began as an advertising copywriter and eventually was part of a team of 3 supervising a staff of 26. Next I was associate manager of advertising at Random House, where I marketed our books to schools, colleges, and libraries. Then I became director of advertising and publicity for Liveright, a small literary publisher with a remarkable history and backlist. They were the first to publish Sigmund Freud, e. e. cummings, Ezra Pound, William Faulkner, and on and on. Today Liveright is an imprint of Norton, one of the last independent publishers. I moved to Los Angeles when my husband became CEO of Nash Publishing, which was then the largest trade publishing company west of Chicago but has now been merged into extinction.

Since we had extensive publishing experience, both marketing and editorial, we launched an independent imprint from Los Angeles with Houghton Mifflin, which is based in Boston. Our imprint focused on commercial fiction (several *New York Times* bestsellers) and travel guides, a series that grew to over 20 titles. At the same time, we were reading many excellent manuscripts that we had to pass on because they didn't fit the profile of our imprint. This led to the creation of the LA Literary Agency. Today we represent a wide range of authors. Many of our clients have very different day jobs — athletes, actors, musicians, physicians, attorneys, chefs, food experts, and historians.

What do you like to do when you're not working? I've had some interesting side trips from agenting. When I moved to Los Angeles, I learned how to fabricate jewelry — mostly in silver. Invited to a party in New York, I wore as much of my new jewelry as I could put on — earrings, two silver cuffs, three rings, a necklace, and a belt buckle. A woman approached me to inquire where I had purchased the pieces. Her name was Vera Wang, then accessories editor at *Vogue*. For the next year, my jewelry was featured every month on the editorial pages of *Vogue* and was sold in major department stores such as Bloomingdale's. I enjoyed designing and making jewelry but didn't see it as a career, so I returned to publishing. I've been knitting since I was 10, and a few years ago I coauthored a knitting book, *Teen Knitting Club* (Artisan). To me, knitting is a creative outlet and a form of meditation.

Knowing what you do now, would you do it again? If not, what might you do instead? I would do it all over again. I've always been in love with books, so publishing was a natural direction for me. When our daughter graduated from college, she wanted to be a television writer. We knew she was talented but wanted her to continue her education. She could become a lawyer, a plastic surgeon, or maybe a veterinarian. Today she's a successful writer/producer for television, from CW's *Gossip Girl* to HBO's *Togetherness*. Lesson learned: do what you love.

Interesting coincidence: one of the *Gossip Girl* episodes she wrote featured the publisher of Simon & Schuster; they cast Jonathan Karp, who really is the publisher of Simon & Schuster, and he was wonderful in the role.

What do you want to tell new/unpublished writers? The internet has opened the floodgates and made it more complicated for writers and agents to find each other. When it's obvious to me that I'm one of hundreds of agents who have received the same email, I'm reluctant to spend any time on it. Nevertheless, I have connected with writers on the internet. I got an email from an academic who remembered me from a writers' conference where we met years ago. He's an international expert on Antarctica who lives in Great Britain, and we're working on his book. I'm also representing several novelists who emailed me blind inquiry letters and sample pages. One is a suspense novel set in Amsterdam, where the author lives. The second is in development with a producer whose last movie was nominated for an Academy Award.

Don't give up on the internet, but here's some advice on how to use it. Try to personalize your approach to an agent. Read the acknowledgments in books that are like yours, and email a note to the agent referred to in the book. Ask everyone you know if they know someone in the publishing world and try to get an email introduction. Look at your college alumni/ae listings and use that shared experience as an introduction. I always respond to undergraduates or graduates from Brown.

Study this book and write to the agent or agents whose entries resonate with you. Make your inquiry personal. We've signed several excellent clients who found us in the 2015 edition of Jeff Herman's book. One of these writers had previously published two books that together have sold over 3.5 million copies.

How would you describe the "writer from hell"? This is an extreme example, but it happened. Eric and I were scheduled to be on an agent panel in Los Angeles sponsored by New York–based Volunteer Lawyers for the Arts. The event was widely publicized. Then we and the Volunteer Lawyers group in New York received anonymous letters explaining why he and I weren't qualified to be on the panel. The letter was also filled with anti-Semitic rhetoric and threats of physical harm. The authorities, thankfully, took it seriously. They had a plan. Two FBI agents went to the conference and when the moderator said that we couldn't be there, a man walked out, clearly angry. The FBI agents followed him and brought him in for questioning. He revealed that months before we had turned down his novel. If the person is already a client and I want to take a Valium before each phone conversation, I try to end the professional relationship as quickly as possible. Today, it's easy for someone who feels ignored or insulted or unhappy to use the internet to vent his or her anger. We try to spot that kind of person early and not get involved.

Describe your job and what you like about it. With fiction and nonfiction I work as an editor, and that's what I truly enjoy. For nonfiction, it's essential to have a stellar, best-on-the-editor's-desk proposal. I work editorially with our clients on the book proposal, which is harder to write than the book. However, when you have it right, you will have a blueprint for your book. In 20 or 30 or 40 pages, the proposal has to do it all. What's the best way to define your book? What will you cover in each chapter? Is the overview effective? What is the best structure for the book? Are the sample chapters good enough? What qualifies you to write the book?

Working with fiction is quite different. Publishers make their decisions based on reading the complete novel. I'm working with several novelists I met through the internet. There was no personal connection, but I was taken by their submission letter. We've done extensive editorial work together to get the novels ready to submit. Communication takes two forms: on the phone and on the computer. I'm not copyediting (punctuation, spelling, etc.), but working on plot, characters, structure, dialogue, and pacing.

Truthfully, I never know where I will find a wonderful book. When our daughter was in college, she went to a lecture given by Norma McCorvey (a.k.a. Jane Roe of *Roe v. Wade*). Surprised that nobody had ever asked Norma to tell her story, we paired her with a writer, and HarperCollins published *I Am Roe*. A small slice of history: Norma learned about the historic Supreme Court decision, *Roe v. Wade*, when she opened up the Dallas daily newspaper lying on her doorstep and read the front page article about herself.

What are your feelings about self-publishing? If all you care about is to see your book in print, go for it. If you believe that when your book is published, the world will find it, reevaluate your conclusion. If you have a huge success, you won. Winners are rare.

Do you think Amazon is good or bad — or both — for the book business? Answering as a customer: Yes, I like Amazon. I buy from them constantly. I'm a member of Amazon Prime and joined audible.com many years ago — before Amazon bought them.

I also go to the Barnes & Noble at the Grove in LA about once a week. Their children's section is a playground with books. You can sit in the café with a cappuccino and look through a pile of new titles. Their display tables highlight books by category like historical fiction or biography. Every year I renew my membership card. If Barnes & Noble closes, I'll be devastated.

Answering as an agent: The publishing business is changing, but I don't have a clue how it will sort itself out. Amazon is a major force. It will be a huge loss to book lovers and the publishing industry if Barnes & Noble can't survive because of Amazon. Books aren't going away.

LEVINE GREENBERG ROSTAN LITERARY AGENCY ❖

www.lgrliterary.com

307 Seventh Avenue, Suite 2407, New York, NY 10001, 212-337-0934

Agent's name and contact info: Danielle Svetcov, dsvetcov@lgrliterary.com

Describe the kinds of works you want to represent. The bald answer is novels, graphic novels, journalism, science, reported memoir, food/cooking, and humor. More specifically, I want to represent novels like *I Capture the Castle*, *The Truth According to Us*, *The Shipping News*, and, er, *Jane Eyre*; I want to represent graphic novels like *Roller Girl*; I want to rep journalism/history like *Devil in the White City* and journalism/science like *The Immortal Life of Henrietta Lacks*; I want to rep memoir like *Don't Let's Go to the Dogs Tonight*; food and recipe books like *Blood, Bones & Butter* and *Twelve Recipes*; and, as for humor, anything, so long as it's yours and no one else's and you've thought long and hard about how to deliver humor in book form.

Describe what you definitely don't want to represent. Self-help, erotica, and other extreme sports.

How do you want writers to pitch you? Write me a letter. Be yourself. Keep it economical, i.e., short. Try to convey your abilities as a writer. Tell me who you are and why you have written what you've written; don't try to tell me everything in the query; just create enough drama in the note to get me interested in hearing more. Include an attached proposal and/or a small sample from the book.

Describe your education and professional history. California public schools, followed by four years at Northwestern University's J-school, followed by three-month culinary "camp" certificate program at Boston University, followed by two and a half years earning an MFA at Warren Wilson College — in that order, but with lots of interstitial years.

How did you become an agent? I answered an ad on Craigslist, which led to a 5-hour-a-week job assisting an agent who'd just moved from New York to San Francisco to start her agency's West Coast office. The 5 hours turned into 10, then 20, then however many hours it took to get the job done. I began selling my own books about five years into the gig. I still work for the agency I began assisting in 2002. I'm the only agent at LGR based in California.

Knowing what you do now, would you do it again? If not, what might you do instead? Yes.

Do you charge fees? If yes, please explain. Not fees, just commissions on sales, 15 percent, the standard commission charged by agents.

When and where were you born, and where have you lived? Born in northern California, 1973. I've lived in Marin County, California; Evanston, Illinois; Albuquerque; Chicago; Oxford (England); New York City; Boston; and Washington, DC, not in that order.

What do you like to do when you're not working? Read, hike, cook, talk through existential and world crises with smart friends.

List some of the titles you have recently placed with publishers. *How to Be Depressed* by Dana Eagle (Knock Knock), *Broad Strokes* by Bridget Quinn (Chronicle), *This Is How They Tell Me the World Ends* by Nicole Perlroth (Portfolio), *Dandelion Chocolate Book* by Dandelion Chocolate, LLC (Potter), *Fermentation on Wheels* by Tara Whitsitt (Bloomsbury).

Describe your personality. Conscientious, practical, encouraging, impatient, occasionally stormy, with a tendency to eye-roll.

What do you like reading/watching/listening to on your own time? I'm a big fan of Newbery-quality middle grade books and tend to shake down our local kids' librarian for the candidates each year; I spend a lot of free time reading those titles and feeling 12, my favorite age. I love a good British mystery (the *Matthew Shardlake* series, the *Flavia de Luce* series, and the Sherlock spin-offs by Laurie R. King have kept me busy over the years though; the last is actually an American doing a mean impression). I chase laughs in my free time, too. David Sedaris, Louis C.K., Zach Galifianakis, Bill Murray are favorites. I miss Gilda Radner. TV taste runs to *Game of Thrones* (though the violence tips my scales some days), *Catastrophe*, *The Wire*, *Man in the High Castle*, and pretty much anything made by the BBC (*Jewel in the Crown*, *The Forsythe Saga*, et al.). You can frequently find me parked in my driveway, listening to a chapter of *Ramona the Brave*, *The Secret Garden*, an episode of the Longform podcast, or Serial.

Do you think the business has changed a lot over the past few years? If yes, please explain. It doesn't seem drastically different from when I began. Still have to find talent. Still have to edit and shape proposals and manuscripts. Still have to cultivate relationships with editors. There are certain kinds of projects — spin-offs from blogs, Vine, Instagram, etc. — that seem to sell faster than ever before; but those are the pop-culture projects. They've always been freaks of nature.

What do the "Big 5" mean to you? The publishers who pay the most and have the greatest ability to distribute a book, here and abroad.

How do you feel about independent/small presses? I think they're wonderful and absolutely essential at this moment when so few "biggies" exist. They are the presses that often find the next generation of great writers, take the first risk on them, launch them.

What are your feelings about self-publishing? I feel it's a lot harder than it looks and that you'd better love to glad-hand and market if you have a desire to succeed as a self-published author.

Do you think Amazon is good or bad — or both — for the book business? Both. Like marriage, it's complicated.

What do you like and dislike about your job? I like that it's an ongoing education, that I'm in contact with talented and creative people, and that I can help them navigate this world. I don't like the feeling I sometimes get — that it's impossible to be heard anymore. I suppose that comes from a discomfort and generalized worry about the pace and habits of the modern world, specifically the modern media cycle, which publishing is part of or at least depends on. I'd like to find new ways to spread the gospel of books.

Describe a book you would like to write. So many, and one will be published in 2017, *Park, Place* (Dial Books for Young Writers).

Do you believe in a higher and/or lower "power"? Sometimes.

Agent's name and contact info: Victoria Skurnick, vskurnick@lgrliterary.com

Describe the kinds of works you want to represent. Fiction: literary, suspense, book-club. Nonfiction: politics, history, narrative, anything with a great narrative voice.

Describe what you definitely don't want to represent. Science fiction, fantasy, romance.

How do you want writers to pitch you? Query letter by email.

Describe your education and professional history. BA, University of Wisconsin, Madison; worked in promotion and advertising at Avon Books, Pocket Books, and Holt, Rinehart & Winston; senior editor at Pocket Books and St. Martin's Press; editor in chief, Book-of-the-Month Club. Also coauthor of seven novels written under the name Cynthia Victor. An agent at LGR since 2007.

How did you become an agent? Switched careers when I left the book club. Figured I'd done everything else and that my experience might lend itself to being an agent.

Knowing what you do now, would you do it again? If not, what might you do instead? I might have started as an agent a few years earlier, but love what I'm doing now. (If someone wanted to star me in a Broadway musical, I might switch — oh so unlikely!)

Do you charge fees? If yes, please explain. No, we do not.

When and where were you born, and where have you lived? Born in NYC, live in NYC (evidently not known for my geographical range).

What do you like to do when you're not working? Music: play it, sing it, and listen to it; read; work out.

List some of the titles you have recently placed with publishers. *All the Time in the World* by Caroline Angell (Holt), *The Queen's Accomplice* by Susan Elia MacNeal (Bantam), *Biography of Chester Arthur* by Scott Greenberger (Da Capo), *Real Impact* by Morgan Simon (Nation Books).

Describe your personality. Outgoing, warm, forthright, opinionated.

What do you like reading/watching/listening to on your own time? Elizabeth Strout, Josephine Tey, Jhumpa Lahiri, Michael Lewis.

Do you think the business has changed a lot over the past few years? If yes, please explain. If you're reading this book, you don't need me to explain everything that has changed — the Web, Amazon, conglomeration, on and on and on.

What do the "Big 5" mean to you? The five large conglomerates remaining.

How do you feel about independent/small presses? Love them, though their contracts can be unforgiving.

What are your feelings about self-publishing? Too complex to go into in this space. Democratic, also fraught.

What do you like and dislike about your job? Love doing it, hate how tough on good new fiction the market has become.

What are ways prospective clients can impress you, and what are ways they can turn you off? Write a great book. Don't text me on my cell. Write a great book. Write a great book.

Describe a book you would like to write. I would have loved to have written *Olive Kitteridge*.

LINDA KONNER LITERARY AGENCY ❖

www.lindakonnerliteraryagency.com

10 West 15th Street, Suite 1918, New York, NY 10011

Agent's name and contact info: Linda Konner, ldkonner@cs.com

Describe the kinds of works you want to represent. I represent adult nonfiction, especially prescriptive nonfiction (health, self-help, relationships, parenting, personal finance, popular psychology). Also some pop culture, celebrity memoir, popular science, business narrative, cookbooks. All of the above *must* be written by or with a top expert in the field with a substantial author platform.

Describe what you definitely don't want to represent. I do not represent fiction, children's, religion, or memoir.

How do you want writers to pitch you? Email, including a brief author bio and a brief book summary. If I'm interested, I will request a full proposal plus one or two sample chapters.

Describe your education and professional history. Brooklyn College (BA), Fordham University (MA). Served as a features editor at *Seventeen*, *Redbook*, and *Woman's World*; editor in chief of *Weight Watchers Magazine* and founding editor/editor in chief of *Richard Simmons & Friends* newsletter. Author or coauthor of eight books, including *The Last Ten Pounds* and *Why Can't a Man Be More Like a Cat?*

How did you become an agent? I was tired of being an author and an editor yet wanted to remain in publishing. I had also negotiated a couple of my own book deals and had many friends who were authors.

Knowing what you do now, would you do it again? If not, what might you do instead? Would definitely do it again; it's been my best career of all.

Do you charge fees? If yes, please explain. One-time expenses fee collected only if/when I sell the book to a publisher.

When and where were you born? Brooklyn, New York, in the 1900s.

What do you like to do when you're not working? Theater, travel, poker, *Law & Order* reruns.

List some of the titles you have recently placed with publishers. What to Eat When You're Pregnant (Ten Speed Press), *Harvard Medical School Guide to Yoga* (Da Capo), *Body Intelligence* (Beyond Words/Simon & Schuster), *Morgue: A Life in Death* (St. Martin's).

Describe your personality. Fun-loving but serious about my work.

What do you like reading/watching/listening to on your own time? Early-20-century fiction; *Law & Order* reruns; Springsteen, WQXR.

How do you feel about independent/small presses? Like them and work with them all the time.

What are your feelings about self-publishing? It's proven successful for a small number of writers, but I'm wedded to the traditional model of author-agent-publisher, and most authors are still eager to be a part of that arrangement.

What do you like and dislike about your job? I love the independence of making decisions on behalf of my clients and myself. I love most of the authors and editors I work with. I love seeing good books come together. Not very much I don't like.

How would you describe the "writer from hell"? Doesn't follow directions; emails incessantly; doesn't meet publisher's deadlines; worries needlessly; has unrealistic expectations about what his or her book is worth.

Describe a book you would like to write. Living Apart and Loving It, based on my successful 36-year relationship.

Do you believe in a higher and/or lower "power"? No.

LIPPINCOTT MASSIE MCQUILKIN ❖ lmqlit.com

27 West 20th Street, New York, NY 10011, 212-352-2055, fax: 212-352-2059

Agent's name and contact info: Laney Katz Becker, laney@lmqlit.com

Describe the kinds of works you want to represent. I love fiction that makes me think and is appropriate for book clubs. I'm also drawn to novels of historical fiction, stories with well-drawn characters, racially charged topics, and writers with a great voice. I'm also always on the lookout for psychological thrillers and domestic suspense. On the nonfiction side, I especially enjoy narratives by journalists (and of course, an established platform is always preferred).

Describe what you definitely don't want to represent. I don't represent children's, middle grade, young adult, fantasy, sci-fi, romance, paranormal, cozy mystery, or dystopian fiction.

How do you want writers to pitch you? I only accept electronic queries. Please query me at laney@lmqlit.com and include the word *Query* in the subject line. Tell me about yourself, your project, your writing background. For fiction, include the word count and your first chapter. For nonfiction, attach your proposal. You should expect to hear back from me within two to four weeks.

Describe your education and professional history. I'm a graduate of Northwestern University. My background is as a writer. I started as a copywriter at the ad agency J. Walter Thompson. Over the next two decades I also worked as a freelance journalist; my articles appeared in more than 50 magazines, including *Self, Health, Seventeen, First for Women.* I'm also an award-winning author (*Dear Stranger, Dearest Friend*; *Three Times Chai*). Somewhere along the way, I decided that spending seven hours a day in my basement writing books was too solitary for me. I wanted to use my marketing, writing, and reading skills in a new and different way. The agenting world allows me to do just that — and it's never, ever solitary! Prior to joining LMQ I was an agent at Folio and Markson Thoma.

Do you charge fees? If yes, please explain. Never.

List some of the titles you have recently placed with publishers. *The Nazi Titanic* (history, Da Capo); *Modern Girls* (historical fiction, Penguin Random House/NAL); *Two Across* (upmarket fiction, Grand Central); *Since She Went Away* (suspense, Penguin Random House/NAL).

What are your feelings about self-publishing? I don't represent self-published authors.

What are ways prospective clients can impress you, and what are ways they can turn you off? I'm always impressed by a talented writer who is also a wonderful, thoughtful person, someone who understands that revision is part of the writing process and is willing to go the distance to make their project the very best it can be. Besides the obvious (a poor query letter that includes typos, is addressed to half the publishing world, and greets me as "Dear Agent"), other turnoffs are queries that say, "My manuscript is ready for publication," or tell me that their project is going to make me a million dollars. Writers with unrealistic expectations are nothing but trouble.

How would you describe the "writer from hell"? Defensive writers who don't want to revise, don't want to listen, and view agents simply as gatekeepers to editors. I'm also not a fan of writers who fail to say thank you. Writers who, because of my writing background, expect me to do their work for them because, "You know how to do this," are also writers I try to avoid. And finally, writers who immediately send back revisions rather than taking time to let things sit, reread what they've written, and then — only then — once they're certain their work can't be any better, send it back to me for my review.

Agent's name and contact info: Rayhané Sanders, rayhane@lmqlit.com

Describe the kinds of works you want to represent. Literary and historical fiction, upmarket women's fiction, narrative nonfiction, select memoir. I like projects that are voice-centered, include specific cultural settings or cross-cultural themes, and illuminate a corner of our world or society too often neglected. I am drawn to works that celebrate the resilience of the human spirit while also depicting the experience of "the other."

Describe what you definitely don't want to represent. Cozies, commercial thrillers, commercial mystery, children's books, romance.

How do you want writers to pitch you? See lmqlit.com for instructions.

Describe your education and professional history. I attended NYU and began my publishing career at *Newsweek* magazine. I then moved to book publishing, working first for Penguin's Dutton and Gotham Books and then for William Morris Endeavor, where I worked with *New York Times* bestselling authors and recipients of such honors as the PEN/Hemingway Award, PEN/New England Award, Guggenheim and Wallace Stegner Fellowships, and National Endowment for the Arts grants, among others. I began to represent authors at WSK Management, where I worked with a slew of bestselling authors and added a *New York Times* bestseller and winners of, among others, the Hopwood Award, Northeastern Minnesota Book Award, Oregon Book Award, Pacific Northwest Booksellers Association Award, and Foreword IndieFab Award to my client list.

How did you become an agent? See above.

Do you charge fees? If yes, please explain. No.

When and where were you born, and where have you lived? Los Angeles, New York.

List some of the titles you have recently placed with publishers. The Small Backs of Children, The Mad Feast, Preparing the Ghost, The Jaguar Man, A House for Happy Mothers, Fishing with RayAnne, God Is an Astronaut, Heart Attack Watch, No. 4 Imperial Lane.

How do you feel about independent/small presses? They are important taste-makers.

What are your feelings about self-publishing? It's rarely a good idea.

THE LISA EKUS GROUP ❖ www.lisaekus.com

57 North Street, Hatfield, MA 01038, 413-247-9325

Agents' names and contact info: Lisa Ekus, Owner and Principal Agent, lisaekus@lisaekus.com; Sally Ekus, Manager and Literary Agent, sally@lisaekus.com

Describe the kinds of works you want to represent. Culinary nonfiction including cookbooks, health, nutrition, women's health.

Describe what you definitely don't want to represent. We don't represent fiction.

How do you want writers to pitch you? Reaching us via email is the best way, though we do still accept hardcopy submissions.

Describe your education and professional history. Lisa: BA from Barnard College (1979). Worked at Random House Crown Publishers. Have owned the Lisa Ekus Group, LLC, for the past 33 years. Represent hundreds of culinary writers through our Literary Agency, PR, Media Training, Talent, and À la Carte divisions.

How did you become an agent? I love to make dreams come true and find the right match of publisher and author. My passion for books made me an English major at Barnard, and I worked for a literary agent while still in college. There was never any question I would embark on a publishing career.

Knowing what you do now, would you do it again? If not, what might you do instead? I would do it all over again!

Do you charge fees? If yes, please explain. We operate on a 15 percent commission for the books our agency represents. There are no fees. We do offer hourly consulting for nonclients who are interested in learning about agenting, publishing, or have other industry-related questions.

When and where were you born, and where have you lived? I was born in Augusta, Georgia, and have lived in New York and Massachusetts.

What do you like to do when you're not working? Reading. Reading. Reading. Novels. Cookbooks. Antiquing and going to flea markets. Dining out. Cooking in. My daughter, now a coagent at the company, and I share a deep love of travel and spicy food. We're both advocates and supporters of charitable organizations and dedicate our "free" time to giving back to the community. I house a personal library of over 8,000 culinary titles and 3,000 novels.

List some of the titles you have recently placed with publishers. We proudly list our titles in a catalog each season on our website, www.lisaekus.com.

Describe your personality. I am a high-energy, outside-the-box thinker. I love to jump on opportunities and adore matchmaking between writers and publishers, writers and media, writers and other literary professionals. Ethical, honest, highly communicative, and compassionate are other adjectives that describe my work ethic and life.

Do you think the business has changed a lot over the past few years? If yes, please explain. Having been in the publishing business more than 35 years, I've seen extensive change. I see a great deal of opportunity in small, independent publishing, hybrid publishing, and deals outside of the proverbial "traditional box." The sky's the limit in terms of the types of deals, the creativity of agents, and the ability to expand in services offered to clients.

What do the "Big 5" mean to you? The top publishing conglomerates, soon to be top 3 perhaps? Consolidation of negotiating and buying power.

How do you feel about independent/small presses? Love them! They present different, creative types of opportunities, and often one can be a very big fish in a small, focused, and dedicated pond. The right fit is very important and, although the advances are lower, the ability to launch the right type of book and author is invaluable. There is a place for all size presses and publishers. It is not always "just about the money."

What are your feelings about self-publishing? Self-publishing has become a great option for authors who have the means and desire to wear the many hats it takes to write, edit, design, print, and promote a book. We often consult with authors on self-publishing.

Do you think Amazon is good or bad — or both — for the book business? Good in its ability to offer the diversity of books from all sorts of authors far and wide. Bad in that it is draining authors' and agents' profits by its deep discounts. The reader/consumer has a major advantage in saving money on books, but at the literal expense of the authors' earning a fair amount for their work. There is no soul in the company. Amazon is interested in much more than the book business, but the authors suffer the most.

What do you like and dislike about your job? Agents are advocates, friends, therapists, and cheerleaders. Our agency loves finding the right match between an author and a publishing house. The biggest downside of our industry right now is that the talent is still thriving, but the advances and monies are significantly lower.

What are ways prospective clients can impress you, and what are ways they can turn you off? Authors who present professionally and respectfully to us are always going to have an advantage. Respecting our terms and our time is imperative. Don't complain about how hard you work and how little your publisher does for you. We want partners in the publishing process and will work long and hard to grow you and your career accordingly. Appreciate us — we appreciate our clients.

How would you describe the "writer from hell"? Someone who does not trust me and our agency, who is not a team player, who goes behind our backs. Don't waste my time. Don't second-guess us. We always listen and confer closely with all our clients.

Describe a book you would like to write. Which one? There are so many rolling around in my head. It won't be fiction though — I leave that to the hugely talented novelists out there.

Do you believe in a higher and/or lower "power"? Of course.

Is there anything you wish to express beyond the parameters of the preceding questions? I believe in always trusting myself and asking, "What's good about it?"

LISA HAGAN LITERARY ❖ www.lisahaganbooks.com

110 Martin Drive, Bracey, VA 23919, 434-636-4138

Agent's name and contact info: Lisa Hagan, lisahaganliterary@yahoo.com, www.publishersmarketplace.com/members/LisaHagan

Describe the kinds of works you want to represent. Popular business, mind-body-spirit, health, science, women's studies, pop culture.

Describe what you definitely don't want to represent. Crime, fiction, dry academic.

How do you want writers to pitch you? Please email your query and include a brief synopsis, your audience, bio, and why you think I would be your best representation.

Describe your education and professional history. Virginia Commonwealth University, major in psychology. Literary agent for 24 years so far.

How did you become an agent? My mother, Sandra Martin, was a well-known literary agent in the field of mind-body-spirit. She was and continues to be my mentor.

Knowing what you do now, would you do it again? If not, what might you do instead? I love being an agent! Discovering new and old authors with forward-thinking ideas, creating brands, and touching people's lives — it is the best career choice ever. I can't wait to turn on my computer in the mornings to see what new and exciting pitches/queries are in my inbox. They are like little gifts every day.

Do you charge fees? If yes, please explain. No.

When and where were you born, and where have you lived? Richmond, Virginia; lived there until I was 30, moved to Manhattan, and then to London; now I live on a farm in southeast Virginia.

What do you like to do when you're not working? Travel, gardening, boating, and reading for pleasure. My grandmother is currently 90. For the last 12 years I have spent time with her every day, and that is something that I will always cherish. Life goes by fast; I want to make the most of every moment.

List some of the titles you have recently placed with publishers. *The E-Word: Ego, Enlightenment & Other Essentials* by Cate Montana (Enliven Books), *The New Alpha: A Roadmap to Unleashing Your Leadership and Human Potential* by Danielle Harlan, PhD (McGraw-Hill), *501 Ways to Roll Out the Red Carpet for Your Customers* by Donna Cutting (Career Press), *The Whole Heart Solution: Halt Heart Disease Now with the Best Alternative and Traditional Medicine* by Joel K. Kahn, MD (Reader's Digest).

Describe your personality. Optimistic and even-tempered.

What do you like reading/watching/listening to on your own time? Historical nonfiction, pop culture, and novels. I enjoy going to the movies, and I am addicted to *The Voice*. I listen to a wide variety of music from classical to country.

Do you think the business has changed a lot over the past few years? If yes, please explain. There is too much focus on social media to sell books.

What do the "Big 5" mean to you? I have enjoyed working with a myriad of editors at all of the Big 5 these last 20 years. I am mostly appreciative of them. When a manuscript comes across my desk, the book turns out beautifully, and the PR and marketing campaign are top-notch, I am thrilled.

How do you feel about independent/small presses? Love them. I have one.

What are your feelings about self-publishing? I've read many well-written self-published books that would never have been picked up by a traditional publisher because of the content. I'm okay with self-publishing.

Do you think Amazon is good or bad — or both — for the book business? Amazon is necessary; it is where we sell books. If they had not instigated the ranking system, I'm not sure we would be as enthralled with it as we are.

What do you like and dislike about your job? I do not enjoy being rejected on behalf of my authors. Even after 24 years, it still stings a little.

What are ways prospective clients can impress you, and what are ways they can turn you off? When an author listens to advice. It takes a team to get published. Listening is super important.

How would you describe the "writer from hell"? The one who calls me every day.

LITERARY MANAGEMENT GROUP, LLC ❖

literarymanagementgroup.com

PO Box 41004, Nashville, TN 37204, 615-812-4445

Agent's name and contact info: Bruce R. Barbour, Founder, brucebarbour@literarymanagementgroup.com

Describe the kinds of works you want to represent. Evangelical Christian adult nonfiction.

Describe what you definitely don't want to represent. We do not represent unpublished authors or children's, illustrated, gift, poetry, reference, or previously published and self-published books.

How do you want writers to pitch you? Query letter, proposal, and two sample chapters.

Describe your education and professional history. BA, cum laude, in business from Pepperdine University, Malibu, CA (1976); various editorial, sales, and marketing positions at Fleming Revell (1976–84); cofounder, Barbour Books (1984–86); VP publisher at Thomas Nelson after selling Barbour Books (1986–93); VP publisher at Random House (1994–96); founder and owner of Literary Management Group, a full-service literary consulting firm specializing in author representation, packaging, and consulting (1996–present).

How did you become an agent? After 20 years on the publisher's side of the desk, I saw an opportunity to help authors and publishers work more effectively and efficiently together.

Knowing what you do now, would you do it again? If not, what might you do instead? I love what I do and can't imagine doing anything else.

Do you charge fees? If yes, please explain. Agency fee is 15 percent for contracts negotiated, packaging fee for projects developed and produced (negotiated), consulting fee for work performed (negotiated).

When and where were you born, and where have you lived? Born December 22, 1953, in Ridgewood, New Jersey, and have lived in New Jersey (NY metro area), Chicago, Nashville, and Ft. Myers.

What do you like to do when you're not working? Read, work out, and spend endless hours with the love of my life, author Karen Moore.

List some of the titles you have recently placed with publishers. A collection of previously unpublished works by Laura Ingalls Wilder (WaterBrook, a division of Random House), *Two Chairs* by Bob Beaudine (Worthy Publishers), *The Smile Prescription* by Dr. Rich Castellano (Morgan James), *Every Day Is Mother's Day* by Karen Moore (BroadStreet), *Thanks for Being You* and *The Gift of Giving* by Karen Moore (Bristol Park), *Simple Giving* by Jen Iacovelli (Tarcher).

Describe your personality. Fun-loving and dedicated to doing my very best for my clients, so they can't stop telling their author friends what a great job I did for them.

What do you like reading/watching/listening to on your own time? Sports (NFL and college football), news, biographies, history, and travel.

Do you think the business has changed a lot over the past few years? If yes, please explain. Not really, if by "business" we mean developing new ideas. If we mean how those ideas are marketed and produced, nearly everything has changed since I started 40 years ago. The secret is keeping the focus on the simple truth that "content is king"; how folks want to learn about new books and read them will always be changing as technology and reading habits develop.

What do the "Big 5" mean to you? Publishers, fiction/nonfiction bestsellers, retailers, and media hits.

How do you feel about independent/small presses? For the right book and author, regional and specialty independent and small presses are oftentimes the best choice.

What are your feelings about self-publishing? I'm really turned off by service companies like Author Solutions, who masquerade as publishers and end up ripping authors off. I think Create Space at Amazon is a great resource for authors who want ebooks and print-on-demand copies of their work and don't want to spend a fortune.

Do you think Amazon is good or bad — or both — for the book business? Since they sell one in three print books and probably a higher portion of ebooks, whether I like them or not is irrelevant. For some consumers, that's their source of choice. Since I want books available everywhere, I'm happy that Amazon offers the services and selection it does.

What do you like and dislike about your job? I love my job, all facets of it. Some parts are more tedious than others, but all in all it's a blast working with authors and publishers.

What are ways prospective clients can impress you, and what are ways they can turn you off? I like prospective authors who have done their homework and can explain why I might be best to help them with their book. When I get a chain letter pitching a children's book that starts out, "My research indicates you are the perfect agent for me," it really ticks me off, because it says such authors haven't taken a nanosecond to check me out. If they had, they would know I don't do children's books. A waste of my time and theirs.

How would you describe the "writer from hell"? Arrogant, proud, contentious, self-absorbed, and narcissistic would be a good start!

Describe a book you would like to write. I'm an editor, not a writer. I break into a cold sweat with a blank page.

Do you believe in a higher and/or lower "power"? I am a Jesus follower and do believe in good and evil.

Is there anything you wish to express beyond the parameters of the preceding questions? If anybody would like to chat, I'd be happy to share how my faith affects every decision I make and, I hope, everything I do.

LITERARY SERVICES, INC. ❖ www.literaryservicesinc.com

PO Box 888, Barnegat, NJ 08005

Agent's name and contact info: John Willig, jwlitagent@msn.com

Describe the kinds of works you want to represent. Fresh, provocative, counterintuitive, contrarian, well-researched, and well-written presentations that "shine a new light" on a topic, event, company, or person. I work primarily in nonfiction categories with a strong interest in history, science, psychology, business, politics, current events, food and cultures, reference, and personal growth. I've also started to represent historical fiction in the mystery/crime and literary categories.

Describe what you definitely don't want to represent. Science fiction, fantasy fiction.

How do you want writers to pitch you? A one-page synopsis (rather than a full proposal) via email (only) per the submissions section on our company website.

Describe your education and professional history. I graduated from Brown University in 1976 and have worked in publishing for 38 years (2016 marks the 25th anniversary of our agency). I started in academic publishing as a college "traveler" (sales rep) with Texas, Oklahoma, and Arkansas as my territory, i.e., "The sun has riz, the sun has set, and here I is in Texas yet." I became an editor at then Harper & Row, a senior editor at WGL, and then executive editor for business professional/trade books at Prentice Hall. That's pretty much the résumé. I sincerely believe, though, that my "professional history" began when I became an avid reader as a teenager. I would see my mother (God bless her Irish soul) come home from the library smiling, happy that she was able to get her favorite writers' new books without having to go on the waiting list. Who were these people who could make her so happy? To find out, I, too, became a reader and lover of "stories well told."

How did you become an agent? Thanks to a restructuring at Prentice Hall, which was then owned by Simon & Schuster, and "creative differences," I decided to start my own literary-services company representing authors and editing journals and professional reference handbooks, etc.

Knowing what you do now, would you do it again? If not, what might you do instead? Yes, ever onward.

Do you charge fees? If yes, please explain. No.

When and where were you born, and where have you lived? New York, New York.

What do you like to do when you're not working? Spending as much time as possible with my now-grown-up sons; cycling; outdoor festivals of all types; exploring new towns, city neighborhoods, and "parts unknown"; movies and theater; and, of course, quiet time reading while enjoying "the sweetness of doing nothing."

List some of the titles you have recently placed with publishers. *John Lennon vs. the U.S.A.* by Leon Wildes, *The Amazing Cell* by Josh Rappaport, PhD, *Winning the Brain Game* by Mathew May, *Rethinking the Future Workplace* by Jeanne Meister, *Make Your Own Waves* by Louis Patler, *Amazing Stories of the Space Age* by Rod Pyle, *Life after the Diagnosis* by Steve Pantilat, MD, *Energy Investing and Trading* by Davis Edwards, *The First CEO: Julius Caesar* by Phillip Barlag, *The Drinkable Globe* by Jeff Cioletti, *Friendly Fire: The D-Day Battles of the Normandy Commanders* by Edward Gordon and David Ramsay.

Describe your personality. Each day trying to be a good man, father, partner, friend, neighbor, and colleague living a compassionate, interesting, and honest life.

What do you like reading/watching/listening to on your own time? I enjoy a wide variety of reading interests from historical fiction (e.g., *The Paris Wife*) to mystery/crime (e.g., authors like Colin Harrison, Michael Connolly, Harlan Cobin). Same for the watching (even though I try to do less watching and more doing each year!): very eclectic interests ranging from political shows to *Homeland* to *Antiques Roadshow* and *American Pickers*, always searching for the diamond-in-the-rough type of shows. Same for listening: from classical to rock to contemporary and country.

Do you think the business has changed a lot over the past few years? If yes, please explain. Yes, the change in the marketplace for our sources of information and entertainment has dramatically changed the book business. Books are now competing with all of the information available on the Web, content and entertainment by major media providers like HBO, Showtime, even Amazon now.

What do the "Big 5" mean to you? All of the Big 5 companies are comprised of many individual imprints with talented publishing professionals working very hard to ensure the quality of their books and brands, which, in turn, garners the respect of distributors and bookbuyers.

How do you feel about independent/small presses? I admire and work with many indies who (per above) are respected throughout the industry for the quality of their books and dedicated focus.

What are your feelings about self-publishing? Walt Whitman self-published/printed the original version of *Leaves of Grass* and with each new printing added new poems based on the reactions of his readers, a lesson in quality oftentimes lacking with self-publishers or self-funders. It's a very crowded marketplace, and to stand out I think many writers can benefit by seeking out professionals providing editorial, design, production, and marketing (which begins with the writing/developing) expertise and experience. Recognizing this need through the many conferences I have attended, I established a Content Coaching & Strategy service for writers considering self-publishing. It has led many writers to rethink their approaches (i.e., broad vs. narrow/focused), titles, subtitles, contents, planned expenses, etc.

Do you think Amazon is good or bad — or both — for the book business? Amazon is now 20 years old and thriving.

What do you like and dislike about your job? On a good day it's discovering a fresh writing voice or presentation, receiving a client's newly published book, or selling a new project to a respected editor. As agents and trusted advisers for our clients, we wear many hats, some days too many, especially when processing delays that can occur in decision making, contracts, payments, and respect.

What are ways prospective clients can impress you, and what are ways they can turn you off? Impress: be a student, do your homework and research, put your hours in, be respectful of those who have "earned their stripes," study the craft, attend conferences, get articles published in journals and magazines (establishing validation of your work), and display at least a whiff of grace and humor. Turn off: exhibit none of the above and expect an agent to spend time reviewing your work and, in accord with today's narcissism on steroids, expect immediate attention.

How would you describe the "writer from hell"? Publishing is a very humbling business (or should be). "Writers from hell" think nearly everything they are proposing will be a *New York Times* or *Wall Street Journal* bestseller and demand that same misguided thinking/passion from their agent and editor.

Describe a book you would like to write. The Sun Also Rises.

LIZA DAWSON ASSOCIATES ❖ www.lizadawsonassociates.com

350 Seventh Avenue, Suite 2003, New York, NY 10001, 212-465-9071

Agent's name and contact info: Liza Dawson, queryliza@lizadawsonassociates.com

Describe the kinds of works you want to represent. In fiction, thrillers and mystery of all types, women's fiction, literary fiction, romance, and historical fiction as well as the occasional young adult or middle grade novel. I like twisty plots and emotionally driven stories. I don't make a distinction between literary and commercial categories. It's all about narrative tension, distinct characters, and strong, confident sentences.

In nonfiction, history, psychology, women's interest, politics, narrative nonfiction, and memoirs by people who either have survived living in closed societies or happen to be very funny. I am drawn to academics who want to move beyond the university-press world and to journalists who have tripped over a singular story that needs a long format.

How do you want writers to pitch you? Query letter only, via email.

Describe your education and professional history. I established Liza Dawson Associates following a successful career in corporate book publishing. I was executive editor at Putnam and executive editor at William Morrow before I launched the agency in 1996. I received my BA in history from Duke University and am a graduate of the Radcliffe Publishing Procedures course.

Knowing what you do now, would you do it again? If not, what might you do instead? Wouldn't it be so much fun to do it again!

Do you charge fees? If yes, please explain. No.

When and where were you born, and where have you lived? I was born in NYC, moved to San Francisco in high school, and went to college in North Carolina.

List some of the titles you have recently placed with publishers. *The Promise Sisters* by Marie Bostwick, *What We Find* by Robyn Carr, *Angels Burning* by Tawni O'Dell.

Describe your personality. I'm an optimistic nurturer with an unexpected passion for methodical planning.

Do you think the business has changed a lot over the past few years? If yes, please explain. It is still all about the book. All the other things — the importance of social media, changes in distribution, the rise of epublishing, and the dominance of the Big 5 publishers — are just tweaks in a stable system in which agents discover talented authors, make sure their manuscripts are strong enough for submission, place said authors with editors, negotiate strong deals, and then systematically ask publishers the right questions, so that when publication day arrives, everything has been done that can be done to give a book the best chance at success.

What are your feelings about self-publishing? It has opened up so many opportunities for writers. (But it's still all about the book.) As an agency we've epublished about 30 books. Most of these were books whose rights have reverted. We've learned a lot in the process: self-publishing is a labor-intensive strategy, but it can revitalize careers and make money.

Agent's name and contact info: Caitie Flum, querycaitie@lizadawson.com

Describe the kinds of works you want to represent. Fiction: adult mystery and thrillers of all kinds, book-club fiction, contemporary romance, and historical fiction; science fiction and fantasy that have a strong young adult crossover; young adult and middle grade mystery and thrillers, contemporary romance, historical, science fiction, and fantasy, all with diverse characters. Nonfiction: memoirs that make people look at the world differently; narrative nonfiction, especially history, that's impossible to put down; books on pop culture, theater, current events, women's interest, and humor.

Describe what you definitely don't want to represent. Literary fiction, paranormal or historical romance, inspirational fiction, adult science fiction and fantasy without crossover audience. Anything that is racist, sexist, or homophobic.

How do you want writers to pitch you? By sending the query only to querycaitie@liza dawson.com.

Describe your education and professional history. I went to Hofstra University and majored in English with a concentration in publishing studies. I interned at Hachette Book Group in ebooks, and after graduating I interned at Writers House. I worked at the book clubs for two and a half years and was the buyer for the Children's Book of the Month Club. I started at Liza Dawson Associates as assistant and audio rights manager.

Do you charge fees? If yes, please explain. No.

What are ways prospective clients can impress you, and what are ways they can turn you off? They can impress me by writing a great book and following guidelines. It isn't about social-media numbers or platform when it comes to fiction. It just matters if the book is great.

They *will* turn me off by sending snail mail queries, calling, or sending more than just the query in their email. Following the guidelines shows that writers value my time. Trying to go around them makes writers stand out in a bad way.

Additional agents at Liza Dawson Associates: Caitlin Blasdell, querycaitlin@ lizadawsonassociates.com; Hannah Bowman, queryhannah@lizadawson associates.com; Jennifer Johnson-Blalock, queryjennifer@lizadawson associates.com

LIZA ROYCE AGENCY, LLC ❖ www.lizaroyce.com

1049 Park Avenue, New York, NY 10028, 212-722-1950

Agents' names: Liza Fleissig, Ginger Harris Dontzin

Describe the kinds of works you want to represent. From picture books through adult projects, fiction and nonfiction, LRA welcomes strong voices and plot-driven works.

How do you want writers to pitch you? We prefer to receive queries via email at submissions@lizaroyce.com. Please include a brief synopsis and a little information about yourself, including any social-media platform and/or marketing ideas you may have, but do not send any attachments, as they will not be opened at this stage in the process.

Describe your education and professional history. Liza: I graduated from the Wharton School of Business at the University of Pennsylvania and later went to Cardozo School of Law, where I graduated magna cum laude. I have practiced law for 20 years and was a partner in a litigation firm before founding LRA with Ginger. Prior to that, I worked in construction development and the banking industry.

How did you become an agent? I have always had a strong sphere of influence from friends in the publishing industry, and had been searching for something creative to do for a long time after my children were born. Besides, I guess when you come from an entrepreneurial family, it's in your blood to take risks and try new things!

Knowing what you do now, would you do it again? If not, what might you do instead? Yes — just maybe wish I had started sooner!

Do you charge fees? If yes, please explain. No.

When and where were you born, and where have you lived? I am a New Yorker from start to finish. I don't discuss age, since it's a meaningless number, but I was at Woodstock when I was *very* young.

What do you like to do when you're not working? Spending time with my family is the most important thing. Whether skiing in Vermont, summering on the Cape, or just doing jigsaw puzzles, we are a pretty tight crew, and I am grateful every day for the life I live.

List some of the titles you have recently placed with publishers. *Clever Little Witch* (McElderry), *Secret to Hummingbird Cake* (Thomas Nelson), *Hildie Bitterpickles Needs Her Sleep* (Creston), *A Final Ace* (Berkley/Penguin), *Grace Hopper* (Sterling Children's), *Between Black and White* (Thomas & Mercer), *How Does That Make You Feel?* (Seal Press).

Describe your personality. Determined, honest, fiercely loyal, and detailed oriented. I don't really follow "signs," but I've been told it's no surprise I was born a Scorpio.

What do you like reading/watching/listening to on your own time? Lately there's been little time for anything outside of LRA books, but I do lean toward suspense/thrillers. As for what I'm watching, I enjoy decompressing to anything from *The Walking Dead* to *NCIS* to *The Big Bang Theory* and tons of junk in between.

Do you think the business has changed a lot over the past few years? If yes, please explain. Incredibly so! Between the Borders chain closing, Amazon's presence, and the fact that *self-publishing* is no longer considered a dirty word, let alone the surge of ereaders, the last few years have proved to be a learning curve for everyone.

What do the "Big 5" mean to you? To me, they are like the Ivy League. Fantastic, strong, long-standing publishers — but not the only game in town. Stanford and MIT are not Ivy League schools but certainly have cachet. I think the Big 5 can be amazing places, and to be sure I love the editors there I work with, but independent and smaller presses can be just as alluring, especially for debuts, because there they have less of a chance of being lost in a huge list.

How do you feel about independent/small presses? I think they can be wonderful opportunities for some authors, especially debuts, who can get a little more hand holding and attention. They can also provide stronger marketing in some cases, since a smaller list means more focus per book. The first LRA book to receive *New York Times* praise and multiple-starred reviews was published by a small press.

What are your feelings about self-publishing? In this crowded marketplace, many books that would have been published 5 to 10 years ago are being passed over as not being "different enough to stand out," and for those authors, self-publishing can be a great way to jump-start a career. But caution: the writing still needs to be super-strong, and you need to constantly work sales and marketing if you expect to later break out to a traditional publisher. With that said, we took on a self-published book that later went on to be optioned for film, won the IPPY Gold Medal for Literary Fiction, was picked up for audio, had great foreign sales, and whose author catapulted to a recent appearance on *Good Morning America*. So anything is possible.

What do you like and dislike about your job? *Love* my job but hate to disappoint, and this business is not for the faint of heart. There is a lot of waiting and many near misses on the route to success.

What are ways prospective clients can impress you, and what are ways they can turn you off? LRA truly works like a family, and although we don't expect clients to hold hands and sing "Kumbaya," we do expect them to cross-support each other. We also expect them to understand the importance of marketing and doing for themselves, instead of waiting for a publisher to do it. And we *love* the creative self-promoter. Can't afford an outside PR team? No issue — we had one client who handmade a ton of swag and even found a way to get college students to help with a trailer project. So basically, if you want to impress us, be graciously supportive and think outside the box.

How would you describe the "writer from hell"? Those who are legends in their own mind, who are way too entitled and can't appreciate the importance constructive criticism.

Do you believe in a higher and/or lower "power"? I believe in the power of positive thinking, taking risks, refusing to accept "no" as a fait accompli, and the ability to change anything for the better.

LYNN SELIGMAN, LITERARY AGENT

400 Highland Avenue, Upper Montclair, NJ 07043, 973-783-3631

Agent's name and contact info: Lynn Seligman, Sole Proprietor, seliglit@aol.com

Describe the kinds of works you want to represent. I represent both commercial and literary fiction and nonfiction as well as young adult fiction. I particularly like women's fiction, romance, and historical fiction as well as memoir, narrative nonfiction, biography, history, entertainment, health, medicine, psychology, and science in the nonfiction areas.

Describe what you definitely don't want to represent. I do not want to represent illustrated or nonillustrated books for young readers or middle grade, thrillers, or mysteries.

How do you want writers to pitch you? I used to ask only for hardcopy with an SASE, which is still fine, but I now get email requests as well. However, I do not open attachments from unknown sources and will not respond to email requests unless I want to follow through on the submission.

Describe your education and professional history. I have a BA from Goucher College and an MA from Columbia University (as well as ABT for my doctorate) in French Literature. In addition to French, I speak Spanish and German. After getting the MA, I taught ESL in a NYC elementary school, but soon decided to enter publishing. I worked at two small houses, Hawthorn Books and Crowell, in editorial and then subsidiary rights, which is what I continued in, first at Doubleday in foreign rights and then as manager of serial rights, and then at Simon & Schuster in the same capacity until I became associate rights director.

How did you become an agent? Although I loved my job at Simon & Schuster, I missed the direct contact with writers and decided that an agent could have the best of both worlds, editorial and negotiation, so I found a job at Julian Bach Literary Agency, where I worked for 5 years until going out on my own, working from a home office, which I am still doing over 30 years later.

Knowing what you do now, would you do it again? If not, what might you do instead? The simple answer is yes. I love what I do, I can make it as interesting as I want, and I love having it all in my own hands.

Do you charge fees? If yes, please explain. No.

When and where were you born, and where have you lived? I was born in NYC, raised in Queens, and lived in New York my entire life (with the exception of college in Baltimore) until I moved to New Jersey around 30 years ago.

What do you like to do when you're not working? I love going to the movies, museums, theater, opera, and especially ballet and dance performances. I like to walk for exercise. I listen to music, mostly classical, and of course love to read. Why else would I do what I do?

List some of the titles you have recently placed with publishers. Alexandra Hawkins, *Masters of Seduction* trilogy (St. Martin's); Dee Ernst, *Stealing Jason Wilde* (Lake Union, a division of Amazon Publishing).

Do you think the business has changed a lot over the past few years? If yes, please explain. I certainly think ebooks have changed the financial picture of the business as well as the kinds of books published. Self-publishing has grown substantially, but publishers, both large and small, seem to have held their own, and even hardcovers are recovering ground. In the end, however, a good book is a good book, and many, fortunately, find their audience.

Do you think Amazon is good or bad — or both — for the book business? I think any company that has that much control over sales can be detrimental to a business, but on the other hand, they sell a lot of books, which is good. I have also done some business with the publishing arm of Amazon and have found them to be very professional and savvy, especially about marketing ebooks. I have often said that major publishers could learn a lot from them on this topic.

What do you like and dislike about your job? I really love finding something wonderful and being able to sell it and see it sell in the marketplace. After all these years, that is still thrilling. I don't like where the contract process has gone and how hard I have to fight with publishers to get terms for my authors that are fair and were not difficult to get just a short time ago.

What are ways prospective clients can impress you, and what are ways they can turn you off? There is nothing as great as an enticing submission letter that is literate and grammatically correct and presents a project in an interesting light. Once I take on a client, I am hard to turn off, but if a client makes unreasonable demands and won't listen to what works and what doesn't and why, that does make my job harder.

How would you describe the "writer from hell"? The chemistry has to be right for me, even if I have to turn down a project I like because I feel I can't work with the client. The only thing that really bothers me once I do is when a client disappears and won't answer my (or the editor's) calls, letters, or emails. I think that is rude and childish.

Describe a book you would like to write. I have no desire to write a book. That's why I do what I do.

MARCIL-O'FARRELL LITERARY, LLC ❖ www.marcilofarrellagency.com

86 Dennis Street, Manhasset, NY 11030, 516-365-6029

Agent's name and contact info: Anne Marie O'Farrell, annemarie@marcilofarrellagency.com

Describe the kinds of works you want to represent. Nonfiction areas of human potential, personal growth, spirituality, health and fitness, business, sports, cooking, travel, gift, quirky books.

Describe what you definitely don't want to represent. Children's books.

How do you want writers to pitch you? Query to annemarie@denisemarcilagency.com.

Describe your education and professional history. Owner of three successful businesses in the areas of publishing, theater, and adult education.

How did you become an agent? I began representing authors in 1986 through the Denise Marcil Literary Agency. Some of these authors had previously worked for me as teachers in my adult education program.

Knowing what you do now, would you do it again? If not, what might you do instead? I love what I do. I'm very happy where I am.

Do you charge fees? If yes, please explain. No fees.

List some of the titles you have recently placed with publishers. *The Thinnest Line* (Center Street), *Exponential Living* (NAL), *We Are Women* (Andrews McMeel), *Virginia Plantations* (Globe Pequot), *A Widow's Guide to Healing* (Sourcebooks).

Describe your personality. Honest, vivacious, down to earth, insightful, and creative.

What do you like reading/watching/listening to on your own time? I like to read business and philosophy books. I love to watch basketball and tennis.

Do you think the business has changed a lot over the past few years? If yes, please explain. Yes. A new communication paradigm has been, and continues to be, created through the internet, and publishing is still struggling to find its place.

What are your feelings about self-publishing? I'm not a fan unless you can't find a publisher. So much of authors' time needs to be spent promoting themselves and their book. Once the book is written, let the publisher do the distribution. This allows authors to focus on expanding their outreach.

What are ways prospective clients can impress you, and what are ways they can turn you off? I enjoy working with authors who are flexible and responsive and appreciate the idea of a team. It's also helpful when authors understand the realities of the publishing landscape.

MARSAL LYON LITERARY AGENCY, LLC ❖

www.marsallyonliteraryagency.com

PMB 121, 665 San Rodolfo Drive, 124, Solana Beach, CA 92075

Agent's name and contact info: Jill Marsal, jill@marsallyonliteraryagency.com

Describe the kinds of works you want to represent. I am looking for all types of women's fiction, especially Southern fiction; stories of family, friendships, secrets, interesting relationships, or multigenerations; and all types of romance, including romantic suspense, historical, contemporary, and category romance. I am also looking for mystery, cozies, suspense, psychological suspense, and thrillers that keep the pages turning and have an original hook. I also like general commercial fiction and welcome a dramatic story line and compelling characters in interesting situations or relationships. If you have a novel that has a highly original concept or voice, I would love to see it.

On the nonfiction side, my areas of interest include current events, business, health, self-help, relationships, psychology, parenting, history, science, and narrative nonfiction.

I am particularly drawn to projects that will move readers or leave them thinking, make provocative arguments or share interesting research, or offer useful, new advice.

How do you want writers to pitch you? Email a query letter to jill@marsallyonliterary agency.com.

Describe your education and professional history. I am a founding partner of the Marsal Lyon Literary Agency and have been in the publishing industry for over 15 years. Previously, I worked as a literary agent with the Sandra Dijkstra Literary Agency for 8 years. I also have a strong legal background, hold a JD from Harvard Law School, and practiced as an attorney with Wilson Sonsini, Goodrich & Rosati for 5 years in the Bay Area.

How did you become an agent? I started as an intern at a literary agency back in high school, then went to work at a publishing house, and then eventually moved back into agenting, which is what I really enjoy. I became an agent because I love reading and editing, and it is so exciting to see a story idea become a book. I love working with authors to help make their stories as strong as possible, so that I can find the perfect publisher for their projects.

Knowing what you do now, would you do it again? If not, what might you do instead? Yes, I love being an agent and working with terrific writers.

Do you charge fees? If yes, please explain. No.

When and where were you born, and where have you lived? I was born in Baltimore and have lived in Denver, New York, San Francisco, San Diego, and Sweden.

What do you like to do when you're not working? I like reading, hiking, animals, music, the beach, and eating ice cream.

List some of the titles you have recently placed with publishers. Fiction: *Forgetting August* by *USA Today* bestselling author J.L. Berg (Grand Central), *With Love from the Inside* by Angela Pisel (Putnam), *Edge of Danger* by *New York Times* bestselling author Katie Reus (Signet Eclipse/NAL), *Counting Stars* by Kathleen Long (Lake Union), *Trigger Yappy* by *USA Today* bestselling author Diana Orgain (Thomas Dunne), *What the Waves Know* by Tamara Valentine (William Morrow), *Accidentally Hers* by Jamie Beck (Montlake). Nonfiction: *The Challenger Customer* by *Wall Street Journal* bestselling authors Brent Adamson, Matthew Dixon, Pat Spenner, and Nick Toman (Portfolio), *The Superhuman Mind* by Berit Brogaard and Kristian Marlow (Hudson St. Press), *China's New Red Guard* by Jude Blanchette (Oxford University Press), *Surviving and Thriving with an Invisible Chronic Illness* by Ilana Jacqueline (New Harbinger), *The Tao of Running* by Gary Dudney (Meyer & Meyer), *Spam Nation: The Inside Story of Organized Cybercrime — from Global Epidemic to Your Front Door* by *New York Times* bestselling author Brian Krebs (Sourcebooks), *Pill City* by Kevin Deutsch (St. Martin's).

Describe your personality. I'm sure this will come as no surprise, given that I am a literary agent, but I love reading — fiction, nonfiction, all types of books. I start my days early and first thing turn on the computer to go through emails and reading. Also, because I can be reading for such long periods, one of my authors convinced me to get a treadmill desk, and I love using that when I am reading manuscripts. I also like to exercise or go outdoors, walk my dog, and get some sunshine (when it's nice weather).

What do you like reading/watching/listening to on your own time? I like reading women's fiction, page-turning suspense stories, and nonfiction.

What do the "Big 5" mean to you? The Big 5 makes me think of the larger, traditional New York publishing houses.

How do you feel about independent/small presses? I think they offer great opportunities for writers, especially as we see more and more consolidation with the big New York houses.

What are your feelings about self-publishing? I think self-publishing offers many writers another opportunity for getting their work out there. It is important for authors to identify their goals in publishing when they are evaluating whether to go with a traditional publisher or epublisher or to self-publish. We have authors who have chosen each of those paths, and many do a combination — I think hybrid authors are very common these days. It really depends what an author is looking for from the publishing experience.

Do you think Amazon is good or bad — or both — for the book business? I think Amazon has really helped the growth of ebooks and opened up new publishing opportunities for many authors.

What do you like and dislike about your job? I love reading and editing and working with authors to make their manuscripts as strong as possible. It is such an exciting process to be able to work on a manuscript and take it from idea/concept to completed book. And, of course, it is such a great thing to take a manuscript on submission, then get "the call" from an editor, and then be able to make "the call" to the author. I like being a part of the process that brings readers books that can impact their lives, offer intriguing stories, take them to places they would never otherwise experience, and entertain and inspire.

What are ways prospective clients can impress you, and what are ways they can turn you off? Prospective authors can impress me with a strong query letter that includes a few paragraphs giving a strong summary of their project (like what you would find on the back of a book) and then a closing paragraph about the author. I want to see in the letter that the story has a strong hook and interesting characters.

How would you describe the "writer from hell"? I think it is really important to have good communication and be responsive, so you can build a relationship. Warning signs for me would be a client who doesn't respond to phone calls or emails and doesn't seem excited about their work and taking steps to move forward in the publishing process.

Describe a book you would like to write. I would write a book with a great voice, original story concept, great hook, fast pacing, interesting characters, and compelling plot.

Is there anything you wish to express beyond the parameters of the preceding questions? Write. Rewrite. And keep writing. But also read and study books that are successful in the area you want to publish in, so you know what is working on the market. If you really want to make this happen, do everything you can to make your work as strong as possible. And then when you believe your manuscript is ready, send it out to agents and try not to get discouraged. It can be a long and trying process, but there are so many stories of writers who received tons of rejections before they found the right agent/editor/publisher who had the passion for their project and made it happen. It only takes one — you just have to find the right one for your book.

Agent's name and contact info: Shannon Hassan, shannon@marsallyonliteraryagency.com, www.marsallyonliteraryagency.com /the-agents/shannon-hassan

Describe the kinds of works you want to represent. I represent authors of literary and commercial fiction, young adult and middle grade fiction, and select nonfiction. With respect to fiction, I am drawn to fresh voices, compelling characters, and crisp prose and enjoy both contemporary and historical settings. For nonfiction, I am interested in exceptional narratives from authors with strong platforms. Based in Boulder, Colorado, I am also eager to hear from authors with a unique perspective on the West.

Describe what you definitely don't want to represent. Genre fiction for adults in the areas of horror, sci-fi, or high fantasy; picture books.

How do you want writers to pitch you? I look forward to receiving queries by *email only* at shannon@marsallyonliteraryagency.com. You can read more about my interests at: www .publishersmarketplace.com/members/sejohnso. Please include a query, short bio, and 10 sample pages.

Describe your education and professional history. I have worked in publishing and law for more than a decade and joined Marsal Lyon in 2013. Prior to becoming an agent, I was acquisitions editor at Fulcrum Publishing and before that a corporate attorney at Arnold & Porter in New York. I have a JD from Harvard and a BA from George Washington University, where I studied journalism and economics.

How did you become an agent? I started my career as a corporate and licensing attorney and then decided to follow my heart into publishing, where I learned the ropes and worked as an acquisitions editor. Becoming an agent was a natural progression for me, as it combines my skills and lifelong passion for books.

Knowing what you do now, would you do it again? If not, what might you do instead? Yes! I have done other things, and this is exactly what I want to do until I retire. There is nothing better than helping an author achieve his or her publishing dreams.

Do you charge fees? If yes, please explain. No.

When and where were you born, and where have you lived? I was born in Arlington, Texas, and have lived in Washington, DC, Boston, and New York. I now live in Boulder, Colorado.

What do you like to do when you're not working? I love to ski, bike, hike with my husband and 11-year-old twins. We also love to travel and have been to South America, Europe, and Asia.

List some of the titles you have recently placed with publishers. A few of my recent or soon-to-be-published books include *Die Young with Me*, a memoir by Rob Rufus of the Blacklist Royals (Touchstone); *The World's Greatest Adventure Machine*, a middle grade adventure by Frank L. Cole (Delacorte); *Let the Good Prevail*, a thriller by Logan Miller and Noah Miller being adapted as a feature film (Rare Bird Books); *The Moon in the Palace*, a historical series by Weina Dai Randel (Sourcebooks); *Almost Anywhere*, a nature memoir by Krista Schlyer (Skyhorse); *Dial Em for Murder*, a young adult suspense novel by Marni Bates (Merit Press/F+W Books); *In Another Life*, a historical/time-slip novel by Julie Christine Johnson (Sourcebooks).

Describe your personality. Hardworking, thoughtful, and passionate about books and publishing.

What do you like reading/watching/listening to on your own time? I'll admit I have eclectic tastes in my TV viewing — from grittier series like *Justified*, *Sons of Anarchy*, and *Fargo* to period pieces like *Mad Men* and *Downton Abbey*. I just love complex and compelling characters and great storytelling (and a little humor).

Do you think the business has changed a lot over the past few years? If yes, please explain. Yes, in several ways, but I'll focus on one for now: authors, along with their agents, need to be very motivated and committed to marketing and publicity. This applies no matter whether you go with a large house or a small house or if you self-publish. There are so many books on the market, and you need to work hard to stand out.

What do the "Big 5" mean to you? To me, it means the five large publishing conglomerates and all of their imprints. I have been fortunate to work with editors at a range of publishing houses from the Big 5 to the independents and the smaller presses, and all can be wonderful homes for authors and their work. It's a matter of finding the right fit for each individual project.

How do you feel about independent/small presses? See above.

What are your feelings about self-publishing? It is often misunderstood by first-time authors as an easy thing to do or a quick fix. Publishing a book and, just as important, reaching your target audience, no matter what route you take, is a long road that requires a lot of hard work, teamwork, and commitment.

What do you like and dislike about your job? I enjoy editing and contributing to the creative process as much as I do negotiating the deal. And of course making calls to authors to tell them they have a book deal is always fun! I don't enjoy giving rejections to authors (or receiving them from editors on my projects!), but it's all about finding the right fit and a passionate advocate for their work.

What are ways prospective clients can impress you, and what are ways they can turn you off? Once I read and fall in love with a manuscript, I always call (or meet) a potential client and become acquainted before I extend an offer. I am looking for authors who are talented, committed to their careers, willing to take criticism, and pleasant to work with.

Is there anything you wish to express beyond the parameters of the preceding questions? Thanks for reading this, and I look forward to your queries!

Agent's name and contact info: Deborah Ritchken, deborah@marsallyonliteraryagency.com, 858-337-0292

Describe the kinds of works you want to represent. I am currently looking for narrative nonfiction, memoir, biography, women's interest, food, including cookbooks, and all things French, including fiction.

Describe what you definitely don't want to represent. I am not looking for genre fiction (thrillers, science fiction) or children's or young adult fiction.

How do you want writers to pitch you? I'd like to be pitched with a query letter by email. If I am interested, I will ask for the proposal and sample chapters.

Do you charge fees? If yes, please explain. I do not charge a fee.

Describe your education and professional history. I have a degree in English from Ohio State University. I began as a bookseller in the Midwest before moving to southern California, where I worked for both Prentice Hall and Harcourt Brace Jovanovich. I began agenting at the Sandra Dijkstra Literary Agency and then with the Castiglia Agency until Julie Castiglia retired.

List some of the titles you have recently placed with publishers. I love my recent French cookbooks that I've worked on and I'm especially proud of those I prop- and food-styled! That brought a new dimension to the work that goes into producing high-quality cookbooks. I'm looking forward to Jeanne Kelley's new cookbook, *Portable Feasts*, from Rizzoli, which is a beautifully shot cookbook full of delicious, healthy dishes you can take to work, on planes, picnics, etc. Also looking forward to *Ernesto: Hemingway's Years in Cuba*, from Melville House, because I'm considering a trip to Havana in 2016.

What do you like reading/watching/listening to on your own time? In my spare time, I read. My favorite novel this year was *A Little Life* by Hanya Yanagihara, a novel that is at once brilliant and disturbing and one I think of almost daily. I cook almost every night, so I devour food magazines and cookbooks. Binge-watching television series with high drama is a welcome respite from all the reading I do, and I especially love *Rectify*.

MARTIN LITERARY & MEDIA MANAGEMENT ❖ www.martinlit.com

Seattle, WA, 206-466-1773 (no query calls, please)

Agent's name and contact info: Sharlene Martin, President, sharlene@martinliterarymanagement.com

Describe the kinds of works you want to represent. As always, we have our long-standing devotion to great narrative nonfiction when it is written with such depth of style and visual clarity that it is naturally adaptable to film. I love to read meaningful memoirs, fun pop-culture subjects, true crime books, and business books (and this even includes how-to books along with self-help or prescriptive books, provided that they are original in tone and do not rehash familiar material). And of course, I love doing celebrity bios if and when they reach for levels of insight and empathy that readers will not get from the tabloid culture.

Describe what you definitely don't want to represent. No scripts, poetry, or revenge books against former spouses, bosses, lovers, etc. No political or religious hate speech or defamation. No whistleblower books that will get me killed.

How do you want writers to pitch you? A standard, businesslike query letter will work, but since we're a "green" agency, we prefer all queries and submissions be made via email. Please think about the level of competition in the commercial book market and plan your query accordingly. There is plenty of good information out there about writing effective query letters, and in my own book (duck — plug approaching), *Publish Your Nonfiction*

Book (Writer's Digest Books), the importance of the query was stressed. Nothing has changed since then.

Consider the contestants on one of my favorite TV shows, *Shark Tank*, all coming in to make their big pitch. Every one of them has polished their delivery down to the line, to the word. They do it like they mean it. I am seeking writers who do it like they mean it, and you would be amazed at how often this is not apparent in queries. We *never take phone pitches* because we are not testing your ability to speak; we are interested in your ability to write in a compelling fashion.

Describe your education and professional history. I was a business major in college and, upon graduation, moved to NYC. I've always been eclectic and entrepreneurial. In fact, I was awarded *Entrepreneur Magazine*'s Homebased Entrepreneur of the Year for a business I started and sold to a competitor in 1989. I then moved to Los Angeles, started a production company with a former network journalist/broadcaster, and was an independent producer for a number of years in addition to doing freelance casting for independent and feature films. Because of that experience, I was invited to join a reality-television production company and spent time doing acquisitions and talent management. It was there that I realized my love of show business found its greatest strength in working with passionate and highly skilled writers. I left to start Martin Literary Management in 2002, which has since expanded to become Martin Literary & Media Management, and the lovely success that has followed seems a natural result of the fact that I've never been happier in any line of work.

How did you become an agent? Simple: I love the written word. Although I was editor of my high-school literary magazine, I never realized my passion for books until later in my career. I want to make a difference in writers' lives by helping them realize their dreams.

Knowing what you do now, would you do it again? If not, what might you do instead? No regrets. I am happy in this work.

Do you charge fees? If yes, please explain. Writers pay nothing unless their book sells; then they pay the traditional 15 percent agency commission on money earned.

When and where were you born, and where have you lived? Born in Fairfield County, Connecticut, grew up on the East Coast, and have been a happy "Left Coast" resident for many years now. After living in Los Angeles for over 20 years, I now live in the Pacific Northwest (Seattle) and love it here! People love books here, and there are wonderful libraries and bookstores galore.

What do you like to do when you're not working? What's "not working"?

List some of the titles you have recently placed with publishers. *Breakthrough: How One Teen Innovator Is Changing the World* by Jack Andraka (HarperCollins), *Dark Heart* by

Kevin Flynn and Rebecca Lavoie (Berkley), *Frientimacy* by Shasta Nelson (Seal Press), *The Art of the Con* by Anthony Amore (St. Martin's), *Finding My Shine* by Nastia Liukin (Amazon), *Maximum Harm* by Michele McPhee (ForeEdge), *Too Pretty to Live* by Dennis Brooks (Diversion), *Impossible Odds: The Kidnapping of Jessica Buchanan and Her Dramatic Rescue by SEAL Team Six* by Anthony Flacco with Jessica Buchanan and Erik Landemalm (Atria), *Honor Bound: My Journey to Hell and Back with Amanda Knox* by Raffaele Sollecito (Gallery), *Newtown: An American Tragedy* by Matthew Lysiak (Gallery), *Picture Perfect: The Jodi Arias Story* by Shanna Hogan (St. Martin's), *Walking on Eggshells* by Lyssa Chapman with Lisa Wysocky (Howard), *In the Matter of Nikola Tesla* by Anthony Flacco (Diversion), *Hidden Girl: The True Story of a Modern-Day Child Slave* by Shyima Hall with Lisa Wysocky (Simon & Schuster Young Readers).

Describe your personality. One of my clients who has had the chance to get to know me gave me a lovely little gift to celebrate her book release. It's a dried and tanned bull scrotum mounted on a frame. Another gave me a beautiful silver bracelet engraved with "TENACIOUS S."

What do you like reading/watching/listening to on your own time? TV shows I love include *Ray Donovan*, *Homeland*, and *The Affair*. Love good films, hiking, visiting my grown kids and their families, especially my toddler grandson, here in Seattle. I enjoy listening to all kinds of music — a few favorites are Adele, Amy Winehouse, the Eagles, Josh Groban, Andrea Bocelli. I enjoy occasional travel, provided it is first class and four stars! Yes, I am a material girl. You will catch me camping out on the same day that you, oh, forget it. It's not going to happen.

Do you think the business has changed a lot over the past few years? If yes, please explain. The changes are of two varieties: (1) The internet sped up the submission and acquisition process, so that's good, but meanwhile the cultural shift is away from having the time and the attention span to read anything in a long form. (2) I hate seeing desperate wannabe authors being taken advantage of by all the self-publishing scams out there. It's tough to fight your way through the maze of publishing "opportunities" and determine what's real and what isn't.

What do the "Big 5" mean to you? The Big 5 are the current top group of traditional publishers, the A list. As with the major Hollywood studios, the largest financial advances are made with the top-tier publishers, but the competition for a slot on their lists is getting more and more intense.

How do you feel about independent/small presses? They definitely have their place in the publishing industry and can usually provide more personalized attention to authors who are able to bet that their book will be successful from a royalty standpoint and not worry as much about the size of the advance.

What are your feelings about self-publishing? For people who have a speaking career, it can be a lucrative way to have "back of the room" sales. If you do not have such a built-in sales opportunity, you must trust your work to somehow find an audience on its own. Once in a great while, this actually happens, and it is wonderful for that author. The rest of them stay home and feel the slow creep of despair as the world turns a blind eye to their work. Those few who do find legitimate financial success in self-publishing are akin to lottery winners — I feel the odds are about the same.

Do you think Amazon is good or bad — or both — for the book business? Amazon is inevitable. I don't decry the organization, but I despise their reviewer policy, which allows trolls who want to trash authors to log on and write disparaging comments, even if their words indicate that they never actually read the book. Amazon won't allow you to review a friend's work, but they have no problem allowing trolls to try to ruin an author's reputation. It's a shameful policy.

I love the convenience of ordering from Amazon as a Prime member, but most of my hardcover books I buy from our independent bookstore here. When I do buy ebooks, I download to my Kindle.

What do you like and dislike about your job? I represent wonderful writers and help to make their literary dreams come true. I do lots of reading, plenty of persuasive selling, and creative career counseling. My greatest joy comes from finding effective ways to market my writers and their work. I love working with smart and creative people. I love working with editors and publishers who share my passion for a great read. As for things I don't like about it, there aren't many, none worth mentioning here.

What are ways prospective clients can impress you, and what are ways they can turn you off? Take the time and spend the effort to craft a great, concise query letter, and *do not* send it out until your book proposal is ready to go. Don't try to "test the waters" by sending out query letters before your book proposal or book manuscript is done. Also, nothing turns me off quicker than a "spam query," in which dozens of agents are all cc'd on the same query and the salutation reads "To Whom It May Concern."

How would you describe the "writer from hell"? Self-entitlement is like a bad flu virus moving through our society. It manifests in the writing world in the form of half-baked written work accompanied by explanations for the unfinished condition and a tale of woe about the author's struggles in the task of getting the work to this stage. These people fail to appreciate the truth that everybody struggles if they endeavor to write truly and well, and writers who believe themselves unique in that regard have already revealed a cautionary tale about their lack of insight toward others. Such people seldom deliver meaningful work.

Describe a book you would like to write. Wrote it already — *Publish Your Nonfiction Book: Strategies for Learning the Industry, Selling Your Book, and Building a Successful Career* (Writer's Digest Books). If you're serious about becoming an author, I highly suggest reading it before you do anything further! Nothing gets my attention quicker than reading a query that starts, "I read your book."

Do you believe in a higher and/or lower "power"? I certainly used to, but now that we're all getting green and taking more responsibility about energy consumption, I tend to keep the setting on "medium power" while I'm away from home and at "lower power" while everyone is asleep.

Is there anything you wish to express beyond the parameters of the preceding questions? Be a voracious reader of the biographies of writers who struggled before they found acceptance. Their stories will make you stronger. And remember, no one has ever come out of the womb a published author. Someone has been every published author's advocate. Maybe I'm yours?

Agent's name and contact info: Clelia Gore, clelia@martinliterarymanagement.com

Describe the kinds of works you want to represent. I acquire everything under the children's books umbrella — from picture books to middle grade fiction and nonfiction to young adult fiction and nonfiction. I'm looking for works that feel thoroughly modern and appropriate for the current marketplace.

Describe what you definitely don't want to represent. I don't represent writers in the adult market. I also don't do genre fiction. I'm not interested in new adult, hard fantasy, sci-fi, or rhyming picture books.

How do you want writers to pitch you? All of our submission instructions are carefully detailed at www.martinlit.com. You can email me at clelia@martinliterarymanagement.com.

Describe your education and professional history. I have a BA in English from Boston College. I also received a law degree from American University and an MA in publishing and writing from Emerson College.

How did you become an agent? I practiced as an attorney in New York, but was unhappy in that career. I decided to transition to a career in the publishing industry because I have always loved books and writing. A career as an agent appealed to me because it combined things that I loved and skills that I had — talent acquisition, networking, editing and writing, and contract negotiation. I moved to Seattle with my husband just after I wrapped up a master's program at Emerson College in publishing and writing. I was lucky enough to connect with Sharlene Martin, who took me under her wing and taught me everything I know about agenting.

Knowing what you do now, would you do it again? If not, what might you do instead? This is my dream job. I could have started out my life a hundred different ways, and I would have always wanted to end up here.

Do you charge fees? If yes, please explain. No. No reputable agent does. It's a commission-based job.

When and where were you born, and where have you lived? I was born on the Upper East Side of Manhattan. I grew up in Tenafly, New Jersey, a little suburban hamlet across the river from New York City. I went to school in Boston and Washington, DC, and before I moved to Seattle, I lived back in my home city, New York.

What do you like to do when you're not working? Books are my favorite medium for storytelling, but I also love television and movies. I think television has gotten so good in the last couple of years with streaming services and cable networks putting out awesome shows. Movie dates are the best — as long as I have a bowl of popcorn, get to see all the trailers beforehand, and have a great discussion about the film afterward. My favorite activity is joining friends to go out to dinner to a great restaurant with great wine. I'm also a big traveler.

List some of the titles you have recently placed with publishers. Some of the books I sold in 2015 include *The Kraken's Rules for Making Friends*, a picture book about a lonely kraken who is tired of having no friends; *Yoga Bunny*, a picture book about a yoga-loving bunny; *Philanthroparties*, a DIY book for teens about incorporating social activism into their social life by teen philanthropist Lulu Cerone; a young adult nonfiction book about geoengineering and climate change; and the second book in the Horace j. Edwards and the *Time Keepers* time-travel series for middle grade readers. I sold to major, boutique, and educational publishers in 2015.

Describe your personality. I'm a smart, considerate, and bubbly professional who takes her career very seriously, even when it involves unicorns and time-traveling machines.

What do you like reading/watching/listening to on your own time? I read gobs of books every year, including many recently published books in all of the genres I represent. I find time to read adult books for pleasure — I try to mix in some classics with contemporary books. My favorite adult fiction book of 2015 was *In the Unlikely Event* by Judy Blume. I consume a lot of media — I love television and movies, too. I am an unabashed lover of pop music (Adult Directioner, Swiftie), but also like indie bands. I go to about 20 concerts, big and small, every year.

Do you think the business has changed a lot over the past few years? If yes, please explain. Of course, the publishing industry has had to adapt to the digital era in lots of ways. As an example, a social-media platform has become a very important factor to publishers

— a huge social-media reach has real meaning to publishers, and they are interested in internet/social-media celebrities more than ever before.

What do the "Big 5" mean to you? The Big 5 are publishers with a long, celebrated history, a wide national and international reach, and a reputation for quality and commercialism — they are the dream publishers of every client.

How do you feel about independent/small presses? Love them! I've had excellent experiences with small presses. I find they provide authors with great support and put out wonderful products. I can't imagine the marketplace without them.

What are your feelings about self-publishing? I think it is an excellent resource for authors who may not be able to get published by a traditional publisher. It also offers readers a wider selection of books, often at low cost. There are problems with quality control in self-publishing, but ultimately I think it's a great way to create a satisfying experience for writers.

Do you think Amazon is good or bad — or both — for the book business? I admire how Amazon's launch of the Kindle established the ereader as a ubiquitous consumer device. I also think Amazon has helped make books accessible to readers in a way they weren't before. I know people have some major qualms about Amazon, but, ultimately I think they cater their business to readers, are willing to innovate, and, when the dust settles, will be known as a positive contributor to publishing and the book business overall.

What do you like and dislike about your job? My favorite part about being an agent is the fact that there is so much potential in this job — potential to find new, amazing talent, potential to bring beautiful, meaningful books to the marketplace, potential to find fresh viewpoints and stories, and potential to have real successes. All of this potential makes this a really unique job, and I find it very exciting and satisfying. The bad part of the job is that I have to disappoint so many hopeful authors who have queried me along the way.

What are ways prospective clients can impress you, and what are ways they can turn you off? I always appreciate professionalism and showing me that you are a serious writer — you've done your research and have a thoroughly edited work and a fine platform. I am turned off by writers who don't abide by guidelines set out on our agency website or who don't treat a query or pitch as a professional interaction.

How would you describe the "writer from hell"? The client from hell does not understand the way the publishing industry works — and doesn't really care to know. He or she has unreasonable expectations and doesn't fulfill my own expectations by missing deadlines, not taking my notes, or not putting the work in. Luckily, I've never had a writer from hell as a client!

Describe a book you would like to write. One inspired by the summers I spent at my French grandparents' beach house in Normandy.

Do you believe in a higher and/or lower "power"? Yes.

MAX GARTENBERG LITERARY AGENCY ❖ www.maxgartenberg.com

912 North Pennsylvania Avenue, Yardley, PA 19067, 215-295-9230

Agent's name and contact info: Anne G. Devlin, agdevlin@aol.com

Describe the kinds of works you want to represent. Nonfiction, current affairs, education, parenting, health, fitness, food, how-to, self-help, business, women's interest, celebrity, true crime, sports, politics, history, music, biography, memoir, environment, pets, narrative nonfiction, historical fiction.

Describe what you definitely don't want to represent. No poetry, science fiction, New Age, fantasy.

How do you want writers to pitch you? Writers desirous of having their work handled by this agency should first send a one- or two-page query letter. Simply put, the letter should describe the material being offered as well as relevant background information about the writer. If the material is of interest, we will request a proposal and sample chapters. Queries are accepted by both email and post. Please include an SASE for a reply via post.

Describe your education and professional history. Max Gartenberg Literary Agency has long been recognized as a source for fine fiction and nonfiction. One of the oldest and most prestigious agencies in the US, it was established in 1954 in New York City and has since migrated to the Philadelphia area.

How did you become an agent? I was offered the opportunity to join this firm because of my background in writing, editing, and marketing.

Knowing what you do now, would you do it again? If not, what might you do instead? It is a most interesting career. Every day is different, and every day I learn something new from the authors I work with.

Do you charge fees? If yes, please explain. No reading fees.

When and where were you born, and where have you lived? I was born in Cleveland, Ohio, and have lived in New York City, Boston, and Philadelphia.

What do you like to do when you're not working? I am interested in (of course) reading, writing, movies, antiquing, traveling, and cooking.

List some of the titles you have recently placed with publishers. *Killers in the Family* (Berkley), *Emote: Using Emotions to Make Your Messages Memorable* (Career Press), *Ogallala Blue* (Norton), *You Should Be Dancing: My Life with the Bee Gees* (ECW Press), *Ecology or Catastrophe* (Oxford University Press), *The New Senior Woman* (Rowman & Littlefield), *Everything a New Elementary Teacher Really Needs to Know* (Free Spirit Publishing), *Jack and Lem* (Da Capo), *What Patients Taught Me* (Sasquatch Books), *Beethoven for Kids* (Chicago Review Press), *Your Guide to the Jewish Holidays* (Rowman & Littlefield), *Charles*

Addams: A Cartoonist's Life (Random House), *Arthritis: What Exercises Work?* (St. Martin's), *The Chocolate Trust* (Camino Press).

Describe your personality. Creative and hardworking.

What are your feelings about self-publishing? Self-publishing is a last resort, as it lacks the support an author receives from a traditional publishing house's production department, marketing department, sales staff, and distributors. Authors who self-publish need to understand that they will need to promote and publicize themselves in every possible venue and medium.

What do you like and dislike about your job? I love being an agent because it allows me to learn and discover. As a former newspaper writer and editor as well as a marketing entrepreneur, I enjoy being part of the creation of a great book. I enjoy discovering authors, pitching book ideas, negotiating deals, and being part of an exciting and dynamic industry. I love getting excited about a new book project that I can pitch to editors. I help authors shape proposals and manuscripts to interest editors, so that they will make an offer. I submit materials to a publisher, negotiate contracts, and generally act as a business manager for authors and intercede whenever necessary throughout the publishing process.

What are ways prospective clients can impress you, and what are ways they can turn you off? To be considered, write a brilliant query letter and, when asked, follow it up with a proposal and sample chapters or a manuscript that is even better. Be sure to include your qualifications and experience along with a synopsis of the work.

How would you describe the "writer from hell"? A client who demands unceasing attention and is never satisfied with the deal the agent brings (this client always has friends who got twice as much) and then delivers the manuscript late and in such disrepair that it is unacceptable. This is not an imaginary character.

MOVABLE TYPE MANAGEMENT ❖ www.movabletm.com

244 Madison Avenue, Suite 334, New York, NY 10016, 646-431-6134

Agent's name and contact info: Adam Chromy, achromy@movabletm.com

Describe the kinds of works you want to represent. Adult commercial and literary fiction; narrative and expertise-based nonfiction.

Describe what you definitely don't want to represent. Middle grade or young adult, heavy genre.

How do you want writers to pitch you? Via email query.

Describe your education and professional history. A BS from NYU's Stern School of Business and a decade in tech start-ups give me a unique business perspective, and over a decade of being a literary agent gives me the storytelling acumen to be a great representative for the right authors.

How did you become an agent? In 2002, I started my own agency because I loved books and wanted to rep authors, but no one would hire me.

Knowing what you do now, would you do it again? If not, what might you do instead? Yes. Every day I wake up and decide to keep doing this because I love it.

Do you charge fees? If yes, please explain. No.

When and where were you born, and where have you lived? Early 1970s in Queens, New York, just like the guys from *Entourage*. Now I split my time between Manhattan and Los Angeles.

What do you like to do when you're not working? I'm almost always working, but I make time for my family and traveling.

List some of the titles you have recently placed with publishers. *The Forever Summer* by Jamie Brenner (Little, Brown), *Café Leila* by Donia Bijan (Algonquin), *The Harrows of Spring* by James Howard Kunstler (Grove/Atlantic), *Dirty Rocker Boys* by Bobbie Brown (Gallery), *GlowKids* by Dr. Nicholas Kardaras (St. Martin's), *What Your Financial Advisor Isn't Telling You* by Liz Davidson (Houghton Mifflin Harcourt), *50 Years, 50 Moments: The Most Unforgettable Plays in Super Bowl History* by Jerry Rice and Randy O. Williams (Dey Street), and *The New Democrats* by Al From (Palgrave).

Describe your personality. Determined and hard-charging yet highly curious with eclectic tastes. One of the things I love about my job is working with the smartest people in the room.

What do you like reading/watching/listening to on your own time? I try to experience real life as much as possible, since I read and watch so much for work — true experiences are the best inspiration for me and my authors.

Do you think the business has changed a lot over the past few years? If yes, please explain. Yes. It has become a hit business like the music industry and will probably only become more so. There will be megasuccessful authors who will be the Taylor Swifts and Adeles of publishing, making a huge percentage of the revenue. And the rest will split less money between more authors — there won't be a midlist middle class. Therefore, I think it's my responsibility to help create as many hits and hit makers as possible. One way I do that is by focusing on the exploitation of the performance rights of my clients' work. Having a TV series or film adapted from your book is a great shortcut to that level of success.

What do the "Big 5" mean to you? The Big 5 are the well-financed hit makers. If you can get a big advance and a big push from them, you have a greater chance of becoming a hit. This is the best road if you have the right kind of book that fits into their hit-making apparatus.

How do you feel about independent/small presses? If you do not have an obvious hit, you might have to work with a small or independent press to create a new kind of success narrative. This is a different road, with a different speed limit, but it can get you there, too.

What are your feelings about self-publishing? This is yet another potential path to success with a hit. But it's DIY. So it takes the most work from the author. And it offers more freedom of choice to the author to experiment and potentially higher rewards when those experiments pay off.

Do you think Amazon is good or bad — or both — for the book business? Amazon is neutral to my authors. I try to convince authors that they are storytellers and they have to sell their story and brand through every available channel and medium. If you have a hit, Amazon is only one revenue stream.

What do you like and dislike about your job? I like helping to tell the stories that make the world go round. I hate rejecting people I like because I cannot help them on their storytelling journey.

What are ways prospective clients can impress you, and what are ways they can turn you off? I'm looking for a very sophisticated approach to storytelling, branding, and tapping into an audience — then I get excited. When someone just wants to tell a story for selfish reasons, like, "Wouldn't it be cool if…(some crazy thing)," then I get immediately turned off.

How would you describe the "writer from hell"? I don't rep any — at least not for long.

Describe a book you would like to write. I recently came up with a narrative methodology that seems to be helping my clients reach their goals. I may write about it eventually, but for now it's exclusive content for my authors.

Do you believe in a higher and/or lower "power"? The ambition to be creative and contribute to the greater good is my higher power; the lower/base desire wants to tear things down. I want to lean toward the positive and build something, no matter how much fear and anger tempt.

NEW LEAF LITERARY & MEDIA, INC. ❖ www.newleafliterary.com

110 West 40th Street, Suite 2201, New York, NY 10018, 646-248-7989

Agents' names and contact info: Mackenzie Brady, Peter Knapp, Kathleen Ortiz, Jaida Temperly, Suzie Townsend, Joanna Volpe; assist@newleafliterary.com, query@newleafliterary.com

Describe the kinds of works you want to represent. Picture books, middle grade, young adult, adult, genre fiction, women's fiction, thrillers, romance, nonfiction of all kinds — basically everything.

Mackenzie: I got my start in publishing as an intern at Farrar, Straus and Giroux and FinePrint Literary Management. I then cut my teeth as an agent at Charlotte Sheedy Literary Agency before moving to New Leaf in 2014.

I was a microbiologist in my prepublishing life, so I'm always on the hunt for projects that bring new or wild facets of science to light. I am endlessly fascinated by the human body, especially the heart. My taste in nonfiction extends beyond science books to memoir, lost histories, investigative journalism, epic sports narratives, and gift/lifestyle books. I am particularly interested in projects that move the cultural conversation forward and have a lasting impact on readers. If you've written the next *Brain on Fire*, *The Power of Habit*, *Random Family*, *The Boys in the Boat*, *The Immortal Life of Henrietta Lacks*, *Autobiography of an Execution*, or *Young House Love*, I want to see it.

On the fiction side, I represent a very select list of upmarket commercial/literary adult and young adult novels (think: *Everything I Never Told You*, *Station Eleven*, and *The Spectacular Now*). I also represent illustrators with or without book projects of their own.

Peter: I joined New Leaf as an agent in July 2015. Previously I worked at the Park Literary Group, where I represented authors of middle grade and young adult fiction; prior to that I was a story editor at Floren Shieh Productions, consulting on book-to-film adaptations for Los Angeles–based movie and TV entities. I graduated from NYU summa cum laude and live in Brooklyn.

At New Leaf, I will continue to represent authors of middle grade and young adult fiction across all genres, and I'm also seeking out smart, high-concept adult fiction. I am genre-agnostic, as long as the writing is great — meaning a standout voice, complex characters (not just the protagonist), and plotting that keeps the reader hooked from the first page through to the very end. In middle grade, I like literary-award contenders, epic adventures (fantastical or not), and everything in between. I have a special place in my heart for middle grade that is spooky, funny, irreverent — or all three. In young adult, I want character-driven contemporary, magical realism, epic fantasy (but it must feel fresh), and realistic stories with some type of twist (speculative, fantastical, or otherwise, such as *The Raven Boys*, *Bone Gap*, and *We Were Liars*). For adult fiction, I want high-concept, voice-driven stories ranging from the highly commercial (such as *The Martian* or Blake Crouch's books) to the more literary (*The Age of Miracles*, *The Language of Flowers*). For all ages, I am always on the lookout for character-driven horror and suspense.

Kathleen: I am the director of subsidiary rights, overseeing audio, translation, and digital rights for the agency's titles. I regularly attend book trade shows around the world to sell titles to translation publishers and look for new medium opportunities for our clients' books.

Also a literary agent, I am actively seeking to sign more authors and illustrators, specifically fresh, new voices in young adult and animator/illustrator talent. In young adult I gravitate more toward beautiful and exceptional world building as well as contemporary stories whose main characters stay with the reader far beyond the pages. I would love to see a beautifully written young adult story set within other cultures and experiences. On the illustration side, I love animator/illustrators and their unique way of storytelling. I am not currently seeking middle grade, screenplays, or adult projects not listed above.

Jaida: After a brief stint in medical school at University of Wisconsin–Madison, I moved to NYC for an internship at Writers House. After five months, I joined New Leaf Literary & Media, assisting Joanna Volpe for the past three years before starting to build my own list of clients. My clients include Kody Keplinger, Kirsten Hubbard, Eric Telchin, Amber McRee Turner, and Maggie Heinze. I also represent illustrators Betsy Bauer, James Lipnickas, and Genevieve Santos.

For children's, middle grade, and young adult titles, I am drawn to quirky, dark stories (*The Mysterious Benedict Society*, *Coraline*, *Escape from Mr. Lemoncello's Library*, *I Don't Like Koala*, etc.). For adult fiction, I love those with strong mystery, high fantasy, or religious undertones (*The Westing Game*, *A Discovery of Witches*, and *The Da Vinci Code*).

Suzie: I represent all brands of children's and adult fiction. Actively looking to build my list, in adult I am specifically looking for new adult, romance (all subgenres), fantasy (urban fantasy, science fiction, steampunk, epic fantasy), and crime fiction (mystery, thrillers). In children's I love young adult (all subgenres) and am dying to find great middle grade projects. I love strong characters and voice-driven stories that break out of the typical tropes of their genres.

Joanna: I represent all brands of fiction from picture books to adult novels. My picture-book taste is the most eclectic, ranging from sweet to fun to smart to quirky. For other fiction (both adult and children's), I have an affinity for stories that have a darker element to them, whether they are horror, drama, or comedy. I'm not the kind of reader who needs a romance in my novels, though I do appreciate a good one.

On the nonfiction side my tastes are much more specific. For children's, I look for topics that captivate kids: biographies, animal-related stories, all sciences and history, etc. I also have an affinity for morbid, weird, or offbeat topics. In my adult nonfiction tastes I tend toward all things geek-related, foodie books, travel books, and general pop culture and popular science. Overall, I'm looking for anything that highlights underrepresented characters. More diversity, please!

How do you want writers to pitch you? Send us a query and your first five pages to query@newleafliterary.com. Submission guidelines are on our website.

List some of the titles you have recently placed with publishers. *Six of Crows* by Leigh Bardugo, *Red Queen* by Victoria Aveyard, *The Little World of Liz Climo* by Liz Climo, *Daughters unto Devils* by Amy Lukavics, *A Key to Extraordinary* by Natalie Lloyd.

PAUL S. LEVINE LITERARY AGENCY ❖ www.paulslevinelit.com

1054 Superba Avenue, Venice, CA 90291, 310-450-6711, fax: 310-450-0181

Agent's name and contact info: Paul S. Levine, paul@paulslevinelit.com

Describe the kinds of works you want to represent. Commercial fiction and nonfiction for adults, children, and young adults (35 percent fiction, 15 percent children's, 50 percent nonfiction).

Describe what you definitely don't want to represent. Science fiction, fantasy, horror.

How do you want writers to pitch you? Query letter *only* by snail mail, email, fax, carrier pigeon (use street address, train pigeon well), or strippergram (must be gorgeous and have a great routine).

Describe your education and professional history. Born: March 16, 1954, New York, NY. Education: BCom, Concordia University, Montreal (1977); MBA, York University, Toronto (1978); JD, University of Southern California, Los Angeles (1981). Career history: attorney for more than 31 years.

How did you become an agent? I have loved the book business ever since I started practicing law in 1981. My first client was a major book publisher in Los Angeles.

If you were not an agent, what might you be doing instead? Practicing entertainment law, reading good books.

Do you charge fees? If yes, please explain. No.

What are some of the most common mistakes writers make when pitching you? Telling me that they're writing to me because they're looking for a literary agent. Duh!

What, if anything, can writers do to increase the odds that you will become their agent? Be referred by an existing client or colleague.

How would you describe the "writer from hell"? One who calls, faxes, emails, or sends carrier pigeons or strippergrams every day. One who constantly needs reassurance that each rejection letter does not mean that the client's project lacks merit and that the client is an awful person.

PEN & INK LITERARY, LLC ❖ www.penandinklit.com

917-740-9498, www.facebook.com/PenInkLiterary, Twitter: twitter.com/PENandINKlit

Agents' names and contact info: Anne Bohner, all domestic deals, ab@penandinklit.com; Taryn Fagerness, coagent for foreign rights; Susan Schulman, coagent for all other subrights including audio and film

Describe the kinds of works you want to represent. *Anne:* I'm currently most focused on women's fiction but will accept romance, young adult, memoir, and some popular nonfiction with an outstanding platform.

Describe what you definitely don't want to represent. Science fiction, erotica.

How do you want writers to pitch you? Email only please.

Describe your education and professional history. I graduated from Villanova University with a major in English. After college I became an editorial assistant at Bantam Dell (Random House), where I went on to become an assistant editor. From there I moved to New American Library (Penguin), where I rose in the ranks to senior editor. I've worked with multiple *New York Times* and *USA Today* bestselling authors.

How did you become an agent? After having a child, I was looking for more work flexibility and stimulation. Creating my own business became a very attractive idea. Considering my wonderful insider contacts as an editor, becoming an agent was a natural next step. I absolutely love it.

Knowing what you do now, would you do it again? If not, what might you do instead? Do it over! It's exciting, engaging, creative, and fabulous.

Do you charge fees? If yes, please explain. No.

When and where were you born, and where have you lived? I was born and raised in New York, but now live in the Philadelphia area.

What do you like to do when you're not working? I'm in the trenches with three small children. If I had hobbies before kids, I can't remember. If I had a moment to myself I would likely read for pleasure, meditate, bike, or run.

List some of the titles you have recently placed with publishers. *Princely Advice for a Happy Life* by H.S.H. Prince Alexi Lubomirski (Andrews McMeel; we've also sold this to about six or seven foreign markets); *One More Day* by Kelly Simmons (Sourcebooks Landmark); *Will You Won't You Want Me?* and *Semi-Charmed Life* by Nora Zelevansky (St. Martin's); *Yes, You Can Get Pregnant: Natural Ways to Improve Your Fertility Now and into Your 40s* by Aimee Raupp (Demos Health/Springer); *The Witch of Persimmon Point*, *The Witch of Little Italy*, *The Witch of Belladonna Bay*, and *The Witch of Bourbon Street* by Suzanne Palmieri (St. Martin's); *Empire Girls* and *I'll Be Seeing You* by Suzanne Hayes and Loretta Nyhan (Mira); *Left* by Tamar Ossowski (Skyhorse).

Describe your personality. Professional, warm, *not* a control freak. Someone once called me "buttoned-up." I'm really just trying to be professional. I strive to be warm but am very much a straight shooter who believes in being accessible but with a degree of formality.

What do you like reading/watching/listening to on your own time? In my downtime I like to read thoughtful women's fiction and some nonfiction about parenting/education (really enjoyed *How to Raise an Adult* and *Growth Mindset*, for example) or history such as David McCullough. Still loving *Downton Abbey*, *Vikings*, and *Game of Thrones*. Big fan of Florence and the Machine, the Beatles, the Rolling Stones, and Strauss waltzes.

Do you think the business has changed a lot over the past few years? If yes, please explain. There have been changes, and the industry has evolved and is more digitized, but at its core book publishing is still the same as it's always been. We will always be lamenting its difficulty and how it's shrinking or changing. Yes, it's changing but the concerned conversations that I have with editors now are similar to ones I had 10 or 15 years ago. Is anyone out there reading anymore? Will we ever make any money? The answer is yes. Change isn't always for the worse. The old standards hold true: if your work is well done, competitive, fresh, and can find a market, then there's a place for you in the publishing world.

What do the "Big 5" mean to you? The publishers with the most resources. I have many friends at those places. Sometimes a tough nut to crack, but definitely worth trying.

How do you feel about independent/small presses? I don't have a lot of experience with indie presses and, honestly, that limited experience has been a bit of a mixed bag so far. Some good and some bad.

What are your feelings about self-publishing? Self-publishing is another avenue for writers who want options. It has certainly helped to launch several major careers in the last few years, but it's hard to beat the prestige of a major publisher and all of its resources, such as packaging, distribution, and promotion. If you don't have knowledge of the ins and outs of the publishing world, it can be difficult to find success. But if you have the verve, vision, and cash, then this is an option. Each author/situation is different.

Do you think Amazon is good or bad — or both — for the book business? Amazon is forward thinking and sometimes does unpopular things. But in the big picture it keeps the market competitive and forces the publishing world to stay on its toes. Everyone is worried about creative destruction, which is a valid concern, but we don't have to fail as an industry. We can grow and evolve. We need to find a way to capitalize on Amazon's strong platform and exploit it to authors' benefit.

What do you like and dislike about your job? I have a small agency and, by design, work with only a handful of clients. This allows me to be totally available to those clients whose works I love. It's not uncommon for me to have a call with an author at 8 AM or on the weekends. Whatever works best for their schedule. I often provide editorial feedback, work to sell the projects, and then manage any business issues that may crop up with the publisher after the sale. I make sure the contracts are in order and take seriously my fiduciary responsibility to the client, maintaining and selling rights if possible and maximizing advances. These are the aspects of the job that I really enjoy. I love the flexibility but sometimes miss the social aspects of being in a large office. I wish I had more of a sounding board sometimes, though there are other very generous agents out there who've graciously picked up the phone to give me advice on occasion.

What are ways prospective clients can impress you, and what are ways they can turn you off? I like to surround myself with smart, self-assured authors who clearly communicate but can also take the initiative when it comes to their own writing and promotion. I feel strongly that authors should follow their own instincts regarding their project. However, I have an editorial background and feel that it's important to provide constructive criticism for projects. I don't expect authors to run with every suggestion, but I do expect them to take them into consideration. Kid gloves are always used in providing this feedback, so it is a huge turnoff when an author gets offended by it. That's a red flag that the client is too sensitive.

How would you describe the "writer from hell"? I hope to never have to use the term, but I do not appreciate overly needy writers or those who don't take it upon themselves to try to understand the publishing world, how to promote themselves, and what is appropriate contact between an author and the publisher. A true client from hell would be one who misrepresents him- or herself, lies, or plagiarizes.

Describe a book you would like to write. Something book-club worthy.

Do you believe in a higher and/or lower "power"? I do but don't expect others to. We are all entitled to our own beliefs, and I respect that.

Is there anything you wish to express beyond the parameters of the preceding questions? Pen & Ink is a boutique literary agency defined by our love for books, dedication to the author, solid relationships with editors, and insider knowledge of the business. We are friends to many in the industry. Importantly, we know the market and what the publisher wants, allowing us to contour the material to make it more marketable. This gives us a distinct competitive edge.

PETER LAMPACK AGENCY, INC. ❖ www.peterlampackagency.com

350 Fifth Avenue, Suite 5300, New York, NY 10118, 212-687-9106, fax: 212-687-9109

Agents' names and contact info: Peter Lampack, President; Andrew Lampack, Agent, andrew@peterlampackagency.com; Rema Dilanyan, Foreign Rights, rema@peterlampackagency.com; Christie Russell, Office Manager, christie@peterlampackagency.com; general queries: andrew@peterlampack agency.com

Describe the kinds of works you want to represent. Commercial and literary fiction as well as nonfiction by recognized experts in a given field.

Describe what you definitely don't want to represent. Horror, New Age, science fiction, children's and young adult fiction.

Do you charge fees? If yes, please explain. We do not charge a reading fee or any fee for office services.

List some of the titles you have recently placed with publishers. *Police State* by Gerry Spence, *The Pharaoh's Secret* by Clive Cussler and Graham Brown, *The Good Story* by J. M. Coetzee and Arabella Kurtz, *Patriot* by Ted Bell.

PROSPECT AGENCY ❖ www.prospectagency.com

551 Valley Road, PMB 377, Upper Montclair, NJ 07043, 718-788-3217

Agent's name and contact info: Emily Sylvan Kim, esk@prospectagency.com

Describe the kinds of works you want to represent. Our agency represents authors who write in a wide array of genres, from romance, to children's books, to nonfiction, to commercial fiction. We are looking for voice-driven stories with fantastic, high-concept hooks and memorable characters. Personally, I am always on the lookout for great contemporary and erotic romance! I love strong female characters and vivid settings and, of course, steamy relationships. I am also seeking strong, edgy young adult and middle grade stories.

Describe what you definitely don't want to represent. I am not looking for paranormal romance and am not a huge sci-fi/fantasy fan in general. I do not represent nonfiction.

How do you want writers to pitch you? Writers should pitch me by going to the Prospect Agency submission form and filling out the necessary information to send their queries.

Describe your education and professional history. I graduated from Carleton College with a degree in English. After a few missteps including a year at law school and a stint teaching test prep for the SATs, I moved to NYC to pursue my dream of working in publishing. I was lucky enough to get a job at Writers House, where I learned the craft. I left to open my own agency, Prospect Agency. Now a decade old, the agency has grown to include 6 other agents and represents over 100 clients!

How did you become an agent? After working as an assistant, I started to take on my own clients. I remember my first deal was with Kensington Zebra for Regina Scott's *To Marry a Duke*!

Knowing what you do now, would you do it again? If not, what might you do instead? I have loved every minute of my career! I am so proud of the agency I have built and the way it has grown and changed over the years, so I can't say I would change a thing (though I might have skipped law school!).

Do you charge fees? If yes, please explain. No, Prospect Agency never charges any sort of fee.

When and where were you born, and where have you lived? I grew up in Denver, Colorado, and attended college in beautiful Northfield, Minnesota. In New York I was lucky enough to live near Prospect Park for many years, thus inspiring the name of the agency. I now live in New Jersey!

What do you like to do when you're not working? I have three amazing children, so whenever I have time to step away from my laptop, I love playing and reading with them and taking them on adventures. I also love taking walks and cooking.

List some of the titles you have recently placed with publishers. Susan Lyon's *Blue Moon Harbor* (Kensington), Serena Bell's *Grizzlies* series (Loveswept), Geri Krotow's *Silver Valley PD* series (Harlequin), Lia Riley's *Stay* (Grand Central), Arin Greenwood's *Wag* (Soho Teen), Julia Kelly's *Governess* series (Pocket Star).

Describe your personality. I am definitely a very high-energy and passionate person. I know one of the things my clients really appreciate about working with me is that I am always there to help them every step of the way in their careers. I also definitely have a sense of humor and use that to help find the bright side in even the toughest situations.

What do you like reading/watching/listening to on your own time? I really enjoy watching *Downton Abbey,* and one of my colleagues has been pushing me to start watching *Outlander* as well. As for reading, I'm a big fan of Jane Smiley's books and have been enjoying those during my downtime. I love folk rock, too, and have a Pandora station dedicated to Dar Williams!

Do you think the business has changed a lot over the past few years? If yes, please explain. The business has gone through some major changes in the last few years, but I think that the heart of the industry is finding and promoting good stories, which is something that will never change.

What do the "Big 5" mean to you? I think the Big 5 bring an impressive power to any project they approach. Most recently, I have been so excited to see how the major publishers are adapting to the changing digital landscape. I love working with the Big 5 because at every turn I see them doing all they can to support and nurture the publishing industry.

How do you feel about independent/small presses? Of course there are small presses I feel are more effective than others, but the right small press can bring a very special energy to the publishing industry, and I highly encourage new presses to launch and continue to shape and grow this literary landscape.

What are your feelings about self-publishing? If you have the time and knowledge, self-publishing can be a great avenue to pursue. A lot of my romance authors enjoy hybrid careers and have had great success! I will say, though, that in order to self-publish successfully, one should have a great knowledge of the market, publicity, and how to utilize subrights in order to build a sustainable career.

Do you think Amazon is good or bad — or both — for the book business? I think that Amazon is a major force in the industry and must be understood and utilized effectively.

What do you like and dislike about your job? My favorite part of the job is helping my wonderful authors find the success they deserve. I take it hard when they have setbacks, so that is definitely my least favorite part. But I am working around the clock to ensure that each and every one finds the success and readership they deserve!

What are ways prospective clients can impress you, and what are ways they can turn you off? When I talk to prospective clients, the ones I click with right away are the ones who are friendly and relaxed and very open to discussing what works and doesn't work with their writing. I know it can be hard to have that sort of attitude when talking about your novel, but when you are very resistant to ideas for changes or when it seems that you aren't willing to think about your project commercially, that can turn me off.

How would you describe the "writer from hell"? Oh, boy! Honestly, I think the writer from hell is one who isn't willing to listen or to try something a different way. The author-agent relationship is a very collaborative one, and if you have someone who is pushing back at every point, it can be difficult to have a positive working relationship.

Describe a book you would like to write. I would love to write a book about two sisters who fall in love with the same person. Wouldn't that be a mess?

Do you believe in a higher and/or lower "power"? Is this book related? When I read a great book, I feel connected to humanity and the world in a special way.

Agent's name and contact info: Linda Camacho, linda@prospectagency.com

Describe the kinds of works you want to represent. I'm interested in middle grade, young adult, and adult fiction across all genres (particularly romance/women's fiction, horror, fantasy, and contemporary). I also seek select literary fiction (preferably with a commercial bent) and picture book writer-illustrators. Diversity of all types welcome (ethnicity, disability, sexuality, etc.)!

Describe what you definitely don't want to represent. I'm pretty open, so I don't like to limit myself. What I can say is that my focus is on trade publishing, so anything outside of that (i.e., academic texts) wouldn't be a good fit for me.

How do you want writers to pitch you? I'm accepting queries through Prospect Agency's submissions page. Please include three chapters and a brief synopsis. Don't query by email or letter mail and don't submit unsolicited manuscripts or inquire about the status of submissions via email.

Describe your education and professional history. At Cornell, I majored in communication and graduated unsure of what I wanted to do with my life. Luckily, a kind soul pointed out that I loved to read, so why not try publishing? So I did. My first job at Penguin was in production under the Berkley/Jove/Ace/Riverhead imprints, so that was a healthy dose of genre fiction with some literary fiction. After some time, I left Penguin when I briefly toyed with the idea of law school. I missed publishing, however, so to get back in, I worked and rotated through the departments at Dorchester, Simon & Schuster, Random House, and Writers House Literary Agency. In the middle of that, I earned an MFA in creative writing from the Vermont College of Fine Arts. Then I made the move to agenting in 2015 and am really glad I did!

How did you become an agent? I was working in marketing at Random House Children's and, although it was an interesting job, I wished I could work more closely with our authors. I wanted the chance to nurture talent from the ground up. A previous internship at Writers House initially piqued my interest, and I knew I wanted to pursue agenting when the right opportunity came. After many informational interviews, I got a few offers to join agencies, but I connected most with Prospect Agency owner Emily Sylvan Kim, a former Writers House person. So I made the leap and haven't looked back.

Knowing what you do now, would you do it again? If not, what might you do instead? It was a 10-year road to agenting, but honestly I'd do it the same way. Because of all the jobs I took to get here, I learned how every department of a publishing house functions. I find it very helpful as an agent, because I better understand how everything works as a whole.

Do you charge fees? If yes, please explain. No.

When and where were you born, and where have you lived? I was born in the Bronx in 1983 and lived there until I went upstate to college. Then my parents moved to the New Jersey suburbs and I lived there while I saved up money to get my own place in the city (ah, the glamorous publishing salary). Now I live in Manhattan, which makes it all the more convenient for all the editor lunches I have!

What do you like to do when you're not working? I love traveling abroad (the last place I went was China) and going to Broadway shows as much as possible! I also binge-watch Netflix and have recently taken up racquetball, so that's a lot of fun.

List some of the titles you have recently placed with publishers. I'm a newer agent, so I'm currently building my list. I'm happy to say that I recently made my first sale, a middle grade contemporary to Scholastic called *Family Game Night and Other Disasters*.

Describe your personality. I can be a bit of a control freak (ha). Yet I'm patient and flexible to work with. I have a sense of humor and am very loyal. I strive to build close relationships with my clients as I advocate for them.

What do you like reading/watching/listening to on your own time? I'm one of those people who doesn't have favorites, but besides the obvious fact that I love to read, I also *love* to watch TV. Netflix allows me to watch new shows and binge-watch older ones, like *The Walking Dead*, *Parks and Recreation*, *The Office*, *Breaking Bad*, *Jessica Jones*, *Friends*, etc.

Do you think the business has changed a lot over the past few years? If yes, please explain. The business has changed a lot in the last few years, given the emergence of ebooks and their implications for the industry. I could write a thesis about it, but let's just say that ebooks have raised a lot of questions in regard to people's roles in publishing and whether the big business of it is still valid. I still believe we're relevant, since printed books will never go away in the end. And even if they did, there's so much that goes into the creation of the ebook beyond the editorial side that even in a world of digital-only I don't live in fear of losing my job.

What do the "Big 5" mean to you? I've only ever worked at the Big 5, so I've seen what an amazing machine it all is. The Big 5 are a force to be reckoned with, since when they truly get behind a book, it's a miraculous thing to see. They have incredible resources and influence, so that if you're lucky to be an author who's a priority at one of these houses, it's almost impossible not to do well in your career.

How do you feel about independent/small presses? Small presses can do big things as well. Some of my favorite publishing houses are small presses, like Candlewick, which is amazing. The beauty of the small press is that they have a much smaller list, so they can really advocate for their authors and not have them fall through the cracks. The smaller press is also more of a risk taker with regard to acquisitions. They have fewer bureaucratic hoops to jump through when acquiring a book and it can make a world of difference, since they can give authors a chance that they might not have been given elsewhere.

What are your feelings about self-publishing? I don't have a problem with self-publishing, as it may work better for some authors. There are authors who are very hands-on and want to handle every single aspect of their career and publishing process. If that's the case, I encourage smart self-publishing and indie press publishing. It might work better for some genres than others (namely, romance), but it can be a good option. I don't advise rushing into it, though, because it's more intense than collaborating with a publisher. Still, if authors like the idea of complete creative and marketing control, then they should go for it.

Do you think Amazon is good or bad — or both — for the book business? I don't like to demonize folks in the industry, but Amazon isn't doing the publishing business and its already underpaid authors much good. As a consumer, I get why it's appealing to have a drastically cheap price for an ebook, but the question doesn't so much lie in the production value. It's a bit cheaper to produce an ebook, but not by a whole lot, given how many people are still involved in the creation. The production value question is solely what's being considered by the consumer, as opposed to the fact that it's also the cost of the intellectual property itself. Are we paying for the paper or the story?

What do you like and dislike about your job? As corny as it sounds, I get to discover talent and make authors' writing dreams come true. A colleague once said it was like being a fairy godmother, which I find to be the case. Conversely, I dislike the feeling that I'm crushing a writer's dreams by rejecting a manuscript. If I could say yes to all the wonderful writers out there, I would. Alas, I'm but one person in this crazy business.

What are ways prospective clients can impress you, and what are ways they can turn you off? Research. It all comes down to research. If an author writes a great targeted query to me and then blows me away with the pages, I'm impressed. If an author doesn't bother to do the research and (1) writes a query that's outright sloppy or (2) queries me in an email sent to maybe 50 other agents like a spam eblast, then I'm definitely turned off.

How would you describe the "writer from hell"? A writer from hell is one who is completely inflexible and refuses to collaborate in the process. A writer from hell also has very unrealistic expectations about the process and has more than a bit of ego on top of it.

Describe a book you would like to write. If I were to write a book? I don't know, given that I love so many genres. Maybe something that's gut wrenching, if I were skilled enough to do it. I do love a good cry. *Atonement* is one of my favorite books, so if I could make a reader cry like that, I'd be set!

Do you believe in a higher and/or lower "power"? In regard to publishing, I believe that the industry relies mostly on luck, if you want to consider that a higher power! So much of it is dependent on timing and subjective tastes that sometimes I'm surprised books ever get published.

Additional agents at Prospect Agency: Kirsten Carleton, kirsten@prospectagency.com; Teresa Kietlinski, tk@prospectagency.com; Rachel Orr, rko@prospectagency.com; Carrie Pestritto, carrie@prospect agency.com; Becca Stumpf, becca@prospectagency.com

P.S. LITERARY AGENCY ❖ www.psliterary.com

20033-520 Kerr Street, Oakville, Ontario L6K 3C7, Canada, 416-907-8325 (Toronto), 212-655-9276 (New York)

Agent's name and contact info: Maria Vicente, maria@psliterary.com, www.mariavicente.com

Describe the kinds of works you want to represent. In fiction, I am looking for literary fiction (especially magical realism), young adult (any genre), middle grade (any genre), and illustrated picture books. For nonfiction, I am looking for projects in the pop-culture, geek-culture, pop-science, design, and lifestyle categories.

Describe what you definitely don't want to represent. I do not represent poetry or screenplays. Adult speculative fiction is not for me.

How do you want writers to pitch you? A query letter that outlines your project should be sent to query@psliterary.com. Do not send attachments or full-length manuscripts or proposals unless requested.

List some of the titles you have recently placed with publishers. *The Fangirl's Guide to the Galaxy* by Sam Maggs (Quirk Books), *Definitions of Indefinable Things* by Whitney Taylor (HMH Books for Young Readers).

What are ways prospective clients can impress you, and what are ways they can turn you off? There are two things I look for when signing a new client: that the writer is always working on something new, and that the writer has a clear idea of the sort of writing career they want to have. When sending a query letter, it makes a huge difference if you simply follow the submission guidelines outlined on the agency's website.

Agent's name and contact info: Carly Watters, query@psliterary

Describe the kinds of works you want to represent. Smart book-club fiction, women's fiction, upmarket adult fiction, commercial adult fiction, domestic suspense, literary mystery and thrillers, historical fiction, contemporary romance, popular science, business and psychology, cookbooks, unique memoir, lifestyle nonfiction (health, wellness, relationships, parenting, design, pop culture), narrative nonfiction (platform-based nonfiction: must have demonstrable expertise and a quantifiable market).

Describe what you definitely don't want to represent. No sci-fi, fantasy, children's (picture books, chapter books), religious texts, poetry, screenplays, or novellas.

How do you want writers to pitch you? P.S. Literary only accepts submissions via email. They should be sent to query@psliterary.com. Please limit your submission to a query letter that consists of three paragraphs: (1) introduction: title and category of your work (i.e., fiction or nonfiction and topic), estimated word count, and brief general introduction; (2) brief overview: should read similar to back-cover copy; (3) writer's bio: tell us a little bit about yourself and your background (awards and affiliations, etc.).

Do not send attachments. Please place text within the body of your email. Please do not submit a full-length manuscript/proposal unless requested. Always let us know if your manuscript/proposal is currently under consideration by other agents or publishers. Address your query to the attention of the agent you feel is the best match for your work. Please do not query multiple agents at the agency simultaneously. If you don't receive a response to your query within four to six weeks, it means a no from the agency. We have "a no response means no" agency policy.

Describe your education and professional history. I began my publishing career in London at the Darley Anderson Literary, TV and Film Agency. I have a BA in English literature from Queen's University and an MA in publishing studies from City University London. I worked at Bloomsbury in the UK and Kids Can Press in Toronto, both in the rights departments, before joining PSLA in 2010. Bestselling, award-winning, and debut clients include Taylor Jenkins Reid, Karen Katchur, Andrea Dunlop, Jay Onrait, Larry Smith, Jennifer Carlson, Allison Day, Jael Richardson, and many more.

How did you become an agent? It was the only job in publishing that encompassed everything: editorial, sales, marketing, rights, and publicity. As soon as I discovered what a literary agent was, I knew it was the job for me.

Do you charge fees? If yes, please explain. No reading fees.

Where have you lived? I have lived in Canada and the UK.

What are your hobbies? Reading, podcasts, yoga, interior design, fashion.

List some of the titles you have recently placed with publishers. *The Seven Husbands of Evelyn Hugo*, *One True Loves*, and *Maybe in Another Life* by Taylor Jenkins Reid (Atria); *Losing the Light* by Andrea Dunlop (Atria); *The Secrets of Lake Road* by Karen Katchur (Thomas Dunne/St. Martin's); *No Fears, No Excuses: What You Need to Do to Have a Great Career* by Larry Smith (Houghton Mifflin Harcourt); *The Mentor Myth* by Debby Carreau (Bibliomotion); *Baby Gourmet* by Jennifer Carlson (Atria); *Whole Bowls* and *Pumpkin* by Allison Day (Skyhorse); *Number Two* by Jay Onrait (HarperCollins).

Describe your personality. Passionate, dedicated, loyal, curious, perceptive, honest.

What are your feelings about self-publishing? I don't represent self-published books, but I represent authors who have self-published in the past.

What do you like about your job? I like that every day is different and the fascinating people I get to work with. I divide my time between fiction and nonfiction, so I meet an array of talented writers who inspire me daily.

What are the qualities you look for in a client? Professionalism online and in person, passion, persistence, respect, patience, talent, and a strong vision that matches mine.

THE PURCELL AGENCY, LLC ❖ www.thepurcellagency.com

847-702-6945
Submissions: tpaqueries@gmail.com

Agents' names and contact info: Tina P. Schwartz, Founder and Literary Agent, querytinap@gmail.com; Kim McCollum, Associate Literary Agent, querykimmc@gmail.com

Describe the kinds of works you want to represent. *Tina*: Chapter books for children; middle grade and young adult fiction and nonfiction; women's fiction.

Describe what you definitely don't want to represent. Please *no* fantasy or picture books.

How do you want writers to pitch you? I love face-to-face pitches at conferences or speaking engagements, but otherwise you can send a query and three sample chapters to tpaqueries@gmail.com.

Describe your education and professional history. BA from Columbia College Chicago in marketing communications and advertising. I was a media buyer, then national radio sales rep for many years while being a writer.

How did you become an agent? Once I gained some success as a children's book author (10 traditionally published books) and helped several friends get published, I decided to marry my two careers — sales/negotiating contracts *and* books. That's how I decided to become an agent. Chicago doesn't have too many literary agencies, so when there were no job openings at the already established agencies, I decided to just go for it and open my own literary agency.

Knowing what you do now, would you do it again? If not, what might you do instead? Sure, I'd do it again in a minute! But there are times that I wish I would have had some sort of formal introduction to it all versus just learning as I go. It's all good, though. I'm happy to report the agency is growing by leaps and bounds, and I appreciate all the lessons I've learned along the way.

Do you charge fees? If yes, please explain. Never.

When and where were you born, and where have you lived? Suburbanite my whole life, living 30 miles north of Chicago (except for the first two years of college in a cornfield, before transferring to a city school!). And I'm an "80s girl," i.e., I'm in my forties.

What do you like to do when you're not working? I love hanging out with my family, dates with my husband (of 20 years), or going to my kids' sporting events; I love hanging with my siblings, too. *Very* close family ties. Hobbies are playing or watching sports, going to movies, and of course — reading!

List some of the titles you have recently placed with publishers. The Strand Murder by Renee James, *The Hound Hotel* series (books 5–8) by Shelley Swanson Sateren, *Berry Road* by Cara Sue Achterberg.

Describe your personality. Half the time I'm high energy (high strung), then the other half of the time I'm very chill and laid-back. I'm usually pretty happy-go-lucky and take things in stride as best as I can. But no matter what, you will *always* find me with a smile on my face!

What do you like reading/watching/listening to on your own time? I'm a total movie buff. I go to the theater whenever I can. Some women collect shoes; I collect DVDs! I have over 500, which is probably too many, but I can't help myself! ☺ My two favorite authors are S. E. Hinton and David Levithan. I read anything and everything I can of theirs.

Do you think the business has changed a lot over the past few years? If yes, please explain. Yes, I think more big houses are requiring an agent's representation, which helps my business. But it will force authors to be very choosy in finding a partner, which is ultimately the best thing possible. I think more boutique agencies will pop up, so authors will have to really do their homework when submitting to see if someone is a legit agent.

What are your feelings about self-publishing? I think it is *very* hard to do well and be successful at, but is a great option for those willing to put in the time and attention to detail.

Do you think Amazon is good or bad — or both — for the book business? Good.

What do you like and dislike about your job? I *love* telling authors that I'd like to represent them and then making those calls to say offers have been made on their manuscript. One thing I dislike is feeling pulled in a hundred directions sometimes and not having enough hours in the day to finish all that I need to!

What are ways prospective clients can impress you, and what are ways they can turn you off? Authors can impress me in simple ways by just following submission guidelines, being respectful, and not treating me rudely. (Some people get very demanding and are not polite about their wishes!)

How would you describe the "writer from hell"? Someone who's unsympathetic to the process when you are very busy working around the clock and things sometimes *still* fall through the cracks. When a writer is negative or slams you (publicly) for taking too long to reply or gets mad for needing a "nudge" for an update, that upsets me. We all try to do the best we can, and some patience is always appreciated. Saying negative things online, while hiding behind a screen name, is a little pet peeve of mine. It doesn't happen to me very often, but when I'm on a writer's online board and see snippy little comments, I really feel for the person being spoken about. I try to be respectful, even when upset with someone, as I know the slight is usually unintentional.

Describe a book you would like to write. I would love to write a women's friendship story, a.k.a. chick lit. I usually only write for teens and younger, so branching out into the adult audience would be fun! But ultimately, I just want to write a book that people read until dawn, something they literally cannot put down!

Do you believe in a higher and/or lower "power"? Yes, I do. And I believe in angels as well. ☺

RED FOX LITERARY, LLC ❖ redfoxliterary.com

129 Morro Avenue, Shell Beach, CA 93449, 805-459-3327, info@redfoxliterary.com

Agent's name and contact info: Karen Grencik, karen@redfoxliterary.com

Describe the kinds of works you want to represent. We are a children's book agency. I represent everything from picture books to young adult, both fiction and nonfiction. I am looking for beautifully written, meaningful, and heartfelt work, or something really fun or funny.

Describe what you definitely don't want to represent. Nothing too dark or edgy; no science fiction or high fantasy; no poetry; no straight nonfiction or concept books.

How do you want writers to pitch you? We are closed to unsolicited submissions and only accept submissions, via email, from conference attendees where we present or through industry referrals.

Describe your education and professional history. I graduated from high school at 16 and traveled the world on my own until age 22. I then got an AA and my stenographer's license. I worked as a court reporter for 24 years, then retired due to a physical disability. I started agenting full-time in 2011, and I'm now living my life's purpose.

How did you become an agent? I had a friend with an amazing life story, and I wanted to memorialize it for him. Once a week for six weeks we got together, and I took his words down on my court reporting machine, then transcribed them for him to review for accuracy. When we were finished, I decided his story needed to be told to the world, so I set out to learn how to be a literary agent. I studied everything I could about publishing. I began attending writers' conferences to find an author to take the verbatim notes and make them publishable. Ha! It was my postman's fiancée who finally took on the project. I called nine agents on the West Coast to see if I could take someone to lunch, so they could teach me what to do. When Linda Allen answered, I told her I would do anything to learn how to sell the manuscript I had, that I would work for her, pay her, send her gifts, and let her use our home in Costa Rica. She laughed and told me to call her in the morning. I flew to NYC to meet with editors, then sold the manuscript, *Double Luck: Memoirs of a Chinese Orphan*, by Lu Chi Fa with Becky White, to Holiday House in 2000. I had no intentions of doing it again, but doors kept opening for me, and I couldn't help but follow the signs.

Knowing what you do now, would you do it again? If not, what might you do instead? I was born to do this.

Do you charge fees? If yes, please explain. No.

When and where were you born, and where have you lived? Born in Orange County, California. I've lived in California, Montana, and Costa Rica.

What do you like to do when you're not working? Hug and kiss my sweetheart and two dogs, spend time with friends and family, hike, do yoga, make videos, and read.

List some of the titles you have recently placed with publishers. Most-recent sales that have been posted include Erica Silverman's *Lana Goes to the Moon*, Brenda Sturgis's *Still a Family*, Diane Ohanesian's *Hugga Bugga Love*, Michelle Houts's *Lucy's Lab*, Brenda Maier's *Little Red Fort*, and Ann Ingalls's *Twelve Days of Christmas in Missouri*. There are many that have not yet been announced.

Describe your personality. I present as an extravert, but I am very much an introvert. I love people and care too much about everything, which wears me out.

What do you like reading/watching/listening to on your own time? I'm always trying to learn, so anything that can provide growth or make me laugh.

Do you think the business has changed a lot over the past few years? If yes, please explain. Because I am fairly new to the industry, I haven't seen a lot of change. For me, as I gain experience, it just keeps getting better and better.

What do the "Big 5" mean to you? To me they symbolize opportunity. I am grateful for each and every imprint and each and every member of their team.

How do you feel about independent/small presses? Some are good, some are bad. I think many have good intentions but do not have the staff to fulfill their promises. I've had very good luck with smaller presses, and I love working with them.

What are your feelings about self-publishing? I'm thrilled that it is available for people who are not able to place their work with a traditional publisher. It's an open door for all writers with a dream.

Do you think Amazon is good or bad — or both — for the book business? I would say both.

What do you like and dislike about your job? I love making people happy, and I hate disappointing them.

What are ways prospective clients can impress you, and what are ways they can turn you off? I like gracious and polite authors. I do not like self-centered people who never stop promoting themselves.

How would you describe the "writer from hell"? Someone who is rude in communications, entitled, demanding, and unappreciative.

Describe a book you would like to write. I wish I could write a memoir.

Do you believe in a higher and/or lower "power"? Without a shadow of a doubt. I live my life by following the signs that present, and they always lead me in the right direction.

Agent's name and contact info: Danielle Smith, danielle@redfoxliterary.com

Describe the kinds of works you want to represent. Children's books, from picture books through to young adult novels, both fiction and nonfiction.

Describe what you definitely don't want to represent. No adult material, cookbooks.

How do you want writers to pitch you? Our agency is open to submissions from attendees of conferences where we present or through industry referrals. We are not currently accepting unsolicited submissions.

Describe your education and professional history. My formal education was in mechanical engineering and classics (emphasis on Latin and Greek studies), but after over six years reviewing children's literature for both online and print publications, I transitioned successfully into the agenting side of children's publishing. After a successful year at Fuse Literary, I moved to Red Fox Literary, where I have been for two years.

How did you become an agent? As I mentioned above, I began reviewing children's books almost 10 years ago. It began on my review site, theresabook.com, and within a few years I added print reviews to my résumé. I served as a judge for numerous awards panels, including as a judge for the fiction picture-book category for the Cybils awards. Prior to joining Fuse Literary in 2013, I had the good fortune of interning under one of the partners at the time. When the agency began, they brought me on as the children's-focused agent. During this time I also considered Karen Grencik a close friend and mentor. After a very successful first year I felt the need to transition to an agency focused on children's literature. Fortunately for me, both Karen and Abigail were looking to expand Red Fox Literary and made the offer to bring me over to the agency; it was an offer I couldn't refuse, and I've loved working with them both ever since!

Knowing what you do now, would you do it again? If not, what might you do instead? Without a doubt. I've had enough life and work experience to know that this is where I'm meant to be. I feel very fortunate to have found this work.

Do you charge fees? If yes, please explain. No. Outside of the typical industry standard agency fees, there no additional fees.

When and where were you born, and where have you lived? I was born and raised in southern California between the beach and the mountains. I've traveled and lived all over the United States; my favorite destination would have to have been the picturesque state of Alaska.

What do you like to do when you're not working? I'm a mom to two talented and incredible children as well as a wife to one of the most supportive and creative husbands a person could hope for. Most of the free time I have is spent with them doing the things we love like being outdoors, going to the movies, playing games, and reading.

List some of the titles you have recently placed with publishers. *A Clown Walked into a Ballpark*, illustrated by Jenn Bower; *Walk Your Dog* by Elizabeth Omlor and illustrated by Neesha Hudson; *Twinderella*, illustrated by Deborah Marcero; *The Evaporation of Sofi Snow* by Mary Weber; *Can You Canoe?*, illustrated by Brandon Reese; *Ursa's Light* by Deborah Marcero; *Bunny's New Friends*, *Help Wanted: One Rooster*, and *Snappsy the Alligator (Did Not Ask to Be in This Book)* by Julie Falatko; *The Backyard Witch*, books 1–3, illustrated by Deborah Marcero.

Describe your personality. Honest, kind, hardworking, dependable, and passionate. I'm a champion for the people and things I love, from my work to my personal life; if it's something I value, I will fight for it. What this means for my work life is that I will pour my heart and soul into work with and for my clients. I do strive to have a good work-life balance, but often those two lines blur a bit, and the people I work with need to be comfortable with that.

What do you like reading/watching/listening to on your own time? I'm a huge fan of all things Sherlock, *Star Wars*, *Star Trek*, and anything generally pop culture. Because I also have a background as a formally trained musician, I most often can be found listening to music, even while I read! I love exploring all types of music to find new artists almost as much as I enjoy finding new authors and illustrators. Some of my favorite musicians at the moment are Nickel Creek, the Hunts, William Fitzsimmons, Adele, Kari Kimmel, Lily Kershaw, and Mat Kearney. I've also been known to pick up a coloring book or two while listening to music or a great audiobook. My guilty pleasure reads recently have been by Brené Brown, Dasha Tolstikova, Beth Kephart, and Cassie Beasley.

Do you think the business has changed a lot over the past few years? If yes, please explain. Yes and no. What's not changed is that this business is very much about the children we're making these books for and the people we work with. Those things simply don't change. Yes, the business is changing as the way our civilization views and incorporates books into their lives, but we adapt and continue to push forward.

What do the "Big 5" mean to you? The five main "big" publishing houses; they're buying and selling my clients' books, and I couldn't be more grateful!

How do you feel about independent/small presses? Independent and small presses can be a great resource in today's market for writers and illustrators. Some of them are creating award-winning literature and publishing books that may have a hard time making it with one of the Big 5. Not all are created equally though, and I strongly recommend writers and illustrators do their research before signing a contract with a press that may not be able to offer valuable distribution, editing, marketing, and other important qualities found at bigger houses.

What are your feelings about self-publishing? Self-publishing is a great option for some writers who have had a difficult time breaking out, and I'm happy that writers have many options open to them.

Do you think Amazon is good or bad — or both — for the book business? I'm a big supporter of indie bookstores and would prefer that all readers do their shopping at their local independent store to support their community. Unfortunately, that isn't always an option, and I'm glad there are a variety of buying options available for all readers, including Amazon. Book buying, in any form, is great for the book business.

What do you like and dislike about your job? There are so many things I *love* about my job, from reading over contracts to writing pitches for submissions, but my favorite aspect of being an agent is calling authors or illustrators to let them know there's an offer on their book. That joy can't be duplicated, except for perhaps when the book is out and in the world for the first time. As for what I dislike about the job, that would have to be when it's just not the right fit with a client for whatever reason. I'm someone who wants to be able to make every relationship work, but that's simply not always possible. In those situations I do my very best to leave each relationship amicably, so that we can continue to cheer each other on as we go our separate ways.

What are ways prospective clients can impress you, and what are ways they can turn you off? I appreciate writers who do their "homework" and show me professionalism in their query letters as well as throughout other stages of the process. A proactive nature balanced with a healthy dose of patience goes a very long way toward a successful career as a writer.

How would you describe the "writer from hell"? Someone unwilling to recognize that an agent is an advocate, a partner, in this sometimes difficult business. Agents are partners in sharing both the joy and the burdens that come with this work, and writers unwilling to recognize this are very difficult to work with. A lack of gratitude at any stage is a huge indication of this, but the opposite quality describes someone I'd expect to see huge success from.

Describe a book you would like to write. I've written books in the past, but right now I'm in full-agent mode. So no books that I can think of at the moment.

Do you believe in a higher and/or lower "power"? Yes.

Is there anything you wish to express beyond the parameters of the preceding questions? Love what you do, but be grateful for every hand involved in your success along the way. Gratitude, humility, and kindness go a long way in this business.

Additional agent at Red Fox Literary: Abigail Samoun, abigail@redfoxliterary.com

RED SOFA LITERARY ❖ www.redsofaliterary.com

PO Box 40482, St. Paul, MN 55104, 651-224-6670 (no queries by phone, please)

Agent's name and contact info: Dawn Frederick, Owner and Literary Agent, dawn@redsofaliterary.com, Twitter: @redsofaliterary

Describe the kinds of works you want to represent. Our categories are described in detail at redsofaliterary.com/representative-categories. I am always in search of a good work of nonfiction that falls within my categories (see my specific list on our website). I especially love pop culture, interesting histories, social sciences/advocacy, humor, and books that are great conversation starters. As for fiction, I am always in search of good young adult and middle grade titles. For young adult I will go a little darker on the tone, as I enjoy a good gothic, contemporary, or historical young adult novel. For middle grade, I will always want something fun and lighthearted, but would love more contemporary themes, too.

Describe what you definitely don't want to represent. Memoir (it seems everyone ignores this request). I also prefer to represent books that aren't overly sappy or romantic or any type of didactic/moralistic material.

How do you want writers to pitch you? Outside of the correct way to query me (see our website), I want a pitch that is engaging and reflective of what I'm looking for and provides the who/what/why perspective on why the author believes it's a good fit for the agency.

Describe your education and professional history. Before publishing I was a bookseller in the independent, chain, and specialty stores. I ended up in Minnesota for my first job at a publishing house and eventually become a literary agent at Sebastian Literary Agency. I have a BS in human ecology and an MS in information sciences from an ALA-accredited institution. I'm also the cofounder of the MN Publishing Tweet Up, the news chair for the Twin Cities Advisory Council for MPR, and a teaching artist at Loft Literary.

How did you become an agent? While working at a publisher, I realized how much I missed selling the finished books, let alone the chance to meet so many authors beyond the completed book. The bookstore life had left this impression, and I realized that, when a friend in grad school suggested I become an agent, that was in fact the best idea. I mentioned this to a friend, who it turns out knew Laurie Harper. And I haven't looked back since. It was meant to be. ☺

Knowing what you do now, would you do it again? If not, what might you do instead? My only change? I would have cut to the chase and became an agent straight out of grad school rather than waiting longer.

Do you charge fees? If yes, please explain. No.

When and where were you born, and where have you lived? I was born in Atlanta, grew up in Tennessee, and moved to the Twin Cities upon completing my graduate degree.

What do you like to do when you're not working? I love to check out indie flicks, roller-skate, cross-stitch obsessively, tend to my pets, do volunteer work, and continue to get more ink (yes, I love a good tattoo project).

List some of the titles you have recently placed with publishers. *Branded* by Eric Smith (Bloomsbury Spark), *Welcome Home* (young adult anthology) edited by Eric Smith (Jolly Fish Press), *Ten Years an Orc: A Decade in the World of Warcraft* by Tony Palumbi (Chicago Review Press), *Behind the Books: How Debut Authors Navigate from the Idea to the End* by Chris Jones (University of Chicago Press), *Caring for Creation: The Evangelical's Guide to Climate Change and a Healthy Environment* by Paul Douglas and Mitch Hescox (Bethany House), *Some Hell* by Patrick Nathan (Graywolf Press), *Choose Your Own Misery: An Office Adventure* by Jilly Gagnon and Mike MacDonald (Diversion).

Describe your personality. I'm happily an ambivert. I have many moments of enjoying the company of others. It's always a treat to meet new people and hear their stories. Yet I am also very protective of my quiet time (away from people). I'm naturally curious, will get along with most personalities, and will happily admit that I'm obsessively organized (which benefits our team). ☺

What do you like reading/watching/listening to on your own time? I am always going to enjoy a good Showtime, HBO, or Netflix series. I find that these shows are always great ways to clear the palate when needing a break from reading. My musical tastes are all over the place. I was classically trained (I played oboe into my second year of college), but the internal "me" is a punker. I'm obsessed with Joy Division and the Talking Heads, thereby making me a New Wave fan. Yet my happiest pleasure is hearing some good bluegrass, too, as it harkens back to my Southern roots.

Do you think the business has changed a lot over the past few years? If yes, please explain. Where do I start? In the "old" days, business was done by phone and post. Yes, we sent materials by mail (crazy, huh?). In this current era, it's mainly done electronically and via social media. Ironically when I see my favorite editors, they claim their phones barely ring anymore. When someone mentions this, I know I'm not the only one who remembers the "old" days.

What do you like and dislike about your job? Finding a new idea and getting the chance to work with an author whose writing I connect with emotionally and intellectually. The only thing I dislike is that there are only 24 hours in a day and that apparently my body requires sleep.

What are ways prospective clients can impress you, and what are ways they can turn you off? Showing a knowledge of my categories and helping me know *they* are the ones to write the book ideas being shared. This will always stand out. Additionally always keeping our interactions personal and professional. Lacking any of the things I find important will generally not leave the best impression.

How would you describe the "writer from hell"? Diva. If someone is bringing too much ego or shows signs of being a difficult client to work with, I will run (not walk) away from this person.

Agent's name and contact info: Jennie Goloboy, Literary Agent, jennie@redsofaliterary.com

Describe the kinds of works you want to represent. I mostly represent adult science fiction and fantasy. Within that genre, I'm looking for work that's progressive, innovative, and most of all fun. I loved *Childhood's End*, but I'd never want to represent something that bleak.

How do you want writers to pitch you? I would like them to send a query letter (no attachments!) to jennie@redsofaliterary.com. Alternately, if you see me at a conference, come say hello!

Describe your education and professional history. In addition to working as an agent, I also write history — my book *Charleston and the Emergence of Middle-Class Culture in the Revolutionary Era* is forthcoming from University of Georgia Press in the fall of 2016. I write sci-fi and fantasy under my pen name, Nora Fleischer.

How did you become an agent? Dawn Frederick took me on as an intern in the fall of 2011. When I found a book I really wanted her to represent, she said, "Why don't you do it?"

Knowing what you do now, would you do it again? If not, what might you do instead? Of course I'd do it again — I love being an agent!

When and where were you born, and where have you lived? I was born near Boston in 1971. I've also lived in Connecticut, Texas, California, and Minnesota.

What do you like to do when you're not working? I'm an avid, if slow-moving, jogger. I also like to cook and do embroidery.

List some of the titles you have recently placed with publishers. Foz Meadows's *An Accident of Stars* and *A Tyranny of Queens* (Angry Robot), Chris Bucholz's *Freeze/Thaw* (Apex), Dan Koboldt's *The Rogue Retrieval* (Harper Voyager Impulse).

What do you like reading/watching/listening to on your own time? Recently I've enjoyed watching *Mad Men* and (most of) the *Marvel* movies. My favorite new toy is my record player — I love buying old records at the bargain store and seeing if I like them!

What are your feelings about self-publishing? I have self-published as Nora Fleischer, and it was a lot of fun. It's a great way to publish a quirky book.

What do you like and dislike about your job? I love my clients — their work always inspires me!

What are ways prospective clients can impress you, and what are ways they can turn you off? To survive in this industry, you not only have to be able to write a great book; you have to have some ideas about how to publicize it. You also have to know that you'll hear no a lot, and you'll have to be okay with that.

How would you describe the "writer from hell"? In a word: impatient.

Describe a book you would like to write. Well, it's coming out from the University of Georgia Press in fall of 2016…

Agent's name and contact info: Stacey Graham, Associate Literary Agent, stacey@redsofaliterary.com

Describe the kinds of works you want to represent. Dark middle grade horror, humor, and humorous memoir, New Age with a strong platform, history (Colonial US and British history are favorites), fiction and nonfiction for adults or middle grade, quirky nonfiction for adult, middle grade, and young adult.

Describe what you definitely don't want to represent. At this time, I do not want to represent young adult fantasy, sci-fi, or romance.

How do you want writers to pitch you? A short query to stacey@redsofaliterary.com. If I feel that we're a good fit, I'll request the first three chapters or a finished book proposal.

Describe your education and professional history. I have BS degrees in history and archaeology/anthropology from Oregon State University. I am the author of four books and multiple short stories, a screenwriter, ghostwriter, and editor.

How did you become an agent? After years of working in the field as a writer, I wanted to be a part of the business side of publishing. After speaking with my agent about working as an agent, she invited me to join her agency.

When and where were you born, and where have you lived? Born in Michigan. Lived in Michigan, California, Oregon, Wyoming, New York, and Virginia.

What do you like to do when you're not working? Raise five children and hide my nervous twitch.

Describe your personality. Organized, hardworking, quirky, funny, and curious.

What do you like reading/watching/listening to on your own time? Jane Austen and Shirley Jackson with a little Erma Bombeck thrown in for flavor.

What do the "Big 5" mean to you? The Big 5 mean an opportunity to reach a broader audience.

How do you feel about independent/small presses? Small presses can give an author more attention and involve the author in the process more than the Big 5 may be able to do.

What are your feelings about self-publishing? Self-publishers are workhorses. They learn the best part of publishing — and the ugliest. It can be an excellent education for authors if they stick it out.

What do you like and dislike about your job? I love the chance to work with writers to develop a career and not just a title.

What are ways prospective clients can impress you, and what are ways they can turn you off? To impress me, show that you've researched how the business of publishing works. Be proactive in the publishing community, either online or locally, and be open to constructive criticism to make the project stronger.

How would you describe the "writer from hell"? A writer who rejects without consideration solid edits in favor of his or her own vision.

Describe a book you would like to write. I'd love to write a coffee-table book on the history of the Ouija.

Agent's name and contact info: Erik Hane, Associate Literary Agent, erik@redsofaliterary.com

Describe the kinds of works you want to represent. Literary fiction, nonfiction (no memoir).

Describe what you definitely don't want to represent. I definitely don't want to represent fiction that sets out at the start to be "genre." I like reading it, but I don't think it's for me as an agent. Bring me genre elements, but I think I'd rather let the classification happen naturally. I also don't want memoir unless you've really, really got something unique and accessible. I also don't want to represent children's lit; that's another thing I really do love and appreciate but don't quite connect with professionally.

How do you want writers to pitch you? For fiction, I'd love to see a pitch letter (perhaps one that includes some comp titles) and a first chapter and will request more if interested. For nonfiction, a proposal that includes an overview of the project, a table of contents, a clear sense of who the author is and why he or she is the one to write the book, comparable titles, and some sample writing.

Describe your education and professional history. I graduated from Knox College with a major in writing and went from school to the Denver Publishing Institute. My first publishing job came soon after, as an editorial assistant and then assistant editor at Oxford University Press. I then moved to the Overlook Press as an acquiring editor, working on primarily upmarket nonfiction (history, biography, popular science), but I was lucky enough to work on some novels as well. Overlook's broad trade-publishing range combined with my experience at OUP has me comfortable with a wide variety of projects, and I look forward to seeing and representing this variety at Red Sofa.

How did you become an agent? I joined up with Red Sofa after moving from NYC to join the literary scene in Minneapolis in late 2015.

Knowing what you do now, would you do it again? If not, what might you do instead? Knowing what I do now, I would certainly go through the work and publishing experiences I've been lucky enough to have. Working in editorial departments at two vastly different houses has provided a frame of reference for the industry and has helped me learn what sorts of books I'd love to work on moving forward.

When and where were you born, and where have you lived? I was born in Naperville, Illinois, but grew up in Littleton, Colorado. I went to college in Galesburg, Illinois (Knox College), and moved from there to Manhattan. And now I'm here in the Twin Cities!

What do you like to do when you're not working? When not working, I play a lot of tennis (and table tennis when I can find it), and I actually write a fair amount of my own fiction. I follow the NFL and professional tennis pretty closely, so if there's football or tennis on, I'm probably watching it. And of course, I read for pleasure whenever I can.

List some of the titles you have recently placed with publishers. N/A; this is my first stretch both with Red Sofa and as an agent. I worked in-house as an editor the last few years.

Describe your personality. I'm pretty excitable. I'm pretty calm and quiet right up until I read or see or hear something that gets my creative muscles working and then I want to write about it, text everyone I know about it, learn as much as I can about it, and so forth. I've got a fairly dry sense of humor, too.

What do you like reading/watching/listening to on your own time? I love reading contemporary fiction. A few of my all-time favorite authors are Karen Russell, Marilynne Robinson, Michael Chabon, and Jonathan Safran Foer. I watch much more television than movies. Like everyone, I loved *Breaking Bad* and *Mad Men*, but I also really enjoy recent shows with polished, dry humor like *Archer* or *Bojack Horseman*. I listen mainly to podcasts: Bomani Jones is doing fantastic work right now, and the *New Yorker* has a few different podcasts I listen to regularly.

Do you think the business has changed a lot over the past few years? If yes, please explain.
Well, I've only been in the business three years, so my perspective is still limited, but from the in-house side, it felt like we were always trying to print more and more conservatively and to-order in any way that we could. Most changes I saw were in promotion/publicity: it now means less, I think, to have a good print review in a newspaper than to generate sustainable buzz on social-media platforms. Word of mouth is always most important, and the way we're talking about books is now changing. So will publicity campaigns.

What do the "Big 5" mean to you? Though I worked at first at an academic house (albeit a large one) and then a tiny independent press, I really like the Big 5. Someone in our industry has to command enough size and power to balance out Amazon's sometimes difficult influence, at least in part. And obviously, some of the best books and some of the best editors I know are at Big 5 houses.

How do you feel about independent/small presses? I love, love small presses. Worked as an editor at them, feel strongly about their mission. Small/independent presses can take risks or publish great books that wouldn't make sense for a larger house. Melville House, Soho Press, Gray Wolf, and my former employer, Overlook, are all examples of houses successfully doing things that wouldn't be possible at larger houses.

What are your feelings about self-publishing? I like self-publishing as long as it's situational. I don't think it's a substitute for traditional publishing: houses have too many resources and sales channels that are simply unavailable to most self-published authors. I do think self-publishing can work if authors have a clear platform or a base for promotion of their book. I also think it's important that those who are willing to pay to have a book produced have the option of doing so. But in most cases that should not be treated as the equivalent, as far as expectations go, of being published by a house.

What do you like and dislike about your job? I've always liked finding authors and projects most of all. The act of commissioning or searching or acquiring, whether I'm in-house or now working on the agency side, feels like the most exciting thing I could do. Reading something in Word-document form that I can absolutely see as a finished book is a terrific feeling, as is having a conversation with a whip-smart author who you can see is starting to put a book idea together.

What are ways prospective clients can impress you, and what are ways they can turn you off? Clear vision impresses me. What is your book, and why should someone pay to read it? And I think something that turns off anyone in the publishing industry is oversized bluster or expectations. It's not that I don't think your book could do really, really well, but if from the outset all you want to talk about is how many copies printed, how many sold, etc., I think that's starting off on the wrong foot and doesn't do justice to the process.

Telling me you expect your book to be a bestseller is a bit empty; obviously I want that, too! I'd rather focus on the book until it's truly time to talk commercial performance.

How would you describe the "writer from hell"? The writer from hell tries to be overly ornate rather than focusing on telling a good story and letting strong prose naturally develop. He or she also doesn't like edits and doesn't trust me. If we're working together, I trust you as the author; I like your book and can picture it doing well. Trust me to do what I can to make it a success on my end as well!

Describe a book you would like to write. As a fiction writer, I of course have the obligatory half-finished novel. That's my writing dream, probably. On nonfiction, I would love to write essays like Marilynne Robinson does (except about tennis). There's a certain kind of sports writing that I see barely any of and it looks nothing like what we typically call "sports writing." I hope I can write that someday. From my OUP days, I love evolutionary biology; there's an 800-page illustrated taxonomy/tree of life book I'd love to see, but I am in no way qualified to write. Guess I'll have to find that one.

Agent's name and contact info: Bree Ogden, Literary Agent, bree@redsofaliterary.com

Describe the kinds of works you want to represent. Highly artistic picture books (highbrow art, think *Varmints*). Young adult: anything *except* sci-fi, fantasy, paranormal, or dystopian. New adult: any genre as long as it has a strong romantic element. Adult: any genre, but preferred genres are transgressive, horror, noir, crime, mystery, thriller, bizarro, gothic, romance, erotica. Graphic novels. Some select nonfiction (*except* memoir or academia, humor, pop culture, art books).

Describe what you definitely don't want to represent. There are not a lot of genres that I completely close myself off to, but I won't represent any type of religious fiction or nonfiction or anything with paranormal elements. I'm not extremely keen on high fantasy or hard sci-fi, but if I find the right one…

How do you want writers to pitch you? Respectfully, coming from a place of professionalism, knowledge, and understanding. Always via email (unless in person at a place and time designated for pitching).

Describe your education and professional history. I have a bachelor's in philosophy and a master's in journalism with an emphasis in editing. I've been working in various areas of journalism for the past nine years. I started agenting in 2011 (after having interned at a literary agency for a year).

How did you become an agent? I began interning with Sharlene Martin at Martin Literary Management right out of my master's program and was promoted to agent a year later after training with and assisting Sharlene.

Knowing what you do now, would you do it again? If not, what might you do instead? I would absolutely do it again. I would have a better understanding of the genres I wanted to represent earlier in my career, but nothing else would change.

When and where were you born, and where have you lived? I was born and raised in Phoenix, Arizona. I attended college in California, Virginia, and Boston. I've since lived in Seattle and Salt Lake City.

What do you like to do when you're not working? Bubble baths and Netflix. I also still work as a freelance journalist on the side.

List some of the titles you have recently placed with publishers. Abigail Larson's *The Cats of Ulthar* (One Peace Books), Kate Watson's *Seeking Mansfield* (Jolly Fish Press), Christina Saunders's *Bad Bitch* series (St. Martin's), and Bonnie Burton's *Crafting with Feminism* (Quirk Books).

Describe your personality. Being able to successfully self-describe my personality is definitely not a personality trait that I possess.

What do you like reading/watching/listening to on your own time? Comics, anything in the horror or thriller genres, a lot of nonfiction, and classics (I prefer old gothic tales or dark fairy tales).

Do you think the business has changed a lot over the past few years? If yes, please explain. There is a constant ebb and flow to the publishing industry, but I'm not sure that in my time anything has drastically changed.

What do the "Big 5" mean to you? They are five of the largest, longest-standing publishers. They are filled with intelligent, hardworking individuals who put out fantastic reading material. That last sentence also applies to non–Big 5 publishers.

How do you feel about independent/small presses? I've had both wonderful and not-so-wonderful experiences with indie presses. The wonderful experiences outweigh the bad, but they've taught me that research is everything when considering selling to a small press. In my wonderful experiences with independent/small presses, I've seen that their attention to detail and utter devotion to their authors are paramount.

What are your feelings about self-publishing? Every author takes a different path to publication, and if self-publishing is the path that works for a certain author, that's wonderful. It frankly doesn't really concern me or my career unless it's my own client who wants to self-publish.

What do you like and dislike about your job? Every day brings different triumphs and struggles. But I will always love being able to call a client with news of an offer from a publisher, and I will always hate having to "shelf" a client's manuscript.

What are ways prospective clients can impress you, and what are ways they can turn you off? Talent always impresses me. Thinking outside of the box is very attractive, and having an understanding of the industry is a definite plus. Being too aggressive, whether it's via social media or email or in a query, will always be a turnoff.

How would you describe the "writer from hell"? Entitlement. I can't work with writers who feel entitled to being published. There is a lack of work ethic hidden inside entitlement.

Describe a book you would like to write. I always wanted to be a social analyst when I was younger. I love predicting social trends. If I ever wrote a book, I'd like to write a nonfiction book in the sociology arena.

Agent's name and contact info: Amanda Rutter, Associate Literary Agent, amanda@redsofaliterary.com

Describe the kinds of works you want to represent. Science fiction/fantasy, the non–young adult ideas; young adult and middle grade science fiction/fantasy.

Describe what you definitely don't want to represent. I am definitely not a nonfiction person. I rarely read it myself, so I wouldn't know where to start to represent it! Also, although I enjoy middle grade fiction and would be happy to represent it, I won't take on picture books.

How do you want writers to pitch you? With an email (to amanda@redsofaliterary.com) stating the genre, the word count, and a brief pitch of the novel. I don't like being approached via social media unless I am taking part in a specific contest.

Describe your education and professional history. I have no formal qualifications in literary arts; in fact, my degree subject was accounting. But my professional history includes acquisitions editor for Strange Chemistry, freelance editor for Bubblecow and Wise Ink Publishing, and book blogger.

How did you become an agent? I was approached when I left Strange Chemistry and asked if I had ever considered a role as a literary agent. I hadn't before then, but gave the matter a great deal of thought and was pleased to accept a position with Red Sofa when offered.

Knowing what you do now, would you do it again? If not, what might you do instead? Ha, well, I suppose I could go back to accounting! I wouldn't change a thing. I love working with authors and publishers and discovering new stories and voices.

When and where were you born, and where have you lived? I was born in Iserlohn, Germany, in 1980. Since then I have lived in over 20 houses in 3 different countries.

What do you like to do when you're not working? I am a complete yarn fiend! I knit and crochet and can be found on Ravelry under the name *magemanda*.

List some of the titles you have recently placed with publishers. I am still new to this and am preparing my clients' manuscripts for submission to publishers early in the new year!

Describe your personality. Absolutely passionate about reading and words, enthusiastic about what I love, sulky about things I don't (exercise key in that!), dedicated, and focused.

What do you like reading/watching/listening to on your own time? Reading: fantasy and science fiction of all flavors. Also partial to women's fiction, a little crime, and historical fiction. I am a Netflix addict and am currently working through the third season of *Orange Is the New Black*. Music-wise I am a rock chick — Slipknot are a love of mine.

Do you think the business has changed a lot over the past few years? If yes, please explain. Massively, and continues to do so. There is a lot of adjustment, thanks to the rise in ebooks and self-publishing, and now bookstores are coming up with new ways to entice customers. It's definitely exciting, but also means it's hard to know where the future lies.

How do you feel about independent/small presses? Very positive. I think they are able to take risks and focus on particular subjects and areas that perhaps the larger publishers aren't able to.

What are your feelings about self-publishing? Again, positive in general. I think that the increasing trend of authors treating it as a business and producing quality products is excellent and has introduced some really talented individuals to a wider readership.

What do you like and dislike about your job? I like discovering a brand-new voice, that feeling of excitement as you read a book and realize it is something special. I dislike the fact that "inbox, zero" is basically a pipe dream now!

What are ways prospective clients can impress you, and what are ways they can turn you off? They can impress me with a sharp and concise pitch for their novel that conveys, without going on for paragraphs and paragraphs, enough to entice me to read the novel. I dislike authors who feel as though they don't need to follow the rules — don't finish a novel before submitting, don't include the information I ask for, etc.

Describe a book you would like to write. I think the one series I would absolutely love to have written is the *Kushiel* books by Jacqueline Carey, starting with *Kushiel's Dart*. Those books are so clever, so progressive, so lushly written. I think they are genuine fantasy masterpieces.

Agent's name and contact info: Laura Zats, Associate Literary Agent, laura@redsofaliterary.com

Describe the kinds of works you want to represent. Adventurous, fun, STEM-inspired middle grade fiction. Diverse young adult of all kinds, especially smart, geeky manuscripts. Feminist romance and erotica with high-quality writing and fresh takes on tropes. Adult science fiction and fantasy that pass the Bechdel Test and/or the Mako Mori Test. Please note that I am actively searching for *diverse and feminist books* and *diverse and feminist authors* across all of my representative categories.

Describe what you definitely don't want to represent. Nonfiction, including memoir. Adult mystery, thriller, literary fiction. Fiction without quirky or distinctive hooks. Books that follow or fit in trends.

How do you want writers to pitch you? A simple query sent to my email address.

Describe your education and professional history. I received my BA from Grinnell College in English and anthropology. In 2011, I held my first editorial position at a publishing house in London. I've worked as an editor ever since and became an agent in 2013 quite by accident.

How did you become an agent? I was preparing to move to NYC in 2013 to begin my New York publishing career in editorial when I decided I needed to learn more about what an agent did. On a whim, I applied for an internship at Red Sofa Literary, the only agency in my hometown of St. Paul, Minnesota. Dawn hired me, and I signed my first author three months later.

Knowing what you do now, would you do it again? If not, what might you do instead? 10/10 would do again! I can't imagine my life being any different. I love being an author's biggest fan for a living.

When and where were you born, and where have you lived? I was born and raised (and still live) in St. Paul, Minnesota. I went to college in Grinnell, Iowa, and spent a short time living in London.

What do you like to do when you're not working? I craft, bake, watch copious amounts of geeky TV on Netflix, read (yes, really), kickbox, play pool, single-handedly support several microbreweries in the Twin Cities, and change the words of popular songs so that they are about my cats.

List some of the titles you have recently placed with publishers. *Kojiki* and *Kokoro* by Keith Yatsuhashi (Angry Robot), *The Dirty Secret* by Kira A. Gold (Carina).

Describe your personality. Nerdy INTJ. Type A with the ability to roll with the punches.

What do you like reading/watching/listening to on your own time? For books, I mostly just consume the same types of books I represent, although I do throw in some literary fiction every now and again. I listen to audiobooks and whatever album catches my eye from my record collection. For TV, everything and anything, *New Who*, Joss Whedon shows, media in the Marvel cinematic universe, *Drunk History*, and more.

What do the "Big 5" mean to you? An excuse to travel to New York and eat cheese with amazing editors! But in all seriousness the Big 5 represent one particular way of getting a book to its ideal readers. It doesn't mean anything beyond that unless both the publisher and the author work hard to get the book out there.

How do you feel about independent/small presses? I love small presses — I believe that every book has its own highest path, and some books might be better served being a big fish in a small pond and getting more attention. For me, success does not have anything to do with the size of a press.

What are your feelings about self-publishing? I am energized and excited about self-publishing. I think it's a great way to expand the market's definition of a "sellable" book. Many of my authors are hybrid authors, meaning they self-publish some books and go traditional with others.

What do you like and dislike about your job? I love everything about it except for two things: (1) saying no to people and (2) the fact that I will never again have a clean email inbox.

What are ways prospective clients can impress you, and what are ways they can turn you off? They can impress me by knowing about my list and what my goals are as an agent before they query me. Essentially, doing research puts you ahead of 95 percent of everyone who queries me. I am turned off when authors don't follow submission guidelines or don't want to hear my advice.

How would you describe the "writer from hell"? Hardheaded, aggressive, suspicious of me, and wanting to dictate how I do my job. A troll on social media and a general loose cannon where their public image is concerned.

REGINA RYAN PUBLISHING ENTERPRISES, INC. ❖

www.reginaryanbooks.com

251 Central Park West, 7 D, New York, NY 10024, 212-787-5589

Agent's name and contact info: Regina Ryan, reginaryan@reginaryanbooks.com

Describe the kinds of works you want to represent. I like to work on books that have something new and meaningful to say and are well written in a fresh, smart, stimulating way. I love a good story, so adventure stories are most welcome; also books that explore nature in all its variety but especially birds. Other areas I am interested in include fossils, paleontology, geology, architecture, history, science (particularly the brain), the environment, women's interest, cooking, psychology, health and wellness, diet, pets, lifestyle, sustainability, popular reference, true crime, and leisure activities including food, travel, and gardening.

Describe what you definitely don't want to represent. Fiction, screenplays, plays, poetry, or political tracts. I also don't like "woe is me" memoirs.

How do you want writers to pitch you? Please send a brief query letter to queries@ reginaryanbooks.com. If appropriate, attach a few pages of the actual text.

Describe your education and professional history. I was an English major at a small but rigorous Catholic women's college: Trinity in Washington, DC. After a brief stint in advertising, I began my publishing career at Alfred A. Knopf as an assistant. I became an editor and stayed there for 11 years. After that, I became editor in chief of the Adult Trade Division of Macmillan Publishing (I was the first woman to hold the position of editor in chief in a major hardcover house). I then went on my own and have worked as both a book packager and literary agent, eventually focusing more on agenting. I handle mainly adult nonfiction and some middle grade and picture books.

How did you become an agent? I was a book packager, but people came to me for agenting, and I eventually decided that I preferred that for a lot of reasons, but mainly because I really enjoyed interacting with people and their ideas rather than living on ideas out of my own head as a packager does.

Knowing what you do now, would you do it again? If not, what might you do instead? Might have become an agent earlier. I like being an agent!

Do you charge fees? If yes, please explain. Yes. I have charged fees as a consultant on a contract, for example, or for general advice and analysis for nonclients. I may have to charge a fee if I have to do a great deal of work on a proposal for a client, though I haven't yet. I don't charge a fee for reading submissions.

When and where were you born, and where have you lived? I was born in New York and grew up in Larchmont in Westchester. I've lived in Manhattan since shortly after I graduated from college.

What do you like to do when you're not working? I love to be outdoors, where I hike, take pictures, watch birds, and collect mushrooms and rocks. I love dinner with friends. I also read a great deal (mainly fiction), make lots of soup, and watch British mysteries on TV. I love baroque music and the opera and go to concerts often. I'm also a fan of dance and movies. And I spend a lot of time at the Metropolitan Museum, also MOMA, the Morgan, the NY Historical Society, and the AMNH.

List some of the titles you have recently placed with publishers. *Peterson's Guide to the Bird Sounds of North America* by Nathan Pieplow (Houghton Mifflin Harcourt, 2017), *Listening to a Continent Sing: Birdsong by Bicycle from the Atlantic to the Pacific* by Donald Kroodsma (Princeton University Press, 2016), *Dr. Petty's Pain Relief for Dogs: The Complete Medical and Integrative Guide to Treating Pain* by Michael Petty (Countryman Press, 2016), *Hair: A Human History* by Kurt Stenn, MD (Pegasus, 2016), *The Friendly Orange Glow: The Untold Story of the Plato System and the Dawn of Cyberculture* by Brian Dear (Pantheon, 2017), *Persuade the Lizard: Seven Secrets of Persuasion Based on the New Science of the Mind* by Jim Crimmins, PhD (Career Press, 2017), *What's Wrong with My Weed?* by David Deardorf, PhD, and Kathryn Wadsworth (Ten Speed Press, 2017), *Craft Wine* by Richard Bender (Storey Press, 2017), *The Boy Who Became Buffalo Bill: Growing Up Billy Cody in Bleeding Kansas* by Andrea Warren (Two Lions Press).

Describe your personality. I am a basically happy, optimistic soul, always looking for the positive. I'm quite social but on the quiet side. I love to laugh and aim to have fun. I'm a good organizer.

What do you like reading/watching/listening to on your own time? After a long day's work, I like to veg out watching British mysteries (preferably) on TV, but almost any mystery will do. I mainly read fiction: read all three Ferrante novels this summer in one go, loved Anthony Doerr's *All the Light We Cannot See*. All that said, I have really been enjoying the great nonfiction book *The Invention of Nature: Alexander von Humbolt's New World* by Andrea Wolff. Also the very beautiful and moving *The Hare with Amber Eyes* by Edmund de Waal. I'd be thrilled to represent books like these!

When I can get outdoors, I love to hike and observe nature. And when in my office, and no one else is around, I happily play my Pandora radio station based around Paul Simon. I love discovering "new" artists on there like Steve Winwood or J. J. Cale.

Do you think the business has changed a lot over the past few years? If yes, please explain. It has changed tremendously. There are fewer publishers, they publish fewer books, and they pay less money (for the most part). It has gotten a lot tougher for everyone.

What do the "Big 5" mean to you? Huge publishers who demand huge platforms of authors.

How do you feel about independent/small presses? I say thank God for them.

What are your feelings about self-publishing? I think it's a very, very hard way to go, and I don't encourage people to do it, but sometimes it's the only way.

Do you think Amazon is good or bad — or both — for the book business? Definitely both. It keeps books available that would otherwise not be, but it also constrains publishers as to what they publish, much as Barnes & Noble used to. I guess that's just the way the business goes, but it can be very frustrating.

What do you like and dislike about your job? Because I choose my projects based on what interests me and also take great care to avoid annoying authors, I love my books and my authors. I treasure the constant arrival of exciting new ideas. I dislike having to deal endlessly with so many pesky problems — often on ancient books — with royalty departments, foreign contracts, options. There is no end to the work. I also dislike having to turn down so many projects, disappointing so many hopeful would-be authors.

What are ways prospective clients can impress you, and what are ways they can turn you off? I am really impressed by savvy authors who have taken the time to understand the business of publishing, especially how to write a good proposal and how much authors have to do these days as partners with the publisher. I am turned off by authors who may have a good idea but don't make the effort to figure out how to develop it into a selling proposal. I am also very turned off by authors who resent the fact that they are expected to do publicity as part of the deal or who always feel they are being cheated somehow.

How would you describe the "writer from hell"? Someone who apparently has a tickler file that results in my being bugged on a constant and regular basis for answers I don't have. Or worse, someone who has such a sense of entitlement to my services that they expect everything from me and give nothing in return — not even thanks.

Describe a book you would like to write. I had begun a book some years back when I first got married to my husband, who is Jewish, and realized how my Catholic education had given me a very limited and warped — even biased — view of Jews. Never had the time to finish it. But the world has changed, and I don't think the book is needed any longer. I have another idea, but I'm not telling. Besides, I still have no time!

Do you believe in a higher and/or lower "power"? I believe in the power of evolution and the big bang.

RENAISSANCE LITERARY & TALENT ❖ renaissancemgmt.net

PO Box 17379, Beverly Hills, CA 90209, 323-848-8305

Agent's name and contact info: Eddie Pietzak, eddie@renaissancemgmt.net

Describe the kinds of works you want to represent. Biography, memoir, historical fiction, science fiction, pop culture, business, culinary, political, self-help, humor.

Describe what you definitely don't want to represent. Fantasy, erotica.

How do you want writers to pitch you? In a clear, concise manner that gives me a complete picture of what your story is about.

Describe your education and professional history. Graduate of Ithaca College, originally worked at Abrams Artists Agency before working at Renaissance Literary & Talent.

Do you charge fees? If yes, please explain. No.

When and where were you born, and where have you lived? New York; currently reside in Los Angeles.

What do you like to do when you're not working? Music, cooking, volunteering at my favorite animal shelter.

List some of the titles you have recently placed with publishers. The Best Cat Book Ever by Kate Funk, *The Best Cat Book Ever: Part II* by Kate Funk, *A Carlin Home Companion* by Kelly Carlin.

What are ways prospective clients can impress you, and what are ways they can turn you off? I'm always impressed first and foremost by authors' talent and passion for their craft.

RICHARD CURTIS ASSOCIATES, INC. ❖ www.curtisagency.com

200 East 72nd Street, Suite 28J, New York, NY 10021, 212-772-7363, fax: 212-772-7393

Agent's name and contact info: Richard Curtis, President, rcurtis@curtisagency.com

Describe the kinds of works you want to represent. Women's fiction, science fiction and fantasy, thrillers, pop culture, middle grade and young adult, nonfiction in the fields of business, science, history, and biography.

Describe what you definitely don't want to represent. Graphic fiction, kiddie books, cozy romances, horror.

How do you want writers to pitch you? One-page letter with SASE.

Describe your education and professional history. Master's degree in English and American studies, worked for literary agency, then worked as a freelance writer, then started my own agency in 1980s. Started first independent ebook publisher in 1999, sold it in 2014. Author of over 50 published books.

How did you become an agent? Worked for an agent and discovered it suited my soul.

Knowing what you do now, would you do it again? If not, what might you do instead?
Yes, I'd do it all over again, but I sometimes fantasize I might have become a humorist, a playwright, a rabbi, a catcher, or a linebacker.

Do you charge fees? If yes, please explain. No.

When and where were you born, and where have you lived? Born in Bronx, New York; raised in Forest Hills, New York; moved to suburban South Shore as a teen; now live in Manhattan.

What do you like to do when you're not working? I write plays.

List some of the titles you have recently placed with publishers. *The Drafter* by Kim Harrison, *Chainsaw Confidential* by Gunnar Hansen, *War Dogs* by Greg Bear, *Love Her Madly* by Elizabeth Lee.

Describe your personality. A Renaissance dilettante.

What do you like reading/watching/listening to on your own time? Read biographies (especially lives of composers), military history, and plays; love watching sports.

Do you think the business has changed a lot over the past few years? If yes, please explain.
I could write volumes, and I have. We have shifted from a business run by entrepreneurial individualists to one run by committees of nervous middle-management executives.

What do the "Big 5" mean to you? Only that tomorrow they will be the Big 4.

How do you feel about independent/small presses? God bless them.

What are your feelings about self-publishing? More power to the authors.

Do you think Amazon is good or bad — or both — for the book business? Good, bad, both.

What do you like and dislike about your job? Love the people, hate the cash flow.

What are ways prospective clients can impress you, and what are ways they can turn you off? Just tell me a good story, and I'm all ears.

How would you describe the "writer from hell"? Read my book *The Client from Hell and Other Publishing Satires* and find out: www.amazon.com/Client-Hell-Other-Publishing -Satires-ebook/dp/B00J52G4EU/ref=sr_1_1?s=books&ie=UTF8&qid=1449765155&sr=1 -1&keywords=the+client+from+hell+by+richard+curtis.

Describe a book you would like to write. A personal history of the ebook revolution.

Do you believe in a higher and/or lower "power"? I believe in intelligent design. I just don't know who the designer is.

THE RIGHTS FACTORY ❖ therightsfactory.com

1902 Seventh Avenue, #2A, New York, NY 10026

Agent's name and contact info: Natalie Kimber, Associate Agent, natalie@therightsfactory.com

Describe the kinds of works you want to represent. I like to represent works that encompass great storytelling while providing a new way to see and experience a topic through the medium of literature. Works that are about risky topics and works that are experimental in form excite me. I like to represent works that provide progressive insight and challenge a traditional, possibly outdated, worldview. I love literary fiction, LGBT writing, memoir, international writers, lifestyle, pop culture, history, music, science and sustainability, peace studies, graphic novels, and spiritual writing that remains intellectual.

Describe what you definitely don't want to represent. I usually don't want to represent books about ghosts, goblins, vampires, werewolves, or witches. I also don't usually go for anything involving finance, politics, or sports.

How do you want writers to pitch you? Please send a query describing your book as effectively as possible, and do include a sample or whatever you've got in lieu of a proposal or manuscript. *Do* always provide an author biography and links to any platform-related material across the Web.

Describe your education and professional history. I am a graduate of Georgetown University (2010), and I began my literary career working for a traditional boutique agency, Literary and Creative Artists, Inc., in 2007. I next worked as the operations and client manager for Georgetown University's Booklab (Office of Scholarly and Literary Publications), where I helped fiction and nonfiction projects find representation and/or publication by academic and trade presses. I started an independent agency, the Sun Rae Agency, in 2010 and joined with the Rights Factory as their NYC-based agent in 2014.

Do you charge fees? If yes, please explain. No.

When and where were you born, and where have you lived? I grew up in the west-side suburbs of Denver, Colorado, and I have since lived in Washington, DC; Albuquerque and Santa Fe, New Mexico; and New York City.

What do you like to do when you're not working? I love to experience nature and culture via walking and exploring parks and places of interest. I enjoy cooking, especially Southwest cuisine, and I always enjoy time with friends and family. I also love films, especially prior to the year 2000.

Describe your personality. I am an aesthete and a theist. I find myself moved by all forms of art, and I appreciate compassion, sincerity, and awareness. I have a very nostalgic side, always curious about the past and what it has to teach us. My other side loves modernity, appreciating intrepid vision and the progressive beauty of form and intellect across life-style and art.

What do the "Big 5" mean to you? Only a small percentage of books make it through to be published by the Big 5, but they are always professional, beautiful products and always worth reading. The people at the Big 5 are real people who absolutely love books and everything about literary life, and they commit their experience and skills to creating and maintaining the traditional publishing industry.

How do you feel about independent/small presses? Although they are smaller, independent presses offer the traditional publishing experience with distribution, vision, and talent. Often, the people running independent presses are just as skilled and talented at creating beautiful and compelling books as the Big 5, and any writer should be as enthusiastic about working with them as they would the larger operations. Smaller presses take on more risk, and one will find the people running them are astonishingly dedicated to their vision and their writers.

What are your feelings about self-publishing? Self-publishing can offer writers a way to get their book out, but there is most often no match for having an experienced publisher, large or small, produce your book. They will give you the best possible product and distribution, which self-publishing cannot offer in most circumstances. As with many things, the more skilled people involved in creating a product, the better the product. When a team of people who love creating books help to create yours, you'll love it much more than anything you could do on your own.

RITA ROSENKRANZ LITERARY AGENCY ❖

www.ritarosenkranzliteraryagency.com

440 West End Avenue, #15D, New York, NY 10024-5358, 212-873-6333

Agent's name and contact info: Rita Rosenkranz, rrosenkranz@mindspring.com

Describe the kinds of works you want to represent. All areas of adult nonfiction.

How do you want writers to pitch you? Via email or regular mail.

Do you charge fees? If yes, please explain. No.

Describe your education and professional history. Former editor at major New York publishing houses. Started agency in 1990.

List some of the titles you have recently placed with publishers. How Ordinary and Extraordinary People Have Transformed Their Lives through Learning — And You Can Too by Barbara Oakley (Tarcher), *On the Verge: Wake Up, Show Up, and Shine* by Cara Bradley (New World Library), *Lost Science* by Kitty Ferguson (Sterling), *Power to the Poet* by Diane Luby Lane (Beyond Words/Atria Books), *Bulletins from Dallas* by William P. Sanderson (Skyhorse).

RLR ASSOCIATES, LTD. ❖ www.rlrassociates.net

7 West 51st Street, New York, NY 10019, 212-541-8641

Agent's name and contact info: Scott Gould, sgould@rlrassociates.net

Describe the kinds of works you want to represent. We represent literary and commercial fiction (including genre fiction) and all kinds of well-written, narrative nonfiction, with a particular interest in history, pop culture, humor, food and beverage, biography, and sports. We also represent all types of children's literature.

Describe what you definitely don't want to represent. Screenplays.

How do you want writers to pitch you? Email me a query letter explaining the book, along with your writing credits. If it's fiction, paste the first chapter in the email.

Describe your education and professional history. As a literary agent for RLR, I oversee all book development within the firm. I began my career in the editorial department of *Playboy* magazine and later in publicity at Tor/Forge. I am a graduate of New York University, where I received a BA in English and American literature.

How did you become an agent? I wanted to be a part of publishing books. I got a taste of agenting while interning for a small agency in SoHo (shout-out to Ethan Ellenberg, great guy!), moved around a bit in the industry, and found my way back.

Knowing what you do now, would you do it again? If not, what might you do instead? You're getting rather existential here, my man.

Do you charge fees? If yes, please explain. No.

When and where were you born, and where have you lived? Born and raised in Baltimore, lived the last half of my life in NYC.

What do you like to do when you're not working? I love reading (obviously), and it's probably my number-one hobby. And not just books, but all kinds of media (I had at one point, I think, 17 magazine subscriptions). Second to that is trying to live a robust social life — eating, drinking, traveling with friends and family. Is there anything better than hearing a good story at the table after the dessert is cleared away and you're still sipping on the last glass of bourbon?

List some of the titles you have recently placed with publishers. *Dodge City Days: Wyatt Earp, Bat Masterson, and the Taming of the American West* by Tom Clavin (St. Martin's), *Candy Cane Lane* by Scott Santoro (Simon & Schuster Children's), *Big Blue Wrecking Crew: LT, Simms, Parcells, and the '86 Champs* by Jerry Barca (St. Martin's), *American Wino: A Story of Reds, Whites, and One Writer's Blues* by Dan Dunn (Dey Street), *Kicks* by *Slam* magazine (Rizzoli), *Great American Craft Beer* by Andy Crouch (Running Press).

Describe your personality. Even-tempered, a listener, a critic.

What do you like reading/watching/listening to on your own time? Slightly unhinged fiction: Sam Lipsyte, Martin Amis, Michael Kimball, et al.; essays: Tim Kreider, Geoff Dyer; comics: Frank Miller, Alan Moore; history; true crime. The list goes on. TV: I believe we are in the golden age of TV: *The Wire, The Sopranos, Eastbound and Down, Louis, Breaking Bad.*

Do you think the business has changed a lot over the past few years? If yes, please explain. Not too much. That electronic shift happened more than a few years ago.

What do the "Big 5" mean to you? Curation, structure, money, the power center of trade publishing. And now that we're 5, we hope even stronger to keep Amazon's terms in line.

How do you feel about independent/small presses? The ones that know their identity and care deeply about their authors can be great. But it's tough to make a living with small presses.

What are your feelings about self-publishing? I think it can be fantastic for a very small number of writers.

Do you think Amazon is good or bad — or both — for the book business? It's kind of like love in an abusive relationship. They're incomparable at many things, especially making books available and easy to buy for absolutely everyone, but there seems to be a tendency to treat book culture like a soulless widget.

What do you like and dislike about your job? My job is finding and shaping compelling work and shepherding it out into the world. Then putting out countless fires.

What are ways prospective clients can impress you, and what are ways they can turn you off? Impress by having a clear vision of one's work and its place in the world. Turn off by calling to pitch a book.

How would you describe the "writer from hell"? Crazy is crazy. You can't really give it a definition, can you?

Describe a book you would like to write. That's your job!

Do you believe in a higher and/or lower "power"? Let me refer you to an old friend of mine, Mr. Hitchens.

ROBIN STRAUS AGENCY, INC. ❖ www.robinstrausagency.com

229 East 79th Street, Suite 5A, New York, NY 10075, 212-472-3282, fax: 212-472-3833

Agent's name and contact info: Robin Straus, info@robinstrausagency.com

Describe the kinds of works you want to represent. High-quality literary fiction and non-fiction. The subject is of less importance than fine writing and research.

Describe what you definitely don't want to represent. Most "genre" fiction, screenplays, juveniles.

How do you want writers to pitch you? Please see our website for submission information. We like a great query letter and sample material that speaks for itself. Caution: we are a very small agency and take on very few new clients.

Describe your education and professional history. BA, Wellesley College; MBA, NYU School of Business.

How did you become an agent? I started at Little, Brown, thinking I'd become an editor, but I became very interested in the business end, so I moved to subsidiary rights at Doubleday and then Random House. But I missed working with authors, and agenting seemed the best way to combine everything. I spent four years at Wallace & Sheil Agency and then started my own agency in 1983.

Knowing what you do now, would you do it again? If not, what might you do instead? I love my work being an advocate for writers, working with them on many books over many years. I would also have probably been happy being a doctor or raising horses and dogs.

Do you charge fees? If yes, please explain. Commission.

When and where were you born, and where have you lived? I was born in New Jersey and have lived in NYC since graduation from college.

List some of the titles you have recently placed with publishers. Works by Alexander McCall Smith, Antony Beevor, Jimmy Connors, Andrew Hacker, Sheila Kohler, David Doubilet, Peter Watson, and Simon Callow.

What do you like reading/watching/listening to on your own time? I'm an eclectic reader, watcher, and listener! A good writer can make his or her work captivate even when I'm not initially drawn to the subject. Ditto for movies and music. I don't like violence, however.

What do the "Big 5" mean to you? I work with the Big 5 and with independent/small presses.

What are your feelings about self-publishing? I think authors benefit most from working with skilled editors and publishers. There is a ton of junk being self-published.

What do you like and dislike about your job? If you don't like to read, if you aren't organized and detail-oriented, and if you are not a people person who enjoys matchmaking and selling, I wouldn't recommend agenting. When I represent an author, I work with him or her to help shape proposals and manuscripts to entice editors to make an offer. I submit material to publishers, negotiate contracts, vet royalty statements, and sell translation, serial, film, and audio rights on behalf of clients. I generally act as the business manager for the author and intercede whenever necessary throughout the entire publishing process. I view my relationship with my clients as a continuum that extends over many books. I like helping to shape a writer's career, and I like the fact that I have my hand in all aspects of the publishing process.

What are ways prospective clients can impress you, and what are ways they can turn you off? Blow me away with your prose and ideas. Watch your grammar, avoid clichés, and don't overstate claims that a book is revolutionary. Be receptive to suggestions on how to improve your work and understand that publishing works best as a collaborative effort. Be imaginative about how to market yourself and your books.

How would you describe the "writer from hell"? Someone who calls to complain every morning at 9.

THE ROHM LITERARY AGENCY ❖ therohmliteraryagency.com

New York, NY, 646-845-0185

Agent's name and contact info: Wendy Goldman Rohm, wendy@rohmliterary.com

Describe the kinds of works you want to represent. Literary fiction, narrative nonfiction, investigative journalism, poetry, plays, and screenplays. We also work with memoir, commercial fiction, inspirational, young adult, and business authors.

In addition to representing our author clients to top publishers, the agency offers ghostwriting services, developmental editing, and collaborative projects between authors and subjects. At a time when the publishing world is changing greatly, we have taken an innovative approach to nurturing individual talent as well as developing collaborations between writers, artists, publishers, and producers across many platforms.

How do you want writers to pitch you? Query letter by email *only*; no paper mail or packages or email attachments unless we ask to see your manuscript based on your query letter.

Describe your education and professional history. As a *New York Times* bestselling author, I have taught and lectured for MediaBistro, Yale University, onboard the QEII, and at numerous universities and organizations in the US, Europe, and Asia. I am in the unusual position of understanding the publishing world from the creative side as well as the business side, having worked in publishing as an author as well as an agent and developmental editor for more than two decades.

I am adept at promotion and public appearances, having personally been a commentator on numerous national and international television and radio broadcasts, including *Nightline*, the *Today* show, *NBC Nightly News*, and *Good Morning America*. I have also been an expert researcher for Townsend & Crew, Skadden Arps, and Conlin Associates, among many others.

How did you become an agent? I learned both sides of the business, having decades of experience as an author myself. I'd been invited to speak at universities and for media organizations worldwide and to present at a series of Master's Teas at Yale. When I had time, I began to teach a writing workshop based on those very popular presentations at Yale. I began getting my best students book contracts and became an associate agent at a couple of major NY agencies. From there, I launched my own agency.

Knowing what you do now, would you do it again? If not, what might you do instead? Yes, I love what I do. I work with marvelous, talented people around the world. Great books will always be published, and great writers need nurturing now, as they always have throughout history. Ignore all the noise about what can or can't be done in book publishing these days. Show me a great piece of work — that's all that matters. The rest will be addressed. Writers should write, not worry about marketing or money issues. Leave that up to the businesspeople.

Do you charge fees? If yes, please explain. No fees for representing our clients. Like all agents, if we offer to represent you, you pay us nothing. We get paid by the publisher when we get you a book contract — 15 percent, as is customary. We use the standard agency contract in use by most major literary agencies in the US.

For some clients, we do ghostwriting or developmental editing. These are high-end services for which there is a fee. If you need extensive help restructuring and rewriting your book, you need a developmental editor. A quote for a project will be given upon request. (Light copyediting of your manuscript is done at no charge before we submit your work to publishers.)

List some of the titles you have recently placed with publishers. The Rohm Agency currently provides literary representation and management for a wide range of authors including novelists, journalists, politicians, scientists, business leaders, screenwriters, and playwrights. Among these are Parisian author, artist, and filmmaker Hélène Guétary; Italian literary journalist/author Livia Manera Sambuy (*Philip Roth: Unmasked*); poet/novelist Taiye Selasi; novelist Bruno Garel; quant genius Igor Tulchinsky; and author and Fulbright scholar Dr. Bhaswati Bhattacharya. Global clients have included author and guru Linus Torvalds (*Just for Fun*, HarperCollins), novelist Sarayu Srivatsa (*The Last Pretence*, HarperCollins India), and many others.

THE RUDY AGENCY ❖ rudyagency.com

449 West 56th Street, Suite 7A, New York, NY 10019, 917-497-9906

Agent's name and contact info: Maryann Karinch, Founder, mak@rudyagency.com

Describe the kinds of works you want to represent. In nonfiction, I look for books in these categories: advice/relationships, biography, business/investing/finance, health, history, politics/current affairs, how-to, lifestyle, memoir, narrative, pop culture, science, sports, and true crime. In the area of fiction, I prefer literary fiction, particularly books that explore the psyche. I am also open to quirky fiction and nonfiction, which might be funny, irreverent, macabre, and/or outrageous.

Describe what you definitely don't want to represent. Poetry, religious works (except those that are historical in nature).

How do you want writers to pitch you? For nonfiction, I'd like a roughly 300-word email query stating specifically what the book is about and why the author is the ideal person to write it. For fiction, a slightly longer query is fine. The query should display the writing ability of the author.

Describe your education and professional history. I have a BA and MA in speech and drama from the Catholic University of America in Washington, DC, and am certified as a personal trainer by the American Council on Exercise. My early career involved managing a professional theater and then doing corporate fund-raising for a museum. I spent a decade in high-tech in marketing communications and then went into publishing, first as a nonfiction author, then as an agent/author.

How did you become an agent? My agent didn't pay attention to me after she had a baby, so I considered who would be the best person to represent me and decided I was that person. And I seemed to be helping other writers all the time anyway, so I thought I would turn that into a business.

Knowing what you do now, would you do it again? If not, what might you do instead?
Absolutely, I would do it again.

Do you charge fees? If yes, please explain. No.

When and where were you born, and where have you lived? I was born in rural Pennsylvania the day of the first public performance of Samuel Beckett's *Waiting for Godot*. I have lived in Karinchville, Pennsylvania (seriously); Washington, DC; Youngstown, Ohio; Bethesda, Maryland; Marion, Massachusetts; Fairfax and Alexandria, Virginia; Mill Valley, El Granada, and Half Moon Bay, California; and Estes Park, Colorado.

What do you like to do when you're not working? Read fun books like *The Bully Pulpit*, exercise, golf, travel, and cook.

List some of the titles you have recently placed with publishers. Golf pro Ji Kim's *Circle of Golf* to help new and experienced golfers find their best swing; *Saving Delaney, Saving Me* by Keston Ott-Dahl and Andrea Ott-Dahl, the first-person surrogacy story of how the authors tried to help another lesbian couple have a baby only to be faced with heartache and the threat of lawsuits for not terminating the pregnancy when they learned the fetus had Down syndrome; and *Snipers*, which features profiles and stories of single-shot warriors, by former military interrogator Lena Sisco, author of *You're Lying!*

Describe your personality. Curious, adaptable, playful, hopeful, determined, resilient, loving.

What do you like reading/watching/listening to on your own time? I like reading/watching/listening to things that stimulate opinions, entertain, and often lead to lively discussion. My idea of good TV, for example, is *Modern Family* and my favorite radio program is *Wait, Wait Don't Tell Me!* on NPR. (I aspire to be a panelist.) I also love the classic songs written by people like the Gershwins, Cole Porter, John Kander and Fred Ebb, and other greats of Broadway.

Do you think the business has changed a lot over the past few years? If yes, please explain.
Yes. Many editors don't have the time to engage in the give-and-take with authors that I benefitted from early in my writing career. The strong emphasis on having something "ready to publish" disappoints authors who had hoped to receive guidance and nurturing from a professional. I find myself trying to fill the void.

What do the "Big 5" mean to you? They mean opportunity when the author has a strong platform and a product with broad consumer appeal. They mean nothing when the author is in the building phase of platform development, regardless of the project. I'm not saying that's bad; it's business.

How do you feel about independent/small presses? Glad they exist. I've had extremely good experiences with a few of them, who did far more to support the author with aggressive promotion than larger publishers.

What are your feelings about self-publishing? It's perfect for authors who want maximum control, have plenty of cash on hand, and know something about marketing. It's also perfect for authors who think more of their work than anyone else does.

Do you think Amazon is good or bad — or both — for the book business? Because I've made some deals with commercial publishing arms of Amazon, I have a very favorable impression of their editorial staff. I also think their practice of monthly reporting and payment of royalties is laudable. If I look at Amazon as a bookseller only, I have mixed feelings, but understandably I don't want to criticize a bookseller that has contributed a lot to my success as an author.

What do you like and dislike about your job? I like the flood of new ideas that comes into my inbox every day. I dislike the way some people can't take no for an answer and haunt me for weeks.

What are ways prospective clients can impress you, and what are ways they can turn you off? Authors who do their homework about the agency impress me. Authors whose confidence about their work might best be described as narcissistic turn me off. The best authors I've known are professionals who balance confidence and humility.

How would you describe the "writer from hell"? It's the person who acts like he or she is the center of my life and how dare I take time to visit my mother when I should be out there trying to get a six-figure deal.

Describe a book you would like to write. I want to write a psychological thriller set in the late 19th or early 20th century.

Do you believe in a higher and/or lower "power"? As much as I like to give a "yes" or "no" to a yes-or-no question, I'm simply going to say that I respect legitimate hierarchies.

Is there anything you wish to express beyond the parameters of the preceding questions? Gratitude. Especially gratitude to Dr. Joan S. Dunphy, my first editor at New Horizon Press and the first person who encouraged me to be an agent. She is someone I will hold close in my heart forever. She passed away October 3, 2015, and heaven is a better place now.

Agent's name and contact info: Jak Burke, jak@rudyagency.com

Describe the kinds of works you want to represent. Children's and young adult. I remember a famous DJ at the BBC talking about why he loved what he did. "I want to discover the next Beatles." It was that simple. As an agent you want to scout that next genius and to help gift the world of literature with a classic timeless work of art.

Describe what you definitely don't want to represent. I don't want to represent badly written, overly didactic, dull stories that are not applicable to a child's world.

How do you want writers to pitch you? I ask for a concise query email that contains a sales-pitch synopsis of the submission and a short bio. If I am interested, I will request the first 50 pages for young adult, the first 20 pages for middle grade, and the entire manuscript plus illustrations for picture books, by mail.

Describe your education and professional history. Green Card holder as an illustrator of "exceptional ability." I have a BA with honors degree in English literature and a teaching diploma (TEFFLA) and am a graduate of Sergio Ruzzio's (School of Visual Arts) course on children's literature. I am a published author and CEO of a parent hub, Baby Does NYC. I have spent 10 years directly working within the juvenile sector and, as such, know oodles about which books stick with kids and which books do not — and why.

How did you become an agent? I saw an opportunity to represent children's literature at the Rudy Agency (Maryann represents me for my nonfiction work), and I proposed myself.

Knowing what you do now, would you do it again? If not, what might you do instead? Yes! I would have done it sooner. I love what I do.

Do you charge fees? If yes, please explain. No.

When and where were you born, and where have you lived? I was born in London. I have lived in London, Wales, Ireland, and France, and now I live in NYC.

What do you like to do when you're not working? I like to read books, watch movies, doodle, write, hike, sing, and jump in puddles.

List some of the titles you have recently placed with publishers. I'm too new to the game at this point; however, I have had tremendous response to our first properties.

Describe your personality. I am positive, sensitive, and curious.

What do you like reading/watching/listening to on your own time? I love to watch classic sci-fi movies or thrillers. I read a lot of nonfiction, usually about historical events and big personalities. I indulge in New Age titles that deal in fringe topics. I also binge-watch Netflix shows and movies, plus I also like to relax to reality TV and *Masterpiece Theatre* on PBS.

Do you think the business has changed a lot over the past few years? If yes, please explain. I am entering the business now with huge progress in digital and self-publishing platforms, and yet I also see trends of parents reading traditional printed books to their children and turning away from digital media. I am optimistic about how the market will sort itself out.

What do the "Big 5" mean to you? Opportunity.

How do you feel about independent/small presses? Niche is here to stay. Small presses keep the publishing industry fresh and relevant.

What are your feelings about self-publishing? I believe that with the right voice and platform anyone can become famous. Self-publishing has evened the playing field. That's good for everyone.

Do you think Amazon is good or bad — or both — for the book business? It is necessary.

What do you like and dislike about your job? I like opening my mailbox and receiving a surprise submission — something that takes my breath away and makes me forget to eat. I don't dislike anything.

What are ways prospective clients can impress you, and what are ways they can turn you off? When they follow the guidelines. When they don't follow the guidelines.

How would you describe the "writer from hell"? It is someone who is rigid and won't listen to constructive criticism.

Describe a book you would like to write. I would like to write a book about time travel that felt plausible.

Do you believe in a higher and/or lower "power"? Yes — both.

Is there anything you wish to express beyond the parameters of the preceding questions? To write for children requires a belief in magic, because children still have one foot in the realm of all-possibility.

Agent's name and contact info: Hilary Claggett, claggett@rudyagency.com

Describe the kinds of works you want to represent. I most enjoy representing books that seek to make a meaningful impact on the world in the areas of current events, politics, foreign policy, international relations, diplomacy, counterterrorism, military studies, veterans' issues, global issues, human rights, civil rights, social and political movements, environment, energy, health, psychology, and journalism/news/media. I especially love a well-written memoir, even though they are tough to sell. I also like travel, individual sports (e.g., marathoning, motorcycling), adventure, and motivational books. Music, fashion, social media, and pop culture are also keen interests.

Describe what you definitely don't want to represent. No fiction, children's books, business books.

How do you want writers to pitch you? An emailed proposal with a sample chapter would be fine. Please don't forget to include the anticipated word count and completion date.

Describe your education and professional history. I have a master's degree in international affairs from Columbia University's School of International and Public Affairs with dual specializations in national security policy and Russian/Soviet studies. My BA is from the University of California, Santa Cruz, where I completed dual majors in politics and Russian. I have worked in the publishing industry for nearly three decades.

How did you become an agent? I began freelancing for the Rudy Agency in 2013 because I had worked with Maryann Karinch for several years in an editorial capacity, and I respected her business acumen, knowledge of the publishing industry, and professionalism.

Knowing what you do now, would you do it again? If not, what might you do instead? I love being a literary agent, and I plan to do it in some capacity for the foreseeable future. It's a little too late for me to become a rock star, although I'm not swearing off the idea of starting the oldest all-girl garage band in history.

Do you charge fees? If yes, please explain. No.

When and where were you born, and where have you lived? This is not a short answer. Born in Concord, Massachusetts, I've lived in 11 states on both coasts and in between; I've lived in San Francisco, Washington, DC, Dallas, New York City, Arkansas, Minneapolis, Cincinnati, Chicago, and various towns in New Jersey and Connecticut.

What do you like to do when you're not working? Run races and train for races, from 5K to 50K, including destination half marathons and full marathons. I also love to socialize. "Networking" is considered an ugly term by millennials for some reason, but I happily combine a very active social life with meeting new friends and expanding my networks. My favorite part of being an agent is meeting new people and learning new things. My nonnetworking volunteer work is centered on homeless people and homeless pets. Maybe because I move around so much. ☺

List some of the titles you have recently placed with publishers. *Own Your Cancer* by Dr. Peter Edelstein (Lyons Press).

Describe your personality. Straightforward, no BS, but not too blunt. I am fun to be around.

What do you like reading/watching/listening to on your own time? This is beginning to look like a Facebook profile, but here goes. Reading: For the past few years I've been obsessed with running and racing, so I've been reading running memoirs. The best are those by Scott Jurek and Kathrine (this is the correct spelling) Switzer. I also like "biographies" of cities such as Detroit and Chicago. I recently went to Cuba for a half marathon and read half a book (about Cuba, not half marathons) in preparation. When I was obsessed with motorcycles, I read motorcycle memoirs, like *Purple Mountains* and *The Perfect Vehicle*.

Watching: Comedy, comedy, comedy, from stand-up (Amy Schumer) to sitcoms (*Broad City*) to animated series (*Archer*, *Bojack Horseman*). Favorite shows: *Mad Men* and any of Anthony Bourdain's series.

Listening: Anything rock-related from the 1950s to the present, including rockabilly, surf guitar, 1960s garage bands, 1960s psychedelic, 1970s–80s punk and New Wave, 1990s grunge, 2000s Euro-lounge world trance, and currently the Black Keys. I also love the sitar and "yoga music," which is rarely played in yoga classes anymore for some reason.

Do you think the business has changed a lot over the past few years? If yes, please explain. It has changed tremendously over the past three decades, although mergers and acquisitions have been a constant, even in the 1980s. Ten years ago all the talk was about ebooks. Now I think ebooks are almost irrelevant as a factor of concern — they are really just a different format. A book is a book is a book in terms of content, whether it's hardcover, paperback, or ebook. Just like an album is a collection of music released at once, whether it's a 45, an LP, a cassette, a CD, or an MP3 file.

What's really changed in the past few years is the coming-of-age of self-publishing. A lot of people equate ebooks with self-publishing, and that's why we still hear so much about ebooks. But most traditional publishers are offering their books as hardcovers and ebooks, so the real distinction that exists is between traditional publishing, where editors have some control over quality, and self-publishing, which is paid for. The quality of self-published books is getting better and better, as many self-publishing companies now offer an à la carte menu of services, including editing, production values (e.g., a decent-looking cover and interior design), and even marketing and publicity.

The other gigantic change we must recognize is that people are reading fewer books. But this does not mean they are reading less. On the contrary, people are reading more, but their material is coming from a stunning variety of sources, including articles that are tweeted or posted on Facebook or LinkedIn. In a way, we're back to the prenewspaper era of getting news from our friends and neighbors. We are so consumed with keeping up with what everyone else is reading and talking about that we have very little time left for traditional media like newspapers in print form (although they do seem to have found new life in social media) and books in any form.

What do the "Big 5" mean to you? The Big 5 publishers currently comprise so many formerly independent publishers that it's hard to generalize about them. Their capabilities vary widely. Therefore I pay more attention to individual imprints than to their parent companies.

How do you feel about independent/small presses? Their one big advantage is that they can take greater intellectual risks, because if a book flops, it's only a loss of a few hundred copies rather than hundreds of thousands.

What are your feelings about self-publishing? See my answer to the question, above, about change in the industry.

Do you think Amazon is good or bad — or both — for the book business? It's good. For many authors, Amazon is the only way individual readers get exposed to them. Many bookstores have closed, and few people go to libraries anymore. I have done all my book shopping on Amazon for years. But I understand why publishers have disputes based on pricing and other things, and Amazon is shooting themselves in the foot by making it very hard to get incorrect data corrected. They also discourage sales by listing books as "out of stock" when they are not, confusing editors, and causing consternation for publishers. (They say a book is "out of stock" just because they don't have any pending orders. Customers then think they mean the book is out of stock at the publisher, so they don't place an order, which means the "out of stock" message remains. I cannot understand why they don't realize they are losing untold sums of money when you add it all up.) But I would not want them to disappear.

What do you like and dislike about your job? I love connecting with new authors and editors, and I love it when a book is finally released into the world. There's nothing in particular I dislike about the job.

What are ways prospective clients can impress you, and what are ways they can turn you off? You can impress me by sending a complete book proposal and being willing to trust my advice. Do not assume that I don't need a book proposal just because you've written a manuscript. And don't assume that you don't need any sample chapters just because you've written a complete book proposal with long chapter summaries.

Turnoffs are people who write email messages using texting shortcuts like *u* and *r* (please use complete sentences) and people who call me incessantly.

How would you describe the "writer from hell"? I try to avoid them as clients, so this is hypothetical, but someone who is too precise about wording would be difficult during the copyediting stage and someone who thinks he or she could design the interior, the cover, etc., would be difficult during production. People who sign with me need to be willing to be published and to let the publisher do what the publisher does best. Because of the prevalence of self-publishing today, I'm finding that some authors don't understand the difference between self-publishing and traditional publishing.

LITERARY AGENTS

Describe a book you would like to write. I do not want to write a book. Honestly, I think this is what makes me a great partner as an editor and an agent. So many people end up in publishing because they wish they were authors, and such people are more likely to have ego-based battles with their authors. I respect my authors' expertise, and I want them to respect mine.

Do you believe in a higher and/or lower "power"? I am not going to answer this one because it may needlessly alienate some people either way. Our mothers taught us not to discuss religion, politics, money, or sex in public for a good reason. If you want to see your networks shrink overnight, give it a whirl.

Is there anything you wish to express beyond the parameters of the preceding questions? Authors should take extra care when preparing the marketing and promotional section of their book proposals. More and more publishers are insisting upon a strong marketing platform, even for specialized books with smallish print runs.

Agent's name and contact info: Fred Tribuzzo, fred@rudyagency.com

Describe the kinds of works you want to represent. Psychological thrillers and historical mystery/crime.

Describe what you definitely don't want to represent. Everything that's not described above.

How do you want writers to pitch you? Email queries are best.

Describe your education and professional history. I've had two years journalism and English studies at Kent State University, including feature writing for the *Kent Stater*.

How did you become an agent? Maryann was kind enough to give me the opportunity.

Knowing what you do now, would you do it again? If not, what might you do instead? I wouldn't change a thing.

Do you charge fees? If yes, please explain. No.

When and where were you born, and where have you lived? I was born in Cleveland and have been a northeastern Ohio resident ever since.

What do you like to do when you're not working? I get back to the several novels I'm working on and occasionally getting short stories published at *Liberty Island Magazine*. And then, if there are a few minutes left, I spend time on next week's guitar lesson.

List some of the titles you have recently placed with publishers. I'm very excited for Mary

Lawrence's second novel, *Death of an Alchemist*, at Kensington, out in January 2016, and Michael Helms's Mac McClellan series at Camel Press. *Deadly Dunes*, Michael's third book, will be released in March 2016.

Describe your personality. Quiet.

What do you like reading/watching/listening to on your own time? I love all the Dean Koontz books, especially his recent creations. I enjoy Hillsdale College's online courses on the Constitution, literature, economics, and much more. And I'm a fan of *The Walking Dead*.

Do you think the business has changed a lot over the past few years? If yes, please explain. There's much more competition in publishing, but editors are still very receptive to a strong pitch.

What do the "Big 5" mean to you? Nothing to fear here. I contact whoever would be best for my client. The editors I've approached among the Big 5 have all been professional and gracious.

How do you feel about independent/small presses? I'm very fond of the small presses. I have an author currently placed in two different independent houses.

What are your feelings about self-publishing? It's a welcomed reality, crowding the writer field, but also bringing opportunity for those writers who stay in the game.

Do you think Amazon is good or bad — or both — for the book business? It's like everything else in publishing — lots of competition for everyone from writers to bookstores. So we have to be innovative and find or create new niches.

What do you like and dislike about your job? I like the writers I've found and the thrill of getting them the best publishing deal I can.

What are ways prospective clients can impress you, and what are ways they can turn you off? The best way to impress me is send a very short pitch that's well written. Writers sending me a synopsis or the first chapter won't get my attention.

How would you describe the "writer from hell"? A badly formatted manuscript is a real disappointment after asking to see a manuscript and signals more problems ahead.

Describe a book you would like to write. I'm working on it right now.

Do you believe in a higher and/or lower "power"? Absolutely.

Is there anything you wish to express beyond the parameters of the preceding questions? Dear Writer: Please keep writing and keep submitting!

SANDRA DIJKSTRA LITERARY AGENCY ❖ www.dijkstraagency.com

1155 Camino del Mar, PMB 515, Del Mar, CA 92014

Agents' names and contact info: Elise Capron, queries@dijkstraagency.com; Andrea Cavallaro, andrea@dijkstraagency.com (only handles subrights); Sandra Dijkstra, queries@dijkstraagency.com; Roz Foster, roz@dijkstra agency.com; Jennifer Kim, jennifer@dijkstraagency.com; Thao Le, thao@dijkstraagency.com; Jill Marr, jmsubmissions@dijkstraagency.com; Jessica Watterson, jessica@dijkstraagency.com

Describe the kinds of works you want to represent. *Elise*: adult literary fiction, narrative-driven history, cultural studies, occasionally memoir.

Sandra: literary and commercial fiction, history, current events, politics, science, self-help, some memoir.

Roz: literary fiction, politics, history, current affairs, business, technology, sociology, cultural studies, urban studies, science, design.

Jennifer: literary fiction, historical fiction.

Thao: adult sci-fi/fantasy, young adult, middle grade; selectively open to romance, and picture books by authors who are also illustrators.

Jill: commercial fiction (mystery, thrillers, romantic suspense, and horror), women's commercial fiction and historical fiction, history, sports, politics, current events, cookbooks, health and nutrition, pop culture, humor, music, very select memoir.

Jessica: all genres of romance, especially historical, contemporary, romantic suspense, paranormal.

Describe what you definitely don't want to represent. *Elise*: fantasy, young adult/middle grade, picture books, romance, sci-fi, business books, cookbooks, poetry, religious/spiritual books, screenplays, self-help.

Sandra: romance, young adult, children's, Christian.

Roz: sports, cookbooks, screenplays, poetry, romance, fantasy, sci-fi, new adult, young adult, children's books.

Jennifer: self-help, romance, Christian.

Thao: adult literary fiction, mystery/thriller (unless it has a speculative element or is young adult), nonfiction, memoir, poetry, religious/spiritual books, screenplays, short stories.

Jill: young adult, children's books, sci-fi, romance, screenplays, graphic novels.

Jessica: middle grade, cookbooks, poetry, short stories, screenplays, self-help, religious/spiritual books.

How do you want writers to pitch you? Our submission guidelines can be found on our website: www.dijkstraagency.com/submission-guidelines.html.

Describe your education and professional history. Sandra: PhD in French literature; founded SDLA over 30 years ago.

Do you charge fees? If yes, please explain. No.

SAVVY LITERARY SERVICES ❖ www.savvyliterary.com

3 Griffin Hill Court, The Woodlands, TX 77382, 281-465-0119, cell: 281-682-7518

Agent's name and contact info: Leticia Gomez, Founder and CEO, savvyliterary@yahoo.com, savvyliterary@gmail.com

Describe the kinds of works you want to represent. Seeking book proposals and manuscripts written in English or Spanish in the following genres. Fiction: suspense thrillers, mystery, women's commercial fiction, fantasy, historical, humor, multicultural, paranormal, romance, erotica, young adult, middle grade. Nonfiction: advice/relationship, biography, business, cooking, diet, health, history, politics/current affairs, how-to, humor, lifestyle, memoir, pop culture, parenting, religion/spirituality, sports, true crime.

Describe what you definitely don't want to represent. Not seeking children's picture books, horror, poetry, short story collections, graphic novels.

How do you want writers to pitch you? Please send me your best query via email and include a synopsis and the first three chapters or a completed book proposal.

Describe your education and professional history. I have been working in the publishing industry as a publisher, acquisitions editor, literary agent, and published author since 1993. During this span of time, I have published my own newspaper, authored and published three books, and edited numerous fiction and nonfiction manuscripts written in both English and Spanish that have gone on to publication. Thus far in my career I have placed approximately 100 books and counting with independent and mainstream publishers.

As founder and CEO of Savvy Literary Services, one of the few minority-oriented publishing firms, I am a literary agent who can communicate effectively with the authors I am representing. Recently, I partnered with Ascendant Group to offer an even greater level of support to aspiring authors. As Director of Ascendant Publishing, I serve as the company's in-house publishing consultant and literary agent. Blending my experience as an author, literary agent, publishing consultant, and acquisitions editor, I am now truly excited to spearhead my very own Hispanic book division, Café con Leche Books, which is an imprint of the Virginia-based independent publisher Koehler Books.

How did you become an agent? When I first launched my literary agency back in 2007, the prime directive was to help as many Latino and other ethnic minority writers as possible get their literary works published. Let's face it — these are the writers who are oftentimes underrepresented, misrepresented, or, worse yet, not represented at all. However, the landscape of publishing has changed so much since I first opened my doors. It seems as though, these days, any writer who has a pulse falls into the category of being an "underdog writer." Although continuing to champion the works of the "underdog writer" will always be high on my priority list, I have expanded my client list to writers who come to me from a more mainstream pool.

Knowing what you do now, would you do it again? If not, what might you do instead? I honestly don't think I would have done anything different, because it has been a truly incredible journey.

Do you charge fees? If yes, please explain. I do not charge any reading or representation fees. However, during those times I am fortunate enough to have lunch or dinner with a client, there is a good chance that I will break down and ask him or her to buy me a Lady Godiva Chocolate Martini (or two).

When and where were you born, and where have you lived? On January 24, 1966, in a cold, sterile, and impersonal hospital in the once booming oil town of Odessa, Texas, I sprung forth from my mother's womb and made my grand entrance into this world as an underdog. When I was six, my father and mother decided to move the family to a small town in New Mexico named Portales, and that is where I grew up. Portales is located in the southeastern part of the state, a hop, skip, and jump away from the Texas Panhandle area. If you happen to drive through Portales on your way to Albuquerque or Santa Fe, the first thing you'll see is a huge billboard sign that reads: "Welcome to Portales, home to 13,000 of the friendliest people you'll ever meet . . . and three or four old grouches." Then the love bug bit me and I got married and relocated to the Houston area. I currently reside in a beautiful master-planned community 20 minutes south of downtown Houston known as the Woodlands, TX. I guess you might say I am a geographically challenged literary agent and have to work harder than most to get noticed.

What do you like to do when you're not working? Let the record show that I am an incurable workaholic. However, once in a blue moon I do have to take time off to decompress and I usually do it by having wine with close personal friends, listening to Latin pop music, or watching rerun episodes of *How I Met Your Mother* alongside my faithful and loving husband of 20 years.

List some of the titles you have recently placed with publishers. Former NBA player turned inventor Jonathan Bender's *The Courtside CEO: Transforming Your Business and Life*, about how to tap into our own faith to overcome fear, which prevents so many people from following their passions and dreams (Cedar Fort); Sara Villanueva's *The Angst of Adolescence: How to Parent Your Teen — and Live to Laugh about It*, advocating for a new view on adolescence, moving from one of sheer survival to one of learning to enjoy the ride with your teen as he or she moves through this critical stage of development — full of positive advice and practical tips from a mom who's been there and from an adolescent psychologist who knows best (Bibliomotion); Tony Castro's *Looking for Hemingway*, about the literary giant's setting out in the twilight of his life on a quixotic quest to recapture the sentimental Spain of his early success in the 1920s only to sadly confront mano a mano a final rite of passage that tests all the credos of bravery and grace under pressure that he had lived by (Lyons Press); psychologist and executive/organizational adviser Dr. Rob Fazio's *Simple Is the New Smart: 26 Success Strategies to Build Confidence, Inspire Yourself, and Reach Your Ultimate Potential*, a fusion of best practices in business thinking, counseling psychology, and sports psychology to make work — and life — simpler (Career Press); evangelist John Ramirez's *Unmasking the Devil: Exposing Eternity's Greatest Deceiver*, in which he teaches what role Satan occupies in the modern world and how Christians today can combat and outsmart him (Destiny Image); Senior Pastor of World Overcomers Christian Church Andy Thompson's *Make It Rain*, in which he teaches readers to look upon and utilize faith as a "way of life" versus merely being a spiritual and practical concept, and his follow-up book *Handle with Care*, which will focus on helping couples keep their marriage relationship strong (Destiny Image); William Hazelgrove's *The Presidency of Edith Wilson*, which tells all about the secret presidency of Edith Wilson and how she actually became the first woman president of the United States, and his follow-up book *The Last Cowboy: How the West Created Teddy Roosevelt*, which narrates the Wild West adventure lived by our nation's twenty-sixth president after having lost his wife, mother, and political career all in a short span of time (Regnery); business trainer, business and behavioral strategist, and nationally syndicated talk-show host Josh Tolley's *Abuse of the Badge: America's Epidemic of Police Corruption and Brutality* (Prometheus); Marissa Monteihl writing as Anita L's *The Taming of Valencia*, a multicultural erotica chock-full of hot sex and drama, with a love triangle that will keep you on your toes (Samhain Publishing); sports writer Tony Castro's *Gehrig and the Babe: The Friendship, the Feud*, a dual biography that begins with the eventful first day they met in 1923, and on through their glory years and the feud between them that began in the early 1930s and continued until Gehrig's famous farewell address thawed out their stone silence (Triumph); mental-health expert Blake LeVine's *The Depression Diet*, which contains simple, life-changing solutions that teach readers how to impact their own physical and mental well-being to obtain happiness (Skyhorse); former San Diego Charger and founder/Senior Pastor of City of Hope Church Terrell Fletcher's *The Book of You: Discovering Your Purpose and Transforming Your Future*, helping readers tap into God's creative intent for them so they can live a meaningful life whereby they are empowered to make deep, significant contributions that have lasting effects on this generation and the next (Waterfall Press).

Describe your personality. I pride myself on being an equal-opportunity literary agent, meaning that I treat all my clients as if they are my own flesh and blood. When my clients wish to speak with me, all they have to do is pick up the phone, and chances are I will answer it live. If I don't happen to be available when they call, I will normally return their call within 24 to 48 hours. I sometimes joke with them by saying that if more than a week goes by without my returning their call, it means something has gone terribly wrong in my life or I am lying unconscious in a ditch somewhere. And like my own children, they are always in the back of my mind. Good communication is the key to a healthy author-agent relationship. Without it, chances are this kind of working relationship isn't going to amount to much. Authors should feel as though they can speak freely to their agent and vice versa.

In a nutshell, I have a sunny disposition and wicked sense of humor (imagine finding that quality in a literary agent) and have been told that I have a heart the size of the Grand Canyon. My son once described me as an "explosion of sunshine" in a poem he wrote in the sixth grade.

Do you think the business has changed a lot over the past few years? If yes, please explain. The landscape of publishing has definitely changed. It is not as glamorous a business as it used to be. Because it is so author platform— and social media—driven, I no longer feel that the best high-quality literature is being published. In regard to paying advances, most publishers have become really stingy and are even requiring their authors to commit to doing buybacks. Most editors are also so overworked and underpaid that they just don't have the time to roll up their sleeves and edit as they did in the good ole days of publishing. The manuscripts they acquire must be absolutely flawless upon submission and anything less will be rejected on the spot.

What do the "Big 5" mean to you? I revere the Big 5 as the publishing gods that every aspiring author dreams of being able to appease.

How do you feel about independent/small presses? I thoroughly enjoy working with and bringing books to independent publishers and small presses because they are more receptive and open-minded about publishing talented emerging authors. Sometimes they are more willing than the bigger, conglomerate publishers to take risks when it comes to content, and they're not so obsessed with name recognition. Although making money is high up on their agenda, in my experience independent publishers and small presses are driven more by their passion to publish and distribute high-quality books. Bigger, conglomerate publishers are missing the boat by rejecting high-quality and out-of-the-box books because they are not written by a high-profile celebrity, professional athlete, or religious or political leader. The smaller publishers now seem to be taking the lead. For example, in the last few years, independent publishers and small presses have been publishing the most talked-about and widely read memoirs. Last but certainly not least, when dealing with these kinds of publishers, the chances of getting to speak to a warm human being on the phone versus a cold automated voice recording is far greater.

What are your feelings about self-publishing? I used to strongly advocate that authors should only self-publish their works as a last resort, when all hope of landing a traditional publishing deal had been lost. In my opinion, the two greatest challenges of self-publishing were (1) the requirement that authors promote and market their books to the point of physical exhaustion and practically going broke and (2) the lack of national print and ebook distribution. The chances of self-publishing success were extremely slim. However, the publishing landscape has changed dramatically. The larger, mainstream, traditional publishers are no longer giving away any "Get Published Free" cards, as they did in the good ole days, leaving aspiring and emerging authors with no choice but to take matters into their own hands.

In recent years a new model of publication known as independent/entrepreneurial publishing has been gaining more and more traction. The beauty of this new model is that it allows authors to keep all creative control of their content. In other words, they call all the shots while keeping the majority of the royalties. The best part of all is that national print and ebook distribution services that were once an elusive dream for self-published authors are now so easy to obtain. Of course, the best-case scenario for any author is to get published by the likes of Penguin Random House, HarperCollins, Simon & Schuster, the Hachette Book Group, and others like them. But for any author who has been forsaken by these publishing gods, independent/entrepreneurial publishing makes for a great consolation prize.

What do you like and dislike about your job? To begin, all the negativity, cold-hearted rejection, and disheartening bureaucracy in this business really leaves a sour taste in my mouth. One has to be really tough-skinned to deal with all of it. I also don't like how long it takes to get things accomplished and the fact that most editors in the business are being overworked and underpaid, although I respect them and the work they do very much. Now let me tell you what balances it out for me. The one singular, yet powerful motive that keeps me turning on my computer day after day to read new submissions is that I believe in the power of the written word with all my heart and soul. For me the undeniable, beautiful virtue of words when published is their ability to immortalize the person who wrote them.

What are ways prospective clients can impress you, and what are ways they can turn you off? I have a very strong work ethic when it comes to representing my authors and their works. I am willing to put in extra hours to make sure I have explored every publishing avenue for their manuscript and in return I expect them to be flexible in their availability when the need arises. Sometimes an editor will request additional information that only the author can provide. I need to be able to reach out to any authors of mine on a dime and know that they will provide me with the ammunition I need in a timely manner, so I can land them a publishing deal. All authors I choose to represent must be willing to work collaboratively with me toward publication. But more important, they must trust and have confidence in my abilities as a literary agent.

How would you describe the "writer from hell"? For me there is no bigger turnoff than when a prospective author pastes a large portion of his or her manuscript in the body of an email. Chapters pasted in the body of the email are hard to read, especially on my ereader, and I end up getting frustrated enough that I lose interest. Like most agents today, I prefer to receive a well-thought-out query letter and synopsis during the initial contact. I am especially appreciative and impressed when authors give me their best elevator pitch for the work they want me to represent.

Describe a book you would like to write. Funny you should ask that! Recently I partnered with a longtime client and dear friend of mine to write a trilogy of humorous erotica novels. Our current work-in-progress is about an international playboy and serial adulterer who is diagnosed with stage-four lung cancer. Since his days seemed to be numbered, he spends them recounting all of his sexual escapades to the feisty Latina live-in personal assistant he's hired to help him cross over to the other side. In the interim he ends up falling madly in love with her and at the last minute decides to enroll in a promising clinical study with the hope that he can prolong death long enough to pursue true love. Think: "The English Patient Meets How I Met Your Mother."

Do you believe in a higher and/or lower "power"? Of course I do!

Is there anything you wish to express beyond the parameters of the preceding questions? During the harsh economic times we're living in what literary agent doesn't dream of negotiating six-figure advance deals and laughing all the way to the bank? I for one daydream about this more than I care to admit. But at the risk of being taken out of the village and stoned to death by my peer literary agents, sometimes it is not about the money at all. Sometimes it's about making someone's dream come true. To illustrate my point, I'd like to share one of the most rewarding experiences I've had since becoming a full-time literary agent.

 Back in January of 2012, I was contacted by a wonderful woman by the name of Patricia L. Aust. Patricia had just finished writing a young adult novel that takes place in a domestic violence shelter, narrated by a sufficiently likable young Hispanic male protagonist. My first gut reaction to the novel was that it gave readers a chilling ground-floor view of domestic and dating violence. I strongly believed it was a must-read for any teen girl or boy.

Not long after signing Patricia, I came to learn that her life revolved around helping others. She recognized that, as many children as there were in the battered women's shelter where she volunteered as a children's counselor, there were many more who still were being abused. After months and months of submitting the manuscript to prospective editors, I received an offer of publication from Tracy Richardson, publisher of Luminis Books. Patricia was ecstatic, and so was I. We were in the middle of contract negotiations when I received a distress call from Patricia's daughter, Laura, whom I had never communicated with before. Laura was calling to let me know her mother had just died from cervical cancer. Needless to say, the news blew me away. I had no idea that Patricia was ill. She had never mentioned it to me.

Laura asked me what the chances were that the publisher would want to proceed with the acquisition and publication of her mother's novel. I told Laura that I honestly did not know. But I did promise her that I would do everything I could to finalize the deal. It was extremely fortunate that Tracy Richardson really loved and believed in the novel enough to publish it even though the author would not be available to promote it. Arrangements were made for Patricia's husband to sign the contract on her behalf. It was also decided that Laura would take over the editorial duties for her mother. I'm happy to report that *Shelter*, written by Patricia L. Aust, was released in the spring of 2014. It was Patricia's hope that her young adult novel might help victims of domestic violence to break the cycle.

SCHIAVONE LITERARY AGENCY, INC.

236 Trails End, West Palm Beach, FL 22314-2135, 561-966-9294

Agent's name and contact info: James Schiavone, EdD, profschia@aol.com

Describe the kinds of works you want to represent. All genres except children's picture books, anthologies, collections, poetry, previously published work in any format (i.e., self-published, POD, online, etc.).

How do you want writers to pitch you? We only accept one-page email query letters, no attachments. No phone calls or faxes. No USPS letters.

When and where were you born, and where have you lived? New York City.

Do you charge fees? If yes, please explain. No.

Describe your education and professional history. BS, MA, New York University; EdD, Nova University; professional diploma as reading specialist in secondary school and college, Columbia University; advanced studies, University of Rome, Italy. Reading Specialist, Miami-Dade (FL) Public Schools; Director of Reading, K-12 Monroe County (FL) Public Schools; Professor of Developmental Skills, City University of New York.

Why do you think you became an agent and how did you become one? Upon early retirement from CUNY, I made the move from academia to publishing when I established my agency in 1996.

Knowing what you do now, would you do it again? If not, what might you do instead? Yes.

List some of the titles you have recently placed with publishers. *Trust Me: A Memoir* by George Kennedy, *The Unofficial Downton Abbey Cookbook* by Larry Edwards, *Beautiful Old Dogs* edited by David Tabatsky.

What are your feelings about self-publishing? My position on representation for previously published work in any format may be found at: Schiavoneliteraryagencyinc.blog spot.com.

Do you think Amazon is good or bad — or both — for the book business? Yes, I have a Prime membership with them and enjoy the numerous benefits they offer. Every book brokered by my agency is available at deep discount via Amazon. Highly recommended.

Do you believe in a "higher power"? Yes.

What will agenting be like in 2020? Publishing is a dynamic industry that keeps up with the latest technology. I envision exciting times for authors, agents, editors, and publishers.

Describe your job and what you like and don't like about it. Selling important books to major publishers is the main thrust of my work. I always look forward to receiving outstanding submissions from prospective clients.

Do you miss the way the business "used to be"? Not at all.

What do the "Big 5" mean to you? The major conglomerates in the Big Apple and their numerous imprints. I keep up with all of them.

What do you want to tell new/unpublished writers? Believe in your abilities and your writing.

Do you like that everything has become largely digitized? Yes, technology requires this.

What do you like reading/watching/listening to on your own time? Fiction, cable news, classical music.

Describe a book you would like to write. I have published five trade books and three textbooks.

THE SCHISGAL AGENCY, LLC ❖ www.theschisgalagency.com

98 Riverside Drive, 2B, New York, NY 10024

Agent's name and contact info: Zach Schisgal, zach@theschisgalagency.com

Describe the kinds of works you want to represent. My focus is on commercial nonfiction in areas including but not limited to business (leadership, management), self-help, humor, politics, pop culture, health and fitness, media tie-in, cookbooks, narrative, memoir, biography. I am also interested in fiction, mainly series-based genre mystery, thriller, sci-fi. I am interested in anything I think is a good work that I can help in the process.

How do you want writers to pitch you? Anyone should feel free to email me by way of introduction.

When and where were you born, and where have you lived? I am a native and lifelong New Yorker.

Do you charge fees? If yes, please explain. I work on a commission basis based on sales and charge no fees above and beyond.

Describe your education and professional history. I am a graduate of the Collegiate School in Manhattan and Wesleyan University in Connecticut. I have spent my professional career in publishing, starting as an editorial assistant at William Morrow and working my way up the ladder there to senior editor. I held positions at HarperCollins, Rodale, Random House, and Simon & Schuster. As an editor, I acquired *New York Times* bestsellers by LL Cool J, Bethenny Frankel, Ken Blanchard, Dan Rather, Ivanka Trump, and Heather McDonald.

What do you like to do when you're not working? I devote the bulk of my free time to my family. I have two elementary-school-age children and draw enormous gratification and enjoyment out of everything I learn from them. I cook, and I spend a fair amount of time at the gym. I enjoy running greatly, but I run just so I can eat ice cream.

Why do you think you became an agent and how did you become one? After about 20 years on the corporate editorial side of the business, I wanted to take control of my career; I didn't want people off in meetings in other rooms making decisions about how I'd spend my time. I wanted new challenges. And I also wanted to be a stakeholder in the success of the projects on which I worked.

Knowing what you do now, would you do it again? If not, what might you do instead? I'm delighted to have been able to have all the wonderful experiences and meet the incredible people I have along the way. I'd just try and do everything a little better next time around.

List some of the titles you have recently placed with publishers. *The New Vote* by Kristen Soltis Anderson, the conservative pollster *Time* magazine named as one of the 30 people under 30 changing the world in 2013; *Mint Juleps with Teddy Roosevelt*, historian Mark Will-Weber's look at presidential drinking; and books by leading vegan Julieanna Hever and retired Navy SEAL and business consultant Rob Roy.

Describe your personality. One of the most flattering things a boss once said about me was that I took my work seriously, but I didn't take myself too seriously. I run a transparent business, respond to every email and phone call, and am an overcommunicator.

How would you describe the "writer from hell"? We work in a business where you live and die by your word, and I value honesty above all else. It's also a deadline-driven business, and you have to be serious about the work.

What are your feelings about self-publishing? It's a great opportunity for many authors as long as they realize that simply making the work available as an ebook is about half the work. Publishers bring enormous resources to the process, for which they don't get their share of credit.

Do you think Amazon is good or bad — or both — for the book business? I have enormous respect for Amazon, and publishers have allowed them to exploit every weakness built into the traditional publishing construct. That said, their fight against local sales tax gives some insight into what the corporation values.

Do you believe in a "higher power"? Only if it believes in me.

What will agenting be like in 2020? There will be consolidation on all sides of publishing. Retail opportunities will fracture, and more agents will also be ebook publishers. The fundamentals will be the same — work hard for each client and collect a commission.

Describe your job and what you like and don't like about it. I love my job. If there weren't headaches, authors wouldn't need agents.

Do you miss the way the business "used to be"? When I started 25 years ago, everyone complained about the business just as much as they do now.

What do the "Big 5" mean to you? Hardworking intelligent people who want to publish good books that do well.

What do you want to tell new/unpublished writers? Follow your passion. Be realistic. Good work gets published. Sometimes it's not a book; it's an app.

Do you like that everything has become largely digitized? Yes. We used to waste so much paper.

What do you like reading/watching/listening to on your own time? I am an odd blend of high and low. I like stupid humor and Pulitzer Prize–winning writing. Sometimes you really can have it all.

Describe a book you would like to write. I am the author of one of the bestselling tailgating cookbooks, *A Man, a Can, a Tailgate Plan*. I would — and did — write that.

Is there anything you wish to express beyond the parameters of the preceding questions? Thanks for reading this far. This book is filled with amazing opportunity, and I wish you the best of luck on your journey. Please be in touch if you'd like to talk more.

SECOND CITY PUBLISHING SERVICES, LLC ❖

www.secondcitypublishing.com

Madison, WI, 608-819-6063

Agent's name and contact info: Cynthia A. Zigmund, Founder and President, cynthia@secondcitypublishing.com

Describe the kinds of works you want to represent. Nonfiction including but not limited to business, self-help, inspirational, narrative, biography, history, memoir. Fiction (mystery).

Describe what you definitely don't want to represent. Children's, erotica, science fiction, horror, fantasy, short stories, poetry.

How do you want writers to pitch you? By email. For fiction, a query is fine. For nonfiction, please submit a complete proposal following the guidelines posted on our website.

Describe your education and professional history. Before founding Second City Publishing Services in 2006, I spent more than 20 years in New York and Chicago publishing including positions at Wiley, Van Nostrand Reinhold (a technical and reference publisher), and Irwin Professional (now McGraw-Hill). In 1996, I joined Dearborn Trade Publishing (now Kaplan Publishing) as executive editor. Six months after joining Dearborn I was promoted to editorial director and was named vice president and publisher in 2000. During my 10 years with Kaplan, I expanded the organization's program beyond real estate and finance to include management, general business, sales, marketing, and architecture. Under my leadership, the organization published a number of business bestsellers and became a leading publisher of business books. I hold a business degree, summa cum laude, from Monmouth University.

How did you become an agent? After leaving Kaplan, I wanted to remain in the publishing industry but was ready for a new challenge. As an independent agent, I am able to focus on helping authors — what I loved most about being an editor — and continue to remain in an industry that I love, but on my own terms.

Knowing what you do now, would you do it again? If not, what might you do instead? I would do it again, but sooner.

Do you charge fees? If yes, please explain. In limited circumstances. For example, if an author comes to us with an offer from a publisher, and he or she does not require representation, we may agree to review the contract for a flat fee instead of a percentage of royalties.

When and where were you born, and where have you lived? I'm a Jersey girl who has lived and worked in the tristate (NYC) area, Boston, Chicago, and now Madison, Wisconsin.

What do you like to do when you're not working? When I'm not working, my husband (and business partner) and I bike, hike, bird-watch, and enjoy living in one of the country's best small cities.

List some of the titles you have recently placed with publishers. *Death on the Sapphire* by Richard Koreto (Crooked Lane), *The Right Wrong Thing* by Ellen Kirschman (Oceanview), *The Difference* by Subir Chowdhury (Crown Business), *You Can Retire Sooner Than You Think* by Wes Moss (McGraw-Hill).

Describe your personality. Intense and detail-oriented — but with a sense of humor. My feedback to authors is straightforward and comprehensive, which clients find helpful and refreshing. It's not unusual for authors I work with to go through several rounds of revisions before we present to publishers.

What do you like reading/watching/listening to on your own time? When I'm not reviewing manuscripts, I tend to have eclectic tastes and, like most people, read based on recommendations. I almost always have the radio on — either public radio or Pandora.

Do you think the business has changed a lot over the past few years? If yes, please explain. This business is always changing. Ebooks were going to be the death of the industry, replacing print and audio. Instead, the mix has changed — and will continue to change.

What do the "Big 5" mean to you? For authors, the Big 5 mean prestige and distribution, though not necessarily big sales (or even big advances). There are some great people working in the larger houses, but they tend to be more risk-averse than those in the smaller, independent houses.

How do you feel about independent/small presses? I love independent presses — they are often the ones who are willing to take the risks the larger houses can no longer afford to. Whether an author is with a large or small house, his or her experience will vary based on timing, editor, and overall support.

What are your feelings about self-publishing? We represent authors who publish commercially and on their own. Depending on the genre and the author's approach, it's a very viable option — if not the right way. The biggest mistake authors make is taking shortcuts — poor design, no editing, no marketing support once the book is published. Authors should not confuse printing with publishing.

Do you think Amazon is good or bad — or both — for the book business? Both; we all know it's a love/hate relationship.

What do you like and dislike about your job? I love working with authors to help them fine-tune proposals and manuscripts. I love telling authors we have a publisher interested in their project — there is nothing more satisfying than placing a book. I hate not being able to place a project (no agent has a 100 percent track record). I really dislike authors who don't listen.

What are ways prospective clients can impress you, and what are ways they can turn you off? Do your homework — about prospective agents and books that will compete against yours. Understand that writing a book is a huge commitment. Understand the importance of your ability to market and sell your book beyond what your publisher will do. Listen to your agent when he or she gives you feedback — even if it's hard to swallow. Don't always second-guess your agent, but do ask lots of questions so you understand the process. Don't commit to a book and then not follow through.

How would you describe the "writer from hell"? The one who is always second-guessing the agent, doesn't want to put the time into fine-tuning a proposal or manuscript, and doesn't want to market or promote the book. In other words, a writer who doesn't take writing a book seriously.

Describe a book you would like to write. I have no interest in writing a book myself — that's why I'm an agent and not an author.

SEVENTH AVENUE LITERARY AGENCY ❖ www.seventhavenuelit.com

2052 124th Street, South Surrey, BC, Canada V4A 9K3, 604-538-7252

Agent's name: Robert Mackwood, Principal Agent and Owner

Describe the kinds of works you want to represent. Strictly nonfiction — main areas: narrative history, business, prescriptive how-to, memoir, health, sports, travel.

Describe what you definitely don't want to represent. Fiction, children's, young adult.

How do you want writers to pitch you? Email query to queries@seventhavenuelit.com — with no attachments, please.

Describe your education and professional history. Originally in broadcasting after a degree in broadcast news, but joined publishing in 1982 and have never left.

How did you become an agent? After six years at Bantam/Doubleday Canada in the early 1990s, my wife and I wanted to return to our West Coast roots, and I teamed up with an old colleague who owned a large speakers' bureau with a smaller literary management division. I took over that division in 1996, bought it out from him in 2005, and have owned Seventh Avenue with my wife ever since.

Knowing what you do now, would you do it again? If not, what might you do instead? Yes, I would do it again.

Do you charge fees? If yes, please explain. No fees on the agency side, but we do offer publishing consulting through Mackwood Publishing Consultants, www.mackwood publishingconsultants.com.

When and where were you born, and where have you lived? New Westminster, BC, in 1955, and have lived in Vancouver and Toronto.

What do you like to do when you're not working? Crazy about tennis and home renovations.

List some of the titles you have recently placed with publishers. *Thrive Diet, 10th Anniversary Edition* by Brendan Brazier (Penguin Random House Canada), *The Idea of Canada: Letters to a Nation* by His Excellency Governor General David Johnston (McClelland & Stewart/Signal Canada), *Full Moon over Noah's Ark: An Odyssey to My Ararat and Beyond* by Rick Antonson (Skyhorse NYC).

What do you like reading/watching/listening to on your own time? Read British and American mystery writers, watch PBS and Canadian television occasionally, listen to YouTube singers' greatest hits.

Do you think the business has changed a lot over the past few years? If yes, please explain. I'll address the Canadian market only, which has been reduced to three main multinational conglomerates, a few midlist Canadian publishers, and a lot of small independent Canadian houses. Add it up and it makes for a much smaller pool with more Canadian agents looking for dance partners. So you have to adapt. We built up our consulting business and launched Brilliant Idea Books, a publishing imprint/service for self-published business authors. We differ from most as we produce the proverbial $20 business card for business entrepreneurs and stay away from brick-and-mortar distribution.

What do the "Big 5" mean to you? The inevitable shift to who controls most of the commercial market. The great divide between them and the huge self-published author and the independent presses will continue to grow.

How do you feel about independent/small presses? Love them, and they are absolutely necessary, but don't do any business with them particularly.

What are your feelings about self-publishing? It is the only real option for a growing segment of writers and categories. Many pitfalls but many successes, too.

Do you think Amazon is good or bad — or both — for the book business? Good, as it makes all books available 24/7 on our globe. That is remarkable. Bad, as it continues a fractured relationship with book publishers. That might prove disastrous down the road.

What do you like and dislike about your job? Love it most days. It's extremely hard but, equally, extremely gratifying. Calling a client to say we have an offer or a book deal is the best feeling. There are times when nothing much seems to be happening and it's easy to despair, but then that one email comes in and your day and journey are whisked off in a new and interesting direction.

What are ways prospective clients can impress you, and what are ways they can turn you off? Give me the facts. Don't elaborate unnecessarily. Don't promise me we will be rich if I take your book on.

How would you describe the "writer from hell"? Someone who takes gobs of my time with something that seemed promising and then falls apart or someone who is only using me to find another agent.

SHEREE BYKOFSKY ASSOCIATES, INC. ❖ shereebee.com

PO Box 706, Brigantine, NJ 08203

Agents' names and contact info: Sheree Bykofsky, Founder and President, shereebee@aol.com; Janet Rosen, janetellenrosen@gmail.com

Describe the kinds of works you want to represent. *Janet*: Very wide-ranging list: health, business, adult nonfiction in all categories (hardcovers and trade paperbacks), quality literary and commercial fiction, mystery.

Describe what you definitely don't want to represent. Please do not query me with horror, occult, poetry, fantasy, or picture books.

How do you want writers to pitch you? Submit a query, pasted into the body of your email, to submitbee@aol.com or shereebee@aol.com. No attachments will be opened.

Describe your education and professional history. BA with honors, State University of New York, Binghamton; MA in English and comparative literature, Columbia University. Career history: executive editor/book producer, Stonesong Press (1984–96); freelance editor/writer (1984); general manager/managing editor, Chron Press (1979–84); author and coauthor of more than two dozen books, including three poker books with coauthor Lou Krieger and *The Complete Idiot's Guide to Getting Published*, 5th ed., with Jennifer Basye Sander.

How did you become an agent? The career matched my skill set. I love reading books and negotiating contracts, multitasking, reviewing royalty statements, helping authors. I was born to do this.

Knowing what you do now, would you do it again? If not, what might you do instead? I would do it again. I lead a charmed life (see Victoria Moran's *Creating a Charmed Life*). Completely blessed and meant to be.

Do you charge fees? If yes, please explain. No.

When and where were you born, and where have you lived? I was born in New York City and lived most of my life in Manhattan. I now happily reside on the Jersey Shore. I have traveled around the world and to all 50 states. I love meeting writers where they live.

What do you like to do when you're not working? I love to walk on the boardwalk, play competitive Scrabble and poker. Twice I won seats in the World Series of Poker.

List some of the titles you have recently placed with publishers. *The Promiscuous Vegan* by Amy Cramer and Lisa McComsey (Perigee), *Working with the Emotional Investor* by Chris White with Richard Koonce (ABC-CLIO), *The Essential Executor* by David Hoffman (Career), *Virtual Billions* by Eric Geissinger (Prometheus), *Calculus for Dummies* by Mark Ryan (Wiley), *ADHD Does Not Exist* by Dr. Richard Saul (HarperCollins), *Idea to Invention* by Patricia Nolan-Brown (McGraw-Hill), *Be Bold and Win the Sale* by Jeff Shore (AMA-COM), *King of the Worlds* by M. Thomas Gammarino (Chin Music), *Jellyfish Dreams* by M. Thomas Gammarino (Kindle), *Mimi Malloy at Last!* by Julia Chang Macdonnell (Picador), *Sell Your Business for an Outrageous Price* by Kevin Short (AMACOM), *Shell Shocked: My Life with the Turtles, Flo and Eddie and Frank Zappa* by Howard Kaylan (Hal Leonard), *Sneaky Math* by Cy Tymony (Andrews McMeel). Many international sales for the following books: *The Melt Method* by Sue Hitzmann; *Fail Fast, Fail Often* by Ryan Babineaux and John Krumboltz; *The Breakthrough Challenge* by John Elkington and Jochen Zeitz; *How to Become CEO, How to Become a Rainmaker*, and *How to Be a Great Boss* by Jeffrey J. Fox; *The 3% Signal* by Jason Kelly; *How NASA Builds Teams* by Charles Pellerin.

Describe your personality. I love fun and games but enjoy the responsibility and details of owning a business. I am rewarded by helping people (and animals). I am very practical and logical, yet I have had several deep intuitive experiences that I can only describe as psychic. I love brilliant, creative people and people who make me laugh, and I appreciate good grammar and original writing. I love technology and fixing things, and my iPhone! My mom taught me to "think positive," and I live to honor her and my dad's memory.

What do you like reading/watching/listening to on your own time? Every cooking show on TV; every show that shows people how to be better in business such as *The Profit*. What happened to Tabitha? I love the series *Fargo* as much as I loved the movie. I prefer talk radio to music, but I enjoy music with an edge and opera. My favorite singer of all time is Louis Armstrong.

Do you think the business has changed a lot over the past few years? If yes, please explain. I miss Borders and Peter Workman and the frequent six-figure deals, but I don't miss the Selectric typewriter too much. My phone used to ring nonstop and now mostly everything is done by email. If I remembered the name of my typing teacher, I would erect a statue to her. I type 90 words per minute, which was the solution to my *Wheel of Fortune* puzzle when I won $34,000. Publishers and agents still need authors, and everyone is still looking for quality books that inform and entertain.

What do the "Big 5" mean to you? Publishing used to be conducted in "publishing houses" — literally rows of brownstones in midtown Manhattan. With all the consolidations and merging of these houses, there are now about five big conglomerates left that are the publishers, and they understandably don't compete with themselves in book auctions.

How do you feel about independent/small presses? Power to them. They are keeping publishing alive.

What are your feelings about self-publishing? It has become a viable option, but most of the time the standard route will still prove more profitable for most authors.

Do you think Amazon is good or bad — or both — for the book business? If I can't wave a magic wand and return to the old days when there were so many mom-and-pop bookshops, I would say Amazon is now far more good than bad. Imagine if they went away!!

What do you like and dislike about your job? I love that you can't hire me to represent you — that I get to choose those projects that make me passionate. I love making my own hours. I love the people I get to work with. I love when my work is appreciated. My favorite thing is to travel to writers' conferences and teach an all-day preconference pitch workshop.

What are ways prospective clients can impress you, and what are ways they can turn you off? This is not to sell you a book, but reading a book such as *The Complete Idiot's Guide to Getting Published*, 5th ed., will help you understand the industry, so that you can get a leg up in securing an agent and a publishing deal. When you are writing a book, the readers' needs have to come first. If you show me that you know the publishing ropes when you approach me, you will impress me. If you break all of the rules to stand out, I call that a "moose call." If you attend one of my publishing workshops, you will learn what I mean by a moose call.

Describe a book you would like to write. I've written over 30 books, including *Secrets the Pros Won't Tell You about Winning Hold 'Em Poker* and *Put Your House on a Diet* (with Ed Morrow and fellow friend and agent Rita Rosenkranz).

Do you believe in a higher and/or lower "power"? I am constantly reminded that there is a realm beyond our comprehension that I don't presume to understand but marvel at.

Is there anything you wish to express beyond the parameters of the preceding questions? I won $34,000 on *Wheel of Fortune*!

SIGNATURE LITERARY AGENCY ❖ signaturelit.com

4200 Wisconsin Avenue NW, #106-233, Washington, DC 20016

Agent's name and contact info: Gary Heidt, gary@signaturelit.com

Describe the kinds of works you want to represent. Nonfiction: history, science, biography, memoir, reference. Fiction: literary.

Describe what you definitely don't want to represent. Children's books, romance, fantasy, historical fiction, health, how-to, cookbooks.

How do you want writers to pitch you? Email a query. For fiction, include a one- to five-page sample pasted into the body of the email as well.

Describe your education and professional history. I have a bachelor's degree from Columbia College in New York. I have been an agent since 2003.

How did you become an agent? I apprenticed with an established agent.

Do you charge fees? If yes, please explain. No.

When and where were you born, and where have you lived? Houston, Texas, 1970; since college, NY metropolitan area; recently, Greensboro, North Carolina.

What do you like to do when you're not working? Play music.

List some of the titles you have recently placed with publishers. *The Insides* by Jeremy Bushnell (Melville House); *Sacred Geometry of the Earth* by Mark Vidler and Catherine Young (Inner Traditions).

Describe your personality. That is not for me to do.

What do you like reading/watching/listening to on your own time? History.

Do you think the business has changed a lot over the past few years? If yes, please explain. I like to think independent booksellers are getting stronger these days.

What do the "Big 5" mean to you? $$$.

How do you feel about independent/small presses? I love them dearly.

What are your feelings about self-publishing? I read a lot of self-published works. There are geniuses out there whose work would not be available otherwise.

Do you think Amazon is good or bad — or both — for the book business? I would never have guessed that the internet would lead to huge monopolies, but in retrospect it seems obvious. It would be nice if there were at least two companies in the Amazon business.

What do you like and dislike about your job? Like: getting to work with authors. Dislike: dunning publishers.

What are ways prospective clients can impress you, and what are ways they can turn you off? Impress me with clarity, precision, and beauty in language. I dislike bombast, vulgarity, and pretentiousness.

How would you describe the "writer from hell"? A writer who writes poorly.

Describe a book you would like to write. I'm working on a book of already completed crosswords.

Do you believe in a higher and/or lower "power"? There are all kinds of higher and lower powers, within an individual, within a society. Some people believe they're alone; these people might be horrified to think that someone else knew all their thoughts; so why do they think and go about their lives with this strange, subtle quality of performance? Consciousness is the fundamental stuff from which the world is made. Matter is an epiphenomenon of mind. The physicists recognize this, but many religious people are still catching up.

SIMENAUER & GREEN LITERARY AGENCY, LLC ❖

www.sgliteraryagency.com

(formerly Simenauer & Frank; Christine Frank has retired)
PO Box 112735, Naples, FL 34108-0416

Agent's name and contact info: Carol H. Green,
carol@sgliteraryagency.com, 303-886-6531

Describe the kinds of works you want to represent. Both fiction and nonfiction manuscripts submitted to us must tell a well-structured story or point of view and must be well written and well researched. Yes, nonfiction also tells a story or presents a point of view, so the preceding is meant to describe both. If the plot or story line fails, the manuscript fails. If the writing fails, the manuscript fails.

In fiction, I like thrillers, mysteries, and historical novels, but I also love almost any story on any other subject that captures my attention and touches my heart from the opening paragraph and never lets go. As for nonfiction, the subject matter should have a new and creative angle that offers insight or needed information to the reader. Health, spirituality, diet, science, the brain, neuroscience, genetics, women's interest, true crime, travel narrative, humor, relationships, aging, and corporate success stories are a few of the nonfiction subjects we like.

Describe what you definitely don't want to represent. Our agency is not interested in crafts, poetry, cookbooks, children's books, science fiction, horror, religion, or pulp-fiction mystery/romance.

How do you want writers to pitch you? Tell us the title, genre, and word count of your manuscript. Give us a brief synopsis of what the story line is about and whether it is fiction or nonfiction. For fiction, you should include at least three chapters or similar sample of your work — enough to tell us you have strong writing and storytelling skills. Many authors attach complete manuscripts. A publisher will require a proposal for a nonfiction work (see Jeff Herman's website for information on how to write a killer nonfiction proposal), but will want a completed manuscript for fiction.

Describe your education and professional history. I am a former newspaper reporter and editor who at mid-career became an attorney and advanced to senior management. I retired from the *Denver Post* after also working at *Newsday* on Long Island, the *Shreveport Times*, and a small daily in Agana, Guam. I attended the Yale Law School under a Ford Foundation Fellowship to study law in a one-year master's degree program and completed my JD degree at the University of Denver. I joined Jacqueline Simenauer to form the Simenauer & Green Literary Agency in 2014.

Do you charge fees? If yes, please explain. We do not charge fees.

What do you like to do when you're not working? I love to read, mostly literary fiction (of course!), am an avid outdoor and nature photographer, and whack away with golf clubs. I also love to travel and recently enjoyed Turkey, Italy, Ireland, Ontario, and Playa del Carmen, Mexico, as well as extensive photography road trips through the American Southwest and to Yellowstone National Park.

Describe your personality. I'm perpetually curious, introverted, spiritual, and committed. I love to solve practical and business-related problems and help others achieve their goals.

List some of the titles you have recently placed with publishers. Most recently, our agency placed *Overwatch* and *First Shot* by Matthew Betley (Emily Bestler Books/Simon

& Schuster). Also *The Caterpillar Way: Lessons in Leadership, Growth, and Shareholder Value* by Craig T. Bouchard and James V. Koch (McGraw-Hill; made the *New York Times* bestseller list); *The New Legions: American Strategy and the Responsibility of Power* by Major General Edward B. Atkeson (Rowman & Littlefield); *The Garage Sale Stalker* by Suzi Weinert (sold to Hallmark Hall of Fame channel for a movie, which garnered the biggest audience in network history; the series is continuing); *Passion's Race* by Christine Mazurk (Lachesis); *Raging Skies* by William Halstead (Blue Water Press); *River of Madness* by William Halstead (Blue Water Press); *Jade's Treasure* by Ana Krista Johnson (Crimson Romance/Adam's Media); *The Insulin Resistant Diet*, rev. ed., by Dr. Cheryle Hart and Mary Kay Grossman (McGraw-Hill; sold more than 150,000 copies).

How would you describe the "writer from hell"? We haven't met one yet, but we do try to ensure the "fit" by getting to know the author and by explaining clearly how agency representation works before establishing a contractual relationship.

Do you think the business has changed a lot over the past few years? If yes, please explain. Just as the internet has revolutionized our lives, it has drastically changed publishing with the advent of ebooks. Although we market to mainstream publishers, many writers who seek our services have already self-published and are now seeking the marketing and distribution support that mainstream publishers provide.

Another major change is the consolidation of the industry into a small number of large publishers, following a merger trend that we have seen in other industries. Publishers are protecting their bottom lines by allocating fewer resources to marketing. Our best advice to authors is that they need to learn to self-promote, so that they can bring an established audience (call it "platform," if you will) to the publisher along with their work. An author who brings sheer talent alone has a much more difficult time getting his or her work accepted.

What do the "Big 5" mean to you? The literary agent has to market more effectively because there are fewer publishers out there. Many imprints overlap at the top of the corporate pyramid, and there is much duplication.

How do you feel about independent/small presses? They may be the seed for the growth of a new trend in creativity and innovation in the market.

Do you think Amazon is good or bad — or both — for the book business? Amazon was inevitable. It offers more access to the market for authors, while it lowers the revenue that authors may expect. Those of us who market to mainstream publishers have to become more innovative in our sales efforts and have to learn how to negotiate better electronic rights for our authors, where possible.

Describe a book you would like to write. A tale that inspires people to find meaning in their lives.

Do you believe in a higher and/or lower "power"? I believe a connecting spirit resides in all of us. What that is, I do not know, but it is a universal force for good.

Agent's name and contact info: Jacqueline Simenauer, jackie@sgliteraryagency.com, 239-597-9877

Describe the kinds of works you want to represent. I like a wide range of strong nonfiction books that include medical, health, nutrition, popular psychology, how-to, self-help, parenting, women's interest, spirituality, men's interest, relationships, social sciences, beauty, and controversial subjects.

Describe what you definitely don't want to represent. Our agency is not interested in crafts, poetry, cookbooks, children's books, science fiction, horror, religion, or pulp-fiction mystery/romance.

How do you want writers to pitch you? My contact of choice is through email. I am open to all well-written nonfiction queries. Please write a really good query letter. This is important. If you can't get your idea across effectively, then you have lost the agent.

Describe your education and professional history. I was born in New York City. After working as an articles editor for a national publication, I decided to start my own literary agency, and, as a result, I coauthored a number of books with my clients. Some of the six books that I was involved with include *Husbands and Wives* (Times Books); *Singles: The New Americans* (Simon & Schuster), which gained the attention of the White House; the bestselling *Beyond the Male Myth* (Times Books), which was featured on *Oprah*; and *Not Tonight, Dear* (Doubleday). They went on to sell more than 200,000 copies. My work also has been featured in most of the nation's magazines and newspapers, including *Time, Reader's Digest, Ladies' Home Journal,* the *New York Times,* and the *Washington Post.* In addition, I have appeared on more than 100 radio and TV shows, including *Good Morning America* and *Today.*

Do you charge fees? If yes, please explain. We do not charge fees.

What do you like to do when you're not working? I have always worked so hard that I have never found time to even think about a hobby. However, I do love classical concerts. I am a member of travel and music groups and a wine society; I love Broadway theater and great fiction.

Describe your personality. Type A, warm, kind, giving.

List some of the titles you have recently placed with publishers. See the list provided above by my colleague, Carol Green (page 514).

How would you describe the "writer from hell"? I haven't encountered what I would call the "writer from hell." Luckily, the writers that I have represented over the years have been a joy to work with.

Do you think the business has changed a lot over the past few years? When I started my agent business, there were no ebooks, and publishers were buying and publishing more hard- and softcover books. Selling was easier then. They weren't afraid to take a chance. The fact that everything has become largely digitized gives writers more opportunity to get their works out there. Books will still be selling in the future, but the sale of ebooks will be climbing right behind them. Agents will probably be selling as many digitized works as hard- and softcover books.

What do the "Big 5" mean to you? The Big 5 mean to me that selling is going to be harder because of the mergers between publishers, and we won't have the choices that we had years ago.

Do you think Amazon is good or bad — or both — for the book business? Amazon has its place.

Describe a book you would like to write. I would love to write the story of my husband's life. He was born in Germany, grew up in China, spent part of his life in Israel, and then went on to a great symphonic career.

STEELE-PERKINS LITERARY AGENCY

26 Island Lane, Canandaigua, NY 14424, 585-396-9290

Agent's name and contact info: Pattie Steele-Perkins, pattiesp@aol.com

Describe the kinds of works you want to represent. Romance and women's fiction, all genres, for example, romantic suspense and inspirational.

Describe what you definitely don't want to represent. Nonfiction and anything that does not meet the guidelines of romance and women's fiction.

How do you want writers to pitch you? Email a query that includes a synopsis. Use the term *Query* in the subject line and paste the synopsis in the email. We do not open attachments.

Describe your education and professional history. Prior to becoming an agent, I was the creative director of a television production company. Prior to that I was a producer/director.

How did you become an agent? I mentored with an established agent who introduced me to the major publishing houses and editors in the romance genre. When I retired, I opened up my own agency.

Do you charge fees? If yes, please explain. No.

STEPHANIE TADE AGENCY ❖ www.stephanietadeagency.com

PO Box 235, 105 County Line Road, Durham, PA 18039, 610-346-8667

Agents' names and contact info: Stephanie Tade, stade@stadeagency.com;
Colleen Martell, cmartell@stadeagency.com

Describe the kinds of works you want to represent. *Stephanie*: Popular nonfiction, particularly in the areas of wellness and well-being — physical (diet/health), emotional, psychological, spiritual — primarily Eastern-based spirituality. National platforms or high credentials with moderate platform.

Describe what you definitely don't want to represent. Children's books, history, true crime, how-to. No fiction at the moment — there can be exceptions but very rare, and no first fiction.

How do you want writers to pitch you? Query, but most through referral.

Describe your education and professional history. Graduated from Cornell University in 1982 and went straight into publishing. Worked at Bantam 2 years (PR and subrights), at Jane Rotrosen Agency 17 years, at Rodale (executive editor of Rodale General Books) 4 years. Opened STA in 2005.

How did you become an agent? Linda Grey (remember her?) recommended me to Jane Berkey (Jane Rotrosen). Linda thought I was smart and needed to escape where I currently was. I fell in love with agenting right away. I was practically an apprentice at first and worked my way up through international and domestic rights for the entire agency and represented my own smaller list at JRA.

Knowing what you do now, would you do it again? If not, what might you do instead? Believe it or not, sometimes I wish I'd gone to law school. I have a thing for contracts and negotiating; I think it's a really creative process and enjoy it. But for the most part, I really wouldn't change a thing. I love being an agent.

Do you charge fees? If yes, please explain. Nope. Just 15 percent commission.

When and where were you born, and where have you lived? Born and raised in western New York. After college I lived and worked in New York City for 12 years; then Taos, New Mexico, where I maintained my office for the JRA for 3 years; now in Bucks County, Pennsylvania. I'm in NYC as needed, usually once or twice a week.

What do you like to do when you're not working? I have a family, one daughter (12 years old) still at home. I do lots of meditation, including retreats (I'm a practicing Buddhist and teach introductory meditation), yoga, reading, running. I have spent years with horses, though I do not currently have one. Not sure what else, but I seem to be constantly busy.

List some of the titles you have recently placed with publishers. Amy Myers, MD, *The Thyroid Connection* (Little, Brown); Leah Weiss, PhD, *Heart at Work* (Harper Wave); Tererai Trent, PhD, *Forgotten Women* (Enliven!); Roshi Joan Halifax, *Standing at the Edge* (Flatiron); Lodro Rinzler, *How to Hold Your Broken Heart* (Shambhala); Frank Lipman, MD, *10 Reasons You Feel Old and Get Fat* (Hay House); Deanna Minich, PhD, *Whole Detox* (HarperOne).

Describe your personality. I suppose I'm a mix, like most people. My practice and my dedication to it contribute to my best attempts to be compassionate. I'm a pretty good listener. I also love to laugh, and really love to negotiate — I find the whole "catastrophe," as they say, an awful lot of fun.

What do you like reading/watching/listening to on your own time? This might seem at odds with the "niceness" that a lot of people associate with me (to my dismay), but *The Walking Dead, Breaking Bad, Game of Thrones* — you get the picture. Also loved *Mozart in the Jungle.* I listen to just about everything music-wise, tend to blast NPR on a sunny day, and read all. the. time. I love fantasy, British historical novels, smart books, commercial books, lots of dharma reading.... Right now I'm reading *Dark Money* and wow. Chilling.

Do you think the business has changed a lot over the past few years? If yes, please explain. Of course, in almost every superficial way — with ebooks and how books are marketed, how brands are built. But basically we're still selling content that deserves to be in book form and finding the best ways to do so.

What do the "Big 5" mean to you? I do most of my business with the bigger publishers.

How do you feel about independent/small presses? It depends upon the book. Sometimes a smaller press is just the thing, but I have less and less time for working with projects that have to be "made," which is really where independent/small presses come in.

What are your feelings about self-publishing? I think it can be a great outlet, and sometimes it helps authors find a way to get their message out when no conventional agent or publisher can do it for them. I think probably some books don't really need to be published, even if the author needs to write them — it's really all about what the author is looking for. Self-publishing can also wreck someone's chances at finding a publisher later, if they can't find an audience.

Do you think Amazon is good or bad — or both — for the book business? Uck, can I just pass on this? I suppose the answer is both. Obviously they sell massive numbers of books — that's a good thing. Publishing needs Amazon, but the problem is, Amazon doesn't really need publishing. So there's an inequity built into the whole partnership that delivers both good and bad to publishers and authors and agents.

What do you like and dislike about your job? I love learning, I love working creatively, I enjoy all the components of what I do. I don't enjoy disappointment (which happens).

Sometimes there are some bad players in the mix. Not everyone plays nice or is trustworthy, and that means dealing with situations that are unpleasant — somewhat rare, but still, that's the one part of my job that I don't like much. But I'm learning to let that just be part of the game and feel fortunate that I can keep my own side of the street clean!

What are ways prospective clients can impress you, and what are ways they can turn you off? You can impress me by knowing what you want, developing what's needed to be successful, and being willing to learn or develop in the areas that need work. Show me your community, your fans, and how you interact with them. You can turn me off by just not doing your homework, or not appreciating what an incredibly cool thing it is to be able to write a book, get it published, and have a readership love what you have to say.

How would you describe the "writer from hell"? Lack of boundaries, narcissist.

Describe a book you would like to write. No thanks. I like writing but I have no desire to write a book. ☺

Do you believe in a higher and/or lower "power"? What a funny question. With a Buddhist answer. I'm a nontheist. I believe in basic goodness (*bodhichitta*), because I experience it every day and I see it everywhere. But that's different from God. I'm not religious, and I don't believe in evil, though I do think profound confusion is at the root of some terrible thoughts and actions.

THE STEVE LAUBE AGENCY ❖ www.stevelaube.com

24 West Camelback Road, A-635, Phoenix, AZ 85013

Agents' names and contact info: Steve Laube, President, krichards@stevelaube.com; Karen Ball, pwhitson@stevelaube.com; Dan Balow, vseem@stevelaube.com; Tamela Hancock Murray, ewilson@stevelaube.com

Describe the kinds of works you want to represent. We work primarily with books intended for the Christian market, both fiction and nonfiction, plus selected children's books.

How do you want writers to pitch you? Please follow the guidelines found on our website. There we give specific methods for making the best pitch to us.

Describe your education and professional history. Steve: I have been in the book industry for over 35 years, first as a bookstore manager (awarded the National Store of the Year by CBA). I then spent over a decade with Bethany House (named the Editor of the Year). I later became an agent and have represented nearly 1,000 new books (named Agent of the

Year by ACFW). I was also inducted into the Grand Canyon University Hall of Fame by the college of theology. In addition, I am the president and owner of Enclave Publishing (enclavepublishing.com). Information on each of the other agents in the firm is available on our website.

How did you become an agent? In 2003 I was approached by an agency to join them and since, at that time, Bethany House was being sold, I made the jump. A little more than a year later (in May 2004) I formed my own agency.

Knowing what you do now, would you do it again? If not, what might you do instead? It was a good decision, which I have never regretted.

Do you charge fees? If yes, please explain. Never.

What do you like to do when you're not working? When asked, "What do you do for a living?" I say, "I read." When asked, "What do you do for fun?" I smile and say, "I read."

List some of the titles you have recently placed with publishers. In 2015 our agency placed over 130 new books with publishers. To choose one or two would leave other worthy titles off that list. I prefer to point to the list of our clients displayed on our website. We are proud to work with some of the best and brightest our industry has to offer.

What do you like reading/watching/listening to on your own time? I am a die-hard science fiction and fantasy reader, but I also enjoy reading thrillers and suspense. They are my "mind candy." In addition I am a voracious reader of nonfiction (history, business, and theology).

Do you think the business has changed a lot over the past few years? If yes, please explain. Economic pressures have caused every publisher, big and small, to change. What used to be a selection process based on "Is this a good book?" has become an exercise in "risk management." Good books still get published, but the economic threshold has skyrocketed for making investments in those books.

How do you feel about independent/small presses? There has always been a place for the strong independent/small presses. The challenge is discerning which ones have the strength to successfully bring a book to market. What we call "micropublishers" seem to crop up on a regular basis, mostly with a digital-first or digital-only focus. A few have staying power and provide a great service, but others stumble or eventually disappear.

What are your feelings about self-publishing? Self-publishing is a great outlet for authors who have been stymied by the risk-aversion mentality of the major publishers (see my above comment). It can be the first-time author who cannot get a foot in the door or it can be the veteran author whose recent sales have slowed and who can no longer get a new contract. In addition, there are many authors who are very prolific, to the point that their traditional publishers cannot fully support the number of books they write. These become "hybrid" authors, which allows them to do some books traditionally and some independently. We fully support the efforts of authors to get their books to market, but we hope that those who do it independently are getting their books properly edited and are using top-level production (meaning covers and interior design) to maintain a high-quality end product.

Do you believe in a higher and/or lower "power"? Absolutely. Our agency is focused on books intended for the Christian market. The agency's motto is, "To help change the world, word by word," and we strive to meet that goal. Included on our website is a statement of faith that expresses our commitment to Jesus Christ.

STIMOLA LITERARY STUDIO ❖ www.stimolaliterarystudio.com

308 Livingston Court, Edgewater, NJ 07020, 201-945-9353, fax: 201-490-5920

Agent's name and contact info: Rosemary Stimola, info@stimolaliterarystudio.com

Describe the kinds of works you want to represent. Preschool through young adult fiction and nonfiction.

How do you want writers to pitch you? See our website for submission guidelines. We will respond within two weeks only to those queries we wish to pursue further with a request for material.

Describe your education and professional history. Education: BA in elementary education and theoretical linguistics, Queens College; MA in applied linguistics, NYU; PhD in applied linguistics and educational psychology, NYU.

How did you become an agent? Career history: professor of language and literature; children's bookseller; literary agent.

Knowing what you do now, would you do it again? If not, what might you do instead? My years as an academic combined with my years as a bookseller laid the perfect foundation for my agenting life. All led me to this profession, which I am proud and pleased to be a part of. I could never see myself doing anything else.

Do you charge fees? If yes, please explain. We do not charge any fees and work on a commission-only basis per the AAR Canon of Ethics.

When and where were you born, and where have you lived? Born November 6, 1952, Queens, New York. Have lived in Queens, Brooklyn, and Leonia, New Jersey. Currently live in Edgewater, New Jersey, and West Tisbury, Massachusetts.

What do you like to do when you're not working? Hobbies: beachcombing, Latin dance, cockapoos.

List some of the titles you have recently placed with publishers. *The Conjurers* by Brian Anderson, *My Diary from the Edge of the World* by Jodi Lynn Anderson, *Simon Thorn* series by Aimee Carter, *Black Wolf in the Snow* by Matthew Cordell, *A Few Red Drops* by Claire Hartfiled, *One Amazing Elephant* by Linda Oatman High, *How to Hang a Witch* by Adriana Mather, *A Tale of Highly Unusual Magic* by Lisa Papademetriou, *The Remnant* trilogy by Mary E. Pearson, *Liberty* by Andrea Portes, *Just Seen Leaving* by Caleb Roehrig, *Are You a Princess or a Dragon?* by Barney Saltzberg, *Girl Rising* by Tanya Lee Stone, *Rude Cakes* by Rowboat Watkins.

Describe your personality. Disciplined, fair-minded, no-nonsense, team builder. Prefer collaboration to confrontation, but can go to the latter when needed. A firm but reasonable negotiator.

What do you like reading/watching/listening to on your own time? I am a very eclectic reader, so anything goes. I tend to read "authors," so any book written by the likes of John Irving, Margaret Atwood, and Amy Tan, and I am always adding to the list. I am also hooked on many of the BBC crime/drama series on Netflix and will binge-watch episodes — sort of like viewing multiple chapters in a book when my eyes are tired.

What will agenting be like in 2020? I would imagine that changes in technology and business will demand ever-evolving knowledge of contractual matters, so that authors' rights are protected and they are duly compensated for their creative work, whatever the format or channels of distribution. I do hope, however, that the core personal relationships of agent, author, and editor remain intact.

Do you miss the way the business "used to be"? I miss the opportunity to "seal a deal" when an editor says "I love this." The bureaucracy of acquisition can sometimes kill a good book's chances of being published. I do not appreciate the use of "tracking," using an author's past sales to determine if a new book will be acquired. The past is not always a prediction of the future, and sometimes a few modestly sold novels lead the way to that bestseller.

What do the "Big 5" mean to you? Just that more and more mergers are likely to take place. I fear we may end up with the Big 1 down the road.

How do you feel about independent/small presses? Small and independent presses play a very crucial role in the current publishing climate, providing titles of interest and importance in the wider spectrum.

What are your feelings about self-publishing? Self-publishing has a place and offers "opportunity," but it can be overinflated, creating an illusion of achieving success that is more the exception than the rule and a vast pool of unedited, unvetted "slush."

Do you think Amazon is good or bad — or both — for the book business? Amazon has changed the climate of publishing and business in general. Whether it is for the ultimate good remains to be seen. I do hope there is a comfortable partnership to be struck between Amazon and publishers as we move forward, one that does not penalize authors.

What do you like and dislike about your job? My job is fulfilling in many ways. Nothing is more exciting than finding and nurturing new talent. Nothing is more exciting than seeing a book you've helped to shepherd find its wings and fly high. Work hours can sometimes be demanding, but in the end it's all for a good cause.

What are ways prospective clients can impress you, and what are ways they can turn you off? I am impressed by a query letter that is well voiced, succinct, and avoids hyperbole.

How would you describe the "writer from hell"? The "writer from hell" has unrealistic expectations and a major ego, is resistant to editor guidance and revision, and always misses deadlines.

Describe a book you would like to write. I don't really think about writing a book. I leave that to my authors.

Do you believe in a higher and/or lower "power"? I do believe in a higher power. I just don't subscribe to institutional religious beliefs about that power.

THE STORY MERCHANT LITERARY MANAGEMENT ❖

storymerchant.com

400 South Burnside Avenue, #11B, Los Angeles, CA 90036, 323-932-1685

Agent's name and contact info: Ken Atchity, atchity@storymerchant.com

Describe the kinds of works you want to represent. Books that can also make commercial films, especially true stories about heroic men or women.

Describe what you definitely don't want to represent. Niche market projects.

How do you want writers to pitch you? *Brief* queries by *email* only.

Describe your education and professional history. BA, Georgetown; PhD, Yale University. Former professor of comparative literature, Fulbright professor to Italy. Regular reviewer, *Los Angeles Times Book Review.*

How did you become an agent? I worked as a professor to help students develop their storytelling skills, so it was a natural progression to the commercial side of the story marketplace.

Knowing what you do now, would you do it again? If not, what might you do instead? I would do exactly what I do: develop stories, sell them to publishers, produce them as movies, and publish new voices under my Story Merchant Books imprint.

Do you charge fees? If yes, please explain. No fees for representation; a launch fee if we assist with direct publishing.

When and where were you born, and where have you lived? Eunice, Louisiana, in the last century. I've lived in the Midwest, on the East Coast, and now for most of my life in Los Angeles.

What do you like to do when you're not working? Wish I were working! I travel all over the world to find interesting places to work from.

List some of the titles you have recently placed with publishers. *Nobody Nowhere* by Dennis Walsh (Thomas Dunne; now a coproduction at MGM with Marc Platt Productions); *Mrs. Kennedy and Me* by Clint Hill and Lisa McCubbin (Gallery); *Dracula: The Un-Dead* by Dacre Stoker (Dutton).

Describe your personality. Optimistic, grateful, determined to turn dreams into realities.

What do you like reading/watching/listening to on your own time? Discovering exciting new stories is my favorite read; addicted to series like *House of Cards*, *Homeland*, *Orphan Black*, *Outlander*, etc.

Do you think the business has changed a lot over the past few years? If yes, please explain. There is *nothing* the same about it, from five years ago *except* the need for great new stories with global appeal.

What do the "Big 5" mean to you? Since I live in both worlds, Fox, Universal, Sony, Paramount, Weinsteins; and Hachette, Viacom, Penguin Random House, Macmillan, and HarperCollins.

How do you feel about independent/small presses? I feel admiration for them, though from our clients' point of view I'd often recommend direct publishing instead.

What are your feelings about self-publishing? For new voices in fiction especially, it's my preferred advice, because it puts the writer in direct touch with both the business and the audience.

Do you think Amazon is good or bad — or both — for the book business? It is as revolutionary and good as Gutenberg's invention of the printing press. The bad comes from its growing monolithic character. But one way or the other it is the *future*.

What do you like and dislike about your job? I love the discovery of a great new story and writer. I dislike the time it takes to find the right path to the audience.

What are ways prospective clients can impress you, and what are ways they can turn you off? Impress me with a well-composed, focused email query that indicates strong writing and thinking as well as awareness of the market. Turn me off with the opposite of that as well as "entitlement," being demanding, being misleading about credentials, or just plain vagueness.

How would you describe the "writer from hell"? Relentless emailing or phoning with even the smallest questions, not taking the time to investigate their own questions, over-the-top expectations, thinking agents are doing *them* a favor, and the worst: clients who blame everyone but themselves.

Describe a book you would like to write. An up-to-the-minute book about the changes in the industry, one that would have to be continually updated every month!

Do you believe in a higher and/or lower "power"? Higher yes, in tune with the universe. Lower is usually within our own nature.

Is there anything you wish to express beyond the parameters of the preceding questions? Here's to peace in our time and an end to religious fanaticism and intolerance.

STRACHAN LITERARY AGENCY ❖ strachanlit.com

PO Box 2091, Annapolis, MD 21404

Agent's name and contact info: Laura Strachan, query@strachanlit.com

Describe the kinds of works you want to represent. I like anything that is a "compelling story, well told." In general that means literary fiction and narrative nonfiction. I also handle some young adult fiction. I tend not to take on genre fiction, but that's not hard and fast. If it's beautifully written, I am interested.

Describe what you definitely don't want to represent. I never say never, but I'm not terribly interested in business books, political books, hard nonfiction. It's all about the narrative.

How do you want writers to pitch you? These days I get most new authors from referrals, but I can be contacted through my website. I want a brief idea of what the book is about and a brief bio.

Describe your education and professional history. I studied English lit as an undergrad and then attended law school. I practiced law for a year and decided it was the wrong career path. I hit upon agenting as a way to combine my legal education with what I loved, namely, books and good writing. How I got there is a long story, but I was able to make the transition with the help and advice of lots of very smart and talented people in the industry — other agents, writers, and a particular publisher to whom I am indebted for his help and friendship.

How did you become an agent? See previous question.

Knowing what you do now, would you do it again? If not, what might you do instead? I wish that I had had the courage to go to New York and jump headfirst into publishing. My law-school education has been helpful to me, but I think that it would have served me just as well to go straight into a publishing career. Coming to the industry from outside of it was a challenge. Alternately, perhaps I would have stayed in the legal profession and focused on intellectual property.

Do you charge fees? If yes, please explain. I do not charge fees, apart from the standard commission. I used to charge for expenses, but they have by and large disappeared, as the business has become electronic and files and paperwork are easily transferred by email. There are the occasional bank transfer fees.

When and where were you born, and where have you lived? I was born in Baltimore, Maryland. I spent some time in Washington, DC, before moving to Annapolis.

What do you like to do when you're not working? My favorite thing to do is read, luckily. But I also enjoy art and the theater. And good food.

List some of the titles you have recently placed with publishers. In Search of Wild Edibles by Jeffrey Greene (University of Virginia Press), *Like the First Morning* by Michael Ortiz (Ave Maria Press), *Café Oc* by Beebe Bahrami (Shanti Arts), *Café Neandertal* by Beebe Bahrami (Counterpoint).

Describe your personality. A recovering perfectionist. It took me a long time to learn that things are what they are. You do what you can, then accept it and move on. Related, I try not to get too worked up about things. I've learned only recently that challenges make us more creative, so I try to see the gift in them.

What do you like reading/watching/listening to on your own time? I like to read what I represent: literary fiction and well-written narrative nonfiction. I watch very little television. I like *Downton Abbey* and I've grown to like *Shameless*. I like the reality competition shows: *Project Runway* and *Top Chef*, etc., because I like watching talented people be creative, and pretty much anything on HGTV. My musical tastes are wide-ranging, from classical to indie.

Do you think the business has changed a lot over the past few years? If yes, please explain. Yes and no. I think it's always been a tough business. The consolidation of smaller publishers into the megacorporations certainly changed the business — and put the focus on the business part of the industry. But I see more and more new, small presses stepping in to fill the void, and I think that's a positive thing.

What do the "Big 5" mean to you? The Big 5 means tradition, and in most cases more financial wherewithal. But the Big 5 doesn't necessarily mean the best placement for a project or even the best publication support.

How do you feel about independent/small presses? I love them. The small indies can take risks that the Big 5 can't, or won't.

What are your feelings about self-publishing? I am not at all against self-publishing. The sad truth is that many deserving books will never be published simply because of certain economic realities, so self-publishing provides an avenue for getting that work out into the world. But just because one *can* self-publish doesn't mean that one *should*. An author should not self-publish something that isn't ready to be published. It's a far different thing to publish a book that has gotten good feedback from industry professionals who regret that circumstances prevent them from taking it on than to self-publish 30 seconds after typing "The End." Any author who chooses to self-publish needs to do the homework and research necessary to understand how the business works and to recognize that publishing is only the beginning of the process (something that traditionally published authors need to understand as well).

Do you think Amazon is good or bad — or both — for the book business? Both. The detrimental effects of Amazon have been well documented and don't need to be repeated here. And it is yet to be seen how Amazon will affect the industry if it really goes into bricks and mortar. But it is also true that Amazon makes my job much easier. It is a great research and reference tool for me to see what else is out there and who is publishing it. And if reduced pricing means someone will purchase one of my author's books that they may not have purchased at full price, I see it as an opportunity.

What do you like and dislike about your job? I love helping my authors find a way to have their voices heard. I'm as excited as they are to see a book I represented on the shelf in the bookstore. But it's a frustrating business. It's not selling widgets. I tell my authors when they are frustrated by a rejection that I deal with rejection in multiples. As much as I love helping to bring a book into the world at large, I hate being unable to place a book that's wonderful but just isn't the right thing at the right time.

What are ways prospective clients can impress you, and what are ways they can turn you off? Authors who have done their homework, who understand, at least on a rudimentary level, how the business works, and who don't have unrealistic expectations will impress me. Authors who want to tell me how to do my job, who are unwilling to listen to advice or criticism (or who "know" a book is going to be a bestseller) are a definite turnoff.

How would you describe the "writer from hell"? Bringing a book to market is a collaborative effort. Understandably, the author has a vested interest in the process and should have a say in it, but an author also needs to let the agent and publisher do what they do.

The client from hell believes he or she knows best and refuses advice or direction. Likewise, the author who needs constant reassurance and updates. Being an agent does entail a great deal of hand-holding, and authors should expect reasonable updates, but there is a balance. The wheels of publishing can turn excruciatingly slowly. Patience is a virtue!

Describe a book you would like to write. In the past I've said that I have no desire to write a book, which isn't really true. If I could, I'd write a novel. But just as I am incapable of painting like Leonardo, I'm incapable of writing the type of novel that I would wish to write. So I leave that to others and am happy to do my part.

Do you believe in a higher and/or lower "power"? I do. I was raised Protestant, so my "higher power" is the more traditional one, but I am not arrogant enough to think that my beliefs are the only true or right ones. Who's to say that the higher power can't choose to present or reveal itself in multiple ways?

THE STUART AGENCY ❖ www.stuartagency.com

New York, NY

Agent's name and contact info: Rob Kirkpatrick, rob@stuartagency.com

Describe the kinds of works you want to represent. Memoir, biography, history, sports, pop culture, music, current events/politics, popular science.

Describe what you definitely don't want to represent. No religious/devotional. No unsolicited fiction.

How do you want writers to pitch you? Submissions should be emailed directly to rob@stuartagency.com. Include a query letter in the body of the email along with an attached proposal that provides a description, table of contents, sample chapter or full manuscript (if available), and any relevant professional credentials, including publication and sales data (if available) for any previously published books.

Describe your education and professional history. I completed my PhD in English while working full-time in the publishing industry and was a senior editor at multiple publishing houses (both Big 5 and independent) for a dozen years.

Do you charge fees? If yes, please explain. No.

What do you like to do when you're not working? Spend time with my wife and our baby son.

What do the "Big 5" mean to you? I worked for almost eight years at an imprint of St. Martin's Press at Macmillan, where I published the books I'm most proud of, and I also met my wife there.

How do you feel about independent/small presses? In some cases, an established independent press can be the right match for an author.

What are ways prospective clients can impress you, and what are ways they can turn you off? An author can impress me by submitting a clear and well-organized proposal for a compelling book that also outlines his or her unique credentials and/or promising sales track.

TESSLER LITERARY AGENCY ❖ www.tessleragency.com

27 West 20th Street, Suite 1003, New York, NY 10011

Agent's name and contact info: Michelle Tessler, Web query form at www.tessleragency.com

Describe the kinds of works you want to represent. High-quality fiction (literary and commercial) and nonfiction (narrative, popular science, memoir, history, psychology, business, biography, food, travel).

Describe what you definitely don't want to represent. Genre fiction, children's books, screenplays.

How do you want writers to pitch you? Via www.tessleragency.com.

Describe your education and professional history. I have a master's degree in English literature and am a member of the Association of Authors' Representatives and Women's Media Group.

How did you become an agent? Having previously worked at the prestigious literary agency Carlisle & Company (now Inkwell Management) and at the William Morris Agency, I founded my own agency in 2004. In addition to my agenting experience, I worked as an executive of business development and marketing in the internet industry. In 1994, just as the internet was becoming a mainstream medium, I was hired by bestselling author James Gleick to help launch the Pipeline. I later worked at Jupiter Communications, an internet market-research company, and at Screaming Media, an online content-syndication company, before returning to publishing. In light of the digital opportunities that are transforming publishing, my experience in the internet world is of great benefit to my authors, both as they navigate ebook and app opportunities and as they look for creative and effective ways to market their books to niche communities that can be targeted online.

Do you charge fees? If yes, please explain. No.

List some of the titles you have recently placed with publishers. *Murder of the Century* by Paul Collins, *Are We Smart Enough to Know How Smart Animals Are?* and *The Bonobo and the Atheist* by Frans de Waal, *The Sleepwalker's Guide to Dancing* by Mira Jacob, *Girl Waits with Gun* and *The Drunken Botanist* by Amy Stewart, *The Same Sky* and *How to Be Lost* by Amanda Eyre Ward.

TONI LOPOPOLO LITERARY MANAGEMENT ❖ lopopololiterary.com

1071 Casitas Pass Road, Suite 104, Carpinteria, CA 93013-2124, 215-353-1151

Agent's name and contact info: Toni Lopopolo, toni@lopopololiterary.com

Describe the kinds of works you want to represent. I love good genre: mystery, cozies (with a hobby), noir (my favorite genre), novels that have a touch of the paranormal, e.g., second sight, a little woo-woo's always good. Understandable, believable magic. (Hey, my father came from southern Italy.) Fiction for today's women. New adult, young adult, and middle grade fiction. I like historicals as well, with proactive female protagonists. I like ancient Rome. Italian Renaissance noir, like Sarah Dunant works. I read James Lee Burke, Dennis Lehane, Robert Crais (big Joe Pike fan), his latest, *Suspect*, and *Promise*, which features a police dog with PTSD. Astonish me. I've been successful with LGBTQ fiction, a growing market. Nonfiction: today's headlines, good narrative nonfiction, even memoir if the subject promises a wide market. I need a terrific nonfiction book proposal with at least three sample chapters. Try me.

Describe what you definitely don't want to represent. Writers who have not mastered the skills needed for book-length fiction and nonfiction. I do not accept screenplays or poetry.

How do you want writers to pitch you? Refer to my website for those instructions, pretty please? Lopopololiterary.com.

Describe your education and professional history. I started working in book publishing as a publicist at Bantam Books, then library promotion director at Harcourt Brace, then paperback marketing director at Houghton Mifflin, then executive editor for paperback books at Macmillan. I spent the last 10 years in book publishing as an executive editor at St. Martin's Press. I graduated from San Francisco State, plus the publishing school of hard knocks.

How did you become an agent? After more than 20 years working in book publishing in New York City, the perfect segue became opening a literary agency in my native state, California, in 1991.

Knowing what you do now, would you do it again? If not, what might you do instead? What and leave show biz? Fantasy career: raising dogs, Italian Greyhounds and calm Jack Russells. I love dogs' faces. I relish editing manuscripts and leading writers' workshops.

Do you charge fees? If yes, please explain. No, not as an agency. However, in November we created Editorial Services. We now offer to edit fiction and narrative nonfiction with a fee schedule of options. See lopopololiterary.com, Editorial Services.

When and where were you born, and where have you lived? Born in Los Angeles on a hot July day. Lived in San Francisco, Fresno, San Fernando, Roscoe, now called Sun Valley, California. I lived in Manhattan during my book-publishing career. I now live in Santa Barbara County in a beach town.

What do you like to do when you're not working? Never enough time for reading. I do, however, never drive without an audiobook sounding off in my red Jeep Liberty gas burner. Actually listened to the entire 800-page novel *Goldfinch* by Donna Tartt. Why doesn't she hire an editor? I'm busy giving Tea With Toni workshops on weekends: one in Thousand Oaks, Saturdays, on Skype site on Sundays with writers scattered around the US, and a great small group of writers on Mondays at an outdoor restaurant called Crushcakes. I have one dog left of six: a little Italian Greyhound named Francesca Saverio Cabrini, a.k.a. Puppy Girl, who's now nine and a half years old. I'm Nonnie Toni to my grandchildren, Zak (film critic studies) and Christina (so beautiful she takes my breath away). I'm learning to make jewelry.

List some of the titles you have recently placed with publishers. *Culture War* by Telly Davidson (McFarland); Manuel Ramos's latest Chicano noir, *My Bad*, featuring Gus Corral and Luis Montez (Arte Publico); Robin Winter's new horror thriller, *Watch the Shadows*, with Chris Meeks (White Whiskers); Shelly Lowenkopf's short story collection, *Love Will Make You Drink and Gamble, Stay Out Late at Night* (same publisher, award-winning volume).

Describe your personality. Changed a lot, more mellow, but passionate about good editing for fiction due to mentoring by Tom McCormack, who wrote a book for publishing editors called *The Fiction Editor*, because he saw a lack of skill. See too many editing errors in published novels by the Big 5 editors. Violation of point of view. Big grammar mistakes even in a famous novelist's nonfiction book. I named one of my Italian Greyhounds Santini. See? I've got a short fuse. Been taught by masters. Shelly Lowenkopf, Sol Stein, Tom McCormack, Renni Browne (though she and I disagree often). I don't accept omniscient POV. Not for today's market. Any writer who wants to become a client of this agency must first own and read: *Stein on Writing* by Sol Stein, *Self-Editing for Fiction Writers* by Renni Browne and Dave King, and *The Fiction Writer's Handbook* by Shelly Lowenkopf. I correct people when they misuse the direct object pronoun, though my daughter Roseanna tells me, "Mom. Cool it. The language keeps changing." Sigh. I cannot bear to the point of hives on my neck when a writer uses the "as" parallel, e.g., "As I walked into the room, she shot me." That particular "as" has an idiot brother named "-ing": "Walking into the room, she shot me."

Two actions happening at once (whether probable or not) dilute the impact of the stronger phrase. See Renni Browne's book, in the chapter entitled "Sophistication," p. 192.

What do you like reading/watching/listening to on your own time? I love Alice Hoffman, Denise Mina, Sarah Dunant, Kate Atkinson (before she went woo-woo on us, though I read those two of hers, one being *Life After Life*). But I love her character Jackson Brodie. I teach from her wonderful POV. I'm reading Sinclair Lewis now. Interesting how Lewis had to create in the 1920s his own techniques to express, for example, Sam Dodsworth's thoughts both in omniscient first person and intimate thirds, which would be unacceptable now because 21-century conventions for writing are so different. We don't have the patience or time for all that detail. Denise Mina, though she hasn't learned some basic skills, is a thrilling writer. I don't own a TV anymore, but I stream like crazy as my reward for so much editing: great writing and acting in series like *The Fall*, *Peaky Blinders*, *Ray Donovan*, *Luther*, *Wolf Hall* (how 'bout that Mark Rylance), anything with Benedict Cumberbatch, whom I saw in the filmed version of *Hamlet* (National Theater); went back to see the filmed play again — exciting. Sent me back to read the play. Other series: *Dicte*, *Fargo*, *True Detective*, even the terrible second one; *Homeland* (getting tired, a bit but straight out of today's headlines about terrorism); I miss *Dexter*. Good writing hard to find anywhere. I never pick up on Network shows. Canned. But I followed *Empire* on Fox. Huh. Really like *Jesse Stone* films with Tom Selleck. Astonished by *American Sniper*, *Bird Man*, not *Gone Girl*. Loved *Girl on the Train*, a drunken Nancy Drew, which means the story kept my interest. *Luckiest Girl Alive* by Jessica Knoll. I liked the main character because she proved more interesting than Gone Girl. My student writers study scenes of dialog from good shows. I'm getting a clip of the film *Spotlight* for that first scene of dialog between Michael Keaton and Liv Schreiber. Whew! Charged dialog rules! *Bridge of Spies*, oh that Mark Rylance, and Tom Hanks's eyes. Bored by *Carol*, so overstylized a film I started to say aloud, "I paid. I have to watch foggy glass forever?" *Room*. *Brooklyn*, which way beat out *Carol* for a story of magnetism. Will see *The Big Short*, maybe *Relevant*. My fave films to rewatch often: *The Third Man* (perfect dialog throughout); *Dodsworth* (1936), Walter Huston, makes me happy; *The Searchers*; *Moonstruck*; and a few others.

Do you think the business has changed a lot over the past few years? If yes, please explain. Conglomerates rule now. Books I published as an editor for 20 years, then later sold as an agent since 1991 can now be classified as "niche"; therefore "we can't do niche anymore." "No instruction books anymore" — like books for writers. So yes, the Big 5 houses buy what they're selling well. Like frontlist.

What do the "Big 5" mean to you? I still go to them but depend on smaller publishers to get the books out faster, market longer, and not stop marketing after the catalog's published for that particular Big 5 season. Big 5, Big Business. Edit as little as you can and leave in all kinds of mistakes, multiple habit words like dead nonverbs "was" and "were" and every form of the infinitive "to be" instead of nice juicy active verbs. "It," "it is," "it's," "there's": all meaningless words. Nouns? What're those?

How do you feel about independent/small presses? I like a few who know what they're doing. I tested a certain "small" publisher with bad manuscripts I kept on hand. They bit. Ugh. They'll take on anything, throw against a wall, and see what sticks. On the other hand, I respect several who know the business because they'd worked in publishing or experienced publishing as authors, like Imajin in Edmonton, Canada. Publishing started with small independent publishers and publishing's headed there again; Mr. Simon and Mr. Schuster started with crossword puzzle books. Bennett Cerf rented an office that had Random House printed on the door. I'll give you an example of a good small publisher who, when Big 5 refused, picked up an "instructional" book: Shelly Lowenkopf's *The Fiction Writer's Handbook: The Definitive Guide to McGuffins, Red Herrings, Shaggy Dogs, and Other Literary Revelations*, from a master, an *a*-to-*z* guide of every literary skill and term a writer should know. I took the project to Chris Meeks and his White Whisker publishing house. Result? To date, 20,912 books sold. Not even found in bookstores; on Amazon or from the publisher.

What are your feelings about self-publishing? Self-publish only if you know why. Most "writers" don't bother to hire any editor, let alone one with a publishing background. Please, never hire an English teacher, no matter what grade level, to edit your fiction. Or your narrative nonfiction. Most selfies clog the market. Very few survive.

Do you think Amazon is good or bad — or both — for the book business? So far good.

What do you like and dislike about your job? I dislike those who come to my agency knowing nothing about writing or the book-publishing business. Do your research. Do your homework. Study the skills you need for your genre. I dislike those queries that bluster about how talented the writer is. Do not write in omniscient POV for my agency. The writer hasn't learned intimacy with the characters. At least for my eyes. I like books. I like to see a book go from a manuscript to a fully bound book. I like the art of the deal. I love to read, to listen to audiobooks. Books R Us.

What are ways prospective clients can impress you, and what are ways they can turn you off? Read the previous question. Please. Be professional in your writing and your attitude, have a passion for your work, be well read, have patience and knowledge.

How would you describe the "writer from hell"? All ego, no skills mastered. I'm old and mellow enough to represent no bad actors.

Describe a book you would like to write. *Fiction Editing for Dummies.*

Do you believe in a higher and/or lower "power"? Agnostic: "Oh God, if there is a God, save my soul, if I have a soul." Covers all bases. If a higher power, a single entity exists, he or she got some splainin' to do.

Is there anything you wish to express beyond the parameters of the preceding questions?
Well, I named my Italian Greyhound after Mother Cabrini, who founded the order of nuns who raised me, incarcerated for eight years in a not-elite boarding school: Villa Cabrini Academy. Must mean something.

TRIADAUS LITERARY AGENCY ❖ www.triadaus.com

PO Box 561, Sewickley, PA 15143

Agent's name and contact info: Laura Crockett, laura@triadaus.com

Describe the kinds of works you want to represent. I'll read just about any genre in young adult if it has a compelling voice and an excellent, unique hook. I'm quite particular about adult fiction, but if the historical fiction, soft fantasy, or women's fiction piece feels fresh, I'll grab for it.

How do you want writers to pitch you? Send a polished query (one worthy of a book jacket!) along with the first 10 pages of the manuscript in the body of the email.

Describe your education and professional history. BS in psychology, MA in publishing, bookseller, librarian, writing tutor, and blogger.

How did you become an agent? While I was working on my MA, I edited several MFA students' manuscripts. One of them told me about her experience with TriadaUS and mentioned an internship. I contacted Uwe, and within a week of the internship I realized just how involved I wanted to be on this side of the publishing process! Discovering great manuscripts that will one day be in the hands of thousands of readers is absolutely thrilling.

Knowing what you do now, would you do it again? If not, what might you do instead? I would still become an agent, of course! In my alternate life I may have continued on to get a PhD in Victorian and Romantic literature (because that's my ultimate weakness), but I've no doubt I would've become an agent after receiving that degree as well.

Do you charge fees? If yes, please explain. Nope. How absurd.

What do you like to do when you're not working? When I'm not working, I'm singing in choir, running a choir alumni association, traveling, hanging out with my fluffy kitty Rossetti, and catching up on life with my friends.

List some of the titles you have recently placed with publishers. *Timekeeper* by Tara Sim (the first of a trilogy).

What do you like reading/watching/listening to on your own time? A lot of what I read on my own time is similar to what I'm looking to represent. Books like *Night Circus*,

Daughter of the Forest, *House at Riverton*, *At the Water's Edge*, *Fangirl*, *Anna and the French Kiss*, *Serafina*, *Jackaby*, and *Outlander*, to name a few. Absolutely love just about anything on British TV, especially modern ones like *Sherlock*, *Endeavour*, *Call the Midwife*, *Merlin*, *Poldark*, *Downton Abbey*, and US comedies like *Big Bang Theory* and *New Girl*. My favorite musicians include Adele, Sam Smith, John Mayer, Mumford & Sons, Coldplay, She & Him, and Hozier.

What do you like and dislike about your job? I love discovering new, fantastically creative writers and their brilliant stories and worlds! I do not like being pushy with others — editors who need to get back to me, the accounting division regarding payments, etc. It feels rude, but my fantastically creative writers deserve the best, and I will deliver!

What are ways prospective clients can impress you, and what are ways they can turn you off? I'm impressed with tight queries, ones that feel like the client put thought and research into who I am and what I represent before they hit the "send" button. My clients all had queries that mimicked the style/voice of their manuscripts, which was extra impressive. I haven't had any particular experience or pattern of experiences of clients turning me off. Be kind and be thoughtful is all that can be said.

How would you describe the "writer from hell"? I'm blissfully ignorant of this sort of person, thank goodness.

Is there anything you wish to express beyond the parameters of the preceding questions? Keep writing, keep querying, keep persevering! There is an agent out there looking for your exact manuscript and voice and style.

Agent's name and contact info: Uwe Stender, uwe@triadaus.com

Describe the kinds of works you want to represent. I am open to pretty much any project that truly excites me the moment I hear the hook or the scope/topic of the project, except for adult sci-fi and fantasy.

How do you want writers to pitch you? Send me a well-written and error-free email or pitch me in person at a conference.

Describe your education and professional history. PhD in German literature, literary agent since 2004, university lecturer (German, film, writing).

How did you become an agent? I have always loved literature (thus I went all the way to a PhD in the academic field), and after years of researching the field from a publishing perspective, I decided to become an agent (with the mentoring and support from several well-connected publishing insiders). I simply love the thrill of discovering a *great* book.

Knowing what you do now, would you do it again? If not, what might you do instead? I would do it over again. The only other thing I would consider doing would be to become a music producer.

Do you charge fees? If yes, please explain. No! And no legitimate agent should.

When and where were you born, and where have you lived? In Germany during the last millennium.

What do you like to do when you're not working? I enjoy biking, swimming, and strength training. I usually hang out with my two Hovawarts, but love to travel without them. I listen to any kind of music except for heavy metal.

List some of the titles you have recently placed with publishers. Who's That Girl by Blair Thornburgh, *Thieving Weasels* by Billy Taylor, *Land of 10,000 Madonnas* by Kate Hattemer, *The Restaurant Critic's Wife* by Elizabeth LaBan, *My Seventh-Grade Life in Tights* by Brooks Benjamin, *Plants You Can't Kill* by Stacy Tornio.

Describe your personality. I am passionate and work hard and am still *very* European after all these years in the US.

What do you like reading/watching/listening to on your own time? Great books, great TV/movies, and great music! For example, in books: *Huckleberry Finn*, *The Big Sleep*, and *Eleanor and Park*; in TV/films: *The Sopranos*, *Cinema Paradiso*, *Sherlock Holmes* (with Benedict Cumberbatch), and *How to Get Away with Murder*; in music: anything by Ellie Goulding, Rihanna, Adele, and Brian Wilson.

What do the "Big 5" mean to you? They are dimensions of personality. The Big Five Factors are openness, conscientiousness, extraversion, agreeableness, and neuroticism. And I know that is not what you implied with your question. In reference to publishing, isn't it a Big 4 now?

How do you feel about independent/small presses? I *love* them.

What are your feelings about self-publishing? It is a great way to be discovered, if for some reason you have not been discovered yet.

Do you think Amazon is good or bad — or both — for the book business? Bad, if they are truly trying to be a monopoly; good, if they are not trying to do that.

What do you like and dislike about your job? It is all about discovering really creative and brilliant people and projects, and I find all of that supremely exciting. I don't like waiting for the advance payments. They should be paid promptly.

What are ways prospective clients can impress you, and what are ways they can turn you off? First question: Don't bore me. Second question: Bore me.

How would you describe the "writer from hell"? I wouldn't know. I avoid signing them.

Describe a book you would like to write. It would be a young adult novel about heartbreak, longing, and redemption, told in reverse.

Do you believe in a higher and/or lower "power"? Yes.

Is there anything you wish to express beyond the parameters of the preceding questions? As writers, agents, and human beings: be humble!

Agent's name and contact info: Brent Taylor, brent@triadaus.com

Describe the kinds of works you want to represent. Upmarket fiction (books that are well-written and robust with emotion and appeal to a commercial audience) across a wide range of categories: middle grade, young adult, graphic novels, women's fiction, crime fiction.

Describe what you definitely don't want to represent. Adult fiction, fantasy, romance.

How do you want writers to pitch you? By pasting their query letter and first 10 pages into the body of an email to brent@triadaus.com with *Query* in the subject line.

How did you become an agent? I interned at a handful of literary agencies before landing at TriadaUS, where I was promoted from intern to literary assistant to associate agent.

What do you like to do when you're not working? Run, read, and bake.

List some of the titles you have recently placed with publishers. *You're Welcome, Universe* by Whitney Gardner (Knopf Children's), *Perfect Ten* by L. Philips (Viking Children's), *The Hemingway Thief* by Shaun Harris (Seventh Street Books), *Call Me Sunflower* by Miriam Spitzer Franklin (Sky Pony Press), *The Gravedigger's Son* by Patrick Moody (Sky Pony Press).

Describe your personality. My boss calls me a "piece of work."

What do you like reading/watching/listening to on your own time? I love to watch anything crime related. I love *How to Get Away with Murder*, *The Following*, and cheesy blockbuster thrillers.

How do you feel about independent/small presses? They can be truly fantastic options for authors. They bring certain qualities to the table that the Big 5 can't offer.

What do you like and dislike about your job? I like everything and dislike nothing.

What are ways prospective clients can impress you, and what are ways they can turn you off? By doing their research and knowing what books I'm selling, what books I like, and keeping up-to-date on my clients. It's a turnoff when a prospective client has no sense of what you're looking for or hasn't done any preliminary research about your tastes.

UNION LITERARY ❖ www.unionliterary.com

30 Vandam Street, Suite 5A, New York, NY 10013, 212-255-2112

Agents' names and contact info: Christina Clifford, christina@unionliterary.com; Shaun Dolan, sd@unionliterary.com; Jenni Ferrari-Adler, jenni@union literary.com; Trena Keating, tk@unionliterary.com; Sally Wofford-Girand, swg@unionliterary.com

Describe the kinds of works you want to represent. We specialize in literary fiction, popular fiction, narrative nonfiction, memoir, social history, business, general big-idea books, popular science, cookbooks, and food writing.

Christina: I worked for many years as an agent at Melanie Jackson Agency, where I represented several award-winning authors and found US homes for the works of international authors. A lifelong New Yorker and lover of the written word, I am looking for both seasoned authors and new voices in fiction and nonfiction. I specialize in literary fiction and have a soft spot in my heart for international fiction hailing from the homeland of authors like William Trevor, Edna O'Brien, and Zadie Smith, not to mention Rohinton Mistry, Mario Vargas Llosa, J. M. Coetzee, and Nadine Gordimer. I am also interested in continuing to build a narrative nonfiction list in the genres of historical biography, memoir, business, and science. I have three children and live in New York City.

Shaun: I am interested in both muscular and lyrical literary fiction, narrative non-fiction, memoir, pop culture, and sports narratives. I'm willing and able to dive into the trenches editorially and look to foster new, exciting voices.

Jenni: I represent the agency's award-winning food writers and food shops; exciting fiction writers including Mo Daviau, Aya De Leon, Rebecca Dinerstein, Chris McCormick, Eileen Pollack, and the estate of Pamela Moore; young adult and middle grade; narrative nonfiction; and other categories.

Trena: I represent authors with bold voices, clever stories, and cutting-edge ideas, including novelists, journalists, and experts writing for a popular audience such as professors, doctors, artists, and scientists. Next, I hope to find a literary novel set in an exotic place or time, a journey or transformation novel for young readers, a distinctly modern novel with a female protagonist, a creepy page-turner, a quest memoir that addresses larger issues, or a nonfiction work based on primary research or a unique niche. I'd also welcome hearing from a great essayist or any voicy writer on any subject who is a great storyteller or makes me laugh.

Sally: My particular areas of interest are history, memoir, women's interest, cultural studies, and, most of all, fiction that is both literary and gripping. I am a hands-on agent with a passion for great storytelling. I love the thrill of discovery in working with debut novelists.

How do you want writers to pitch you? Interested writers should read and consider the agent bios when submitting to the agency and should only query the agent they feel would best respond to their work. If we think someone else in the agency would be a better fit, we will happily refer it to them.

We prefer to receive submissions by email with sample pages attached in doc or docx format. Please do not send PDFs. Nonfiction submissions should include a query letter, a proposal, and a sample chapter. Fiction submissions should include a query letter, a synopsis, and either sample pages or a full manuscript.

Please note that, due to the high volume of submissions we receive, we will only be in contact regarding projects that appear to be matches for our agents. Rest assured, every incoming query is read and evaluated. Please do not call regarding submissions.

WALES LITERARY AGENCY, INC. ❖ www.waleslit.com

1508 10th Avenue East, #401, Seattle, WA 98102, 206-284-7114

Agents' names and contact info: Elizabeth Wales, President; Neal Swain, Assistant Agent; general email: waleslit@waleslit.com

Describe the kinds of works you want to represent. We represent quality mainstream fiction and narrative nonfiction. In fiction and nonfiction, we look for talented storytellers, both new and established, and we're especially interested in projects that could have a progressive cultural or political impact. Clients are from all over the country; as well, we represent a strong group of Northwest, West Coast, and Alaskan writers.

Describe what you definitely don't want to represent. We don't represent the following: children's books, how-to, self-help, and almost all genre projects (romance, true crime, horror, action-adventure, most science fiction/fantasy, thrillers).

How do you want writers to pitch you? Writers should send their queries without attachments to waleslit@waleslit.com. We do not accept queries by phone or mail.

Describe your education and professional history. *Elizabeth*: BA, Smith College; graduate work in English and American literature, Columbia University. Member, AAR. Founded the agency in 1990 with Dan Levant.

Do you charge fees? If yes, please explain. We do not charge fees. Our agency works only on commission: 15 percent domestic sales, 20 percent foreign sales/film/TV.

List some of the titles you have recently placed with publishers. *Mozart's Starling* by Lyanda Lynn Haupt (Little, Brown, 2017), *The Witness Tree* by Lynda Mapes (Bloomsbury

USA, 2017), *Honeybees Can't Pollinate Tomatoes* by Paige Embry (Timber Press, 2017), *Gaining Lost Ground* by David Montgomery (Norton, 2017).

THE WALLACE LITERARY AGENCY, INC. ❖ wallaceliteraryagency.com

229 East 79th Street, Suite 5A, New York, NY 10075, 212-472-3282

Agent's name and contact info: Robin Straus, robin@wallaceliteraryagency.com

Describe the kinds of works you want to represent. We are a long-established literary agency with a distinguished client list.

How do you want writers to pitch you? We are not taking on new clients.

List some of the titles you have recently placed with publishers. Works by, for example, Don DeLillo, Jack Weatherford, Marge Piercy, R. K. Narayan, William F. Buckley.

WATERSIDE PRODUCTIONS, INC. ❖ www.waterside.com

2055 Oxford Avenue, Cardiff, CA 92007, 760-632-9190

Agent's name: Bill Gladstone

Describe the kinds of works you want to represent. How-to nonfiction, business, and technical titles. Mostly working with established bestselling authors and well-known business leaders, visionaries, and celebrities.

Describe what you definitely don't want to represent. First-time authors should work with other Waterside agents.

How do you want writers to pitch you? Must have existing relationship with a Waterside client I already represent or be referred by an editor or publisher with whom I have a professional relationship.

Describe your education and professional history. Degrees from Yale University in Hispanic civilization and Harvard University in cultural anthropology. Former editor in chief of Arco Publishing, senior editor for Harcourt Brace, and founder of Waterside since 1982.

How did you become an agent? Serendipity.

Knowing what you do now, would you do it again? If not, what might you do instead? Have loved every minute of it for the past 34 years.

Do you charge fees? If yes, please explain. No.

When and where were you born, and where have you lived? Born in New York City; have lived in Barcelona and San Diego.

What do you like to do when you're not working? Enjoy golf, tennis, walking on the beach, playing with my grandson.

List some of the titles you have recently placed with publishers. Titles by Daniel Pincheck, Barbara DeAngelis, Neale Donald Walsch, Melissa Ambrosini, Jake Ducey, Napoleon Hill Foundation, Bob Proctor, Brian Tracy, Dr. and Master Sha.

Describe your personality. Outgoing, focused, energetic, demanding of self and others. Super good guy to have watching out for your interests.

What do you like reading/watching/listening to on your own time? *The Good Wife, Game of Thrones, Downton Abbey.*

Do you think the business has changed a lot over the past few years? If yes, please explain. Yes. Digital has changed the industry and continues to do so. Consolidation continues to limit opportunities for new authors. Self-publishing has become more viable.

What do the "Big 5" mean to you? Big advances, great distribution for established authors.

How do you feel about independent/small presses? Love them and bless them. Most of our success over the past 30 plus years has come from them. They remain the starting point for most authors.

What are your feelings about self-publishing? Too much is being published without proper editing or marketing. We have developed our own hybrid press in partnership with Amazon to assist authors who want quality self-publishing with professional guidance.

Do you think Amazon is good or bad — or both — for the book business? More good than bad, though not an ideal situation when a single entity controls more than 50 percent of all book-publishing revenues generated.

What do you like and dislike about your job? Love it all. The best is taking new authors and helping them reach wide audiences and fulfill their dreams. Representing books that create a better world is our goal and gives us joy. Mistakes happen and are never fun to have to correct. Do not enjoy authors who cannot go with the flow or overreact to the inevitable disappointments from the often irrational and illogical world of book publishing.

What are ways prospective clients can impress you, and what are ways they can turn you off? It turns me off when authors tell me they have the next great bestseller. No one knows for certain what the next bestseller will be, and new authors should be enthusiastic but humble. I am more impressed with why a book will make this a better world than the amount of money I might make as the agent for a book.

How would you describe the "writer from hell"? Calls constantly to complain about the mistakes the publisher is making.

Describe a book you would like to write. Have written several. *The Twelve* sold about 500,000 copies and has just been released through Waterfront Press as an ebook with print on demand. My biography *Dr. and Master Sha: Miracle Soul Healer* is an interesting read, and my cowritten books *Tapping the Source* (Tarcher) and *The Golden Motorcycle Gang* (Hay House) are worth a look.

Do you believe in a higher and/or lower "power"? We are all connected to a higher power.

Is there anything you wish to express beyond the parameters of the preceding questions? Each day is a gift and a blessing. Write if you have something important to share or if writing brings you joy. Whether you get published and whether your book sells well are to a certain extent beyond your control. Work with professionals and treat everyone with courtesy and good will and you may enjoy some of the happy accidents that have helped our agency generate more than $3 billion in retail book sales in North America alone.

Agent's name and contact info: Margot Maley Hutchison, Senior Literary Agent, Director of Online Courses, mmaley@waterside.com

Describe the kinds of works you want to represent. Wide range of nonfiction, some fiction, and online courses.

Describe what you definitely don't want to represent. Religion, romance, horror.

How do you want writers to pitch you? With a well-written query letter sent by email.

Describe your education and professional history. I have a degree in literature from University of San Diego. I spent a year studying Spanish literature at the University of Barcelona. I've been an agent with Waterside since 1992 and have worn many hats. I was the foreign rights agent for several years, have represented hundreds of books to publishers, and have worked with several online education companies to create opportunities for our authors.

How did you become an agent? Growing up, I always had a book or a phone in my hand, so I was a natural.

Knowing what you do now, would you do it again? If not, what might you do instead? I might have been an international spy but, really, I would do it all again.

Do you charge fees? If yes, please explain. No.

When and where were you born, and where have you lived? I was born in Troy, New York, grew up in northern New Mexico, and have been accused of secretly working for the New Mexico Chamber of Commerce. I've also lived in Barcelona and currently live in San Diego.

What do you like to do when you're not working? I play tennis and live the crazy life of a traveling soccer mom to growing boys.

List some of the titles you have recently placed with publishers. Bone Broth Diet, Talking to Crazy, Survival Strategies for Parenting, The Screen-Dependent Child, Self-Confidence for Dummies, Grant Writing for Dummies. Courses: SAT Prep, PSAT Prep at Lynda.com, Writeriffic, Creativity Training for Writers, Photographing People, Photographing Nature, Social Media Marketing with Udemy.

Describe your personality. Creative, tenacious, problem solver.

What do you like reading/watching/listening to on your own time? Literary fiction, memoirs, quality nonfiction, Modern Family, House of Cards.

Do you think the business has changed a lot over the past few years? If yes, please explain. Yes, it has changed quite a lot, though I'm very happy to report that print is not dead, as some predicted, and independent bookstores are enjoying a huge comeback.

How do you feel about independent/small presses? I love them and can't say enough good things about most of them.

What are your feelings about self-publishing? I think it is a very viable avenue for many authors. Authors need to understand that self-publishing does not mean "If you build it, they will come." You really have to develop a platform and have a way to reach your target market.

Do you think Amazon is good or bad — or both — for the book business? I think Amazon is both good and bad. Some of their policies have hurt and changed the industry, but overall I think they've been a good thing for authors.

What do you like and dislike about your job? I love helping authors find the right home for their book. I like helping take an idea and shaping it into something interesting and compelling. I don't like dealing with irrational people, but even the parts of my job I don't like make for great stories.

What are ways prospective clients can impress you, and what are ways they can turn you off? They can impress me with a professional and well-written manuscript and a kind and respectful attitude. They can turn me off with a "Do you know who I am?" attitude.

How would you describe the "writer from hell"? Someone whose ego is not consistent with their accomplishments.

Describe a book you would like to write. Something funny. If I'm dreaming big, the next *Catcher in the Rye.*

Is there anything you wish to express beyond the parameters of the preceding questions? I'd like to remind authors to appreciate the journey. I'm of the Ferris Buehler philosophy: "Life moves pretty fast. If you don't stop and look around once in a while, you could miss it."

Agent's name and contact info: Jill Kramer, Encinitas, CA, editorjk2@aol.com, 760-201-5737

Describe the kinds of works you want to represent. Fiction of all types, including young adult. No children's, unless it's a celeb. Nonfiction of all types, as long as the author has a platform or a story so unique that it would interest a publisher.

Describe what you definitely don't want to represent. Books with violent themes, speculative fiction.

How do you want writers to pitch you? Via email: editorjk2@aol.com.

Describe your education and professional history. BS in broadcasting and film, with a minor in English, Boston University; editorial director at Hay House for 17 plus years.

How did you become an agent? I worked with Bill Gladstone when I was an editor; after I left Hay House, I asked him if I could be an agent in his agency.

Do you charge fees? If yes, please explain. No.

When and where were you born, and where have you lived? Born in Philadelphia, college in Boston, lived in LA for 10 years, now in the San Diego area.

What do you like to do when you're not working? Tennis, pickleball, beach, libraries, travel, movies, TV, playing with my cats, hanging out with friends.

List some of the titles you have recently placed with publishers. *What's Stressing Your Face?, I Don't Know What to Believe, The Aha! Moment, Beating the Workplace Bully, The Raging Hormone Myth, A Year of Living Mindfully.*

Describe your personality. Perfectionistic, even-tempered, detail-oriented, dedicated.

What do you like reading/watching/listening to on your own time? All types of books, fiction and nonfiction; *Homeland, The Affair,* all news magazine shows.

Do you think the business has changed a lot over the past few years? If yes, please explain. Yes. Publishers are less apt to take on first-timers. Self-publishing is huge, as is digital.

What do the "Big 5" mean to you? Big advances, great distribution for established authors.

How do you feel about independent/small presses? A good starting point for new authors.

What are your feelings about self-publishing? Can be a good option for authors who can't find a traditional publisher, but the quality of editing, etc., needs to be maintained.

What do you like and dislike about your job? I love calling an author to tell him or her that a book deal has been offered. I don't like chasing money — trying to track down checks. And if authors have unreasonable expectations about the money they will earn, it can be frustrating.

What are ways prospective clients can impress you, and what are ways they can turn you off? A well-written, fascinating book, a finely tuned proposal, and an author who is realistic about expectations impress me. I don't want to hear that someone has the next "great American novel" (that's an eye-roller). Also, I don't like when authors try to "interview" me for the position. After all my years in the publishing industry, I don't feel I have to "sell" myself.

How would you describe the "writer from hell"? Those who keep calling and asking when they're going to get their check and those who want me to interfere with the publisher's processes (that are not related to contractual matters, etc.). Having been on the other side for so many years, I can attest to the fact that editors do not take kindly to agents getting involved in areas that are none of their business (such as cover copy and art, who's going to be their editor, the publisher's PR/marketing plans).

Do you believe in a higher and/or lower "power"? I believe in both physics and metaphysics. There is definitely a positive force in the universe, and I'm fine with calling this power God, but I do not believe in the white-haired guy in the sky. I am also a devotee of Yogananda. There is also definitely negative energy in our world, but that is human-created, and I try to avoid it.

Is there anything you wish to express beyond the parameters of the preceding questions? I love books, libraries, reading; I've always been a bookworm…and still am. I feel grateful that my professional career has always involved publishing, editing, writing, etc., as I have always loved what I do; and I know that not everyone feels that way about his or her profession.

WELLS ARMS LITERARY, LLC ❖ www.wellsarms.com

info@wellsarms.com

Agent's name: Victoria Wells Arms

Describe the kinds of works you want to represent. I represent mostly children's books — fiction and nonfiction, for all ages. I represent artists who also write, but I am not an illustration agency; that is, I don't take on artists who don't write their own material or who do covers or editorial work only.

Describe what you definitely don't want to represent. I don't do much that isn't aimed at the children's market.

How do you want writers to pitch you? By email, short and sweet.

Describe your education and professional history. I have a BA in English from Middlebury College and a degree in culinary arts. I have been an editor at Penguin (Dial and Putnam) and was founding editorial director at Bloomsbury USA's children's imprint. I founded Wells Arms Literary Agency in 2013.

How did you become an agent? After 20 years as an editor it was a natural step.

Knowing what you do now, would you do it again? If not, what might you do instead? Might have stayed in cooking. Or been a veterinarian. But I love what I do.

Do you charge fees? If yes, please explain. I don't charge fees; I do take a 15 percent commission.

When and where were you born, and where have you lived? I am a fifth-generation New Yorker, but I have also lived in the UK, Chicago, Vermont, and Washington, DC.

What do you like to do when you're not working? I enjoy cooking and reading, hiking and skiing, traveling and hanging out with my family.

List some of the titles you have recently placed with publishers. The Christmas Fox by Anik McGrory (Knopf); six books by E. D. Baker (Bloomsbury); *Bossy Flossy* by Paulette Bogan (Holt); *Violet and the Woof* by Rebecca Grabill (Harper); *Prairie Dog Song*, illustrated by Susan Roth (Lee & Low); *Billy Cabritos Gruff* by Susan Middle Elya (Penguin/Putnam).

How do you feel about independent/small presses? There is much to love about the passion of independent publishers, and the attention they sometimes can bring to a book and author is really invigorating.

What do you like and dislike about your job? I love working with so many talented authors and editors every day, being involved in lots of unique projects. I dislike being told something is "not for my list" when it is so clearly awesome.

What are ways prospective clients can impress you, and what are ways they can turn you off? I look for good writing first and art with a wow factor to it. Seeing that someone treats the creative process professionally and passionately but with a minimum of ego also helps.

WENDY SCHMALZ AGENCY ❖ www.schmalzagency.com

402 Union Street, #831, Hudson, NY 12534, 518-672-7697

Agent's name and contact info: Wendy Schmalz, wendy@schmalzagency.com

Describe the kinds of works you want to represent. Young adult and middle grade fiction and nonfiction, adult narrative nonfiction and literary fiction.

Describe what you definitely don't want to represent. Romance, science fiction, fantasy, books for very young children.

How do you want writers to pitch you? I accept only email queries. The query letter should include a brief synopsis and information about the author. Any query letter that includes an attachment will be deleted unread. Because of the number of queries I receive, I reply only to the authors whose work I want to read. If I have not responded to a query within two weeks of the date it was sent, it means I'm not interested.

Describe your education and professional history. BA in American studies from Barnard College. Right after college, I spent a year in the film department of Curtis Brown, Ltd. I then went to the film department of Harold Ober Associates and also began building my own list of authors. I was a principal in the firm. I opened my own agency in 2002.

How did you become an agent? I read Tennessee Williams's memoir when I was in high school. That was the first time I'd ever heard of a literary agent, and I made up my mind then that that's what I wanted to be.

Knowing what you do now, would you do it again? If not, what might you do instead? There is nothing I'd rather be.

Do you charge fees? If yes, please explain. No.

What do you like to do when you're not working? Refinishing furniture, cooking.

List some of the titles you have recently placed with publishers. The Girl I Used to Be and Boy, Stolen by April Henry (Holt), Threads by Ami Polonsky (Hyperion), Everything All at Once by Katrina Leno (HarperCollins), The Train I Ride by Paul Mosier (HarperCollins), The Borden Murders by Sarah Miller (Random House).

Describe your personality. I have a good sense of humor. I'm loyal. I have a bit of a temper. I can be terse.

What do you like reading/watching/listening to on your own time? I read a lot of nonfiction. My favorite books of all time are Robert Caro's volumes on LBJ. I loved Breaking Bad and House of Cards.

What do you like and dislike about your job? The thrill of selling someone's first book never gets old. On the flip side, telling someone whom you've represented for a while that their manuscript isn't sellable is always difficult.

What are ways prospective clients can impress you, and what are ways they can turn you off? I like a query letter that's concise. It should give the impression of confidence, but not arrogance. A good writer takes criticism well and is willing to revise. I detest disingenuous self-deprecation.

Describe a book you would like to write. If I were a writer, I'd be a biographer.

WORDSERVE LITERARY AGENCY ❖ www.wordserveliterary.com

7061 South University Boulevard, Suite 307, Centennial, CO 80122, 303-471-6675

Agents' names and contact info: Greg Johnson, greg@wordserveliterary.com; Sarah Freese, sarah@wordserveliterary.com; Nick Harrison, nick@wordserve literary.com

Describe the kinds of works you want to represent. We're looking for books that will fit in either the general market or the Christian market. Nonfiction: history, military, biography, health, self-help, memoir, family, current affairs, money, pop culture, psychology, women's interest, and various other topics; acceptable word counts: 40,000 to 100,000 words depending on topic. Fiction: women's, historical, suspense/thriller, legal, literary, mainstream, supernatural, romance; acceptable word counts: 60,000 to 120,000.

Describe what you definitely don't want to represent. Gift books, poetry, short stories, screenplays, graphic novels, children's picture books, science fiction, fantasy.

How do you want writers to pitch you? Via email, by following the submission guidelines on our website: www.wordserveliterary.com/submission-guidlines.

Describe your education and professional history. Greg: I have been in publishing for more than 25 years. Before becoming a full-time literary agent in 1994, I wrote and published 20 works of nonfiction with traditional publishers; I was also an editor for a teenage boys' magazine for 5 years. In my years as an agent, I have personally represented more than 2,300 books and negotiated more than 1,800 contracts with over 85 publishing houses. These works include adult trade books (nonfiction and fiction), children's books, specialty Bibles, movie options, video curricula, audio products, gift books, and greeting cards.

How did you become an agent? I loved the business and proposal portion of the book industry more than the writing and promoting. It was a natural progression from author to agent.

Knowing what you do now, would you do it again? If not, what might you do instead? I love serving authors and watching great ideas and writing be turned into books that make a difference in someone's life.

Do you charge fees? If yes, please explain. No.

When and where were you born, and where have you lived? Grew up in Oregon, but have also lived in Washington and California, and Colorado since 1991.

What do you like to do when you're not working? Golf, traveling.

List some of the titles you have recently placed with publishers. Steve Arterburn and Becky Johnson, *The Mediterranean Love Plan* (Zondervan); Kara Powell, *Current Church* (Baker); Julie Parker, *Sex Savvy* (BroadStreet); Steve Arterburn and David Stoop, *Take Your Life Back*, three books (Tyndale); Debora Coty, *Too Blessed to Be Stressed Daily Devotional* (Barbour); Leslie Leyland Fields, *Crossing the Waters* (NavPress); Jonathan Sandys, great-grandson of Winston Churchill, *God and Churchill* (Tyndale).

Do you think the business has changed a lot over the past few years? If yes, please explain. The loss of retail has most definitely changed the way people find out about books. More reliance on author platform has hurt the creative effort. Not sure if that will ever change.

What are your feelings about self-publishing? Doesn't matter much what I feel; it's here to stay in a big way.

Do you think Amazon is good or bad — or both — for the book business? Both. Capturing markets is bad for business, but they've created a model where it is easy to buy, so that helps authors. We can't curse what we used to praise just because they've developed a good business. We have to live and work within it.

What are ways prospective clients can impress you, and what are ways they can turn you off? Read my website about submissions, so that no one is wasting their time.

Do you believe in a higher and/or lower "power"? Both. I'm a man of faith. About 80 to 90 percent of the books we represent are for the Christian market.

WORDWISE MEDIA SERVICES ❖ www.wordwisemedia.com

4083 Avenue L, Suite 255, Lancaster, CA 93536, 661-382-8083, get.wisewords@gmail.com

Agent's name and contact info: Steven Hutson, steve@wordwisemedia.com

Describe the kinds of works you want to represent. I handle a broad range of fiction and nonfiction works for children and adults. See our website for examples of books we've sold.

Describe what you definitely don't want to represent. Don't send me *Fifty Shades*, and don't send me *Chucky*. No poetry, short stories, or picture books. And if your story has abundant foul language or graphic sex, it probably isn't for us.

How do you want writers to pitch you? Please use the query form on our website, and follow the instructions carefully. Better yet, meet me at a writers' conference.

Describe your education and professional history. Majored in business at Los Angeles City College. Former director of a writers' conference; 12 years' experience in book editing, 5 years as an agent. Frequent speaker and instructor at writers' events.

How did you become an agent? I ran an advertisement for my editing service and received an inquiry from a film producer. He asked me to help him adapt several screenplays into books and then pitch the books to publishers. As it turned out, I already had all the right connections and persuasion skills, and the editors didn't tell me to get lost. Who knew? Those projects never came to fruition, but the effort inspired me to go into business as an agent.

Knowing what you do now, would you do it again? If not, what might you do instead? I would have started the process at least 20 years earlier.

Do you charge fees? If yes, please explain. I might charge you for printing and postage on a manuscript submission. But almost all publishers require emailed submissions these days, so to date, I've never billed a client for anything.

When and where were you born, and where have you lived? Born in Hollywood and lived in southern California all my life.

What do you like to do when you're not working? Swimming, gardening, bicycling.

List some of the titles you have recently placed with publishers. *The Sword and the Song* by Carla Laureano (NavPress), *The Disposable Visionary* by Bill Jerome and Curt Powell (Praeger), *Free to Be Fabulous* by Debbie Hardy (Morgan James), *Surviving Haley* by Brenda Baker (Pelican Book Group), *The Breeding Tree* by J. Andersen (Brimstone Fiction).

Describe your personality. Lifelong introvert, building a career as a public speaker. Non-conformist.

What do you like reading/watching/listening to on your own time? My parents raised me on an eclectic mix of music, from show tunes to Frank Sinatra to Roberta Flack to Blood, Sweat & Tears. My taste in books and movies is similarly unpredictable.

Do you think the business has changed a lot over the past few years? If yes, please explain. Count me among the minority who think the business has not fundamentally changed.

Good writing, professionalism, and decent platform will always bring the best chance of success.

What do the "Big 5" mean to you? Wish we had a Big 20. Too much power in too few hands is never a good thing.

How do you feel about independent/small presses? Wish we had a few hundred more of them, to make the marketplace more competitive. They're more likely to take a chance on a new writer.

What are your feelings about self-publishing? Self-pub works spectacularly well for a tiny percentage. But it gives false hope to most, because the authors aren't prepared to treat it like a business. It's not the empowering, liberating experience they expected. If anything, the rise of self-pub has flooded the market with hundreds of thousands of lousy books. This makes it ever harder for the good stuff to stand out.

Do you think Amazon is good or bad — or both — for the book business? I believe Amazon needs to learn how to play nice with others. Gotta leave something on the table for the other guy. I surely hope that free markets will fix this imbalance, before any government agency has to get involved.

What do you like and dislike about your job? Good: I love it when I call a client to give her the news that her book was accepted for publication. I helped her dreams come true. Bad: The world is full of good stories, but short of teachable writers. I recently gave an author three chances to resubmit her work in a form that I could work with, and she kept sending me the same old stuff. Her book might be fantastic, but I can't tell. This record doesn't fill me with confidence that she will be a client who cooperates with me.

What are ways prospective clients can impress you, and what are ways they can turn you off? You can impress me by presenting yourself as a professional. Make it easy for me to say yes. Give me the information I need in order to make an intelligent decision about your work. You can turn me off by getting defensive when I give feedback on your work or (OMG!) ask you to participate in your own success.

How would you describe the "writer from hell"? Won't follow instructions. Not interested in learning.

Describe a book you would like to write. I've been getting a lot of ideas recently, on topics in politics and religion. We'll see if they ever come to fruition.

Do you believe in a higher and/or lower "power"? I suppose you mean, "Do I believe in God and a Devil?" The answer is yes. This belief system informs everything I do.

WRITERS HOUSE, LLC ❖ www.writershouse.com

21 West 26th Street, New York, NY 10010, 212-685-2400

Agent's name and contact info: Stephen Barr, sbarr@writershouse.com, 212-685-2663

Describe the kinds of works you want to represent. I've got a consistent hankering for unexpected memoirs with itchy voices, narrative nonfiction that tackles hard-to-tackle issues, wry and rarely paranormal young adult, laugh-until-you-squirt-milk-out-of-your-nose middle grade (with heart!), sweet and wacky (but still logical) picture books from innovative author-illustrators, and any fiction that rewards readers line-by-line and lets them get to know at least one character really, really well (recent favorites include *Jeff in Venice*, *The Lazarus Project*, *Diary of a Bad Year*, and *Horns*, which was awesome). I'm also willing to be a sucker for mysteries that bend reality, ghost stories that blow reality to hell, humor that's more than just an infinitely repeated gag in sheep's clothing, and Secret Book X (I don't know what Secret Book X is, but suffice it to say, I'm open to the occasional curveball).

Describe what you definitely don't want to represent. There's very little I'll categorically refuse to represent, but it's hyper unlikely that I'll ever work on any unflinching self-help, unflinching romance, or unflinching religious fiction. But everyone flinches every now and then.

How do you want writers to pitch you? Far and away the best approach is just to send me an honest, conversational email describing the book, the author, and some hopes and dreams and then letting the first 10 or 15 pages do the talking.

Describe your education and professional history. In short, I was always obviously going to be an English major, and then I was (at UCLA). Then I moved to New York 12 seconds after graduating, failed to get about 17 jobs, landed an internship at an awesome, intimate film/literary agency called Hotchkiss & Associates, landed a simultaneous internship at an awesome, intimate literary agency called Writers House, and I'm so fond of my job that I'll probably do it even after I become a skeleton.

How did you become an agent? I think I became an agent because my favorite thing in the world is talking to people about things that don't exist (or don't exist yet), and writers' brains are full of things that don't exist (or don't exist yet). I became one (an agent, that is, not a thing that doesn't exist) by thinking that I was supposed to be an editor, and then — while chasing a job as an editorial assistant — discovering that there was a job that could often put me even closer to the germination moment of a book.

Knowing what you do now, would you do it again? If not, what might you do instead? I would do it all over again, but with a different haircut.

Do you charge fees? If yes, please explain. Nope! No fees, no how.

What do you like to do when you're not working? I should maintain *some* element of mystery about myself, shouldn't I? I'm interested in mysteries. My hobby is being a mystery. Also playing the guitar and the drums and the piano and kitchen instruments (which is a stupid way of saying I like to cook).

List some of the titles you have recently placed with publishers. Staff writer for Rookie and author/illustrator of the graphic memoir *Honor Girl* Maggie Thrash's first two books in the *Mystery Club* series (Simon & Schuster); *Here Is Real Magic* by Nate Staniforth, the memoir of a curiously philosophical magician (who's lectured at Oxford University and the Mayo Clinic) following his evolution from obsessed wunderkind to disillusioned wanderer, and telling the story of his rediscovery of astonishment — and the importance of wonder in everyday life — during his trip to the slums of India, where he infiltrated a 3,000-year-old clan of street magicians (Bloomsbury); debut author/illustrator Shelley Johannes's first three books in the *Beatrice Zinker, Upside Down Thinker* series, charting the adventures of a plucky third grader whose topsy turvy-point of view turns the world sunny-side up (Disney/Hyperion); National Book Award finalist and Printz Medal winner John Corey Whaley's next two young adult novels (Dial); *Blue Chicken* and *The Story of Fish and Snail* author and illustrator Deborah Freedman's *Shy*, in which the protagonist is nearly too bashful to appear in his own book, let alone confront the object of his affection (Viking Children's).

Describe your personality. Excited and excitable, warm and warmable, pretty jokey, sporadically obsessive, creative and happy, and an appreciator of well-timed solitude.

What do you like reading/watching/listening to on your own time? Idiosyncratic but still grounded fiction; inventive, gorgeous picture books; TV shows with emotionally weird protagonists; songs with that "Everything's sad but that's okay" vibe to them.

What do the "Big 5" mean to you? I know what it's supposed to mean, but it first reminds me of a sporting-goods chain, Big 5, and how I got my soccer cleats there every year before the season started. I hope they will both be around for many big years to come.

What are your feelings about self-publishing? It's perfect for some, the same way that traditional publishing is perfect for others!

Do you think Amazon is good or bad — or both — for the book business? They are obviously very creative, very ambitious, and capable of many incredible things. I just think they could be all those things while simultaneously being much, much, much more sensitive to their peers in the bookselling industry, succeeding by being the best when they can be the best, not by preying on others who might be better sometimes.

What do you like and dislike about your job? I love being a sounding board/brainstorming partner for my clients' ideas, sometimes being present at the very moment their inspiration finally clicks into place. I hate giving bad news.

How would you describe the "writer from hell"? Pitchfork, horns, tail, hooves, carrying a memoir about how hard it is to date.

Describe a book you would like to write. Inevitably long-winded, but good for a few laughs, I'd hope, with a main character who talks about his feelings too much, probably.

Do you believe in a higher and/or lower "power"? Objection: irrelevant!

Agent's name and contact info: Brianne Johnson, bjohnsonsubmissions@writershouse.com

Describe the kinds of works you want to represent. I represent mainly children's books, everything from character-driven picture books to funny middle grade to beautiful and exciting young adult. I like both contemporary and fantasy. I also represent some select adult work — mostly historical fiction, although I'd love to find a psychological thriller. Check out my website at www.publishersmarketplace.com/members/bjohnson for a more detailed breakdown.

Describe what you definitely don't want to represent. I don't want to see a cute poem that "might work as a children's book." Writing children's books is very difficult. Even shorter work demands careful plotting and character development. I'm not interested in erotica or straight romance.

How do you want writers to pitch you? I only accept digital submissions — no snail mail. Please send a query letter, with the first 10 pages of your manuscript pasted in, to bjohnsonsubmissions@writershouse.com. I respond to everyone.

How did you become an agent? Prior to coming to Writers House in 2008, I worked in three different independent bookstores for six years. I have also worked for a book warehouse, a literary magazine, and in publishing here in NYC. I love books!

Do you charge fees? If yes, please explain. No. We take 15 percent on domestic sales and 20 percent on foreign sales (10 percent for us and 10 percent for our foreign coagents).

When and where were you born, and where have you lived? I'm from Oswego, New York, and went to school in the Hudson Valley.

What do you like to do when you're not working? I moonlight as a pottery teacher and have been a potter for most of my life. I also love quilting while listening to audiobooks and exploring Prospect Park in Brooklyn.

List some of the titles you have recently placed with publishers. *Adrift* by Jessica Olien (picture book, Balzer + Bray, 2017), *The Skeleton Tree* by Kim Ventrella (middle grade, Scholastic, 2017), *The Crown's Game* by Evelyn Skye (young adult, Balzer + Bray, 2016), *Roses and Rot* by Kat Howard (adult, Saga Press, 2016), *The Violinist of Venice* by Alyssa Palombo (adult, St. Martin's Griffin).

Agent's name and contact info: Stacy Testa, stesta@writershouse.com

Describe the kinds of works you want to represent. I'm looking for literary fiction and upmarket women's fiction, particularly character-driven stories with an international setting, historical bent, or focus on a unique subculture. Although I am not partial to genre thrillers (no international spies, please), I would like to see well-crafted psychological thrillers. I am also open to realistic young adult fiction, but please know that this does comprise a very small portion of my list. In nonfiction, I'm looking for voice-driven narratives, particularly stories about little-known historical moments and/or strong pioneering women as well as urgent, relevant narratives of social justice. I also represent prescriptive, practical nonfiction, preferably with a great sense of humor and geared toward a younger audience. Finally, I represent a great deal of memoir; I tend to be drawn to stories that are as startling and unique as they are relatable.

Describe what you definitely don't want to represent. I'm not interested in representing romance, erotica, paranormal, horror, fantasy, middle grade, or picture books.

How do you want writers to pitch you? Please email your query letter with the first five pages of your manuscript pasted into the body of the email to stesta@writershouse.com.

Describe your education and professional history. I graduated with a BA cum laude in English from Princeton University. Prior to joining Writers House, I interned at Farrar, Straus and Giroux and Whimsy Literary.

How did you become an agent? I joined Writers House in 2011 as an assistant to senior agent Susan Ginsburg. Under her mentorship, I began building my own client list in 2013 and now represent a wide range of adult fiction and nonfiction.

Knowing what you do now, would you do it again? If not, what might you do instead? There was a time when I thought I would pursue a career in the performing arts, as an actor/singer, but my natural inclination toward structure and stability ultimately convinced me that this was not the right path. So I turned to a career in my other great love: reading! And knowing what I know now, I can confidently say that I would absolutely make the same choice again if given the chance. I feel so lucky to have found a career that is endlessly entertaining, enlightening, and challenging. It's really a perfect fit.

What do you like to do when you're not working? Outside of work, yoga is my greatest passion. I think the physical nature of the practice provides a wonderful contrast to the often sedentary nature of a life in the publishing industry. I am planning on pursuing yoga teacher training over the course of the coming year.

List some of the titles you have recently placed with publishers. *Always a Bridesmaid (For Hire)* by Jen Glantz (Atria), *The Sisters of Glass Ferry* by Kim Michele Richardson (Kensington), *No Baggage: A Minimalist Tale of Love and Wandering* by Clara Bensen (Running Press).

What do you like reading/watching/listening to on your own time? Some of my recent favorite reads include *Modern Romance* by Aziz Ansari, *Americanah* by Chimamanda Ngozi Adichie, *Tiger, Tiger* by Margaux Fragoso, *The Likeness* by Tana French, *A Little Life* by Hanya Yanagihara, *The Secret History* by Donna Tartt, and *Tiny Beautiful Things* by Cheryl Strayed.

I also watch quite a bit of TV. Some of my favorite all-time series are *Six Feet Under*, *The Jinx*, *Arrested Development*, *Black Mirror*, and *Twin Peaks*. I also have a soft spot for crime procedurals like *Law & Order* and *CSI*; they're just so very reliable! I'm currently watching *The Good Wife*, *Master of None*, *The Leftovers*, and *The Mindy Project*.

THE ZACK COMPANY, INC. ❖ www.zackcompany.com

Agent's name: Andrew Zack, President

Describe the kinds of works you want to represent. Serious narrative nonfiction; history and oral history, particularly military history and intelligence services history; politics and current affairs works by established journalists and political insiders or pundits; science and technology and how they affect society, by established journalists, science writers, or experts in their fields; biography, autobiography, or memoir by or about newsworthy individuals, individuals whose lives have made a contribution to the historical record; personal finance and investing; parenting by established experts in their field; health and medicine by doctors or established medical writers; business by nationally recognized business leaders or established business writers, for example, from the *Wall Street Journal*; relationship books by credentialed experts, that is, psychiatrists, psychologists, therapists with prior publishing credits. Commercial fiction (but not women's fiction); thrillers in every shape and form — international, serial killer, medical, scientific, computer, psychological, military, legal; mysteries and not-so-hard-boiled crime novels; action novels, but not action-adventure; science fiction and fantasy, preferably hard science fiction or military science fiction (I was a huge Robert Heinlein fan when I was younger) and big, elaborate fantasies (not coming-of-age fantasies) that take you to a new and established world; horror novels that take you on a roller-coaster ride; historical fiction (but not Westerns).

Describe what you definitely don't want to represent. Westerns; nonfiction religious works; Christian fiction or nonfiction; gay or lesbian fiction; humor (unless by an established humorist, columnist, or comedian); any work of nonfiction in a specialized field that is not by a qualified expert in the field; anything that is supposed to be a novel but is less than 65,000 words; previously self-published books that have sold less than 20,000 copies.

How do you want writers to pitch you? Please use the eQuery form on our website.

Describe your education and professional history. I have an extensive publishing background, beginning as the evening manager of an independent bookstore in a suburb of Boston. While attending college, I continued working at the university's bookstore, served as an editor on several student publications, and was managing editor of the university yearbook. I graduated in 1988 with a BA in English and political science and then attended the Radcliffe Publishing Course.

In September of 1988, I began work at Simon & Schuster's trade division as a foreign rights assistant. Not long thereafter, I moved to Warner Books as an editorial assistant, where I edited a number of titles and began acquiring on my own. I was substantively involved in the editing of several bestsellers, including the Batman movie tie-in and two *Headlines* titles by Jay Leno.

I next worked at Donald I. Fine, Inc., as an assistant editor and rights associate. Within six months, I was promoted to associate editor and rights manager. I acquired numerous titles and also sold subsidiary rights to the entire Fine list, including serial, bookclub, reprint, large print, film, and television. I also served as liaison with Fine's British and foreign sub-agents. The Berkley Publishing Group became my next home, after they recruited me as an editor. I was eventually responsible for acquiring more than 40 titles and brought several first-time authors to the list. I left Berkley during a corporate downsizing and entered the world of freelance.

As a freelance editor, I worked with literary agencies and publishers including Berkley, Donald I. Fine, Inc., Avon, Dell, and Tom Doherty Associates. I also reviewed for Kirkus and the Book-of-the-Month Club.

I became a literary agent in September 1993, joining the then recently formed Scovil Chichak Galen Literary Agency. I was immediately joined by several former authors whom I had edited, and proceeded to build my list of fiction and nonfiction authors. I founded the Zack Company, Inc., in March 1996 as the Andrew Zack Literary Agency.

I also served as chairperson of the AAR Royalty Committee, which regularly meets with publisher's royalty departments to discuss how statements and policies might be improved to better meet the needs of agents and authors. I have long advocated better communication between publishers and authors.

How did you become an agent? I had been an editor but was laid off. A number of authors asked me to represent them. I was wary of launching my own firm, but when I had an opportunity to join an agency and work with veteran agents, I took it.

Knowing what you do now, would you do it again? If not, what might you do instead? I would likely still be an editor or perhaps a copyright or entertainment attorney.

Do you charge fees? If yes, please explain. Certain out-of-pocket expenses (primarily postage) are charged back to the client.

When and where were you born, and where have you lived? A long time ago in a hospital far, far away. Many places.

What do you like to do when you're not working? When am I not working?

List some of the titles you have recently placed with publishers. Generally speaking, any answer to this will be outdated by the time you read this. Publishers Marketplace or my own website would be a better resource for this information.

Describe your personality. Detail-oriented and persistent. Sarcastic. Pragmatic.

What do you like reading/watching/listening to on your own time? I follow a number of television series, read a number of magazines, such as *Esquire* and *Wired*. I often listen to audiobooks of my clients' works while driving.

Do you think the business has changed a lot over the past few years? If yes, please explain. Anyone interested in my thoughts on the business should visit my blogs at www.zack company.com and www.authorcoach.com.

What do the "Big 5" mean to you? Simon & Schuster, Macmillan, HarperCollins, Hachette, Penguin Random House.

How do you feel about independent/small presses? There are some that are quite good, but a lot feel like "amateur hour." Their contracts are terrible, they don't understand the terms of traditional publishing, and they can't really get the copies out. Most authors would be better off self-publishing.

What are your feelings about self-publishing? If you are willing to do the work to produce a quality book, meaning investing the thousands of dollars for professional editorial services, cover design, interior design, and more, you can produce a great book yourself these days for far, far less than in the predigital age.

Do you think Amazon is good or bad — or both — for the book business? Overall, I think it has been good, but it now has far too much power over our industry.

What do you like and dislike about your job? Too much paperwork and not enough time to read.

What are ways prospective clients can impress you, and what are ways they can turn you off? It's all about the writing. Impress me with your creativity and writing. I am most turned off by repeated follow-ups that turn into nagging.

How would you describe the "writer from hell"? The writer from hell has probably published two or three, or maybe three or four, books. These are likely fiction, but might be nonfiction. Although the writer from hell is not always male, let's just say "he." He has "fired" his previous agent because his career is going nowhere, and that is, of course, the agent's fault. He is looking for an agent who can "make things happen." And just to make sure those things happen, he calls a minimum of three or four times a week for updates. He attempts to micromanage me as though I am an employee whom he is paying a six-figure yearly salary (but likely the commissions are far short of even five figures). This writer is convinced that his ideas are future bestsellers and can't understand why no one agrees with him. He wants instant feedback from me and never once considers that I may have other clients.

Clients from hell send proposals via email and don't understand why there isn't an instant response (the one downside to email is that it creates a presumption that, because it's almost instantaneous in delivery, the reply to it should be instantaneous). Bottom line: writers from hell believe that their needs outweigh everyone else's: their agent's, their editor's, their publicist's, and the needs of all the other writers the agent represents.

Describe a book you would like to write. I could, but then I'd have to kill you.

Do you believe in a higher and/or lower "power"? The Federal Reserve System, a.k.a. The Fed. Also, J. J. Abrams.

Is there anything you wish to express beyond the parameters of the preceding questions? The agent-author relationship is a business partnership. Agents have their role, and authors have their role. Neither is an employee of the other. Interestingly enough, I never hear about agents or authors hiring each other, but I hear about them firing one another all the time. Agents, obviously, are businesspeople. Authors need to be businesspeople, too. Authors should do their best to be as informed as possible about the nature of the publishing business. They should talk to their local independent bookseller (and if they really want to learn a few things, they should get a part-time job working in a bookstore). My best client is an educated client. I find that the hardest thing about the agent-author relationship is communication. Email has become an important mode of communication for me. It's quick and easy and almost instantaneous as a form of communication. Authors should be able to ask their agents all the questions they want, and if an author's agent disagrees with that, it's time to find another agent. But authors also need to recognize that every minute spent on the phone with them is a minute that could be spent selling their projects. As long as authors understand the job they have and the job agents have in the author-agent relationship, the business partnership will flourish and be profitable.

ZIMMERMANN LITERARY ❖ www.zimmermannliterary.com

Agent's name and contact info: Helen Zimmermann, submit@zimmagency.com

Describe the kinds of works you want to represent. Nonfiction: memoir, relationships, health/wellness/nutrition, pop culture, sports, music, women's interest. Fiction: *very* simple criteria — strong characters and a plot that keeps me up at night!

Describe what you definitely don't want to represent. Science fiction, poetry, romance.

How do you want writers to pitch you? Email queries only, please. For fiction, I like to see a single paragraph summary, a bio, and a bit about the audience/readership/marketing. Please don't attach chapters to the email unless I request them, but you can put the first chapter into the *body* of the email. For nonfiction, again, brief summary, bio, and a bit about the audience/readership/marketing. As it's just me who reads these, please understand that I can't answer every query. Sorry! I do read them with enthusiasm, and if I have interest in seeing more material, you will hear from me within two weeks.

Describe your education and professional history. After graduating from SUNY Buffalo with a double major in psychology and English literature, I started my publishing career in the marketing department of Random House. I soon became the director of advertising and promotion for one of its divisions, Crown Publishing. After 12 years I moved to New York's Hudson Valley, where I was the author-events director at a successful independent bookseller. I founded the agency in 2003 and enjoyed early success with the *New York Times* bestseller *Chosen by a Horse*. My experience working at a large publishing house and an independent bookseller gives me unique and invaluable insight into each project that I work on. I am well aware of the value of in-house buzz, online marketing, store placement, social media, author platform, etc., and I work hard to make sure all these components are in place for each and every project. I have been a member of the AAR since 2007.

How did you become an agent? As an events director, I spoke with many aspiring writers at the readings. They would always ask me, "How do I get published?" to which I would always reply, "You need an agent." After this conversation took place about a dozen times, I offered to show a writer's material to some publishers, since I still had many contacts. I never did sell that first project, but the next one I went out with became a bestseller. Voilà, an agent is born! Even though I became an agent kind of by default, I wouldn't have kept with it all these years unless I truly loved it. Being a part of making writers' dreams come true is pretty darn awesome.

Do you charge fees? If yes, please explain. No.

When and where were you born, and where have you lived? Born in Bronxville, New York, in 1964. I've lived in Hartsdale, Briarcliff Manor, New York City, and the Hudson Valley. I am in the process of building a yurt in the Adirondacks.

What do you like to do when you're not working? I'm an avid hiker; I recently completed all 46 of New York's Adirondack High Peaks. Took me 10 years, but I did it! I'm a runner, skier, and an occasional Netflix binge-watcher. Oh! And I read. *A lot.*

List some of the titles you have recently placed with publishers. *Goodnight L.A.: Untold Tales from Inside Classic Rock's Legendary Recording Studios* by Kent Hartman (Da Capo), *The Champion's Comeback* by Jim Afremow (Rodale), *The Normal Bar: Where Does Your Relationship Fall?* by Chrisanna Northrup (Crown), *Choices for Change: How to Make the Right Healthcare Decisions* by Archelle Georgiou (Rowman & Littlefield), *Pocket Paleo* by Nell Stephenson (Harlequin Nonfiction), *Chosen by a Horse* by Susan Richards (Soho/Harcourt).

Describe your personality. I'm affable, smart, compassionate, and athletic. And I go to bat for my clients like a parent at a PTA meeting.

What are your feelings about self-publishing? Self-publishing is great as long as you do it right, which is a *full-time job* on the part of the writer.

How would you describe the "writer from hell"? Someone who doesn't listen to my advice! That's what I'm here for — because I know the industry inside and out!

Part 7

INDEPENDENT EDITORS

INTRODUCTION
EDITORS VS. SCAMMERS

Jeff Herman

What Is an Independent Book Editor?

Someone who is qualified to make your proposal and/or manuscript better than you could do by yourself.

Why Might You Want to Retain an Editor?

Because even "perfect" writers are imperfect and can greatly benefit from an objective and qualified edit. Selling your work to agents and publishers is extremely competitive, so you want your editorial product to be as strong as possible. Typos, grammatical errors, and missed opportunities to say it better can mean the difference between "yes" and "no." The high-end editors and consultants listed here offer years of specialized experience along the lines of what one would expect from any other high-end consultant, whether legal, medical, or financial. Their services are not about copyediting and proofreading. Most editors of this ilk not only ensure that the text is as strong as it should be for the given market but also guide writers on navigating the publishing arena. Even if you already have a publishing deal, the reality is that in-house editors are not necessarily going to do a pristine editing job, and what gets published is a reflection on you not them. Self-publishers should be especially vigilant about having their work professionally vetted and edited prior to publication.

What Kind of Editor Should You Retain?

Someone who has a genuine history of editing the kind of work you are writing. It's best if you actually read some of the works they have edited and communicate with some of the people who have used their services.

Where Can You Find Qualified Editors?

This section lists 31 of the most experienced and qualified independent editors in America. Most of them have many years of traditional in-house publishing experience, and they may have even edited one or more of your favorite books. The editors in this section are members of small, informal organizations that enable freelance editors to network, teach, and support each other in mutually beneficial ways. For instance, an editor who specializes in romance novels can refer science fiction writers to an appropriate editor, and vice versa. The editors prefer to keep their groups no larger than the number of people that can comfortably fit in a Manhattan living room, which is why new groups keep forming.

Most affiliated members reside in and around New York City, which is only natural since almost all of them have worked for New York publishers. However, there surely are many excellent editors throughout the country who don't belong to one of these organizations and haven't worked for a New York publisher. They can be found through Google, Editcetera (www.editcetera.com), or the Editorial Freelancers Association (www.the-efa .org) and by networking with fellow writers. No editor should be dismissed simply because they aren't listed in this section. I was only able to list the editors I have personal confidence in, and membership in one of these groups gives me that confidence. I welcome your suggestions for additional editors to include in future editions (jeff@jeffherman.com).

What Does It Cost to Hire an Editor?

Frankly, I'm not sure. It obviously depends on what type or level of editing you need, who you use, and when you use them. More experienced editors, and those with some "big hits" on their résumés, will presumably charge more than others. Even stated rates might be negotiable. The best thing to do is ask experienced people and shop around.

What about Scams?

Unfortunately, scams are legion. You need to be careful and discerning. Here are some tips.

- Only retain the actual person who will be working with you, not a company that will randomly assign someone to you.
- Avoid anyone who makes outlandish promises before they have even seen your work. Actually, don't give anyone money before they see your work and give you a proposal for what they will do and what it will cost.
- Check references and the internet for complaints.

An independent editor isn't a literary agent or a publisher. If they are offering to represent and/or publish you for money (you pay them), it's likely a scam. If someone is promising to fulfill your most cherished publishing dreams for a fee, it's probably too good to be true.

AN EDITOR OF ONE'S OWN

Members of Words into Print
(For information about Words into Print, see page 581)

Are book doctors really worth it? What do they do that agents and in-house editors might not? With all the help a writer can get on the journey from manuscript to published book, why hire an editor of one's own?

Before the Age of the Independent Editor, literary agents and publishing staff were the first publishing insiders to read a proposal or manuscript. Today, however, the focus on business interests is so demanding and the volume of submissions so great — agents alone take in hundreds of query letters a month — that a writer's work has to be white-hot before receiving serious consideration. In light of these developments, a writer may turn to an independent editor as the first expert reader in the world of publishing's gatekeepers.

What Else Do Independent Editors Do, and How Much Do They Charge?

Services. Not every writer and project will call for the services of an independent editor. However, if you are looking for the kind of personalized and extensive professional guidance beyond that gained from workshops, fellow writers, online sources, magazines, and books, hiring an editor may well be worth the investment. An editor of your own can provide a professional assessment of whether or not your project is ready to submit, and to whom you should submit it; expert assistance to make your manuscript or book proposal as good as it should be; help with preparing a convincing submissions package; and an advocate's voice and influence to guide you in your efforts toward publication.

Another key role an independent editor plays is to protect writers from querying their prospects before their material is irresistible. Premature submissions cause writers needless disappointment and frustration. Your editor can zero in on the thematic core, central idea, or story line that needs to be conveyed in a way that is most likely to attract an agent and a publisher. In short, an editor of your own can identify the most appealing, salable aspects of you and your work.

Rates. "Good editing is expensive," our venerable colleague Jerry Gross, editor of the book *Editors on Editing*, prudently notes. What kind of editing is good editing and how expensive is it? The internet and other sources quote a wide range of rates from a variety of editors. The numbers are not necessarily accurate or reliable. We've seen hourly rates ranging from about $50 to well above $200. Several factors account for this spread: the type of editing, the editor's level of experience, and the publishing venue. For example, rates for copyediting are lower than those for substantive editing. Moreover, standards in book publishing are particularly rigorous because books are long, expensive to produce, made to last, and vulnerable to the long-term impact of reviewer criticism.

Process. Book editors are specialists. Every book project arrives on the desk of an independent editor at a certain level of readiness, and the first task is to determine what the project needs. A deep book edit is typically a painstaking, time-consuming process that may move at the pace of only three or four manuscript pages per hour — or, when less intensive, eight to twelve pages per hour. Occasionally a manuscript received by an independent is fully developed, needs only a light copyedit, and may well be ready to submit as is. In other cases, the editorial process may require one or more rounds of revisions. If you are hiring an editor to critique your work, you should be aware that reading the material takes considerably more time than writing the critique. Sometimes a flat fee, rather than an hourly rate, may be appropriate to the project. Sometimes an editor will offer a brief initial consultation at no charge. A reputable independent book editor will be able to recommend a course of action that may or may not include one or more types of editorial services, and give you a reliable estimate of the time and fees involved.

But Won't the In-House Editor Fix Your Book?

Sometimes. Maybe. To an extent. Independents and in-house editors are, in many ways, different creatures. For starters, in-house editors spend much of the day preparing for and going to meetings. Marketing meetings. Sales meetings. Editorial meetings. Production meetings. The mandate for most of these in-house editors is to acquire new book projects and to shepherd those that are already in the pipeline. With so many extended activities cutting into the business hours, the time for actually working on a manuscript can be short.

Many in-house editors have incoming manuscripts screened by an already overworked assistant. (The days of staff readers are long gone.) The only quiet time the editor has for reading might be evenings and weekends. We have known editors to take a week off from work just to edit a book and be accessible to their authors. These days, too, the acquiring editor may not do any substantive work on a book project under contract, leaving that task to a junior editor. There is also a distinct possibility the acquiring editor may leave the job before that book is published, and this can occur with the next editor, too, and the next, threatening the continuity of the project. All of which doesn't mean that there aren't a lot of hardworking people at the publishing house; it means that editors have more to do than ever before and must devote at least as much time to crunching numbers as to focusing on the writer and the book.

Independent editors, on the other hand, spend most of their business days working exclusively with authors and their texts. They typically handle only a few manuscripts at a time and are free from marketing and production obligations. An independent editor's primary interest is in helping you to get your book polished and published. An editor of your own will see your project through — and often your next book, too.

What Do Agents Say about Independent Editors?

"As the book market gets tougher for selling both fiction and nonfiction it is imperative that all submissions be polished, edited, almost ready for the printer. Like many other agents I do as much as possible to provide editorial input for the author, but there are time constraints. So independent editors provide a very valuable service these days in getting the manuscript or proposal in the best shape possible to increase the chances of impressing an editor and getting a sale with the best possible terms."   — **Bill Contardi**

"Agents work diligently for our clients, but there are situations in which outside help is necessary. Perhaps a manuscript has been worked on so intensively that objectivity is lacking, or perhaps the particular skill required to do a job properly is not one of an agent's strong suits. Maybe more time is required than an agent can offer. Fortunately, agents and authors are able to tap into the talent and experience of an outside editor. The outside editors I've worked with offer invaluable support during the editing process itself and for the duration of a project. Their involvement can make the difference between an author getting a publishing contract or having to put a project aside, or the difference between a less- or more-desirable contract."   — **Victoria Gould Pryor**

"The right editor or book doctor can make all the difference in whether a manuscript gets sold. A debut novelist, for example, may have a manuscript that is almost there, but not quite. With the input of a good editor, the novel can reach its full potential and be an attractive prospect to a potential publisher. Similarly, someone writing a memoir may have had a fascinating life but may not really have the god-given writing talent that will turn that life into a compelling and readable book. An editor can take that person's rough-hewn words and thoughts and turn them into a memoir that really sings on the printed page."   — **Eric Myers**

"Occasionally a novel will land on my desk that I feel has talent or a good concept behind it but for whatever reason (the writing, the pacing) needs an inordinate amount of work. Instead of just rejecting it flat out I may then refer the author to a freelance editor, someone who has the time and expertise to help the author further shape and perfect their work."   — **Nina Collins**

"I have had several occasions to use the help of freelance editors and think they provide incalculable good service to the profession. In these competitive times, a manuscript has to be as polished and clean as possible to garner a good sale to a publisher. If it needs work, it simply provides an editor with a reason to turn it down. My job is to not give them any excuses. I do not have either the time or the ability to do the editorial work that may be required to make the manuscript salable. Paying a freelance professional to help shape a book into its most commercially viable form ultimately more than pays for itself."

— **Deborah Schneider**

So How Can You Find the Right Editor?

You've searched online. You've looked in directories such as this one. You've asked around. A personal recommendation from a published writer-friend who has used an independent editor for his or her work may or may not do the trick. Every author has different needs, every author-editor dynamic a different chemistry.

Although sometimes an author and editor "click" very quickly, many editors offer free consultations, and it's fine to contact more than one editor at this stage. A gratis consult may involve an editor's short take, by phone or in writing, on sample material the editor asked you to send. But how to distinguish among the many independent editors?

Some editorial groups are huge, and they are open to all who designate themselves as editors; it might take some additional research to identify the members who are most reputable and best suited to your work. The smaller groups consist of editors who have been nominated, vetted, and elected, which ensures the high quality of the individual professionals. They meet with regularity, share referrals, and discuss industry developments. Your consultation, references offered, and the terms of any subsequent agreement can tell the rest.

Another way to find the right editor is to prepare your manuscript to its best advantage — structurally, stylistically, and mechanically. Asking the opinion of one or more impartial readers — that is, not limiting your initial reviewers to friends and relatives — is a great strategy as well. If you have the benefit of a disinterested reader, you may be able to make some significant changes before sending an excerpt to an independent editor. One more element to consider: editors often will take your own personality and initial written inquiry into account as carefully as they do your writing. Seasoned independents do not take on every project that appears on their desk; they can pick and choose — and, working solo, they must.

Tales from the Trenches

We hope we've given you a sense of what an editor of your own can do for you and where we fit into the publishing picture. But next to firsthand experience, perhaps nothing communicates quite as sharply as an anecdote. Here are a few of ours from the past and present members:

"An in-house editor called me with an unusual problem. He had signed up an acclaimed author for a new book project. She had written a number of stories — nonfiction narratives about her life in an exotic land. The problem was this: some of the stories had already been published in book form in England, and that collection had its own integrity in terms of theme and chronology; now she had written another set of stories, plus a diary of her travels. How could the published stories and the new ones be made into one book?

"I decided to disregard the structure of the published book altogether. As I reexamined each story according to theme, emotional quality, geographical location, and people involved, I kept looking for ways in which they might relate to each other. Eventually, I sensed a new and logical way in which to arrange them. I touched not one word of the author's prose. I did the same thing I always try to do when editing — imagine myself inside the skin of the writer. A prominent trade book review had this to say about the result: 'One story flows into the next....'"   — **Alice Rosengard**

"A writer had hired me to help with his first book after his agent had sold it to a publisher because he wanted to expedite the revisions and final approval of his manuscript. As a result of our work together, the book came out sooner than anticipated; it also won an award and the author was interviewed on a major TV news program. The same author hired me a year later for his second book, purchased by a larger publisher, and this book, too, entailed some significant developmental editing. At that point we learned the in-house editor had left the publisher and a new one had come aboard. This editor not only objected strongly to one whole section of the book; she also gave the author a choice: revise the section in one week or put the project on hold for at least six more months.

"From halfway across the world, the writer called me on a Friday to explain his publishing crisis, which was also coinciding with a personal crisis, and asked if we could collaborate closely on the fifty pages in question over the weekend. I agreed and cancelled my weekend plans, and we camped out at each end of the telephone and emailboxes almost nonstop for three days. He resubmitted the book on Tuesday, the book received all requisite signatures in-house, and a month later it went into production. This hands-on and sometimes unpredictable kind of collaboration with writers helps illustrate the special nature of independent editing."   — **Katharine Turok**

"A writer with a truly astonishing story to tell received only rejections when he sent his query letter to agents. He had an informal proposal and assumed that his extraordinary experiences on the Amazon River would be enough to get him a book deal for his memoir. I could see right away that the query letter was confusing and didn't present him or his story in a powerful-enough light.

"I culled the most effective parts of his story and reworked the book proposal so that his enthusiasm and vivid tales dominated. We hammered out a succinct and compelling query letter. I offered the names of several agents I thought might be interested, and this time it worked. He signed with an agent who sold his manuscript to a major publisher."

— **Linda Carbone**

"My work on a book about a near-extinct bird species was greatly enhanced when the author gave me a tour of a California estuary. Guided by his passion and on-site expertise, I was able to spot exquisite birds, hear bird-watching lingo, and see his high-end scope in action. Now I understood the thrill of what he was writing about and was better able to help him communicate it.

"One of my most challenging assignments was to add action scenes to a memoir by an Olympic fencing champion. Here was a subject I knew nothing about. I tried to bone up in advance through reading, but my author had a better idea. Working his way across my living room floor, he sparred with an invisible opponent, demonstrating what he wished to describe in his book. I wrote down what I saw.

"As an independent editor, I have the time and freedom to work 'outside the book,' to literally enter the worlds my authors are writing about."   — **Ruth Greenstein**

"An author seeking help with her debut novel presented a specific challenge: a knock-out story to tell along a recently well-trodden road. After several rounds that involved radically restructuring the point of view and making subtle style shifts, we produced an originally crafted, unique result that, to our mutual chagrin, could not be placed with an agent. (This often happens when a hot title kicks off a zeitgeist craze and the niche market is flooded.) Believing in the value of what we had, I encouraged my client — who was on the verge of giving up — to pursue an alternate route to publishing. Using an independent platform, not only did she manage to garner the coveted Kirkus star, but her novel went on to be named one of *Kirkus Reviews*' Best Indie Books of 2012."   — **Michael Wilde**

THE LISTINGS

BOOK DEVELOPMENT GROUP ❖ www.bookdevelopmentgroup.com

Book Development Group (BDG) is an alliance of independent New York City publishing professionals. All the BDG editors have at least 25 years of experience, and they work with first-time and seasoned writers in both fiction and nonfiction. The editors work independently of one another with services that range from developing a strong book concept to completely editing a manuscript and — for authors who wish to self-publish — producing a printed book.

The editors of Book Development Group can help you with:

- idea and concept development
- manuscript evaluation
- in-depth manuscript editing
- query letters and book proposals for agents
- project management for self-publishing books and ebooks
- coaching throughout the writing process
- assistance and advice for related publishing services

Whether you are a writer of fiction or nonfiction, BDG editors can help you transform your manuscript into a polished and professional book.

Janet Spencer King, janet@bookdevelopmentgroup.com

Specialties: Fiction — most genres in commercial/mainstream fiction including, among others, mystery, women's, and young adult. Nonfiction — health/fitness/nutrition, relationships, medical, narrative, self-help/popular psychology, business, spirituality, travel, women's interest.

Janet Spencer King has been an editor and writer for more than 25 years and was previously a literary agent, placing both nonfiction and fiction with key publishing houses. King has been the author or coauthor of five books published by major houses. She started her career in magazine publishing, eventually becoming editor in chief of three national magazines. Today she works one-on-one with writers, providing them with professional guidance throughout the entire book-writing process; she also specializes in managing production of self-published books.

Diane O'Connell, diane@bookdevelopmentgroup.com

Specialties: Fiction—commercial/mainstream, thriller/mystery/suspense, fantasy/science fiction, women's, young adult. Nonfiction — business, biography/memoir, health/fitness/nutrition, narrative, self-help/popular psychology, spirituality/New Age, true crime.

Diane O'Connell has over 25 years' publishing experience as a Random House editor and author of six books, including the award-winning *The Novel-Maker's Handbook: The No-Nonsense Guide to Crafting a Marketable Story*. She specializes in working with first-time authors and has helped numerous authors get deals with major publishers, including some that have become bestsellers. She edits manuscripts, coaches writers, writes and edits book proposals, and is available to work in person with authors. She welcomes authors at any stage of the book-writing process.

Olga Vezeris, olga@bookdevelopmentgroup.com

Specialties: Fiction — commercial/mainstream, general, thriller/mystery/suspense, historical novels and sagas. Nonfiction — narrative, self-help/popular psychology, health/fitness/nutrition, art/architecture, business, food/entertaining, illustrated and gift books on all subjects, lifestyle/decorating, travel, true crime.

Olga Vezeris has extensive experience in the publishing industry, having held senior editorial and subsidiary rights positions at companies including Simon & Schuster, Grand Central Publishing (Warner Books), Workman, HarperCollins, and the Bertelsmann Book Club group, where she has acquired, edited, or licensed many commercial fiction and non-fiction titles and illustrated books. Currently she works with authors, editing proposals and manuscripts and guiding them in all aspects of traditional and ebook publishing.

THE EDITORS CIRCLE ❖ www.theeditorscircle.com

This group of independent book editors has more than 100 years of collective experience on-staff with major New York publishers. They have come together to offer their skills and experience to writers who need help bringing their book projects from ideas or complete manuscripts to well-published books, whether the authors choose to work with traditional publishers or self-publish.

As publishing consultants (or "book doctors"), they offer a variety of editorial services that include:

- defining and positioning manuscripts in the marketplace
- refining book ideas
- evaluating and critiquing complete or partial manuscripts and book proposals
- editing, ghostwriting, or collaborating on proposals, manuscripts, and Web content
- offering referrals to agents and publishers
- helping authors develop platforms and query letters
- guiding authors through the publishing process
- consulting on publicity and marketing

If you need help with your book project, the publishing professionals of The Editors Circle can offer you the editorial services you seek, a successful track record of projects placed and published, and the behind-the-scenes, hands-on experience that can help you take your idea or manuscript wherever you want it to go.

Bonny V. Fetterman, 718-739-1057, bonnyfetterman@theeditorscircle.com

As a professional Judaica editor with an MA in Jewish studies from Brandeis University and a former senior acquisitions editor of Schocken Books for 15 years, Bonny edits both popular and scholarly books in the fields of Jewish history, literature, religious thought, biblical studies, biography, memoir, and pop culture. In addition to editing, she critiques manuscripts, writes book proposals, and serves as a publishing consultant from contract negotiations to publication. Her most recent projects are *Stars in the Ring: Jewish Champions in the Golden Age of Boxing* by Mike Silver (Lyons Press); *Raising Secular Jews: Yiddish Schools and Their Periodicals for American Children* by Naomi Prawer Kadar (Brandeis University Press); *Holocaust, Genocide, and the Law* by Michael Bazyler (Oxford University Press); and *Exit Berlin: How One Woman Saved Her Family from Nazi Germany* by Charlotte Bonelli (Yale University Press). Based in New York City, she has been an independent editor for 16 years and held editorial positions at Harper & Row, Basic Books, and *Reform Judaism* magazine.

Rob Kaplan, 914-736-7182, robkaplan@theeditorscircle.com

As an editor, ghostwriter, and collaborator on nonfiction book proposals and traditionally published and self-published books, Rob specializes in the areas of business, self-help, popular psychology, parenting, history, and other subjects. Among his recent projects are *Imagine That! Igniting Your Brain for Creativity and Peak Performance* by James Mapes (Greenleaf Book Group Press); *Rethinking Public Administration* by Richard Clay Wilson, Jr. (Mill City Press); *The Facts of Business Life* by William McBean (Wiley); and *By the Grace of God: A 9/11 Survivor's Story of Love, Hope, and Healing* by Jean Potter (AuthorHouse).

Prior to becoming an independent editor, he held senior editorial positions at Amacom Books (American Management Association), Macmillan, Prentice Hall, and HarperCollins. He is currently based in Cortlandt Manor, New York.

Beth Lieberman, 310-403-1602, bethlieberman@theeditorscircle.com

Beth has acquired, edited, and published more than 500 books, including a number of *New York Times* bestsellers. She is a skillful writing coach for novelists and memoirists, a dedicated developmental editor of book proposals, and a keen navigator in the world of independent publishing. Beth is also an ordained rabbi, and her not-so-secret passion is working with Jewish wisdom texts. Beth has worked on-staff at New American Library, Warner Books, Kensington Publishing, Dove Books and Audio, and NewStar Press. She lives and works in both Los Angeles and New York. Her most recent projects include *Enchantress* by Maggie Anton (Penguin/Plume); *The Invitation* by Clifton Taulbert (New-South Books); and *Wise Aging* by Rachel Cowan and Linda Thal (Behrman House).

John Paine, 973-783-5082, johnpaine@theeditorscircle.com, www.johnpaine.com

Among the services John offers are developmental editing, line editing, fiction evaluations, and nonfiction proposals. He helps authors both within traditional publishing and with ebooks. Areas of interest in fiction include thriller, mystery, historical, and African American. Trade nonfiction specialties include health, memoir, true crime, and business. Among his recent projects are the bestselling *Calorie Myth* by Jonathan Bailor (Harper); *Assassination Generation* by Lt. Col. Dave Grossman (Little, Brown); and *Murder in the Courthouse* by Nancy Grace (BenBella). He developed his editing skills at Dutton and New American Library, imprints of Penguin Books USA, and he now works in Montclair, New Jersey.

Susan A. Schwartz, 212-877-3211, susanschwartz@theeditorscircle.com

Susan has developed and edited *New York Times* bestsellers and ghostwritten eight nonfiction books. She specializes in women's fiction and medical, legal, and political thriller, as well as fitness and health books, memoir, business, relationships, and popular reference books (all subjects), and has extensive experience developing book proposals for writers, publishers, and literary agents. Her current focus is on editing and producing corporate reference, conference, and marketing publications (histories, biographies, essays, and website content). Susan is based in Manhattan, where she is a member of Women's Media Group and maintains her contacts with the industry's movers and shakers. Her previous on-staff experience includes Random House (2 years), Doubleday (15 years), Facts On File

(4 years), and NTC/Contemporary Books (3 years). Her latest accomplishments include editing Suzanne Morris's new novel, *Aftermath* (SFA Press), and Cathy Curran's memoir, *Secondhand Scotch* (Ant Press), an Amazon Top 10 Hot Pick.

THE INDEPENDENT EDITORS GROUP ❖ www.bookdocs.com

The Independent Editors Group is the longest-running continuous professional affiliation of New York City–based independent editors (sometimes called "outside editors" or "book doctors") who work with writers, editors, publishers, and agents in trade book publishing. Years of distinguished tenure at major publishing houses qualify them to provide the following editorial services on fiction and nonfiction manuscripts and book proposals:

- thorough evaluations and detailed critiques
- plot restructuring
- developmental and line editing
- reorganization, revision, and rewriting
- consultation, conceptual development, and sample chapter writing on book proposals
- ghostwriting and collaboration
- salvaging of endangered or orphaned book projects
- project guidance and assistance on all aspects of self-publishing
- author coaching

If an editor is unavailable, referrals will be made to other appropriate IEG members. Résumés and references can be found at www.bookdocs.com. For fees, consult editors individually.

Sally Arteseros, 212-982-3246, sarteseros@bookdocs.com

Having worked as an editor and then senior editor at Doubleday for more than 25 years, Sally edits all kinds of fiction: literary, commercial, women's, historical, and contemporary, as well as short stories. And in nonfiction: biography, history, science, psychology, anthropology, business, religion, inspiration, essays, academic books.

Harriet Bell, 212-249-5625, harrietbell@verizon.net, www.bellbookandhandle.com

Specializes in nonfiction categories such as memoir, lifestyle, cookbooks, self-help, illustrated books, business, health and fitness, diet, and fashion. Writes proposals and website copy, ghostwrites books, edits manuscripts, and packages books. See her website for more information.

Toni Burbank, 718-499-3993, toniburbank@bookdocs.com

Former vice president and executive editor at Bantam Dell/Random House, with particular interest/expertise in psychology, health, women's interest, spirituality, and self-help. She has edited more than 10 *New York Times* bestsellers; authors include Daniel Goleman, Christiane Northrup, MD, Miriam E. Nelson, Daniel Siegel, MD, Tara Brach, Jack Kornfield, and Brian Wansink. Offers developmental and line editing, manuscript evaluation, and proposal writing. Nonfiction only.

Susan Dalsimer, 212-496-9164, susan.dalsimer@gmail.com

Former vice president and publisher of Miramax Books, specializing in editing literary and commercial fiction and young adult fiction. In nonfiction, areas include memoir, spirituality, biography, psychology, theater, film, and television.

Paul De Angelis, 860-672-6882, pdeangelis@bookdocs.com, www.pauldeangelisbooks.com

Manuscript evaluations, rewriting or ghostwriting, and editing. Thirty-five years' book-publishing experience in significant positions at St. Martin's Press, E. P. Dutton, and Kodansha America. Special expertise in history, current affairs, music, biography, literature, and translations. Authors have included the Delany sisters, Mike Royko, and Jorge Luis Borges.

Michael Denneny, 212-362-3241, mldenneny@aol.com

Thirty years' editorial experience at the University of Chicago Press, Macmillan, Crown, and St. Martin's Press. Edits commercial, literary, and mystery fiction; in nonfiction, works with biography, history, current affairs, memoir, psychology, and almost any narrative nonfiction. Also works with writers on book-proposal packages.

Paul Dinas, 646-932-4916, dinas.paul@gmail.com, www.pauldinasbookeditor.com

As an editor for more than 30 years in trade book publishing, Paul has enjoyed being part of the creative process, helping to develop and shape manuscripts from inception through final publication. His experience embraces nearly every genre of book-length work, both fiction and nonfiction. He works with many experienced authors but finds great satisfaction in helping develop and shape the works of first-time writers. Many have gone on to find publishers or to have great success in the vibrant self-publishing arena. See his website for more details about his career and services.

Emily Heckman, 917-837-3817, emilyheckman@aol.com

Editor of adult and young adult fiction and nonfiction. In fiction, areas of interest include women's, suspense, thriller, and horror. Areas of interest in nonfiction include memoir, health, psychology, pop culture, history, and spirituality. Writer of nonfiction books (coauthor, ghostwriter) including bestselling memoirs. Training includes senior editorial positions at major publishing houses (Simon & Schuster, Random House, etc.).

Susan Leon, 914-833-1422, scribe914@gmail.com

Editor specializing in concept development, manuscript evaluation and editing, book proposals, collaborations, and heavy rewrites. Ghostwrote two *New York Times* bestsellers and edited multiple award-winning titles. Fiction interests: historical novels of all kinds and contemporary relationship-driven stories with compelling, affirmative themes. Nonfiction interests: history (special expertise), memoir, biography, politics, adventure and travel, women/family themes, film, television and theater, design, and lifestyle. Especially enjoys working with new and emerging writers.

Richard Marek, 203-341-8607, rwmarek@earthlink.net

Former president and publisher of E. P. Dutton. Specializes in editing and ghostwriting, both fiction and nonfiction. Edited Robert Ludlum's first nine books, James Baldwin's last five, and Thomas Harris's *The Silence of the Lambs*. Ghostwrote 14 books, including Trisha Meili's *I Am the Central Park Jogger* and James Patterson's *Hide and Seek*.

Sydny Miner, 914-391-8665, sydny.miner@gmail.com

Sydny has extensive experience as an editor at major publishing houses (Crown Publishing Group, Simon & Schuster), working primarily in nonfiction, with a special emphasis on cookbooks, food and nutrition, health and wellness, diet, fitness, exercise, psychology, and self-help. She has worked closely with high-profile authors (including two First Ladies) and edited numerous bestselling and award-winning titles, taking projects from concept to outline to finished book. She sees herself as a midwife, helping authors to put their unique voice and vision on the page, deconstructing their expertise and making it accessible to the layperson.

Beth Rashbaum, 212-228-9573, bethrashbaum@gmail.com

A veteran of over 35 years in publishing, Beth was an editor most recently at Bantam Dell/Random House. She edits all kinds of nonfiction — including memoir, biography, investigative journalism, Judaica, health and wellness, yoga, psychology, and popular science. She also edits and writes proposals, has ghostwritten one *New York Times* best-seller, and was coauthor, with Olga Silverstein, of *The Courage to Raise Good Men.* Authors she has worked with include Gretchen Rubin, Gloria Steinem, Leonard Mlodinow, Stephen Hawking, Mildred Kalish, Daniel Coyle, Luke Barr, Alexander Masters, and Candace Pert.

Betty Kelly Sargent, 212-486-1531, bsargent@earthlink.net

Founder and CEO of BookWorks.com — The Self-Publishers Association, and former editor in chief of William Morrow, specializing in collaborations and developmental editing for both literary and commercial fiction as well as general nonfiction including memoir, health, humor, psychology, and spirituality. Coauthor of seven published books and recent consultant for those who want to self-publish and take advantage of social media for book promotion.

James O'Shea Wade, 914-962-4619, jwade@bookdocs.com

With 30 years' experience as editor in chief and executive editor for major publishers, including Crown/Random House, Macmillan, Dell, and Rawson-Wade, James edits and ghostwrites in all nonfiction areas and specializes in business, science, history, biography, and militaria. Also edits all types of fiction, prepares book proposals, and evaluates manuscripts.

MARVELOUS EDITIONS ❖ www.marvelouseditions.com, www.facebook.com/MarvelousEditors

Marvelous Editions is the partnership of respected independent editors Marlene Adelstein and Alice Peck. They each have over two decades of expertise in developmental and line editing as well as ghostwriting, proposal drafting, and screenplays. They provide comprehensive guidance for writers from the first inspiration to the published work — be it through a mainstream publisher, independent press, self-publishing venture, periodical, or website. When appropriate, they also provide referrals to reliable and talented designers, copyeditors, proofreaders, publicists, and agents. Marlene and Alice usually work independently but have joined forces when appropriate, editing authors including Kristen Wolf, Nicole Bokat, and Kim Powers.

Marlene Adelstein, marlene@fixyourbook.com, www.fixyourbook.com

Provides thorough, constructive critiques, developmental and line editing, advice on a book's commercial potential, and agent referrals when appropriate. Over 20 years' experience in publishing and feature-film development. Specializes in commercial and literary fiction: mystery, thriller, women's, romance, historical; young adult; memoir; screenplays. Recent authors include Karan Bajaj, Peter Golden, Beth Hoffman, Douglas Carlton Abrams, Kim Powers, Antoinette May, Anne Serling, Jeanne Bogino, and Amanda McTigue.

Alice Peck, alicepeck@alicepeck.com, www.alicepeckeditorial.com

Evaluates and edits memoir, narrative nonfiction, psychology, spirituality/religion, and fiction; writes and edits proposals; ghostwrites. Acquired books and developed them into scripts for film and television before shifting her focus to editing in 1998. Recent authors include E. A. Aymar, Nadine Bjursten, Lama Surya Das, Gretchen Grossman, Chris Grosso, Jeri Parker, Dr. Jeffrey B. Rubin, Mark Schimmoeller, Joanie Schirm, Hannah Seligson, and Bonnie Myotai Treace.

WORDS INTO PRINT ❖ www.wordsintoprint.org

Words into Print is one of New York's top networks of independent book editors, writers, and publishing consultants. Founded in 1998, WiP is a professional alliance whose members provide editorial services to publishers, literary agents, and book packagers, as well as to individual writers. Members of WiP have extensive industry experience, averaging 20 years as executives and editors with leading trade book publishers. As active independent professionals, members meet individually and as a group with agents and other publishing colleagues; participate in conventions, conferences, panels, and workshops; and maintain affiliations with organizations that include PEN, AWP, the Authors Guild, the Women's Media Group, Lambda Literary Foundation, the CLMP, the Modern Language Association, and the Academy of American Poets.

The consultants at Words into Print are committed to helping established and new writers develop, revise, and polish their work. They also guide clients through the publishing process by helping them find the most promising route to publication. WiP's editors and writers provide:

- detailed analyses and critiques of proposals and manuscripts
- editing, cowriting, and ghostwriting
- expert advice, ideas, and techniques for making a writer's project the best it can be
- assistance in developing query letters and synopses for literary agents and publishers
- referrals to literary agents, publishers, book packagers, and other publishing services
- guidance in developing publicity and marketing strategies

- project management — from conception through production
- inside information writers need to make their way successfully through the publishing world

Words into Print's editors are nominated, vetted, and elected to membership. Members conform to group guidelines, so potential clients can be confident of the highest caliber of skills and conduct. Each member has his or her own contracts, fee structures, and business arrangements. The range of rates is in keeping with market rates for independent editors with longtime experience at major publishing houses. Estimates and individualized agreements will be provided, as appropriate, on a project-by-project basis. Brief profiles appear below. For more information, please visit www.wordsintoprint.org.

Jeff Alexander, alexandereditorial@gmail.com

Twenty years of editing experience in magazines and book publishing, editing nonfiction with a focus on science, history, politics, sociology, technology, and current events. Has edited books for Vintage/Anchor, Pantheon, Knopf, and the Penguin Press. Has worked with Robert Reich, Jaron Lanier, David Grann, Alice Dreger, Charles C. Mann, Michael Dobbs, and Simon Critchley. Offers a full range of editorial services for manuscripts and proposals, including ghostwriting.

Becky Cabaza, rtcbooks@gmail.com

Becky Cabaza has more than 20 years of full-time publishing experience as an acquisitions editor and editorial director and an additional 11 years as a freelance editor, ghostwriter/collaborator, and consultant to numerous authors. Freelance services include writing and restructuring from idea/proposal phase through finished manuscript, as well as thorough project evaluation and editing at any level. Specialties: self-help, practical nonfiction, health and wellness, parenting/family, book proposals, ghostwriting, collaboration.

Jane Fleming Fransson, jffeditor@gmail.com

More than 15 years of experience editing narrative nonfiction and fiction (both adult and young adult). Former editor at Penguin Press. Has worked with Frank Bruni, Novella Carpenter, Pamela Druckerman, Deanna Fei, Camilla Gibb, Paul Greenberg, Emma Larkin, Marina Lewycka, Christine Montross, Craig Mullaney, Ann Napolitano, Georgia Pellegrini, Jim Sheeler, Sadia Shepard, Jane S. Smith, and Dana Thomas. Offers manuscript critiques, proposal editing and writing, developmental and line editing of manuscripts, ghostwriting, project management, and general publishing consulting.

Ruth Greenstein, rg@greenlinepublishing.com

Editing independent voices since 1989. Literary fiction, biography/memoir, social issues, arts and culture, nature and popular science, travel, religion/spirituality, poetry, photography, media companions. Founding member of WiP; formerly with Harcourt and Ecco; longtime associate of Turtle Point Press and its imprints. Has worked with Anita Shreve, Erica Jong, John Ashbery, Gary Paulsen, Alice Walker, Sallie Bingham, and Dennis Lehane. Offers a wide range of editorial and consulting services, plus synopsis writing, submissions guidance, career strategy, and Web presence development.

Emily Loose, emilylooselit@gmail.com

Twenty-five years' experience editing nonfiction for Random House, Penguin, Simon & Schuster, and Cambridge University Press. Seventeen *New York Times* bestsellers. Has worked with Lawrence Wright, Ross Douthat, Arianna Huffington, Charles Fishman, Gillian Tett, Peter Sims, and Nicholas Wade. Offers proposal development, detailed critiques, developmental and line editing, and consultation about agents, building a promotional platform, marketing, and self-publishing. Specializes in narrative nonfiction, business, politics, history, science, social science, women's interest, memoir, biography, psychology.

Julie Miesionczek, julie@writewithjulie.com

Ten years' experience with literary to commercial fiction, including historical, thriller, women's fiction, and select narrative nonfiction and memoir. Worked at Doubleday Broadway, the Crown Publishing Group, Pamela Dorman Books/Viking, and Viking Books at Penguin Random House. Has worked with Jojo Moyes, Luanne Rice, Jasper Fforde, Paolo Giordano, Anne M. Fletcher, and Beth Hoffman. Offers detailed critique, developmental editing, and line editing services as well as submissions/publishing guidance.

Anne Cole Norman, acole157@gmail.com

Specializing in nonfiction projects including self-help, how-to, health, relationships, lifestyle, parenting, personal finance, and memoir. Offers developmental and detailed editing, rewriting/book doctoring, manuscript evaluation, proposal writing, and ghostwriting. Fifteen years' experience as an acquiring editor at Hyperion, Doubleday, and HarperCollins. Can assist in finding an agent when appropriate.

ACKNOWLEDGMENTS

Georgia Hughes, my remarkable editor at New World Library, deserves my eternal gratitude for her confidence in this book and in me. She was one of my very first editors more than 15 years ago. Since then this book has experienced many publishers and editors, so it felt like a homecoming to be embraced by her once again.

I was extremely fortunate to have Kristen Cashman, the managing editor at New World Library, on my side. She is smart and incredibly patient, and got me to do a better job than I would have without her.

For more than 20 years, Deborah Herman, my partner in life and work, has contributed more than she knows to this book throughout its history with her perfectly timed comments and words of encouragement.

Finally, a huge "thank you" to all the people who taught me to be humble and appreciative — even if I'm frequently appointed to learn it all over again.

GLOSSARY

abstract   A brief sequential profile of chapters in a nonfiction book proposal (also called a synopsis); a point-by-point summary of an article or essay. In academic and technical journals, abstracts often appear with (and may serve to preface) the articles themselves.

adaptation   A rewrite or reworking of a piece for another medium, such as the adaptation of a novel for the screen. (*See also* **screenplay**.)

advance   Money paid (usually in installments) to an author by a publisher prior to publication. The advance is paid against royalties: if an author is given a $5,000 advance, for instance, the author will collect royalties only after the royalty moneys due exceed $5,000. A good contract protects the advance if it should exceed the royalties ultimately due from sales.

advance orders   Orders received before a book's official publication date, and sometimes before actual completion of the book's production and manufacture.

agent   The person who acts on behalf of the author to handle the sale of the author's literary properties. Good literary agents are as valuable to publishers as they are to writers; they select and present manuscripts appropriate for particular houses or of interest to particular acquisitions editors. Agents are paid on a percentage basis from the moneys due their author clients.

American Booksellers Association (ABA)   The major trade organization for retail booksellers, chain and independent. The annual ABA convention and trade show offers a chance for publishers and distributors to display their wares to the industry at large and provides an incomparable networking forum for booksellers, editors, agents, publicists, and authors.

American Society of Journalists and Authors (ASJA)   A membership organization for professional writers. ASJA provides a forum for information exchange among writers and others in the publishing community, as well as networking opportunities. (*See also* **Dial-a-Writer**.)

anthology   A collection of stories, poems, essays, and/or selections from larger works

587

(and so forth), usually carrying a unifying theme or concept; these selections may be written by different authors or by a single author. Anthologies are compiled as opposed to written; their editors (as opposed to authors) are responsible for securing the needed reprint rights for the material used, as well as supplying (or providing authors for) pertinent introductory or supplementary material and/or commentary.

attitude A contemporary colloquialism used to describe a characteristic temperament common among individuals who consider themselves superior. Attitude is rarely an esteemed attribute, whether in publishing or elsewhere.

auction Manuscripts a literary agent believes to be hot properties (such as possible best-sellers with strong subsidiary rights potential) will be offered for confidential bidding from multiple publishing houses. Likewise, the reprint, film, and other rights to a successful book may be auctioned off by the original publisher's subsidiary rights department or by the author's agent.

audiobooks Works produced for distribution on audio media, typically MP3, other downloadable electronic formats, or audio compact disc (CD). Audiobooks are usually spoken-word adaptations of works originally created and produced in print; these works sometimes feature the author's own voice; many are given dramatic readings by one or more actors, at times embellished with sound effects.

authorized biography A history of a person's life written with the authorization, cooperation, and, at times, participation of the subject or the subject's heirs.

author's copies/author's discount Author's copies are the free copies of their books that the authors receive from the publisher; the exact number is stipulated in the contract, but it is usually at least 10 hardcovers. The author may purchase additional copies of the book (usually at 40 percent discount from the retail price) and resell them at readings, lectures, and other public engagements. In cases where large quantities of books are bought, author discounts can go as high as 70 percent.

author tour A series of travel and promotional appearances by an author on behalf of the author's book.

autobiography A history of a person's life written by that same person, or, as is typical, composed conjointly with a collaborative writer ("as told to" or "with"; *see also* **coauthor; collaboration**) or ghostwriter. Autobiographies by definition entail the authorization, cooperation, participation, and ultimate approval of the subject.

B

backlist The backlist comprises books published prior to the current season and still in print. Traditionally, at some publishing houses, such backlist titles represent the publisher's cash flow mainstays. Some backlist books continue to sell briskly; some remain bestsellers over several successive seasons; others sell slowly but surely through the years. Although many backlist titles may be difficult to find in bookstores that stock primarily current lists, they can be ordered either through a local bookseller or internet retailer or directly from the publisher.

backmatter   Elements of a book that follow the text proper. Backmatter may include the appendix, notes, glossary, bibliography and other references, lists of resources, index, author biography, offerings of the author's and/or publisher's additional books and other related merchandise, and colophon.

bestseller   Based on sales or orders by bookstores, wholesalers, and distributors, best-sellers are those titles that move the largest quantities. Lists of bestselling books can be local (as in metropolitan newspapers), regional (typically in geographically keyed trade or consumer periodicals), or national (as in *USA Today*, *Publishers Weekly*, or the *New York Times*), as well as international. Fiction and nonfiction are usually listed separately, as are hardcover and paperback classifications. Depending on the list's purview, additional industry-sector designations are used (such as how-to/self-improvement, religion and spirituality, business and finance); in addition, best-seller lists can be keyed to particular genre or specialty fields (such as bestseller lists for mysteries, science fiction, or romance novels, and for historical works, biography, or popular science titles) — and virtually any other marketing category at the discretion of whoever issues the bestseller list (for instance, African American interests, lesbian and gay topics, youth market).

bibliography   A list of books, articles, and other sources that have been used in the writing of the text in which the bibliography appears. Complex works may break the bibliography down into discrete subject areas or source categories, such as General History, Military History, War in the Twentieth Century, or Unionism and Pacifism.

binding   The materials that hold a book together (including the cover). Bindings are generally denoted as hardcover (featuring heavy cardboard covered with durable cloth and/or paper, and occasionally other materials) or paperback (using a pliable, resilient grade of paper, sometimes infused or laminated with other substances such as plastic). In the days when cloth was used lavishly, hardcover volumes were conventionally known as clothbound; and in the very old days, hardcover bindings sometimes featured tooled leather, silk, precious stones, and gold and silver leaf ornamentation.

biography   A history of a person's life. (*See also* **authorized biography**; **autobiography**; **unauthorized biography**.)

blues   (or bluelines) Once photographic proofs of the printing plates for a book with a telltale blue hue, these are now more likely delivered as PDF format electronically. Plates and bluelines have been rendered archaic by current techniques. Blues are reviewed as a means to inspect the set type, layout, and design of the book's pages before it goes to press.

blurb A piece of written copy or extracted quotation used for publicity and promotional purposes, as on a flyer, in a catalog, or in an advertisement (*see also* **cover blurbs**).

book club A book club is a book-marketing operation that ships selected titles to subscribing members on a regular basis, sometimes at greatly reduced prices. Sales of a work to book clubs are negotiated through the publisher's subsidiary rights department (in the case of a bestseller or other work that has gained acclaim, these rights can be auctioned off). Terms vary, but the split of royalties between author and publisher is often 50 percent/50 percent. Book club sales are seen as blessed events by author, agent, and publisher alike.

book contract A legally binding document between author and publisher that sets the terms for the advance, royalties, subsidiary rights, advertising, promotion, and publicity — plus a host of other contingencies and responsibilities. Writers should therefore be thoroughly familiar with the concepts and terminology of the standard book-publishing contract.

book distribution The method of getting books from the publisher's warehouse into the reader's hands. Distribution is traditionally through bookstores but can include such means as telemarketing and mail-order sales, and of course online via websites, as well as sales through a variety of special-interest outlets such as health-food or New Age venues, sports and fitness emporiums, or sex shops. Publishers use their own sales forces as well as independent salespeople, wholesalers, and distributors. Many large and some small publishers distribute for other publishers, which can be a good source of income. A publisher's distribution network is extremely important, because it not only makes possible the vast sales of a bestseller but also affects the visibility of the publisher's entire list of books.

book jacket *See* **dust jacket**.

book producer or **book packager** An individual or company that can assume many of the roles in the publishing process. A book packager or producer may conceive the idea for a book (most often nonfiction) or series, bring together the professionals (including the writer) needed to produce the book(s), sell the individual manuscript or series project to a publisher, take the project through to manufactured product — or perform any selection of those functions, as commissioned by the publisher or other client (such as a corporation producing a corporate history as a premium or giveaway for employees and customers). The book producer may negotiate separate contracts with the publisher and with the writers, editors, and illustrators who contribute to the book.

book review   A critical appraisal of a book (often reflecting a reviewer's personal opinion or recommendation) that evaluates such aspects as organization and writing style, possible market appeal, and cultural, political, or literary significance. Before the public reads book reviews in the local and national print media, important reviews have been published in such respected book-trade journals as *Publishers Weekly*, *Kirkus Reviews*, *Library Journal*, and *Booklist*. A gushing review from one of these journals will encourage booksellers to order the book; copies of these raves will be used for promotion and publicity purposes by the publisher and will encourage other book reviewers nationwide to review the book.

Books in Print   Listings published by R. R. Bowker, of books currently in print; these were once yearly printed volumes (along with periodic supplements such as *Forthcoming Books in Print*). Now they exist more online than in print; they provide ordering information, including titles, authors, ISBNs, prices, whether the book is available in hardcover or paperback, and publisher names. Intended for use by the book trade, *Books in Print* (www.booksinprint.com) is also of great value to writers who are researching and market-researching their projects. Listings are provided alphabetically by author, title, and subject area. Most libraries subscribe to their service or have access to some form of the metadata.

bound galleys   Copies of uncorrected typesetter's page proofs or printouts of electronically produced mechanicals that are bound together as advance copies of the book (*compare* **galleys**). Bound galleys are sent to trade journals (*see* **book review**) as well as to a limited number of reviewers who work under long lead times.

bulk sales   The sale, at a set discount, of many copies of a single title (the greater the number of books, the larger the discount).

byline   The name of the author of a given piece, indicating credit for having written a book or article. Ghostwriters, by definition, do not receive bylines.

C

casing   Alternate term for binding (*see* **binding**).

category fiction   Also known as genre fiction. Category fiction falls into an established (or newly originated) marketing category (which can then be subdivided for more precise target marketing). Fiction categories include action-adventure (with such further designations as military, paramilitary, law enforcement, romantic, and martial arts); crime novels (with points of view that range from deadpan cool to visionary, including humorous capers as well as gritty urban sagas); mysteries or detective fiction (hard-boiled, soft-boiled, procedurals, cozies); romances (including historical as well as contemporary); horror (supernatural, psychological, or technological); thrillers (tales of espionage, crisis, and the chase); Westerns; science fiction; and fantasy. (*See also* **fantasy**, **horror**, **romance fiction**, **science fiction**, **suspense fiction**, and **thriller**.)

children's books Books for children. As defined by the book-publishing industry, children are generally readers ages 17 and younger; many houses adhere to a fine but firm editorial distinction between titles intended for younger readers (under 12) and young adults (generally ages 12 to 17). Children's books (also called juveniles) are produced according to a number of categories (often typified by age ranges), each with particular requisites regarding such elements as readability ratings, length, and inclusion of graphic elements. Picture books are often for very young readers, with such designations as toddlers (who do not themselves read) and preschoolers (who may have some reading ability). Other classifications include easy storybooks (for younger schoolchildren), middle grade books (for elementary to junior high school students), and young adult (sometimes abbreviated YA, for readers through age 17).

coauthor One who shares authorship of a work. Coauthors all have bylines. Coauthors share royalties based on their contributions to the book. (*Compare* **ghostwriter**.)

collaboration Writers can collaborate with professionals in any number of fields. Often a writer will collaborate in order to produce books outside the writer's own areas of formally credentialed expertise (for example, a writer with an interest in exercise and nutrition may collaborate with a sports doctor on a health book). Though the writer may be billed as a coauthor (*see* **coauthor**), the writer does not necessarily receive a byline (in which case the writer is a ghostwriter). Royalties are shared, based on respective contributions to the book (including expertise or promotional abilities as well as the actual writing).

colophon Strictly speaking, a colophon is a publisher's logo; in bookmaking, the term may also refer to a listing of the materials used, as well as credits for the design, composition, and production of the book. Such colophons are sometimes included in the backmatter or as part of the copyright page.

commercial fiction Fiction written to appeal to as broad-based a readership as possible.

concept A general statement of the idea behind a book.

cool A modern colloquial expression that indicates satisfaction or approval, or may signify the maintenance of calm within a whirlwind. A fat contract for a new author is definitely cool.

cooperative advertising (co-op) An agreement between a publisher and a bookstore. The publisher's book is featured in an ad for the bookstore (sometimes in conjunction with an author appearance or other special book promotion); the publisher contributes to the cost of the ad, which is billed at a lower (retail advertising) rate.

copublishing Joint publishing of a book, usually by a publisher and another corporate entity such as a foundation, a museum, or a smaller publisher. An author can copublish with the publisher by sharing the costs and decision making and, ultimately, the profits.

copyeditor   An editor, responsible for the final polishing of a manuscript, who reads primarily in terms of appropriate word usage and grammatical expression, with an eye toward clarity and coherence of the material as presented, factual errors and inconsistencies, spelling, and punctuation. (*See also* **editor**.)

copyright   The legal proprietary right to reproduce, have reproduced, publish, and sell copies of literary, musical, and other artistic works. The rights to literary properties reside in the author from the time the work is produced — regardless of whether a formal copyright registration is obtained. However, for legal recourse in the event of plagiarism or other infringement, the work must be registered with the US Copyright Office, and all copies of the work must bear the copyright notice. (*See also* **work-for-hire**.)

cover blurbs   Favorable quotes from other writers, celebrities, or experts in a book's subject area, which appear on the dust jacket and are used to enhance the book's point-of-purchase appeal to the potential book-buying public.

crash   Coarse gauze fabric used in bookbinding to strengthen the spine and joints of a book.

curriculum vitae (abbreviated **CV**)   Latin expression meaning "course of life" — in other words, the résumé.

D

deadline   In book publishing, this not-so-subtle synonym is used for the author's due date for delivery of the completed manuscript to the publisher. The deadline can be as much as a full year before the official publication date, unless the book is being produced quickly to coincide with or follow up on a particular event.

delivery   Submission of the completed manuscript to the editor or publisher.

Dial-a-Writer   A project-referral service of the American Society of Journalists and Authors, in which members, accomplished writers in most specialty fields and subjects, list their services.

direct marketing   Advertising that involves a "direct response" (which is an equivalent term) from a consumer — for instance, an order form or coupon in a book-review section or in the back of a book or mailings (direct-mail advertising) to a group presumed to hold a special interest in a particular book.

display titles   Books that are produced to be eye-catching to the casual shopper in a bookstore setting. Often rich with flamboyant cover art, these publications are intended to pique bookbuyer excitement about the store's stock in general. Many display titles are stacked on their own freestanding racks; sometimes broad tables are laden with these items. A book shelved with its front cover showing on racks along with diverse other titles is technically a display title. Promotional or premium titles are likely to be display items, as are mass-market paperbacks and hardbacks with enormous best-seller potential. (Check your local bookstore and find a copy of this *Guide to Book Publishers, Editors, and Literary Agents* — if not already racked in "display" manner, please adjust the bookshelf so that the front cover is displayed poster-like to catch the browser's eye — that's what we do routinely.)

distributor   An agent or business that buys or warehouses books from a publisher to resell, at a higher cost, to wholesalers, retailers, or individuals. Distribution houses are often excellent marketing enterprises, with their own roster of sales representatives, publicity and promotion personnel, and house catalogs. Skillful use of distribution networks can give a small publisher considerable national visibility.

dramatic rights   Legal permission to adapt a work for the stage. These rights initially belong to the author but can be sold or assigned to another party by the author.

dust jacket (also **dustcover** or **book jacket**)   The wrapper that covers the binding of hardcover books, designed especially for the book by either the publisher's art department or a freelance artist. Dust jackets were originally conceived to protect the book during shipping, but now their function is primarily promotional — to entice the browser to actually reach out and pick up the volume (and maybe even open it up for a taste before buying) by means of attractive graphics and sizzling promotional copy.

dust-jacket copy   Descriptions of books printed on the dust-jacket flaps. Dust-jacket copy may be written by the book's editor but is often either recast or written by in-house copywriters or freelance specialists. Editors send advance copies (*see also* **bound galleys**) to other writers, experts, and celebrities to solicit quotable praise that will also appear on the jacket. (*See also* **cover blurb**.)

E

ebook   Refers to any book that exists in digital form, regardless of whether or not it also exists in a traditional physical form.

editor   Editorial responsibilities and titles vary from house to house (often being less strictly defined in smaller houses). In general, the duties of the editor in chief or executive editor are primarily administrative: managing personnel, scheduling, budgeting, and defining the editorial personality of the firm or imprint. Senior editors and acquisitions editors acquire manuscripts (and authors), conceive project ideas and find writers to carry them out, and may oversee the writing and rewriting of manuscripts. Managing editors have editorial and production responsibilities, coordinating and scheduling the book through the various phases of production. Associate and assistant editors edit; they are involved in much of the rewriting and reshaping of the manuscript and may also have acquisitions duties. Copyeditors read the manuscript and style its punctuation, grammar, spelling, headings and subheadings, and so forth. Editorial assistants, laden with extensive clerical duties and general office work, perform some editorial duties as well — often as springboards to senior editorial positions.

Editorial Freelancers Association (EFA)   This organization of independent professionals offers a referral service, through both its annotated membership directory and its job phone line, as a means for authors and publishers to connect with writers, collaborators, researchers, and a wide range of editorial experts covering virtually all general and specialist fields.

el-hi   Books for elementary and/or high schools.

endnotes   Explanatory notes and/or source citations that appear either at the end of individual chapters or at the end of a book's text; used primarily in scholarly or academically oriented works.

epilogue   The final segment of a book, which comes "after the end." In both fiction and nonfiction, an epilogue offers commentary or further information but does not bear directly on the book's central design.

F

fantasy   Fantasy is fiction that features elements of magic, wizardry, supernatural feats, and entities that suspend conventions of realism in the literary arts. Fantasy can resemble prose versions of epics and rhymes or it may be informed by mythic cycles or folkloric material derived from cultures worldwide. Fantasy fiction may be guided primarily by the author's own distinctive imagery and personalized archetypes. Fantasies that involve heroic-erotic roundelays of the death dance are often referred to as the sword-and-sorcery subgenre.

film rights   Like dramatic rights, these belong to the author, who may sell or option them to someone in the film industry — a producer or director, for example (or sometimes a specialist broker of such properties) — who will then try to gather the other professionals and secure the financial backing needed to convert the book into a film. (*See also* **screenplay**.)

footbands   *See* **headbands**.

footnotes   Explanatory notes and/or source citations that appear at the bottom of a page. Footnotes are rare in general-interest books, the preferred style being either to work such information into the text or to list informational sources in the bibliography.

foreign agents   Persons who work with their US counterparts to acquire rights for books from the United States for publication abroad. They can also represent US publishers directly.

foreign market Any foreign entity — a publisher, broadcast medium, etc. — in a position to buy rights. Authors share royalties with whoever negotiates the deal or keep 100 percent if they do their own negotiating.

foreign rights Translation or reprint rights that can be sold abroad. Foreign rights belong to the author but can be sold either country by country or en masse as world rights. Often the US publisher will own world rights, and the author will be entitled to anywhere from 50 percent to 85 percent of these revenues.

foreword An introductory piece written by the author or by an expert in the given field (*see* **introduction**). A foreword by a celebrity or well-respected authority is a strong selling point for a prospective author or, after publication, for the book itself.

Frankfurt Book Fair The largest international publishing exhibition — with 500 years of tradition behind it. The fair takes place every October in Frankfurt, Germany. Thousands of publishers, agents, and writers from all over the world negotiate, network, and buy and sell rights.

Freedom of Information Act A federal law that ensures the protection of the public's right to access public records — except in cases violating the right to privacy, national security, or certain other instances. A related law, the Government in the Sunshine Act, stipulates that certain government agencies announce and open their meetings to the public.

freight passthrough The bookseller's freight cost (the cost of getting the book from the publisher to the bookseller). It is added to the basic invoice price charged the bookseller by the publisher.

frontlist New titles published in a given season by a publisher. Frontlist titles customarily receive priority exposure in the front of the sales catalog — as opposed to backlist titles (usually found at the back of the catalog), which are previously published titles still in print.

frontmatter The frontmatter of a book includes the elements that precede the text of the work, such as the title page, copyright page, dedication, epigraph, table of contents, foreword, preface, acknowledgments, and introduction.

fulfillment house A firm commissioned to fulfill orders for a publisher — services may include warehousing, shipping, receiving returns, and mail-order and direct-marketing functions. Although more common for magazine publishers, fulfillment houses also serve book publishers.

G

galleys Typeset proofs (or copies of proofs) on sheets of paper, or printouts of the electronically produced setup of the book's interior — the author's last chance to check for typos and make (usually minimal) revisions or additions to the copy (*see also* **bound galleys**).

genre fiction   *See* **category fiction**.

ghostwriter (or **ghost**)   A writer without a byline, often without the remuneration and recognition that credited authors receive. Ghostwriters often get flat fees for their work, but even without royalties, experienced ghosts can receive quite respectable sums.

glossary   An alphabetical listing of special terms as they are used in a particular subject area, often with more in-depth explanations than would customarily be provided by dictionary definitions.

H

hardcover   Books bound in a format that uses thick, sturdy, relatively stiff binding boards and a cover composed (usually) of a cloth spine and finished binding paper. Hardcover books are conventionally wrapped in a dust jacket. (*See also* **binding; dust jacket.**)

headbands   Thin strips of cloth (often colored or patterned) that adorn the top of a book's spine where the signatures are held together. The headbands conceal the glue or other binding materials and are said to offer some protection against accumulation of dust (when properly attached). Such bands placed at the bottom of the spine are known as footbands.

hook   A term denoting the distinctive concept or theme of a work that sets it apart as being fresh, new, or different from others in its field. A hook can be an author's special point of view, often encapsulated in a catchy or provocative phrase intended to attract or pique the interest of a reader, editor, or agent. One specialized function of a hook is to articulate what might otherwise be seen as dry, albeit significant, subject matter (academic or scientific topics; number-crunching drudgery such as home bookkeeping) into an exciting, commercially attractive package.

horror   The horror classification denotes works that traffic in the bizarre, awful, and scary in order to entertain as well as explicate the darkness at the heart of the reader's soul. Horror subgenres may be typified according to the appearance of werecreatures, vampires, human-induced monsters, or naturally occurring life-forms and spirit entities — or absence thereof. Horror fiction traditionally makes imaginative literary use of paranormal phenomena, occult elements, and psychological motifs. (*See* **category fiction; suspense fiction.**)

how-to books   An immensely popular category of books ranging from purely instructional (arts and crafts, for example) to motivational (popular psychology, inspirational, self-awareness, self-improvement) to get-rich-quick (such as in real estate or personal investment).

imprint   A separate line of product within a publishing house. Imprints run the gamut of complexity, from those composed of one or two series to those offering full-fledged and diversified lists. Imprints also enjoy different gradations of autonomy from the parent company. An imprint may have its own editorial department (perhaps consisting of only one editor), or the house's acquisitions editors may assign particular titles for release on appropriate specialized imprints. An imprint may publish a certain kind of book (juvenile or paperback or travel books) or have its own personality (such as a literary or contemporary tone). An individual imprint's categories often overlap with other imprints or with the publisher's core list, but some imprints maintain a small-house feel within an otherwise enormous conglomerate. The imprint can offer the distinct advantages of a personalized editorial approach while availing itself of the larger company's production, publicity, marketing, sales, and advertising resources.

index   An alphabetical directory at the end of a book that references names and subjects discussed in the book and the pages where such mentions can be found.

instant book   A book produced quickly to appear in bookstores as soon as possible after (for instance) a newsworthy event to which it is relevant.

international copyright   Rights secured for countries that are members of the International Copyright Convention (*see* **International Copyright Convention**) and that respect the authority of the international copyright symbol, ©.

International Copyright Convention   Countries that are signatories to the various international copyright treaties. Some treaties are contingent upon certain conditions being met at the time of publication, so an author should, before publication, inquire into a particular country's laws.

introduction   Preliminary remarks pertaining to a piece. Like a foreword, an introduction can be written by the author or an appropriate authority on the subject. If a book has both a foreword and an introduction, the foreword will be written by someone other than the author; the introduction will be more closely tied to the text and will be written by the book's author. (*See also* **foreword**.)

ISBN (International Standard Book Number)   A 13-digit number that is linked to and identifies the title and publisher of a book. It is used for ordering and cataloging books and appears on the dust jackets of hardcovers, the back covers of paperbacks, and all copyright pages.

ISSN (International Standard Serial Number)   An 8-digit cataloging and ordering number that identifies all US and foreign periodicals.

J

juveniles *See* **children's books**.

K

kill fee A fee paid by a magazine when it cancels a commissioned article. The fee is only a certain percentage of the agreed-on payment for the assignment (no more than 50 percent). Not all publishers pay kill fees; a writer should make sure to formalize such an arrangement in advance. Kill fees are sometimes involved in work-for-hire projects in book publishing.

L

lead The crucial first few sentences, phrases, or words of anything — be it a query letter, book proposal, novel, news release, advertisement, or sales tip sheet. A successful lead immediately hooks the reader, consumer, editor, or agent.

lead title A frontlist book featured by the publisher during a given season — one the publisher believes should do extremely well commercially. Lead titles are usually those given the publisher's maximum promotional push.

letterhead Business stationery and envelopes imprinted with the company's (or, in such a case, the writer's) name, address, and logo — a convenience as well as an impressive asset for a freelance writer.

letterpress A form of printing in which set type is inked, then impressed directly onto the printing surface. Now used primarily for limited-run books-as-fine-art projects. (*See also* **offset**.)

libel Defamation of an individual or individuals in a published work, with malice aforethought. In litigation, the falsity of the libelous statements or representations, as well as the intention of malice, has to be proved for there to be libel; in addition, financial damages to the parties so libeled must be incurred as a result of the material in question for there to be an assessment of the amount of damages to be awarded to a claimant. This is contrasted to slander, which is defamation through the spoken word.

Library of Congress (LOC) The largest library in the world, located in Washington, DC. As part of its many services, the LOC will supply a writer with up-to-date sources and bibliographies in all fields, from arts and humanities to science and technology. For details, write to the Library of Congress, Central Services Division, Washington, DC 20540.

Library of Congress Catalog Card Number An identifying number issued by the Library of Congress to books it has accepted for its collection. The publication of those books, which are submitted by the publisher, is announced by the Library of Congress to libraries, which use Library of Congress numbers for their own ordering and cataloging purposes.

Literary Market Place (LMP)   An annual directory of the publishing industry that contains a comprehensive list of publishers, alphabetically and by category, with their addresses, phone numbers, some personnel, and the types of books they publish. Also included are various publishing-allied listings, such as literary agencies, writers' conferences and competitions, and editorial and distribution services. *LMP* is published by Information Today and is available in most public libraries.

literature   Written works of fiction and nonfiction in which compositional excellence and advancement in the art of writing are higher priorities than are considerations of profit or commercial appeal.

logo   A company or product identifier — for example, a representation of a company's initials or a drawing that is the exclusive property of that company. In publishing usage, a virtual equivalent to the trademark.

M

mainstream fiction   Nongenre fiction, excluding literary or avant-garde fiction, that appeals to a general readership.

marketing plan   The entire strategy for selling a book: its publicity, promotion, sales, and advertising.

mass-market paperback   Less expensive smaller-format paperbacks that are sold from racks (in such venues as supermarkets, variety stores, drugstores, and specialty shops) as well as in bookstores. Also referred to as rack (or rack-sized) editions.

mechanicals   Typeset copy and art mounted on boards to be photocopied and printed. Also referred to as pasteups.

middle grade   Just like the name implies, books for fourth to eighth graders.

midlist books   Generally mainstream fiction and nonfiction books that traditionally formed the bulk of a publisher's list (nowadays often by default rather than intent). Midlist books are expected to be commercially viable but not explosive bestsellers — nor are they viewed as distinguished, critically respected books that can be scheduled for small print runs and aimed at select readerships. Agents may view such projects as a poor return for the effort, since they generally garner a low-end advance; editors and publishers (especially the sales force) may decry midlist works as being hard to market; prospective readers often find midlist books hard to buy in bookstores (they have short shelf lives). Hint for writers: Don't present your work as a midlist item.

multimedia   Presentations of sound and light, words in magnetically graven image

— and any known combination thereof as well as nuances yet to come. Technological innovation is the hallmark of the electronic-publishing arena, and new formats will expand the creative and market potential. Multimedia books are publishing events; their advent suggests alternative avenues for authors as well as adaptational tie-ins with the world of print. Meanwhile, please stay tuned for virtual reality, artificial intelligence, and electronic end-user distribution of product.

multiple contract   A book contract that includes a provisional agreement for a future book or books. (*See also* **option clause/right of first refusal**.)

mystery stories or **mysteries**   *See* **suspense fiction**.

N

net receipts   The amount of money a publisher actually receives for sales of a book: the retail price minus the bookseller's discount and/or other discount. The number of returned copies is factored in, bringing down even further the net amount received per book. Royalties are sometimes figured on these lower amounts rather than on the retail price of the book.

New Age   An eclectic category that encompasses health, medicine, philosophy, religion, and the occult — presented from an alternative or multicultural perspective. Although the term has achieved currency relatively recently, some publishers have been producing serious books in these categories for decades.

novella   A work of fiction falling in length between a short story and a novel.

O

offset (offset lithography)   A printing process that involves the transfer of wet ink from a (usually photosensitized) printing plate onto an intermediate surface (such as a rubber-coated cylinder) and then onto the paper. For commercial purposes, this method has replaced letterpress, whereby books were printed via direct impression of inked type on paper.

option clause/right of first refusal   In a book contract, a clause that stipulates that the publisher will have the exclusive right to consider and make an offer for the author's next book. However, the publisher is under no obligation to publish the book, and in most variations of the clause the author may, under certain circumstances, opt for publication elsewhere. (*See also* **multiple contract**.)

outline   Used for both a book proposal and the actual writing and structuring of a book, an outline is a hierarchical listing of topics that provides the writer (and the proposal reader) with an overview of the ideas in a book in the order in which they are to be presented.

out-of-print books   Books no longer available from the publisher; rights usually revert to the author.

P

package   The package is the actual book; the physical product.

packager   *See* **book producer**.

page proof   The final typeset copy of the book, in page-layout form, before printing. Proofs are read and reviewed by the author and the publisher's proofreader for errors.

paperback   Books bound with a flexible, stress-resistant, paper covering material. (*See also* **binding**.)

paperback originals   Books published, generally, in paperback editions only; sometimes the term refers to those books published simultaneously in hardcover and paperback. These books are often mass-market genre fiction (romances, Westerns, Gothics, mysteries, horror, and so forth) as well as contemporary literary fiction, cookbooks, humor, career books, self-improvement, and how-to books — the categories continue to expand.

pasteups   *See* **mechanicals**.

permissions   The right to quote or reprint published material, obtained by the author from the copyright holder.

picture book   A copiously illustrated book, often with very simple, limited text, intended for preschoolers and other very young children.

plagiarism   The false presentation of someone else's writing as one's own. In the case of copyrighted work, plagiarism is illegal.

platform   Refers to the author's professional connections and popularity, measured by internet and media presence, and the extent to which such can be leveraged to sell books.

preface   An element of a book's frontmatter. In the preface, the author may discuss the purpose behind the format of the book, the type of research upon which it is based, its genesis, or an underlying philosophy.

premium   Books sold at a reduced price as part of a special promotion. Premiums can thus be sold to a bookseller, who in turn sells them to the bookbuyer (as with a line of modestly priced art books). Alternatively, such books may be produced as part of a broader marketing package. For instance, an organization may acquire a number of books (such as its own corporate history or the biography of its founder) for use in personnel training and as giveaways to clients; or a nutrition/recipe book may be displayed along with a company's diet foods in nonbookstore outlets. (*See also* **special sales**.)

press agent   *See* **publicist**.

press kit   A promotional package that includes a press release, tip sheet, author biography and photograph, reviews, and other pertinent information. The press kit can be put together by the publisher's publicity department or an independent publicist and sent with a review copy of the book to potential reviewers and to media professionals responsible for booking author appearances.

price There are several prices pertaining to a single book: the invoice price is the amount the publisher charges the bookseller; the retail, cover, or list price is what the consumer pays.

printer's error (PE) A typographical error made by the printer or typesetting facility, not by the publisher's staff. PEs are corrected at the printer's expense.

printing plate A surface that bears a reproduction of the set type and artwork of a book, from which the pages are printed.

producer *See* **book producer**.

proposal A detailed presentation of the book's concept, used to gain the interest and services of an agent and to sell the project to a publisher.

publication date (or **pub date**) A book's official date of publication, customarily set by the publisher to fall six weeks after completed bound books are delivered to the warehouse. The publication date is used to focus the promotional activities on behalf of the title — so that books will have had time to be ordered, shipped, and available in the stores to coincide with the appearance of advertising and publicity.

public domain Material that is uncopyrighted, whose copyright has expired, or that is uncopyrightable. The last category includes government publications, jokes, titles — and, it should be remembered, ideas.

publicist (press agent) The publicity professional who handles the press releases for new books and arranges the author's publicity tours and other promotional venues (such as interviews, speaking engagements, and book signings).

publisher's catalog A seasonal sales catalog that lists and describes a publisher's new books; it is sent and/or emailed to all potential buyers, including individuals who request one. Catalogs range from the basic to the glitzy and often include information on the author, on print quantity, and on the amount of money slated to be spent on publicity and promotion. Now also available online.

publisher's discount The percentage by which a publisher discounts the retail price of a book to a bookseller, often based in part on the number of copies purchased.

Publishers' Trade List Annual A collection of current and backlist catalogs arranged alphabetically by publisher, available in many libraries.

Publishers Weekly (***PW***) The publishing industry's chief trade journal. *PW* carries announcements of upcoming books, respected book reviews, interviews with authors and publishing-industry professionals, special reports on various book categories, and trade news (such as mergers, rights sales, and personnel changes).

quality   In publishing parlance, the word *quality* in reference to a book category (such as quality fiction) or format (quality paperback) is a term of art — individual works or lines so described are presented as outstanding products.

query letter   A brief written presentation to an agent or editor designed to pitch both the writer and the book idea.

remainders   Unsold book stock. Remainders can include titles that have not sold as well as anticipated, in addition to unsold copies of later printings of bestsellers. These volumes are often remaindered — that is, remaining stock is purchased from the publisher by specialty distributors at a huge discount and resold to the public. Both online and physical bookstores have high-discounted sections where these books can be bought for pennies on the dollar.

reprint   A subsequent edition of material that is already in print, especially publication in a different format — the paperback reprint of a hardcover, for example.

résumé   A summary of an individual's career experience and education. When a résumé is sent to prospective agents or publishers, it should contain the author's vital publishing credits, specialty credentials, and pertinent personal experience. Also referred to as the curriculum vitae or, more simply, vita.

returns   Unsold books returned to a publisher by a bookstore, for which the store may receive full or partial credit (depending on the publisher's policy, the age of the book, and so on).

reversion-of-rights clause   In the book contract, a clause that states that if the book goes out of print or the publisher fails to reprint the book within a stipulated length of time, all rights revert to the author.

review copy   A free copy of a (usually) new book sent to electronic and print media that review books for their audiences.

romance fiction or **romance novels**   Modern or period love stories, always with happy endings, which range from the tepid to the torrid. Except for certain erotic specialty lines, romances do not feature graphic sex. Often mistakenly pigeonholed by those who do not read them, romances and romance writers have been influential in the movement away from passive and coddled female fictional characters to the strong, active modern woman in a tale that reflects areas of topical social concern.

royalty   The percentage of the retail cost of a book that is paid to the author for each copy sold after the author's advance has been recouped. Some publishers structure royalties as a percentage payment against net receipts.

sales conference　A meeting of a publisher's editorial and sales departments and senior promotion and publicity staff members. A sales conference covers the upcoming season's new books, and marketing strategies are discussed. Sometimes sales conferences are the basis upon which proposed titles are bought or not.

sales representative (sales rep)　A member of the publisher's sales force or an independent contractor who, armed with a book catalog and order forms, visits bookstores in a certain territory to sell books to retailers.

SASE (self-addressed stamped envelope)　It is customary for an author to enclose SASEs with query letters, proposals, and manuscript submissions sent via snail mail. Many editors and agents do not reply if a writer has neglected to enclose an SASE with correspondence or submitted materials.

satisfactory clause　In book contracts, a publisher will reserve the right to refuse publication of a manuscript that is not deemed satisfactory. Because the author may be forced to pay back the publisher's advance if the complete work is found to be unsatisfactory, the specific criteria for publisher satisfaction should be set forth in the contract to protect the author.

science fiction　Science fiction includes the hardcore, imaginatively embellished technological/scientific novel as well as fiction that is even slightly futuristic (often with an after-the-holocaust milieu — nuclear, environmental, extraterrestrial, genocidal). An element much valued by editors who acquire for the literary expression of this cross-media genre is the ability of the author to introduce elements that transcend and extend conventional insight.

science fiction/fantasy　A category-fiction designation that actually collapses two genres into one (for bookseller-marketing reference, of course — though it drives some devotees of these separate fields of writing nuts). In addition, many editors and publishers specialize in both these genres and thus categorize their interests with catchphrases such as *sci-fi/fantasy*.

screenplay　A film script — either original or based on material published previously in another form, such as a television docudrama based on a nonfiction book or a movie thriller based on a suspense novel. (*Compare with* **teleplay**.)

self-publishing　A publishing project wherein an author pays for the costs of manufacturing and selling his or her own book and retains all money from the book's sale. This is a risky venture but one that can be immensely profitable (especially when combined with an author's speaking engagements or imaginative marketing techniques); in addition, if successful, self-publication can lead to distribution or publication by a commercial publisher. (*Compare with* **subsidy publishing**.)

self-syndication　Management by writers or journalists of functions that are otherwise performed by syndicates specializing in such services. In self-syndication, it is the writer who manages copyrights, negotiates fees, and handles sales, billing, and other tasks involved in circulating journalistic pieces through newspapers, magazines, or other periodicals that pick up the author's column or run a series of articles.

serialization   The reprinting of a book or part of a book in a newspaper or magazine. Serialization before (or perhaps simultaneously with) the publication of the book is called *first serial*. The first reprint after publication (either as a book or by another periodical) is called *second serial*.

serial rights   Reprint rights sold to periodicals. First serial rights include the right to publish the material before anyone else (generally before the book is released, or coinciding with the book's official publication) — either for the United States, a specific country, or a wider territory. Second serial rights cover material already published, in either a book or another periodical.

series   Books published as a group either because of their related subject matter (such as a series on modern artists or on World War II aircraft) and/or single authorship (a set of works by a famous romance writer, a group of books about science and society, or a series of titles geared to a particular diet-and-fitness program). Special series lines can offer a ready-made niche for an industrious author or compiler/editor who is up-to-date on a publisher's program and has a brace of pertinent qualifications and/or contacts. In contemporary fiction, some genre works are published in series form (such as family sagas, detective series, fantasy cycles).

shelf life   The amount of time an unsold book remains on the bookstore shelf before the store manager pulls it to make room for newer incoming stock with greater (or at least untested) sales potential.

short story   A short work that is more pointed and more economically detailed as to character, situation, and plot than a full novel. Published collections of short stories — whether by one or several authors — often revolve around a single theme, express related outlooks, or comprise variations within a common genre.

signature   A group of book pages that have been printed together on one large sheet of paper that is then folded and cut in preparation for being bound, along with the book's other signatures, into the final volume.

simultaneous publication   The issuing at the same time of more than one edition of a work, such as in hardcover and trade paperback. Simultaneous releases can be expanded to include (though rarely) deluxe gift editions of a book as well as mass-market paper versions. Audio versions of books are most often timed to coincide with the release of the first print edition.

simultaneous (or **multiple**) **submissions**   The submission of the same material to more than one publisher at the same time. Although simultaneous submission is a common practice, publishers should always be made aware that it is being done. Multiple submissions by an author to several agents is, on the other hand, a practice that is sometimes not regarded with great favor by agents.

slush pile The morass of unsolicited manuscripts at a publishing house or literary agency, which may fester indefinitely awaiting (perhaps perfunctory) review. Some publishers or agencies do not maintain slush piles per se — unsolicited manuscripts are slated for instant or eventual return without review (if an SASE or email address is included) or may otherwise be literally or figuratively pitched to the wind. Querying a targeted publisher or agent before submitting a manuscript is an excellent way of avoiding, or at least minimizing the possibility of, such an ignoble fate.

software Programs that run on a computer. Word-processing software includes programs that enable writers to compose, edit, store, and print material. Professional-quality software packages incorporate such amenities as databases that can feed the results of research electronically into the final manuscript, alphabetization and indexing functions, and capabilities for constructing tables and charts and adding graphics to the body of the manuscript. Software should be appropriate to both the demands of the work at hand and the requirements of the publisher (which may contract for a manuscript suitable for electronic editing, design, composition, and typesetting).

special sales Sales of a book to appropriate retailers other than bookstores (for example, wine guides to liquor stores). This classification also includes books sold as premiums (for example, to a convention group or a corporation) or for other promotional purposes. Depending on volume, per-unit costs can be very low, and the book can be custom designed. (*See also* **premium**.)

spine That portion of the book's casing (or binding) that backs the bound page signatures and is visible when the volume is aligned on a bookshelf among other volumes.

stamping In book publishing, the stamp is the impression of ornamental type and images (such as a logo or monogram) on the book's binding. The stamping process involves using a die with a raised or intaglioed surface to apply ink stamping or metallic-leaf stamping.

submission guidelines An agent or publisher's guidelines for approaching them about publication of a work. Usually can be found on the agency or publisher website.

subsidiary rights The reprint, serial, movie and television, and audiotape and videotape rights deriving from a book. The division of profits between publisher and author from the sales of these rights is determined through negotiation. In more elaborately commercial projects, further details such as syndication of related articles and licensing of characters may ultimately be involved.

subsidy publishing A mode of publication wherein the author pays a publishing company to produce his or her work, which may thus appear superficially to have been published conventionally. Subsidy publishing (alias vanity publishing) is generally more expensive than self-publishing, because a successful subsidy house makes a profit on all its contracted functions, charging fees well beyond the publisher's basic costs for production and services.

suspense fiction　Fiction within a number of genre categories that emphasize suspense as well as the usual (and sometimes unusual) literary techniques to keep the reader engaged. Suspense fiction encompasses novels of crime and detection (regularly referred to as mysteries). These include English-style cozies, American-style hard-boiled detective stories, dispassionate law-enforcement procedurals, crime stories, action-adventure, espionage novels, technothrillers, tales of psychological suspense, and horror. A celebrated aspect of suspense fiction's popular appeal — one that surely accounts for much of this broad category's sustained market vigor — is the interactive element: the reader may choose to challenge the tale itself by attempting to outwit the author and solve a crime before detectives do, figure out how best to defeat an all-powerful foe before the hero does, or parse out the elements of a conspiracy before the writer reveals the whole story.

syndicated column　Material published simultaneously in a number of newspapers or magazines. The author shares the income from syndication with the syndicate that negotiates the sale. (*See also* **self-syndication**.)

syndication rights　*See* **self-syndication**; **subsidiary rights**.

synopsis　A summary in paragraph form, rather than in outline format. The synopsis is an important part of a book proposal. For fiction, the synopsis portrays the high points of story line and plot, succinctly and dramatically. In a nonfiction book proposal, the synopsis describes the thrust and content of the successive chapters (and/or parts) of the manuscript.

T

table of contents　A listing of a book's chapters and other sections (such as the front matter, appendix, index, and bibliography) or of a magazine's articles and columns, in the order in which they appear; in published versions, the table of contents indicates the respective beginning page numbers.

tabloid　A smaller-than-standard-size newspaper (daily, weekly, or monthly). Traditionally, certain tabloids are distinguished by sensationalism of approach and content rather than by straightforward reportage of newsworthy events. In common parlance, *tabloid* is used to describe works in various media (including books) that cater to immoderate tastes (for example, tabloid exposé, tabloid television, the tabloidization of popular culture).

teleplay　A screenplay geared toward television production. Similar in overall concept to screenplays for the cinema, teleplays are nonetheless inherently concerned with such TV-loaded provisions as the physical dimensions of the smaller screen and formal elements of pacing and structure keyed to stipulated program length and the placement of commercial advertising. Attention to these myriad television-specific demands is fundamental to the viability of a project.

terms The financial conditions agreed to in a book contract.

theme A general term for the underlying concept of a book. (*See also* **hook**.)

thriller A thriller is a novel of suspense with a plot structure that reinforces the elements of gamesmanship and the chase, with a sense of the hunt being paramount. Thrillers can be spy novels, tales of geopolitical crisis, legal thrillers, medical thrillers, techno-thrillers, domestic thrillers. The common thread is a growing sense of threat and the excitement of pursuit.

tip sheet An information sheet on a single book that presents general publication information (publication date, editor, ISBN, etc.), a brief synopsis of the book, information on relevant other books (sometimes competing titles), and other pertinent marketing data such as author profile and advance blurbs. The tip sheet is given to the sales and publicity departments; a version of the tip sheet is also included in press kits.

title page The page at the front of a book that lists the title, subtitle, author (and other contributors, such as translator or illustrator), as well as the publishing house and sometimes its logo.

trade books Books distributed through the book trade — meaning bookstores and major book clubs — as opposed to, for example, mass-market paperbacks, which are often sold at magazine racks, newsstands, and supermarkets as well.

trade discount The discount from the cover or list price that a publisher gives the bookseller. It is usually proportional to the number of books ordered (the larger the order, the greater the discount) and typically varies between 40 percent and 50 percent.

trade list A catalog of all of a publisher's books in print, with ISBNs and order information. The trade list sometimes includes descriptions of the current season's new books.

trade (quality) paperbacks Reprints or original titles published in paperback format, larger in dimension than mass-market paperbacks, and distributed through regular retail book channels. Trade paperbacks tend to be in the neighborhood of twice the price of an equivalent mass-market paperback version and about half to two-thirds the price of hardcover editions.

trade publishers Publishers of books for a general readership — that is, nonprofessional, nonacademic books that are distributed primarily through bookstores.

translation rights Rights sold either to a foreign agent or directly to a foreign publisher, either by the author's agent or by the original publisher.

treatment   In screenwriting, a full narrative description of the story, including sample dialogue.

U

unauthorized biography   A history of a person's life written without the consent or collaboration of the subject or the subject's survivors.

university press   A publishing house affiliated with a sponsoring university. The university press is usually nonprofit and subsidized by the respective university. Generally, university presses publish noncommercial scholarly nonfiction books written by academics, and their lists may include literary fiction, criticism, and poetry. Some university presses also specialize in titles of regional interest, and many acquire projects intended for commercial book-trade distribution.

unsolicited manuscript   A manuscript sent to an editor or agent without being requested by the editor/agent.

V

vanity press   A publisher that publishes books only at an author's expense — and will generally agree to publish virtually anything that is submitted and paid for. (*See also* **subsidy publishing**.)

vita   Latin word for "life." A shortened equivalent term for *curriculum vitae* (*See also* **résumé**).

W

word count   The number of words in a given document. When noted on a manuscript, the word count is usually rounded off to the nearest 100 words.

work-for-hire   Writing done for an employer, or writing commissioned by a publisher or book packager who retains ownership of, and all rights pertaining to, the written material.

Y

young adult books   Books for readers generally between the ages of 12 and 17. Young adult fiction often deals with issues of concern to contemporary teens.

young readers or **younger readers**   Publishing terminology for the range of publications that address the earliest readers. Sometimes a particular house's young-readers program typifies books for those who do not yet read, which means these books have to hook the caregivers and parents who actually buy them. In certain quirky turns of everyday publishing parlance, young readers can mean anyone from embryos through young adults (and *young* means you when you want it to). This part may be confusing (as is often the case with publishing usage): sometimes *younger adult* means only that the readership is allegedly hip, including those who would eschew kids' books as being inherently lame and those who are excruciatingly tapped into the current cultural pulse, regardless of cerebral or life-span quotient.

Z

zombie (or **zombi**)   In idiomatic usage, a zombie is a person whose conduct approximates that of an automaton. Harking back to the term's origins as a figure of speech for the resurrected dead or a reanimated cadaver, such folks are not customarily expected to exhibit an especially snazzy personality or be aware of too many things going on around them; hence some people in book-publishing circles may be characterized as zombies.

INDEX

Agents and Agencies

Independent Editors

Publishers, Imprints, and Agents by Subject

INDEX

ABOUT THE AUTHOR

Jeff Herman opened his literary agency in the mid-1980s while in his mid-20s. He has made nearly 1,000 book deals, including many bestsellers. His own books include *Jeff Herman's Guide to Publishers, Editors & Literary Agents* (more than 500,000 copies sold) and *Write the Perfect Book Proposal* (coauthored with Deborah Herman). He has presented hundreds of workshops about writing and publishing and has been interviewed for dozens of publications and programs.

In 1981, shortly after graduating from Syracuse University, Herman was riding the subway on a hot summer day when he spotted an ad stating: "I found my job in *The New York Times*." He promptly bought a copy and answered some Help Wanted ads. A few days later he was summoned for an interview with the publicity director at an independent publishing house and was hired on the spot as her assistant for $200 a week. Showering, shaving, wearing a suit, saying little, and promising to show up were the clinchers.

The publicity department comprised Herman and his boss, who took her summer vacation his first week on the job. He was left "in charge," though he knew nothing about publicity, publishing, or how an office functioned. But he was a quick study and soon helped make *When Bad Things Happen to Good People* a massive bestseller.

In time, Herman followed the money into corporate marketing, where he worked on various product-promotion campaigns for Nabisco, AT&T, and many other large and small brands. But books were his passion and calling.

Today, Jeff Herman is an exceptionally successful veteran literary agent, entrepreneur, and author. His areas of editorial expertise include popular business, spirituality, and most other areas of nonfiction. "If I feel I can sell it, I'll represent it," says Herman.

The Jeff Herman Agency, LLC
PO Box 1522 • 29 Park Street • Stockbridge, MA 01262
413-298-0077 • jeff@jeffherman.com • www.jeffherman.com